Kant and the Capacity to Judge

Kant and the Capacity to Judge

SENSIBILITY AND DISCURSIVITY IN

THE TRANSCENDENTAL ANALYTIC OF

THE *CRITIQUE OF PURE REASON*

• *BÉATRICE LONGUENESSE* •

Translated from the French by Charles T. Wolfe

PRINCETON UNIVERSITY PRESS

PRINCETON AND OXFORD

The Library of Congress has cataloged the cloth edition of this book as follows
Longuenesse, Béatrice
[Kant et le pouvoir de juger.   English]
Kant and the capacity to judge : sensibility and discursivity in the transcendental
analytic of the Critique of pure reason / Béatrice Longuenesse.
p.   cm.
Includes bibliographical references and index.
ISBN 0-691-04348-5 (alk. paper)
1. Judgment. 2. Kant, Immanuel, 1724–1804—Contributions in doctrine of judgment.
3. Kant, Immanuel, 1724—1804. Kritik der reinen Vernunft. I. Title.
B2779.L6613 1997 121—dc21
97-15848 cip

This book has been composed in Times Roman

Revised English version of *Kant et le pouvoir de juger: Sensibilité et discursivité dans
l'Analytique transcendentale de la* Critique de la raison pure
(Presses Universitaires de France, 1993)

The paper used in this publication meets the minimum requirements of
ANSI/NISO Z39.48-1992 (R 1997) (*Permanence of Paper*)

www.pup.princeton.edu

Printed in the United States of America

3 5 7 9 10 8 6 4 2

• *A JEAN-CLAUDE PARIENTE* •

EN TÉMOIGNAGE D'ADMIRATION

ET D'AMITIÉ

· C O N T E N T S ·

THIS BOOK is the translation, with some revision, of my *Kant et le pouvoir de juger*, Presses Universitaires de France, 1993. I am grateful to Presses Universitaires de France for having allowed the translation. My thanks go also to Alexander Nehamas, who encouraged me to have the book translated; and to Ann Wald, of Princeton University Press, who saw the project through with exemplary patience and good humor. The translation was made possible by grants from Princeton University and from the Presses Universitaires de France. I am grateful to both these institutions for their support.

A first version of the translation was provided by Charles T. Wolfe. The translation then underwent extensive revision, which also provided me with an occasion to introduce a number of amendments into the text for the English-language edition.

The English and French versions differ in the following ways:

1. I have added a chapter on "Judgments of Perception and Judgments of Experience" (chapter 7), which means that the numbering of the suceeding chapters has changed accordingly. The new chapter 7 was in fact part of the original version of the book, but had to be cut from the French published version for reasons of length. My thanks to Princeton University Press for allowing me to restore it to its original place. A slightly different version of this chapter was published, in French, in *Kant-Studien* (1995). My thanks to the editors of *Kant-Studien* for allowing the translation in the new format, as a chapter of the book.

2. In an effort to help orient the English-language reader, I have added a discussion of recent anglophone literature. One exception is Michael Wolff's *Die Vollständigkeit der Kantischen Urteilstafel* (Frankfurt am Main: Klostermann, 1995), which appeared as I was revising this translation and whose topic is in some respects close to mine. I hope to undertake a more extended discussion of Wolff's important contribution elsewhere.

3. I have sometimes reformulated the argument and attempted to make the thematic unity of the book clearer by adding opening or closing paragraphs to some chapters. Readers wishing to compare the English to the French will find that the two texts sometimes diverge. These divergences remain rare, however, and never affect the substance of the positions I defend. All in all, the book remains a translation: I have forestalled any temptation, however great, to forget the French book altogether and write a new one!

The translation and revision were brought to completion thanks to a sabbatical leave from Princeton University in 1995–1996, the second part of which was spent in Berlin. While I was there, Rolf-Peter Hortsmann organized a biweekly colloquium during the summer semester, under the joint sponsorship of the Humboldt-Universität and the Wissenschaftskolleg. We discussed chapters of the book in English as I finished their revision. I benefited from these discussions enormously, and express my gratitude to all the participants in the colloquium.

My particular thanks, for their penetrating comments and criticisms, to David Bell, Hans-Friedrich Fulda, Rolf-Peter Horstmann, Georg Mohr, Marcus Otto, Bernhard Thöle, Wayne Waxman, and Michael Wolff.

Among the many friends and colleagues, in France and in America, whose advice and comments have helped me bring the project to completion, my special thanks go to Richard Aquila, Paul Benacerraf, Jean-Marie Beyssade, Bernard Bourgeois, Jean-Louis Chédin, Michael Friedman, Paul Guyer, Mark Johnston, Jean-Claude Pariente, Robert Pippin, Gideon Rosen, Olivier Schwartz, Bas Van Fraassen, Margaret Wilson, and Allen Wood.

David Martin helped enormously during the initial phase of the revision, proof-reading my own translation of several chapters and making countless stylistic suggestions. David also prepared the index of cited works. I would also like to thank Karen Verde, of Princeton University Press, for her help in editing the printed proofs. Thanks also to Allen Wood, who generously proofread the finished typescript.

Most of all, my deepest gratitude goes to Wayne Waxman, who once again saw me through, d'un bout à l'autre. The time and care he took to read the typescript, the corrections and improvements he suggested, and the unfailing support he provided are beyond the measure of any possible thanks.

WORKS OF KANT

References to Kant's works are given in the German Academy edition: *Gesammelte Schriften*, herausgegeben von der Königlich Preußischen Akademie der Wissenschaften, 29 vols. (Berlin: 1902–83; 2d ed., Berlin: De Gruyter, 1968, for vols. I–IX).

They are indicated as follows: abbreviation of the title of the work, followed by Ak., volume, and page. For the *Critique of Pure Reason*, the references are shortened, in keeping with current practice, to the pagination of the original edition indicated by A for the 1781 edition, and B for the 1787 edition.

Reference to the Academy edition is followed, after a semicolon, by reference to an English trnaslation, if a current English translation is available. I indicate which editions have been used in the list of abbreviations given here. Only the page will be indicated in the footnotes. For example: *Anfangsgründe*, Ak. IV, 503; 48.

Particular sections of the *Critique of Pure Reason* are mentioned with capital letters, without quotations marks, for example, the Transcendental Aesthetic, the Transcendental Deduction of the Categories. When mentioning the argument developed in the section rather than the section itself, I use no capital letters, for example, the transcendental deduction of the categories.

I have sometimes modified existing translations. I bring attention to these modifications only when they have important consequences for the interpretation of the text. Unless otherwise stated, and except for the German or Latin original given in brackets, the italics in quotations are always Kant's.

Anfangsgründe	*Metaphysische Anfangsgründe der Naturwissenschaft* (1786). *Metaphysical Foundations of Natural Science*, in *Philosophy of Material Nature*, trans. J. W. Ellington (Indianapolis: Hackett, 1985).
Anthr.	*Anthropologie in pragmatischer Hinsicht* (1798). *Anthropology from a Pragmatic Point of View*, trans. V. L. Dowell, rev. and ed. H. H. Rudnick (Carbondale: Southern Illinois University Press, 1978).
Beweisgr.	*Der einzig mögliche Beweisgrund zu einer Demonstration des Daseins Gottes* (1763). *The Only Possible Argument in Support of a Demonstration of the Existence of God*, in *Theoretical Philosophy, 1755–1770*, ed. and trans. D. Walford and R. Meerbote (Cambridge: Cambridge University Press, 1992), 107–203.
Corr.	*Philosophical Correspondence, 1759–1799*, ed. and trans. Arnulf Zweig (Chicago: University of Chicago Press, 1967).

Deutlichkeit	*Untersuchung über die Deutlichkeit der Grundsätze der natür-lichen Theologie und der Moral* (1764). *Inquiry Concerning the Distinctness of the Principles of Natural Theology and Morality*, in *Theoretical Philosophy, 1755–1770*, ed. and trans. D. Walford and R. Meerbote (Cambridge: Cambridge University Press, 1992), 1–45.
Dilucidatio	*Principiorum cognitionis metaphysicae nova dilucidatio* (1755). *A New Elucidation of the First Principles of Meta-physical Cognition*, in *Theoretical Philosophy, 1755–1770*, ed. and trans. D. Walford and R. Meerbote (Cambridge: Cam-bridge University Press, 1992), 1–45.
Diss.	*De mundi sensibilis atque intelligibilis forma et principiis* (1770). *Inaugural Dissertation*, in *Theoretical Philosophy, 1755–1770*, ed. and trans. D. Walford and R. Meerbote (Cam-bridge: Cambridge University Press, 1992), 1–45.
Entdeckung	*Über eine Entdeckung, nach der alle neue Kritik der reinen Vernunft durch eine ältere entbehrlich gemacht werden soll* (1790). *On a Discovery According to Which Any New Critique of Pure Reason Has Been Made Superfluous by an Earlier One*, in *The Kant-Eberhard Controversy*, ed. and trans. H. Allison (Baltimore: Johns Hopkins University Press, 1973), 107–160.
Erste Einl.	*Erste Einleitung in die Kritik der Urteilskraft* (1790). "First Introduction," in *Critique of Judgment*, trans. W. Pluhar (Indianapolis: Hackett, 1987).
KpV	*Kritik der praktischen Vernunft* (1788). *Critique of Practical Reason*, trans. Lewis White Beck, 3d ed. (New York: Mac-millan, 1993).
KrV	*Kritik der reinen Vernunft* (1781). *Critique of Pure Reason*, trans. N. Kemp Smith (New York: St. Martin's Press, 1965; originally published, London: Macmillan, 1929).
KU	*Kritik der Urteilskraft* (1790). *Critique of Judgment*, trans. W. Pluhar (Indianapolis: Hackett, 1987).
Logik	*Logik* (1800). *Logic*, ed. J. B. Jäsche [*Jäsche Logic*], in *Lec-tures on Logic*, ed. and trans. J. Michael Young (Cambridge: Cambridge University Press, 1992), 521–640.
Logik Blomberg	ed. and trans. J. Michael Young (Cambridge: Cambridge University Press), *The Blomberg Logic*, in *Lectures on Logic*, 15–246.
Neg. Gr.	*Versuch den Begriff der negativen Größen in die Weltweisheit einzuführen* (1763). *Attempt to Introduce the Concept of Negative Magnitudes into Philosophy*, in *Theoretical Philos-ophy, 1755–1770*, ed. and trans. D. Walford and R. Meerbote (Cambridge: Cambridge University Press, 1992), 203–41.

Prol.   *Prolegomena zu einer jeden künftigen Metaphysik, die als Wissenschaft wird auftreten können* (1783). *Prolegomena to Any Future Metaphysics That Will Be Able to Come Forward As Science*, in *Philosophy of Material Nature*, trans. J. W. Ellington (Indianapolis: Hackett, 1985).

Refl.   *Reflexionen (Kants handschriftlicher Nachlaß)*. These *Reflexionen* are quoted according to the numbering of the Akademie edition, with the date suggested by Adickes. On the method of this dating, see Adickes's introduction to volume XIV of the Akademie edition.

WORKS BY OTHER AUTHORS

G   G. W. Leibniz, *Die philosophischen Schriften*, ed. G. J. Gerhardt (Berlin, 1882; repr. Hildesheim: Georg Olms Verlag, 1978), 7 vols.

GW   G. W. F. Hegel, *Gesammelte Werke*, in Verbindung mit der Deutschen Forschungsgemeinschaft, ed. Rhein. Westfäll.Akad.d. Wiss. (Hamburg: Felix Meiner, 1968–).

For citations of all other works I use an unambiguous abbreviation of the full title given in the bibliography at the end of this volume. For works in foreign languages, page numbers refer first to the edition in original language, then to the English translation mentioned in the bibliography. For instance, Arnauld et Nicole, *Art de penser*, 37; 23.

NOTE ON MY USE OF QUOTATION MARKS

Throughout the text, I have used single quotation marks when mentioning terms, concepts, or propositions; double quotation marks when mentioning terms or concepts *as used by Kant*; and double quotation marks for citations and scare quotes.

Kant and the Capacity to Judge

IN SECTIONS 9 and 10 of the Transcendental Analytic in his *Critique of Pure Reason,* Kant claims to establish an exhaustive table of the pure concepts of the understanding, or categories, according to the "guiding thread" provided by the logical forms of judgment. This enterprise has long stood in ill-repute. Hegel himself already disparaged the merely empirical character of Kant's list of the logical forms of judgment and his derivation of the categories from them.[1] And indeed, it seems that Kant's only justification for his table of logical forms was its adoption from "the logicians," that is, its conformity to the Aristotelian heritage as Kant found it in German academic textbooks:

> Here, then, the labors of the logicians were ready at hand, though not yet quite free from defects; and with this help I was enabled to exhibit a complete table of the pure functions of the understanding, which were however undetermined in regard to any object. I finally referred these functions of judgment to objects in general, or rather to the condition of determining judgments as objectively valid; and so there arose the pure concepts of the understanding, concerning which I could make certain that these, and this exact number only, constitute our whole cognition of things from pure understanding.[2]

Even this explanation is dubious, however, since neither Kant's precise list of logical forms nor their grouping under the headings of quantity, quality, relation, and modality is in direct conformity with any of the logic textbooks that preceded the *Critique of Pure Reason.*

Hermann Cohen, who a century after the first *Critique* proclaimed that the time had come for a "return to Kant," could seem justified when he meanwhile denied any pertinence to the idea of a "metaphysical deduction" of the categories according to the guiding thread of the logical forms of judgment. He proposed instead to read the Transcendental Analytic in reverse order, interpreting the Analytic of

---

[1] Cf. Hegel, *Logik* II, in *GW* XII, 253–54 (*Science of Logic*, 613): "Kantian philosophy . . . *borrows* the categories, as so-called root notions for *transcendental logic*, from subjective logic in which they were adopted empirically. Since it admits this fact, it is hard to see why transcendental logic chooses to borrow from such a science instead of directly resorting to experience."

[2] *Prol.*, §39, Ak. IV, 323–24; 65–66. (For explanation of references to German and English editions of Kant's works, see my note on sources and abbreviations). Note that in this text, Kant speaks of logical *functions* rather than logical *forms*. The term "function" is explained at A68/B93: "I understand by function the unity of the act of bringing different representations under a common representation." By "unity of the act," I think we should understand the way in which the act is structured, which makes it apt to achieve a specific result. A few lines later Kant goes on to explain that the "act" here described is that of judgment. The understanding thus "brings different representations under a common representation" according to fundamental *forms* (modes of combination of representations), which are forms of *judgment.* I say more later on Kant's notions of logical function and logical form of judgment. On Kant's notion of form, see also chapter 6. For a very detailed analysis of Kant's notions of *form* and *function* of judgment, see Wolff, *Vollständigkeit*, 9–32; cf. my introduction to part II, note 10. For possible origins of Kant's notion of *function*, see Schulthess, *Relation*, 2–4, 217–59.

Principles as an epistemology of Newtonian science, which thus became the true source of the table of categories.[3] When Heidegger in turn claimed Kant's heritage for himself and, in opposition to the neo-Kantian reduction of the *Critique of Pure Reason* to an epistemology of the natural sciences, interpreted Kant's doctrine of transcendental imagination as an analytic of finitude, he too rejected the idea that the categories might originate in the logical functions of judgment. Their origin, according to him, is to be found rather in the synthesis of imagination as the relation of human being (*Dasein*) to time.[4]

Finally, one last example, which appears to be a coup de grâce: Strawson's work, a major inspiration for the renewal of Kantian studies in the analytic tradition, has reinforced the suspicion of Kant's claim to a strict parallelism between his table of categories and a table of the logical forms of judgment. Strawson observes there are fewer "primitive" logical forms than Kant's table would have us believe. He points out, for example, that Kant's table includes, as two distinct forms of relation in judgment, the hypothetical and the disjunctive forms, when in fact each is definable in terms of the other together whith negation. In any case, the choice of the "primitive" logical forms is up to the logician, and from it we can draw no conclusion as to how the objects of experience should be thought. Not formal logic but the analysis of what counts for us as an experience illuminates the framework of categories, or primitive concepts, necessary to all experience.[5]

Despite their considerable differences, the interpretations just mentioned have at least one thing in common: all agree that the relation Kant claims to establish between the categories and the logical forms of judgment is, at best, not especially enlightening and, at worst, downright wrong. That any experience of objects (whether it be understood in the narrow sense of scientific experience or in the broader sense of our relation to a world of objects in general) presupposes the use of concepts which not only do not result from experience, but are themselves the very condition of experience, is agreed by all to be a thesis still deserving of

[3] Cohen, *Erfahrung*, 345–46. Recall that in section 26 of the B Deduction, Kant uses the expression "metaphysical deduction" of the categories to designate the exposition of the table of categories according to the guiding thread of the logical forms of judgment (achieved in §10 of the Transcendental Analytic, and unchanged from the first to the second edition of the *Critique*). This deduction is "metaphysical" in the sense that Kant gave to this adjective when he presented the "metaphysical exposition" of the concepts of space and time: the exposition of a concept is "metaphysical" when it "contains that which exhibits the concept as given *a priori*" (A23/B38). Thus the exposition of the table of categories according to the guiding thread of the logical forms of judgment is *metaphysical* because it presents what makes these categories a priori concepts: it shows that their origin is in the a priori forms of our thinking, the logical forms of our judgments. It is a *deduction* in the legal sense of "legitimation" (cf. A84/B116–17). What is legitimated in the metaphysical deduction of the categories is the claim to see them as concepts whose origin is in the understanding, and not in the associations of imagination (as Hume claimed). As for the *transcendental* deduction, it legitimates or justifies (*deduction*) the relation of the categories to any object of cognition, by showing that they are a priori conditions of any representation of an object (*transcendental* deduction). For an interesting analysis of the idea of a "metaphysical deduction" of the categories, and its relation to *transcendental* deduction, see Horstmann, *Deduction*.

[4] Heidegger, *Kant*, §12; *Phän. Int.*, §21e.

[5] Strawson, *Bounds of Sense*, 74–82.

interpretation and debate. But, they go on to say, the parallelism between these concepts and a corresponding table of the logical forms of judgment is merely the result of Kant's architectonic mania. Retaining what is fruitful and innovative in Kant's "Copernican revolution" with regard to the categories means repudiating the alleged metaphysical deduction of the categories according to the guiding thread of the logical forms of judgment.

In what follows, I shall defend the opposite thesis: neither the argument of the Transcendental Deduction of the Categories, that is, the demonstration of the role of the pure concepts of the understanding in any representation of an object, nor the System of Principles of the Pure Understanding, can be understood unless they are related, down to the minutest details of their proofs, to the role that Kant assigns to the logical forms of our judgments, and to the manner in which he establishes the table of categories or pure concepts of the understanding according to the "guiding thread" of these logical forms.

One needs, however, to be quite clear about what Kant means by the expression "logical form of judgment." Kant's notion of logical form is not that of modern logic, in which the form refers to the logical constants and the rules of composition and derivation adopted in a given calculus. In the name of the latter notion, Strawson rejects Kant's table and underscores the arbitrary character of the forms adopted as primitive in a logical calculus. But for Kant "logical form" refers to something different, namely the universal rules of discursive thought. He understands logic in much the same way as the Port-Royal logicians did, as the "reflection that men have made on the . . . operations of their mind."[6] What Kant claims to display in his table of the logical forms of judgment are forms of mental activities, and the transcendental deduction of the categories consists in showing that these mental activities are necessary for any representation of an object. Perhaps it would be enlightening to be able to analyze Kant's table in terms of those logical languages we have at our disposal. But this can come only as a second step. Such an analysis can be relevant only if one has already elucidated the nature and role of the logical procedures whose table Kant claims to draw up.

One might reply that the idea of founding the argument of the transcendental deduction on the analysis of mental activities is precisely what is objectionable, and what the various positions mentioned here intended to challenge. Cohen's epistemological reading, Heidegger's phenomenological reading, and Strawson's analysis of "transcendental arguments" have one thing in common, as paradoxical as such an agreement may seem: they all stand firmly under the banner of antipsychologism. For Cohen, to explain the possibility of the relation of our cognitions to an object by elucidating the mental acts that are supposed to give rise to these cognitions is to confuse psychological genesis and epistemic evaluation, to confuse a question of fact (*quaestio facti*) with a question of right (*quaestio juris*). For Heidegger, it is to confuse the analytic of *Dasein* with psy-

---

[6] Cf. Arnauld and Nicole, *Art de penser*, 37; 23 (translation modified). I discuss this connection at greater length in the introduction to part II.

chology or anthropology, however "philosophical" they may claim to be. For Strawson, it is to launch oneself into a mysterious "transcendental psychology" lacking any criteria of verification whatsoever.

Unfortunately, to disclaim any "psychological" or "mental" dimension to the transcendental deduction of the categories, and to the transcendental analytic as a whole, is to forgo from the outset any chance to grasp their coherence or meaning. Indeed, both in the Transcendental Deduction of the Categories and in the Analytic of Principles, which the Deduction is meant to ground, Kant's argument for the applicability of categories to objects rests on the relation he tries to establish between *discursive* syntheses or combinations (combinations of concepts in judgments) on the one hand, and syntheses or combinations of our *sensible* perceptions on the other. Such an argument is undeniably "mentalist" or "psychological," even though Kant's procedure is quite the opposite of an introspective procedure, and even though the *psychological* hypotheses are always guided by a *logical* analysis of the conditions of truth or falsity of our judgments. Refusing to follow Kant on his own terrain all too often results in attributing to him surprisingly weak or even blatantly untenable arguments, such as the famous "*non sequitur* of numbing grossness" Strawson denounces in the Second Analogy of Experience.[7]

I do not mean to imply, however, that the present work is the first to consider Kant's argument as resting on the presentation and the analysis of mental activities. One may think, for instance, of the works of Lachièze-Rey, Hansgeorg Hoppe, Patricia Kitcher. But none of these authors has given central place to Kant's doctrine of the logical forms of judgment. A metaphysics of subjectivity (for Lachièze-Rey) or a phenomenological psychology (for Hoppe) seem sufficient to ground the doctrine of the categories. It is particularly surprising that Patricia Kitcher, who attempts to relate what she calls Kant's "transcendental psychology" to contemporary cognitive psychology, should remain silent about what in Kant's argument belongs to the analysis of the *logical forms* of judgment.[8] In Germany on the contrary, since the pioneering study of Klaus Reich, important work has been devoted to Kant's table of judgments. The line of the present work is perhaps closest to the one defended by Lorenz Krüger. In a discussion of Reich's book he gives a forceful account of the architectonic function of the logical forms of judgment, understood as acts of the understanding.[9] And in an essay written in collaboration with Michael Frede he explores the relation between logical forms of judgment and categories in the case of the three headings of quantity.[10] More recently, important studies have been devoted to Kant's logic and his table of logical functions of judgment.[11] But I am unaware of any systematic

[7] Strawson, *Bounds of Sense*, 28, 136–38.

[8] See Lachièze-Rey, *Idéalisme*; Hoppe, *Synthesis*; Kitcher, *Transcendental Psychology*.

[9] Krüger, "Urteilstafel." Cf. Reich, *Vollständigkeit*. I shall discuss some of Reich's views in the following chapters. Important recent works on Kant's table of judgment include Schulthess, *Relation*; Brandt, *Urteilstafel*; Wolff, *Vollständigkeit*.

[10] Frede and Krüger, "Quantität."

[11] See in particular Schulthess, *Relation*; Brandt, *Urteilstafel*; Wolff, *Vollständigkeit*. Brandt's book appeared as I was proofreading the French version of this book. Wolff's appeared two years after mine, while I was working on this English version. Extended discussion of their results as compared with mine will have to await a different publication.

investigation of the relation between logical functions of judgment and categories, and of the import of this correlation for Kant's principles of pure understanding. Such an investigation is what I am presenting in this book.

Just before expounding his table of logical functions of judgment in section 10 of the Transcendental Analytic, Kant defines the understanding as a "capacity to judge": "We can reduce all acts of the understanding to judgments, and the understanding may therefore be represented as a *capacity to judge* [*Vermögen zu urteilen*]" (A69/B94). This description of the understanding appears again in the next section, right after Kant has laid out the table of categories according to the guiding thread provided by the logical forms of judgment: "This division [of the categories] is developed systematically from a common principle, namely, the capacity to judge [*nämlich dem Vermögen zu urteilen*] (which is the same as the capacity to think [*Vermögen zu denken*])" (A81/B106).

Compare this *Vermögen zu urteilen* with Kant's distinction between *Vermögen* and *Kraft* in his *Lectures on Metaphysics*, inspired by Baumgarten. The *Vermögen* (*facultas*) is the possibility of acting, or tendency to act, that is proper to a substance. Following Baumgarten, Kant writes that a *conatus* is associated with every *Vermögen*. This *conatus* is a tendency or effort to actualize itself. For this tendency to be translated into action, it must be determined to do so by external conditions. Then the *Vermögen* becomes a *Kraft*, in Latin *vis*, force.[12] Following this line, the *Vermögen zu urteilen*, specified according to the different logical forms presented in Kant's table, can be considered as a *possibility* or *potentiality* of forming judgments. The *Urteilskraft* which Kant describes in the Analytic of Principles and in the *Critique of Judgment* (*Kritik der Urteilskraft*) is the actualization of the *Vermögen zu urteilen* under sensory stimulation.

To be sure, one should approach this parallel with caution. First of all, the *Critique* warns us not to consider the *Gemüt* or mind, the whole of our represen-

---

[12] Cf. *Met. Volckmann* (1784–85), Ak. XXVIII-1, 434: "*Capacity* [*Vermögen*] and *power* [*Kraft*] must be distinguished. In capacity we represent to ourselves the possibility of an action, it does not contain the sufficient reason of the action, which is power [*die Kraft*], but only its possibility. . . . The *conatus*, effort [*Bestrebung*] is properly speaking the determination of a capacity *ad actum*." *Refl.* 3582 (1775–77), Ak. XVII, 72: "The internal possibility of a power [*einer Kraft*] (of acting) is capacity [*das Vermögen*]." In the original French version of this work I translated *Vermögen* by *pouvoir* (hence the French title of the book, *Kant et le pouvoir de juger*). And I adopted the usual translation of *Urteilskraft* by *faculté de juger*. I would have liked to keep the same pair in English: *Vermögen zu urteilen* as *power of judgment* and *Urteilskraft* as *faculty of judgment* (even though *Vermögen*, as we have seen from the texts of Baumgarten I have quoted, translates the Latin *facultas*!). But *power* seems not to have as clearly, in English, the connotation of "mere potentiality" that *pouvoir* has in French. Allen Wood indicated to me that in the new translation of the *Critique* he is preparing with Paul Guyer, they have translated *Vermögen zu urteilen* by *faculty of judging*, and *Urteilskraft* by *power of judgment*. I have preferred *capacity to judge* for *Vermögen zu urteilen*, again to preserve as much as possible the idea of unactualized potentiality. And I have adopted Guyer and Wood's translation of *Urteilskraft* by *power of judgment*, thus sacrificing the parallel with my French use. Translating is a difficult task, and no solution will ever be completely satisfactory. In any case, as I say later, the distinction between the terms *Vermögen* and *Kraft* is interesting and illuminating in some contexts (I am convinced it is in the present one), but not always.

tational capacities, as a substance.[13] This being the case, it would then be incorrect to identify the meaning of *Vermögen* and *Kräfte* when applied to the mind with the meaning these terms have in the metaphysics of substance set forth in the *Vorlesungen zur Metaphysik*. Second, the distinction between the *Vermögen zu urteilen* (the understanding) and the *Kraft (Urteilskraft*, the "power" at work in the activity of judgment) is not always entirely clear. Not only does Kant sometimes refer to the *Urteilskraft* (power of judgment) itself as a *Vermögen zu urteilen*[14] but, furthermore, he generally applies the term *Vermögen* to all the higher cognitive faculties: the understanding, the power of judgment (*Urteilskraft*), and reason. The vocabulary is thus far from fixed, and it would be a mistake to expect it to sustain overly sharp distinctions. Even so, *in the context I have mentioned*—that is, the establishment of the table of the logical forms of judgment as the guiding thread for the table of categories—I think the relation between the terms *Vermögen* and *Kraft* is significant. It is important for the understanding of Kant's argument to consider the *Vermögen zu urteilen* as a *capacity for discursive thought*, and the power of judgment, *Urteilskraft*, as its actualization in relation to sensory perceptions. In any case, when I use the expression "capacity to judge" in the title of this work, this is how it should be taken. It should not be taken as referring to the power of judgment discussed in the System of Principles or in the third *Critique* (although it remains true that the *Urteilskraft*, in English *power of judgment*, expounded in these two texts depends on the *Vermögen zu urteilen*, the *capacity to judge*). My main concern shall be the *Vermögen zu urteilen*, the capacity for discursive thought, the specific forms of which are delineated by Kant in his table of the logical functions of judgment. I intend to show that Kant's attempt to elucidate this capacity is the key to the argument of the Transcendental Analytic, and thereby one of the cornerstones of the critical system.

Such an interpretive orientation agrees with the program Kant announced in a famous footnote in the preface to the *Metaphysical Foundations of Natural Science* (published in 1786). He declared that he could reformulate the argument of his transcendental deduction of the categories by deducing it from the "precisely determined definition of a judgment in general."[15] He did what he announced and presented, in the second edition of the *Critique,* a completely new version of the transcendental deduction. The pivot of this new version is the definition of judgment stated in section 19: "A judgment is nothing but the manner in which given cognitions are brought to the objective unity of apperception" (B141).

[13] Kant develops this view in his criticism of the Paralogisms of Pure Reason, that is, his criticism of the rationalist notion of a soul. Cf. A341/B399–40.

[14] Cf. *KU*, §35, Ak. V, 287; 151: "The subjective condition of all judgments is our very capacity to judge [*Vermögen zu urteilen selbst*], i.e., the power of judgment [*oder die Urteilskraft*]. When we use this power of judgment in regard to a representation by which an object is given, then it requires that there be a harmony between two representational powers [*zweier Vorstellungskräfte*], imagination (for the intuition and the combination of its manifold) and understanding (for the concept that is the representation of the unity of this combination)."

[15] *Anfangsgründe*, Ak. IV, 476n; 13n.

The new presentation of the argument thus relies on a definition of judgment, where the issue is indeed judgment considered *in its logical form*, as indicated by the title of section 19: "The logical form of all judgments consists in the objective unity of the apperception of the concepts which they contain." The transcendental deduction of the categories is then directly related to the role of guiding thread assigned to the table of the logical forms of judgment in the metaphysical deduction. The present work, therefore, will give pride of place to the Transcendental Deduction in its second edition, so much so that in a way, parts II and III of my study could be read as an extended commentary on a few sections of this deduction: sections 19 and 20, in which Kant moves from the consideration of the merely logical definition of judgment to the conclusion that all sensible intuitions must necessarily conform to the categories; and sections 24 and 26, where he explains that such a subordination of appearances to the logical functions of judgment, and thereby to the categories, presupposes the activity of a "transcendental synthesis of imagination" or *synthesis speciosa*, combining our sensible intuitions.

However, to acknowledge the superiority of the B Deduction argument is not to say that the argument in the A edition should be dismissed as superfluous. On the contrary, I think the latter is the indispensable prerequisite of the former. In particular, the exposition of the "threefold synthesis" that opens the A Deduction is an indispensable *via negativa* by which Kant attempts to establish that a Humean empiricopsychological genesis of our perceptions and their combinations cannot provide an account of our capacity to subsume singular intuitions under general concepts. This *via negativa* prepares the way for the positive argument of the B edition, where the *logical* argument takes over from the *psychological* argument of the A Deduction. The Deduction no longer rests mainly on a genetic psychological account of the combinations of sensible perceptions and their relation to an object, but on the consideration of the logical form of judgment as the form of an original capacity, that is, the form of the *Vermögen zu urteilen* or form of the "objective unity of apperception."

The structure of the present work should be understood against the background of the general argument just developed.

Part I ("The Guiding Thread") sets the stage for the main argument. In chapter 1, I discuss the problem of the categories as Kant formulates it after the *Inaugural Dissertation* of 1770. I analyze the emergence of two main themes in Kant's attempt to solve this problem: the role of the logical function of judgment in relating concepts to objects; and the role of synthesis in generating the representation of manifolds in sensibility. I show that the latter theme is closely linked to Kant's reflection on the nature of mathematical concepts and reasoning.

In chapter 2, I analyze the initial sections of the A Deduction, where the theme of synthesis and the mathematical model are predominant. I show that the necessity of bringing the logical function of judgment more explicitly into the argument of the transcendental deduction results from the shortcomings of Kant's argument in these sections.

In chapter 3, I discuss the manner in which the B Deduction preserves some main results of the A Deduction while setting the transcendental deduction of the categories on its proper terrain, that of the activity of judgment.

By thus bringing together the different themes that led to the perfected formulation of the problem of the categories and its solution, I hope to clarify the vocabulary in which they are stated, and thereby the philosophical horizon in which they are situated. I explicate notions whose meanings are supposedly well known but often remain insufficiently determined—for example, *experience, synthesis, appearance,* and lastly the: "I think," which, Kant asserts at the beginning of the B Deduction, "must be able to accompany all my representations"[16] and leads to consideration of the logical forms of judgment.

In part II ("The Logical Forms of Judgment, As Forms of Reflection"), I elucidate the role Kant assigns to the logical forms of judgment.

In chapter 4, I examine Kant's definitions of judgment considered in its logical form. I focus more particularly on three definitions, borrowed from the *Critique* and from Kant's published and unpublished texts on logic. I stress two important points in Kant's characterization of the logical form of judgment. (1) He calls logic "formal" or "general" insofar as it is concerned merely with "all thought in general, without regard to objects."[17] (2) He relates the combinations of concepts in a judgment to something represented by "x" or "x, y, z," *thought under* the concepts. Each of these points plays a major role in the "revolution in the way of thinking," which must lead, according to Kant, to the refutation of rationalist metaphysics. (1) By assigning to logic the task of laying out the "mere form of thought," Kant dissolved the link which the *Schulphilosophen* saw between logic and ontology. The various ways in which we combine our concepts in judgments and syllogisms are not the more or less adequate expression of ways in which essential and accidental marks are combined in things, but merely the implementation of the rules proper to our discursive activity. And (2) by making explicit the relation that concepts, combined in a judgment, have to something represented by "x" (or "$x, y,$ and z"), thought *under* them, Kant's explanation of the logical form of our judgments is meant to show why this form is proper to a *discursive* and not an *intuitive* understanding, an understanding whose activity is dependent on its relation to singular intuitions that must be given to it by a distinct faculty of sensibility and are irreducible to the concepts under which they are thought.

How then does discursive thought relate to what is given in sensibility? Kant's answer has two aspects. The first concerns the ways we form general concepts from sensible objects (or "reflect upon" what is given in sensibility). The second concerns the ways we first generate sensible objects *as objects of representation,* so that they *can* be so reflected upon—that is, *can* provide instances for the terms "x, y, z" in our judgments. This second aspect is at the heart of the "revolution in the way of thinking," which Kant claims to bring about with his *Critique of Pure Reason.*

In chapter 5, I examine the first aspect of Kant's answer. This aspect is actually not developed in the *Critique of Pure Reason,* not because it is unimportant,

[16] Cf. *KrV,* §16, B131–32.
[17] *Logik,* introd. I, Ak. IX, 13; 528.

but because it raises no particular difficulty in Kant's eyes. The logical forms of judgment guide the activity by which understanding elevates given representations to a discursive form—that is, reflects them under concepts. In the first *Critique,* Kant calls this activity *analysis.*[18] In the *Logic,* Kant specifies that this *analysis* consists of the operations of "comparison, reflection, and abstraction," *and that these operations are performed with a view to forming judgments.*[19]

A major reason for the general misunderstanding concerning the role of the logical forms of judgment as "guiding thread" for the table of categories is that commentators neglect their function in the activities of "comparison, abstraction, and reflection." If we take this function into account, it illuminates each step of the argument of the first *Critique.* Indeed, one could summarize this argument as follows: consider the forms of the *analysis* of what is given in sensibility (the forms of "comparison, abstraction, reflection"—the logical forms of judgment) and you will have the key to the forms of the *synthesis that must occur prior to analysis,* namely the synthesis required for the sensible representation of the *x*'s that can be reflected under concepts according to the logical forms of our judgments. Consequently, you will also have the key to the meaning and role of the categories, concepts that "universally represent" the different forms of this synthesis.[20]

In chapter 6, I undertake to confirm my interpretation by laying out the contribution of each and every one of Kant's logical functions of judgment to the activity of "comparison, reflection, abstraction." For this I make extensive use of a very important, although rarely studied chapter of the Transcendental Analytic, the appendix on the Amphiboly of Concepts of Reflection.

I am aware that stressing in this way a primarily "reflective" role of judgment and its logical forms—one in which the movement of thinking is "from the bottom up," from sensible representations to concepts formed by "comparison, reflection, and abstraction"—may strike some as quite contrary to the fundamental orientation of the *Critique of Pure Reason,* to Kant's proclaimed "revolution in the way of thinking." Does Kant not present the idea that the objects of our experience "conform to our concepts" as one of the two major propositions of this "revolution"?[21] Does such a proposition not entail that the movement of thinking

[18] A77/B103: "Before we can analyze our representations, they must themselves be given"; A78/B104: "By means of *analysis* different representations are brought under one concept—a procedure treated of in general logic."

[19] Cf. *Logik,* §5: "This *logical* origin of concepts—the origin as to their mere form—consists in reflection, whereby a representation common to several objects . . . arises, as that form which is required for the power of judgment." In section 6, Kant specifies that this "reflection whereby a representation common to several objects arises" includes the three operations of "comparison, reflection, and abstraction."

[20] Cf. *KrV,* §10, A78/B104: "Pure synthesis, *universally represented,* gives us the pure concept of the understanding."

[21] Cf. Bxvii–xviii: "For experience is itself a species of cognition which involves understanding; and understanding has rules which I must presuppose as being in me prior to objects being given to me, and therefore as being *a priori.* They find expression in *a priori* concepts to which all objects of experience necessarily conform, and with which they must agree." The thesis that the object of experience must conform to our concepts is preceded by the thesis that the object of our senses conforms to our faculty of sensible intuition; the two a priori forms of this faculty are space and time.

depicted in the first *Critique* is essentially "from the top down," from the a priori concepts (the categories) to a set of sensible representations that must somehow be constrained to conform to our conceptual schemes? Is this not quite contrary to the line of interpretation I am suggesting?

In response to such a possible objection, I argue that Kant's thesis that appearances conform a priori to the categories can be understood correctly only in light of the objectifying role that Kant grants *to the logical forms of judgment as forms of reflection*. Again, our motto should be: use the forms of analysis (the logical functions of judgment) as your guiding thread to the "universal representations of synthesis" (the categories). This is because *synthesis* of what is given in sensibility is achieved *in order to make analysis possible*. Categories *before* synthesis are *nothing but* mere forms of analysis, logical functions of judgment. But these "mere forms of analysis" *govern the synthesis* of what they are to analyze. And only when the analysis is carried out can full-fledged categories, "pure concepts of the understanding" (causality, quantity, interaction, etc.) be applied to appearances.

In chapter 7, I further sustain this point by examining Kant's famous distinction in the *Prolegomena* between "judgments of perception" and "judgments of experience." In addition, I argue that my analysis reveals a greater continuity than is generally recognized between Kant's theory of judgment in the first *Critique* and its further development in the *Critique of Judgment*.

Thus in part II I will have considered in detail Kant's analysis of the discursive activity of judgment, from the exposition of its "mere logical forms" to the examination of their function of *reflection* on the sensible given. In part III ("*Synthesis Intellectualis, Synthesis Speciosa*: Transcendental Imagination and the Foundation of the System of Principles"), I consider the *syntheses* of imagination that must occur *prior to* the discursive activity of judgment. I argue that according to Kant, the function of these syntheses is to generate in the sensible given the forms of unity (singular intuitions, the "*x*" or "*x,y,z*" of judgment) susceptible to being reflected under concepts—that is, to provide the extension of the concepts combined in judgments. Here the "guiding thread" described earlier takes on its full meaning. Elucidate the forms of *discursive analysis*—the logical forms of judgment—and you will have the key to the universal forms of the *sensible synthesis* that is prior to analysis, and therefore also prior to the categories in their proper role as full-fledged concepts, "universal representations" of these forms of sensible synthesis.

In chapter 8, I show that the doctrine of transcendental imagination both presupposes the doctrine of the a priori forms of intuition developed in the Transcendental Aesthetic, and furnishes a new reading of it. According to the Transcendental Aesthetic, space and time are a priori forms of our receptive capacity, and singular intuitions. According to the Transcendental Analytic, they are forms in which singular objects are presented to sensible cognition. As such, they are themselves the result of that figurative synthesis or "affection of inner sense by the understanding" which Kant calls *synthesis speciosa*. This completes the transcendental deduction: appearances, being given in space and time, are given in accordance with the forms of *synthesis speciosa*, of which the categories are "universal representations."

In chapter 9, I show how the "Schematism of the Pure Concepts of Understanding" is then clarified: the mere enumeration of the schemata, which in the Schematism chapter Kant deems sufficient, loses its apparent arbitrariness when the schemata are interpreted as just those rules of synthesis which provide the discursive forms with the substitutional instances for the "*x*" of judgment.

This interpretation clarifies, in the first place, the relation between the logical form of quantity in judgment, the schema of quantity, and the "principle of the Axioms of intuition" resulting from the latter. I argue that if we follow, as Kant recommends we should, the "guiding thread" of logical forms and their relation to sensible syntheses generating the extension of concepts, Kant's view of mathematics and its relation to the forms of discursive thought appears far more subtle and sophisticated than is generally acknowledged. New light is shed on Kant's conception of arithmetic and geometry, and on the ways in which this conception relates to later developments in philosophy of mathematics.

In chapter 10, I examine the relation between logical forms of quality in judgments (affirmative, negative, "infinite" judgments), schemata of quality, and the ill-reputed "principle of intensive magnitudes" that is supposed to follow from these schemata. I argue that following Kant's "guiding thread" is the only way to understand not only his categories of reality and negation but also, and most importantly, his category of *limitation* (the third category of quality, corresponding to infinite judgment). Understanding this category is in turn a necessary step in understanding Kant's argument concerning the applicability of mathematics not only to the form of appearances (space, time, and movement: this was handled in the Axioms of Intuition) but also to their matter (reality). Such an approach is an important advance toward understanding the exact nature of the relation between Kant's critical endeavor and the Newtonian model of science.

In chapter 11, I argue that the schemata for the categories of substance, causality, and interaction must be understood in light of their relation to the logical forms of categorical, hypothetical, and disjunctive judgment. I also argue that this approach sheds new light on Kant's argument in all three Analogies of Experience: for instance, on Kant's argument for the permanence of substance, on his response to Hume on causality, on the Lovejoy-Strawson misunderstanding of this argument, on Kant's argument for the universal interaction of substances and the role played by our own body in our experience of this interaction.

I do not devote a specific chapter to the modal categories, even though I discuss Kant's account of the modalities of judgment at some length in part II (in the last section of chapter 6), and on that occasion I offer some clarification of Kant's view of modal categories. A fuller treatment of these categories must be reserved for another work.

By developing, in the chapters that follow, the argument that I have here only sketched out, I would like to convince the reader that taking Kant's "guiding thread" seriously reveals both an unsuspected unity and a remarkable diversity in the modes of thinking analyzed in the course of the Transcendental Analytic. (1) Unity: the logical argument weaves through the whole Transcendental Analytic, stitching together its different elements. (2) Diversity: just as each of the titles of the logical forms of judgment refers to a different aspect of the act of judging or subsuming the object represented by the term "*x*" in our judgments under concepts, so the acts of combination of the sensible perceptions by which substitutional instances for "*x*" are first generated for judgment—and, subsequently, so too the "applications" of the corresponding categories—are each different. Far from resulting in excessive architectonic rigidity, taking Kant's logical guiding thread seriously turns out to be the best way to avoid an overly petrified notion of the various parallelisms Kant emphasized. For behind the deceptive fixity of the numerous tables (of logical forms, of categories, of schemata, of principles), we can discern the acts of thought that give them their meaning. What then comes to the fore is the remarkable combination of stubborn determination and imaginative insight with which Kant undermines the forms of the school logic he inherited, and reinvents the meaning of *philosophia prima sive ontologia*: first philosophy, or ontology.

My effort in the present book has been mainly devoted to elucidating Kant's intentions and results. I also endeavored, especially in part III of the work, to offer some elements for a critical evaluation of his conclusions. But certainly in this regard a lot more can and should be said. My hope is that the case I offered for Kant's systematic endeavor will contribute to further developments in our understanding and evaluation, not only of Kant's project, but also of our own.

PART ONE

The Guiding Thread

Synthesis and Judgment

THE TRANSCENDENTAL Deduction of the Categories is meant to answer the question, How can a priori concepts be applied to objects that are given? This question concerns primarily the concept of cause, by means of which we think a necessary connection between distinct existences. Such a concept cannot be drawn inductively from experience, and yet we apply it to objects whose connections we know only empirically. Even more suspiciously, metaphysicians make use of this concept beyond the realm of what is given in any experience at all, and take the principle of causality as universally applicable to the existence of things in general, whether they can be given to our senses or not. Kant calls the problem posed by the concept of cause "Hume's problem," but he claims credit for its generalization: there are many other concepts besides that of cause which cannot have been acquired by mere empirical generalization, which we nevertheless use in our cognition of empirical objects, and which moreover constitute the framework of a metaphysics that purports to proceed by means of pure reasoning, independently of any experience.[1]

Kant's first formulation of the problem which eventually becomes that of the transcendental deduction of the categories in the *Critique* is to be found in his Letter to Marcus Herz of February 21, 1772. The problem of the relation between a priori concepts and given objects is the occasion for a more general inquiry into the relation between a representation and its object, an inquiry taken up again, almost word for word, nine years later in the Transcendental Deduction. However, the two texts differ in a fundamental respect. While the Letter to Herz presents the relation between a representation and its object as a causal relation between two heterogeneous entities, the representation that is "within" the mind and the object which is "outside" it, the *Critique internalizes* the relation between the representation and the object *within representation itself*, so that the problem assumes a new meaning. This fundamental shift is what I now want to examine.

---

[1] Kant calls the problem of causality "Hume's problem," and claims credit for its generalization, in the preface to the *Prolegomena* (Ak. IV, 259–60; 4). In the first edition of the *Critique*, he discusses Hume's position at some length in the Transcendental Doctrine of Method (A764/B792–93). Only in the second edition does he specifically mention Hume's name in the Transcendental Deduction itself (B 127). For an account of Kant's relation to "Hume's problem" in the precritical period, and of the emergence of the Transcendental Deduction of the Categories, see Carl, *Der schweigende Kant.*

REPRESENTATION AND OBJECT OF REPRESENTATION

The Letter to Herz of February 21, 1772, and the Causal Relation between Representation and Object of Representation

In the Letter to Herz, Kant brings up a difficulty he admits he took no account of in his 1770 *Inaugural Dissertation*: how can concepts that depend only on "the very nature of the pure understanding"[2] agree with objects that are quite independent of our understanding? This problem leads Kant to examine more generally the relation between representations and objects of representation. "I noticed that I still lacked something essential, something that in my long metaphysical studies I, as well as others, had failed to pay attention to and that, in fact, constitutes the key to the whole secret of hitherto still obscure metaphysics. I asked myself: What is the ground of the relation of that in us which we call 'representation' to the object?"

Kant then considers two possible cases. In the first case, the representation "is only a way in which the subject is affected by the object." Then "it is easy to see how the representation is in conformity with this object, namely, as an effect in accord with its cause [*als eine Wirkung seiner Ursache gemäß sei*], and it is easy to see how this determination of our mind can *represent* something, that is, have an object."[3]

All our sensible representations are of this kind. Since they are only "the way in which the subject is affected" by the object, they do not resemble this object, as the *Dissertation* already stated, but they still have a regular correspondence with it: for the object causes them, and same cause, same effect. This relation to the object, not one of resemblance but of conformity "as an effect in accord with its cause," is true not only of the data of the five senses, but also of the spatiotemporal relations between sensory data. Indeed, if space and time are, as Kant stated in the *Dissertation*, "not an outline or any kind of schema [*adumbratio aut schema*] of the object, but only a certain law which is inherent in the mind and by means of which it co-ordinates for itself that which is sensed from the presence of the object,"[4] then the spatiotemporal coordinations of our sensations are dependent on what we might call the "disposition to representation" of the affected subject, and therefore have no relation of resemblance to external things. Like sensations, they nevertheless have a constant relation to the presence of these things, and their variations, just like those of sensations, are determined by that presence. Thus Kant is merely reiterating the doctrine of the *Dissertation* when, in the Letter to Herz, he claims that all sensible representations without exception have "a

[2] Cf. *Diss.*, §8, Ak. II, 395; 387.

[3] Letter to Herz, Ak. X, 130; 71.

[4] *Diss.*, §4, Ak. II, 393; 385. "Law inherent in the mind" translates *lex quaedam menti insita*. Kant never rejects this innatism, which is not an innatism of representations, but of *faculties* or representational capacities, involving sensible forms (dependent on the receptive, sensible faculty) as much as the categories (dependent on the spontaneous, intellectual faculty: cf. *Diss.*, 8).

conceivable relation to objects": "Thus the *passive* or sensible representations have an understandable relation to objects, and the principles that are derived from the nature of our soul have an understandable validity for all things insofar as those things are supposed to be objects of the senses."[5]

The second possible case of correspondence between a representation and its object is when the representation creates the object that it represents: "In the same way, if that in us which we call 'representation' were *active* with regard to the *object*, that is, if the object itself were created by the representation (as when divine cognitions are conceived as the archetypes of things), the conformity of these representations to their objects could be understood." In this case, the "conformity" would not just be the regular correspondence of the effect (the object) to its cause (the representation), but also, to one degree or another, the resemblance of the object to the representation that is its archetype.

Kant concludes that we are then able to understand the agreement between a representation and its object both in the case of an *intellectus archetypus*, such as the divine intellect, and in the case of an *intellectus ectypus* such as the human intellect, in which sensible representations are caused by the objects affecting the senses and give rise in turn to logically coherent empirical concepts.[6] But the problem posed by the "pure intellectual concepts" allowed by the *Dissertation* is that they do not correspond to either of these two cases. They do not emerge from the objects of the senses by comparison and abstraction, nor do they create their object, since they are not concepts of an *intellectus archetypus*, but of our finite understanding.

Therefore the pure concepts of the understanding must not be *abstracted* from sense perceptions, nor must they express the receptivity of representations through the senses; but though they must have their origin in the nature of the mind, they are neither caused by the *object* nor bring the object itself into being. In my *Dissertation* I was content to explain the nature of intellectual representations in a merely negative

---

[5] Letter to Herz, Ak. X, 130; *Corr.*, 71.

[6] One might be surprised that Kant, in the letter, should seem to consider only the problem of the agreement of *sensations* with given objects, and not that of the agreement of *empirical concepts* with given objects. But this is because the doctrine of the *Dissertation* appears to be sufficient concerning empirical concepts: all that is required of them is that their formation should not lead to contradictory judgments, or there must always be agreement between the predicate and the subject of empirical judgments. The agreement of concepts with *things* can, for its part, only be mediate: it is mediated by the (causal) agreement with things of the sensations and intuitive (spatiotemporal) sensible representations from which the concepts are then formed: see *Diss.*, II, §11: "[Insofar as phenomena] are sensory concepts or apprehensions, they are, as things caused, witnesses to the presence of an object, and this is opposed to idealism. Consider, however, judgments about things which are sensitively cognized. Truth in judging consists in the agreement of a predicate with a given subject. But the concept of a subject, insofar as it is a phenomenon, would be given only through its relation to the sensitive faculty of cognizing, and it is in accordance with the same relation that predicates would be given which were sensitively observable. It is, accordingly, clear that representations of a subject and a predicate arise according to common laws; and they thus furnish a foot-hold for cognition which is in the highest degree true" (Ak. II, 397; 389).

way, namely, to state that they were not modifications of the mind brought about by the object. However, I silently passed over the further question of how a representation that refers to an object without being in any way affected by it can be possible.[7]

Kant rejects divine guarantee as a solution, finding it riddled with both a vicious circle and empty mysticism.[8] One might then expect him to hold fast to the only relation between representation and object that he found comprehensible with regard to our finite understanding: the causal determination of our minds by external things. One might accordingly expect him to deny, in the end, the possibility of any "pure intellectual concept." But it is clear from what follows in Kant's letter that for him such a move is out of question. He announces that he is about to establish a classification of pure concepts inspired by "a few fundamental laws of the understanding." He evidently has no doubt as to the possibility of such "purely intellectual" concepts, and this seems to indicate that he is also on the verge of proposing a solution to the problem of the relation of such concepts to given objects.

Kant's definitive statement of the principle for this solution is to be found in section 14 of the Transcendental Deduction of the Categories, in 1781. This principle depends on the radical change in the formulation of the problem that I shall now explain.

Section 14 of the Transcendental Deduction of the Categories, and the Internalization, within Representation, of the Relation between Representation and Its Object

In section 14 of the Transcendental Deduction, Kant formulates alternatives analogous to those he stated in the Letter to Herz. But his vocabulary has changed. He no longer speaks of a causal relation between the object and the representation, but of a relation where the former "makes [the latter] possible," or conversely, where the latter "makes [the former] possible." Now, this shift from causality to conditions of possibility is only a manifestation of a more fundamental shift: Kant is no longer examining the relation of two heterogeneous elements (one "within" and the other "outside" representation), but the relation of two elements both internal to representation.[9] We are thus no longer faced with an alternative

[7] Letter to Herz, Ak. X, 130; 72.

[8] Ibid., Ak. X, 132; 74.

[9] This might mean one of two things. (1) The object now considered is an independently existing object, but considered "as" object-of-representation, that is, "as" it appears to a cognitive subject. What I call here "internalization of the object to representation" would then simply mean internalization to the point of view of (human) representing subjects. Such an interpretation would be sympathetic to Allison's interpretation and defense of Kant's transcendental idealism as an elucidation of "epistemic conditions," that is, of universal conditions under which cognition of objects is possible: see Allison, *Idealism*, chap. 1; (2) The object now considered is *internal to (mental) representation itself*: appearances are "mere representations," that is, *mental* intentional correlates of our representational capacities and activities. As most commentators have noted, Kant's expressions, when he talks, in the *Critique*, of the objects of experience, or appearances, as opposed to things in themselves, sometimes encourage the first interpretation (most notably in the B preface to the *Critique of Pure*

between two causal relations opposite in direction, but with the cooperation of two complementary relations, which together constitute the "relation of a representation to its object." Reformulating the problem in this way, Kant has already set the terms of its solution.

There are only two possible cases in which a synthetic representation and its objects can establish connection, relate to one another with necessity and, as it were, meet one another: either if the object alone makes the representation possible, or the representation the object [*entweder wenn der Gegenstand die Vorstellung, oder diese den Gegenstand allein möglich macht*]. In the former case, this relation is only empirical, and the representation is never possible *a priori*. This is true of appearances, as regards that in them which belongs to sensation. In the latter case, representation in itself does not produce its object insofar as *existence* is concerned, for we are not speaking here of its causality by means of the will. Nonetheless the representation is *a priori* determinant of the object, if it be the case that only through the representation is it possible to *cognize* anything *as an object*. (A92/B125–26, translation modified)

The first of the two relations concerns the case in which "the object makes the representation possible": "such is the case with appearances with regard to what in them belongs to sensation." This "case" is ambiguous: must "appearances, with regard to what in them belongs to sensation" be considered as the *representations* "made possible" by the object, or as the *objects* "making [the representation] possible"? Both interpretations are plausible. In fact, Kant's ambiguity might be deliberate. The first reading, in which appearances are "*representations* made possible by the object" (with regard to what in them belongs to sensation), recalls the doctrine of the Transcendental Aesthetic: we have representations of objects only insofar as the latter "affect the mind in a certain manner"; sensation is the "effect of an object on the representational capacity inasmuch as we are affected by it," and appearances, the "matter" of which is constituted by "what corresponds to sensation," are "mere modifications of our sensible intuition" (in the forms of our receptivity, space, and time).[10] The appearance, "as to what in it

---

Reason: see Bxxvi–xxviii), sometimes the second (see, e.g., A372–73, A491–92/519–20). I think the overall evidence is in favor of the second interpretation: objects "as" objects-of-representation are appearances "in us," either as "undetermined objects of empirical intuition" or as appearances moreover "determined under concepts" (phenomena). This view is not incompatible, in fact, with Kant's formulations in the B preface cited in favor of the first interpretation: Kant can say that the very same things that "as" things in themselves, exist outside us, appear to us only "as" appearances, *namely by means of representations "in us."* We should then conclude that Kant's conception of perception is an indirect realist one (things do exist in themselves outside us, but we perceive them only by means of states of consciousness in us) combined with what he calls a "formal idealism," namely the view that space and time are *nothing but* ways in which we intuit things, and nothing outside our way of intuiting them. Needless to say, I am here anticipating much more than I should explanations I shall give in more detail in the course of this book. I would like at least to give an idea of what I mean by "internalization within representation." I mean that in Kant's reasoning in §14 of the Deduction the object is considered "as" object-of-representation *and*, as such, it is the intentional correlate of states of consciousness "in us." This will become clearer, I hope, in the detailed explanation I now proceed to give.

[10] Cf. Transcendental Aesthetic, §1 (A19–20/B33–34), §8 (A46/B63).

belongs to sensation," may then be described as a *representation* made possible by the *object* that affects our representational capacity. On this reading, the "object" with which we start is thus still an object "outside representation," and the relation described remains close to the first alternative stated in the Letter to Herz. But the very notion of a causal connection has been put into question, and indeed as a result of the Transcendental Deduction Kant will be led to exclude any cognitive use of the categories (and thus of the concept of cause) beyond the realm of appearances. This explains the cautious formulation he adopts here, as opposed to what he allowed himself to say in the *Dissertation*: now the object is said to "make [the representation] possible" rather than being described as its "cause," to which, as an effect, the representation would "conform."

But this is not the only possible interpretation of the relation considered here (where the object "makes possible" the representation). True, the Transcendental Aesthetic has to start with the reference to an object in itself as the ground of all representation—since it describes our capacity for intuitions as merely "receptive," thus not possibly the source of its own representations. However, the problem of the "relation of a synthetic representation to its objects" as stated in the Transcendental Analytic no longer involves any direct relation to an object *outside representation*. Since Kant established in the Transcendental Aesthetic that an object is present to our representation only insofar as it "affects us in a certain manner," the object he discusses in the Transcendental Deduction of the Categories is no longer the object "in itself," but the object of *a sensible intuition*, or the appearance. The problem of the "relation of a synthetic representation to its objects" can then be posed only in relation to this object "as appearance."[11]

If this is so, one may interpret the relation in which "the object makes the representation possible" in a new way. Appearances, "with regard to what in them belongs to sensation," are now themselves the *objects* that "make possible" certain "synthetic representations"—for example, representations of succession, juxtaposition, constant conjunction, and maybe even of causal connection. In such a case, the relation of such synthetic representations to their object "would always be empirical, and the representation would never be possible *a priori*." If the con-

---

[11] Vaihinger gives a detailed account of the difficulties raised by the fact that Kant admits an object "affecting sensibility" at the beginning of the Transcendental Aesthetic, and then restricts all talk of objects to *appearances*, namely to what is *given in sensibility*. He recounts the various attempts, in post-Kantian philosophy (particularly on the part of Maïmon, Fichte, and later the Neo-Kantians), to rid Kant's philosophy of such a presupposition, which was deemed incompatible with the results of the Transcendental Analytic (cf. *Commentar*, II, 26–55). There is no doubt that Kant himself never gave up this presupposition, even if the conclusions of the Transcendental Analytic doom any characterization of the relation between the object "considered in itself" and our representational capacities to remain problematic. One main objection to Kant's talk of things in themselves is the apparent incoherence of the notion of "affection" by a thing in itself. Affection seems to be precisely the kind of causal notion Kant, on his own critical teaching, should not allow himself to use in such a context. I shall argue in what follows that a minimal meaning *can* be given to the notion of "affection" in the case of things in themselves: to say that we are "affected" by things in themselves is merely to say that things in themselves are a condition for representation "external" to our representational capacities (where "external" has no spatial meaning but is a mere "concept of reflection" associated to the logical form of hypothetical judgment: see chapter 6).

cept of cause was "made possible" by appearances in this way, no other universality would be possible for it than "comparative" universality, as Kant said earlier, at the end of section 13 of the Transcendental Deduction.[12]

In such an interpretation the relation in which "the object makes the representation possible" is indeed internal to the very realm of representation. It is no longer a causal relation between things existing "in themselves" and (mental) representations, but a relation between appearances as ("internalized") objects of empirical intuition and representations formed by what Kant called in the *Dissertation* "the logical use of the understanding," that is by discursive reflection on what is given in sensibility. Objects (appearances) are said to "make possible" synthetic representations, but not to "cause" them, because they are necessary but not sufficient conditions of such representations; for these representations to be formed, mental activities must process the appearances. It will suffice for now to say that these mental activities are discursive activities of comparison and generalization.

Now, consideration of these acts of the mind explains the second case of the relation between representation and object Kant considers: the case in which "the representation makes the object possible." In this second case, "representation in itself does not produce its object insofar as *existence* is concerned, for we are not here speaking of its causality by means of the will. Nonetheless the representation is *a priori* determinant of the object, if it be the case that only through the representation is it possible to *know* anything *as an object*" (A92–93/B125).

The relation considered here no longer has anything in common with the second term of the alternative stated in the Letter to Herz. The object is an object-of-representation which representation alone "makes possible," not in its existence (which continues to be dependent on the presence of an in-itself outside representation), but in its character as a represented object. But this clause presupposes a new meaning of the term "representation" itself. Representation here is no longer a *result* (as the synthetic representations "made possible by the object" were in the previous case), but an *act* of representation, or at least a *disposition to* represent. If representation is considered in this way, one may say that the object (e.g., the *appearance* that in the previous case "made possible" representation) is possible only if there is a representation or "disposition to representation," which constitutes it *as* an object of representation: the preposition *as* signals the internalization of the object within the representation. But perhaps, then, the disposition to representation has its own characteristics that determine the features of the object "as" internalized within representation.

In the Transcendental Aesthetic, Kant offered the first example of such a dependence of the object "as" represented object, on our disposition to representation: the object, Kant there said, is made possible "as" appearance by our *receptive* capacity for representations, of which space and time are the *forms*. And in

---

[12] A91–92/B124: "Appearances do indeed present cases from which a rule can be obtained according to which something usually happens, but they never prove the sequence to be *necessary*. . . . This strict universality of the rule is never a characteristic of empirical rules; they can acquire through induction only comparative universality, that is, extensive applicability."

section 14, Kant again refers to these forms as the first illustration of the case where "representation alone makes the object possible":

> Now there are two conditions under which alone the cognition of an object is possible, first, *intuition*, through which it is given, though only as appearance. It is evident from the above that the first condition, namely, that under which alone objects can be intuited, does actually lie *a priori* in the mind as the ground of the objects considered in their form. All appearances necessarily agree with this formal condition of sensibility, since only through it can they appear, that is, be empirically intuited and given. (A92–93/B125)

Space and time, being forms of receptivity, impart spatial and temporal character to appearances because through them alone the object is possible "as" appearance: as "the undetermined object of an empirical intuition."[13]

But intuition, or the *capacity for* sensible intuition, is only the first of the "two conditions under which the cognition of an object is possible." When Kant, in the text quoted previously, writes that "the object is given, *but only as appearance*," this restrictive formula may first be intended to distinguish the appearance from the object in itself, outside all representation, and thus to restrict spatial and temporal forms to appearances or "indeterminate objects of empirical intuition." But it is also intended to distinguish, *within the realm of representation*, between the object "only as" appearance and the object "as" object. In other words, it is intended to distinguish the object that might be called "preobjective" (the indeterminate object of empirical intuition, prior to any distinction between the representation and the object of representation) from the "objective" object, or the object "corresponding to" intuition. For this distinction to be possible, and therefore "for the cognition of an object *as object*," a second type of representation is required: concepts. We must now consider this second condition, which I omitted in the preceding quotation: "There are two conditions under which alone the cognition of an object is possible, firstly *intuition*, by which the object is given, but only as appearance; *secondly* concept, *by which an object which corresponds to this intuition is thought.* (The emphasis mine; Kant emphasizes "concept," as he had previously emphasized "intuition.")

The distinction between the object "given in intuition, but only as appearance"

---

[13] This is Kant's definition of appearance in §1 of the Transcendental Aesthetic (A20/B34). An intuition is a "singular and immediate representation" (see *Jäsche Logic*, §1), as opposed to a concept that is a "general and reflected representation." Intuition is "singular" in that it relates to a single object. In what sense it is "immediate" is a matter of controversy (see Parsons, "Aesthetic," 64–66). I suggest that its "immediate" character means for Kant at least that intuition is the only representation that relates to an object *without the mediation of another representation* (unlike a concept, which in its cognitive use relates to an object only by the mediation of intuitions). "Undetermined" here means as yet undetermined *by concepts*. That space and time are forms *of our receptivity*, and thus imposed on appearances *by our own representational capacities*, is a thesis Kant already defended in the 1770 *Inaugural Dissertation*, and which he takes up again in the Transcendental Aesthetic. This is the core of Kant's transcendental idealism, and is also a matter of heated controversy (cf. note 9). Since my main objective in this chapter is to explain how Kant arrived at his guiding hypothesis concerning the relation of logical functions of judgment and categories, I shall not dwell on his explanation of space and time. It will be examined in some detail in chapter 8.

and the object "corresponding to intuition," which concepts alone allow one to *think*, was already present in the *Inaugural Dissertation*. Kant called the imme-diate object of sensible intuition *apparentia* and the object "corresponding to intuition," *phaenomenon*. He argued that in order to think an object correspond-ing to sensible intuition (an object distinct from the object immediately present to intuition, or *apparentia*), "the logical use of the understanding" was required. Comparing our intuitions, we notice identities and differences, subsume our intu-itions under general concepts that are subordinated to one another, and thus dis-tinguish what Leibniz would have called the *phaenomena bene fundata* from mere appearances (*apparentiae*). Kant called *experience* the cognition of *phaeno-mena* by systematic discursive reflection on the *apparentiae*:

> But in the case of sensible things and phenomena [*phaenomenis*], that which pre-cedes the logical use of the understanding is called *appearance* [*apparentia*], while the reflective cognition, which arises when several appearances are compared by the understanding, is called *experience*. Thus, there is no way from appearance to expe-rience except by reflection in accordance with the logical use of the understanding. The common concepts of experience are called *empirical*, and the objects of experi-ence are called *phenomena* [*phaenomena*], while the laws both of experience and generally of all sensitive cognition are called the laws of phenomena.[14]

This reminder from the *Dissertation* is helpful to understand the distinction Kant makes in section 14 of the Transcendental Deduction, between the object of intuition, that is, the object "as appearance," and the object "as object," or "cor-responding to intuition." The "concept by which an object is thought correspond-ing to intuition" is any of the empirical concepts formed by what Kant calls "reflection." These make it possible to distinguish between *apparentia* and *phaenomenon*, the object "simply as appearance" (the indeterminate object of an empirical intuition) and the object "as object," "corresponding to intuition." For example, informed by experience (the systematic comparison of our sensible intuitions), we recognize the shape seen from afar as an object (*phaenomenon*) that we thus think under the concept "tower," and which we thereby distinguish from the *apparentia* immediately present to our intuition (a rectangular shape of various shades of brown standing out on the surrounding horizon . . .).

---

[14] *Diss.*, §5, Ak. II, 394; 386. A distinction analogous to that made in the *Dissertation* between *apparentia* and *phaenomenon* occurs once in the *Critique*, and only in the first edition, in chapter 3 of the Transcendental Analytic (The Ground of the Distinction of All Objects in General into Phe-nomena and Noumena), A248–49: "*Erscheinungen, sofern sie als Gegenstände nach der Einheit der Kategorien gedacht werden, heißen Phaenomena.*" In the *Critique*, it is often necessary to rely on the context in order to determine whether by *Erscheinung*, Kant means *apparentia* or *phaenomenon*. Moreover, the distinction at A248–49 is not exactly that of the *Dissertation*, since Kant speaks not of "reflection in accordance with the logical use of the understanding," but of "unity in conformity with the categories." But in fact, these two ways of determining the *phaenomenon* are tightly linked. The new formulation in the *Critique* indicates the resolution of the problem overlooked by the *Disserta-tion*: how do we apply pure concepts of the understanding to given objects? The solution to this prob-lem is made possible, as we shall see, by the identification of the function of the understanding at work (1) in synthesis according to the categories, and (2) in "reflection in accordance with the logical use of the understanding" by which empirical objects are thought "as" objects.

One may then ask whether this capacity to represent the object no longer merely "as appearance" but "as object," also has a priori conditions, just as space and time, the forms of our receptivity, were a priori conditions for the capacity to represent the object "as appearance." If this were the case, then just as the object "as appearance" was made possible by the form of our disposition to represent in its *receptive* aspect, so would the object "as object" (distinguished from the appearance) be made possible by the form of our disposition to represent in its *active* aspect. This active aspect of our disposition to representation is manifest in what Kant called, in the *Dissertation*, the "logical use" of the understanding— that is, its use in the empirical generalization of our sensible representations. Precisely, Kant wants to examine the hypothesis that this role of a priori conditions for the representation of an object "as" object is held by the *categories*—by those pure concepts of understanding which have been in question as to their possibility ever since the Letter to Herz: "The question now arises whether *a priori* concepts do not also serve as antecedent conditions under which alone anything can be, if not intuited, yet thought as object in general. In that case all empirical cognition of objects would necessarily conform to such concepts, because only as thus presupposing them is anything possible as *object of experience*" (A93/B125–26).

THE "LOGICAL USE OF THE UNDERSTANDING"
AND THE CATEGORIES

The strategy of the Transcendental Deduction of the Categories now takes shape. The solution to the problem Kant posed in the Letter to Herz will consist in bringing together two aspects of the understanding that had remained separate in the *Dissertation*: on the one hand, the "laws of the mind" from which the pure concepts of understanding arise, and on the other hand, the "logical use of the understanding" in the subordination of sensible representations under "common concepts," a use by means of which "an object is thought for appearances." Kant indeed outlines such a solution in section 14 of the Transcendental Deduction: "The objective validity of the categories as *a priori* concepts rests, therefore, on the fact that, so far as the form of thought is concerned, through them alone does experience become possible. They relate of necessity and *a priori* to objects of experience, for the reason that only by means of them can any object of experience be thought" (A93/B126).

The term "experience" should be understood as it was defined in the *Dissertation*: "reflexive cognition, which arises when several appearances are compared by the understanding."[15] In the *Dissertation*, Kant argued that, on the one hand,

---

[15] The introduction to the *Critique* confirms this definition: "There can be no doubt that all our knowledge begins with experience. For how should our faculty of knowledge be awakened into action, did not objects affecting our senses partly of themselves produce representations, partly arouse the activity of our undertanding to compare these representations, and by combining or separating them, work up the raw material of the sensible impressions into *that knowledge of objects which*

we have empirical cognitions in which we generate our concepts inductively from experience and subordinate them to one another in accordance with the rules of the "logical use of the understanding"; and, on the other hand, we possess "pure concepts" arising from "the laws of the mind alone, when we reflect on the sensible." By means of these pure concepts, we make a "real use" of our understanding in metaphysics, that is, in an intellectual cognition proceeding by analysis of pure concepts alone. But pure concepts, he added, can also be applied to the sensible by means of the "logical use" of the understanding. In this way, concepts such as cause, substance, possibility, necessity could be applied to appearances.[16] The Letter to Herz puts each of these two uses of pure concepts into question. For it is difficult to see how concepts having their source in our intellect alone could be applied to given objects, no matter what kind of objects we consider, objects of pure intellect or appearances. But, Kant now suggests, if the "laws of the mind" from which the pure concepts of the understanding emerge are none other than the laws from which *its logical use* itself emerges, we might have the key to the problem of the relation of these concepts to objects. For every object of experience (every *phaenomenon* corresponding to our sensible intuition) is thought according to the rules of the "logical use" of the understanding (immediate subordinations, in judgments, and mediated subordinations, in syllogisms, of "common concepts"). If it can be shown that the pure concepts of the understanding are originally nothing other than the very functions of the understanding that generate *these very rules*, then the *phaenomena* will thereby be necessarily subject to them.

---

is entitled experience?" (B1, my emphasis). Kant never abandons this definition, but following the Transcendental Deduction of the Categories, completes it in this way: experience presupposes a synthesis of perceptions according to the categories (A177/B218–19). The first definition is open to several interpretations, a rationalist one (in which the function of the understanding is to make clear intelligible connections that are confusedly perceived in the sensible given), a moderate empiricist one "*à la* Locke" (in which the understanding is considered as abstracting general concepts from the sensible given), and a skeptical-empiricist one "*à la* Hume" (in which the concepts of understanding are only the generalized idea of the connections of imagination). By grounding the possibility of any discursive combination of sensible representations on the prior synthesis of perceptions in conformity with the categories, Kant shuts off all of these interpretations, and replaces them with his own, grounded by the *Critique*. The *Critique* starts with the first definition of experience stated previously, the one that is relatively neutral (open to multiple interpretations); its completion by A177/B218, also stated previously, is what requires a proof.

[16] One may object that in §12 of the *Dissertation*, Kant writes "*Thus there is a science of sensory things*, although, since they are phenomena, *the use of the understanding is not real but only logical*" (Ak. II, 398; 390; second emphasis mine. The first is Kant's). However, that does not mean we cannot, according to the *Dissertation*, apply the pure concepts of the understanding to appearances, but just that we may do so only through the logical use of the understanding, which subordinates our various empirical concepts to one another until they are eventually also subsumed under the pure concepts of understanding. Section V of the *Dissertation*, devoted to delimiting the usage of sensitive cognitions and intellectual cognitions, specifically indicates that it is illegitimate to attribute a predicate including a sensible condition to an object "in itself," but on the other hand it is perfectly legitimate to attribute intellectual concepts to sensible objects (cf. §25–30). Furthermore, section III ("On the Principles of the Form of the Sensible World") applies pure concepts to appearances (cf., e.g., §14.5, in which appearances are determined as *substances* and *accidents*).

But this first step toward a possible solution is not sufficient. For the suspicion applying to the "pure concepts" can be transferred to the "logical use of the understanding" itself: why should appearances conform to it? Why would the application of the logical forms of our discursive thinking to appearances not be completely arbitrary? Or again—retreating to skeptical empiricism—how could one claim it does more than result from the same subjective tendencies born of imagination and habit, which Hume viewed as the source of the idea of causality? If the solution proposed is to be at all plausible, something *in the nature of appearances themselves* must make them agree with the forms of the logical use of the understanding and, if the categories are originally nothing else but the logical functions according to these forms, with the categories. It must therefore be shown that these functions are not only conditions of the subordination of concepts according to logical use, but conditions *of the very presentation of appearances in sensible intuition*, a presentation that generates for these appearances objects reflected under concepts. This is precisely the solution announced in section 14 as the "principle of the transcendental deduction of all *a priori* concepts":

> The transcendental deduction of all *a priori* concepts has thus a principle according to which the whole enquiry must be directed, namely, that they must be recognized as *a priori* conditions of the possibility of experience, *whether of the intuition which is to be met with in it, or of the thought.* Concepts which yield the objective ground of the possibility of experience are for this very reason necessary. (A94/B126, my emphasis)

Thus what I have called "the internalization within representation" of the relation between the representation and the object enabled Kant to reformulate the problem of the relation between pure concepts of the understanding and given objects. And this reformulation sketches the path to a possible solution. The paradox, however, is that this solution, whose proof is supposed to be given in the Transcendental Deduction of the Categories, is actually asserted *before* the transcendental deduction is achieved. Indeed, it is not only asserted in the introduction to the Transcendental Deduction proper (section 14, which I just quoted), but even as early as the metaphysical deduction of the categories, in section 10 of the Transcendental Analytic.

In this very complex section, Kant justifies the parallelism between the table of the categories and that of the logical forms of judgment by asserting that "the same function" presides over the unity of concepts in a judgment on the one hand, and the a priori unity of the sensible given "universally represented" by the categories on the other. This assertion is itself the culmination of a series of earlier assertions, each of which Kant will attempt to demonstrate in the Transcendental Deduction of the Categories. First, Kant asserts that prior to any concept, a synthesis (combination) of the manifold of a priori sensible intuition is necessary (paragraphs 1 and 2 of section 10): this will be argued for in the exposition of the "threefold synthesis" in the A Deduction, and restated more briefly at the beginning of the B Deduction.[17] Second, Kant asserts that the unity of this synthesis is

---

[17] A99–110 (the "threefold synthesis" in the A Deduction), B129–31 (§15 in the B Deduction).

represented by the a priori concepts, the categories (paragraphs 3, 4, and 5 of section 10): a proof for this assertion will be expounded in both versions of the Transcendental Deduction.[18] Last, Kant asserts that these concepts are none other than the functions of unity in judgment applied to the a priori synthesis of the manifold of intuition (paragraph 6): this is to be shown in sections 19 and 24 of the Transcendental Deduction in the B edition. But the original identity of categories with logical functions of judgment remains unrestated in the A edition. This is, in my view, the main reason why Kant rewrote his deduction for the B edition.

Now these successive theses lead up to the exposition of the parallelism between the table of categories and the table of judgments. It seems therefore that in stating this parallelism Kant already presupposes the transcendental deduction of the categories. Conversely, in the transcendental deduction he assumes from the outset that the logical functions of judgment and the pure concepts of the understanding are originally the same, and he seems to hold the mere parallelism of the two tables to be a sufficient argument for this assumption.

There may well be room to deplore the extreme difficulty occasioned for us by Kant's circular presentation of an argument which is already difficult enough to follow. Yet we must acknowledge that Kant's method here agrees with his announcement in the second preface to the *Critique* that "reason has insight only into that which it produces after a plan of its own" (Bxiii). Before attempting his transcendental deduction of the categories, Kant asserts that the "pure concepts of the understanding" depend on the same "laws of the understanding" as the logical forms of judgment do. This assertion, which solves the major difficulty Kant discovered in his *Dissertation*, is expounded before being justified and fully explained. This is also why the parallelism of the categories and the logical forms of judgment is asserted in the metaphysical deduction only as a "guiding thread" or a "clue" (*Leitfaden*). It will be justified as a genuine identity of the "function of the understanding" at work in the synthesis of the sensible and in the logical forms of judgment only after the transcendental deduction of the categories has been completed.[19]

---

[18] Particularly point 4 of the second section, and all of the third section, in the A Deduction (A110–28); §20–23 in the B Deduction.

[19] Most commentators have acknowledged the fact that §10 anticipates the Transcendental Deduction of the Categories. Adickes speculated that the first five paragraphs of this section were probably added after the fact, and that the initial version of the section had begun directly by stating the functional identity between the logical forms of judgment and the categories (para. 6, A79/B105; cf. Adickes, *Kritik*, 119n). Without going as far as granting such a hypothesis, De Vleeschauwer describes the construction of this section as "defective and unbalanced," and suggests that one go straight from §9 ("The Logical Form of the Understanding in Judgments") to para. 6 of §10 ("The same function . . .": see De Vleeschauwer, *Déduction*, II, 70–71). In my opinion, this is making short shrift of the real source of the difficulty, which resides in Kant's method. Heidegger is closer to the truth when he asserts that at that point of the Transcendental Analytic, it is too early for the categories to be derived from the logical functions of judgment, and that the idea of a *mere guiding thread* attached to the statement of the parallelism should be taken literally (Heidegger, *Kant*, §12). I disagree with him, however, when he goes so far as to claim that the origin of the categories is not in the logical functions of judgment at all. To my mind, the metaphysical deduction announces, with the parallelism of the two tables, an original identity of the categories and the logical functions, for which the transcendental deduction must provide the proof and completed explanation.

Synthesis

The most important term in section 10 of the Transcendental Analytic is "synthesis." It is defined right at the opening of the section:

> Space and time contain a manifold of pure *a priori* intuition, but at the same time are conditions of the receptivity of our mind—conditions under which alone it can receive representations of objects, and which therefore must also always affect the concept of these objects. But if this manifold is to be cognized, the spontaneity of our thought requires that it be gone through in a certain way, taken up, and connected. This act I name *synthesis*.
>
> By *synthesis*, in its most general sense, I understand the act of putting different representations together, and of grasping [*begreifen*] what is manifold in them in one cognition. Such a synthesis is *pure*, if the manifold is not empirical but is given *a priori*, as is the manifold in space and time. (A77/B102–3)

Here Kant clearly indicates that the conception of *synthesis* he intends to expound is inseparable from the doctrine of space and time he put forth in the Transcendental Aesthetic. Now, the term "synthesis" is related to a model of thinking whose fruitfulness has engaged Kant ever since his precritical writings: mathematical thinking.[20]

The first significant occurrence of the term "synthesis" is in Kant's 1764 *Preisschrift: Inquiry Concerning the Distinctness of the Principles of Natural Theology and Morality*, in the context of a discussion of the difference between mathematical and philosophical thinking. Mathematics, Kant writes, forms its concepts arbitrarily by the synthesis of simple concepts, whereas philosophy can proceed only by the analysis of complex concepts, whose confusedly perceived marks it must make clear.[21]

To be sure, the *synthesis* that Kant held to form mathematical concepts is quite different from the synthesis discussed at the beginning of section 10 of the Tran-

[20] Strawson neglects this aspect of the notion of synthesis, when he declares it to be foreign to a transcendental procedure understood as an analysis of experience, and argues that it falls under the "completely imaginary" procedure of a transcendental psychology (*Bounds of Sense*, 32). There is no doubt that synthesis is a psychological notion, in that it refers to a mental act. But the psychological aspect of the notion is inseparable from its epistemological aspect, and from the context of a logical investigation in which the model of synthesis is the counterpart of that of analysis. On his part, Hoppe, who defends the psychological dimension of Kant's transcendental procedure against Strawson, interprets the notion of synthesis in terms of a phenomenologically inspired psychology (in which transcendental synthesis is the originary act of thinking by which we relate ourselves to the world in general), and sees it as the instrument of a polemic against empiricist associationism (*Synthesis*, esp. 82–112). I shall try to show that even when the polemic against associationism is indeed in the foreground, namely when Kant puts forth the "threefold synthesis" in the A Deduction, the mathematical model is constantly present (cf. chapter 2).

[21] *Deutlichkeit*, §§1, 2, Ak. II, 276–79; 248–51. This text is the answer to the 1763 prize question of the Berlin Academy (therefore its usual designation as *Preisschrift*), which bore on the respective evidence of mathematical and metaphysical truths, most particularly theological and moral truths. Gottfried Martin provides an illuminating account of the terms *analysis* and *synthesis*, starting with

scendental Analytic (in the A edition): the issue in the *Preisschrift* is not the combination of a sensible manifold, but the discretionary combination of concepts in the understanding. Thus Kant conceives of synthesis on the model of a Leibnizian-type combinatoric. Similarly, the idea that the clarity and simplicity of mathematical concepts allow sensible signs to be used in order to display their combinations is of Leibnizian inspiration. Nonetheless, this text contains the first seed of the critical use of the mathematical model of synthesis.

This model acquires a new significance in the *Inaugural Dissertation*, where the discretionary combination or composition of concepts in mathematics becomes inseparable from the generation of their object in pure sensible intuition. This anticipates the use of the term "synthesis" characteristic of section 10 of the Transcendental Analytic: "synthesis" no longer means only the combination of concepts for the arbitrary formation of a complex concept, but also the composition of a manifold given in the a priori forms of sensible intuition. According to the *Dissertation*, it is by means of such a composition that the concept of number, but also all mathematical concepts, insofar as they are always concepts of quantities, are formed: "And we can make the *quantity* of space itself intelligible only by expressing it numerically, having related it to a measure taken as a unity. This number itself is nothing but a multiplicity which is distinctly known by counting, that is to say, by successively adding one to one in a given time."[22]

However, this composition is not yet called "synthesis." Kant does not call it so until the *Critique*, where he then goes on to distinguish combination by *composition* and combination of the empirical manifold by *nexus*, under the regulation of dynamical categories.[23] But in the *Dissertation*, Kant uses the term "synthesis" only to elucidate (in section 1) the concept "world," namely, the combination of individual substances into a whole. The concept "world" is to be thought either by the pure intellect ("intelligible world") or under the spatiotemporal conditions of sensible intuition ("sensible world"). But we can already make out the relation of parentage between the synthesis that generates an object for the concept of world, and the synthesis that generates a manifold under the guidance of a mathematical concept. Indeed the former is called *quantitative* synthesis, whether it is purely intellectual or realized under sensible conditions. And it is thereby distinguished from *qualitative* synthesis, the *synthetic method* of the ancients.[24] Moreover, the quantitative synthesis of the concept of world *under sensible conditions* is expressly viewed as similar to the synthesis governed by mathematical concepts. Kant notes that one can no more complete such a synthesis than one can

the Euclidean distinction between analytic and synthetic method and then moving to its Cartesian and Leibnizian reformulations: see Martin, *Kant*, 245–312. The opposition Kant states in the *Preisschrift* between mathematical thinking, which generates its concepts synthetically, and philosophical thinking, which proceeds only by analyzing given concepts, is present again in the *Critique*, in the Transcendental Doctrine of Method; but the *synthesis* of mathematical concepts is then inseparably linked, not only to the use of sensible signs but, more important, to the *construction* of concepts, that is, to their presentation in a priori sensible intuition (A713/B741–42).

[22] *Diss.*, §15, Ak. II, 406; 399–400.
[23] Cf. A162/B201n.
[24] *Diss.*, §1n, Ak. II, 388; 378n.

generate an infinite number, since the generation of the manifold may in both cases be pursued indefinitely.[25]

In the Letter to Herz of February 21, 1772, when discussing the difficulty of relating the pure concepts of the understanding to given objects, Kant notes that mathematical thinking is free of this problem. Its concepts are a priori, and nevertheless related to objects without any difficulty. But this is so because mathematical objects, unlike the objects of metaphysics, are not given outside of thought but generated in pure intuition:

> If . . . *intellectual* representations depend on our inner activity, whence comes the agreement that they are supposed to have with objects—objects that are nevertheless not possibly produced thereby? And the axioms of pure reason concerning these objects—how do they agree with these objects, since the agreement has not been reached with the aid of experience? In mathematics this is possible, because the objects before us are magnitudes, and can be represented as magnitudes only because it is possible for us to produce their mathematical representations (by taking numerical units a given number of times). Hence the concepts of magnitudes can be spontaneous [*selbsttätig*], and their principles can be determined *a priori*. But in the case of relationships involving *qualities*—as to how my understanding may form for itself concepts of things completely *a priori*, with which concepts the things must necessarily agree, and as to how my understanding may formulate *real* principles concerning the possibility of such concepts, with which principles experience must be in exact agreement and which nevertheless are independent of experience—this question, of how the faculty of understanding achieves this conformity with the things themselves, is still left in a state of obscurity.[26]

Section 13 of the Transcendental Deduction offers the same contrast between mathematical concepts, which do not require a deduction for their a priori validity, and the pure concepts of the understanding, whose objective validity is difficult to justify:

> In geometry . . . the objects, so far as their form is concerned, are given, through the very cognition of them, *a priori* in intuition. In the case of the *pure concepts of the understanding*, it is quite otherwise; it is with them that the unavoidable demand for a transcendental deduction first originates. . . . Also, not being grounded in experience, they cannot, in *a priori* intuition, exhibit any object such as might, prior to all experience, serve as ground for their synthesis. (A87–88/B120)

The example of mathematics suggests at least that the possibility of a relation between pure concepts and given objects would become understandable if one presupposed that a relation existed between these concepts and appearances—a relation that would at least be comparable with, if not similar to, that found between mathematical concepts and their objects, which are generated by the successive addition of unit to unit in pure intuition—that is, by *synthesis* in the new

[25] Ibid., Ak. II, 389; 379n.
[26] Letter to Herz, Ak. X, 125–26; 72.

sense the term acquires after the *Dissertation*: not merely the discretionary combination of concepts in the understanding, but the combination of a sensible manifold *under the rule of a concept or even of a combination of concepts.*

My goal in this section was to show that the term "synthesis," as used in section 10 of the Transcendental Analytic, must be understood against the background of a very long maturing process in Kant's reflection on the model provided by mathematical thought. As for the relation announced, in the texts I quoted, between the synthesis of the sensible manifold and the categories, it will be understandable with some degree of clarity only when the transcendental deduction of the categories is completed. Here again, the preliminary exposition anticipates the results of a proof, which it only sketches out as a promise to be fulfilled.

SYNTHESIS AND JUDGMENT: THE TWO PATHS OF THE TRANSCENDENTAL DEDUCTION OF THE CATEGORIES

We have followed two lines of argument in Kant's attempt to resolve the problem of the categories. The first concerned what Kant calls, in the *Inaugural Dissertation*, "the logical use of the understanding," that is, the discursive subordination of empirically formed general concepts. Insofar as objects may be thought for intuitions (*phaenomena* for *apparentiae*) only by means of such subordination of concepts, the problem of the relation between the pure concepts of the understanding and empirical objects might be resolved by identifying pure concepts with the very functions of undertanding generating the forms of subordination of empirical concepts. A second line of argument then emerged, which concerned the theme of *synthesis*, associated with another model for the use of the understanding: the model of mathematics and its a priori generation of multiplicities, which may be represented as multiplicities of objects to be thought under concepts. Kant's programmatic exposition in section 10 of the Transcendental Analytic announces that the whole argument of the transcendental deduction of the categories will rest on the attempt to combine these two models: the model of generalizing reflection and the model of the a priori synthesis of the sensible manifold. Each of these two models should be called upon, in one way or another, to regulate *our very perception of appearances*, so that the eventual relation of a priori concepts to empirical objects may be thinkable.

In my opinion, the difficulty that Kant encountered in his attempt to correlate these two models of thinking (the discursive-reflective model of logic, the intuitive-constructive model of mathematics), the problem he encountered in explaining their respective relation to the constitution of our perception of objects, was the main reason why he rewrote the Transcendental Deduction. In the A Deduction, the model of synthesis is almost exclusively privileged over the logicodiscursive model. In the B Deduction, on the other hand, the logical form of judgment (and the a priori synthesis of the sensible given, *geared toward reflection according to the logical forms of judgment*) plays the decisive role. Thus the B deduction appears more likely than the A to clarify the relation of logical forms to sensible syntheses: precisely the relation Kant invoked in section 10 to justify the exposition of the table of categories according to the "guiding thread" of the table of logical forms of judgment. And yet, there are good reasons why we should follow Kant's advice, and view the A Deduction as a useful complement to the B Deduction.[27] First of all, granting the exposition of the "threefold synthesis" in the A Deduction the attention it deserves means considering the transcendental deduction on its proper terrain, which is Kant's confrontation with the empiricist conception of perception and its objects—specifically, with Hume's skeptical empiricism. Second, the mathematical model of *construction*, which Kant opposes to the empiricist model of the *association* of sensible representations, plays a key role in this confrontation, becoming more prominent as one progresses from the first to the third of the "syntheses" expounded in A.

This prevalence of the mathematical model is both a strength and a weakness in Kant's argument. It is a strength because it emphasizes the continuity between the Transcendental Analytic and the Transcendental Aesthetic, between the doctrine of the categories and the doctrine of space and time as forms of intuition. It is a strength also because, by linking the transcendental deduction of the categories to Kant's longtime reflection on the nature of mathematical thought, it makes clear that the exposition of the "threefold synthesis" is not just a psychological argument (the description of mental acts), but also an epistemological one (the analysis of a specific mode of cognition). But the predominence of the mathematical model is also a weakness, because the particular solution it provides to the problem of the relation of a concept to its object is not adequate, as Kant himself pointed out in the Letter to Herz, to solve the specific problem Kant announces in sections 13 and 14 of the Transcendental Deduction: the problem of the relation between *a priori* concepts and *empirical* objects. However, this very weakness sheds light, by contrast, on the importance of the methodological change in the B Deduction, in which the main emphasis is placed on the logical form of judgment considered as the form of the relation of our representations to an *empirical* object.

In the following chapter, I will offer an analysis of the "threefold synthesis" in the A Deduction, in order to clarify precisely the strengths and weaknesses I just outlined, and thus the reasons for Kant's rewriting of the Transcendental Deduction. In chapter 3, I shall analyze the first few sections of the B Deduction, which mainly serve to introduce the core of the argument as Kant, on his own admission, reformulated it: the argument that explains how the logical forms of judgment are the forms of the "objective unity of self-consciousness," that is, the forms of a consciousness that is able to relate its representations to objects.

[27] Cf. Bxlii.

The "Threefold Synthesis" and the Mathematical Model

IN SECTION 10 of the Transcendental Analytic, Kant mentions only *one* synthesis of the manifold of intuition.[1] But the A Deduction introduces not one, but *three* acts of synthesis: the "synthesis of apprehension in intuition," the "synthesis of reproduction in imagination," and the "synthesis of recognition in a concept." Why this multiplication of syntheses? Notice first that the three elements "in" which there is an act of synthesis are representations, not faculties carrying out three distinct syntheses. The intuition "in which" there is synthesis of apprehension is what Kant defines elsewhere as a "singular and immediate representation," whose "matter," when the intuition is empirical, is sensation.[2] The imagination "in which" there is reproduction is not the imagination as a faculty or power (*Einbildungskraft*), but the *representation produced by* this faculty (*Einbildung*).[3] And finally, the concept "in which" there is synthesis of recognition is what Kant defines elsewhere as a "universal or reflected representation."[4] Kant's list of the three syntheses seems thus to follow the order of the empirical genesis of representations, from sensible impressions (apprehended in empirical intuition) to their representations in imagination, then from these to concepts. Considering these representations in sequence, Kant shows that each requires an act of empirical synthesis (respectively: of apprehension, of reproduction, of recognition). But, moreover, he shows that these acts of combination can contribute to the cognition of a *phaenomenon*, an object distinct from the "indeterminate object of empirical intuition" (*Erscheinung*), only if they all belong to one and the same act of synthesis of the spatiotemporal manifold. The form of this act is determined a priori by the nature of our mind, and its outcome is threefold: the manifold of intuition represented "as" manifold, the representation of imagination (*Einbildung*)

---

[1] A77/B102.

[2] For Kant's definitions of intuition and concept, cf. *Logik*, §1, Ak. IX, 91 (589). *KrV* A320/B377.

[3] Therefore translating *Einbildung* by *imagination* is somewhat confusing. The word *Einbildung* means the *representation* stemming from imagination, not imagination as a faculty: cf. Baumgarten, *Metaphysica*, §557, Ak. XV, 19: "Repraesentatio status mundi praeteriti, hinc status mei praeteriti, est phantasma (imaginatio, visum, visio)" [The representation of a past state of the world, and therefore of one of my past states, is [a] phantasm (imagination, vision)]. Kant adds "*Einbildung*" for "*phantasma*" in the margin. Cf. also Tetens,*Versuche*, I, 37: ". . . sensory representations recalled once again, which one calls phantasms or images [*Phantasmata oder Einbildungen* . . .]"; Kant, *Anthr.*, §28: "Imagination, insofar as it involuntarily generates images [*Einbildungen*], is called *phantasmagoria*" (Ak. VII, 167; 56). I shall generally translate Kant's *Einbildung* by *representation of imagination* but also sometimes, for short, by *imagination*. Image (which I used to translate *Einbildung* in the two citations in this note) has the shortcoming that it erases the strongly *active* connotation of the German *Einbildung*. Its proper German counterpart is not *Einbildung*, but *Bild*.

[4] See note 2.

emerging from empirical associations; and finally the universal representation or concept, under which particular representations are subsumed. This act is that very act of synthesis which Kant, in section 10, attributes to the imagination, in the A Deduction more precisely to *transcendental* imagination, and which in the B Deduction he calls *synthesis speciosa*, figurative synthesis.[5]

In the A Deduction, the "threefold synthesis" is expounded three times: first in what Kant presents as a mere propaedeutic to the Deduction properly speaking;[6] then in a brief exposition "descending" from the transcendental unity of self-consciousness to sensible intuition; and finally in a more detailed exposition "ascending" from sensible intuition to the transcendental unity of self-consciousness and thereby to the categories.[7] The mathematical model is mostly emphasized in the first exposition. Kant considers the three empirical syntheses ("in an intuition," "in a representation of imagination," "in a concept") successively and shows that each presupposes an act of "pure" synthesis, namely a synthesis of the pure forms of space and time, for which he gives examples taken from geometry or arithmetic (line, number, triangle). One should not make more of these examples than Kant himself claims for them: they serve the merely propaedeutic function of preparing the reader to understand Kant's argument about the categories. The transcendental deduction proper occurs only at the end of this preparatory exposition and is then repeated more completely in the two reexpositions of the argument. Proceeding in this way, Kant forces us to progress somewhat blindly at first, and to content ourselves with partial, incomplete glimpses into his argument. Nevertheless, this propaedeutic exposition remains the best introduction to what might be called the *theme of synthesis* in the transcendental deduction of the categories. Following this theme as it is gradually developed reveals the limits of the mathematical model on which it is built and hence Kant's reasons for making the *logical form of judgment* the heart of the transcendental deduction in the B edition.

I will now follow the three steps of the "threefold synthesis." I shall then analyze Kant's conception of the relation of concepts to objects, and the relation of both to the "transcendental unity of apperception." My goal, however, will not be to give a complete analysis of the transcendental deduction in the A edition. Rather, I shall use Kant's propaedeutic exposition in order to show what made it necessary for him to introduce more explicitly, in the B Transcendental Deduction, what we might call the "theme of judgment."

THE "SYNTHESIS OF APPREHENSION IN INTUITION"

Every intuition contains in itself a manifold which can be represented as a manifold only insofar as the mind distinguishes the time in the sequence of one impression upon another; for each representation, *insofar as it is contained in a single moment,*

[5] Cf. A78/B103, A118, B151.

[6] A98: "I have found it advisable in the four following passages rather to prepare than to instruct the reader."

[7] Cf. A116 ff. for the exposition starting from "pure apperception;" A119–24 for the exposition "starting from below."

can never be anything except absolute unity. In order that unity of intuition may arise out of this manifold (as is required in the representation of space) it must first be run through, and held together. This act I name the *synthesis of apprehension*. (A99)

Here we encounter again what I called earlier the *internalization* of the object of representation within representation. According to section 14 of the Transcendental Deduction of the Categories, the object was represented "as" appearance by its internalization within our receptivity and its forms; it was then represented "as" the object of the appearance by being reflected under concepts. We now witness an internalization that is, as it were, intermediate between these two. The manifold of intuition received in the forms of sensibility can be perceived "as" manifold only if an act of synthesis is added to receptivity. Thus, where British empiricists and, after them, the psychology textbooks of German *Schulphilosophie* considered the manifold of simple sensations as given, what Kant considers as immediately given is not a manifold of sensory atoms, but *indeterminate empirical intuitions*; the sensations or impressions constituting its "matter" are perceived "as" manifold only if they are actively *distinguished*.[8] This differentiating act presupposes in turn the *distinction of moments in time*, as the first sentence of the text indicates:

> Every intuition contains in itself a manifold *which can be represented as a manifold only insofar as the mind distinguishes the time in the sequence of one impression upon another* [my emphasis] [*wenn das Gemüt ... die Zeit in der Folge der Eindrücke aufeinander unterschiede*]; for each representation, insofar as it is contained in a single moment, can never be anything except absolute unity.

The time mentioned here is not that of a succession of impressions we might suppose to be given "in itself," prior even to the act of apprehension. The temporality we are dealing with here is generated by the very act of apprehending the manifold. As for the manifold of intuition thus generated "as" manifold, it is both the manifold of parts into which any spatial intuition may be divided, and (if the intuition is empirical) the manifold of the *sensory qualities* accessible to the different senses. This qualitative manifold is present in an undifferentiated manner in the *synopsis* of our sensible intuition,[9] before being apprehended "as" manifold

---

[8] The idea that an act of the mind is necessary for the apprehension of sensation itself is already present in Tetens, who distinguishes between sensation or *Empfindung*, and *Nachempfindung*. *Nachempfindung* alone is properly *representation*, which presupposes that the mind remarks or "reflects" sensation. This takes place in a time interval that varies according to the sensations considered (very short for the sensations of touch, longer for those of hearing or sight) (cf. *Versuche*, 32–33). Tetens refers to the capacity of the mind to form *Nachempfindungen* as *Fassungskraft* (*Versuche*, 105), and views it as the first seed of the activity of the imagination (157). The importance of Kant's reading of Tetens during his completion of the first *Critique* is well known (cf. De Vleeschauwer, *Déduction* I, 289–90). Nonetheless, relative to Tetens's *Fassung*, the "synthesis of apprehension" has a new meaning, since it generates not only the manifold of sensations "as" manifold, but also the very intuition of time, and since it shows itself to be, not a "weak" activity of the mind prior to the "stronger" activity of the imagination, but an essential aspect of this activity itself. I shall say more about Kant's views on time-consciousness in chapter 8.

[9] On this term, cf. A97: "As sense contains a manifold in its intuition, I ascribe it to a *synopsis*. But to such synopsis a *synthesis* must always correspond; *receptivity* can make cognition possible only when combined with *spontaneity*." For a very detailed analysis of the role Kant assigns to synopsis, see Waxman, *Model*, 218–25.

by the synthesis of apprehension that successively distinguishes the elements of our empirical intuition.[10]

But the act of apprehension is more than an act of *distinguishing*; from the outset it aims at *unifying what is distinguished*. This is what makes the manifold a manifold *of intuition*, of a singular representation: "In order that unity of intuition may arise out of this manifold (as is required in the representation of space) it must first be run through, and held together. This act I name the *synthesis of apprehension*." The "unity of intuition" might be that of any empirical intuition: the intuition, say, of a tree, of a house. But by mentioning "for example, the representation of space," Kant draws attention to the spatial character of any outer intuition and introduces his main thesis: the synthesis of apprehension unifies not only the empirical given, but also the "pure" manifold—the mere forms of space and time.

> This synthesis of apprehension must also be exercised *a priori*, that is, in respect of representations which are not empirical. For without it we should never have *a priori* the representations either of space or of time. They can be produced only through the synthesis of the manifold which sensibility presents in its original receptivity. We have thus a pure synthesis of apprehension.

Thus the manifold of sensations is engendered and unified *qua* manifold in the forms of space and time. The manifold of sensations, the starting point for empiricist accounts of the genesis of representations, is thus taken up into the form of a more fundamental manifold, a "pure form" of manifoldness that alone makes the sensible manifold perceivable *qua* manifold. Sensory elements are not a starting point but already themselves a result, in a continuous process of generating differentiated and conceptualizable representations. In what follows we shall see Kant pursue and amplify his encirclement of empiricist positions by showing that the psychological *data* empiricists assume depend themselves on operations empiricists cannot account for.

THE "SYNTHESIS OF REPRODUCTION IN A REPRESENTATION OF IMAGINATION"

> It is a merely empirical law, that representations which have often followed or accompanied one another finally become associated, and so are set in a relation whereby, even in the absence of the object, one of these representations can, in accordance with a fixed rule, bring about a transition of the mind to the other. (A100)

---

[10] Unlike De Vleeschauwer, I do not believe that it is contradictory to say on the one hand that, insofar as intuition is contained in a moment, it is "absolute unity," and on the other hand that it "contains a manifold." Every intuition, insofar as it is "contained in a moment," is absolute unity, that is, *undivided* unity, not the *unity of a manifold* apprehended "as such," which it can only become by means of the synthesis of apprehension. But it "contains a manifold" because what is given to our intuition is never absolutely *simple*. Space and time, the forms of our intuition, are infinitely divisible (*quanta continua*, as Kant explains in the Axioms of Intuition and the Anticipations of Perception. This point will be explained in part III, chapters 9 and 10). De Vleeschauwer is thus reduced to arguing that the "ab-

The "merely empirical law" stated here is the most important among the associative rules that the psychology textbooks present as rules of reproductive imagination.[11] Kant himself spends some time, in his *Anthropology*, explaining the rules of empirical association.[12] But in the context of the transcendental deduction his concern is less with association itself than with what it presupposes in the constitution of appearances. Appearances must conform to rules if they are to provide occasion for association:

> But this law of reproduction presupposes that appearances are themselves actually subject to such a rule, and that in the manifold of these representations a conjunction [*Begleitung*] or succession takes place in conformity with certain rules. Otherwise our empirical imagination would never find opportunity for exercise appropriate to its powers, and so would remain concealed within the mind as a dead and to us unknown faculty. (A100, translation modified)

The requirement stated here seems reasonable, and agrees to that extent with the doctrine of Hume or of any empiricist, skeptical or not, regarding the association of ideas: representations would not be associated if they had not first presented themselves in relations of constant conjunction or succession, "in conformity with a rule." There must, therefore, be a *given* regularity of representations if imagination is to apply its own rules of reproductive association. Kant gives a variety of examples, the most famous of which is that of cinnabar, its weight and its remarkable red color. If I had encountered this object as now red, now black, now light, now heavy, if in my past perceptions there had been no regular conjunction of the color and the weight, then my imagination would not now associate the red color that I see with the feeling of weight, and it would not induce me to think of the object that I call cinnabar in the presence of that color. Or, to mention another example which is probably an allusion to Hume's *Enquiry Concerning Human Understanding*, if on the longest day of the year the earth were now "covered with fruits," now "covered with ice and snow," the imagination would not associate the length of the days, the state of the climate, and that of the vegetation. In short, we would not form any notion of season.[13] Lastly, if no regular conjunction between words and sensible impressions had ever presented itself,

---

solute unity" discussed in the text I quoted is that of the impression itself as *simple* impression. But this means he identifies unity and simplicity and moreover attributes to Kant an atomism of sense data which in my opinion is quite foreign to him (cf. De Vleeschauwer, *Déduction*, II, 245).

[11] Cf. Hume, *Enquiry*, §3; Wolff, *Psychologia*, §104; Baumgarten, *Metaphysica*, §561; Tetens, *Versuche*, I, 108–9.

[12] Cf. Kant, *Anthr.*, §31*b* (Ak. VII, 176; 66).

[13] Cf. Hume, *Enquiry*, IV-2, 22: "Is there a more intelligible proposition than to affirm that the trees will flower in December and January, and will wither in May and June?" According to Hume, such a proposition is "intelligible," that is, it is not contradictory. The connection between the months of May and June and trees in flower is not a necessary connection founded on the principle of contradiction, but an association founded on a tendency of the imagination, which results from their repeated conjunction in the past. It is precisely this repeated conjunction that Kant insists on here, saying that regularly repeated conjunctions must have been given for the associations of the imagination to be exercised.

our associative imagination would not have any occasion to associate names with things, and all use of language would be impossible. "Nor could there be an empirical synthesis of reproduction, if a certain name were sometimes given to this, sometimes to that object, or were one and the same thing named sometimes in one way, sometimes in another, independently of any rule to which appearances are in themselves subject" (A101).

So far Kant has not departed in the slightest from a quite standard empiricist orthodoxy, whatever the variations might be when it comes to accounting for the source and nature of phenomenal regularities: Locke's realist account (it is reasonable to suppose that these regularities are to be correlated with real relations between the things that our ideas represent), Berkeley's phenomenalist account (these regularities are real uniformities in the combinations of our ideas as God has produced them in us), or Hume's skeptical account (these regularities are radically contingent and manifest nothing more than conjunctions among our impressions, which we have repeatedly witnessed in the past and expect, by a natural propensity of imagination, to see repeated in the future).

But Kant has his own program for explaining these phenomenal regularities: "There must then be something which, as the *a priori* ground of a necessary synthetic unity of appearances, makes their reproduction possible" (A101). I use the phrase "program for explaining" here, because the sentence I just cited can indeed state only a *program*, not a *conclusion*. Nothing that came before entitles Kant to *conclude* that the regularity of the "appearances themselves" reveals the presence of a "ground of a necessary synthetic unity." However, the program of a transcendental deduction of the categories as stated in section 14 could be fulfilled if one could find a ground for the phenomenal regularities that would relate them to "necessary synthetic unities." Such a ground would make it possible to counter Hume's skeptical doubt by considering some pure concepts of the understanding—for instance, that of causality, not as the empirical and contingent *result* but as the a priori and necessary *condition* of the associations of imagination. The clause "there must then be" should therefore read as meaning "let us then search if there is not," for—at least Kant is convinced of this—"there *must* be."

And indeed, we might have evidence that there is such an a priori ground:

What that something is we soon discover, when we reflect that appearances are not things in themselves but are the mere play of our representations, and in the end reduce to determinations of inner sense. For if we show that even our purest *a priori* intuitions yield no cognition save insofar as they contain a combination of the manifold such as renders a thoroughgoing synthesis of reproduction possible, then this synthesis of imagination is likewise grounded, antecedently to all experience, upon *a priori* principles; and we must assume a pure transcendental synthesis of imagination as conditioning the very possibility of experience. For experience as such necessarily presupposes the reproducibility of appearances. When I seek to draw a line in thought, or to think of the time from one noon to another, or even to represent to myself some particular number, obviously the various manifold representations that are involved must be apprehended by me in thought one after the other. But if I were

> always to drop out of thought the preceding representations (the first parts of the line, the antecedent parts of the time period, or the units in the order represented), and did not reproduce them while advancing to those that follow, a complete representation would never be obtained: none of the above-mentioned thoughts, not even the purest and most elementary representations of space and time, could arise. (A101–2)

This explanation is disconcerting for at least two reasons. The first is that Kant gives as ground for the given regularity of appearances, which must provide the occasion for their empirical reproduction, *another reproduction*, though a "pure" one, exercized not on empirical representations but on the successively synthesized elements of a line, a stretch of time, or a number. The second surprise is, instead of a ground for the empirical representation of *conjunction* and *succession* of sensible impressions (which causes them to be associated), we are given a ground for pure representations (line, time, and number), which are certainly insufficient to ground empirical relations of conjunction or succession.

Let us try the following explanation: Kant wants to show that for conjunction or succession to be present in appearances, an act of combination is necessary *prior* to the associative combinations made possible by repeatedly perceived conjunctions or successions. Now, just such an act is exemplified in our representations of "line, number, and time," and the act of combination is already itself an act of *reproduction*. But if a reproductive synthesis is necessary even to generate these representations, then some such synthesis is all the more necessary in order to perceive a succession and even a conjunction of empirical impressions, *prior to any associative reproduction* of that conjunction or that succession. Consider conjunction (*Begleitung*). As we saw with the *synthesis of apprehension*, it is one thing to have present to mind an intuition "containing a manifold," quite another to *apprehend this manifold "as" manifold*. This requires that "the time be distinguished" in which each impression is apprehended. But just as

> if I were always to drop out of thought the preceding representations (the first parts of the line, the antecedent parts of the time period, or the units represented one after the other), and did not reproduce them while advancing to those that follow, a complete representation would never be obtained: none of the above-mentioned thoughts, not even the purest and most elementary representations of space and time, could arise,

In the same way, if I were always to drop out of thought each of the impressions making up the apprehension of a piece of cinnabar or a human figure, I would never form the sensible intuition of a conjunction of impressions—that is, of the unity of a spatial manifold with its various sensory determinations. Therefore I would never form the representation of the conjunctions of impressions, and even less any *repetition* of these conjunctions, which alone can generate the associations of reproductive imagination. Similarly, consider now succession: in order to perceive that two or more representations (impressions or manifolds of impressions apprehended "as" manifolds) succeed each other, each of the elements of the succession must be reproduced as one goes on to the next. Otherwise, no succession and a fortiori no regularly repeated succession would be perceived: the empirical imagination would have no occasion to exercise its associative rules.

Before any associative reproduction, then, the *occasion* for empirical association must be present, that is, the particular form of combination of a phenomenal manifold and its regular repetition. The capacity for presenting such occasions for association manifests itself in its "pure" form in the mental act of drawing a line, representing a number, representing a stretch of time, which itself presupposes a reproduction of each of the elements of the complete representation. Here again, just as in the earlier presentation of the synthesis of apprehension, Kant uses the example of the synthesis of a *mathematical* representation as a model to present the capacity for *mentally constituting a distinct manifold of elements*, whether pure or empirical. True, the examples of line and number do not explain how specific representations of *empirical conjunction* or *succession* are possible. At this point in the argument, we are still far from being able to resolve such a problem, or even to formulate it adequately. For this we must await the Analogies of Experience in the System of Principles of Pure Understanding. But, at the very least, Kant here shows that for any representation of a manifold "as" manifold, it is not enough that the manifold be *given*. An act of mental synthesis analogous to that grounding elementary mathematical constructions is necessary: not only a synthesis of apprehension but also, "inseparably bound up with it," a synthesis of reproduction of each of the elements of an apprehended manifold, performed in order to constitute it as a complete series.

But the mathematical examples can be understood in a different way. Instead of being put in parallel to their empirical counterparts, they should serve to introduce the idea that the *aim to represent a whole* guides every associative reproduction of the imagination. What corresponds to the particular instances of cinnabar, of human figure, of a solstice day are then not the totality of the line, the number or the whole interval of time, but the *elements successively reproduced* in the synthesis of these representations as wholes. The reproduction of the parts of the line, the parts of time, or the numeric units is made necessary by the project of representing the whole line, the whole interval of time, or the number. The reproduction of the elements thus takes place only because the goal of the synthesis is the *representation of a whole* that guides the successive reproduction. One may likewise suppose that the implicit project of constituting *a whole of experience* is what drives us to reproduce the past representations of cinnabar, of a summer solstice, or of a human being when a manifold of impressions respectively analogous to each of them is presently affecting us. The reproduction of past representations *represented as such*, and *represented as belonging to one and the same series of successively reproduced elements*, occurs only if it is called forth by such a goal.

According to this second reading, the mathematical examples are not meant to show that for each singular intuition a reproduction of their manifold is necessary if the intuition itself is to be reproducible according to the associative laws of imagination. Rather, they are meant to show that every reproduction, whether empirical (the reproduction of past representations of cinnabar that we associate with the present representation of a red object) or "pure" (the reproduction of the units in an enumeration, the parts of the line, the parts of the stretch of time), presupposes a *totalizing project*. In the case of empirical reproductions, the goal is the constitution of experience as a whole. In the case of "pure" reproductions, it is the representation of the "time from one noon to another," of the line, or of the denumerated collection. On this reading, it remains true that the quantitative examples have a merely introductory and propaedeutic role, because generating the representation of a whole of experience is a more complex operation than generating a geometrical figure or a number. Indeed, at the beginning of the System of Principles, Kant will carefully distinguish between "mathematical" combination, which is constitutive of its object and arbitrarily produced, and "dynamical" combination, which is only regulative and produced under the condition of an empirical given.[14] But in the transcendental deduction he is not yet in a position to make such distinctions. I suggest that this is an important contributory factor to the obscurity of the argument of the A Deduction.

I have proposed two possible interpretations for the examples of pure synthesis of reproduction. According to the first interpretation, line, number, and interval of time are analogues for any singular intuition insofar as it contains a manifold that can be represented "as" manifold. According to the second interpretation, they are analogues for the *representation of a whole* that conditions all reproductive synthesis, whether empirico-associative or "pure." These two interpretations are not at all incompatible, since each makes the mathematical example the illustration of the conditions of *the intuition of a whole* as the *unity of a manifold*. Either the singular empirical intuition is itself considered as a whole in which the manifold must be apprehended "as" manifold, in which case the mathematical examples serve as a model for the apprehension of such a manifold; or the particular empirical intuition is a unit that may be reproduced in prospect of the constitution of a whole of experience, in which case the mathematical examples serve as models for the anticipation of the whole that is a condition for the reproduction of the particular intuitions. The parts of the line, the units successively synthesized in a number, the parts of time then are equivalent to the empirical units—the particular instances of cinnabar, of human figure, of summer solstice—which for their part can be reproduced to constitute a whole of experience. In both interpretations, the mathematical model serves only to introduce the idea that there are a priori conditions for the representation of an empirical *manifold*. But it is by no means sufficient to ground the possibility of empirically given *regularities* in the manifold.

The obvious difference between what Kant announces (an a priori ground of the associability of appearances) and what he delivers (an act of "pure" reproduction applied to the pure forms of space and time in which every manifold is represented) has confused and exasperated many commentators. Adickes maintained that the first paragraph of the Synthesis of Reproduction in Imagination, which concerns the empirical law of association, is a late interpolation, and that

---

[14] Cf. A160–61/B199–200; also A178–79/B221–22.

the continuity of the argument demands a direct move from the Synthesis of Apprehension in Intuition to the "pure" reproduction as expounded in the second paragraph of the Synthesis of Reproduction in Imagination. Kemp Smith adopted the contrary position and chose empirical association against pure reproductive synthesis, which is (according to him) a useless and confusing addition. De Vleeschauwer refused to allow himself the easy comfort of patchwork hypotheses, but granted the difficulty of relating the two aspects of reproduction considered by Kant.[15] In my opinion, the only way out of this difficulty is to acknowledge that at this point in the argument, Kant does not set out to furnish the ground needed for the associability of appearances but only to indicate a first step in establishing such a ground. In the Synthesis of Recognition, he will show that the "associability" of the empirical given depends on a transcendental synthesis of imagination considered not just as a *reproductive* synthesis whose pure form is the reproduction of pure spatiotemporal manifolds, but as a synthesis *whose act of reproduction, in its pure form, takes its rules a priori from the categories.* This synthesis will then be called the *productive* synthesis of imagination.[16] The merely preparatory character of the first exposition of the "threefold synthesis," which Kant has expressly warned us of, will then be confirmed, and what had been provisional is rectified and fulfilled by the two reiterations of the triple synthesis, "from top down," and "starting from below."[17]

THE "SYNTHESIS OF RECOGNITION IN A CONCEPT"

Without the consciousness that what we think is precisely the same as what we thought a moment before, all reproduction in the series of representations would be useless. For there would be in our present state a new representation which would not in any way belong to the act whereby it must have been successively generated. The manifold of the representation would therefore never form a whole, since it would lack that unity which only consciousness can impart to it. If, in counting, I forgot that the units which are now present to my senses have been successively added to one

[15] Cf. Adickes, *Kritik*, 657; Kemp Smith, *Commentary*, 247–48; De Vleeschauwer, *Déduction*, II, 251. More recently, Hoppe, *Synthesis*, 181–85.

[16] This takes care, I think, of what might otherwise seem like an inconsistency in Kant's terminology. In the propaedeutic exposition, the transcendental synthesis of the imagination is called *reproductive* (A102). Everywhere else, it is called *productive* (see in particular A118), and the adjective *reproductive* is reserved for the empirico-associative synthesis. If my analysis is correct, in fact *every* synthesis of imagination is reproductive: the proper function of imagination is to reproduce the elements of a sensible manifold in order to constitute "whole series of perceptions" (A121). Without this *synthesis*, no discursive *analysis* of appearances would be possible. But this reproduction is termed *productive synthesis* inasmuch as, being exercised on the pure (spatiotemporal) form of the manifold according to the rules provided by the categories, it *produces* the sensible forms in which the appearances turn out to conform to the categories, that is, it produces the *affinity* (A122) of appearances. This explains why subsequently Kant always distinguishes the *transcendental* synthesis from the *empirical* synthesis by calling the first *productive* and the second *reproductive*.

[17] "From the top down": A116ff. "Starting from below": A119–20.

another by me, I would not cognize [*erkennen*] the production of the multiplicity [*die Erzeugung der Menge*] through this successive addition of unit to unit, and so would also not cognize a number. For the concept of a number is nothing but the consciousness of this unity of synthesis. (A103, translation modified)

This presentation of the synthesis of recognition is disconcerting. Familiar with the method adopted before, one would expect Kant to expound an empirical synthesis and then show that this empirical synthesis presupposes a pure synthesis, which he would then illustrate by a mathematical example (number, line, figure). But here Kant dispenses with the exposition of the empirical synthesis, and directly introduces the example of number. As before, the mathematical example accommodates two directions of interpretation: on the one hand it may serve as an analogue for the *whole of experience*, which the empirical reproduction of representations is supposed to generate; on the other hand, it may serve as an analogue for *each of these representations* as a singular intuition, which is itself considered as a whole. I shall begin my analysis considering the case in which the number serves as an analogue for the *whole of experience*, and its units serve for successively apprehended and reproduced empirical representations.

I understand Kant's analysis as follows. The representation of a number is generated by a successive synthesis of numbered units.[18] Each unit is reproduced as we progress in the series from one number to the next. For instance I (mentally) reproduce the unit to which I attach the number one in order to synthesize it with an additional unit that will then be called the number two; I reproduce the latter in turn to synthesize it with an additional unit to which I then attach the number three, and so on. But, of course, the reproduction of any units whose successive synthesis is to generate the representation of a number (say, the number of pearls on this string) would be pointless if I did not know that "the units which are now present to my senses have been successively added to one another," and if I did not recognize them all to belong to *one and the same act of production* of a number ("if we were not conscious that what we are thinking is precisely the same as what we were thinking a moment before").

Similarly, the empiricoassociative reproduction of past representations of cinnabar would be useless (for the process of representing an object) if we were not somehow aware of the generic identity between the reproductive representations (the *Einbildungen*: for instance, the representations conserved in memory of a red and heavy object similar to the one I have now in my hand and before my eyes) and the past perceptions whose repetition induces the present association.[19] Now, the awareness of this generic identity depends on the consciousness (however obscure) of the unity of the act by which these representations are successively apprehended and then reproduced; which is to say, this awareness depends

---

[18] I am here considering only the use Kant makes of the act of denumerating a collection for analyzing what he calls "synthesis of recognition in a concept." Kant's concept of number and arithmetic will be analyzed in detail in chapter 9.

[19] This is indeed how Kant describes empirical recognition, just before the second exposition of the transcendental deduction, "from the top down." Recognition is described as "consciousness of the identity of the reproduced representations with the appearances whereby they were given" (A115).

on the (however obscure) consciousness of the act of constitution of the *complete experience* to which all particular representations of cinnabar belong. Though not conscious that they belong thus to one experience, we might yet reproduce past representations: animals are capable of associative reproductions, and we ourselves rely on unreflected, *merely* associative reproductions for the needs of everyday life. But the *consciousness of the generic identity between the reproductive representation and all those preceding it* would not result from such merely associative reproductions. Consequently, no universal concept would be generated under which the successively apprehended and reproduced representations could be subsumed and thereby taken up in a further network of comparisons.

The recognition of the generic identity of the empirical representations that are apprehended and reproduced depends thus on the consciousness of their belonging to a unified act of synthesis. In the text quoted, Kant calls "concept" the "consciousness of the unity of synthesis":

> If, in counting, I forgot that the units which are now present to my senses have been successively added to one another by me, I would not recognize [*erkennen*] the production of the multiplicity [*die Erzeugung der Menge*] through this successive addition of unit to unit, and so would also not recognize a number. For the concept of a number is nothing but the consciousness of this unity of synthesis. The word "concept" might of itself suggest this remark. For this unitary consciousness is what combines the manifold, successively intuited, and thereupon also reproduced, into one representation. (A103)

This is a very unusual use of the term "concept." It is clear that this "concept" is quite different from the "universal or reflected representation" defined in the *Logic*.[20] Here, the concept is not a universal representation formed by the discursive acts of comparison, reflection, and abstraction, but the (clear or obscure) consciousness of the unity of an act of synthesis, and moreover, of the synthesis of a *whole*. That a concept should thus be understood as *consciousness of an act*, and more precisely of an act of *combining and grasping together*, is what Kant seems to be insisting upon when he calls attention to the word "concept," *Begriff*: for even more explicitly than the Latinate *concept*, the German *Begriff* carries the connotation of *grasping, seizing*.

Let us now consider the other possible interpretation of the mathematical example. In this other interpretation, line or number is to be compared not with the whole of experience generated by means of the reproduction of particular empirical intuitions, but with each singular empirical intuition itself, taken as a whole, which is to say, as the unity of a manifold. Recall that in the Synthesis of Reproduction in a Representation of Imagination, Kant suggested that the reproduction of representations according to the rules of empirical association presupposes a prior reproduction of the manifold contained in every singular intuition. The pure form of this reproduction, determined a priori by the nature of our representational

---

[20] Cf. note 2.

faculties, is the reproduction of a spatiotemporal manifold. I want to suggest, then, that just as the reproductive synthesis "inseparably linked" to apprehension was the prior condition of the associative reproduction of empirical intuitions, so the "consciousness of the unity of synthesis" immanent to any particular intuition is the condition of the empirical recognition of the generic identity of empirical representations reproduced by virtue of the associations of the imagination. If we were not conscious, *for each particular intuition*, that each of the elements of the manifold that we successively apprehend and reproduce in it belonged to one and the same act of apprehension/reproduction of the manifold of intuition, then we would not be capable of subsequently recognizing the *generic identity* of different empirical intuitions. On this reading, the function of the mathematical model is now to exhibit an apprehension, a reproduction, and a recognition *for each particular intuition*, which *condition* the empirical association and reproduction of the conjunctions of impressions, and the recognition of the generic identity of these empirically reproduced conjunctions. In other words, *each particular* intuition is the object of a threefold synthesis, the form of which is provided by the "pure" spatiotemporal syntheses. Consequently, the presentation in intuition of mathematical concepts provides the model (i.e., the pure form) of the relation of any concept to intuition, insofar as it provides the rule for the generating of the unity of a manifold. The generic identity of the empirical intuitions reproduced by associative imagination is shown to be the generic identity of the *acts of successive synthesis* which in turn generate each of these particular empirical intuitions "as" specific unities of a manifold.

We find here again a twofold meaning for the term "concept." On the one hand, it is the "consciousness of the unity of synthesis" of a sensible manifold. On the other hand, it is a discursive concept, a "universal or reflected representation" of the act of synthesis which was common to several particular representations, and thereby made it possible for us to recognize them as generically identical. Only if one carefully distinguishes between these two meanings of the word "concept" does the last sentence of the text quoted previously escape tautology:

> This unitary consciousness [i.e., the concept, according to what Kant said immediately before] is what combines into one representation the manifold which is successively intuited and then reproduced. This consciousness may often be only faint, so that we do not connect it with the act itself, that is, not in any direct manner with the *generation* of the representation, but only with the outcome [that which is thereby represented]. But notwithstanding these variations such consciousness, however indistinct, must always be present; without it, concepts, and therewith cognition of objects, are altogether impossible. (A103–4)

"Without this consciousness," that is, without the concept as consciousness, which "may often be faint," of the unity of an act of synthesis, "concepts, and therewith cognition of objects, are altogether impossible"—the "universal and reflected representations" of one or the other of the forms of "unity of synthesis" of an intuition are impossible.

CONCEPT AND OBJECT: THE CONCEPT AS RULE

Here the limits of Kant's mathematical examples become evident. The "consciousness of the unity of synthesis" of a sensible manifold clearly cannot mean the same thing in both the case of a mathematical concept and the case of an empirical concept whose object is given and somehow constrains the act of mental synthesis.

Notice, however, that mathematical concepts themselves may have an empirical use. They may be not simply the "consciousness of the unity of the act" of arbitrarily generating a figure or a number, but also the "consciousness of the unity of the act" by which we apprehend/reproduce/recognize the object of an empirical intuition. Like any empirical concept, the mathematical concept (e.g., that of a triangle, or a triangular shape) is then the concept of an "object = X," distinct from our representations, and the supposition of which drives us to seek coherence among our representations. This is at least what Kant seems to say when, having remarked that we never have to deal with anything but our own representations, he wonders how the expression "object of our representations" should be understood:

Now we find that our thought of the relation of all cognition to its object carries with it an element of necessity; the object is viewed as that which prevents our cognitions from being haphazard or arbitrary [*was dawider ist, daß unsere Erkenntnisse nicht aufs geratewohl, oder beliebig . . . bestimmet seien*], and which determines them *a priori* in some definite fashion. For insofar as they are to relate to an object, they must necessarily agree with one another, that is, must possess that unity which constitutes the concept of an object. But it is clear that, since we have to deal only with the manifold of our representations, and since that *X* (the object) which corresponds to them is nothing to us—being, as it is, something that has to be distinct from all our representations—the unity which the object makes necessary can be nothing else than the formal unity of consciousness in the synthesis of the manifold of representations. It is only when we have thus produced synthetic unity in the manifold of intuition that we are in a position to say that we cognize the object. . . . Thus we think a triangle as an object in that we are conscious of the combination of three straight lines according to a rule by which such an intuition can always be represented. This *unity of rule* determines all the manifold and limits it to conditions which make unity of apperception possible. The concept of this unity is the representation of the object = X which I think through the predicates, above mentioned, of a triangle. (A104–5)

The "unity of rule" of the synthesis of the sensible, which the concept of triangle reflects, "limits [the manifold] to conditions which make unity of apperception possible" in two ways. On the one hand, it allows the manifold of a sensible intuition to be apprehended "as" manifold and at the same time as *one* intuition; on the other hand, it allows for the recognition of the generic identity of the intuited object with all of the objects whose apprehension depends on the same rule and which thus are reflected as having the same marks (*Merkmale*). The "unity of apperception," then, is not only the unity of the apperception *of this singular object* (consciousness of the act of synthesis of the manifold of its intuition), but also the unity of the apperception of this object *as generically identical to all those whose apprehension depends on the same rule*.

This twofold aspect of the rule appears once again when Kant finally moves to an example of a strictly *empirical* concept: the concept of *body*.

> All cognition demands a concept, though that concept may, indeed, be quite imperfect or obscure. But a concept is always, as regards its form, something universal which serves as a rule. The concept of body, for instance, as the unity of the manifold which is thought through it, serves as a rule in our cognition of outer appearances. But it can be a rule for intuitions only insofar as it represents in any given appearances the necessary reproduction of their manifold, and thereby the synthetic unity in our consciousness of them. The concept of body, in the perception of something outside us, necessitates the representation of extension, and therewith representations of impenetrability, shape, etc. (A106)

The concept of body "serves as a rule in our cognition of outer appearances" because, once formed, this empirical concept guides our apprehension/reproduction of the phenomenal manifold, allowing the associative reproductions to form in order to constitute complete representations of objects from our present impressions. Thus the concept of body "can be a rule for intuitions only insofar as it represents in any given appearances the necessary reproduction of their manifold, and thereby the synthetic unity in our consciousness of them." In my opinion this "necessary reproduction" must be understood both as the reproduction, for a singular given intuition, of the manifold that constitutes it, and as the reproduction of the *past representations* we can associate with it, by virtue of which we henceforth consider the conjunction of characters we attribute to them as "necessary." Thus the concept of body "necessitates the representation of extension, and therewith representations of impenetrability, shape, etc." Here, "necessitates" means *inescapably demands* the association of the character of impenetrability with those of extension and shape, by a tendency of the mind analogous to that which Hume attributed to associative imagination, but which Kant, at the end of the laborious exposition of the "threefold synthesis," will describe as the tendency of an associative imagination *guided by the a priori forms of the unity of apperception*. But "necessitates" also means *reflects as necessary*, inasmuch as the characters that are here considered (extension, impenetrability, shape) are represented as *necessarily belonging* to the singular objects cognized under the concept of body.[21] Past impressions have accustomed me to associate impenetrability with any object presenting itself as extended and delimited in space (I know that I must

---

[21] This means that they are determinations that from an ontological standpoint belong to its essence. The "necessity" evoked here anticipates explanations that Kant gives in full only in the Analogies of Experience, (cf. chapter 11). As I said earlier, this repeated anticipation of explanations that will be completely developed only in the System of Principles greatly contributes to the obscurity of the A Deduction.

not try to go through an unopened door). But to have made a concept of body out of this conjunction is more than the expression of this merely subjective habit. My apprehension of empirically given spatial multiplicities is henceforth guided by the concept. I consider the marks contained in the concept 'body' as necessarily belonging to the given multiplicities I reflect under the concept. If something that appeared to me as extended and limited in space turned out not to possess the character of impenetrability, I would either have to admit that, contrary to my initial assumption, this "something" was not a body, or—and with empirical concepts this is always possible—to correct my concept of body.

Hence the notion of *rule* by means of which Kant defines all concepts has a twofold meaning, parallel to the twofold meaning we earlier found for the term "concept" itself (the concept as "consciousness of the unity of an act of synthesis," and the concept as "universal and reflected representation"). The concept is a rule insofar as it is the consciousness of the unity of an act of sensible synthesis or the consciousness of the procedure for generating a sensible intuition. This first sense of *rule* anticipates what Kant, in the Schematism of the Pure Concepts of the Understanding, calls a *schema*.[22] But the concept is a rule also in another, discursive sense. It is a rule in that thinking an object under a concept provides a reason to predicate of this object the marks that define the concept. Under this second aspect, the term *rule* has the meaning Kant assigns to it in his *Logic* as well as in the *Critique of Pure Reason* when using it to describe the major premise of a syllogism:

> In every syllogism I first think a *rule* (the major premise) through the *understanding*. Secondly, I *subsume* something known under the condition of the rule by means of *the power of judgment* [*Urteilskraft*] (the minor premise). Finally, what is thereby known I *determine* through the predicate of the rule, and so *a priori* through *reason* (the conclusion). (A304/B360–61)[23]

Every concept is a *rule* insofar as its explication (e.g., a body is extended, limited in space and impenetrable) can function as the major premise in a syllogism whose conclusion would be the attribution of the marks belonging to this concept to an object of sensible intuition. The two meanings of "rule," as rule for sensible synthesis (the concept as schema) and as discursive rule (the apodeictic statement of the marks of the concept as a "rule for subsumption" or major premise of a possible syllogism), are indeed linked. Because one has generated a schema, one can obtain a discursive rule by reflection and apply this rule to appearances. Thus, as Kant states at the end of the A Deduction, the understanding is "always occupied in examining [*durchspähen*] appearances in order to detect some rule in them."[24] This must be understood in two ways: on the one hand, the

[22] A140/B180: "This representation of a universal procedure of imagination in providing an image for a concept, I entitle the schema of this concept. . . . The schema of the triangle can exist nowhere but in thought. It is a rule of synthesis of the imagination, in respect to pure figures in space." Similarly, an empirical concept "always stands in immediate relation to the schema of imagination, as a rule for the determination of our intuition, in accordance with some specific universal concept."

[23] Cf. also *Logik*, §57–58, Ak. IX, 120; 614–15.

[24] A126 (translation modified).

understanding is occupied in examining appearances *in search of objects con-forming to the rules it has already formed*; on the other hand, it is occupied in ex-amining appearances *in order to form new rules*, that is, new schemata, which can be reflected in turn as discursive rules or "rules for subsumption."[25]

For such rules to be formed, the whole of our representations must be taken up in one and the same act of synthesis. Thus the *numerical identity* of the function of combination (*one and the same* act at work in all our representations) and the *unity of consciousness* (the combination of all our representations in one space and one time) are necessary conditions for the constitution of a unified experi-ence, and thereby for the relation of our representations to objects.

Against this last claim one might argue that numerical identity and unity of consciousness, far from being *conditions* of the possibility of a unified experi-ence, merely *result*, as Hume claimed, from the reproductive associations of imagination.[26] One might likewise also object that nothing justifies Kant's claim that a "consciousness (however obscure) of the unity of the act" of combining representations *conditions* these combinations and leads to the representation of rules or concepts. But, in fact, the possibility of such an objection has been metic-ulously forestalled throughout the exposition of the threefold synthesis. In each of its first two steps, we saw that sensory receptivity and empirical reproduction, which by themselves would be quite scattered and random, had as their necessary concomitant a (more or less obscurely conscious) *unified and unifying activity* of the mind or faculties of representation. Kant thus prepared the way to show, as he does when we reach the third step, that the recognition of representations under a concept is possible only if the activities described in the first two steps *were al-ways already oriented toward this goal*. In other words, for recognition to occur, not only should the act of apprehension be "inseparably linked" to an act of re-production, but this act of reproduction should itself be accompanied by the "con-sciousness of the unity of the act" to which it belongs. This does not mean that each moment of the "threefold synthesis," *considered in its empirical aspect*, is necessarily conditioned by the next: it would be excessive to suppose that we (empirically) apprehend only if we have already (empirically) reproduced, or re-produce only if we have already (empirically) recognized under a concept. I think that what Kant wants to say is that acts of apprehension/reproduction/recognition lead to empirical concepts and thus to knowledge of objects—are acts of relating

---

[25] As Hoppe remarks, the way in which Kant introduces the idea that concepts function as rules does not make his position very easy to understand. His examples (the concept of triangle, the con-cept of body) are introduced as *already formed* concepts that guide the apprehension of appearances. But the problem is obviously to know *how the concepts are formed* in the first place, what makes pos-sible a recognition of empirical objects under concepts (cf. Hoppe, *Synthesis*, 185–86). At the end of the propaedeutic exposition of the three syntheses, the categories will precisely turn out to be the *rules for forming rules*, or the forms of the effort of the mind to subject its representations to rules. Only then will we get an answer to the question, How do empirical concepts themselves emerge?

[26] Cf. Hume's discussion of personal identity in *Treatise Concerning Human Nature*, bk. I, pt. 4, sec. 6. "Our notions of personal identity proceed entirely from the smooth and uninterrupted progress of the thought along a train of connected ideas, according to the principles above-explained" (the "principles above-explained" are the associations of imagination according to relations of resem-blance, contiguity, and causality).

appearances to *phaenomena*—*only if* one and the same act, unifying our representations, is at work throughout this process. This act is what Kant calls "numerical identity of the act of synthesis," and he claims that the consciousness of such an "identity of the act," however "obscure" it may be, accompanies all of our representations related to objects.

Having thus introduced the requirement of the unity and numerical identity of consciousness (and *self*-consciousness: consciousness of the numerically identical act combining the sensible manifold), Kant finally introduces the categories as the "conditions of thought in a possible experience" or "universal functions of synthesis." Only now can the provisional, merely preparatory exposition of the "threefold synthesis" be retrospectively clarified.

The Transcendental Unity of Self-Consciousness and the Categories

Kant reasons as follows. Perceptions constitute an experience, that is, a combination of representations under empirical concepts, only insofar as they are combined by a numerically identical act of synthesis. The categories are the "conditions of thought in a possible experience" (A111) or "universal functions of synthesis" (A112), namely the very functions at work in the numerically identical act of synthesis that combines perceptions into experience. Therefore appearances, as objects of experience, are under the categories as necessarily as they, as objects of empirical intuition, are in the forms of space and time.

But curiously, Kant gives no justification for this identification of the categories with universal "conditions of thought" or "functions of synthesis." He asserts this identity without any further explanation:

> Now I maintain that the categories, above cited, are nothing but the *conditions of thought in a possible experience*, just as *space and time* are the *conditions of intuition* for that same experience. They are fundamental concepts by which we think objects in general for appearances, and have therefore *a priori* objective validity. This is exactly what we desired to prove.
>
> . . . In original apperception everything must necessarily conform to the conditions of the thoroughgoing unity of self-consciousness, that is, to the universal functions of synthesis, namely, of that synthesis according to concepts in which alone apperception can demonstrate its complete and necessary identity. (A111–12)

Such an abrupt statement is surprising. One would expect Kant to support his claim with the help of his earlier suggestions. In the metaphysical deduction (section 10) he related the categories to the logical functions of judgment, and even before that he had stated the identity between *thinking* and *judging*.[27] But here he makes no explicit use of these earlier developments. He comes closest to explicitly referring to them in the first reexposition of the transcendental deduction

---

[27] A67–68/B92–93, The Logical Use of the Understanding. I will analyze this section in the introduction to part II, and in chapter 4.

("from the top down") when in a note he explains that the relation to the 'I' is what gives logical form to all cognition.

> [T]hat all the variety of *empirical consciousness* must be combined in one single self-consciousness is the *absolutely* first and synthetic principle of our thought in general. But it must not be forgotten that the bare representation *I* in relation to all other representations (the collective unity of which it makes possible) is transcendental consciousness. Whether this representation is clear (empirical consciousness) or obscure, or even whether it actually occurs, does not here concern us. But *the possibility of the logical form of all cognition is necessarily conditioned by relation to this apperception* as a capacity [my emphasis on last sentence—Kant already emphasized *as a capacity*: *als einem Vermögen*]. (A118n)

From what preceded we can understand why "the bare representation *I*" makes the collective unity of all other representations possible. We can suppose that this representation is the (more or less obscure) consciousness of the numerically identical act of synthesis that unifies the empirical given into a whole of experience I can call "mine." This "bare representation" makes the logical form of all cognition—the reflection of singular representations under concepts—possible. Now, as the *Dissertation* already asserted and as we have been reminded in the metaphysical deduction of the categories, the acts of reflecting under concepts are acts of judgment.[28] One would therefore expect Kant to help us with a reminder of the relation he stated in section 10 between the categories and the logical functions of judgment, and to justify in this way his assertion that the categories are "the conditions of thought in a possible experience."

But Kant does not do this, even when such a reminder would seem most natural. This is the case when, after arguing that the transcendental unity of apperception is a necessary condition for the formation of empirical concepts (i.e., for recognizing rules of synthesis of the empirical manifold), Kant dwells once again on the meaning of the expression "object of representation":

> Now, also, we are in a position to determine more adequately our concept of an *object* in general. All representations have, as representations, their object, and can themselves in turn become objects of other representations. Appearances are the sole objects which can be given to us immediately, and that in them which relates immediately to the objects is called intuition. (A108–9)

This text bears a striking resemblance to a passage from the introductory section to the Analytic of Concepts, The Logical Employment of the Understanding:

> Since no representation, save when it is an intuition, is in immediate relation to an object, no concept is ever related to an object immediately, but to some other representation of it, be that other representation an intuition, or itself a concept. Judgment is therefore the mediate cognition of an object, that is, the representation of a representation of it. (A68/B93)

---

[28] Cf. chapter 1, pp. 25–29.

Both texts assert that the only representation that has an immediate relation to an object is an intuition, whose object is the appearance. The other type of representation, besides intuition, that relates to an object, Kant adds in The Logical Employment of the Understanding, is a *concept*, which however never relates to an object directly, but always by the mediation of another representation (intuition or concept). In the Deduction, on the other hand, Kant calls "object" not only the object of intuition or appearance, but any representation (whether intuition or concept) to which another representation relates: thus the object (appearance) to which an intuition intentionally relates, but also the representation (intuition or concept) thought under a concept. If we grant this switch in vocabulary, in both texts Kant states that every representation has an object (thought or, we might say in the case of intuition, "intended" by it) and can in turn be the object of another representation (i.e., be thought under a concept, if it is an intuition; or be thought under a higher concept, if it is a concept). But the ultimate object of all representations is the immediate object of a sensible intuition, that is, an appearance.

However, from this point on, the two texts diverge. The text from The Logical Employment goes on to present *judgment* as the mediating act that relates representations (concepts and intuitions) to one another, and thus also to the "immediately given" object, the appearance:

> Judgment is therefore the mediate cognition of an object, that is, the representation of a representation of it. In every judgment there is a concept which holds of many representations, and among them of a given representation that is immediately related to an object. Thus in the judgment 'all bodies are divisible', the concept of the divisible applies to various other concepts, but is here applied in particular to the concept of body, and this concept again to certain appearances that present themselves to us [*auf gewisse uns vorkommende Erscheinungen*]. (A68–69/B93)

But in the Deduction, Kant introduces a new element to account for the relation of representations to an object: the *transcendental object*. The relation of representations to their object, he writes, cannot stop with their relation to the appearance, since this is still a representation. The latter therefore has itself an object, *which is not itself a representation any more*: the transcendental object = X. Now, in many respects this reference to the transcendental object seems to play the role played by judgment in the previous text: it is supposed to account for the way in which we relate our empirical concepts to objects:

> But these appearances are not things in themselves; they are only representations, which in turn have their object—an object which cannot itself be intuited by us, and which may, therefore, be named the non-empirical, that is, transcendental object = X.
>
> The pure concept of this transcendental object, which in reality throughout all our knowledge is always one and the same, is what can alone confer upon all our empirical concepts in general relation to an object, that is, objective reality. This concept cannot contain any determinate intuition, and therefore refers only to that unity which must be met with in any manifold of cognition [*Erkenntnis*] which stands in

relation to an object. This relation is nothing but the necessary unity of consciousness, and therefore also of the synthesis of the manifold, through a common function of the mind, which combines it in one representation. (A109)

In fact, the difference between the two texts should come as no surprise. In the former, Kant merely characterizes the "logical employment" of understanding, that is, the discursive combination of concepts; he thus considers the object itself only from the point of view of this "logical employment," that is, as *that about which* a judgment is stated.[29] The latter text, on the other hand, belongs to the Transcendental Deduction of the Categories. There Kant questions what we mean by object of representation and relation of representations to an object, when all we have available to us are appearances as the "undetermined objects of an empirical intuition" (cf. A20/B34)—themselves mere representations. His questioning thus goes beyond the analysis of the logical function of judgment provided in The Logical Employment of the Understanding, and leads him to relate the appearance—the "object" of concepts combined in judgment, according to The Logical Employment—to its own object, insofar as it is, itself, a "mere" representation.

But this only confirms my previous remark: when Kant, in the passage from the Transcendental Deduction, asserts that the "pure concept of a transcendental object = X" is what can "confer upon all our empirical concepts in general relation to an object," or again when he adds that "this relation is nothing but the necessary unity of consciousness, and therefore also of the synthesis of the manifold, through a common function of the mind," we would expect him to specify that this "function" is no other than the logical function of judgment. We would

---

[29] This "logical" object is thus characterized in a late *Reflexion*: "What is an object? That which is represented through a totality of several predicates which pertain to it. The plate is round, warm, tin, etc. 'Warm', 'round', 'tin' etc. are not objects, but the warmth, the tin etc. are. An object is that in the representation of which other representations can be thought as synthetically connected. Every judgment has a subject and predicate. The subject of the judgment, insofar as it contains different possible predicates, is the object" (*Refl.* 6350, Ak. XVIII, 676; cf. Henrich, *Identität*, 44–46, 152–55; Allison, *Idealism*, 146–47). An object in the logical sense is thus whatever is thought under the subject-concept of a categorical judgment, where the subject-concept is a *complex* concept, to which many different predicates may be attributed. Now, the "object" discussed in the Transcendental Deduction is not this merely logical notion. What is under discussion in the Deduction is primarily the *empirical* object: the "appearance," or "undetermined object of an empirical intuition," inherited from the Transcendental Aesthetic; and the "object of the appearance," or *phenomenon* (see chapter 1, p. 25): an object we represent "as" distinct from our representations of it (what Strawson calls "object in the weighty sense," as opposed to the mere particular instance of a general concept: cf. *Bounds of Sense*, 73. Strawson, however, finds the project of Kant's Analytic less interesting if it takes the admission of the object "in the weighty sense" as a fundamental premise: see ibid., pp. 73–74; and my chapter 3, at note 3). Whether the object we represent "as" distinct from our representations of it actually has independent existence is a different issue, which Kant treats in the Refutation of Idealism. The issue in the Deduction is only, How do we represent an object "as" an independent object, an object that may remain the same while our representations of it change, or while we have no representation of it at all? Hume reduced the representation of independent existence to a mere result of associations in imagination. Kant wants to argue that this representation is possible only if generated by an original discursive function, under the objective unity of apperception.

expect him to say that this function is what makes it possible to relate our representations to a "transcendental object = X," that is, to that object which "prevents our cognitions from being haphazard or arbitrary" and under the supposition of which we expect our cognitions to "agree with one another, i.e. [to] possess that unity which constitutes the concept of an object" (cf. A104–5, quoted earlier). But no such connection is expressly stated (although one cannot doubt, given the metaphysical deduction of the categories, that Kant had it in mind). Only in the B Deduction will the connection between logical function of judgment and representation of an object take center stage.

In the A Deduction, on the contrary, having simply "maintained" that the categories are "the conditions of thought in a possible experience," Kant goes on to recapitulate his exposition of the "threefold synthesis," first "from the top down," then "starting from below." He thus emphasizes again how each of the empirically distinguished moments (empirical intuition, reproductive representation of imagination, concept) depends upon the "numerical identity of self-consciousness" and thereby on the categories. I will not discuss this twice repeated recapitulation here. I have already indicated some of the ways in which it corrects and completes the first presentation of the "threefold synthesis," and I shall have more to say on the transcendental unity of apperception in the A Deduction when I compare the latter to the B Deduction in the next chapter. Here my principal focus has been the first exposition of the "threefold synthesis," where Kant attempts to show the impossibility of a merely empirical account of the genesis of representations, one that neglects to show how they are made possible "as" representations, and even more "as" representations *which relate to an object* (the "object of the appearance"). The use Kant intends to make of the model provided by the generation of pure multiplicities or manifolds under the guidance of arithmetical and geometrical concepts is seen most strikingly in this first exposition. The true import, and also the limitations of this model, will emerge when the categories are explicitly related to the logical forms of judgment, so that mathematical construction and logical reflection are distinguished more sharply and connected with greater precision. The B Deduction will achieve precisely this.

OBJECTIVE DEDUCTION AND SUBJECTIVE DEDUCTION:
KANT'S REWRITING OF THE TRANSCENDENTAL
DEDUCTION OF THE CATEGORIES

In the first preface to the *Critique of Pure Reason*, Kant insists on the exceptional importance of his transcendental deduction of the categories. But in the same place, even before being chastened by the hostile reception of this first edition, he already admits that his deduction might fail to persuade his reader. He would be satisfied, he says, if at the least the *objective* deduction is granted, whose sole concern is to make "the objective validity of *a priori* concepts" understandable. The *subjective* deduction, which attempts to explain this validity by laying out the activity of the understanding in relation to the other cognitive faculties, need not be so strong a pivot. Its shortcomings should not detract from the main argument: "For the chief question is always simply this: —what and how much can the understanding and reason cognize apart from all experience? not: —how is the *faculty of thought* itself possible?" (Axvii).

But this separation of the two aspects of the argument is a bit surprising. For if one takes it literally, the entire exposition of the threefold synthesis in its three successive versions, which contains the examination of "the pure understanding itself, its possibility and the cognitive faculties upon which it rests" (Axvi), seems reduced to the status of mere opinion. All Kant defends without restriction, then, is the first section of the Deduction of the Pure Concepts of the Understanding in which he puts forth the program of the transcendental deduction as well as its consequences for the limitation of the use of the pure concepts of the understanding (sections 13, 14). But a program is not a proof, and indeed it seems that the very manner in which Kant stated the problem of the categories obliges him to account, in one way or another, for how "the representation makes the object possible," that is to say, how representational activity gives its form to the object of representation.

Kant's fears that his Transcendental Deduction of the Categories might not win the assent of its readers were confirmed, if we trust a famous footnote to the preface to the *Metaphysical Foundations of Natural Science*.[30] To Professor Ulrich, who declared that he was not convinced by the Transcendental Deduction of the Categories, Kant answers basically that weaknesses discoverable in the detail of the proof are unimportant. It is enough if he has convincingly shown that the categories can be applied only to objects of a possible experience. And for this purpose only the doctrine of the pure forms of sensibility and the deduction of the categories from the logical functions of judgment need be granted. For then it is clear that, on the one hand, our cognition can be applied only to appearances and, on the other hand, the combination of these appearances into one experience obeys the system of the categories resulting from the "formal operations of the understanding."

True, Kant acknowledges, if one merely asserted that any cognition of an object depends upon (1) the pure forms of sensible intuition, and (2) the logical functions of our judgments, the agreement of the latter with given objects might well remain a matter of preestablished harmony. It would be perfectly contingent, still open to a skeptical interpretation such as Hume's. An admission like this from Kant is enough to revive our suspicions regarding his assurance in the preface that the examination of "the pure understanding itself, its possibility and the cognitive faculties upon which it rests" is not an essential part of the transcendental deduction. At that point he called this investigation "subjective deduction" but now describes it as "the answer to the question *how*." But, he adds, "this problem has . . . great facility, inasmuch as it can be solved almost by a single conclusion from the precisely determined definition of a *judgment* in general (an act by which given representations first become cognitions of an object)."[31]

---

[30] Kant, *Anfangsgründe*, Ak. IV, 474n; 11, n. 8.
[31] Ibid., Ak. IV, 475n; 13, n. 3.

This heralds the new method in the B Deduction. Instead of the method of the A Deduction that consisted in uncovering the "threefold synthesis" underlying the psychological genesis of our empirical cognitions, Kant will now adopt a positive method that consists in deducing the nature of the acts of thought from the "exactly specified definition of a judgment in general." But if the analyses I proffer here are correct, then this really means that Kant takes up the B Deduction where the A Deduction left off, namely at the point where he should have explained that "the numerical identity of self-consciousness" is the numerical identity of the *act of judging*, which aims to weave its web through the infinite manifold of given perceptions.

In the next chapter I will confirm this point by examining the initial sections of the B Deduction. The setting of the stage complete, I shall be able to consider, in part II, what I take to be the first main component of Kant's Transcendental Deduction of the Categories in the B edition: the role he assigns to what he calls "logical function of judgment" in generating our representation of objects.

The Transition to Judgment

THE FIRST SECTIONS of the B Deduction can be read as an exposition of the bare structure of the "threefold synthesis" and its relation to the unity of apperception, expounded in psychological detail in the A Deduction. All combination of the manifold of sensible representations is the result of an act of synthesis (section 15). This act of combining the manifold depends on the original synthetic unity of apperception (section 16). The latter is therefore the source of the relation of our representations to an object (sections 17, 18). The results of the lengthy propaedeutic exposition of the "threefold synthesis" in the first edition are here stated from the outset, and the new deduction takes up the explanation where the first prematurely left off. Section 19 first introduces us to new material: the objective unity of apperception is none other than the logical form of judgment. This puts the transcendental deduction of the categories in line with the metaphysical deduction, and reveals the full meaning of the parallelism of the two tables set out in section 10. So one cannot too strongly emphasize the complementary character of the two editions of the Transcendental Deduction. Rather than providing a substitute for the demonstration of the A Deduction, the B Deduction takes the initial steps of the demonstration in A for granted and completes the argument where the earlier exposition seemed insufficient or faulty.

Of course, this means that the unity of apperception, which in the A edition was preceded by the exposition of the "threefold synthesis," now appears almost as our starting point. And this gives the entire Transcendental Deduction a different tenor. In the first Deduction, the relation of every representation of object to the unity of apperception was established only after minute examination of the main components in the representation of an object: sensible intuition, representation of imagination, and concept. Here, on the contrary, the proof begins from the place occupied by what in the first Deduction was the reexposition "from the top down" of the Transcendental Deduction (A116). It seems therefore that the various components of representation are from the outset swallowed up into the unity of apperception. As a consequence of this shift in emphasis, readers of the *Critique* have often thought they must choose one or the other version of the transcendental deduction, and they did so depending on what they believed to be the most fruitful orientation of Kant's argument. Cohen and his neo-Kantian followers favored the orientation of the B edition because of what they perceived to be the more epistemological character of its argument, as opposed to the dubious psychologism of the A edition.[1] Heidegger, on the contrary, preferred the A edition because he found that the B edition diminished the fundamental role of transcendental imagination and instead privileged pure understanding, thus "intellectualizing" the

---

[1] Cohen, *Erfahrung*, VIIIc, 315f–16.

transcendental deduction with the ultimate goal of affirming the supremacy of reason in its practical use.[2] In readings of the *Critique of Pure Reason* in the analytic tradition, the issue is no longer that of understanding versus imagination. Such readings focus instead on the question, What is the fundamental premise of the deduction? Does Kant presuppose knowledge of objects and then go on to show that it is possible only under the condition of unity of apperception—which he shows, in turn, to imply the use of the categories? Or does he, on the contrary, admit the unity of apperception as his sole premise and go on from there to show that some form of rule-governedness among objects of consciousness is a necessary condition for self-consciousness? The first way of proceeding is more associated with the A, the second more with the B Deduction.[3] In fact, however, if what I suggested earlier is right there is no fundamental opposition between the two deductions. As far as the Cohen/Heidegger confrontation goes, I shall argue that the role of imagination is not eliminated from the B Deduction, but that the understanding itself becomes more clearly linked, in its transcendental function, to sensibility. For it is more clearly linked to the *productive synthesis* of the sensible given, the fundamental role Kant attributes to transcendental imagination in both editions. As for the alternative premises proposed in analytic readings, I shall argue that it is quite clear from section 15 of the B Deduction that Kant asserts the necessity, *for representation of an object*, of the very same threefold synthesis that he so carefully layed out in the A edition as condition for such a representation; *only after* having asserted this, does he go on to assert that the original synthetic unity of apperception is the necessary condition for this three-fold synthesis (section 16). Nonetheless, in the B Deduction Kant does dispense

---

[2] Heidegger, *Kant*, §§15, 31.

[3] Strawson revives Cohen's mistrust of the A Deduction on grounds of its excessive psychologism. He prefers the B to the A Deduction because, according to him, it is less dependent on the "imaginary topic of transcendental psychology" and in particular on the doctrine of synthesis (*Bounds of Sense*, 31–32). Though an important shortcoming of both, the fabricated drama of what goes on in the mind receives more attention in the A version, whereas the B version is more in the form of an argument with premises and conclusion (86–87). Its "fundamental premise is that experience contains a diversity of elements (intuitions) which, in the case of each subject of experience, must somehow be united in a single consciousness capable of judgment" and whose conclusion is that "this unity requires another kind of unity or connectedness on the part of the multifarious elements of experience" (87). Dieter Henrich has taken up Strawson's suggestion that there are two alternative premises for the Deduction. Either the supposition of experience as knowledge of objects, for which unity of apperception and categories are shown to be the necessary conditions, or the supposition of unity of apperception, for which objective rule-governedness is shown to be the condition. Like Strawson, Henrich claims that only the second argumentative strategy has any chance of success, and he develops it at great length (*Identität*, 54–55). Guyer refines the division of possible argumentative structures by detecting two versions of each fundamental structure (*Claims*, 85–86) and ends up finding a successful argument—not in the Transcendental Deduction itself, whether A or B, but in the Analogies and Refutation of Idealism. My own reading is probably closest to Henry Allison's. Like him, I see Kant clarifying in the B Deduction an argument whose general line was essentially present in the A edition (cf. Allison, *Idealism*, 133). And like him, I take the B Deduction to be structured around judgment as the intellectual activity by means of which representations are related to the objects "of which" they are representations, and the relation of judgment to its sensible conditions: space and time as forms of receptive intuition (ibid.). But as what follows will show, our views differ on the way in which Kant relates *categories* and *forms of judgment*, and on the relation of each to sensible syntheses.

with the point-by-point dialogue with empirical psychology characteristic of the A Deduction, and instead sets out from the culminating point of the A Deduction (the relation of every representation to the transcendental unity of apperception) to expound the heart of the new argument: the relation between logical functions of judgment and sensible syntheses.

In the present chapter I aim to clarify this connection between the A and B Deductions. To do this I shall examine the introductory sections of the B Deduction, whose whole function in my view is to justify the new orientation of the argument while placing it in line with the argument developed in the A Deduction. I will consider first the prima facie surprising statement that all synthesis is to be attributed no longer to imagination (as Kant stated both in the metaphysical deduction, which he left unaltered in B, and in the A edition's transcendental deduction) but rather to the understanding. I will then show how this characterization of synthesis in section 15 should help us understand Kant's explanation of the "original synthetic unity of apperception" or "objective unity of apperception" or "I think," in section 16. Finally, I will explain how, after having elucidated what we mean by "I think," Kant rests his transcendental deduction of the categories on the two interdependent aspects of the act of thinking: the logical function of judgment and the *synthesis speciosa* or transcendental synthesis of imagination.

SYNTHESIS: A FUNCTION OF THE UNDERSTANDING?

In section 15, under the title "Of the Possibility of Combination in General," Kant states that even though the manifold of any representation is given by the senses, any combination of this manifold requires the intervention of an active faculty of synthesis. This is recognizably a thesis already stated in the A Deduction. However, as I have already pointed out, Kant seems to shift its meaning by attributing the combination not to imagination, but to understanding:

> All combination—be we conscious of it or not, be it a combination of the manifold of intuition, empirical or non-empirical, or of various concepts—is an act of the understanding. To this act the general title "synthesis" may be assigned, as indicating that we cannot represent to ourselves anything as combined in the object which we have not ourselves previously combined. (B130)

According to the A Deduction, the synthesis or combination of the sensible manifold (whether it is the manifold of an empirical representation or the manifold of a pure representation, such as that of space or time) was performed by imagination. The *unity* of this synthesis, that is, the "consciousness of the unity of the act" to which each apprehended and reproduced element belongs, was yielded by transcendental apperception, which "in its relation to the synthesis of imagination" is the understanding.[4] Thus the function of synthesis attributed to imagination clearly served as a *mediator* between the sensible given and the unity of understanding.

---

[4] Cf. A119: "*The unity of apperception in relation to the synthesis of imagination* is the *understanding*; and this same unity, with reference to the *transcendental synthesis* of the imagination, the *pure understanding*."

Now, since every appearance contains a manifold, and since different perceptions therefore occur in the mind separately and singly, a combination of them, such as they cannot have in sense itself, is demanded. There must therefore exist in us an active faculty for the synthesis of this manifold. To this faculty, I give the title, imagination. (A120)

The two extremes, namely sensibility and understanding, must stand in necessary connection with each other through the mediation of this transcendental function of imagination, because otherwise the former, though indeed yielding appearances, would supply no objects of empirical cognition, and consequently no experience. (A124)

The imagination, through its acts of synthesis of the sensible manifold, produces "whole series"[5] of representations, which then admit of being reflected under concepts. The understanding, that is, the "unity of apperception in its relation to the syntheses of the imagination," generates the "consciousness of the unity of the act" to which any reproductive synthesis belongs, and thereby "intellectualizes" the synthesis.

It is this apperception which must be added to pure imagination, in order to render its function intellectual. For since the synthesis of imagination connects the manifold only as it *appears* in intuition, as, for instance, in the shape of a triangle, it is, though exercised *a priori*, always in itself sensible. And while concepts, which belong to the understanding, are brought into play through relation of the manifold to the unity of apperception, it is only by means of the imagination that they can be brought in relation to sensible intuition. (A124)

In the A Deduction, the functions of the imagination and understanding were thus clearly distinguished both in their empirical aspect, where associative imagination mediated between the empirical given and concepts as "universal or reflected representations," and in their transcendental aspect, where imagination in its functions, both of "pure" reproduction (applied to the very forms of space and time) as well as of *producing* the affinity of appearances, mediated between any sensible given and the categories as forms of the unity of apperception. Do we not, however, lose this distinction, as well as the mediating function of imagination if, as the B edition says, "every synthesis is an act of the understanding"?

Before answering we should note that Kant goes on to describe the synthesis or combination thus attributed to the understanding as including "the manifold, the synthesis of the manifold, and the unity of this manifold": "But the concept of combination includes, besides the concept of the manifold and of its synthesis, also the concept of the unity of the manifold. Combination is representation of the *synthetic* unity of the manifold" (B130–31).

The synthesis described as an "act of the understanding" thus brings together the three moments of the "threefold synthesis" of the A Deduction: the apprehension of the manifold, its reproduction, and its recognition in the "conscious-

[5] A121.

ness of the unity of the act" to which each apprehended and reproduced element belongs. Now, the A Deduction showed that *these three aspects of synthesis yield the representation of an object*, that is, the formation of concepts, only if all three depend on *transcendental* imagination, that is to say, on productive/reproductive syntheses of the imagination *under the unity of apperception*. Hence even in the A Deduction synthesis (imagination) and consciousness of the unity of synthesis (unity of apperception) were hardly separable within the activity of the representational capacities insofar as this activity must lead to the representation of an object. The activity of reproductive imagination applied to the forms of space and time stood under the unity of apperception, and this was how the imagination could be said to be *productive* of the rules of affinity of appearances.[6] Thus the synthesis Kant describes in section 15 of the B Deduction as an "act of the understanding" is the same as the synthesis of imagination *under the unity of apperception* which was described as the condition of the "synthesis of recognition in the concept." In order for the formulation in section 15 of the B Deduction to be completely coherent with the teaching of the A Deduction, it has only to be specified that every synthesis (inasmuch as it is capable of yielding the representation of objects) is an act of the understanding, that is to say of *the unity of apperception in relation to the synthesis of imagination.*[7]

This reminder also helps us to understand the twofold characterization of synthesis in section 15 quoted earlier: "All combination—*be it a combination of the manifold of intuition . . . or of various concepts*—is an act of the understanding" (my emphasis). To say that the combination *of several concepts* is an act of the understanding raises no particular difficulty. Such a combination may be either a combination of concepts into a complex concept, or a combination of concepts into a judgment. However, it is more surprising that the combination *of the manifold of intuition* should also be an act of the understanding. One would rather have expected, in this case, a combination *by the imagination*—unless one remembered that here, the understanding means nothing other than "the unity of apperception in relation to the synthesis of imagination." One may therefore acknowledge that the combination of the sensible manifold is achieved by the imagination, to be sure, but under the rule (or rules) supplied to it by the unity of apperception, which, again, "in its relation to the synthesis of imagination," is none other than the understanding.

If this is so, then we in fact have here two aspects of the activity of understanding corresponding to the two aspects of *concepts* and *rules* we encountered in the A Deduction. According to the first aspect, the understanding is *a rule giver for the syntheses of imagination*. Its original form is transcendental understanding—that is, the transcendental unity of apperception in relation to synthesis of imagination. In this first aspect the activity of the understanding, or actualizing of its rules, is nothing else than productive synthesis of imagination. According to the second aspect, the understanding is *reflective* or *discursive*. It reflects sensible syntheses under concepts, whether empirical or pure. The understanding said to

---

[6] Cf. p. 44.
[7] Cf. A119, and pp. 48–56.

produce the "combination of the manifold of intuition" in the text quoted previously is the understanding considered in the first aspect. The understanding said to produce the "combination of concepts" is the understanding considered in the second aspect.

In the same section, Kant states the relation between these two aspects of the activity of the understanding when he writes that the understanding can analyze only what it has previously combined:

> It will easily be observed that this act [of combination] is originally one and holds equally for all combination, and that its dissolution [*Auflösung*], namely *analysis*, which appears to be its opposite, nevertheless always presupposes it. For where the understanding has not previously combined, it cannot dissolve [*auflösen*], since only as having been combined *by the understanding* can anything that allows of analysis be given to the faculty of representation. (B130)

What makes the notions of synthesis and analysis presented here original is that while both operations are dependent upon the understanding, they are in no way symmetrical, nor are they "intellectual" (dependent on understanding or intellect, the *intellectus* of the *Dissertation* and Kant's early Latin writings) in the same manner. The *synthesis* the understanding must have effected before it can effect any *analysis* is a "synthesis of the manifold of sensible intuition," that is, a synthesis which is itself sensible and preconceptual. Only under the condition of such a synthesis can the *analysis* of the sensible into empirical concepts, "universal or reflected representations," take place. That is, the understanding can analyze the empirically given into concepts only if, as transcendental understanding/imagination, it has already been at work to guide the syntheses of the sensible manifold— the reproductive syntheses of imagination, whether these reproductive syntheses are empirical (exercized on a manifold of sensory data given in space and time) or pure (exercized on the a priori forms of space and time).

The logical (i.e., discursive) aspect of the functioning of understanding is therefore dependent on its aspect as synthesis of the sensible, a "blind" synthesis that remains mostly unknown to us, as Kant wrote when he introduced the term "synthesis" for the first time (A78/B103). The understanding can combine concepts only on the condition that it has previously guided the combination of the sensible in such a way that the latter may be reflected under concepts. One must bear in mind the original connection thus established between sensible combination and discursive combination if one is to understand at all the meaning of the famous proclamation that opens section 16 of the B Deduction.

The Kantian "Cogito"

> It must be *possible* for the 'I think' to accompany all my representations; for otherwise something would be represented in me which could not be thought at all, and that is equivalent to saying that the representation would be impossible, or at least would be nothing to me. (B132)

There is reason to be surprised here. Kant, unlike Descartes, does not identify representation with conscious representation, and even less does he identify conscious representation with thought. For him not all representations are conscious, and only *representation by concepts* is called *thought*.[8] How can one reconcile these distinctions with the unequivocal assertion that "It must be possible for the 'I think' to accompany all my representations"? That this should be the case for *conceptualized* representations is perhaps acceptable. But what about all the rest? Before answering these queries, I will briefly consider the two distinctions just mentioned: between representation and *conscious* representation, between conscious representation and *thought*.

In his *Anthropology*, Kant devotes a rather long paragraph to explaining that the representations we are conscious of make up only a small part of the "immense map of our mind." Similarly, in the *Logic* and in the introduction to the Transcendental Dialectic of the *Critique of Pure Reason* he distinguishes between representation and representation with consciousness.[9] In light of the A Deduction, it seems the representations "of which we are conscious" are those that have been the object of a "synthesis of apprehension," namely those that have been *distinguished* within a manifold of other representations. Conversely, those "of which we are not conscious" are ones that have not been the object of a synthesis of apprehension. In the *Anthropology*, Kant gives various examples of representations "of which we are not conscious, while we know that we have them," that is, representations we do not apprehend but can conclude are somehow present to our mind: the features of a house seen from afar, the individual notes of a chord struck in the course of a musical improvisation, the representations excluded from our attention in favor of other representations (an exclusion due perhaps to our sense of decency, to operations of abstraction necessary for the formation of general concepts, or any other reason).[10] In these examples, some of the representations considered may certainly become conscious. We may have apprehended them in the past, or may at some future time apprehend them. But others may remain forever unapprehended and thus may never reach the threshold of consciousness.

Moreover, even if we consider only representations "of which we are con-

---

[8] Cf. B94: "Thought is cognition by means of concepts"; B146: "Cognition involves two factors: first, the concept, through which an object in general is thought"; B283: "thought, or cognition through concepts."

[9] Cf. *Anthr.*, §5. *Logik*, introd., VIII, Ak. IX, 64–65; 569. *KrV* A320/B376–77.

[10] *Anthr.*, §5. Notice the similarity between these examples of representations "of which we are not conscious" and Leibniz's "*petites perceptions*" (cf. *Nouveaux Essais*, preface, *G* V, 46–47). The example of the musical keys in the improvised piece is also mentioned in the *Critique* (B144n). But there it is not described as an example of the *absence of consciousness*, but of *obscure consciousness*. A solution to this seeming disagreement between the *Anthropology* and the *Critique* may lie in the fact that, for Kant as well as for Leibniz, there is an infinite multiplicity of insensible degrees between the absence of consciousness and consciousness; the absolute zero of consciousness (for Kant, of apprehension) is thus only a limit, and the "obscure consciousness" of the *Critique* and the "absence of consciousness" of the *Anthropology* would therefore not be radically contradictory. However, it seems to me that the example of musical improvisation should be understood as illustrating the former rather than the latter case.

scious" (which we apprehend), nothing entitles us to assume that they are also *thought*. In the *Jäsche Logic*, Kant grants animals conscious representations and the capacity to perceive generic identities and differences between these representations. Yet he denies them the capacity to be *conscious of their own acts of comparison*. On this basis, Kant writes, animals may surely *know* (*kennen*), but not *cognize* (*erkennen*). That is to say, they cannot form concepts—those concept*s* (in the plural) that according to the A Deduction were dependent on *the* concept (in the singular) as the "consciousness of the unity of the act of synthesis" by which representations of objects are generated.[11] Now it is plausible to think that a great number of *our* representations involve acts of mere apprehension and reproductive associations of the same type as those animals are capable of, and the apprehension/reproduction/recognition *leading to concepts*—that is, to thought—is at work in only a small part of them.

To sum up: according to Kant we certainly have many representations of which we are not conscious; among our conscious representations there are some we just apprehend without reproducing them or reproduce without subjecting them to the rules of synthesis that allow them to be reflected under concepts—that is, to be thought. And indeed, all the opening sentence of section 16 states is that it must be *possible* for the 'I think' to accompany all my representations, not that it *must actually accompany them*. In other words, all of my representations must be such that it is *possible* to combine them (mediately or immediately) within the framework of the "unity of synthesis" of the manifold of my intuition, and to become conscious of such a combination. But this does not mean that such a combination always takes place. And the misleading suggestion—were it not possible for the 'I think' to accompany it, "the representation would be impossible"—is corrected right away by another: "or at least [it] would be nothing to me."[12]

It would be nothing to me, or in other words, it would not be *my* representation. Thus we can understand the assertion that "It must be *possible* for the 'I think' to accompany all my representations" as simply an explication of the thought expressed by the words "*my* representation." Kant means just this when he asserts that "the principle of the unity of apperception is an analytic proposition" (B135, 138).

How could we formulate this "proposition"? Taking into account Kant's previous explanations and their development in the A Deduction, the proposition might be something like: "Each representation I call *my own* is related to the original synthetic unity of apperception." The predicate of the proposition makes explicit what is implicitly thought in the expression "*my* representation," or "a representation I call *my own*." A representation is my own just in case it is taken up in the unified act of synthesis in which the representation 'I' itself originates, being the consciousness of the numerically identical function of unity at work in the synthesis of representations. This is also why, after having asserted that the "principle of the necessary unity of apperception" is an analytic proposition, Kant adds: "nevertheless it reveals the necessity of a synthesis of the manifold given in intu-

---

[11] *Logik*, introd., VIII, Ak. IX, 65; 570. Cf. *KrV* A103, and chapter 2, p. 46.
[12] Cf. B132.

ition, without which the thoroughgoing identity of self-consciousness cannot be thought" (B135).[13]

But the 'I think' cannot simply be identified with the understanding in its function of *synthesis* of the manifold of sensible intuition. For as we have seen, to *think* means to *represent by means of concepts*. The act of synthesis of the sensible manifold is a conscious 'I think' only insofar as the synthesis is directed toward *concept formation*, that is, insofar as it makes *analysis* possible. If this be the case, the 'I think' must be equated with what Kant calls the *analytic* unity of consciousness, which he says "attaches to all general concepts as such" and is possible only "with the presupposition of some synthetic unity."

> The analytic unity of consciousness attaches to all general concepts, as such [*hängt allen gemeinsamen Begriffen, als solchen, an*]. If, for instance, I think red in general, I thereby represent to myself a property which (as a character) can be found in something, or can be combined with other representations; that is, only by means of a presupposed synthetic unity can I represent to myself the analytic unity. (B133n)

Only because I can synthetically combine the manifold of sensible intuition and be conscious of the unity of this act of synthesis can I also analyze this manifold into concepts.

Such dependence of the analytic unity of consciousness on the synthetic unity confirms my remarks earlier in this chapter on the link between discursive thought and sensible synthesis. Discursive thought analyzes intuitive representations into concepts by comparing these representations in order to combine their concepts in judgments. These judgments reestablish the synthesis which first had

---

[13] Both Kant's statement that "the principle of the necessary unity of apperception is itself . . . an identical, and therefore analytic, proposition" and his remark immediately following this statement, that "nevertheless it reveals the necessity of a synthesis of the manifold given in intuition," have been the occasion for much debate. See in particular Strawson, *Bounds of Sense*, 93–97; Henrich, *Identität*, 54–57; Allison, *Idealism*, 137–39; Guyer, *Claims*, 115–17. Two main claims are, I think, distinctive of the interpretation I propose here. (1) The principle of the unity of apperception is "analytic" because it explains the expression "my representation": "my" representation = a representation taken up into one unified consciousness together with all the other representations I call "mine." This "analytic" principle is, like the definition of experience commented earlier (see p. 26), one on which any early modern philosopher would agree, even if they would use quite different vocabulary to make the point. But what they would not agree on is the *nature* of the unity of consciousness in question. For Kant, it is neither the unity of the consciousness of representations that are *each*, as isolated representations, accompanied with the idea of the self (contra Locke, *Essay*, bk. II, chap. 7, §11; cf. *KrV* B133, A107), nor a unity that results from the mere associative combination of ideas in imagination (contra Hume, *Treatise*, bk. I, sec. 6; cf. chapter 2). It is a unity that "reveals the necessity of a synthesis of everything given in intuition." This last point is actually quite cryptic. It finds its explication in the brief recollection of the threefold synthesis in §15 and more extensively in the exposition of the threefold synthesis in the A Deduction, which culminated in the "transcendental unity of apperception." (2) Most important about the "principle of the necessary unity of apperception" in B is the relation it establishes between *synthetic* unity and *analytic* unity of apperception (not to be confused with the description of the principle itself as an "analytic" proposition). This relation is parallel to the relations I stressed earlier between the two aspects of concept(s), of rules, and of the understanding. In all these cases, *synthesis* is the condition for *analysis*. I develop this point in the next few paragraphs of this section.

undergone analysis. It reestablishes it, however, no longer in the form of a combination of the manifold of intuition, but in the form of a combination of *concepts*. Keeping in mind the dynamic relation of the two syntheses, sensible synthesis and synthesis of concepts, we can understand the concluding sentence of section 16: "I am conscious to myself *a priori* of a necessary synthesis of representations—to be entitled the original synthetic unity of apperception—under which all representations that are given to me must stand, but under which they have also first to be brought by means of a synthesis" (B135–36). If it is hard to see how representations, on the one hand, *stand under* a "necessary a priori synthesis," and on the other hand also have to be *brought under* this synthesis, consider that synthesis is, on the one hand, synthesis of the manifold "as" sensible manifold and, on the other hand, discursive synthesis by which this manifold is reflected under concepts. The latter is possible only under the condition of the former, and conversely, the former is oriented toward achieving the latter. Both depend on one single act of synthesis that combines the manifold of representations into one experience; both are to be perpetually regained over the chaotic and contingent manifold of apprehended perceptions and merely associative reproductions of imagination.

For Kant, the proposition 'I think' is thus characteristic of a merely discursive, not an intuitive understanding. It is characteristic of an understanding that can "only" think: "An understanding in which through self-consciousness all the manifold would *eo ipso* be given, would be *intuitive*; our understanding can only *think*, and for intuition must look to the senses" (B135). That our understanding "can only think" means that it can form only discursive concepts, namely universal representations produced by "comparison, reflection, and abstraction" of the manifold given in intuition. Thought here appears to be an oddly inferior faculty. 'I', the 'I think', seems to share this inferior status. An understanding that forms discursive concepts and an understanding as 'I think' are limited in the same way. The 'I' of the 'I think' is nothing other than the "consciousness of the unity of synthesis" of a manifold *given* in sensibility before it is reflected under concepts. The 'I' is nothing other than the reflexivity of the act of *sensible* synthesis. An understanding that would intuit would not form discursive concepts (it would not "think" in the sense of "thinking" we know). But it seems that this understanding would not be an 'I' either, or at least that this 'I' would have nothing in common with what we mean by the word ("the consciousness of the unity of a synthesis" that is made necessary by the fact that representations are *given* as a random and contingent manifold). In the first paragraphs of the *Anthropology*, Kant explains that children acquire the capacity to conceptualize at the same time that they come to have the representation 'I'.[14] Indeed, if we follow the analyses of the Transcendental Deduction, to refer to oneself as 'I' is just to be (however obscurely) conscious of the unique act of synthesis and analysis that makes representations 'mine', and culminates in the formation of concepts.

[14] *Anthr.*, §1, Ak. VII, 127; 9–10.

THE "I THINK" AND THE OBJECT: LOGICAL FORMS OF JUDGMENT
AND TRANSCENDENTAL SYNTHESES OF IMAGINATION

The original synthetic unity of apperception is also called *objective* unity of apperception, or objective unity of self-consciousness. For only through this unified consciousness, or consciousness of the unity of synthesis, is any relation of our representations to an object possible. Kant argued for this point in great detail in the preliminary exposition of the A Deduction, as we saw in chapter 2. I have just argued that section 15 of the B Deduction recalled at least the bare structure of the "threefold synthesis" of A, necessary to introduce the "principle of the original synthetic unity of apperception," expounded in section 16. Section 17, I want to suggest, also relies on the explanations given in A. Indeed, keeping in mind the exposition of the "threefold synthesis," most importantly the "synthesis of recognition in a concept," is a necessary condition for making sense of the definition of an "object" Kant gives in section 17 of the B Deduction: "An *object* is that in the concept of which the manifold of a given intuition is *united*" (B137). If we remember the two aspects of "concept" we encountered in the "synthesis of recognition in a concept," we can understand this characterization of "object" in the following way. A concept (*Begriff*, act of seizing)[15] is (1) the (clear or obscure) "consciousness of the unity of the act" of grasping together a sensible manifold. But it is also (2) the *reflection* of this "unity of the act," namely of the rule for synthesis that, insofar as it is common to many (otherwise different) sensible representations, may be thought as a "universal and reflected representation." The *object* is thus (1) the object of intuition generated by the "consciousness of the unity of the act," and (2) the object of this intuition, *thought under* the discursive concept or "universal and reflected representation." Note that if this is correct, what we have here are the two aspects of "object" (as object-of-representation) I analyzed in chapter 1: the *appearance* (the singular object of an empirical intuition, which is now said to be *synthesized* by a concept—"that, in the concept of which the manifold of a given intuition is united"); and the *object of the appearance*, or *phenomenon* (the object *thought under* a concept—that, we might say, "*under* the concept of which the manifold of an intuition is united").

In the A edition, when he reached this point in his account of the representation of an object, Kant emphatically declared: "Now I maintain that the categories above cited are nothing but the conditions of thought in a possible experience" (A111).[16] But in B, Kant does not content himself with any such declaration. The relation of the categories to the original synthetic unity of apperception, and thereby to the objects of experience, still remains to be *proved*. And this proof is broken down into two steps. In the first step, Kant establishes the identity between the *logical forms of judgment* and the objective unity of apperception (section 19). Since, according to the metaphysical deduction, the categories are themselves

---

[15] See chapter 2, p. 46.
[16] Cf. chapter 2, p. 52.

originally nothing other than the logical functions (manifested in logical forms) of judgment, their own relation to the objective unity of apperception and thus to the objects of experience is thereby established (section 20). The second step answers the question, How do objects given only to the *senses*, in the forms of our receptivity, agree nonetheless with the logical functions of our judgments, and thus with the categories? Kant's answer consists in expounding his notion of "figurative synthesis" (*synthesis speciosa*), also called transcendental synthesis of imagination, and "determination of inner sense by the understanding" (sections 24, 26). By introducing this notion, Kant means finally to clarify the nature of the original synthetic unity of apperception which, according to sections 15 and 16 of the B Deduction, is a necessary condition of any combination of our representations. Hence these initial sections are definitely relegated to the role of a mere introduction to the Transcendental Deduction proper, in which Kant's argument mainly consists in explaining the relation between discursive syntheses (according to the logical forms of judgment) and sensible syntheses (according to the forms of *synthesis speciosa*, the transcendental synthesis of imagination).[17]

Let me now recapitulate the results achieved so far.

My goal in this first part of the book was to show that Kant's "leading thread"—making the logical functions of judgment the guideline for establishing

[17] Kant twice explicitly states that the B Deduction is organized around the two moments I just characterized. He states it first in §21, which closes the first step (B144–45), then in §26, which is the culmination of the second step (B159–60). These two steps have given rise to various interpretations. According to Adickes (*Kritik*, 139–40), then Paton (*Metaphysic*, I, 501), they reproduce the duality between the objective and the subjective deduction stated in the preface to the A edition. But this is not convincing, for in fact, both moments of the argument refer to acts of representation, and both deal with the relation of a priori concepts to objects. Erdmann (*Kritizismus*), and after him De Vleeschauwer (*Déduction*, III, 24–25) read them rather as a deduction "from the top down," followed by a deduction "starting from below," which thus repeats the two recapitulations of the A Deduction. This reading is no more convincing than the first, however, for both moments deal from the outset with the sensible manifold *and* the original synthetic or objective unity of self-consciousness, without presenting either of the progressions of the A Deduction, "from the top down" or "starting from below." Dieter Henrich has argued (*Beweisstruktur*, 95–96) that §§19 and 20 lead only to the *conditional* assertion of the subordination of the objects of intuition to the categories (*if* an intuition is *one, then* it is subject to the categories). On its part, §26 shows that *since* all our intuitions are contained in one intuition of space and time, they are necessarily subject to the categories. For a discussion of Henrich's view, see Wagner, "Argumentationsgang"; and the debate published in Tuschling, *Probleme*, 41–96. None of the commentators mentioned seem to notice the fact that the shift from the first to the second moment of the deduction is a shift from a consideration of the logicodiscursive function of the understanding (in step 1) to a reevaluation, *in light of the first consideration*, of what we learned in the Transcendental Aesthetic about space and time, that is, about "the manner in which things are given to us" (in step 2). Allison comes closest to such a reading, but it seems to me that he confuses it unnecessarily by organizing his interpretation around two senses of "object" which he associates with the German terms: *Objekt* (for the first step) and *Gegenstand* (for the second step), corresponding to which he thinks Kant proved the *objective validity* of the categories on the one hand, their *objective reality* on the other hand (cf. *Idealism*, chap. 7, 133–36, 144–48). These terminological distinctions do not seem to me to be substantiated by the text and, more important, I do not think they are really helpful in understanding the nature of the argument. I shall say more on this point in chapter 5; see in particular note 14.

a table of the categories—far from being an unfortunate architectonic coquetterie, was on the contrary a ground-breaking step for Kant's conception of the categories or "pure concepts of the understanding" and for the transcendental deduction itself.

Kant starts with a question loaded with presuppositions: "how can *a priori* concepts relate to objects that are *given*?" But this initial question leads him to a broader one: "What is the relation between representation and object of representation *in general* (whether the representation is 'pure', or empirical)?" His answer to the broader question is meant to provide both legitimation of, and answer to, the narrower, presupposition-loaded question. This broadening of the scope of the question is what makes Kant's endeavor so interesting.

In chapter 1, I argued that Kant's first important step in answering the broader question, in the *Critique of Pure Reason*, is his giving up the *causal* model still prevalent in the 1772 Letter to Herz to account for the relation between representation and its object, and instead considering strictly the "representational," or we might say "intentional" relation between representation and object-of-representation. So considered, the object-of-representation has two aspects: it is an object-of-sensible-intuition (appearance, the *apparentia* of the 1770 *Inaugural Dissertation*); but it is also the object *thought for* the appearance (for instance, the object thought under the concept 'tower' and thus "recognized" when we perceive patches of brown in the distance, the object thought under the concept 'coach' when we hear the approaching sound, and so on). In the 1770 *Inaugural Dissertation*, Kant argued that we thus recognize objects under concepts when we progress from *apparentia* to *experientia*, from appearance to experience (and the object of experience: *phaenomenon*), by virtue of what he called the "logical use of the understanding": by this he meant, not the use of the understanding *in logic*, but the use of the understanding for empirical knowledge, according to just those forms of concept-subordination (judgments and syllogisms) for which logic codifies the rules.

Kant's essential move, in the Transcendental Deduction of the Categories in the *Critique of Pure Reason*, is to argue that categories are originally nothing other than the functions of intellect at work in the "logical use of the understanding," described in the *Dissertation* as generating our representations of *phaenomena*. This does not mean that all the *Critique* does is take up the theory of the "logical use of intellect" from the *Dissertation*. On the contrary, what it means is that Kant became aware, not only that he had given no account of the application of "pure concepts of the understanding" to objects that are given; but also that his account of the "logical use of the understanding" itself was *not* sufficient to explain the possibility of cognizing even mere *phenomena*. For this "logical use" of intellect to occur at all, appearances must be combined in such a way that they *are* susceptible to being reflected according to this use of intellect. Now, a model for such active, intellect-driven combination of sensible representations was provided by the *synthesis* proper to mathematical thinking. With "logical use of understanding" and (mathematical) "synthesis" Kant thus had in hand the two major tools for answering both his questions: the "narrow" one (how do a priori concepts relate to object that are given?) and the "broad" one (how do representations relate to objects-of-representations in general?).

In chapter 2, I analyzed Kant's use of the model of synthesis in the A Deduction, and his falling just short of relating adequately this mode of combination to the "logical use of the understanding." In the present chapter, I argued that the initial sections of the B Deduction are meant to take up the "threefold synthesis" and its relation to the unity of apperception, which are the bulk of the argument in A, and from there, move to the main argument of the B Deduction: step one, the role of logical functions of judgment in relating representations to objects; step two, the ways in which these logical functions relate to objects *given in sensibility*.

The rest of this book will be devoted to elucidating just these two steps. In part II, I shall examine Kant's claim, in section 19 of the Transcendental Deduction, that "The logical form of all judgments consists in the objective unity of apperception of the concepts contained in it." I will examine what Kant means by "logical form of judgment," and elucidate in great detail what he means when he says that it is the discursive form in which we relate our representations to objects. This will lead me in the end to retrace my steps and return (in part III) to what must occur prior to discursive judgment: to the prediscursive synthesis, *synthesis speciosa*, or transcendental synthesis of imagination. This is the second step in the B Transcendental Deduction (sections 24 and 26). I shall argue that close analysis of these two steps allows us not only to give its full due to Kant's metaphysical deduction of the categories, but also to provide a complete and coherent interpretation of the System of the Principles of Pure Understanding that the Transcendental Deduction of the Categories is supposed to ground.

· PART TWO ·

The Logical Forms of Judgment as
Forms of Reflection

THE PREVIOUS ANALYSES lead me to characterize Kant's claim about judgment as follows. The primary function of the combination of concepts in a judgment is to reflect in discursive form a synthetic unity first present in the sensible given in a form that is intuitive, continuous, indistinct.

This description of the function of judgment depends on Kant's analysis of the conditions of possibility of cognition. Consequently, any attempt on his part at a *logical* definition of judgment depends on the ways in which he characterizes the function of thought in the "Transcendental Doctrine of Elements," the Transcendental Aesthetic and Transcendental Analytic in the *Critique of Pure Reason*. To provide a logical definition of judgment is to define its "mere form," namely the form of the activity of discursive thinking regardless of the object to which it may apply. But Kant's explanation of this activity is provided in his transcendental doctrine of the elements of all cognition. There Kant explains the respective roles of sensibility or a priori receptivity, the original synthetic unity of apperception, and finally the analytic unity of consciousness in which the synthetic unity is "reflected," that is, thought by means of concepts, themselves combined in judgments.

One reason Kant's definitions are so often perplexing is this dependence of logical definition on transcendental critique. Consider, for instance, the definition he gives in section 19 of the Transcendental Deduction: "a judgment is nothing but the manner in which given cognitions are brought to the objective unity of apperception" (B141). Is such a definition logical or transcendental? Kant seems to be claiming it holds from a purely logical point of view, since in the same passage he reproaches the *logicians* for not having been able to formulate it. But the reference to the objective unity of apperception seems to place it squarely in a *transcendental* context, since Kant's discussion of the role and nature of the objective unity of apperception has its proper place in the Transcendental Deduction of the Categories. In fact, these two ways of characterizing the proposed definition (as purely logical, as transcendental) are not incompatible. The definition belongs, indeed, to what Kant calls *general* or *formal* logic, since it defines any judgment, regardless of object or whether the origin of the concepts it combines is a posteriori or a priori. Nonetheless, this purely logical definition depends on an elucidation of procedures of thought that can be carried out only by a transcendental critique.

Let there be no confusion about what "purely logical" means here. Kant calls logic *formal* insofar as it "abstracts from all content of cognition . . . and deals solely with the form of thought in general (that is, of discursive cognition)" (A131/B170). But what he means by this is different from what is meant by contemporary logicians. Today we call "form" the structural features of the proposition that are relevant to truth-preserving inference and are expressed in the language of a logical calculus. In many ways Kant's "formal" logic is even further from such a model than Aristotle's *Prior Analytics*, and a fortiori, further than Leibniz's *calculus ratiocinator* or its developments in Wolff or Lambert.[1] His conception of logic is closer to that of the Port-Royal logicians, for whom logic was the exposition of "the reflections men have made on the four main operations of their mind—conceiving, judging, reasoning, and ordering"; Kant describes logic as "the self-cognition of the understanding and of reason . . . merely as to form."[2]

But this comparison with Port-Royal logic also serves to emphasize the originality of Kant's definition of judgment just quoted. Here is how Arnauld and Nicole define judgment: "After conceiving things by our ideas, we compare these ideas and, finding that some belong together and some do not, we unite or separate them. This is called *affirming* or *denying*, and in general *judging*."[3]

Such a definition presupposes that ideas are prior to judgments. The entire function of judgments is to state the combinations of ideas that follow from comparing them. On the contrary, the definition given in section 19 of the Transcendental Deduction does not presuppose a plurality of already determined ideas that could be combined into judgments when they are compared. Instead, it presupposes an indeterminate manifold of representations, which the judgment must then bring to one and the same "objective unity of apperception." Thus, if for both Port-Royal and Kant the definition of judgment is dependent on a prior notion of

---

[1] For a discussion of Leibniz-inspired works on logical calculus, specifically German works, cf. Blanché, *Logique*, 224. Lambert, for whom Kant's admiration is well known, was the author of many works on logical calculus (cf. especially the *Dianoiologie*, which is the first part of the *Neues Organon* published in 1764, *De universali calculi idea*, and *In algebram philosophicam breves annotationes*, published in the *Acta Eruditorum* in 1764 and 1766, respectively, and *Sechs Versuche einer Zeichenkunst in der Vernunftlehre*, published in 1782 by Bernoulli). For his part, Kant was skeptical early on as to the metaphysical use of a logical combinatoric presupposing completely analyzable concepts (cf. *Nova Dilucidatio*, I-2, scholium, Ak. I, 390; 8). Hence he never showed great interest in projects of logical calculus, though it is worth noting that when he was satisfied with his own "analytic of concepts of the pure understanding," he encouraged Schultz to try to elaborate a combinatoric on this basis, a task Schultz politely declined. Cf. "Letter to Schultz," August 26, 1783 (Ak. X, 351; 109) and Schultz's reply, August 28, 1783 (Ak. X, 354; 111).

[2] Arnauld and Nicole, *Art de penser*, 37; 29. Kant, *Logik*, Ak. IX, 14; 529. I first encountered this parallel between Kant's and Arnauld's characterization of logic in Cavaillès, *Théorie de la science*, 2.

[3] Arnauld and Nicole, *Art de penser*, II-3, 313; 108.

"what it is to think,"[4] for Kant, transcendental philosophy alone can tell us "what it is to think."

This dependence of the "self-cognition of reason merely as to its form" on transcendental philosophy is what gives the particular logical forms—and, in the first place, the forms of judgment—their necessary character. Only because the combinations effected by judgments are identical with the combinations "universally represented" by the categories, as stated in the metaphysical deduction,[5] and because these combinations are necessary for all representation of a sensible object, as shown in the transcendental deduction, may the forms of judgment be termed a priori and thus be considered *necessary* rules for combining our representations. Thus the rules of logic derive their necessary character from their relation to the original synthetic unity of apperception. Kant says as much in section 16 of the Transcendental Deduction: "The synthetic unity of apperception is therefore the highest point to which we must ascribe all use of the understanding, *even the whole of logic*, and conformably therewith, transcendental philosophy" (B133n, my emphasis).

In his essay *Sur la logique et la théorie de la science*, Cavaillès argued that although Kant advocated freeing logic from psychology, he was unfaithful to his own requirement. In this respect, he claimed, Kant's logic is as ambiguous as Arnauld's. It makes the necessity of the rules of thought, as stated in logic, dependent on the self-illumination of a consciousness perfectly transparent to itself.[6] One just "sees" the necessity of the rules of logic by "reflecting upon the main operations of the mind." To be sure, Cavaillès adds, this necessary character of the rules, which makes them genuine laws of thought and gives Kant's notion of *form* its meaning, presupposes that empirical consciousness, with its contingent features, has been overcome in attaining awareness of these rules. But then the only aid to reaching awareness of the pure form (which coincides with the act of thinking in general) is the requirement that thought should be in agreement with itself. But what can such a requirement teach us except the "emptiness of logical identity"? Therefore, Cavaillès claims, when it comes to expressing and combining the four logical elements (concept, judgment, reasoning, and method), Kant ultimately falls back on empirical introspection for any insight into the activity of thinking. He lacks the resources Aristotle and Leibniz had at their disposal for escaping psychologism, since logic for them is grounded in an ontology, whereas for Kant logic is the ultimate source of all ontological concepts. The relation of general logic to transcendental logic does not compensate for this loss, since the forms of general logic are supposed to provide a guiding thread for the concepts of transcendental logic rather than the reverse. Even this supposed derivation is suspicious, however, for the "forms" of general logic seem to be in fact borrowed from the previously admitted concepts of transcendental logic. "During the entire

---

[4] I borrow this expression from Descartes, *Principles of Philosophy*, II, 9.

[5] A79/B104–5: "The same function which gives unity to the various representations in a judgment also gives the mere synthesis of representations in intuition a unity which, expressed universally, is called pure concept of the understanding". This passage will be analyzed later.

[6] Cavaillès, *Théorie de la science*, 2.

course of the transcendental deduction, one senses the discomfort stemming from
the use of general logic as a guiding thread and a prior basis—ready-made to be
used without any critique or justification—while the notions it makes use of,
quality, quantity, and relation, are either of foreign origin, or come after the act of
synthesis." Cavaillès concludes: "In a philosophy of consciousness, either logic is
transcendental, or it does not exist at all."[7]

I reject such a conclusion. True, general logic as Kant defines it ("the self-cognition of the understanding and of reason . . . merely as to form") depends ultimately on transcendental logic (on the analysis of the role of understanding in
providing a priori grounds for any cognition of objects), and more particularly on
the transcendental deduction of the categories in which Kant provides his explanation of the function and nature of discursive thought. But this dependence (1)
does not deprive general logic of its specificity, and (2) does allow it to escape
empirical introspection of operations of the mind in establishing its forms. Let us
briefly examine each of these two points.

1. General logic is not deprived of its distinctness from being dependent on
transcendental logic. Recall Kant's definition of *transcendental* cognition: "I entitle *transcendental* all cognition which is occupied not so much with objects as
with the mode of our cognition of objects insofar as this mode of cognition is to
be possible *a priori*" (B25). Or, again: "Not every kind of knowledge *a priori*
should be called transcendental, but that only by which we know that—and
how—certain representations (intuitions or concepts) can be employed or are
possible purely *a priori*" (A56/B80). Thus transcendental logic shows first how a
priori concepts relate to empirical objects (in the Transcendental Deduction of the
Categories) next how a priori judgments relate to experience in general (in the
Analytic of Principles), and last how the claim to determine an object by reasoning with pure concepts leads only to illusion (in the Transcendental Dialectic).
The domain of transcendental logic, therefore, is quite precisely circumscribed. It
does not provide a characterization of discursive forms *as such*, whether they are
used for a priori or a posteriori, sensible or intellectual cognition. Only general
logic can provide such an exposition.

2. That general logic is dependent on transcendental logic is, however, what allows it to escape the alternatives proposed by Cavaillès, namely the choice between empirical introspection on the one hand, and on the other a deduction of
the forms of thought from the mere requirement of "agreement with itself," that
is, empty identity. Kant's exposition of the forms of thought depends on what the
Critique showed to be the essential function of discursive thinking: namely, to
combine our representations according to the original synthetic unity of apperception, by means of analytic unity (i.e., analysis of representations into concepts,
combined in judgments, connected to each other by inferences). Befitting this
characterization of the function of discursive thought, the central discursive form
in Kant's logic is *judgment*. As we shall see, *concepts* and *inferences* are both in-

---

[7] Ibid., 10. This view is very similar to the Neo-Kantian view mentioned in the introduction to this
book.

volved in Kant's definition of judgment, and both are shown to be generated together with judgment, in the very act of forming judgments.

In my opinion, Kant's discovery of the essential function of discursive thought (we combine our representations according to the original synthetic unity of apperception by means of analytic unity) gave his table of the logical forms of judgment its order. Examination of the *Nachlaß* supports this point. During the 1770s Kant gradually arrived at the systematic exposition of the table of logical forms of judgment we find in the *Critique of Pure Reason* as well as in the *Logic* Jäsche later collated at his request.[8] Thus the discovery of the parallelism between the two tables (of the logical forms of judgment and of the categories), quite probably heralded in the "Letter to Herz" of February 21, 1772, dominates from then on Kant's explication of the forms of discursivity. In other words, if it is true, as Kant says in section 10 of the *Critique*, that one and the same function gives unity both to concepts in judgment and to the mere synthesis of representations in intuition, "universally represented" in a category, then each of the two tables sheds light on the other. The strength and coherence of each is established and buttressed by that of the other.[9]

One might object that in this case, we fall back into the dilemma Cavaillès drew attention to. General logic only escapes psychologism at the cost of being indistinguishable from transcendental logic, and the role of the table of judg-

---

[8] The *Logik Blomberg* and the *Logik Philippi* (of 1771 and 1772, respectively) give a more scattered presentation of judgments, which is closer to the textbooks Kant used (above all, Meier's) than to the systematic organization of the *Critique* (cf. Ak. XXIV-1, 273–79, and 461–65; for the *Blomberg Logic*, see *Lectures on Logic*, 220–25). According to Tonelli, the first appearance of the two tables in an almost identical form to that they have in the first *Critique* is in the 1777 lectures on metaphysics: *Vorlesungen über philosophische Enzyklopädie* (1777–80) and *Metaphysik Pölitz* (1778–80) (cf. Tonelli, *Vorrausetzungen*, 147; Kant, *Met. L1*, Ak. XXVIII-1, 187). In the article quoted, Tonelli gives a detailed inventory of the logic textbooks that might have influenced Kant. On this point, see also Schulthess, *Relation und Funktion*, 11–121. What is perhaps more interesting even than the exposition of the parallelism between the two tables, Schulthess shows how between the 1750s and the 1770s, Kant moved from an intensional conception of logic, which privileges relations of concepts considered in their intension or content, to what Schulthess calls an *extensional-intensional* conception, which privileges the extension of concepts, regardless of whether this extension is made up of concepts or of intuitions, and lastly to a conception which Schulthess calls *extensional-extensional*, in which the extension of concepts is made up of things *which fall under concepts* (i.e., by the singular objects of sensible intuition, in Kantian terms). In what follows I will show how important this transformation is for understanding the role of the categories. The relation between Kant's interpretation of formal logic and his transcendental critique of cognition goes far beyond the parallel exposition of the categories and the logical forms of judgment. Nevertheless, for reasons which will become clear, I think that Schulthess goes too far in drawing Kant's logic toward an extensional logic in the post-Fregean sense.

[9] If one grants that the two tables illuminate each other to an equal degree, any attempt at a systematic deduction of Kant's table of judgments from the mere definition of judgment as the "function of unity in thinking" alone must seem fruitless. This is a major shortcoming of Reich's otherwise pioneering *Die Vollständigkeit der Kantischen Urteilstafel (The Completeness of Kant's Table of Judgments)* one of the works which did the most to draw attention to the importance of Kant's table of the logical forms of judgment. For a critical overview and a summary of the German literature on the topic, see Brandt, *Urteilstafel*, pp. 8–43; and Wolff, *Vollständigkeit*, pp. 1–8.

ments—namely, that of being a "guiding thread" for the table of the categories—is after all an illusion.

But the objection pays insufficient heed to Kant's structure of dependencies, which can be roughly sketched as follows. Kant asked himself which logical forms of judgment should be considered primitive *if* the *original* function of judgment is to "bring given cognitions to the objective unity of apperception," that is, to relate our representations to objects. In this sense, the transcendental question must have had a key role in the establishment of a systematic table of the logical forms of judgment. Having discovered that the objectifying function of these forms provided him with the solution he was seeking to the problem of the categories, Kant retained as primitive only those forms which he thought indispensable for generating the relation of our representations to an object. But this is precisely what led him to describe the logical forms thus selected as the "guiding thread" for the table of the categories. The categories' having their origin in the functions of understanding manifested in the "mere logical forms of judgment" is precisely what makes them liable to a systematic inventory and to a full elucidation of their meaning.[10]

If we disregard the priority of the logical forms of judgment over the categories, Kant's whole argument is rendered incomprehensible. Take for instance Jonathan Bennett's objection to Kant's metaphysical deduction of the categories: "it is just not true that the only task of categorical judgments is to attribute properties to substances. Again, causal judgments are only a sub-class of hypotheticals, and the concept of cause is therefore not just the ability to handle hypotheticals."[11]

Fortunately, Kant never held the position Bennett attributes to him here. He did not argue that every judgment involves the "application" of the categories that correspond to the various aspects of its logical form. Indeed, he expressly maintained the opposite view, for at least two reasons. First, judgments may have no

[10] The relation I suggest here between transcendental logic and general logic seems to me in agreement with Michael Wolff's interesting analysis of the distinction and correlation between *function* and *form* of judgment. I suggest that the discovery in transcendental logic of the original *function* of judgment provides a guideline for identifying primitive *forms* of judgment respectively effecting the various ways in which the function is fulfilled, and thus in turn serving as guideline for establishing a table of the *categories*. Wolff writes: "Very generally Kant wants to say that when a human being judges, and gives his judgment one of the listed *forms*, then a determinate function (corresponding in each case to the form) of human understanding is implemented, which the form respectively exhibits" (*Vollständigkeit*, 20). Wolff then goes on to make a very sophisticated use of the distinction between 'function' and 'form'. According to him, the former notion is *transcendental*, and the latter alone purely *logical*. The four main titles of the table (quantity, quality, relation, modality) are established as the four main logical *functions*, while the subdivisions of each title are established under the guideline of consideration of logical *forms* (see *Vollständigkeit*, 10–43). Only by making use of this distinction, says Wolff, can one discern within the relevant sections of the Transcendental Analytic (sec. 1 and 2 of chap. 1: §§9 and 10) a systematic argument for the completeness of Kant's table of logical functions of judgment. Wolff's work appeared too late for me to be in a position to discuss his impressive analysis in the present book.

[11] Bennett, *Analytic*, 92. Similarly Guyer, *Claims*, 99: "It is hard to see why we should be able to make hypothetical—that is, 'if . . . then————' judgments only if we can detect *causal* connections among objects, and disjunctive judgments—that is, 'either . . . or————.' judgments—only if objects *interact*." Of course. But Kant said nothing of the kind.

relation to a sensible intuition. *In such a case no category is involved.* For instance, the example of a hypothetical judgment Kant gives in the course of his explanation of the table of logical forms is not a causal judgment: 'If there is a perfect justice, the obstinately wicked are punished'. This judgment is a hypothetical combination of propositions founded on the analysis of the concept of 'perfect justice'. Relying on analysis of concepts alone, without synthesis of intuition, it does not express a causal connection.[12] Second, even when judgments do apply to objects of a sensible intuition, causality and substantiality are so far from being equivalent to the *logical* relation in the hypothetical and categorical judgments that, on the contrary, from a "merely logical" standpoint, one can assign the position of subject or of predicate to either term in a categorical proposition, or of ground or of consequence to either judgment in a hypothetical proposition, provided only that the appropriate logical conversions are carried out. So, far from determining the form of judgment, each category, on the contrary, derives its meaning from its relation to the corresponding logical form.[13] *How* this is so certainly needs analysis and explanation. But this need makes it all the more important first to ask how Kant understood the various logical forms of judgment that he set up in his table—not, or at least not first, to ask how we understand the more or less relevant reconstructions we may propose of them. He who dispenses with the former question forgoes all chance of evaluating the fruitfulness or barrenness of Kant's theses in the first *Critique*.

In chapter 4 I will examine some of Kant's definitions of judgment from a "merely logical" standpoint, in order to shed light on the logical function of understanding at work in the discursive forms that are supposed to "bring given cognitions to the objective unity of apperception." In chapter 5 I will focus on the operations by means of which judgment reflects a sensible given supposed in itself to be radically foreign to any conceptual form. In chapter 6 I shall pursue this examination with the help of the appendix to the Transcendental Analytic, The Amphiboly of the Concepts of Reflection. This all-too-neglected chapter of the first *Critique* provides exceptionally fruitful indications as to Kant's conception of the discursive operation he calls "reflection," by means of which the sensible given is

[12] Cf. A73/B98. The difference between this judgment and a causal judgment will be analyzed in chapter 11. See also my: "Logique et métaphysique," 78; and "Kant on Causality," forthcoming.

[13] See B128: "[The categories] are concepts of an object in general, by means of which the intuition of an object is regarded as determined in respect of one of the logical functions of judgment. Thus the function of the categorical judgment is that of the relation of subject to predicate; for example, 'All bodies are divisible'. But *as regards the merely logical employment of the understanding, it remains undetermined to which of the two concepts the function of the subject, and to which the function of predicate, is to be assigned. For we can also say, 'Something divisible is a body'. But when the concept of body is brought under the category of substance, it is thereby determined that its empirical intuition must always be considered in experience as subject and never as mere predicate. Similarly with all the other categories.*" (See also *Prol.* §39, Ak. IV, 323–24.) To be sure, this text is not easy to interpret. But at least it unambiguously shows that the relation of subject and predicate in a judgment does not always express one of substance and accident. The same holds for all other categories. I will develop this point in detail in part III.

thought under concepts combined according to the different logical forms of judgment. In chapter 7 I will show that Kant's much vilified distinction between two types of empirical judgments—judgments of perception and judgments of experience—if properly construed, greatly helps understand in what sense judgment in general is "the act by which representations are brought under the objective unity of apperception."

I will thus have followed Kant's explanation of the forms of discursive analysis as far as seems necessary for a correct evaluation of Kant's first line of argument in the Transcendental Deduction of the Categories. Kant's second line of argument will then remain to be examined. It concerns the question, What prior forms of combination of the sensible given are necessary for discursive analysis to be possible? The answer lies in Kant's doctrine of the *synthesis speciosa* or transcendental synthesis of imagination, which I shall discuss in part III.

Logical Definitions of Judgment

IT MAY SEEM strange that I should mention *definitions* in the title of this chapter rather than *a* (logical) *definition* of judgment. Does the plural betray uncertainty on Kant's part, or his often decried incapacity to give a clear-cut meaning to the most fundamental terms of his system? Actually, the three definitions we shall consider are complementary, each of them describing the form of judgment in a specific aspect.

The first definition Kant provides in section 19 of the Transcendental Deduction of the Categories: "A judgment is . . . the manner in which given cognitions are brought to the objective unity of apperception" (B141). By describing judgment in the terms provided by the Transcendental Analytic, this definition sheds light on the function fulfilled by the discursive forms that general logic expounds in detail.

The second definition can be found in the *Jäsche Logic*. It explains the *discursive* nature of the function of unity in judgment: "A judgment is the representation of the unity of the consciousness of various representations, or the representation of their relation insofar as they constitute a concept."[1] This definition should be compared with what is said in section 10 of the Transcendental Analytic: it is "by means of analytic unity" that the understanding "produces the logical form of a judgment" (A79/B105). "By means of analytic unity" means: by bringing several intuitive representations under one concept, and several concepts under one concept of greater universality.

The third definition we shall consider states the relation of the discursive combination of concepts to *truth*, by defining judgment as assertion *under a condition*.[2] This third definition relates the second one to the first, since in it the discursive combination of concepts (second definition) is considered as potentially true (or false) and as such related to an object (first definition). Moreover, the notion of *condition* makes every judgment an element in a potential syllogistic inference

---

[1] *Logik*, §17, Ak. IX, 101; 597.

The *Logic* Jäsche edited and published at Kant's request, from materials Kant provided (the annotated copy of Meier's *Auszug aus der Vernunftslehre* Kant used for his lectures), is often considered to be almost useless and certainly an unreliable source. See for instance Stuhlmann-Laeisz, *Logik*, 1; Schulthess, *Relation*, 12; and Young, preface, xvii–xviii. It is true that the textbook must be used with caution. Jäsche indiscriminately collected lectures from different periods, some selections are doubtful or even contradict each other. The textbook is in many respects less reliable than the *Nachlaß* on logic (*Reflexionen* and Lectures), since it masks the chronological diversity of the notes collected in it. Nevertheless, it remains a precious source of insight as long as it is read in conjunction with the *Nachlaß* and, above all, with the most surely reliable source: the treatment of logical questions in Kant's own published works.

[2] For the references supporting this definition, cf. pp. 93–97.

where the condition of a given judgment is subsumed under the condition of a judgment of greater universality, or conversely subsumes the condition of a judgment of lesser universality, and in the end subsumes the sensible objects of intuition.

Judgment as "The Manner in Which Given Cognitions Are Brought to the Objective Unity of Apperception"

> I have never been able to accept the interpretation which logicians give of judgment in general. It is, they declare, the representation of a relation between two concepts. I do not here dispute with them as to what is defective in this interpretation—that in any case it applies only to *categorical*, not to hypothetical and disjunctive judgments. . . . I need only point out that the definition does not determine in what the asserted *relation* consists.

Kant then suggests the following "determination":

> But if I investigate more precisely the relation of the given cognitions in any judgment and distinguish it, as belonging to the understanding, from the relation according to laws of the reproductive imagination, which has only subjective validity, I find that a judgment is nothing but the manner in which given cognitions are brought to the objective unity of apperception. (B141)

This explanation seems to display excessive confidence in what the logical function of judgment, according to its logical form, can achieve: how could the mere fact of organizing our representations according to this form render a combination that is merely subjective (because it is dependent upon the vagaries of empirical reproduction) objective (because it occurs "*in virtue of the necessary unity* of apperception")?[3]

In answer to such a question, first note that the "objective" unity of apperception is not the unity of apperception *that conforms to an object* (and thus forms combinations of representations that can be called 'true'), but is instead the unity of apperception *that relates our representations to an object* (and thus forms combinations of representations that *tend* to truth, but may in fact be true *or* false).[4] The two senses of objectivity are of course not independent of one another. To relate representations to an object (in the second sense) *is* to strive toward a combination of representations that would prove to be *in conformity with the object*, that is to say, true. In other words, *objectivity*, in the full sense of a *conformity to the object* of the combination of representations is what the activity of judgment tends to achieve. This is the immanent norm, as it were, of judgment, rather than a state of representations one can suppose to be present in judgment from the outset. Indeed, this is what Kant seems to mean when he continues:

---

[3] B142 (Kant's emphasis).

[4] On this point I agree with Allison, *Idealism*, 72; see also Prauss, *Erscheinung*, 86–87; and Thöle's distinction between objectivity of judgment in the broad sense of *Wahrheitsanspruch* (claim to truth) and in the strict sense of *Wahrheit* (truth) (cf. Thöle, *Gesetzmäßigkeit*, 69–72) .

[To bring given representations to the objective unity of apperception] is *what is intended* by the copula 'is'. It is employed to distinguish the objective unity of given representations from the subjective. It indicates their relation to original apperception and its *necessary unity*, even if the judgment is itself empirical and therefore contingent, as, for example, in the judgment 'Bodies are heavy'. (B142, translation modified)

By means of the logical forms of our judgment we strive to bring about the "objective unity of given representations." The "subjective unity" emerges from the associative combinations of imagination, which are dependent on the contingent conjunctions of our representations. But the objective unity of representations, being the combination of *empirically given* representations, is itself dependent on the empirical associations of imagination and the contingent circumstances in which they occur. Consequently, even though every judgment as such aims at objectivity (in the strict sense, conformity to the object) by means of the combination of representations according to its logical form, the judgment may remain "subjective" to a greater or lesser degree. To use a distinction Kant makes in the *Prolegomena*, it may hold good only "for myself," "in my present state of perception" (Kant calls this kind of judgment, "judgment of perception"), and not "for everyone, always" (which would make the judgment a "judgment of experience").[5] Yet however subjective the judgment may remain—that is, even when it is most dependent on the particular circumstances of my associative combinations—the combination of representations it expresses is possible only because it is required by the unity of apperception that relates sensible representations to objects and thus aims at forming true judgments: in this sense, *every* judgment (and, in particular, every empirical judgment) is "the manner in which given cognitions are brought to the unity of apperception."

For example, a judgment such as 'Bodies are heavy' may be only the empirical generalization of a customary association between impressions of weight and of carrying a body. If it expresses nothing more than such a generalization, the correlation it expresses is contingent. It is quite possible that the combination of the concept of body and that of weight should express a correlation that does not hold of the object itself and therefore "for everyone, always," but only relative to contingent features of my particular physiology and psychology. In that case, there is no necessity to the correlation, and somebody with a psychology and physiology different from mine need not form the same judgment. But *even in this case* the combination occurs only because it is required by the original unity of apperception, the form of which is judgment. The empirical "filling" of this form results from the subjective associations (subjective—that is, occurring "for me, and in the present state of my perception") provided by the reproductive imagination. *But these associations can issue in judgment only if they have themselves been predetermined by the activity of judging, which relates all cognition to the objective unity of apperception.* By virtue of the objectifying function manifested in the very form of judgment, the synthesis of our intuitions takes place

---

[5] Cf. *Prol.*, §§18–20. Ak. IV, 298–99; 41–43. I shall give a detailed analysis of this distinction and its relation to §19 of the Transcendental Deduction in chapter 7.

"according to principles of the objective determination of all representations, insofar as cognition can be acquired by means of these representations—principles which are all derived from the fundamental principle of the transcendental unity of apperception" (B142).

The "principles" mentioned here can be none other than the Principles of Pure Understanding, which Kant expounds in the second part of the Transcendental Analytic. He is therefore anticipating a demonstration that is still to come when he indicates that the logical form of judgment expresses the combination of the sensible given in accordance with the absolutely universal forms of synthesis that will be stated in the "Principles of Pure Understanding." Our intuitions are synthesized according to these principles and reflected in judgments that first depend on our particular empirical associations, and which are therefore unworthy of being considered as anything more than "judgments of perception." Nonetheless, *even these* are acts of relating representations to objects, and this is why they eventually lead to genuine "judgments of experience," with a claim to hold "for everybody, always."[6]

Unfortunately, Kant does not indicate *how* judgment, considered in its logical form, is "the manner in which given cognitions are brought to the objective unity of apperception." Recall the passage just quoted:

> This is what is intended by the copula 'is'. It is employed to distinguish the objective unity of given representations from the subjective. It indicates their relation to original apperception and its necessary unity, even if the judgment is itself empirical, and therefore contingent, as, for example, in the judgment 'Bodies are heavy'. (B142)

One is tempted to turn Kant's reproach to "logicians" against him and declare: "I do not here dispute with Kant as to what is defective in his interpretation of 'what is intended by the copula'—that in any case, it applies only to *categorical*, not to hypothetical and disjunctive judgments. I need only point out that he does not thereby determine in what the asserted relation consists."[7] For on the one hand, Kant gives no indication as to whether and how the role he attributes to the "copula 'is' " might also be that of the other connectives in judgment, 'if . . . then' and 'either . . . or'.[8] On the other hand, the significance of the copula and the nature

---

[6] If the analysis I am proposing here is correct, the present example of empirical judgment, 'Bodies are heavy', could be either a judgment of perception (holding only "for me, in the present state of my perception") or already a judgment of experience (thought under a universal principle and thus expecting a claim to hold "for everybody, always"). In the *Prolegomena* Kant gives a similar example of a judgment one may consider first as a mere judgment of perception, then as a judgment of experience. The example is 'Air is elastic' (cf. *Prol.*, §19, Ak. IV, 299; 43). In any case, *as a judgment* (whether "only" a judgment of perception, or already a judgment of experience), its form is always dependent on the original unity of apperception by means of which our representations are related to objects. I shall give a detailed analysis of Kant's distinction between judgments of perception and judgments of experience in chapter 7. I shall then show how this distinction can further clarify what Kant has to say about judgment in §19 of the Transcendental Deduction.

[7] Cf. B141.

[8] Kant calls these, respectively, *consequence* and *disjunction*. Cf. *Logik*, §§25, 28, Ak. IX, 105–6; 601–2.

of the combination by which it "brings given cognitions to the objective unity of apperception" are left undetermined.

This shortcoming in Kant's explanation is probably due to the fact that, at this point in his argument, his main goal is to assign the forms of judgment to their proper place in the progression of the transcendental deduction, that is, to indicate their relation to the original synthetic unity of apperception. However, in order to understand the precise nature of the combination yielded according to the forms of judgment, and in order to understand why the logical form of judgment can be equated with "the objective unity of apperception of the concepts contained [in judgment]" (B140), one must go further than mere mention of the relation between the discursive unity of representations in judgment and the original synthetic unity of apperception. One must consider the nature of discursive unity itself, and ask what about it makes it "the objective unity of apperception." In this respect, section 19 of the Transcendental Deduction clearly presupposes an analysis of the forms of judgment that is given elsewhere, and with which Kant assumes his readers to be familiar. The characterization of judgment given in section 19 of the Transcendental Deduction thus needs to be complemented by Kant's definition of judgment in the *Logic*.

JUDGMENT AS "REPRESENTATION OF THE UNITY OF THE CONSCIOUSNESS OF VARIOUS REPRESENTATIONS," OR CONCEPT SUBORDINATION

In the *Jäsche Logic*, we find "A judgment is the representation of the unity of the consciousness of various representations, or the representation of their relation insofar as they constitute a concept."[9] Compare this with the section On the Logical Use of the Understanding, in the first *Critique*:

> In every judgment there is a concept which holds of many representations, and among them comprises also a given representation [*auch eine gegebene Verstellung begreift*] that is immediately related to an object. Thus in the judgment 'all bodies are divisible', the concept of the divisible applies to various other concepts, but is here applied in particular to the concept of body, and this concept again to certain appearances that present themselves to us. . . . Accordingly, all judgments are functions of unity among our representations; instead of an immediate representation, a *higher* representation, which comprises the immediate representation and various others, is used in cognizing the object, and thereby many possible cognitions are collected into one. (A68–69/B93–94)

We see here in what sense the "unity of consciousness" in a judgment is a *discursive* unity: it consists in the fact that several concepts, and with them the representations contained "under" them, are thought under one and the same concept of greater universality. Kant says essentially the same thing in section 10, when

[9] Kant, *Logik*, §17, Ak. IX, 101; 597. Cf. *Refl.* 3050 (1776–83), Ak. XVI, 632.

he says that the understanding produces the "logical form" of a judgment *by means of analytic unity* (B105). In section 16 of the Transcendental Deduction, he explains that the analytic unity of consciousness "attaches [*anhängt*] to all universal concepts as such" (B133n). I take him to mean that the analytic unity of consciousness is that unity of consciousness which *results from the analysis of given representations*, by means of which a plurality of representations is thought *under one and the same* concept. Therefore, to say that the *synthesis* of representations in a judgment is performed by means of *analytic* unity is to say that in judgment, various representations are combined in such a way as to be thought under one concept. This concurs with Kant's explanation of the example from the Logical Use of the Understanding just quoted: in the judgment 'All bodies are divisible', the concepts 'body' and 'divisible' are combined (*synthesized*) insofar as the concept of body, together with other concepts, is thought under the concept of the divisible (*analytic* unity). This is also what Kant meant in the *Logic* when he stated that judgment is "the representation of the relation [of various representations] insofar as they constitute a concept." For this is just to say that, in judgment, representations are related in such a way that they constitute the *extension* of one and the same concept.[10]

Judgment as Concept Subordination

To characterize judgment as Kant does in the section On the Logical Use of Understanding is to characterize it as a *subordination of concepts*, by means of which the objects subsumed under the subject-concept are also subsumed under the predicate-concept. In the *Logic*, Kant gives a novel expression to the idea that judgment—that is, subordination of concepts—is ultimately the subsumption of objects under the subordinated concepts. He says that every judgment of the form 'A is B' can be developed into the following form: 'To everything *x*, to which the

[10] Klaus Reich gave a persuasive analysis and commentary of Kant's assertion that in judgment the unity of representations is achieved "by means of analytic unity." Cf. Reich, *Vollständigkeit*, 12–13, 33–34. My comments on this point owe a lot to his work. Brandt has criticized Reich for identifying the notion of "analytic unity" in the metaphysical deduction and that of "analytic unity of consciousness" in §16 of the B Deduction. See Brandt, *Urteilstafel*, 18–20; 18–20. My own view is that on this point Reich is correct. The two notions, it seems to me, are essentially the same and are both to be explained in light of the general relation of synthesis and analysis I have laid out in chapter 3. In any case, there should be no confusion here between *analytic unity* and *analytic judgment*. Even *synthetic* judgments involve what Kant calls "analytic unity," that is, unity of representations *under concepts*, or *by means of analysis*. For an excellent explanation of this point, and of the misunderstandings it has occasioned in the history of Kant commentary, see Reich, *Vollständigkeit*. A related point is, of course, that the logical form of judgment is the form of *synthetic* just as much as of *analytic* judgments. Misunderstanding this point makes nonsense of the whole metaphysical deduction of the categories (cf. again Reich, who gives a very severe account of neo-Kantian mistakes in this regard, 13–14. Also Paton, *Metaphysic* I, 215. And my *Kant et le pouvoir de juger*, 91–96). In fact, Kant's introducing the term "*x*" in his explanation of the logical form of judgments is precisely due to his awareness that contrary to Leibnizian illusions, not all true judgments can be reduced to analytic judgments or judgments that are true by analysis of the subject-concept.

concept A belongs, belongs also the concept B'. Kant then uses this developed form to explain the difference between *analytic* and *synthetic* judgments. "An example of an *analytic* proposition is, To everything x, to which the concept of body $(a + b)$ belongs, belongs also *extension* (b). An example of a *synthetic* proposition is, To everything x, to which the concept of body $(a + b)$ belongs, belongs also *attraction* (c)."[11]

One can see here that even though analytic judgments, unlike synthetic judgments, are true in virtue of the mere content of the concepts combined in the judgment, Kant makes the presence of the x to which the two concepts are attributed explicit *for analytic as well as for synthetic judgments*. This is because in both cases concepts have meaning only if they are "universal or reflected representations" of singular objects (here, the objects of sensible intuition thought under the concept of body).[12] But then for all judgments, even when they are analytic, what ultimately makes the combination of concepts possible is always their relation to an "x of judgment."

If concepts derive their meaningfulness only from being related to singular objects in judgments, they are conversely the *grounds of cognition* of these singular objects. Kant assigns this role to concepts considered in their *extension (Umfang)*.

> Every concept, *as partial concept*, is contained in the representation of things; as *ground of cognition* [*Erkenntnisgrund*], *i.e. as mark* [*Merkmal*], these things are contained *under* it. In the former respect every concept has a *content* [*Inhalt*], in the other an *extension*.[13]

This *extension* of concepts, that is to say the objects thought under the concepts combined in judgments, is sometimes represented in the plural by "x, y, z." For example, in *Reflexion 3042*:

[11] Kant, *Logik*, §36, Ak. IX, 111; 607.

[12] The idea that concepts related to one another in a judgment are ultimately related to the thing whose properties they represent might appear strictly Wolffian. In his introduction to the *Philosophia rationalis* (clxxiv–clxxv), Jean Ecole convincingly shows how Wolff replaced Leibnizian conceptual analysis with what might be termed a 'rational empiricism' in which the relation of the attribute to the subject in a judgment is the expression of the attribution to the *thing* of its *marks*. Hence every judgment expresses the attribution of a mark (*Merkmal*) represented by the predicate-concept to the singular things represented by the subject-concept (cf. Wolff's definition of judgment, *Philosophia rationalis*, §39: "The act of the mind by which we attribute to or withdraw from a thing, something distinct from it, is called judgment [*actus iste mentis, quo aliquid a re quadam diversum eidem tribuimus vel ab ea removemus, judicium appellatur*]"; §240: "The subject is the term indicating the thing with which the judgment is concerned [*subjectum enim est terminus, quo indicatur res, de qua judicium fertur*]." On this point, see Schulthess, *Relation*, 18–20). But for Wolff the thing, even when it is given to our senses, is *in itself* rational or conceptual, so that the correspondence between logical and ontological relations is grounded in the thing itself. I will show at greater length in what follows that for Kant, on the contrary, even if concepts are related to one another in a judgment only by being related to an object, these relations are not *given in the object*, but are *the result of the operation* of judgment; and the object to which concepts are related is not in itself conceptually determined. It is merely what is represented by the "x of the judgment." How the term "x" should be interpreted will be explained in chapter 5.

[13] *Logik*, §7, Ak. IX, 95; 593.

A judgment is a cognition of the unity of given concepts: namely, that what is B [*dasjenige B*], together with other things *x*, *y*, *z*, belongs under the same concept A [*unter denselben Begriff A gehöre*], or again: that the manifold under B is also to be found under A.[14]

In the passage I have already quoted from the Logical Use of the Understanding, Kant describes a subordination of the same type:

Instead of an immediate representation, a *higher* representation, which comprises under itself [*unter sich begreift*] the immediate representation and various others, is used in cognizing the object, and thereby many possible cognitions are collected into one. (A69/B94)[15]

The definition of judgment in the *Logic* then becomes clearer: the "representation of the relation of various representations, insofar as they constitute a concept," means the subsumption of what is thought under a concept A, together with other representations of objects *x*, *y*, and *z*, under a concept B which "represents" all of them.[16]

The form of judgment, then, is the form of the relation of concepts to objects precisely insofar as it is the form of the subordination of concepts, since to say that concepts are subordinated in judgment is to say that objects *x*, *y*, and *z*, which are subsumed under the subject-concept, are also subsumed under the predicate. This is how, by virtue of its logical form alone, a judgment lays a claim to holding for any consciousness, whereas a mere coordination of representations might only hold for my subjective consciousness.

We can find an interesting elaboration of this point in *Reflexion* 3051. Here is how the beginning of this *Reflexion* appears in Kant's notes: "The representation of the manner in which various concepts (as such)* belong to a consciousness** (in general, not only my own) is judgment." The asterisks refer to the end of the

[14] *Refl.* 3042 (1773–77), Ak. XVI, 629. The judgment presupposed here is obviously 'B is A' or rather 'All Bs are A'. I intentionally left out the conclusion of the *Reflexion*: "such that the concepts A and B can be represented by a concept B." I think that Kant mixed up A and B, so that one should actually read "concepts A and B can be represented *by a concept A*." According to the explanations he gives everywhere else, it is indeed the *predicate* (the concept of greater extension) which "represents" the concept of lesser extension, and thereby the objects thought under it.

[15] Here Kant calls the concept of body in the judgment 'All bodies are divisible' an "immediate representation," while it obviously is a concept. The "immediacy" here is relative and means only that this concept is related to objects without the mediation of another concept, while the predicate 'divisible' is related to objects by the mediation of the concept of body.

[16] It is difficult not to oscillate between the terms '*representation*' and '*thing*' in the explanation of the term '*x*'. This is because *thing* and *representation* are hardly distinguishable in the critical interpretation of "*x*" since the thing is present to us only *as a representation* (cf. chapter 1). One might even add that, if one keeps to the standpoint of general or formal logic alone, the *x*, *y*, and *z*'s subordinated to the subject-concept could be the symbols of an intuition *or* of a concept (a sub-concept of the subject-concept). But transcendental logic teaches us that the forms of our thought are discursive because we can "only" think a *given* sensible intuition. The symbols "*x*, *y*, *z*," Kant introduces into the logical form of a judgment thus ultimately refer to objects of intuition, irreducible to any concept. They indicate the place where logical form reaches its limit, and (as transcendental logic informs us) presupposes the sensible syntheses.

Reflexion, where Kant provides the following explanations. For "concepts (as such)," he specifies "*in a universally necessary manner (empirically or *a priori*)." For "belong to a consciousness," he indicates that "**concepts belong to a consciousness *only insofar as they are thought as subordinated, and not as coordinated with one another* (like sensations) [*nur dadurch, daß sie unter, nicht neben einander (wie Empfindungen) gedacht werden*]."[17] One can see here that the distinction between the *subordination* (of concepts) and the *coordination* (of sensations) marks the difference, in the very form of thought, between what holds "for a consciousness in general, not only my own," and what holds only for my consciousness, which as empirical consciousness is different from all others because of the representations it has empirically acquired and the associations that make up its particular unity. One may compare the distinction Kant makes here between subordination of concepts and coordination of sensations with his distinction, in section 19 of the Deduction, between the formulation of the judgment 'Bodies are heavy' and that of the empirical association 'When I support a body, I feel an impression of weight'. In the former case, the concept of *body* is subordinated to the concept of *weight*, and in this form both are related to the objects *x*, *y*, and *z*, which, being contained under the concept of *body*, are thereby also contained under the concept of *weight*. In the latter case, the sensations reflected under the concept of body are *coordinated* with the feeling of weight in my state. If we then return to the first supplementary explanation of our *Reflexion*, concerning the expression "concepts (as such)," we will conclude that even if concepts are involved in the formulation of empirical association—since sensations themselves are reflected discursively, namely, by concepts—they nevertheless fulfill their proper function as concepts only in the *subordination of concepts*: in judgment. For judgment alone combines concepts "as such, that is, in a universally necessary manner." Now compare this indication to section 19 of the Deduction, where Kant asserts that the connection expressed in a judgment is "necessary, even if the judgment itself is empirical, that is, contingent" (B142). Presumably the connection is "necessary" because it expresses not a contingent association of my sensations, but a connection of properties grounded in the object itself. Expressing such properties is the function of concepts "as such," and this function they perform in judgments.

After having defined judgment as "the representation of the manner in which various concepts belong to a consciousness (not only my own)," Kant continues:

> They [the concepts] belong to a consciousness in part [*teils*] according to the laws of the imagination, and hence subjectively, or [*oder*] according to the laws of the understanding, that is, in a manner which is universally valid for any being possessing an understanding. The subjective combination depends on the particular situation of the subject in experience.

Surprisingly, according to this passage the "laws of the imagination," just as much as the "laws of the understanding," seem to be able to ensure that concepts belong to *a* (not only *my*) consciousness. Would this not jeopardize the foregoing dis-

[17] *Refl.* 3051 (1776–83), Ak. XVI, 633 (my emphasis).

tinction between the subordination (of concepts) and the coordination (of impressions)? Not if we remember our earlier considerations concerning the relation of every judgment to the objective unity of apperception, or the fact that objectivity (in the strict sense of conformity to the object) is a normative propensity rather than an inbuilt character of every judgment. On the one hand, the function, goal, or immanent norm of judgment, in virtue of its very form as a subordination of concepts, is to express "the manner in which concepts belong to a consciousness *in general*" (not only my own empirically determined consciousness). But, on the other hand, a judgment may have been formed in one of two ways. Either it was formed under the influence of the "laws of the imagination" alone, relying uncritically upon empirical associations, or it was determined by the "laws of the understanding," that is, with attention to the norm of coherence between this judgment and all the other judgments (mine and those of "everyone, always") that together make up the general context of our cognition of objects.[18] Thus, as remarked earlier when analyzing section 19 of the Transcendental Deduction, the form of a judgment is not by itself a guarantee that this judgment is the expression of the *objective* (rather than *subjective*) unity of our representations. But at least by dint of its very form—concept subordination, not coordination of impressions—its goal or its immanent norm is to express the relation of concepts by expressing also their relation to objects.

Judgment and Syllogism

In a judgment—that is, in concept subordination—the more general concept "represents" the concepts contained "under it," just as it "represents" all the objects *x*, *y*, *z* contained in its sphere. It is thus a "ground of cognition" (*Erkenntnisgrund*):

> A judgment is the representation of the unity of the relation of the ground of cognition to the possible cognition of an object.

> A concept, thanks to its general validity [*vermöge seiner Gemeingültigkeit*], has the function of a judgment. It applies to other concepts *potentialiter*. The actual relation of a concept to others, as means of their cognition, is judgment.[19]

When we subordinate a concept to one that is more general, we attribute the marks pertaining to the concept of greater generality to all the objects contained under the first concept. But thereby every judgment, as concept subordination, is the potential major premise of a syllogism attributing the genus to the species and thereby the genus to all individuals in the sphere of the species.[20] Consider again the example from the *Critique*:

---

[18] How there is such a norm of coherence in the very characterization of judgment as subordination of concepts, we shall see in the next sections: "Judgment and Syllogism," and "Judgment As Relation between an assertion and Its Condition."

[19] *Refl.* 3045 (1776–79), Ak. XVI, 630.

[20] This alone already makes it quite an interesting fact that Kant should have completed his undertaking of a Critique of reason with a *Critique of Judgment* (*Kritik der Urteilskraft*). According to the conception of judgment already present in the first *Critique*, the activity of reason, namely inference, is involved in the very form of the "capacity to judge" (*Vermögen zu Urteilen*). Every judgment carries within it a potential syllogism. I develop and justify this point in what follows.

Thus in the judgment, 'all bodies are divisible', the concept of the divisible applies [*bezieht sich*] to various other concepts, but here applies in particular to the concept of body, and this concept again to certain appearances that present themselves to us. These objects, therefore, are mediately represented through the concept of divisibility. (A68–69/B93)

From this explication of the judgment 'All bodies are divisible', we may conclude that being able to think such a judgment is being able to make the inference: "The concept of the divisible applies to the concept of body; now, the concept of body applies to objects *x*, *y*, *z*; therefore the concept of the divisible applies to these same objects." Moreover, being a universal representation, the concept of body, like the concept 'divisible', may itself be treated as the major term of a syllogism. Indeed, a few lines later Kant writes: "The concept of body means something, for instance, metal, which can be cognized by means of that concept. It is therefore a concept solely in virtue of the fact that other representations are contained under it, by means of which it can relate to objects" (A69/B94). As before, this means that the judgment "metal is a body" is the potential major premise of a syllogism such as: "The concept of body applies to the concept of metal, the concept of metal applies to objects *x*, *y*, and *z*; therefore, the concept of body applies to these same objects."

This syllogistic function of judgment, as Kant presents it, is so striking that it led Adickes to correct Kant in a note to one of the *Reflexionen* on judgment. This *Reflexion*, Adickes claims, is actually not about judgment, as Kant would have us believe, but about syllogism. The *Reflexion* is quite long; I shall quote only the passage discussed by Adickes:

> In a categorical judgment, the thing whose representation is considered as a part of the sphere of another subordinated representation is considered as subordinated to the latter's higher concept. Hence in the subordination of spheres, the part of the part is compared to the whole.[21]

Adickes devotes an entire note to this sentence and remarks:

> Here Kant seems to have in mind, not relations in the *categorical judgment*, but relations in the *categorical syllogism*. . . . Suppose *the thing* to be the lion; suppose the *representation subordinated to another* (for example, to the concept of predator) as in the major of a categorical syllogism, is the feline species, of which the lion is in the minor *considered as part of the sphere*; then, in the conclusion, the *thing* (the lion), *insofar as it is contained under the middle concept* (the feline species), *is considered as relating to its higher concept* (predator) and *in the subordination of the spheres* (in the categorical syllogism considered as a whole) *the part* (the lion) *of the part* (the feline genus) *is compared to the whole* (predator).[22]

In other words, Adickes claims that instead of the relation of representations in a categorical judgment Kant is really defining the relation of representations in a categorical *syllogism*. For instance 'Felines are predators; now, lions are felines,

21 *Refl.* 3095 (1769–75), Ak. XVI, 656.
22 Ak.XVI, 656n.

therefore lions are predators'. Significantly, Adickes meanwhile substitutes for Kant's *thing* a *concept* ('lion'). And he does so because he fails to see that when Kant says that *das Ding*, as part of the sphere of a subordinated representation, is itself subordinated to the higher concept, his intention is to refer to *the thing as distinct from any concept*.[23] In every judgment, "the thing" is both present and absent: present by means of the term "*x*" that gives the concept subordination its meaning, and absent because it is not itself a discursive representation. If, as Adickes believes, there is a syllogism in what Kant presents as a categorical judgment, this syllogism, first of all, is only a syllogism that we potentially form from the judgment taken as a major premise (we still need to find which things *x,y,z*, the subject of the major premise, might relate to). Second, once formulated the syllogism would look something like: 'Lions are predators; now a certain thing *x* (or: some things *x,y,z*) is (are) a lion, therefore this same thing *x* (these things) is (are) a predator'.

The concept subordination is thus a *rule* in Kant's sense of the term: "an assertion under a universal condition."[24] It is the major premise of a possible syllogism whose minor term is always the object, the appearance. Earlier we saw Kant describe a *concept* as "a rule in our cognition of outer appearances."[25] I added that a concept would be more correctly described as the possible *condition* of a rule. Indeed, the very universality of a concept makes it the condition required by a rule that allows its marks to be attributed to the objects "recognized under" it. In the *Logic* Kant says that concepts are "that form which is required for the power of judgment [*Urteilskraft*]."[26] We can now see two reasons for this striking statement. On the one hand, a concept is formed *in order to be combined* with other concepts in judgments (i.e., concept subordination). On the other hand, it is formed *in order to subsume* the appearances recognized under it. Both these functions make the formation of concepts dependent on the discursive capacity to form judgments. But they also make all judgments, as concept subordinations, potential major premises of syllogisms. This is why Kant insisted that judgment takes precedence over concept formation and inference, the other two "operations of the

---

[23] One might be disturbed here by the fact that Kant seems to be confusing subordination of concepts and subsumption of objects under concepts. And indeed these two relations are not clearly distinguished by him. They were not distinguished at all in eighteenth-century logics, where the extension of a concept was indifferently the concepts (species) subordinated to a given concept or the individuals subsumed under it. In *Refl.* 3095 quoted here, Kant speaks indifferently of *things* or *concepts* being subordinated to a "higher concept." This should not mask the fact, however, that he is aware of the difference between the two relations. This is precisely why he (correctly) restricts the domain of the logic he knows to *concepts* and concept subordination. In my own text I generally use 'subsumption' when talking of objects' falling under concepts, and 'subordination' when talking of lower concepts' falling under higher concepts (but not always—it depends on how closely I am following Kant's usage). Kant generally uses 'subordination' for both relations, and 'subsumption' to refer, in the context of syllogism, either to the relation between the minor term and the middle term or to that between the minor premise and the major premise. Cf. *Logik* §58, Ak. IX, 120–21; 615. §62, Ak. IX, 123; 617. *KrV* A322/B378.

[24] Cf., e.g., *Logik* §58n, Ak. IX, 120; 615.

[25] Cf. A106, and chapter 2, p. 49.

[26] *Logik*, §5, Ak. IX, 94; 592. Cf. *Refl.* 2851, Ak. XVI, 546.

mind" treated in eighteenth-century logic textbooks. Or rather, both of these have their common root in our capacity to form judgments (*Vermögen zu urteilen*).[27]

The analyses given so far have taken into consideration only the predicative form of judgment, 'A is B'. In fact, Kant's explanations of judgment in general (as opposed to his analysis of particular forms of judgment) always give pride of place to categorical judgments. It thus seems that even while chastizing his predecessors for doing so, Kant himself continues to privilege this form. Yet the notion of *rule*, with its two corollaries, the *condition* and the *exponent* of the rule, provides the means for understanding the other forms of relation in judgment.

JUDGMENT AS A RULE, AND THE DIFFERENT TYPES OF RELATION IN JUDGMENT

In section 23 of the *Prolegomena*, Kant defines judgments in the following way: "Judgments, when considered merely as the condition of the unification of given representations in a consciousness, are rules."[28]

If we then consider Kant's definition of a rule ("A rule is an assertion under a universal condition")[29] we may conclude that "judgments, when considered merely as the condition of the unification of given representations in a consciousness, are assertions under a universal condition."

This definition is interesting because we find in it the terms Kant uses to distinguish categorical, hypothetical, and disjunctive judgments. He distinguishes these by the type of connection they express between an assertion and its condition. This connection is what he calls the *relation* in the judgment. However, in the *Logic* this meaning of *relation* is not explained in the chapter on *judgment* but rather when Kant discusses *syllogism*. When explaining the various relations in a judgment, Kant only states that

> As to relation, judgments are either *categorical* or *hypothetical* or *disjunctive*. The given representations in judgment are subordinated one to another for the unity of consciousness, namely, either as *predicate* to *subject*, or as *consequence* to *ground*, or as *member of the division* to the *divided concept*. Through the first relation *categorical* judgments are determined, through the second *hypothetical*, and through the third *disjunctive*.[30]

Clearly, *subordination* here no longer has the meaning we have seen for it earlier, where it was a relation of inclusion between the extensions of concepts (a concept A is subordinated to a concept B just in case the subconcepts and objects

---

[27] Of course, all of this holds, strictly speaking, only of *universal* judgments. Only these are rules. But they are after all the primary forms of judgments for Kant. When we form judgments, we form rules for recognition. Particular and singular judgments are instantiations of these rules, their formation depends on the initial formation of rules. This will, I hope, become clearer in the next chapter, when we move from the logical forms to their epistemic use.

[28] *Prol.*, §23, Ak. IV, 305; 48–49.

[29] *Logik*, §58, Ak. IX, 121; 615.

[30] *Logik*, §23, Ak. IX, 104; 601.

contained under A are also contained under B). It is certainly not in this manner that the predicate is "subordinated" to the subject or the consequence to the ground or the division to the divided concept. However, the text quoted does not make clear how this new type of subordination should be understood. We have to wait until the chapter on syllogism for Kant to provide some indication of this.[31] There the three relations in judgment provide the three possible major premises for a syllogism, and subordination is the *subordination of the assertion to its condition*: subordination of the predicate to the subject insofar as the latter is the *condition* of the assertion of the predicate, or subordination of the consequent to the antecedent insofar as the latter is the *condition* of the assertion of the former, or subordination of the complete division to the divided concept insofar as the latter is the *condition* of the assertion of this division.

> All rules (judgments) contain objective unity of consciousness of the manifold of cognition, hence a condition under which one cognition belongs with one another to one consciousness. Now only three conditions of this unity may be thought, however, namely: as subject of the inherence of marks, or as ground of the dependence of one cognition on another, or, finally, as combination of parts in a whole (logical division). Consequently there can only be just as many kinds of universal rules (*propositiones majores*), through which the *consequentia* of one judgment from another is mediated.[32]

The introduction to the Transcendental Dialectic provides many more examples of this characterization of subordination. I shall give just two of them:

> The proposition 'Caius is mortal' I could indeed derive from experience by means of the understanding alone. But I am in pursuit of a concept (in this case, the concept 'man') that contains the condition under which the predicate (general term for what is asserted) of this judgment is given; and after I have subsumed under this condition taken in its whole extension ('All men are mortal'), I proceed, in accordance therewith, to determine the cognition of my object ('Caius is mortal'). (A322/B378, translation modified)

> Reason, in its logical use, seeks to discover the universal condition of its judgment (the conclusion), and the syllogism is itself nothing but a judgment made by means of the subsumption of its condition under a universal rule (the major premise). (A307/B364)

These texts show that the condition of judgment fulfills a two-sided, or bidirectional function. On the one hand it is the term that, *insofar as it is subsumed under the condition of a judgment of greater generality serving as a rule*, provides a reason for asserting the given judgment. Such is the function of the term 'Caius', in

---

[31] There is one exception to the absence of the notion of condition in the exposition of *judgment* in the *Logic*: the case of hypothetical judgment. Cf. *Logik*, §25–2, Ak. IX, 105; 602. But this exception is deceptive in that it might lead to the conclusion that the hypothetical relation alone links the assertion to a condition. This is clearly not Kant's intention if we consider his treatment of syllogism.

[32] *Logik*, §60, Ak. IX, 121–22; 616.

the judgment 'Caius is mortal'. 'Caius' is the condition of the judgment insofar as it is subsumable under 'man'. Such is also the function of the concept 'metal' in the judgment 'All metals are divisible'. 'Metal' is the condition of the judgment insofar as it is subsumable under 'body'. But on the other hand, the condition is the term *under which* one subsumes the subject of another judgment, thus providing a reason for attributing to it the predicate attributed to the term under which it is subsumed. Such is the function of the term 'men' in the judgment 'All men are mortal', or of the term 'body' in the judgment 'All bodies are divisible'. Therefore the *possibility of a subsumption* is what makes a condition what it is. The condition in a judgment is the *subsuming or subsumed term*, which is a condition precisely through its relation to another subsuming or subsumed term, which in turn derives its function as condition from its relation to the previous term as well as to a third, which subsumes or is subsumed, and so on. Thus the explication of the term 'condition' confirms the conclusion of the previous section of this chapter: syllogism, as the subordination of a given judgment to a general rule that provides the reason for so judging, or as the use of a judgment as a rule that provides the reason for asserting another judgment, is not a function of thought distinct from that of judging. On the contrary, this function is in some sense "encased" in every judgment.[33]

Kant and Wolff on the Condition of Judgment

Kant inherits the term "*condition*" from Wolff and his school. Wolff's notion of a *condition* is related to his explanation of what makes a judgment true. A judgment is true just in case it is in agreement with its object. But it is in agreement with its object just in case the predicate of the judgment is "determined" either by the subject-concept of the judgment or by some condition "added to" the subject-concept. The predicate is "determined" by the subject just in case either it belongs to the subject-concept as one of its marks, or it can be asserted of this concept by virtue of a demonstrative procedure that may be more or less long and complex. Now this means that the determinability of the predicate by the subject is both the criterion of truth (that by which we recognize a judgment as true) and the real definition of truth (what it is for a proposition to *be* true).

---

[33] I introduce here a systematic connection between 'condition' and 'reason' which is not explicitly stated by Kant, but which I think is true to his conception of judgment, and is implicated by the general point I want to make. For Kant, syllogistic reasoning is a function potentially at work in all judgment. The condition of a judgment is the term that, by subsuming or being subsumed, *provides a reason*, that is, typically, generates the minor premise of a syllogism from which a given judgment may be deduced as a true judgment. For instance, the concept 'man' is the *condition* in the rule 'all men are mortal'. This means that it is the condition (sufficient but not necessary) for asserting of any object x the predicate: 'mortal'. Subsuming any object x, or any species, under the concept 'man', is formulating a *reason* for asserting the predicate 'mortal' of the object or species. For instance, 'Socrates is a man' (reason). 'Socrates is mortal' (assertion). This will be important for Kant's analysis and defense of the so-called principle of reason and of the concept of cause. See chapter 11, pp. 358–60. See also Longuenesse, "Logique et métaphysique," and "Kant on Causality."

If a predicate, either affirmative or negative, fits the subject [*subjecto convenit*] either absolutely or under a given condition, the proposition is said to be true. Truth is therefore the agreement of our judgment with the object or the represented thing [*Est itaque veritas consensus judicii nostri cum objecto, seu re repraesentata*].[34]

Truth is the determinability of the predicate by the notion of the subject [*Veritas est determinabilitas praedicati per notionem subjecti*]. . . . You have the real definition of truth if you conceive it as the determinability of the predicate by the notion of the subject.[35]

Whoever perceives how the predicate is determined by what is contained in the subject, knows the truth of a judgment.[36]

The *criterion of truth* is an element which is intrinsic to the proposition [*Criterium veritatis est propositioni intrinsecum*], whereby one knows that it is true; consequently *it presents sufficient marks [notas] in any circumstance to know the truth and therefore to tell a true proposition from a false one*.[37]

The "sufficient marks" to know the truth or falsity of the judgment are what Wolff calls the *condition* of the judgment. Depending on the case, they will be *essentialia* (i.e., marks belonging to the essence of the subject), *attributa* (i.e., marks which, without belonging to the essence of the subject, can be deduced from it), or *relations external* to the subject of the judgment, or again contingent *modes* (external relations and modes depending on the "added conditions" mentioned earlier). But again, in any of these cases one finds either in the subject or in the "added conditions" the marks that, *if asserted of the subject*, provide a sufficient reason to assert the predicate of this same subject. This is why these marks are called the *condition* of the judgment. Meier clearly took his inspiration from Wolff when he wrote, in his *Auszug aus der Vernunftlehre*: "The conditions of a judgment are 1) either sufficient or insufficient; 2) either internal or external; 3) either absolutely necessary or contingent. [In each case], the former are the essence, the essential parts, the properties or the definition of the subject, the latter are its contingent properties and relations."[38]

However, Wolff's characterization of the condition of a judgment is not acceptable to Kant. For, by restricting the role of condition in the judgment to *concepts*, Wolff clearly treats all judgments as if they were all true by *analysis*, whether of the subject, or of its "added conditions," or of a combination of the two. Witness the biting irony with which Kant reacted to Eberhard's allegation that with his distinction between analytic and synthetic a priori judgments he merely gave a new name to Wolff's distinction between judgments predicating of a subject marks belonging to its essence (*essentialia*), and judgments predicating of a subject marks that could be deduced from its essence (*attributa*). Kant retorts

[34] Christian Wolff, *Philosophia rationalis*, §505.
[35] Ibid., §513.
[36] Ibid., §516.
[37] Ibid., §523.
[38] Meier, *Auszug*, §298, Ak. XVI, 642.

that a judgment can be called synthetic only if its ultimate condition is the *intuition* subsumed under the condition of the judgment, whether this intuition is empirical (synthetic a posteriori judgment) or a priori (synthetic a priori judgment). Wolff, in contrast, never looked for the condition of predication outside *concepts*, especially where a priori (i.e., universally necessary) predication was concerned.[39] For Kant, in most cases concepts function as conditions only insofar as they subsume (a priori or empirical) sensible intuitions, which are thus ultimately the true conditions of judgments. This again might well be the reason why, in his logic, Kant introduces developments of the notions of *condition* and of *relation of an assertion to its condition* not in the chapter on judgment, but rather in the chapter on syllogism.

Condition and Exponent of a Judgment

To define relation in judgment as relation of an assertion to its condition is to consider the judgment as a link in a chain of syllogisms that provide reasons for its being true. One further indication of this is Kant's term for the relation of the assertion to its condition: *exponent*. From the 1770s on, Kant uses this term to give a unified account of the three forms of relation in a judgment (*categorical, hypothetical*, and *disjunctive* relations):

> The relation of concepts (*exponent*): subject to predicate; ground-consequence; whole-part (form of judgments: categorical, hypothetical, disjunctive).[40]

> The matter of judgment: *termini*. The form or the relation *has for its exponent* copula. If. Either or. . . . " [*die Form oder das Verhältnis exponiert* copula. *Wenn. entweder oder*].[41]

Klaus Reich has convincingly argued that Kant derived the term 'exponent' (*Exponent*) from mathematics. In eighteenth-century textbooks the notion of exponent is used in the theory of proportions. There it refers to "the number that the first term of a 'relation' [*Verhältnisses*] is to be multiplied by in order to obtain the second term (or the second term itself, when the first is the unit or can be taken as the unit)."[42] Thus defined, the exponent is the *ratio* of a series, in the mathematical sense: the coefficient of proportionality between one term and the next in the series. For instance, says Reich, the exponent of the relation of 3 to 12 would be either 4, or 1/4. Given these two terms one could pursue the series as 3, 12, 48, 172, . . . Or 12, 3, 3/4, 3/16, . . . If a term of the series is given and the exponent is specified, the entire series is thereby defined. In the Introduction to the Transcendental Dialectic Kant refers explicitly to this model of the series:

[39] Cf. *Entdeckung*, Ak. VIII, 241; 152.

[40] *Refl.* 3063 (late 1770s), Ak. XVI, 636.

[41] *Refl.* 3039 (1772–75), Ak. XVI, 628. I interpret 'copula' as the subject of the verb "*exponiert*"; the copula "gives its exponent" to the form or the relation, or these "have as exponent" the copula.

[42] Kästner, *Anfangsgründe der Arithmetik*, V, 26, quoted by Reich (*Vollständigkeit*, 69; *Completeness*, 76). Reich also quotes Klügel, *Mathematisches Wörterbuch*, div. I, pt. II; Euler, *Vollständige Anleitung zur Algebra*, pt. I, sec. III, chaps. 1 and 6.

Now every series the exponent of which is given (in categorical or hypothetical judgment) can be continued; consequently this same activity of reason leads to *ratiocinatio polysyllogistica*, which is a series of inferences that can be prolonged indefinitely on the side either of the conditions (*per prosyllogismos*) or of the conditioned (*per episyllogismos*). (A330/B387)

Each of the relations in a judgment can be considered as the *exponent* of a series in which the given judgment may be contained. Thus in the *Logic*, immediately after defining a *rule* as "an assertion under a universal condition," Kant adds that "The relation of the condition to the assertion, namely how the latter stands under the former, is the *exponent* of the rule."[43]

Our next question, then, is why Kant retains for his three 'exponents' those which define the categorical, the hypothetical, and the disjunctive judgment. None of these three forms of judgment were Kant's discovery. His grouping them under one and the same heading, under that of relation, was nevertheless an innovation. In the logic textbooks of his time, propositions were first distinguished as to their quality and quantity. Then *simple* propositions were distinguished from *composite* propositions. The *simple* propositions are what Kant calls *categoricals* (of the form 'subject-copula-predicate'). Among *composite* propositions were, besides hypothetical (also called 'conditional') and disjunctive propositions, many other propositions Kant does not consider at all. True enough, the *Schulphilosophen* who most directly influenced Kant had already limited the list of composite propositions. Besides hypothetical and disjunctive, most of them only considered "copulative" propositions. But none of Kant's predecessors brought the categorical judgment together with hypothetical and disjunctive under the common heading of relation.[44]

---

[43] *Logik*, §58n., Ak. IX, 121; 615. This explanation of the term 'exponent' also sheds light on the passage in the Analogies of Experience in which Kant explains that the Analogies "portray the unity of nature in the combination of all appearances under certain *exponents* which express nothing save the relation of time . . . to the unity of apperception—such unity being possible only in synthesis according to rules" (A216/B263). For the Analogies, particularly the second, organize appearances into series (or rather into series of series of series, etc.) the exponent of which is provided by the logical form of the hypothetical judgment (on this point, see chapter 11). One may, I think, also relate to this explanation of *exponent* the verb *exponieren* Kant uses in the third *Critique* to describe the move from an intuition to a concept. The aesthetic idea, he says, cannot be *exponiert*, that is, brought to concepts: "in the case of an aesthetic idea the *understanding* with its concepts never reaches the entire inner intuition that the imagination has and connects with a given representation. And since bringing a representation of the imagination to concepts is the same as *expounding* [*exponieren*] it, aesthetic ideas may be called *unexpoundable* [*inexponible*] representations of the imagination (in its free play)" (*KU*, §57, Remark 1, Ak. V, 343–44; 216–17). To say that the idea of the imagination cannot be *exponiert* is to say that it cannot be subsumed under the exponents, the laws of phenomenal series, provided by the categories of relation or logical forms of relation in judgment applied to appearances.

[44] See the long list of composite propositions in Arnauld and Nicole's *Art de penser* (II, chaps. 9–10), which influenced all seventeenth- and eighteenth-century textbooks. Tonelli (*Voraussetzungen*) gives a minute inventory of these textbooks, and their divisions of propositions. Cf. also Reich, *Vollständigkeit*, 72, 80. Wolff restricts composite propositions to disjunctive and copulative ones (*Philosophia rationalis*, §314); Lambert, to hypothetical, disjunctive, and copulative ones (*Neues organon I: Dianoiologie*, §131); see also Meier, *Auszug*, §304. Lambert and Meier interpret the hypothetical proposition as one of the composite propositions, whereas Wolff studies it together with the

Yet, the "triplet" of categorical, hypothetical, and disjunctive forms did appear in discussions of *syllogism*. These three forms are those of the three possible types of major premises in syllogisms. That they have this function is, in my view, the major reason why Kant privileged these three forms and grouped them under the single heading of 'relation'. Each governs a specific way of subsuming a particular case under a general rule. To each of these possible forms of subsumption corresponds a relation of the assertion to its condition. We now must consider this.[45]

Categorical and Hypothetical Propositions According to Wolff

For a better understanding of Kant's conception of the *hypothetical* judgment, we must look once more to the tradition from which he emerged and on whose definitions he implicitly relied. Wolff's *Philosophia rationalis sive logica* provides a helpful starting point. By examining the definitions given in this work, we can appreciate the extent of Kant's debt to it and flesh out his often vague, gap-ridden explications. At the same time, comparing his views with Wolff's reveals how radically Kant transformed the meaning of those very logical forms he says he received "ready to hand" from "the labors of the logicians."[46]

Wolff defines the *categorical* proposition as a proposition "in which the predicate is stated about the subject absolutely, or without any added condition [*nulla adjecta conditione*]." A hypothetical proposition, in contrast, is a proposition "in which the predicate is attributed to the subject under an added condition [*sub adjecta conditione*]." The function of the 'if . . . then' connective is to express the link of the assertion to this *adjectae conditioni*. Wolff's examples of categorical propositions are 'God is the wisest' ('*Deus est sapientissimus*'), and Pythagoras's theorem 'The square of the hypotenuse is equal to the sum of the squares of the remaining sides'. His examples of hypothetical propositions are 'If a man repeatedly performs exercises, he acquires a habit', and 'If a stone falls from a tower, it acquires an increasing speed'. As these examples show, the difference between the two propositions corresponds to the difference between, on the one hand, an

---

categorical proposition as one of the two possible relations of the assertion to its condition, and consequently discusses it before introducing the distinction between simple and composite propositions. Kant retains precisely this aspect of the relation of the assertion to its condition as the common heading of the three *relations* or *exponents* of a judgment. Schulthess (*Relation*, 43–44) draws attention to what seems closest to Kant's notion of relation: Reimarus's notion of *Verbindung*, which includes hypothetical and disjunctive judgments. Furthermore, Reimarus considers these two propositions to be "the most important ones [*die vornehmsten*], because they are also used in syllogisms" (Reimarus, *Vernunftlehre*, §144–45, quoted by Schulthess, 43. Reimarus's *Logic*, inspired by Wolff, went through six editions between 1757 and 1790). Nonetheless, Kant is the first to bring together hypothetical, disjunctive, *and categorical judgments* under the heading of relation (of the assertion to its condition).

[45] On categorical, hypothetical, and disjunctive judgments as forms of the major premise of a syllogism, cf. Wolff, *Philosophia rationalis*, §403–4; Lambert, *Neues Organon* I: *Dianoiologie*, §§262, 278; Meier, *Auszug*, §392, 396.

[46] *Prol.* §39, Ak. IV, 323–24. Cf. my introduction, p. 1.

attribution under the condition of the essence (for which the subject of predication is consequently the sufficient condition of the attribution of the predicate)
and, on the other hand, an attribution under the condition of modes and external
relations. The logical difference between judgments is thus based on an ontological difference in the ways in which properties are related to one another. What is
predicated absolutely, therefore in a categorical proposition, are *essentialia* and
attributa as well as everything belonging to the subject by virtue of them. What
is predicated *conditionally* (*conditionate*), therefore in a hypothetical proposition,
are modes and relations, which can be asserted only if a particular condition, not
contained in the subject-concept or derivable from it, is presupposed.[47]

Since the difference between the two types of propositions has an ontological
grounding, it seems that one should not be able to transform a categorical proposition into a hypothetical one, or conversely a hypothetical into a categorical. But
on the contrary, Wolff argues that every categorical proposition can be formulated
as a hypothetical by making explicit the relation of the assertion to its condition.
Such a transformation is often useful for demonstration. To illustrate this point,
Wolff uses an example from geometry, followed by one concerning the idea of
God.

> 'A regular figure can be inscribed in a circle' is a categorical proposition. Now, by
> 'regular figure' I mean an equilateral plane figure with equal angles. Therefore the
> categorical proposition is equivalent to the following hypothetical proposition: 'If a
> plane figure is equilateral, with equal angles, it can be inscribed in a circle'. This re-
> duction is often made in the demonstration of theorems. . . . 'God created the world'
> is a categorical proposition. But a definition must correspond to the name of God, if
> the word is to have meaning. For example, if along with the Cartesians you define
> God as the most perfect being, the hypothetical proposition shall be 'If God is the
> most perfect being, then He created the world'.[48]

To transform the categorical proposition into a hypothetical, one analyzes the
subject-concept of the initial predication so as to reveal in it, and formulate as an
"added condition," the specific marks on which the predication depends. Thus the
subject 'regular figure' is analyzed into two components, 'plane figure' on the one
hand and 'equilateral, with equal angles' on the other hand. The latter becomes
the added condition under which the predicate 'can be inscribed in a circle' is asserted. The other example is more puzzling. I suggest Wolff might have in mind
something like the following. The subject 'God' may be analyzed into two com-

[47] Wolff, *Philosophia rationalis*, §§215–18, 224–25. Wolff uses the term *propositions* where Kant
says *judgments*. More precisely, in Wolff 'proposition' refers to the linguistic expression of a judgment,
which is a psychological activity. But for Kant, such a distinction is irrelevant because no judgment (as
psychological activity) can take place without linguistic expression. He uses the term 'proposition' to
refer to assertoric judgments. Cf. *Logik*, §§30–33, Ak. IX, 109; 604–5: "On the distinction between
problematic and assertoric judgments rests the true distinction between judgments and *propositions*
[*Sätzen*], which is customarily placed, wrongly, in the mere expression through words, without which
one simply could not judge at all. In judgment the relation of various representations to the unity of
consciousness is thought merely as problematic, but in a proposition as assertoric."

[48] Wolff, *Philosophia rationalis*, §226.

ponents: 'the being we name *God*' and 'the most perfect being'. Making explicit the relation of the assertion to its condition is thus to say: 'If the being we name *God* is the most perfect being, then He created the world'.

Conversely, hypothetical propositions can be reduced to categorical propositions by directly attaching their "added condition" to the subject-concept of their consequent. The main use of such reductions is to allow hypothetical syllogisms to be expressed as categorical syllogisms of the first figure.[49] Wolff adds, however, that replacing a hypothetical form by a categorical one is often a grammatical exercise that fails to do justice to the content of our thought. When a categorical proposition is obtained by means of integrating predicates representing contingent modes or external relations into the subject-concept, what we get is only seemingly a categorical, really a hypothetical proposition:

> If the condition under which the predicate belongs to the subject is expressed by a composite term without a conditional, the proposition has the form of a categorical proposition, even though it is actually hypothetical. Indeed, if the predicate does not belong to the subject absolutely, but under a certain condition, the condition does not cease to hold just because the conditional is not expressly posited. The proposition then remains hypothetical.[50]

The reason for this about-face lies in the ontological grounding of the distinction between categorical and hypothetical propositions. As we saw, the condition of "absolute" predication (or predication *nulla adjecta conditione*) is the essence of the subject. Predication is hypothetical, on the contrary, if its condition is some external relation or a contingent mode added to the essence and attributes. To conceal this conditional character by integrating the condition into the subject through grammatical devices does not, says Wolff, make the proposition any less hypothetical.

Hypothetical Judgments According to Kant

We can now turn to Kant's conception of hypothetical judgments. I devoted time to expounding Wolff's distinction between predication *nulla adjecta conditione* and predication *sub adjecta conditione* because it seems to me that for Kant too this distinction constitutes the difference between categorical and hypothetical judgments. Because Kant inherits from Wolff the distinction between the two types of condition for predication and assumes it is well known, he does not make it explicit. In spite of this, I am convinced it is implicitly present in his treatment of categorical and hypothetical judgments, although clearly it can no longer have the same meaning it had for Wolff. Wolff's distinction had an ontological grounding, whereas Kant's, at least in the *Logic*, concerns the mere form of thought irrespective of its object.

[49] Ibid., §410–15.
[50] Ibid., §227.

What, then, is an "added condition"? It is a condition of predication distinguished from the subject of predication by *the mere form of judgment*. Whether or not this condition is really distinct—that is, whether, when one considers the content of the judgment, the condition belongs or does not belong to what is thought in the subject of the predication—does not matter at all from the point of view of logical form. The judgment is described as hypothetical simply because *its form* separates the *condition* from the *subject* of predication (whereas, in the categorical form, the subject itself contains the condition for the assertion of the predicate). This is what the example Kant gives in the *Logic* is meant to show: "There is an essential difference between the two propositions, All bodies are divisible, and, If all bodies are composite, then they are divisible. In the former proposition I assert the matter [*ich behaupte die Sache*] directly, in the latter only under a condition expressed problematically."[51] In the first proposition, "I assert directly", that is, I assert under the condition thought in the subject. In the second case, "I assert under a condition expressed problematically", that is, I assert under a condition thought as distinct from the subject and which may or may not actually fit the subject. In the example under consideration ("If all bodies are composite, then they are divisible"), if one takes into account the *content* of the judgment—that is, the marks of the concepts combined in the judgment—the condition is in no way added to the subject of the judgment. On the contrary, 'composition' is an analytic mark of the concept of body, a mark that results from the essential mark of extension. Therefore the only thing that makes this condition an "added" condition is the *form* of the judgment.[52]

In Wolff's examples, by contrast, the hypothetical judgment added to the subject of predication a condition that was distinct from it *in content*, distinct *with regard to the marks* (attributes or modes) thought in it. When moving from the categorical judgment 'A regular figure can be inscribed in a circle' to the hypothetical judgment 'If a plane figure is equilateral, with equal angles, it can be inscribed in a circle', one splits up the idea of 'regular figure' so that one could express as *added conditions* (namely, added to the subject: 'plane figure') the marks of equal sides and equal angles, which, if asserted of the subject 'plane figure', provide the reason for asserting the predicate: 'can be inscribed in a circle'. Similarly, when moving from the judgment 'God created the world' to the hypothetical judgment 'If God is the most perfect being, then He created the world', the idea of 'most perfect being' was considered separately from the idea of 'being we name God'; the former idea could then be considered as a mark that, if asserted of the latter, provides a reason for asserting of it the mark 'creator of the world'.

What would Kant think of such examples? If we trust the passage from the *Logic* quoted earlier, he would say that they in no way represent moves from categorical judgments to hypothetical judgments *equivalent* to them, differing only in making the condition of the assertion explicit. Rather, the one form is essentially different from the other *with regard to the act of thinking*; we get *two* quite

[51] Kant, *Logik*, §25, Ak. IX, 105–6; 602.

[52] Cf. Letter to Reinhold, May 12, 1789, Ak.XI, 35–36; 138: "Divisibility is deduced from the concept of the extended (as composite) according to the principle of identity."

different judgments, depending on whether we (1) have *added* to the subject 'plane figure' a condition such as 'the equality of sides and angles', which, *if* asserted of it, allows one to assert of it the predicate 'can be inscribed in a circle', or (2) have directly asserted this predicate of the subject 'regular figure', without any *added* condition. For Wolff, a categorical judgment can be formulated as a hypothetical judgment if *the same content* is expressed in categorical or hypothetical form. Conversely, the reason he expresses misgivings about the reformulation of some hypothetical judgments into categoricals is that *from the point of view of content* it is deceptive to treat as categorical a judgment where the predicate can be asserted only under a condition really external and contingent with regard to the subject. By contrast, Kant's example is intended to show that the two forms of judgment are irreducible to one another because, *irrespective of the content* of the concepts, *the form of thought, that is, the act of discursive combination*, is different. Refusing to confound logic with ontology, Kant emphasizes differences in the logical forms considered as forms of the act of thinking—forms of the discursive combination of concepts.[53]

This in turn might help to illuminate another feature of Kant's distinction between categorical and hypothetical judgments. In explaining this distinction Kant does not remain strictly within the standpoint of what he calls *relation*. Instead, he introduces *modal* considerations into his explanation: "In categorical judg-

---

[53] From the explanation proposed here it follows that a possible formalization for Kant's distinction between categorical and hypothetical judgments might be $(x) (Bx \longrightarrow Dx)$ for the categorical judgment 'All bodies are divisible', and $(x) [(Bx.Cx) \longrightarrow Dx]$ for the hypothetical judgment 'If bodies are composite, then they are divisible'. I am here interpreting the English sentence (or Kant's German: *Wenn Körper zusammengesetzt sind, dann sind sie teilbar*) as having the same meaning as: 'If a body is composite, it is divisible' or, even better, as: 'All bodies, if composite, are divisible'. One might also interpret the English sentence in such a way that it would be formalizable as: $[(x) (Bx \longrightarrow Cx) \longrightarrow (x) (Bx \longrightarrow Dx)]$. However, the formalization I propose is more adequate to the meaning of Kant's hypothetical as I explain it earlier (I am grateful to Paul Benacerraf for bringing to my attention the ambiguity of the English sentence; the same ambiguity exists in German and, for that matter, in French). $\longrightarrow$ represents the conditional of our propositional calculus. This formalization makes explicit how the difference between the two judgments lies in the fact that in the first case Bx (x is a body, or I think x under the concept of body) is, *without any added condition*, the condition for Dx (I think x under the concept of divisibility), while for the second, Bx is a condition for Dx only *under the added condition* of Cx (I think x under the concept of compositeness). To express the categorical proposition as a conditional is not distorting Kant's thought, for he says specifically that in the categorical proposition the subject is the *condition* of the attribution of the predicate, and for him, as I showed earlier, this indeed means that the attribution of the subject-concept to the object = x is the condition of the attribution of the predicate-concept to the same object = x. This presentation of Kant's categorical and hypothetical judgments shows that the *formal* difference between them is merely a difference in the *complexity of the relation of condition to conditioned*. The two thought operations considered here under the heading of relation can both be formalized as uses of the *conditional* connective, combined with conjunction in one case and not in the other. Such an analysis confirms that Kant's table of the logical forms of judgment should not be interpreted as a table of elementary logical operators (which would make it vulnerable to Strawson's criticism; cf. p. 4), but as a table of the forms of thought (the logicodiscursive forms of judgment) universally necessary for relating our sensible representations to objects. This hypothesis will be established by the detailed examination of Kant's argument in the Analogies of Experience, in chapter 11. And see also the conclusion of this book.

ments, *nothing is problematic, everything is assertoric*; whereas in hypothetical judgments, *only the consequence is assertoric*" (my emphasis).[54] Similarly, in a passage cited earlier Kant asserted that in a hypothetical proposition, I assert the state of affairs "under a condition *expressed problematically*" (my emphasis). Now, Kant explains in the *Critique* that modality "contributes nothing to the content of the judgment . . . but concerns the value of the copula in relation to thought in general." And in the *Logic* he says that "[Through] modality, the relation of the whole judgment to the faculty of thought in general is determined." Given this definition of modality, introducing modal determinations into the definition of the hypothetical relation confirms that, for Kant, the difference between the latter and the categorical relation lies wholly in the *form*, that is, in the act of thinking whatever the content of the thought.[55] The hypothetical relation is a relation between two predications (the antecedent and the consequent) both of which are suspended (i.e., problematic). Only the *relation* of the predication, expressed by the consequent to an *external* or *added* condition expressed by the antecedent, is asserted.[56]

Finally, it should now be clear that what Kant calls "relation" in a judgment is quite different from a relation in a modern sense, namely a many-place predicate. What Kant calls "relation" is thought within the context of the classical predicative model, and the hypothetical judgment itself is thought within this context, as the "relation" *of a predication to its condition* (my emphasis)—the condition being, in this case, itself expressed in the form of a predication. This privileging of predication explains the predominant place, in Kant's general consideration of judgment, of concept subordination (in the first sense considered here: the inclusion of the extension of a concept in the extension of another concept). The privileging of predication also explains why the form of the categorical judgment was the predominant model informing Kant's logical definitions of judgment as well as his explanation of syllogism. We shall see presently how important this model is for understanding Kant's views on the relation between discursive forms and sensible intuition, and therefore for understanding the meaning of the categories.

Disjunctive Judgment

Kant sometimes presents disjunctive judgment as functioning in a way symmetrically opposed to that of a categorical judgment. The latter starts from the *thing*, subsumes it under a concept A, and by means of this concept A subsumes it under a concept B that contains the first concept under it. Conversely, disjunctive judg-

---

[54] Kant, *Logik*, 925, Ak. IX, 105–6; 602.

[55] Cf. *KrV*, A74/B10: modality "contributes nothing to the content of the judgment . . . but concerns the value of the copula in relation to thought in general." Cf. also *Logik*, §30, Ak. IX, 108; 604: "[Through] modality, the relation of the whole judgment to the cognitive capacity [*Erkenntnisvermö-gen*] in general is determined."

[56] Note that the terms 'internal' and 'external' which respectively qualify the condition of the categorical and hypothetical judgment are the two "concepts of reflection" corresponding to these two forms of judgment in the Amphiboly of the Concepts of Reflection. I shall comment on this correspondence in detail in chapter 6.

ment starts from a concept and then states all the possible divisions contained under it. Kant draws attention to this symmetry when discussing categorical judgment in a *Reflexion* I analyzed earlier:

> In a categorical judgment, the thing whose representation is considered as a part of the sphere of another subordinated representation is considered as subordinated to the latter's higher concept. Hence in the subordination of spheres, the part of the part is compared to the whole. . . . But in disjunctive judgments, I move from the whole to all of the parts considered together: what is contained under the *sphere* of a concept is also contained under one of the parts of this sphere. Consequently, the *sphere* must first be divided.[57]

And in the the next *Reflexion*:

> Here (in the disjunctive judgment) I think many things with one concept, there (in the categorical judgment), one thing with many concepts.[58]

Thus, the third relation in a judgment is a relation neither between a predication and a condition internal, nor between a predication and a condition external to the subject of predication. It is a relation between a concept and the entire field of cognition possible under it. In this sense, as Kant's analysis of the Transcendental Ideal in the Transcendental Dialectic will confirm, disjunctive judgment is the form of the universal subordination of genera and species toward which cognition tends.[59] It seems, then, that we should not expect this form of relation in judgment to have the same role as the other two in subsuming sensible objects under discursive forms. A disjunctive judgment presupposes that concepts are already formed, and have their assigned place in a unified field of cognition. It may play an essential role in correlating achieved or possible cognitions into one whole, but it does not seem likely to play the role we might expect from categorical and hypothetical judgments in subsuming sensible objects under concepts. What the form of disjunctive judgment may do is contribute to the acts of forming categorical and hypothetical judgments the perspective of their possible systematic unity. But, surely, one must already have engaged in considerable activity of concept formation and concept subordination for disjunctive judgments to occur. This systematic role of disjunctive judgment will be confirmed when we examine Kant's explanation of the use we make of discursive forms in empirical concept formation.[60]

The examination of Kant's three logical definitions of judgment has led us to appreciate how they mutually complement and illuminate one another.

The first—a judgment is "the manner in which given cognitions are brought to the objective unity of apperception"—makes the judgment the mediating element between the *original synthetic* unity of apperception and the *objective* unity of apperception, if one understands the former as producing the synthesis of the man-

---

[57] *Refl.* 3095 (1769–75), Ak. XVI, 656.

[58] *Refl.* 3096 (1769–75), Ak. XVI, 656.

[59] I shall analyze the relation between disjunctive judgment and the Transcendental Ideal in chapter 10, pp. 310–312; and chapter 11, pp. 390–391. See also Longuenesse, *Transcendental Ideal*.

[60] See chapter 6, p. 147n.

ifold of sensible intuitions, and the latter as relating the synthesis to objects. This first definition thus furnishes the proper perspective on the other two: it defines the fundamental function to be fulfilled by the acts of thinking whose discursive form is characterized in the second and third definitions.

According to the second definition, judgment is "the unity of the consciousness of various representations, or the representation of their relation insofar as they constitute a concept." I suggested that complementing this definition with explanations we found in the *Reflexionen* allows us to characterize judgment as *concept subordination*. This characterization emphasizes that the form of conceptual universality, or the "analytic unity of consciousness," is the means by which (synthetic) objective unity of consciousness is realized in judgment.

According to the third definition, judgment is a rule involving an exponent, namely a specific relation between the assertion of a predicate and the condition of this assertion. Under this definition judgment achieves its proper place within the framework of syllogistic inference. Thus, inquiry is directed toward the acts of thought by means of which concept subordination is thought as grounded, and judgment admits of being either true or false.

In this chapter, I have not focused on the table of logical forms of judgment itself. One may nonetheless see how these forms fit into the framework of the definitions I have examined. The quantity and quality of judgments are determinations of the relation of subordination of concepts (in which the extension of a concept is *totally* or only *partially* comprehended in the extension of another concept, or on the contrary is *totally* or *partially* excluded from it: universal and particular judgments, affirmative and negative judgments). Relation and modality are determinations of the relation of the assertion to its condition. A more detailed consideration of the various logical forms will be given in subsequent chapters.

Finally, what I would like to stress most emphatically, upon concluding my examination, is the presence of the term "x" in Kant's analysis of the logical forms of judgment. Concept subordination derives its meaning only from the x to which it is ultimately related. The "condition" of all judgment is ultimately this same "x". Now, the *Critique* tells us that, as a singular object, what is represented by the term "x" can be object only of a *sensible* intuition.[61] The full import of this original relation of all discursive use of judgment to a sensible given will appear as we now examine no longer the mere logical forms of judgment but the formation of judgments in relation to the sensible given. Or, more precisely, as we examine the joint formation of concepts and judgments, or the generation of concepts as "that form required for the power of judgment."[62]

---

[61] In this work I shall not consider the use of discursive forms in the domain of practical reason. At least it is clear that the Typic of the Pure Practical Power of Judgment (*Typik der reinen praktischen Urteilskraft*) expounded in the *Critique of Practical Reason* (Ak. V, 67; 176, translation modified), as well as the symbolic presentation of rational ideas explained in the *Critique of Judgment* (cf. *KU*, §59), obeys the same necessity of relating concepts to *singular objects*, which can for us be represented only as *sensible* objects, even if these objects can have only a symbolic, not a schematic, relation to the concepts under consideration.

[62] Cf. *Logik* §5, Rem. 1, Ak. IX, 94; 592.

How Discursive Understanding Comes to the Sensible Given: Comparison of Representations and Judgment

KANT INDICATED the place of sensible intuition right in the logical form of judgment itself, by means of the term "x"—a sensible intuition that provides the cement holding concepts together. We saw this with Kant's explanation of the difference between analytic and synthetic propositions:

> An example of an *analytic* proposition is, To everything x, to which the concept of body ($a + b$) belongs, belongs also *extension* (b).

> An example of a *synthetic* proposition is, To everything x, to which the concept of body ($a + b$) belongs, belongs also *attraction* (c).[1]

Kant is more explicit still in a *Reflexion* from the *Metaphysik Nachlaß*:

> When I say 'A body is divisible', this means: 'some x, which I cognize through the predicates that together constitute the concept of body, I also think through the predicate of divisibility'.[2]

Kant then specifies that two concepts a and b can be said to belong to the same x in two ways: either b is already contained in the concept a, so that one need only analyze the latter to find b, or b belongs to the x thought under a, without being contained in a. In the *Logic* Kant formulates the distinction between analytic and synthetic judgments in similar terms. In both texts, he relates the combination of concepts to the object represented by the term "x" to which the concepts can be attributed, whether the judgment is analytic or synthetic. At the beginning of the *Reflexion* just quoted, Kant goes so far as to say that every concept, regardless of its position in the judgment, is nothing but a *predicate* of the object $= x$ thought in the judgment:

> We cognize an object only through predicates we express or think of it. Prior to this, those representations we find in us can be counted only as materials [*Materialen*], not as cognition. Consequently, an object is only a something in general [*nur ein Etwas überhaupt*] we think through certain predicates that constitute its concept [*was wir uns durch gewisse Prädikate, die seinen Begriff ausmachen, gedenken*]. In every judgment, therefore, there are two predicates we compare to one another. One, which constitutes the given cognition of the object, is the logical subject, and the other, which is compared with it, is called the logical predicate.

---

[1] Kant, *Logik*, §36, Ak. IX, 111; 607.
[2] *Refl.* 4634 (1772–76), Ak. XVII, 616.

Thus one should look beyond the grammatical form of the judgment for the form proper to the activity of thinking itself, a form in which all concepts are related, as predicates, to what alone is ultimately subject of any judgment: the object = x.

To consider the concepts combined in judgment as the predicates of a subject, which ultimately refers to the individual thing not explicitly represented in the grammatical form of the judgment, is not a particularly original position. Wolff himself held that the universal notions combined in judgment represent, as *essentialia* and *attributa*, the resemblances of the *individuals*, which they classify into genera and species.[3] But what is original about Kant's position is the thesis that neither the concepts, nor the object = x to which they are related, are independent of the act of judging, or prior to it.

Consider, first, *concepts*. In the *Jäsche Logic*, Kant says they are "the form required for the power of judgment [*diejenige Form, die zur Urteilskraft erfordert wird*]."[4] Earlier he had enumerated the various possible origins of a concept as to its *matter*. In this regard, concepts are either empirically given, or made, that is, arbitrarily formed (mathematical concepts), or given in pure understanding (categories). He then adds that "The form of a concept, as that of a discursive representation, is always made."[5] Jules Vuillemin has remarked that with this assertion, Kant "dismisses any realism of universals."[6] This remark is correct insofar as Kant's sentence means that concepts do not refer to universals given independently in things, in the mind, or in some Platonic realm of Ideas. Their universal form is produced by the act of judging itself, in their employment as predicates in judgment. But we shall see that Kant also asserts, albeit in terms unique to the framework of his philosophy, that universality is a form immanent to empirical objects themselves. The originality of Kant's position lies in the combination of these two aspects of his conception of universals, one antirealist and the other, one might say, "immanentist."

I shall have more to say on this point shortly.[7] But I now want to consider Kant's conception of the *object* of judgment. As noted earlier, the object represented by the term "x" in the logical form of judgment is itself, according to Kant, dependent upon the act of judging that relates predicates to it. This takes us back to what I earlier called the "internalization to representation of the object of representation."[8] To understand what the term "x" stands for, in Kant's logical form of judgment, we need to take into account three different but correlated components in Kant's notion of an object. Two of them have already been mentioned in chapter 1. They resulted from the two main aspects of the "internalization to representation" of the object of representation: (1) the object as *appearance* (*apparentia*, according to the *Dissertation*) or the "indeterminate object of an empirical

---

[3] Cf. Wolff, *Philosophia rationalis*, §§44, 54–56.

[4] Kant, *Logik*, §5, n. 1, Ak. IX, 94; 592.

[5] Ibid., §4, Ak. IX, 93; 591.

[6] Vuillemin, "Kants Logik," 312: "*So nimmt Kant Abschied von dem Realismus der Universalien.*"

[7] See the section, "Concept Formation through 'Comparison, Reflection, and Abstraction'."

[8] See chapter 1, p. 20.

intuition"; and (2) the object as *phenomenon*, or the empirical object as *determined by concepts*.[9] (3) The third component in Kant's notion of an object we encountered in chapter 2: it is the "transcendental object," a notion present in the A, but which has disappeared from the B Deduction (although retained in other parts of the B edition *Critique*).[10] I submit that this notion is in fact one of the prime components in the interpretation of the term "*x*" in the logical form of judgment. I shall now consider each of the three components in detail.

1. When relating to a sensible given, the act of judging relates first of all to the appearance (*apparentia*), the "indeterminate object of a sensible intuition." But we saw from Kant's exposition of the first two syntheses in the A Deduction that however undetermined the intuition and the object it immediately, "blindly" relates to (i.e., however undetermined *by concepts*), they are nevertheless products of syntheses of imagination (apprehension and reproduction). The latter will ultimately lead to representations of *determined* objects (*phenomena*) only if they are "brought under" the unity of apperception: if they are synthesized not merely by associative imagination, but by *transcendental* imagination, or imagination *under the unity of apperception*.[11] No intuition without imagination, no intuition *leading to representation of (determinate) object* without *transcendental* imagination—that is, imagination "under the unity of apperception."

2. In the introduction to the *Critique of Pure Reason*, Kant asserts that the "complete experience of the object" is the X on which synthetic judgments can rely to combine concepts. I think we should understand this "complete experience" to be the synthesis of *appearances* (immediate, undetermined objects of empirical intuition), which eventually generates *phenomena*, or objects determined under concepts in judgment:

> In synthetic judgments I must have besides the concept of the subject [of predication] something else (X), upon which the understanding may rely, if it is to cognize that a predicate not contained in this concept nevertheless belongs to it. In the case of empirical judgments, judgments of experience, there is no difficulty whatsoever in meeting this demand. This X is the complete experience of the object which I think through the concept A—a concept which forms only one part of this experience. (A8)

The "complete experience of the object" mentioned here is the same as the "synthetic unity with other representations" Kant claims to be the basis for the formation of "common concepts."[12] From such synthesis and its reflection under concepts emerge the *phenomena* to which the concepts combined in a judgment relate. These *phenomena* are the appearances Kant refers to in his explanation of the "logical use of the understanding" at the beginning of the Analytic:

---

[9] Again a heritage from the *Dissertation*. But, as explained earlier, what the *Dissertation* called *phaenomenon* the *Critique* usually terms *Erscheinung*, so that it is not terminologically distinguished from the *apparentia*, also *Erscheinung* in German. See chapter 1.

[10] See A247/B304, A478/B506, A539/B567.

[11] See chapter 2. And chapter 3 pp. 61–64.

[12] B133n. See chapter 3.

Thus in the judgment, 'all bodies are divisible', the concept of the divisible applies to various other concepts, but is here applied in particular to the concept of body, and this concept again to certain appearances that present themselves to us. These objects, therefore, are mediately represented through the concept of divisibility. (A68–69/B93–94)

3. When expounding the "synthesis of recognition in a concept" in the A edition of the Transcendental Deduction, Kant explained that we strive to find coherence between our representations only if we relate them to a "transcendental object = x" independent of our representations. But, he added, the source of this representation is the transcendental unity of apperception itself.

> Appearances are not things in themselves; they are only representations, which in turn have their object—an object which cannot itself be intuited by us, and which may, therefore, be named the non-empirical, that is, transcendental object = x. The pure concept of this transcendental object, which in reality throughout all our cognition is always one and the same, is what can alone confer upon all our empirical concepts in general relation to an object, that is, objective reality. This concept cannot contain any determinate intuition, and therefore refers only to that unity which must be met with in any manifold of cognition which stands in relation to an object. This relation is nothing but the necessary unity of consciousness, and therefore also of the synthesis of the manifold, through a common function of the mind, which combines it in one representation. (A109)

Shortly after, Kant added: "Now I affirm that the categories are the forms of the transcendental unity of apperception" (A111). When commenting on this passage in chapter 2, I suggested that it would have been helpful here to remind us that categories are originally nothing other than logical functions of judgment.[13] Kant could then have made clear that the unity of apperception is the unity of the act of judging—that is, synthesizing appearances, analyzing the synthesized representations into concepts, and so relating them to objects. This clarification is precisely what he sought to provide in the first part of the B Deduction.

The notion of a transcendental object apparently disappears from the B Deduction. I suggest that it remains implicitly as a component in the interpretation of the term "x" in the logical form of judgment. Relating our sensible representations to an object *represented "as" independent of them* ("the . . . transcendental object = x"), striving thereby to find coherence among our representations, is precisely what we are engaged in doing when forming empirical judgments. *Appearances* become *phenomena*, empirical objects that the terms "x", or "x,y,z," can stand for, in Kant's description of the logical forms of judgments, only insofar as these empirical objects are thought as themselves representing an object *independent of our representations*, which "throughout all our cognition is always one and the same," the transcendental object = x.[14]

---

[13] See chapter 2, pp. 52–56.

[14] On this point I disagree with Henry Allison's analysis of the B Deduction. He holds that the first part of the B Deduction is concerned merely with the object "in sensu logico," and therefore is not at all concerned with the transcendental object of the A Deduction (see Allison, *Idealism*, 135, 147–48).

As we saw earlier, discursive thinking, or *analysis*, would be unable to generate the representation of objects—represented in Kant's logical form of judgment by the term *"x"*—unless a prior *synthesis* made analysis itself possible.[15] We shall give this synthesis detailed consideration in part III of this book. Our present concern is *analysis*. In this chapter and the next, I shall examine the ways in which according to Kant, our discursive capacity relates to the sensible given and thus contributes to generating representations capable of functioning as substitutional instances for the term *"x"* in judgments. For this I shall rely on the conclusions established in the previous chapter concerning the "pure" forms of discursive combinations. My focus here will be on what might be called their "impure" forms. I shall consider how acts of discursive thinking sift the sensible given with an eye to generating, inseparably, concepts to be bound in judgments and thus representation of objects (figured by the term *"x"* in Kant's logical form of judgment) to be reflected under those concepts.

COMPARING

What I call the "impure" form of discursive combinations depends on one basic operation, the *comparison* of representations: comparing *sensible representations* in order to generate *concepts* as "the form required for the power of judgment," and comparing *concepts* in order to form *judgments*.

The term "comparison" (*Vergleichung*) is present everywhere in Kant's explanations of the activity of cognition. We encountered it in the *Reflexion* quoted earlier: "In every judgment, therefore, there are two predicates we *compare* with one

---

I think that in B as in A, *relation to a transcendental object* is essential to the generation of the object of (empirical) judgment or *phenomenon*. To the obvious point of objection that 'transcendental object' is not mentioned in the B Deduction, I can only insist that if we analyze Kant's conception of the logical form of judgment *and its role in empirical knowledge*, as I have tried to do, we cannot but come to the conclusion that reference to an object represented by the term 'x' in the logical form of judgment does have as one of its components reference to an independent object leading us to seek coherence among our representations of it, and allowing us to think the connection of representations in judgment as in some sense necessary, "even if the judgment is empirical and therefore contingent": which is precisely the role Kant assigned to reference to the "transcendental object = x" in the A edition. I might add that, in the absence of *empirical* intuition, the object of judgment remains an "object in general = x," or the mere form of an object. We then have no reference to an object in the full sense of the term (cf. B146–47). My disagreement with Allison on this point is the reason I think neither his distinction between *Objekt* and *Gegenstand*, nor his distinction between *objektive Gültigkeit* and *objektive Realität* of the categories are really helpful in understanding the two steps in the B Deduction (see chapter 3, note 17). I do not believe these two steps are differentiated in the way Allison suggests, namely by the fact that in the first the object is considered only "in sensu logico," and in the second it is considered as an object "in the strong sense." My view is that in both steps what is at stake is the *generating* of the empirical object *as* represented object, or object-of-representation, or object "for the appearance" (*phenomenon* for the *apparentia*). As I understand it, the first part of the deduction considers the role of *discursive forms* (analysis) in the generation of this object. The second part the role of *sensible synthesis* presupposed for any analysis, and thus for judgment, to be possible.

[15] Kant argued for this point in the initial paragraphs of the B Deduction, and in the A Deduction. See chapters 2 and 3.

another."[16] Similarly, in the chapter on the Amphiboly of Concepts of Reflection in the first *Critique*, we find: "Before any objective judgment we compare the concepts" (A262/B317). But Kant also calls upon comparison of representations to explain the empirical genesis of cognitions. The term can be found right at the beginning of the B edition of the *Critique*: "For how should our cognitive faculty be awakened into action did not objects affecting our senses partly . . . arouse the activity of our understanding to compare these representations and, by combining or separating them, work up the raw material of the sensible impressions into that cognition of objects which is entitled experience? (B1).

The term "comparison" and the operations it signifies have been almost unanimously overlooked by Kant's commentators. This negligence may be due to the seeming banality of the term. But I believe that its neglect also stems from a reading of Kant that deliberately privileges the *determination* of the empirical by the a priori (i.e., by the categories and by mathematical concepts), to the detriment of the *reflective* relation between the intellectual forms and the sensible.[17] And finally, the term "comparison" is so closely linked to British empiricism in many readers' mind that, upon encountering it in a text of Kant's, one tends to read it as a residue of precritical empiricist temptation.

It is true that the activity of comparison played a prominent role in empiricist accounts of cognition. For Locke, this activity gives rise to all our ideas of relation. The scope of the capacity for comparing, the ability to apply it not only to particular instances but to general ideas as well, also grounds the human capacity to reason, and distinguishes it from the narrowly circumscribed comparisons of which animals are capable.[18] Similarly, for Hume, all reasoning, as founded on ideas of relation ("qualities, which make objects admit of comparison")[19] can be traced back to comparison of ideas.

However, the importance conceded to comparison as the discursive activity par excellence is not peculiar to empiricism. We also encountered the notion of comparison in the definition of judgment quoted earlier from the Port-Royal Logic: "After conceiving things by our ideas, we compare these ideas . . ."[20] What dis-

[16] *Refl.* 4634, quoted earlier in this chapter.

[17] The distinction between *determinative* and *reflective* use of judgment is made by Kant in the third *Critique*. See *KU*, introd. IV, Ak. V, 179: "The power of judgment [*Urteilskraft*] is in general the power to think the particular as contained under the universal. If the universal (the rule, the principle, the law) is given, then the power of judgment, which subsumes the particular under the universal, is *determinative* (the same holds when, as transcendental power of judgment, it indicates *a priori* the conditions according to which alone one can subsume under this universal). . . . But if the particular is given, for which the power of judgment must find the universal, then the power of judgment is merely *reflective*." See also *Erste Einl.* V, Ak. XX, 211. Because the categories and mathematical concepts are a priori concepts, they are used in *determinative* judgments. So are all empirical concepts once they have been formed as "clear concepts." But I argue that this "application" is itself indissociable from a reflective use of the power of judgment, that is, an activity of comparison/reflection/abstraction.

[18] Locke, *Essay*, bk. IV, chap. i, §2. Cf. also bk. II, chaps. xi and xxv.

[19] Hume, *Treatise*, bk. I, pt. I, sec. 5, 14. Cf. also bk. I, pt. III, sec. 2, 73: "All kinds of reasoning consist in nothing but a *comparison*, and a discovery of these relations, either constant or inconstant, which two or more objects bear to each other."

[20] Arnauld and Nicole, *Art de penser*, II, 3, 313; 82.

tinguishes empiricism is less the importance it grants to the act of comparison than its conviction that this act applies to ideas whose *origin* is ultimately always sensible and empirical. But whether empiricist or rationalist in inspiration, any investigation of the *act of thinking* in judgment emphasizes the comparison of ideas, which generates the discursive combination of concepts. Even in Leibniz's *New Essays on Human Understanding*, Theophilus (Leibniz) does not dispute Philalethes' (Locke's) opinion that judgments are formed through the comparison of ideas and propositions, although he does suggest that the *connection* or *concurrence* of ideas should be distinguished from relations relying merely on comparison (agreement or disagreement, resemblance, equality, etc.).[21] And Kant explicitly declares himself to be in accord with Leibniz when, in the Amphiboly of Concepts of Reflection, he defines judgment as a *comparison of concepts*. However, he adds that one should pay due attention to what exactly is being compared, that is, what kind of representation, resulting from which of our representational capacities:

> Prior to all further treatment of our representations, this question must first be asked: In which of our cognitive faculties are our representations connected together? Is it the understanding, or is it the senses, by which they are connected [*verknüpft*] or compared? . . . All judgments, . . . and indeed all comparisons, require *reflection, i.e.* distinction of the cognitive faculty to which the given concepts belong. (A260–61/B316–17)

Indeed, the first original feature of Kant's notion of 'comparison' consists in his distinction between different representational 'locations' for the act of comparison. In the Amphiboly chapter he maintains that the comparison of *concepts* in the *understanding* needs to be carefully distinguished from the comparison of *objects* given in *sensible intuition*. The first comparison is logical. Kant also terms it *logical reflection*. The *distinction* between (logical) comparison of concepts and comparison of objects in sensibility is effected by *transcendental reflection*, in which we attempt to determine the "relation of given representations . . . to one or the other of the two kinds of cognition" (sensible or intellectual):

> The interrelations of given representations can be determined only through transcendental reflection, that is, through [consciousness of] their relation to one or the other of the two kinds of cognition. Whether things are identical or different, in agreement or in opposition, etc., cannot be established at once from the concepts themselves by mere [logical] comparison (*comparatio*), but solely by means of transcendental reflection (*reflexio*), through distinction of the cognitive faculty to which they belong (A262/B318).[22]

---

[21] Cf. Leibniz, *New Essays*, II, chap. 11, §4; IV, chap. 1, §3.

[22] Kant adds the Latin terms in parentheses next to the German terms: *Vergleichung* (*comparatio*), *Überlegung* (*reflexio*). The meaning of the term 'reflection', so often associated with the term 'comparison', is not univocal. In the first place, it refers to the operation of *universalization*. This is the sense in which Kant uses the term in the *Logic* (§§6–2; 82), as well as in the *Anthropology* (§7). Similarly, in the third *Critique*, he calls *reflective* judgment the operation of "finding the universal for the particular" (see note 16). This first sense is also relevant for what Kant calls *logical reflection*, the

Now, it seems plausible to assume that this transcendental reflection (which Kant also calls transcendental comparison) presupposes a comparison one may call *aesthetic*, by means of which appearances are recognized as identical or different *in sensible perception* and externally related to one another.[23] If this is so, then we should distinguish between three distinct senses of 'comparison': logical, aesthetic, transcendental. But this is not all. In the *Logic*, we find a fourth meaning of 'comparison'. Concepts are *generated as to their form* (universality) through the three operations of the understanding, "*comparison*, reflection, and abstraction." This fourth kind of comparison, associated with reflection and abstraction, is what Kant has in mind when he writes, in the introduction to the *Critique of Pure Reason*, that objects of the senses "partly of themselves produce representations, partly arouse the activity of our understanding to compare these representations, and connect [*verknüpfen*] or separate them."[24]

Leaving aside *transcendental* comparison or reflection, there are then three "natural" activities of comparison: *logical* comparison of concepts in the understanding; *aesthetic* comparison of appearances in sensible perception; and a comparison intermediate between the previous two, by means of which *concepts* are formed through the comparison of *sensible* representations.[25] However, Kant does

comparison *of concepts* that results in the subordination of different concepts to a common concept. Finally, reflection is *transcendental* reflection, "consciousness of the relation of given representations to our different sources of cognition," or the "act by which I confront the comparison of representations with the cognitive faculty to which it belongs" (A260/B 316, A261/B317). Note that even in this case Kant does not use 'reflection' to mean the self-transparency of consciousness. Transcendental reflection is not an introspective procedure at all. Rather, it results from the critical procedure of elucidating the conditions of possibility of cognition, which allows for the exposition of a "transcendental topic"—a determination of the transcendental locations of our various representations (cf. A268/B324).

[23] A *Reflexion* from the 1790s appears to confirm that Kant allows for such an aesthetic comparison: "The faculty of sensible representation in its totality: 1. Sense (*facultas apprehendendi*): a. Apprehension of what is internal (*sensus internus*), b. of the external situation, c. of oneself (*aperceptio*). 2. Imagination (*imaginandi*): a. *facultas reproducendi*, b. *praevidendi* [foresight] c. *fingendi* [production]. 3. Faculty of comparison [my emphasis] (*comparandi*): a. *ingenium* [astuteness] b. *acumen* [perspicacity] c. *facultas signandi* [capacity to represent marks] (*Refl.* 228, on the *Anthro.*, Ak. XV, 87). As one can see, Kant here takes into account a *sensible* faculty of comparison, which only in its third step (*facultas signandi*, capacity to represent marks) leads to concepts. One may be surprised to see "apperception" located in the first division of the "faculty of sensible representation." But note that this is in concordance with the fact that in the *Critique*, Kant describes the 'I think' as an "empirical proposition," which expresses an "indeterminate empirical intuition, i.e. a perception (which shows that sensation, which belongs to sensibility, lies at the basis of this existential proposition)" (B422–23n).

[24] B1, quoted earlier, p. 112; on "comparison, reflection, and abstraction," cf. *Logik*, §6, Ak. IX, 94; 592. I translate *verknüpfen* as 'connect' and *verbinden* as 'combine'. *Verbindung* is a broader concept than *verknüpfen*: combination (*Verbindung*) of representations can be *composition* (*Zusammensetzung*) or *connection* (*Verknüpfung*). Kant associates the first with categories of quantity and quality, the second with categories of relation (cf. B201–2n). Kemp Smith does not systematically respect the distinction in his translation.

[25] Against the intermediate position I attribute to the comparison through which concepts are generated (between *aesthetic* comparison and *logical* comparison), one might object that the *Logic* does not assert the *sensible* character of the representations from which concepts are formed. My response is that this is no objection because the *Logic* does not need to say anything about this. Such consider-

not devote any systematic analysis to these three aspects of comparison. Mention of them is scattered throughout the first *Critique*, the *Jäsche Logic*, the *Anthropology*, and the *Reflexionen*, without being explicitly related to one another. More particularly, the *logical* comparison of the Amphiboly of Concepts of Reflection is, as far as I know, never related to the operations of comparison, reflection, and abstraction discussed in the *Logic*. I shall attempt to establish their relation, not in order to "understand Kant better than he understood himself,"[26] but, on the contrary, in order to show how he must have understood himself. In other words, I want to argue that a correlation that was self-evident for Kant has been unduly neglected by commentators, at the cost of obscuring an essential element of his theory of cognition: the correlation between the logical comparison (of concepts), described in the Amphiboly chapter, and the operation of comparison accompanying those of reflection and abstraction through which concepts are generated in the first place, described in the *Logic*.

Each of these two kinds of comparison illuminates the other. On the one hand, the forms of logical comparison expounded in the Amphiboly shed light on the activity of comparison applied to given representations, which according to both the *Logic* and the *Critique* generates concepts as the "form required for the power of judgment." On the other hand, taking into account the reflective activity of comparison through which the sensible is reflected under concepts serves to alleviate the seeming rigidity of the separation between "transcendental locations," sensibility and intellect, advocated in the Amphiboly. Although in the latter text, Kant counsels us to distinguish between a comparison located in the understanding alone—comparison of concepts—and a comparison of objects as appearances given in sensibility, clearly there must also be a comparison by means of which *sensible* objects are reflected under *concepts*. The latter comparison, which in the *Logic* is associated with reflection and abstraction, will be the main subject of my discussion in the remainder of this chapter and in the next.

CONCEPT FORMATION THROUGH "COMPARISON, REFLECTION, AND ABSTRACTION"

The comparison of sensible representations that gives rise to concept formation is a search for common marks. As such it is inseparably linked to the two other "acts of the understanding," namely reflection and abstraction: "I see, e.g., a spruce, a

---

ations do not belong to it, "the origin of concepts in regard of their *matter* . . . is considered in metaphysics" (*Logik*, §5). The three operations described in the *Logic* (comparison, reflection, abstraction) may indeed be performed on representations which have already been made into concepts. But as far as the initial acquisition of *empirical* concepts is concerned, the three operations of the understanding must originally be applied to sensible intuitions. The *intermediate* character of the comparison at issue here is confirmed by the fact that it seems to exist in embryonic form in sensibility itself: what is the *facultas signandi* [capacity to represent marks], the last aspect of sensible comparison mentioned in *Reflexion* 229 (quoted in note 22), if not a *sensible* capacity to take in marks, preparatory to the formation of concepts?

[26] To borrow a phrase Kant used to refer to his own reading of Plato: cf. A314/B370. This phrase has perhaps too often been raised to the dignity of a method for reading Kant himself.

willow, and a linden. By first comparing these objects with one another I note that they are different from one another in regard to the trunk, the branches, the leaves, etc.: but next I reflect what they have in common, trunk, branches, and leaves themselves, and I abstract from the quantity, the figure, etc., of these; thus I acquire a concept of a tree."[27] Actually, the chronological presentation of these operations is implausible. The "comparison" of trunks, leaves, etc., which takes stock of their differences, is not temporally prior to "reflection" and "abstraction." Rather, it presupposes efforts to *reflect* the similarities among the elements compared and *abstract from* (leave out) their dissimilarities. *Reflection* and *abstraction* are not operations that follow comparison and are dependent on it; rather, each depends on the others and all proceed simultaneously. Indeed, only insofar as comparison is conjoined with the two other operations can it be geared from the outset toward universal representation, that is, the production of a concept. Thus, what we might call "universalizing comparison" differs from merely aesthetic comparison precisely by the fact that it is inseparable from reflection and abstraction. *Aesthetic* comparison is a comparison of intuitions—that is, singular representations, with respect to their spatiotemporal situations. *Universalizing* comparison is a comparison of universal marks *which are generated by the very act of comparison*: "We compare only *what is universal in the rule of our apprehension [das Allgemeine der Regel unserer Auffassung]*. For example, one sees a sapling, so one has the representation of a tree; an elongated rectangle makes one think of a square [*gibt Anlaß zum Quadrat*]."[28]

Now, the "rule of apprehension" is the schema.[29] To compare representations in order to form concepts is therefore to compare schemata. And to compare

[27] Kant, *Logik*, §6, Ak. IX, 94–95; 592.

[28] *Refl.* 2880 (1776–8?), Ak. XVI, 557. My emphasis.

[29] On the schema as "rule of apprehension," cf. A141/B180: "The schema of the triangle can exist nowhere but in thought. *It is a rule of synthesis of the imagination, in respect to pure figures in space.* Still less is an object of experience or its image ever adequate to the empirical concept; for this latter always stands in immediate relation to the schema of imagination, as a *rule for the determination of our intuition, in accordance with some universal concept*" (my emphasis). One may object that according to this text, there is no schema without a concept of which the schema is the "presentation" (*exhibitio*, as the third *Critique* says: see introd. VIII, §§57, 59, etc.), whereas on my analysis, the schemata are acquired *before* the concepts, which reflect them. But this seeming disagreement is due only to the difference between the perspective of the Schematism chapter and that of the Transcendental Deduction. In the Schematism (from which the preceding quotation is taken) Kant is concerned with the conditions under which *a concept already formed* may relate to a sensible object. For this it requires a sensible schema, which is its "presentation." Without such a schema, no use can be made of concepts, whichever they may be (categories, mathematical or empirical concepts). But if one inquires, as the deduction does, into the formation or acquisition both of "rules for the determination of our intuition" and of concepts ("representing" these rules, which in turn "present" them in intuition: are their "schemata"), it seems clear that the "rules for the synthesis of intuition" must first have been *acquired* at the outcome of the operations described in the A Deduction (apprehension, reproduction, and recognition), in order to be *reflected* as discursive concepts, "universal or reflected representations." We are here concerned with this empirical acquisition of "rules for the synthesis of intuition." Of course, for the account to be complete, we would need to consider also the prior activity of *associative imagination, under the guidance of productive imagination.* This will be done only in part III. Here let me simply add that empirical concepts being thus acquired, the discursive operations of the understanding that combine them in judgments and inferences allow other concepts also to be formed,

schemata, by means of the three joint acts of comparison, reflection, and abstraction, is first of all to *generate* these schemata. Thus the schemata result from the very acts of universalizing comparison of which they are the object. Several representations must be compared with one another so that different schemata, rules for apprehension, may arise in them and be reflected as concepts:

> Question: could we, from an intuition alone, without comparison, abstract something [*etwas absondern*] in order to subordinate other things to it if they presented themselves? (We can become conscious solely [*ganz allein*] of the activity of the imagination, i.e., of the combination of representations either with one another, or with our sensibility [*mit unserem Sinne*], without considering what is combined and its own marks, for example, a house. But a concept becomes clear only through its application in a comparison).[30]

Only that differentiation which combines comparison with reflection and abstraction can outline common rules for apprehension and then elevate these rules to the status of universal representations or concepts. One may then "subordinate other things" to these universal representations, that is, subordinate those representations to them in which the same general rule for apprehension may be "recognized" (by means of the "synthesis of recognition" explicated in Deduction A or the *Erkenntnis* mentioned in the *Logic*).[31] Note how both directions of judgment, *reflective* as well as *determinative*, collaborate in relating concepts to objects and allowing concepts to "become clear," reflected explicitly as concepts: "a concept becomes clear only through its [determinative] *application* in a [reflective] *comparison*."

What would a representation be in which these "universal rules of our apprehension," the schemata of empirical concepts, were not delineated by comparing/reflecting/abstracting? What would it mean to "become conscious solely of the activity of the imagination, i.e. of the combination of representations either with one another, or with our sensibility, without taking into account what is combined and its own marks"? Kant's laconic suggestion refers us to "for example, a house." The *Jäsche Logic* sheds light on this:

> If, for example, a savage sees a house from a distance, whose use he does not know, he admittedly has before him in his representation the very same object as someone else who knows it determinately as a dwelling established for human beings. But as to form, this cognition of one and the same object is different in the two cases. In the former it is *mere intuition*, in the latter it is simultaneously *intuition* and *concept*.[32]

Kant's savage intuits a combination of sensations according to relations of contiguity in space, differences in color, light, and shadow, similar in "matter" to those intuited by "someone else" who knows that what he has before him is a house.

---

which in turn are the source of new schemata ("rules for apprehension") that guide the "presentation" (*Darstellung, exhibitio*) of new objects in sensible intuition. The relation of mathematical concepts and of the categories to their schemata will be considered in detail in part III.

[30] *Refl.* 2878 (1776–8?), Ak. XVI, 556–57.
[31] A103–6; *Logik*, introd. VIII, Ak. IX, 64–65; 569.
[32] *Logik*, introd., V, Ak. IX, 33; 544–45.

Thus, in his intuition of the house, the "savage" is conscious of the "combination of representations with each other." He is also conscious of a relation of these representations "to (his) senses," that is, conscious of them not merely as presenting an object to him but as *sensations* within him, perhaps associated with feelings of pleasure or displeasure.[33] But the system of comparisons into which the content of his intuition is channeled has nothing in common with ours. He has never seen anything similar (in the way "a spruce, a willow, and a linden" are similar) from which he could have obtained a common concept by comparing objects according to their similarities and differences, reflecting similar features and abstracting from the differences (in material, size, shape, and so on). In his apprehension there is no rule guiding him to privilege certain marks and leave aside others, so that a concept of house might apply. Should someone point to the object and call it 'house', this might suggest to him a proper name for the singular object he has in front of him, but even this is uncertain: how is he to know what is being referred to—the door, the color, the shape, the site, or what? Only the "application in a comparison," that is, the gradually dawning consciousness of a "rule of apprehension" common to the representation of various objects serving the same purpose, would pick out analogous marks and bring forth the concept of a house. This application alone will complement the intuition of Kant's savage with a discursive form similar to that acquired by the man who throughout his life passed his nights in a warm house in Königsberg.

The "rule of apprehension" of which the concept is the universal representation is both immanent to the sensible, singular representation, and generated by the act of comparison. Comparing representations in order to subsume them under a "unified consciousness" means *generating* the awareness of a rule of apprehension. But the very possibility of such an awareness supposes that the sensible representations *lend themselves* to such a rule: "This community [*Gemeinschaft*] of representations under one mark presupposes a comparison, not of perceptions, but of our apprehension, *insofar as it contains the presentation [Darstellung] of an as yet undetermined concept, and is universal in itself [an sich allgemein ist]*."[34] The act of apprehension is the "presentation" (*Darstellung*) of a *still undetermined concept*. The determination of the concept will *result* from the act of comparison, but the concept must already be present in an "undetermined" state, that is, in an intuitive state, or more precisely, as a still unreflected, "obscure" rule for the synthesis of intuition. This is why the apprehension is said to be "universal in itself": it is *universal* insofar as the rule is already present there, in an unreflected state. It is universal *in itself* insofar as universality is immanent to it. But it is *only* in itself universal as long as "the rule of apprehension" is unreflected and therefore as yet only potentially there. Universality (*Allgemeinheit*) is the form of "clear consciousness," of concept. "A representation that becomes universal as a mark through consciousness [*die durch das Bewusstsein als Merkmal*

---

[33] On sensation as a perception that "relates solely to the subject as the modification of its state," cf. A320/B376–77; on the relation between *sensation* and *feeling* (of pleasure or displeasure), cf. *Anthr.*, §15; *KU*, introd. VII, 188–89, and §3.

[34] *Refl.* 2883 (1776–8?), Ak. XVI, 558 (my emphasis).

allgemein wird] is called a concept."[35] But this universality is brought about only by the act of comparison accompanied by acts of reflection and abstraction. In other words, it has only comparative and differentiating value.

The originality of Kant's view will perhaps be more evident if we confront his conception of the relation between concept and sensible representation with those of his empiricist predecessors. In the first place, Kant turns his back on the Berkeleyan-Humean critique of general ideas. Berkeley held, against Locke, that there are no abstract or general ideas. Every idea is particular. We have no idea of red "in general" or a triangle "in general", but always a determinate shade of red and a triangle of a particular shape and dimension. "General" ideas are nothing other than particular ideas that function as signs "representing" or calling to mind other, equally particular ideas: "Now if we will annex a meaning to our words, and speak only of what we can conceive, I believe we shall acknowledge that an idea which considered in itself is particular becomes general by being made to represent or stand for all other particular ideas of the same sort."[36] In the same vein, Hume says that "a particular idea becomes general by being annexed to a general term—that is, to a term, which from a customary conjunction has a relation to many other particular ideas, and readily recalls them in the imagination."[37] For Hume, as all ideas are images, they are also particular; only in use do they become "general."

On the contrary, if for Kant too the universality of the *concept* lies in its use, that is, in its "application in a comparison," universality is nevertheless its proper *form*, and this form is adequate to what it represents—not a singular image, but a rule of apprehension, the generality of which results from the act of comparison. Does this mean that Kant is content to restore Locke's conception of the abstract idea beyond Berkeley's and Hume's criticisms? One might be inclined to believe so, since Kant hails Locke's "physiology of the human understanding" and goes as far as granting it the dignified status of an *empirical deduction* of the concepts of the understanding.[38] And it is tempting to relate Kant's assertion that "The form of a concept, as that of a discursive representation, is always made" to Locke's: "*general* and *universal* belong not to the real existence of things; but are the inventions and creations of the understanding, made by it for its own use. . . ."[39]

But actually Kant goes well beyond reaffirming a Lockian position on universals. Locke denied any reality to universals: what is general or universal is not in things, but only in how we think them. For Kant, on the contrary, to say that concepts are strictly discursive (that they are never *given* as to their form, but can only result from acts of the understanding) does not mean that they do not represent anything real in things. The sentence just cited from Locke was not complete, as I was then only interested in the similarities between his conception of abstract ideas and Kant's characterization of concepts as to their *form*. In full it

---

[35] *Refl.* 3057 (179?), Ak. XVI, 634.
[36] Berkeley, *Principles*, introd., §§12, 31–32.
[37] Hume, *Treatise*, bk. I, pt. I, sec. 7, 22.
[38] Cf. Transcendental Deduction, §13, A85–86/B117–19.
[39] Locke, *Essay*, bk. III, chap. 3, §11. Cf. Kant, *Logik*, 4, and my p. 110.

reads: "*General* and *universal* belong not to the real existence of things; but are the inventions and creations of the understanding, made by it for its own use, and concern only signs, whether words or ideas."[40] For Kant on the contrary, *universals* do indeed belong to the existence of things (they represent resemblances lending themselves to "rules of apprehension"), but are revealed in things only by the acts of "comparison, reflection, and abstraction" of the understanding. Although it is "made" as to its form, a concept represents something universal "present in itself" in the given object.[41] But as I showed earlier, only the "application in a comparison" makes what is "present in itself" a property reflectable under a "clear concept."[42]

Should we consider that this dependence of concepts on their "application in comparison" holds not only for empirical concepts, but also for a priori concepts—categories and mathematical concepts? Should one say also of the latter that they are generated through "comparison, reflection, and abstraction" from given representations, and that they have no universality other than that generated by these acts? The *Jäsche Logic* clearly maintains that not only empirical but also mathematical concepts and the categories are "made" as to their form, although the three types of concepts differ as to their matter or content. As regards matter, only mathematical concepts are "made," that is, synthetically and arbitrarily formed; by contrast, the pure concepts of the understanding are "given a priori," while empirical concepts are "given a posteriori." All equally are, however, *made as to their form.*[43] Now, the only operations of the understanding to which Kant refers when he explains how the form of concepts is "made" are the three considered earlier: comparison, reflection, and abstraction: "The logical *actus* of the understanding, through which concepts are generated as to their form, are: 1. *comparison* . . . , 2. *reflection*, and 3. *abstraction*."[44]

Since the example Kant gives to illustrate these operations clearly has to do

---

[40] Locke, *Essay*, bk. III, chap. 3, §11.

[41] This is, of course, because the "given" object is in fact not given but produced, synthesized by imagination. What is "in itself present" in the object is the rule for synthesis, or the schema. This will be further analyzed in part III.

[42] Interestingly, C. S. Peirce claimed a Kantian heritage for his own (pragmatist) realism. He wrote, for instance: "What Kant called his copernican step was precisely the move from the nominalistic to the realistic view of reality. It was the essence of his philosophy to *consider the object as determined by the mind*. This meant nothing else than to consider that all conception and all intuition that enters necessarily into the experience of an object and is not transitory and accidental has objective validity" (Peirce, *Collected Papers*, VIII, 15, quoted by Apel, "From Kant to Peirce," 95). Note also that when Kant denies that we cognize *the real essence* of things, he does not say that we cognize only their nominal essence (as Locke does—see *Essay*, bk. III, chap. 3, §18), but their *logical* essence. We cognize only the logical essence of things, that is, the content (*Inhalt*) of the concepts we form (of things) through comparison, reflection, and abstraction. These operations are performed by the "logical use" of the understanding that Kant, in the *Dissertation*, opposed to its "real use" (through which we could doubtless have cognized the real essence of things). Cf. *Logik*, introd. VIII-5, Ak. IX, 61; 566; Letter to Reinhold, May 12, 1789 (Ak. XI-2, 36–37; 139–40).

[43] *Logik*, §4, Ak. IX, 93; 591: "All concepts, *as to matter*, are either *given* [*gegeben*] (*conceptus dati*) or *made* [*gemacht*] (*conceptus factitii*). The former are given either a priori or a posteriori. . . . *Note*: The form of a concept, as that of a discursive representation, is always made [*gemacht*]."

[44] *Logik*, §6, Ak. IX, 94; 592.

with empirical concepts ("I see a spruce, a willow, and a linden . . . "), one may doubt the three operations mentioned are capable of clarifying the "made" character of a priori concepts. Yet, we should not exclude this possibility too quickly. Consider first the categories. Their emergence as "clear representations" will be considered when we examine Kant's explanation of the move from *judgments of perception* to *judgments of experience*.[45] For now I will insist only on the following. To be sure, Kant maintains that the categories are a priori concepts. Yet, like any other concept, they can be recognized in the sensible only through "application in a comparison." Witness Kant's repeated assertion that causal relations are cognized only empirically, even though the origin of the concept of cause is not empirical.[46] Indeed, this is precisely why the categories require a transcendental deduction. For while, like other concepts, they are *made* as to their form (generated as "clear representations" through "comparison, reflection, and abstraction"), it still has to be proved that they are *given a priori* as to their content or meaning.

Second, consider mathematical concepts. To be sure, according to Kant they are *constructed*, that is, presented a priori in sensible intuition.[47] Nevertheless, recognizing figures, volumes, measures, and motions in *empirical* sensibility also depends on operations of comparison, reflection and abstraction. For even if a priori construction complements these operations and makes it possible to anticipate empirical correlations (e.g., when formulating laws of motion), the use of a priori constructions in empirical cognition nevertheless depends on acts of comparison. Moreover, "pure" mathematical constructs themselves undergo these operations of comparison reflection abstraction. Recall the *Reflexion* quoted earlier: "An elongated rectangle makes one think of a square."[48] One might go on to say that a rectangle and a square "make one think" of a trapezoid and thus generate the concept of a quadrilateral, and so on. Thus the operation of comparison/reflection/abstraction is indeed the discursive act par excellence, through which the very form of conceptual universality is produced, whichever kind of concept we consider.[49]

In sum, the act of comparison/reflection/abstraction has these four uses: (1) comparing empirical (or, more broadly, sensible) representations, in order to form concepts, (2) comparing the *schemata* (the general rules of our apprehension) of these representations, (3) generating a *discursive representation* of these schemata, namely *concepts*, and, (4) relating concepts in *judgments* within which they are, again, "compared" (but this time, as purely discursive forms). In the end, all four are but different facets of a single reflective act of the understanding.

The act of comparison is guided by the *Vermögen zu urteilen*, that is, by the ca-

---

[45] See chapter 7.

[46] I will develop this point at length in chapter 11.

[47] Kant's conception of mathematical construction will be examined in chapter 9.

[48] *Refl.* 2880. Cf. note 27.

[49] Of course, I am not claiming that mathematical thought can be reduced to operations of comparison, reflection, and abstraction, but only that these operations also have their place therein. For Kant's conception of mathematics, see chapter 9.

pacity *to form judgments*. In the *Jäsche Logic*, shortly before presenting the three "acts of the understanding" through which concepts are formed, Kant states: "This *logical* origin of concepts—their origin as to their mere form—consists in reflection, whereby a representation common to several objects (*conceptus communis*) arises as the form which is required for the power of judgment [*Urteilskraft*])."[50] Our analysis of Kant's conception of the logical form of judgment in the previous chapter helps us to clarify Kant's meaning. We saw there that every judgment is, as to its form, a subordination of concepts by which the *x, y, z* "thought under a concept A" are also "thought under a concept B." The logical form of judgment may then be regarded as the form of the very act of generating "representations common to several objects." A felicitous formulation of this point was given by Steckelmacher when he said that concepts are generated by "an act of judging carried out silently":

> In the operations of "comparison, reflection, and abstraction," one must recognize an act of judging carried out silently, however incompletely achieved it might be [*ein wenn auch nur unvollkommenes, im Stillen sich vollziehendes Urteilen*], which in this very incompleteness is proper to the first formation of concepts, and which consequently must be taken into account before any consideration of genuine and fully achieved judgments.[51]

But if one admits that a "silent" and "incompletely achieved" act of judging presides over concept formation itself, then one must conclude that the forms of judgment, in which "achieved" concepts will be combined, must regulate even the comparison of those representations "only in themselves universal," the rules of our sensible apprehension, and first contribute to the very *generation* of these rules, ultimately reflected under discursive concepts combined in judgments.[52]

COMPARISON/REFLECTION/ABSTRACTION AND THE COMPARISON OF CONCEPTS IN JUDGMENT

We have good reason, then, to try to specify the acts of comparison/reflection/abstraction described in section 6 of the *Logic* by means of the "concepts of comparison" expounded in the Amphiboly. Examining these concepts might give us some indication as to the "silent judgments" by which our concepts of objects are formed. It is indeed a striking fact, generally overlooked by Kant commentators, that the Transcendental Analytic, which opens with the parallel exposition of

---

[50] *Logik*, §5, n. 1, Ak. IX, 94; 592.

[51] Steckelmacher, *Formale Logik*, 21–22.

[52] If these analyses are correct, a point I stressed in the previous chapter is here confirmed from another angle. The initial form of any empirical judgment is the combination/comparison of *two concepts*, that is, *two universal representations*, discursive representations of the schemata outlined in the sensible given by the very act that compares them, or that compares the "rules for our apprehension." Consequently, for Kant, the canonical form of judgment is universal (and affirmative) judgment, while at the same time the primary function of this form is to subsume singular objects.

forms of judgments and categories, should close with another parallel exposition, that between forms of judgments and "concepts of reflection," or "concepts of comparison." The neglect in which the latter correspondence is held might well be due to a fundamental misunderstanding of the nature and function of judgment according to Kant, the same misunderstanding that leads commentators to disregard the term "comparison" in Kant's characterization of cognition. Yet, in my view, it is only by paying sufficient attention to the acts of comparison in judgment that one can hope to understand how judgments formed by comparison of representations may eventually lead to the subsumption of appearances under categories, and so to what Kant calls "judgments of experience." However, before coming to this last point (in chapter 7), we need to appreciate how Kant's explanation of the comparison of concepts, in the Amphiboly of Concepts of Reflection, illuminates the comparison of representations performed in order to generate concepts, that is, representations whose universality is "the form which is required for the power of judgment."

First in need of explanation are the expressions "concept of comparison" and "concept of reflection." Kant uses them to refer to the four pairs of concepts he examines in the Amphiboly chapter. The term *Vergleichungsbegriff*, "concept of comparison" is applied to them insofar as they function as rules for logical comparison, that is, rules for comparison *of concepts*.[53] But he also characterizes such comparison as "logical reflection,"[54] so that even in this first sense, "concepts of comparison" may be considered "concepts of reflection." Kant introduces the latter expression, however, with the specific aim of criticizing Leibniz's confusion between comparison of concepts and comparison of things, and demanding that logical comparison be supplemented by *reflection on the relation of our representations in general to their sources in our mind*. This reflection is *transcendental*. It is when representations undergo such reflection that "concepts of comparison" are specifically designated as "concepts of reflection."[55] What should one think, then, of the term *"Reflexionsbegriffe"* in the title of the Amphiboly chapter? Presumably there Kant has in mind both senses of the term *Reflexion*: it may

[53] Cf. A262/B318: "Before any objective judgment we compare the concepts to find in them *identity* (of many representations under one concept) with a view to *universal* judgments, *difference* with a view to *particular* judgments, *agreement* with a view to *affirmative* judgments, *conflict* with a view to *negative* judgments, etc. For this reason we ought, it seems, to call the above-mentioned concepts, concepts of comparison (*conceptus comparationis*)."

[54] Cf. A279/B335: "If we reflect in a merely logical fashion, we are only comparing our concepts with each other in the understanding."

[55] Cf. A260/B316: "*Reflection (reflexio)* [*Überlegung*] does not concern itself with objects themselves with a view to deriving concepts from them directly, but is that state of mind in which we first set ourselves to discover the subjective conditions under which [alone] we are able to arrive at concepts. It is the consciousness of the relation of given representations to our different sources of cognition; and only by way of such consciousness can the relation of the sources of cognition to one another be rightly determined." A270/B326: "Having no such transcendental topic, and being therefore deceived by the amphiboly of the concepts of reflection, the celebrated Leibniz erected an *intellectual system of the world*." A276–77/B332–33: "I shall always be obliged to compare my concepts, in transcendental reflection, solely under the conditions of sensibility. . . . The remaining concepts of reflection have to be dealt with in the same manner."

ɪean "logical reflection"; or it may signify the "transcendental reflection"
ɪrough which logical comparison and (aesthetic) comparison of sensible objects
are distinguished.

In this chapter and the next I shall give preference to the expression "concepts
of comparison" so as to emphasize the role of these concepts in *logical* comparison or reflection, which in its fully achieved discursive form is a comparison of
concepts, but in its "silent," or embryonic form, is a comparison of sensible representations in order to form concepts. Concepts of comparison are thus a peculiar kind of concept, since they are in no sense concepts of *objects*; they merely
reflect *acts of comparison of concepts*, that is, "that comparison of representations
which is prior to the concept of things [*die Vergleichung der Vorstellungen, die
dem Begriffe der Dinge vorhergeht*]" (A269/B325).

Thus I argue that by shedding light on the operations of comparison, the chapter on the Amphiboly of Concepts of Reflection can help us to understand Kant's
views on the formation of empirical concepts. To this one might object that the
comparison discussed in the Amphiboly chapter is fundamentally distinct from
the comparison/reflection/abstraction mentioned in the *Logic*. The aim of the appendix to the Transcendental Analytic is to demonstrate that Leibnizian rationalism rests on a deeply rooted illusion. Believing that cognition of objects is possible by concepts alone, independently of any necessary reference to sensibility,
Leibniz confounded relations between concepts with relations between the objects thought under these concepts. To each of the four general titles in the table
of logical forms of judgments there corresponds a specific relation between concepts, and in each case Kant exposes one aspect of Leibniz's fundamental confusion. I shall undertake a detailed examination of these correspondences and
Kant's analysis of Leibniz's confusion in the next chapter. For the present, therefore, a simple review will suffice. Against Leibniz, Kant maintains that: (1) Objects thought under two (generically) identical concepts are *not* therefore numerically identical, since they can still be distinguished by their position in
space. (2) Determinations of an object thought under noncontradictory concepts
may nevertheless be opposed to each other as sensible determinations, as the case
of forces of opposite direction in space shows. (3) Even though a concept is defined by its *internal* marks, an object appearing in space consists of nothing but
external relations. (4) In cognition by pure concepts, the *matter* precedes the
form (i.e., the determinable precedes the determination of its relations), but in appearances the spatiotemporal *form* precedes the phenomenal *matter*, that is, the
appearances. In each of the four cases considered, Kant thus distinguishes the
comparison of *concepts* from the comparison of *objects* thought under them,
claiming that the sensible given is ultimately irreducible to conceptual determination, that appearances are ultimately irreducible to the concepts under which
they are thought.[56]

What, then, do the two species of comparison distinguished in the Amphiboly

---

[56] Cf. A271/B327 to A280/B336.

chapter—that of concepts and that of appearances—have in common with the activity of comparison/reflection/abstraction expounded in the *Logic*? Kant's concern in the latter is to explain how concepts are acquired through a comparison of representations that bestows on them "the form which is required for the power of judgment." By contrast, his aim in the Amphiboly chapter is to remind us that it is essential rigorously to distinguish intellectual concepts from sensible objects (appearances). Hence, not only do these two disparate treatments of comparison seem difficult to equate, one might even be tempted to query whether Kant's emphasis in the Amphiboly on the irreducibility and priority of appearances vis-à-vis concepts is compatible with the relation between the sensible and the intellectual highlighted in my explanation of comparison as a source of concepts. Indeed, this explanation appears to be vulnerable to the same reproach Kant addressed to Locke: "Locke . . . *sensualized* all concepts of the understanding, *i.e.* interpreted them as nothing more than empirical or abstracted concepts of reflection" (A271/B327).[57] Could one not reproach me with having attributed to Kant precisely the "sensualization of the concepts of the understanding" he criticized in Locke? If this were the case, clearly my attempt to explain comparison/reflection/abstraction by means of the concepts of comparison in the Amphiboly would be pointless. Indeed, my entire explanation of concept formation according to Kant would be invalidated.

To answer this objection we need to be clear about just what Kant's criticism of Locke in the passage just cited amounts to. Locke believed that all ideas originate in one way or another from the senses (whether these ideas are simple or complex, particular or abstract, ideas of substances or ideas of relations, and even whether they are ideas of sensation or ideas of reflection, since the latter reflect acts of the mind when it perceives ideas of sensation). Now, Kant holds that while such a conception is surely able to account for the empirical generation of all our concepts, it cannot account for their origin. Though all our cognitive concepts do indeed become clear only through the operations of comparison, reflection, and abstraction performed on empirical, sensible representations, some of them (the categories) do nevertheless originate a priori in the understanding. Kant's reproach against Locke—that he made the concepts of the understanding "sensible"—thus comes down to the charge that he was mistaken about the true origin of the *categories*. But *because* of this mistake, Locke is also accused of misunderstanding the formation of *all concepts* generally. For Locke's failure to acknowledge the a priori origin of the categories is in fact a failure to recognize that a priori forms of thought are essential to all concept formation. He appreciated their role neither in guiding the syntheses of sensible manifolds (which we shall consider in part III) nor in discursive understanding (our present concern). Hence, he could explicate neither the nature of mathematical concepts nor the a priori conditions whereby alone empirical concepts can relate to objects. Nevertheless,

---

[57] What Kant here calls "concepts of reflection" (*Reflexionsbegriffe*) are of course not the concepts of reflexion he analyzes in the Amphiboly chapter. The expression here refers to all concepts insofar as they are supposed to be formed by empirical reflection (comparison/reflection/abstraction).

that he cautions against Locke's mistake does not excuse Kant from giving an account of how empirical concepts are generated from the sensible given. Indeed, it is all the more necessary that he explain how original discursive forms (the forms of judgment) contribute to empirical concept formation. Accordingly, far from invalidating my attempt to relate the concepts of comparison expounded in the Amphiboly, to the operations of comparison/reflection/abstraction expounded in the *Logic*, Kant's criticism of Locke justifies bringing together the two texts in order to understand better, on the one hand the strictly intellectual origin of discursive forms and, on the other hand, their relation to the sensible given in generating empirical concepts.

What makes this clarification all the more important is that, in the context of the Amphiboly, one of the chief aims of Kant's criticism of Locke is to highlight his inverse critique of Leibniz. Whereas Locke thought he could derive all concepts from the sensible given, Leibniz believed that access to the true nature of things is possible only through purely intellectual concepts. Now, here again one should inquire into the exact nature of the alternative Kant proposes to the Leibnizian amphiboly. Clearly Kant cannot answer Leibniz just by making a distinction Leibniz is supposed to have missed—that between comparison of concepts on the one hand, and comparison of objects (as appearances) on the other hand. If these two comparisons are to be distinguished, then the comparison of concepts itself needs to be reconsidered. Indeed, the consequence of the irreducibility of the sensible to the intellectual is that concepts have objective meaning only when they are related to those very sensible manifolds that are rigorously heterogeneous to them. This being so, the comparison of concepts in a judgment can itself no longer be a "merely logical" comparison in the narrow sense, namely a comparison *of concepts alone* (except in the case of analytic judgments formed from purely rational concepts, such as moral judgments). It can no longer be that comparison which, in Kant's words, "*only* compares *our concepts with each other in the understanding*, to find whether both have the same content, whether they are contradictory or not, whether something is contained within the concept or is an addition from outside, which of the two is given and which should serve only as a mode of thinking what is given" (A279/B335).

Such comparison may be the ground of a *calculus ratiocinator*, such as Leibniz tried to develop with his *ars combinatoria*. But if concepts get their meaning from the sensible manifolds they are related to when combined in judgments, then their comparison is quite different from that implemented in a Leibnizian-style combinatoric. What we compare in judgments are no longer marks given in understanding alone, but universal representations of "rules of our apprehension." Such comparison is not directly discussed in the Amphiboly chapter, but Kant does point to it: "I shall always be obliged to compare my concepts, in transcendental reflection, solely under the conditions of sensibility" (A276/B332).

True, the aim of transcendental reflection proper is merely to assert the distinction, overlooked in the rationalist amphiboly, between the relation of concepts in the understanding on the one hand and the relation of appearances in sensibility on the other. Transcendental reflection is a "transcendental topic": a distinction between the (faculty) locations of comparison. But I think that this very distinction entails an expansion of the meaning of "logical comparison" (i.e., comparison of concepts). Besides what I called *merely logical comparison in the narrow sense*, one must take into account *logical comparison in the broad sense*, a comparison of *concepts* (and thus a *logical* comparison), but under *sensible* conditions.[58] Concepts can then be compared in a judgment only insofar as they are "universal or reflected" representations of schemata, rules for the synthesis of sensible objects. I suggested earlier that such rules are generated under the impetus of the very act of comparison. If this is so, the concepts of comparison that govern the comparison of concepts in a judgment also govern the comparison of sensible representations that generates empirical schemata and thus also empirical concepts, as "the form which is required for the power of judgment."

If this is correct, the indications of the *Logic*, according to which concepts are formed as "the form which is required for the power of judgment" may be supplemented with those of the Amphiboly, according to which "Before any objective judgment we compare the concepts to find in them *identity* (of many representations under one concept) with a view to *universal* judgments, *difference* with a view to *particular* judgments, *agreement* with a view to affirmative judgments, *conflict* with a view to *negative* judgments, etc." (A262/B317).[59] The concepts of comparison according to which comparisons of concepts occur, according to the Amphiboly, are also the concepts of comparison according to which comparison/reflection/abstraction, the generation of empirical concepts, occurs, according to the *Logic*. Of course, in the latter case the issue is concept *formation*, for which forms of judgment serve as guides, whereas in the former case, *already formed* concepts are compared in order to be combined in judgments. But if my analysis is correct we may assume that the former case sheds light on the latter. Our rules for comparing concepts in judgment are also rules for forming concepts through comparison/reflection/abstraction.

[58] The distinction I am suggesting here, between "merely logical" comparison (in the narrow sense), and logical comparison (in the broad sense), is equivalent to that between *analytic* and *synthetic* judgments. To state that a comparison, although *logical* (i.e., belonging to the *understanding*), cannot take place in understanding *alone*, is to affirm, against the Leibnizian rationalist, that a major part of our judgments is synthetic. It may seem surprising that a comparison that takes place *under sensible conditions* should be called *logical*. But considered as to its form, the comparison does indeed belong to logic, just as logic is concerned with the form of a judgment in general, whether it is analytic or synthetic. The adjective 'logical' merely serves to distinguish the comparison of *concepts* from the comparison of *sensible perceptions* ('aesthetic' comparison) as well as from 'transcendental' comparison or reflection, the reflection on the relation of our representations to the sensible or intellectual cognitive faculties. I shall therefore use 'logical comparison' to designate a comparison simply insofar as it has discursive form ('logical' here has the same broad sense as in the 'logical use of the understanding', A67–68/B92–93). By 'merely logical comparison (in the narrow sense)' I shall designate a comparison performed in the understanding alone, and by 'logical comparison (in the broad sense)' a comparison performed in the understanding subject to sensible conditions.

[59] Unlike Kemp Smith, I translate *Widerstreit* by *conflict*, and reserve *opposition* for *Entgegensetzung*. Further explanations will be given in the next chapter.

So far I have argued that to say that concepts are generated as "the form which is required for the power of judgment" is to say that the concepts of comparison corresponding to each form of judgment govern the operations of comparison/reflection/abstraction whereby empirical concepts are generated. In the following chapter, I will elaborate this argument in detail by examining each particular concept of comparison in its relation to the corresponding form of judgment. At this point, however, we encounter a difficulty. In the Amphiboly chapter, Kant leaves the exposition of the correspondence between concepts of comparison and forms of judgment unfinished. He explicitly asserts the correspondence of (1) *identity* and *difference* to *universal* and *particular* judgments; and of (2) *agreement* and *conflict* to *affirmative* and *negative* judgments. But the list ends here, with an abrupt "etc." No further indication is given concerning the two correspondences that would normally follow, those between *inner/outer* and *relation* in judgments, and between *matter/form* and *modality* of judgments.[60]

Reich viewed this unfinished exposition as support for his thesis that comparison of concepts accounts only for quality and quantity of judgments. These first two, he claimed, are forms of concept subordination, and comparison of concepts is sufficient to establish such subordination. It determines whether the *extension* of a concept is included or not included, totally or partially, in the extension of another concept; and that the marks belonging to a concept (its *content* or intension) belong or do not belong to the marks of another concept. Together, these comparisons generate the so-called square of oppositions, the four classically recognized possible combinations of quantity and quality in propositions: universal affirmative, universal negative, particular affirmative, particular negative. But where *relation* is concerned, Reich continues, a judgment is no longer a *comparison*, but a *connection* (*Verknüpfung*) of concepts—a relation of condition to conditioned. No comparison of concepts is sufficient to account for that *Verknüpfung*, which is dependent upon the objective unity of consciousness taking up the subordination of concepts in judgment into its own forms of necessary unity. To be sure, comparison and connection (*Verknüpfung*) cannot be completely separated from one another since the requirement of connection accompanies the act of comparison. Reich none the less deems the two operations to be quite distinct. According to him, comparison is dependent only on the analytic unity of consciousness, while connection is dependent also on the objective unity of apperception.[61]

To be sure, distinctions will have to be made between the various concepts of comparison as to the nature and import of the discursive acts they respectively re-

DISCURSIVE UNDERSTANDING ·

flect. It can also be granted that since *relation* refers to *subordination of conditioned to condition* in judgment and is, as such, the aspect of the discursive form by means of which a judgment may be considered as true or false,[62] the corresponding comparison will be the decisive one. But it is a grave mistake to suppose that some determinations of judgment depend on the comparison of concepts while others do not. First, Kant asserts, not once but repeatedly, that there are as many concepts of comparison as there are logical forms of judgments.[63] Second, if, as Kant tells us, the operation of comparison/reflection/abstraction that aims at the formation of judgments is what actually generates the form of all concepts (universality), then it seems clear that all the forms of judgment, and *above all* those determining the connection of concepts—namely, those defining the relation of an assertion to its condition—must guide comparison, whether the comparison of previously formed concepts or the comparison of representations required to form concepts. The notion that quantity and quality are dependent on *comparison*, on the one hand, while relation and modality are dependent on *connection* but *not* on comparison, on the other hand, would imply that concepts are prior to and independent of their use in judgment, which is quite contrary to Kant's thought.[64] Finally, isolating the forms of *connection* from the *comparisons* whereby concepts are formed, and so viewing those forms as superimposed on the *results* of the comparison rather than as involved in the acts of comparison themselves (i.e., as immanent norms engrained in the very activity of comparison), would, as I shall argue, eliminate one of the principal foundations of Kant's transcendental deduction of the categories.

If this is so, why then did Kant not take the trouble to elaborate fully the correspondence he asserted? Likely he met with some difficulty. The nature and role of the concepts of comparison had to be differentiated when moving from the first two to the last two titles in the table of judgments. Kant made such a differentiation in the Analytic of Principles, when he distinguished between "mathematical" and "dynamical" principles.[65] A corresponding difference should have served for the concepts of comparison as well. I think the reason Kant chose to avoid this difficulty by resorting to a cavalier "etc." is that he dealt only with what he took to be his most pressing task. In the Amphiboly this task was to show that the meaning of the concepts of comparison is not the same when they are used to reflect the comparison of *concepts* and when they are used to reflect the comparison of *objects thought under concepts*. Polemical effect won out over meticulous exposition, with the result that we are left with only a partial elucidation of the concepts of comparison and their role in the formation of judgments. Even the half we are offered is put forth in a summary manner. My aim, therefore, will be

---

[62] Cf. chapter 4, pp. 93–99.

[63] Cf. A262/B318, A279/B335; and *Prol.*, §39, Ak. IV, 326; 68.

[64] Indeed, some of Reich's remarks explicitly indicate that he thinks concepts have priority over judgments. Cf. *Vollständigkeit*, 48: "The material given to us before any judgment is concepts alone [*Das vor allem Urteile gegebene Material sind allein—Begriffe*]."

[65] Cf. A162/B201; A178–79/B221–22; *Prol.* §25, Ak. IV, 307; 50.

to expand on and complete Kant's exposition, first by explicating the correspondence in the case of the first two titles, *quantity* and *quality*, and then, more importantly, by extending it to where it is only hinted at: the correspondence of
inner and *outer* to *relation* in judgment, and the correspondence of *matter* and
form to *modality* of judgment.[66]

[66] Hardly any commentaries on the first *Critique* grant any importance at all to the concepts of reflection. Murray Lewis Miles does relate the concepts of comparison in the Amphiboly chapter to the
operations of comparison/reflection/abstraction described in the *Logic*. He contends that much more
than a mere criticism of the rationalist amphiboly can be derived from the appendix to the Transcendental Analytic. Nevertheless, his elucidation of the concepts of comparison remains little more than
a sketch (see Miles, *Logik*, 126–42). See also Parkinson, "Amphiboly," and Hans Graubner's chapter
on the concept of form in the Amphiboly of Concepts of Reflection (*Form und Wesen*, 243–55). On
the other hand Johannes Heinrichs [*Vernunftkritik*] places such emphasis on the concepts of reflection
in the Amphiboly chapter that, for him, they are the real grounding of the metaphysical deduction of
the categories. Yet he does so in light of an interpretation of reflection as *Selbstspiegelung* of the subject that, on his own avowal, is far more Fichtean than Kantian and which, in my opinion, is quite foreign to the problematic of the *Critique*. Lastly, it should be noted that Hegel accurately characterized
Kant's concepts of reflection as mediators between sensible representations and the concepts of the
understanding: "Kant . . . adds also, as an Appendix to transcendental logic or the doctrine of the understanding, a *treatise* on the *concepts of reflection*—a sphere which is in between *intuition* and the
understanding, or *being* and the *concept*" (*Logik* II, *GW* XII, 19, 49).

· C H A P T E R 6 ·

Concepts of Comparison, Forms of Judgment, Concept Formation

IN THIS CHAPTER I shall argue that close examination of Kant's "concepts of reflection" or "concepts of comparison" helps us understand the role Kant assigns to the logical forms of judgment in guiding the generation of empirical concepts. More precisely, I shall attempt to show that to each form of judgment laid out in Kant's table corresponds a specific aspect of the activity of reflection upon the sensible given, geared toward subsuming particular objects under general concepts. I shall thus endeavor to make explicit, for each concept of comparison, a demonstration that remains largely implicit in Kant's text. Kant's main argument, in the Amphiboly, is that the comparison of *concepts* should be strictly distinguished from the comparison of *objects* thought under these concepts. I want to argue that this distinction has two important consequences that Kant left unstated. Only if these consequences are given proper attention can the full significance of this important chapter be appreciated. The first consequence is that one should distinguish not merely between comparison of concepts and comparison of objects, but also, *among comparisons of concepts themselves*, between what I have earlier called a "merely logical comparison (in the narrow sense)" and a "logical comparison (in the broad sense)."[1]

Most of our judgments are based on the latter kind of logical comparison: they are comparisons of concepts under the condition of the sensible given. This being so, the fallacy ascribed to Leibniz in the Amphiboly chapter is not simply to have confounded intellectual comparison (of concepts) with comparison of things, but also to have viewed the comparison of concepts itself as something that can be— at least in principle if not always in practice—strictly intellectual, free from any dependence on sensible representations. This second aspect of Leibniz's error is not explicitly discussed by Kant, because it is not essential to the argument of the Amphiboly chapter. I shall argue that it nevertheless matters to our understanding of Kant's theory of judgment. A second consequence then follows, which like the first is not explicitly drawn in the Amphiboly. If the comparison of concepts in judgments is guided by concepts of comparison (also called concepts of reflection), then so too is the generation of concepts from the sensible given (by comparison/reflection/abstraction). Hence, the concepts of comparison express the rules for the reflective genesis of all concepts, or—what is the same thing—the rules for the reflective genesis of all combinations of concepts, that is, judgments.

Each concept of comparison will therefore be analyzed in four steps. First, we

---

[1] Cf. chapter 5, p. 127, and note 58.

will consider Kant's characterization of the logical comparison corresponding to each form of judgment. Second, we shall analyze Kant's denunciation of the Leibnizian amphiboly in respect of each concept of comparison. These two steps are still within the bounds of Kant's explicit discussion. We shall move beyond this, to what is only implicit in Kant's argument, by, third, distinguishing between a merely logical comparison in the narrow sense and a logical comparison in the broad sense, namely a comparison of concepts that takes place only *under sensible conditions*. Fourth, the examination of judgment as a comparison of concepts under sensible conditions will enable us to determine how concepts of comparison, and, by their means, forms of judgment, guide the very acts of forming concepts from the sensible given.

"IDENTITY" AND "DIFFERENCE" OF REPRESENTATIONS, "QUANTITY" OF JUDGMENTS

Before any objective judgment we compare the concepts to find in them *identity* [*Einerleiheit*] (of many representations under one concept) with a view to *universal* judgments, *difference* [*Verschiedenheit*] with a view to *particular* judgments. (A262/B317)

1. Consider first logical comparison in its most general sense, where concepts are viewed solely in regard to their form, that is as "universal or reflected representations." In the universal judgment, 'All As are B', the representations thought under A are, without exception, also thought under B. They do not *differ* from one another with respect to B—that is, they are (generically) *identical* with one another insofar as they are all thought under the concept B. This does not mean, of course, that they are identical with one another per se, as singular representations. In the judgment 'All As are B' the identity, with respect to B, of the representations thought under A, is not the numerical identity of these representations. They may also *differ* with respect to other concepts and thus be combined in *particular* judgments, for example: 'Some As are C'. The representations thought under A then *differ* insofar as some, but not all, are also thought under C.

From this, it is clear that identity and difference guide the comparison of concepts considered in their *extension*. Kant's formulations make this point quite plain. Rather than the *content* of concepts, it is the "representations (thought) *under* a concept" that are *identical* or *different* (with respect to another concept) and are thereby reflected under concepts in a *universal* or a *particular* judgment. We saw in chapter 4 that the standpoint of *extension*—that is, the consideration of concepts inasmuch as objects are contained *under* them—governs the definition of judgment as concept subordination. The same standpoint is manifest here, in the act of comparison. By contrast, the point of view of *content*, or comprehension, predominates in Kant's account of comparison according to *agreement* or *conflict* (see discussion below).

2. The description of the act of comparison in its most general sense helps clarify the nature of Leibniz's amphiboly. If things were known to us by pure concepts, then all things x, y, and z, thought under a concept A and identical with respect to every other concept (B, C, D, etc.), would ipso facto be *numerically* identical (identity of indiscernibles): "Certainly, if I cognize a drop of water in all its inner determinations as a thing in itself, then I cannot hold any drop to be distinct from any other if the complete concept of the latter is identical with the former" (A272/B328, my translation). By contrast, if things are given to us in a sensible intuition that is irreducible to concepts of the understanding, then things that are identical with respect to every *concept* may still differ as sensible individuals, by virtue of their mere location in space. Thus, for Kant, the complete identity of things with respect to concepts does not entail their numerical identity.

3. As suggested previously, Kant's argument can be taken beyond the characterization of logical comparison (in general) and the denunciation of the Leibnizian amphiboly. If it is true that objects are given only as appearances, and that concepts have no other cognitive use than with respect to these appearances, then we should not rest content with merely distinguishing the comparison of concepts (according to the qualitative identity and difference of what is thought under them) from the comparison of things (according to their numerical identity and difference). We should also acknowledge that the comparison of concepts itself is quite different from what Leibniz supposed—logical comparison in the narrow sense. The latter comparison, if it could be performed systematically and exhaustively, would yield Leibniz's *calculus ratiocinator*. For this presupposes completely analyzed concepts, whose possible combinations one might then rigorously determine according to the possible combinations of their marks. But for Kant, such a logical comparison in the narrow sense makes up only a small part of the comparisons of concepts constituting our judgments, and it is utterly illusory to believe that our knowledge could, even ideally, take on the form of an exhaustive combinatoric of completely analyzed concepts. Comparison of objective concepts occurs always under sensible conditions. Comparing concepts does not mean combining marks and comparing them according to the identities and differences of these combinations, but rather comparing schemata, rules for the synthesis of the sensible given. Comparisons of concepts take place under the condition of the sensible syntheses whose rules they reflect. In other words, the irreducibility of comparisons of *appearances* to comparisons of *concepts* also means the irreducibility of most comparisons of concepts to merely logical comparisons in the narrow sense.

4. Acknowledging the *sensible condition* of comparisons of concepts helps one to understand how concepts of comparison are at work not only in the comparison of concepts already explicitly formed and reflected, but also in the very genesis of concepts. In the previous chapter, we saw that the emergence of concepts, or rather the emergence of their schemata, was regulated by the search for identities

and differences that makes it possible to generate "rules of our apprehension" of the sensible.[2] In section 6 of the *Logic*, Kant assigns to the acts of *comparison* and *reflection* the tasks of showing, for the first, what is *different* in the objects (for instance, "a spruce, a willow, and a linden") and for the second, what is *common* to them, in order to form a common concept (for instance, the concept 'tree').[3] Similarly, in *Reflexion* 2878, he asks: "Could we, from an intuition alone, without comparison, abstract something in order to subordinate other things to it, if they presented themselves?"[4] These two operations of comparison and reflection, being the search for what is *different* and *common* (= *qualitatively identical*), exhibit the first aspect of the "silent judgments" presiding over the genesis of empirical concepts. If, in Kant's own words, "Before any objective judgment we compare the concepts . . . ," we may say also that, *in order* to form concepts, we sift through our sensible representations by means of our concepts of comparison, which thus guide the formation of concepts for judgments. Recognition of the (generic) *identity* of the "rules of our apprehension" in different representations yields a universal judgment. Recognition of the *difference* of the "rules of our apprehension" in various representations yields particular judgments (some As are C, some As are not C).

After (1) the logical comparison of concepts in judgment, and (2) the Leibnizian amphiboly with respect to this comparison, we saw that (3) Kant's denunciation of the amphiboly can be taken a step further by distinguishing between merely logical comparison in the narrow sense and logical comparison under sensible conditions. We then saw that (4) the concepts of comparison 'identity' and 'difference' (*Einerleiheit, Verschiedenheit*) also guide the comparison of representations, which generates concepts from the sensible given. I shall presently argue that the same can be shown concerning the two concepts of comparison guiding the formation of judgment as to its *quality*—that is, the concepts of the *agreement* and *conflict* of concepts (corresponding respectively to affirmative and negative judgments).

Before proceeding, however, I want to make two remarks concerning Kant's reading of Leibniz. The first concerns logical comparison in the narrow sense, to which Kant accuses Leibniz of reducing all judgment, the second Kant's reconstruction of Leibnizian metaphysics from the four pairs of concepts of comparison.

Leibniz would certainly have conceded that many of our comparisons of concepts are possible only in *empirical* judgments, irreducible to logical comparison in the narrow sense. For comparison of concepts in the intellect alone is possible

---

[2] Cf. chapter 5, p. 116.

[3] "To make concepts out of representations one must thus be able *to compare, to reflect*, and *to abstract*, for these three logical operations of the understanding are the essential and universal conditions for generation of every concept whatsoever. I see, e.g., a spruce, a willow, and a linden. By first comparing these objects with one another I note that they are different from one another [*daß sie voneinander verschieden sind*—note that the first pair of concepts of comparison is *Einerleiheit/Verschiedenheit*] in regard to the trunk, the branches, the leaves, etc.: but next I reflect on what they have in common among themselves, trunk, branches, and leaves themselves, and I abstract from the quantity, the figure, etc., of these; thus I acquire a concept of a tree" (§6, n.1, Ak. IX, 94–95; 592).

[4] Ak. XVI, 556–57. Cf. chapter 5, note 30.

only if concepts are completely analyzed (the presupposition of the *calculus ratiocinator*). Thus one might object that Kant failed to take account of the role Leibniz grants to experience.[5] The response to this objection is that the real difference between Kant's and Leibniz's position concerns not the empirical genesis of our cognitions, but their transcendental ground (i.e., their origin in a priori capacities of representation). For Leibniz, even though we in fact depend on experience for many of our cognitions, for an infinite understanding these very same cognitions would be analyzable into combinations amenable to purely logical comparison (logical comparison in the narrow sense). For Kant, on the contrary, comparisons of concepts occurring under sensible conditions cannot possibly occur otherwise. Given the nature of space and time as a priori forms of sensible intuition, no exhaustive analysis could bring comparisons under sensible conditions to purely intellectual comparisons. Of course, it is possible to relate the logical forms of judgment to the four pairs of concepts of comparison without specifying whether the comparison takes place in the understanding alone or under sensible conditions. And there are indeed cases where comparison does occur in the intellect alone, and the comparisons are logical in the narrow sense. But such comparisons are, *and can be*, only a very small portion of our judgments.[6] For Leibniz, by contrast, all combinations which (for us) are dependent on experience are no more than obscure and confused representations of combinations that for an infinite intellect would be purely intellectual. Every logical comparison in the broad sense is a confused representation of a logical comparison in the narrow sense, which, for an infinite intellect, represents things as noumena, objects of pure thought. Kant is therefore justified in saying that, for Leibniz, *comparisons of concepts* and *comparisons of things* ultimately resolve into one and the same kind of comparison.

My second remark is that Kant's use of the list of concepts of comparison as a guideline for his reading of Leibniz is quite idiosyncratic. He derives the four pairs of concepts of comparison from his own theory of judgment, and then forces Leibnizian rationalism into the mold so provided. It is not my purpose to assess the relevance of this Kantian reconstruction of Leibnizianism. My concern in the present chapter is simply to convince the reader that to understand Kant's own conception of discursive thought, one must recognize the importance of the concepts of comparison and the role he assigns to them in the formation of all our judgments.[7]

---

[5] See for example Leibniz, *New Essays*, bk. I, chap. 1, §§1, 5.

[6] In fact, for Kant only some practical judgments could depend on the intellect alone (in this case, practical reason), and, as I pointed out earlier, even practical judgments call for a sensible analogue for us to be able to make sense of them and of their object. Cf. chapter 4, note 61. As for analytic judgments formed from empirical concepts, although the comparison of concepts in them does not rely on further appeal to experience, nevertheless the concepts themselves have been formed by comparison/reflection/abstraction from a sensible given which no amount of analysis could reduce to a combination of purely intellectual representations.

[7] Schulthess calls attention to a source that may have influenced Kant's conception of the activity of judgment as an activity of comparison and reflection, as well as his exposition of concepts of comparison. This source is Reimarus's *Vernunftlehre* cf. for example its first paragraph: "Hence a *power*

"AGREEMENT" AND "CONFLICT" OF CONCEPTS,
"QUALITY" OF JUDGMENTS

> We compare the concepts to find in them . . . agreement [*Einstimmung*] with a view
> to affirmative judgments, [and] conflict [*Widerstreit*] with a view to negative judg-
> ments.[8]

1. Consider once again logical comparison in its most general sense, in relation
to the logical form of judgment. If two concepts are in a relation of logical *conflict* (*Widerstreit*)—if they cannot both be attributed to the same subject—then the
judgment that combines them is negative. If the attribution of one does not logically exclude the attribution of the other, then they are in *agreement* (*Einstimmung*), and the judgment is affirmative. Note that combining the comparisons according to *Einstimmung* and *Widerstreit* with those according to *Einerleiheit* and
Verschiedenheit is combining "affirmative" and "negative" with "universal" and
"particular" judgments, thus producing the classic square of oppositions, A-E-I-O
(universal affirmative, universal negative, particular affirmative, particular
negative).

2. Here what is compared is the *content* of concepts: the marks "contained in",
not the objects "thought under" concepts. The amphiboly Kant denounces is then
the following. If one views the *content* of concepts, that is, the *marks* of which

---

of reflecting [*eine Kraft zu reflectieren*] is nothing other than a faculty and activity of the human understanding, through which it can discern, by comparing the things represented, if and how they are
identical [*einerlei*], contradict each other [*sich widersprechen*] or not." Or again, §15: "Thus the faculty of reflecting on things represented according to the rules of agreement and contradiction [*nach
den Regeln der Einstimmung und des Widerspruchs*] is what we call *reason*" (quoted by Schulthess,
Relation, 39). But of course no one prior to Kant had thought of proposing a systematic list of concepts of comparison correlated to the forms of judgment, and still less the idea of a "Copernican reversal" which makes the acts of comparison the source of the "universalization" of sensible representations, that is, the source of "rules of our apprehension" and their reflection under concepts.

[8] I translate *Widerstreit* by *conflict* and *Entgegensetzung* by *opposition*. In the titles of the Amphiboly, on the second pair of concepts of comparison (A262/B318, A264/B320), Kemp Smith gives *opposition* for *Widerstreit*. In most other places he translates *Widerstreit* and *widerstreiten* by *conflict*
(substantive and verb) (A273/B329, A274/B329, A282/B338). This is certainly preferable. In the Amphiboly Kant uses the adjective *entgegengesetzt, opposed*, when he speaks of the spatial *directions* of
forces. The forces themselves are then in *conflict, Widerstreit. Entgegensetzung* thus applies to the
mathematical magnitudes constructed in intuition (vectors in space), *Widerstreit* to the dynamical
magnitudes (forces). It is important to respect Kant's terminology to preserve the coherence of his
argument, whose general line is as follows. Between determinations of things there are two sorts of
opposition (Entgegensetzung) or *conflict (Widerstreit)*: *logical conflict* (or *opposition*), that is, contradiction, and *real conflict* (*realer Widerstreit*), which depends on *real opposition* (*reale Entgegensetzung*). That there is no logical conflict between two determinations (no contradiction between
their concepts) does not mean that there is also no real conflict between them. This is because their
representations in spatial intuition may still have directions *opposed* (*entgegengesetzt*) to each other
and may thus partly or completely cancel each other. Note, though, that in the 1763 essay on negative
magnitudes, Kant mainly used the term *reale Entgegensetzung* instead of the *Critique's realer Widerstreit*. See note 9.

they are composed, as *realities* which are objects of the intellect alone, independently of any sensible condition, then, like Leibniz, one will conclude that the logical comparison of concepts is in principle sufficient for discovering the relations of agreement or conflict between determinations of things thought under the concepts. This means, first, that if two concepts are not in (logical) conflict with one another, then one may legitimately infer that the determinations of things thought under these concepts also do not conflict (i.e., no determination of the one in any way negates a determination of the other). But according to Kant, just as things identical with respect to all concepts can still be numerically different, so too things whose concepts are not logically contradictory may still be in *conflict* (*Widerstreit*) in respect of their sensible determinations. Moreover, although two concepts whose marks are positive determinations cannot conflict (*widerstreiten*), that is, contradict one another (*einander widersprechen*)—a concept A is in contradiction only with its negation, non-A—two *sensible* realities, each of which are positively defined, may still come into conflict (*Widerstreit*), that is, they can stand, as spatial determinations, in a relation of *real opposition* (*reale Entgegensetzung*), thus cancelling each other out. Conversely, although two *logically opposed* determinations cannot coexist in the same logical subject (by virtue of the principle of contradiction), two *really opposed* determinations may nevertheless coexist in the same real subject and mutually cancel out each other's effects.[9]

3. Once again, Kant's criticism of the Leibnizian amphiboly requires that we not only distinguish the comparison of *concepts* from the comparison of *appearances*, but also rethink the comparison of concepts itself. In particular, just as the distinction between difference *with respect to concept* and *numerical* difference drew our attention to the irreducibility of the object, as sensible object, to the concepts through which it is thought, here the distinction between *logical opposition or conflict* and *real opposition or conflict* draws our attention to the irreducibility of the sensible given to concepts. In consequence, the comparison of concepts itself must also be rethought in relation to its sensible conditioning. Agreement of concepts is neither their analytic identity (the one being analytically contained in the other) nor their mere noncontradiction (no mark of the one being the logical negation of a mark of the other). It may also be—in most cases it is—the agreement of one concept with another *under sensible conditions*, or, in other words, the agreement of the *schemata* corresponding to the concepts. This is the case for instance in the judgments 'All bodies are heavy' or 'In every triangle the sum of the angles is equal to two right angles'. In the first example, the concept 'body' is compared to that of 'weight' under the condition of empirical associations of

[9] Kant first invoked the irreducibility of real oppositions (illustrated by the oppositions of force in nature, and also by the opposition of good and bad in moral motivations of the will) to merely logical contradictions, and asserted the positive reality of suffering and moral evil (as against their interpretation, in Leibnizian rationalism, in terms of mere limitation or privation), in his 1763 essay, *Attempt to Introduce the Concept of Negative Magnitudes into Philosophy*. See *Neg. Gr.*, third sec., Ak. II, 189–97; 227–35. On the confrontation between Kant and Leibniz concerning the opposition of forces and its metaphysical implications, see Gueroult's remarkable analyses (*Leibniz*, 168–71, esp. 169, n. 4).

sensible impressions, themselves embedded in spatiotemporal synthesis. In the second example, the concept 'sum of the angles of a triangle' and that of 'two right angles', are *constructed*—that is, exhibited a priori in sensible intuition. Only under the condition of such constructions can these concepts be compared and acknowledged to be in *agreement* with one another. In both examples, agreement signifies neither analytic identity (too strong) nor noncontradiction (too weak), but rather that two concepts jointly belong to one and the same sensible subject = x. That this is so can be ascertained only by reflection on the sensible synthesis of the object represented by the term x in the logical form of judgment. Similarly, *conflict* is not just *logical contradiction*—'no body is nonextended'— but also the conflict of concepts under sensible conditions—'5 · 3 is not 14',[10] or 'Lead does not float on water'. In other words, just as we saw that most of our comparisons of concepts according to identity and difference can occur only under sensible conditions, not only in fact (de facto), but also by right (de jure) or in virtue of their origin in our representational capacities, so too comparison according to agreement and conflict can be performed, by right no less than in fact, only under sensible conditions (not because of the contingent circumstances under which we have acquired them, but because of the very nature of discursive thinking, which in all cognition is ineluctably paired with sensible synthesis).

Perhaps here I should warn against a possible misunderstanding. I am *not* suggesting that the agreement or conflict of concepts "under sensible conditions" (i.e., in a comparison that does not take place in understanding alone) are *real* agreements or conflicts such as are the agreement or conflict *of appearances*. On the contrary, agreement and conflict *of concepts*, albeit *under sensible conditions*, are still *logical*, *discursive* relations, relations between *concepts*, not between (*realities represented in) intuitions*. They are comparisons between universal representations in judgments, concept subordinations. As *logical* comparisons, they belong to the same general kind as merely logical comparisons in the narrow sense. But they differ from them in that they take place only under sensible conditions. No amount of analysis of the concepts compared could make of these logical comparisons in the broad sense logical comparisons in the narrow sense (yielding a Leibnizian-type *calculus ratiocinator*).

4. The preceding should make clear how comparison according to 'agreement' and 'conflict' can guide the genesis of empirical concepts. For these two concepts of comparison, and the acts of comparison they guide and reflect, are clearly inseparable from identity and difference. Earlier, we saw how judgments such as 'All As are B' presuppose acts of comparison with respect to *identity* (the x's thought under A are *identical* with respect to the concept B). But comparison with respect to *agreement* is clearly involved as well: as to its *content*, B is in agreement with A. Similarly, comparison as to *difference*, which guides particular judgments, involves comparison with respect to the *conflicts* between concepts, or the conflicts between some of their marks. If 'Some As are B', it may also be

---

[10] Why and in what sense there is a 'sensible condition' in this case will be examined in chapter 9.

the case that 'Some As are not B', or that some of the *x*'s thought under concept A may also be thought under marks in conflict with those of concept B (marks that cannot be in the same subject at the same time). Thus, all of these comparisons (according to identity and difference, and according to agreement and conflict) are implicit in the logical description of the operations of comparison/reflection/abstraction.

The astute reader will have noted that although Kant lists concepts of comparison corresponding to *universal* and *particular*, *affirmative* and *negative* forms of judgment, he offers none for the *singular* judgment (even though he lists this form as the third according to quantity) or for the *infinite* judgment (the third form according to quality). This is an interesting omission. I suggest it confirms the relation between logical forms of judgment and concepts of comparison. There is a correlation between the fact that specific acts of comparison do not correspond to *singular* and *infinite* judgments, and the fact that, in Kant's view, these are not properly speaking distinct logical forms. For from a strictly logical standpoint, the singular is not distinguished from the universal judgment because in both alike the predicate is attributed to the totality of what is thought under the subject.[11] Similarly, the infinite judgment is not distinguished from the affirmative because the copula is in both cases affirmative, and logic is not concerned with the content of the concepts combined in judgment but only with the form of the combination itself.[12] We shall see that distinguishing *singular* from *universal* judgments will be of the utmost importance for deriving the categories of quantity (*unity, totality*), and distinguishing *affirmative* from *infinite* judgments will be likewise for deriving the categories of quality (*reality, limitation*). This stems from the fact that, according to Kant, both singular and infinite judgments, considered in their relation to sensibility (in which capacity alone are they the sources of the categories) refer concepts to what is beyond discursive capacity: the singular intuition in the first case, the whole of experience in the second. That no specific concept of comparison—that is, no specific form of *discursive* comparison or comparison *of concepts*—corresponds to them thus seems to me to be an additional manifestation of the peculiar role of these two "forms" of judgment: they outline, at the extremes of discursive thought—the singular intuition, the whole of experience—the limits of discursive thought.

[11] Cf. A71/B96: "Logicians are justified in saying that, in the employment of judgments in syllogisms, singular judgments can be treated like those that are universal. For, since they have no extension at all, the predicate cannot relate to part only of that which is contained under the concept of the subject, and be excluded from the rest. The predicate is valid of that concept without any exception, just as if it were a general concept and had an extension to the whole of which the predicate applied." When he writes that singular judgments "have no extension," Kant probably means that their *subject* "has no extension." Cf. *Logic*, §21: the subject of the singular judgment is "a concept that has no sphere at all" (Ak. IX, 102; 598). I shall say more on this in chapter 9.

[12] Cf. A72/B97: "In like manner, *infinite judgments* must, in transcendental logic, be distinguished from those that are *affirmative*, although in general logic they are rightly classed with them and do not constitute a separate member of the division. General logic abstracts from all content of the predicate (even though it may be negative); it enquires only whether the predicate is ascribed to the subject or opposed to it [*ob dasselbe dem Subjekt beigelegt oder ihm entegegensetzt werde*]."

"Inner" and "Outer," and "Relation" in Judgment

Judgments considered in their *quantity* and *quality*—comparisons of concepts according to *identity/difference* and *agreement/conflict*—are based on the consideration of concepts with respect to their *extension* (representations *thought under* the concepts are identical or different with respect to these concepts) and with respect to their *content* (marks *contained in* the concepts are in agreement or conflict with each other). Both these standpoints, extension and content of concepts, are involved in forming judgments, as concepts-subordinations. Now, when considering Kant's logical definitions of judgment, we saw that concept subordinations are *judgments* properly so called (combinations of representations with a claim to truth) only insofar as they express the relation of a predication to its *condition*. This last characterization allowed us to make sense of the forms of *relation* in judgment according to Kant. With it, the *comparison* (*Vergleichung*) of concepts becomes their *connection* (*Verknüpfung*).[13] Yet, when we reach this third title in the Amphiboly of Concepts of Reflection, Kant's explanation of the correspondence between concepts of comparison and forms of judgment seems to come to a halt: "Before constructing any objective judgment we compare the concepts to find in them *identity* (of many representations under one concept) with a view to *universal* judgments, *difference* with a view to *particular* judgments, *agreement* with a view to affirmative judgments, *conflict* with a view to *negative* judgments, etc." (A262/B317–18).

However, immediately prior to this passage, Kant had included in his list of "relations in which concepts can stand to one another in a state of mind" the concepts of "inner" and "outer" as the third pair of concepts of comparison, corresponding to the third title in his table of logical forms: "Now the relations in which concepts can stand to one another in a state of mind are those of *identity* and *difference*, of *agreement* and *conflict*, of *inner* and *outer*" (A261/B317). Similarly, just before concluding his examination of the Leibnizian amphiboly, Kant writes:

> If we reflect in a merely logical fashion, we are only comparing our concepts with each other in the understanding, to find whether both have the same content, whether they are contradictory or not, *whether something is contained within the concept or is an addition from outside*, which of the two is given and which should serve only as a mode of thinking what is given. (A279/B335, my emphasis)

There is thus no doubt that according to him, comparison of concepts takes place according to the concepts of comparison "inner" and "outer," and that these concepts correspond to the forms of relation in a judgment. However, the precise meaning he gives to this correspondence remains unclear.

Here our elucidation of logical forms in chapter 4 should prove helpful. We saw there that a *categorical* judgment expresses the subordination of a predica-

---

[13] On judgment as the *relation of an assertion to its condition*, cf. chapter 4, pp. 93–99.

tion to a condition *internal* to the subject of predication, whereas a *hypothetical* judgment expresses the subordination of a predication to an *external* condition— a condition *added to* the subject of predication. In my view, this relation of predication to a condition that is either inner or outer (added) with respect to the subject of predication furnishes the key to the correspondence between the forms of *relation* in judgment and the concepts of comparison "inner" and "outer."

It might be suggested that there is a more natural interpretation than mine of Kant's statement that "if we reflect in a merely logical fashion, we are only comparing our concepts with each other in the understanding, to find . . . whether something *is contained within* the concept *or is an addition from outside* [my emphasis]." For might this not simply be an allusion to the difference between *analytic* and *synthetic* judgments? Introducing the notion of *relation* to understand the concepts of comparison "inner" and "outer" would then be quite superfluous. "Something contained within the concept" could be understood simply as what is attributed to it in an analytic judgment, while "an addition from outside" would be what is attributed to it in a synthetic judgment.[14] Yet, accepting such a reading would amount to charging Kant with a very serious inconsistency: it would mean that halfway through his exposition he abandons the correspondence between concepts of comparison and forms of judgment initially announced. But nothing compels us to brand Kant with such inconsistency if we recall that the distinction between categorical and hypothetical judgments *as to their form* is a distinction between predication "without any added condition" and predication "under an added condition," and if we interpret the concepts of comparison "inner" and "outer" accordingly.

Keeping this point in mind, I shall once again propose a four-step analysis of Kant's concepts of comparison: (1) the meaning of logical comparison according to *inner* and *outer*; (2) Kant's criticism of the rationalist amphiboly. These first two steps are explicit in the Amphiboly chapter. I shall argue that they entail two further steps, in which one should consider: (3) the distinction between logical comparison in the narrow sense and logical comparison in the broad sense; and (4) how logical comparison in the broad sense governs the generation of concepts from the sensible given.

Logical Comparison According to "Inner" and "Outer"

To compare concepts in terms of "inner" and "outer" is to attend to the character of the *discursive condition* (the condition expressed in a concept or combination of concepts) under which a predicate can be attributed to a subject. In other words, it is to consider whether a predicate can be attributed *nulla adjecta conditione* (no

---

[14] This is how Reich interprets the distinction. This interpretation is made all the more compelling for him by his conviction that *relation* and *modality* of judgments, contrary to *quantity* and *quality*, cannot possibly have anything to do with comparison of concepts (cf. Reich, *Vollständigkeit*, 83–84; 94–95; and my discussion of his position in chapter 5, pp. 128–29). He therefore has no reason to inquire into a possible meaning for the correspondence between "inner/outer" and "relation" in judgment.

condition being added) or only *sub adjecta conditione* (under an added condition). Examples of the first case include: "All bodies are divisible" (analytic judgment) or "All bodies are heavy" (synthetic judgment). Examples of the second are: "If there is perfect justice, the wicked are punished" (analytic judgment) or "If the sun shines on the stone, it becomes warm" (synthetic judgment). In the first sort of case, the condition for attributing a concept B, as a predicate, to another concept A, as a subject, is expressed by the subject A of the judgment itself ("inner condition" of predication); the judgment is then categorical (As are B). In the second sort of case, a predicate B can be attributed to the subject A only if another concept C is predicated of A, or even perhaps only if a state of affairs quite independent of A obtains, expressed by the attribution of a predicate to another subject. This added condition, or "outer condition" of predication, is expressed in the antecedent of a hypothetical judgment (if As are C, then they are B; or, If Fs are G, then As are B).[15]

Criticism of the Rationalist Amphiboly

If the preceding is the correct way of fleshing out Kant's third set of concepts of comparison, then Kant's denunciation of the rationalist amphiboly can be understood as follows. Because Leibniz held that things could be known by intellect alone—that is, be completely determined (individuated) by concepts—he also believed that the comparison of things could in principle be reduced to the comparison of their concepts. This means that, from the standpoint of an infinite intellect, every judgment attributing to a thing any of its properties or states is a categorical judgment, in which the subject (the complete concept of the individual thing) contains all the conditions for asserting of it any of its predicates. Every determination is thus an *inner* determination, or determination *under internal conditions.* Hypothetical judgments, or predications under *external* or *added* conditions ("If G is F, then A is B"; or "if A is C, then A is B"; and so on) are all reducible in principle to categorical predications, whose conditions are internal to the completely determined concept of the individual thing. Leibniz's metaphysical system of monadology, a system in which all determinations are internal and there are no external relations between substances, is the natural consequence of such a view:

> According to mere concepts the inner is the substratum of all relational or outer determinations. . . . From this it seems to follow that in whatever is a thing (substance) there is something which is absolutely inward and precedes all outer determinations, inasmuch as it is what first makes them possible; and consequently, that this substra-

---

[15] I say '*expressed by* the subject' and not '*contained in* the subject', in order to indicate that the judgment could be synthetic as well as analytic. As we saw in chapter 4, the "inner" or "outer" character of the condition depends on the *mere form* of judgment, irrespective of the synthetic or analytic character of the judgment. In the text cited earlier (A279/B235), Kant describes the "inner" condition as "contained in" the subject because he is there concerned with logical comparison in the narrow sense, namely a comparison of concepts in the intellect alone, as Leibniz conceived it. On the forms of categorical and hypothetical judgment as forms of the relation between a predication and its condition, cf. chapter 4, pp. 99–104.

tum . . . no longer contains in itself any outer relations. . . . And since we are acquainted with no determinations which are absolutely inner except those given through our inner sense, this substratum is not only supposed to be simple, but also to be (in analogy with our inner sense) determined through *representations*; in other words, all things are supposed to be really *monads*, or simple beings endowed with representations. (A283/B339–40)

In this passage, the two steps of the intellectualist amphiboly are clearly laid out. First, if things are in principle completely knowable through concepts alone, every outer condition of predication can be reduced to an inner condition, to a condition contained in the subject of predication. Second, as the relations of substances are reducible to relations between concepts, they are properly thought according to the model of predication under an inner condition, with the consequence that all outer relations can be reduced to strictly inner determinations. *Interiority* here is thus interiority in a logical sense: the interiority of the *condition* of the attribution of any predicate to the subject of the judgment.[16]

For Kant, by contrast, things are individuated not by their completely determined concept in the understanding, but by their situation in space and time as forms of sensible intuition. To Leibniz's *substantia noumenon*, he opposes the *substantia phaenomenon* expounded in his System of Principles. Thus whereas, for Leibniz, inner determinations are the foundation of all seemingly outer determinations, and *outer* determinations are merely the confused appearance of what is always ultimately a system of *inner* determinations, for Kant the "inner determinations" of a thing in appearances *are themselves nothing but (outer) relations*:

[The] inner determinations [of a *substantia phaenomenon* in space] are nothing but relations, and it is itself made up of mere relations. We are acquainted with substance in space only through forces which are active in this or that space, either drawing other objects to it (attraction), or preventing them from penetrating into it (repulsion and impenetrability). (A265/B321)

---

[16] The amphiboly is not always as clearly formulated as it is in the passage just quoted. In other passages, Kant's explanation of Leibniz's use of the concepts 'inner' and 'outer' often occasions shifts in meaning that can be difficult to sort out. Parkinson ("Amphiboly," 311–13) detects two main shifts: from the *interiority* of determinations to the *simplicity* of substance, and from the *interiority* of determinations to the interiority of *inner sense*. Yet, Parkinson seems not to have noticed that the basic thrust of Kant's argument is logical, bearing on the interiority or exteriority of the *condition* or *ground* of predication. Once this is acknowledged, Kant's argument can be granted more coherence than Parkinson was able to recognize in it. As for Kant's knowledge of Leibniz, it should be noted that, apart from the *Discourse on Metaphysics* and the *Correspondence with Arnauld* (which remained unpublished until the nineteenth century and are exceptionally rich sources for Leibniz's views on the problems here discussed), Kant had available to him virtually all of Leibniz's major philosophical writings. He knew the *New Essays* through the 1765 Raspe edition of Leibniz's works, while the Dutens edition (1768) contained in its second volume much important logical and metaphysical works, such as *Meditations on Cognition, Truth and Ideas*; *Of the Improvement of First Philosophy and of the Notion of Substance*; *Principles of Nature and of Grace*; *A New System of the Nature and Communication of Substances*; *Leibniz-Clarke Correspondence*; and *De Arte Combinatoria*. We may therefore assume that it is quite deliberately and in full cognizance of Leibniz's views that Kant, in the Amphiboly, takes on Leibniz himself rather than Wolff's version of Leibnizian rationalism.

Matter is *substantia phaenomenon.* That which inwardly belongs to it I seek in all parts of the space which it occupies, and in all effects which it exercises, though admittedly these can be only appearances of outer sense. I have therefore nothing that is absolutely, but only what is comparatively inward and is itself again composed of outer relations. (A277/B333)

Thus, far from substance being thought as that which has within itself (within its complete concept), independently of any outer condition, the complete set of conditions for asserting of it any of its determinations, we find, on the contrary, that

an abiding appearance in space (impenetrable extension) can contain only relations and nothing at all that is absolutely inward. (A284/B340)

All that we cognize in matter is merely relations (what we call the inner determinations of it are inward only in a comparative sense), but among these relations some are self-subsistent and permanent, and through these we are given a determinate object. (A285/B341)[17]

Two Kinds of Logical Comparison:
Kant's Argument Continued

I want to argue that Kant's denunciation of the Leibnizian confusion between comparison of *concepts* and comparison of *things* calls for another distinction, within logical comparison itself: that between inner/outer as concepts of logical comparison in the narrow sense (concerned with concepts alone) and in the broad sense (under sensible conditions). Thus an *inner* condition of predication, properly formulated in a *categorical* judgment, is by no means necessarily a condition *analytically contained* in the subject-concept. On the contrary, a concept is normally an *inner* condition for the attribution of a predicate only insofar as it is itself related to the object represented by the term '*x*' in the developed form of cat-

---

[17] A typical example of an external or merely relational determination is the property of *impenetrability* under which we recognize objects as falling under the concept 'body'. Although *impenetrability* functions as an inner determination in the judgment 'all matter is impenetrable', it is nevertheless a property we can identify as a property pertaining to all matter only as an *external* determination, a determination recognized under external (added) conditions, and expressed in a hypothetical judgment, such as 'If a body moves into a space filled by matter, matter resists penetration' (cf. *Anfangsgründe*, chap. II def. 1, anm., Ak. IV, 496; 40). The same could be said of the property expressed by the predicate 'heaviness'. It is an *inner* determination in the (synthetic) judgment 'all bodies are heavy'. But this 'inner' determination is identified by means of determinations that are themselves assertable only 'under added conditions': 'If a body is let loose on an inclined plane, it rolls toward the lower part of the plane', 'If I carry a body, I feel an impression of weight', and so on. These points shall be considered again when we discuss judgments of perception and judgments of experience (in chapter 7) and Kant's account of the categories of substance and causality (in chapter 11). It is in many respects premature to try to elucidate the Amphiboly chapter, which is a mere appendix to the Transcendental Analytic, without having first examined Kant's System of Principles. My reason for considering it at this point is that, even if its main argument is bound to remain imperfectly elucidated, it seems to me indispensable to understanding logical comparison in its relation to logical forms of judgment.

egorical judgment: "*x*, which I know under concept A, I also think under concept B."[18] Similarly, it may be the case that a concept or combination of concepts is an *outer* condition for a given predication only if one takes into consideration the sensible given thought under them. In other words, the logical form of judgment may characterize either a synthetic judgment (where the condition, be it inner or outer, is such only under some sensible condition) or an analytic judgment (where the condition, whether inner or outer, is contained in the concepts combined in the judgment). In most cases the comparison of concepts is performed by an understanding whose function is to "represent in a universal manner" the rules for our sensible apprehension. Such an understanding compares its concepts according to the concepts "inner" and "outer" *only in relation to a sensible manifold*, whether this sensible manifold is itself empirical (synthetic a posteriori judgments) or a priori (synthetic a priori judgments).

"Inner" and "Outer", and the Generation of Concepts from the Sensible Given

We have already seen how Kant's example of the generation of the concept 'tree' amounts to a 'silent judgment' according to the concepts of comparison *identity* and *diversity*, *agreement* and *conflict* (the first two pairs of concepts of comparison). The same is true with respect to the concepts "inner" and "outer." For we generate the concept 'tree' by comparison/reflection/abstraction insofar as we learn to attribute to every object thought under the concept 'tree', without any added condition, the predicates 'having a trunk', 'having branches', and so on. But we also recognize an object under the concept 'tree' by learning to attribute to it various characters dependent on *added* conditions: "If the weather gets cold, trees lose their leaves," "If a tree gets no water, it perishes," etc. Generation of concepts by comparison/reflection/abstraction thus includes the discovery of *conditions for rules*. Recall Kant's formula at the end of Deduction A: the understanding is busy "scrutinizing appearances in search for rules."[19] Searching for rules and searching for concepts as conditions for rules (either conditions "internal" to the concept under which an object is recognized, or conditions "added" to it) are one and the same endeavor.

Consider another example. The concept 'freezing' can be formed as a "general and reflected representation" of the state of water under the "external" condition of the surrounding temperature. I am borrowing this example from section 26 of the Transcendental Deduction, where Kant uses it for a different purpose. He argues that the category of causality is necessary if we are to perceive the succession of states of the water we call its 'freezing'. In the third part of this book, I shall consider the conception of the schematism of imagination presupposed in Kant's statement. Here I suggest that according to Kant's conception of the operations of comparison/reflection/abstraction, the concept of comparison "outer"

[18] Cf. chapter 5, note 2.
[19] A126.

guides the formation of the concept 'freezing', in the context of a judgment such as 'if the temperature is very cold, water freezes'. I do not consider here (as Kant does in section 26) the *synthesis* that produces the schema of succession, but the *analysis* that allows the understanding to reflect under the concept 'freezing' the objective succession of states of the water (fluidity, hardness) synthesized by imagination. My claim is that the sensible synthesis described by Kant in section 26 is supplemented by an *analysis* (the operations of comparison/reflection/abstraction) which results, under the guidance of the concept of comparison "outer," in forming the concept 'freezing' together with a silent judgment such as 'if the temperature is very low, water freezes'. This is an example of the two syntheses (sensible synthesis, discursive synthesis) that the metaphysical deduction brought back to "the same function" (B105). The same function, whose act of synthesis produces the sensible schema of objective succession (of the states of water) also produces the discursive form of judgment "by means of analytic unity." This "analytic unity" results in the formation of the concept 'freezing'.

Contrary to Reich's view,[20] not only do the concepts *inner* and *outer* govern the comparison of concepts in judgments, they also play an indispensable role in the original formation of concepts from the sensible given. Reich was correct, however, to the extent that the third pair of concepts of comparison do indeed play a role significantly different from that of the previous two. The first two pairs concern the comparison of concepts only insofar as they involve the "analytic unity of consciousness," whereas the pair outer/inner generates the form of judgment proper, that is, the copula or connective, thus the *synthesis* in judgment. There is thus a hierarchy between the concepts of comparison, which Reich was right to stress when he said that *Verknüpfung*, connection, grounds *Vergleichung*, comparison. But from this he drew the erroneous conclusion that only *quantity* and *quality* of judgment depend on comparison, and thus on concepts of comparison, whereas *relation* depends on *connection* only. I, on the other hand, conclude that the search for connection, that is, the formation of *judgments*, is the determining motivation in *all* comparison leading to representations of objets reflected under concepts. Hence, the concepts of comparison guiding the search for connection have the primary role, the two other pairs merely being means for the the attainment of the end, *Verknüpfung*. Comparison according to *inner* and *outer*, geared toward the formation of rules expressed in *judgments*, govern the comparison according to identity and difference (of objects) and agreement and conflict (of marks) which is geared toward forming *concepts*, "universal and reflected representations" to be combined in judgments. In this way, the form of judgment (the copula or connective by means of which the relation of an assertion to its condition is thought) is determinative with respect to its matter (the concepts combined in judgment), and the distinctive feature of Kant's antirationalist system is secured: the form (determination) is prior to the matter (the determinable).

The third pair of concepts of comparison thus leads us to the fourth and last pair, "form" and "matter." The search for an *inner* or *outer* condition for predica-

---

[20] Cf. chapter 5, pp. 128–29, and chapter 6, note 14.

tion (the search for rules) guides all comparison of representations, and thus all concept formation, just as more generally, according to a Kantian motto that is very famous but insufficiently explained, in representation *form always precedes matter*. One generally understands this Kantian phrase as concerning the relation between form and matter in the sensible given: space and time, the forms of our sensible intuition, precede its matter, that is, sensation. But in fact Kant's phrase has a broader import. As we shall see, his criticism of the rationalist amphiboly involving the fourth pair of concepts of comparison results in his asserting that in representation (and therefore in *objects* of representation) *form*, whether sensible or discursive, precedes *matter.* We shall now consider this last pair of concepts of comparison.[21]

"MATTER" AND "FORM", AND MODALITIES OF JUDGMENT

Judging from the pattern of correspondence between concepts of comparison and forms of judgment, one might expect the fourth pair to be related to the first two forms of judgment under the heading of modality, so that "matter" corresponds to *assertoric* judgment, and "form" to *problematic* judgment. But there is no trace of such a correspondence in the Amphiboly chapter, where reflection on "matter" and "form" seems to be confined to the nature of space and time. Kant's criticism of the rationalist amphiboly may then seem to be the following: Leibniz thought that space and time were the order of intelligible substances, of which *sensible* space and time were merely the confused representation; but since the truth is that space and time are the a priori forms in which appearances are represented in our sensibility, the primacy of *matter* (substances as noumena) over *form* (the order of these substances), characteristic of the intelligible realm, gives way to the primacy of *form* (space and time as a priori forms of sensible intuition) over *matter* (sensations, then objects as appearances) in the sensible realm:

> The intellectualist philosopher could not endure to think of the form as preceding the things themselves and determining their possibility—a perfectly just criticism on the assumption that we intuit things as they really are, although in confused representation. But since sensible intuition is a quite specific subjective condition, which lies *a priori* at the foundation of all perception, as its original form, it follows that the form is given by itself, and that so far is the matter (or the things themselves which appear) from serving as the foundation (as we should have to judge if we followed mere concepts) that on the contrary its own possibility presupposes a formal intuition (time and space) as antecedently given. (A267–68/B323–24)

[21] Note that Kant does not assign any specific concept of comparison to disjunctive judgment. This might be linked to what I suggested in chapter 4 concerning the specific role of this form of relation in judgment: it provides the form of systematic unity of genera and species, which is thinkable only *after* concepts have been formed and correlated. We shall see in chapter 11 that disjunctive judgment, and the corresponding category of community, are indeed strongly dependent on the first two logical forms and categories of relation (categorical judgment and substance, hypothetical judgment and causality), for which they in turn provide the goal of reflecting a totality of correlated determinations.

However, the relation between *matter* and *form* is thus difficult to distinguish from that between *inner* and *outer*. Consider, for example, the following: "In the concept of the pure understanding *matter* is prior to *form*; and for this reason Leibniz first assumed things (monads), and *within* them a power of representation, in order afterwards to found on this their *outer* relation" (A267/B323, emphasis mine on "within" and "outer"). Here we seem to lose sight of any parallelism between concepts of comparison and forms of judgment. Yet a more careful review shows that at least one modal notion is evident throughout the exposition of the fourth pair of concepts of comparison, the notion of the *possible*. Kant's disagreement with Leibniz concerning what is to be understood by *possible* is the background of the dispute on the nature of space and time. To the possible considered as an *ens*, a *being*, given in thought by pure concepts, Kant opposes possible experience, the nature and boundaries of which he had defined in the Transcendental Aesthetic and Analytic. This move from an ontological to a transcendental definition of the possible, in which an object is deemed possible only if it is an object of possible experience, constitutes the context of Kant's treatment of the notions of "matter" and "form." Against the primacy of intelligible "matter" (concepts, as expressions of simple essences) over "form" (the combinations of simple essences according to logical rules in God's intellect), by means of which the possible is characterized as *ens* or purely intelligible essence, Kant affirms the primacy of "form" (the forms of sensible intuition, but also the schemata implementing the synthesis of these forms according to the categories) over "matter" (sensation, and appearances)[22] in experience, and thus also in the *object* of possible experience, appearance. The discussion of space and time is then only an element (albeit an essential one) in the broader confrontation between Leibniz's and Kant's notions of possibility.

We can now get a better grasp of Kant's overall argument concerning matter and form. These two concepts "underlie all other reflection, so inseparably are they bound up with all use of the understanding" (A266/B322). Unlike other concepts of reflection, they do not reflect or guide a particular aspect of the activity of comparison, but characterize thinking in general. "Matter," for Kant, is the "determinable," and "form" its "determination." All thinking is an activity of *determining* (giving *form* to) a *determinable* (*matter*). If thought were a purely intellectual activity, independent of any external (sensible) condition, its matter would consist of purely intelligible concepts, and its form of the various combinations of these concepts. The rationalist amphiboly thus has the same nature here as in the three previous cases. The intellectualist philosopher supposes that all thought can in principle be completely analyzed into its elements—that is, the simple concepts that constitute logic's "matter," and whose possible combinations comprise its "form." He also holds that this relation between matter and form in pure intellect mirrors the relation between matter and form in things (this is how sensible space and time are relegated to the status of confused representations of the intelligible order of essences and substances). Kant's criticism of the amphiboly

---

[22] On this twofold meaning of sensible "matter," cf. note 37.

consists accordingly in showing (1) that the form of the sensible given is irreducibly heterogeneous to any form thinkable by pure intellect, and (2) that in the sensible given (objects of sensible representation) the matter does not determine the form (simple elements are not prior to their combinations), but on the contrary, the form precedes and determines the matter.

To these two steps of the argument, which are explicit in the Amphiboly, may, I shall argue, be added two more: (3) if our thought is not purely intellectual but conditioned by sensible intuition, *the primacy of form over matter holds also for thought itself* (and not merely in the sensible realm, the realm of appearances). This primacy of the *form* of thought over its *matter* results in a completely new definition of the *modalities* of judgment, so that there does, in the end, emerge a correspondence, paralleling the three previous cases, between concepts of comparison and forms of judgment. (4) The primacy of the *form* of thought over its *matter* means that, in the generation of empirical concepts (the *matter* of thought), not only are the *logical forms of judgment*, but also the *form of a system*, at work. In consequence, the conception of judgment resulting from the Amphiboly chapter is surprisingly close to that developed a few years later in the *Critique of Judgment*. Important lessons may be drawn from this proximity.

Let us now consider the four steps of the argument just outlined.

Logical Use of the Concepts "Matter" and "Form"

> *Matter* and *Form*. These two concepts underlie all other reflection, so inseparably are they bound up with all use of the understanding. The one [matter] signifies the determinable in general, the other [form] its determination. (A266/B322)

Such a definition of "matter" and "form" places Kant in direct continuity with the Aristotelian tradition. However, Kant's usage of these concepts bears the mark of what I have called the "internalization within representation" characteristic of transcendental philosophy.[23] For Aristotle, "matter" and "form" are two concepts by means of which change can be thought in all being—matter as the passive, undetermined given, form its principle of determination and actualization; or, at a higher level of determination, generic matter (wood, brass) potentially specified by a particular form (coffin, bed, statue).[24] For Kant, by contrast, "matter" and "form" characterize the two poles of the activity of representation: the given ("determinable"), and the act of combining this given ("determination"). It is significant, in this regard, that in Kant's *Logic* distinctions of matter and form recur at each level of increasing complexity in the exposition of the activity of thinking: "Concept," "Judgment," "Reasoning," "Method." *Objects* are the matter for concepts, *universality* their form. *Concepts* are the matter for judgment, the *combination* of concepts by means of the copula 'is' or the connective 'if . . . then' or 'either . . . or' their form. *Judgments*, in the capacity of premises, are the *matter* for syllogisms, the *mode of inferring (consequentia)* their form. Finally, *com-*

---

[23] See chapter 1, pp. 20–25.
[24] Cf. particularly Aristotle, *Metaphysics* VIII 4, 1044a15–32.

bined and connected cognitions are the matter for the whole of cognition, *system* its form.[25]

We should therefore have no difficulty understanding Kant's claim that these two concepts "underlie all other reflection, so inseparably are they bound up with all use of the understanding." In all activities of thought, we can recognize a relation between matter (determinable) and form (determination). These two concepts reflect all other activities of comparison of concepts, and so too the fundamental structure of any act of thinking. Every act of thinking is the relation of a *form* (an act of determination) to a *matter* (a determinable). But these concepts are themselves merely comparative or relative: as we just saw, the matter for a certain form is, on its part, the form for a matter of lower determination, just as the form is the matter for a form of higher determination. Kant is faithful here to the relational meaning Aristotle himself had granted these concepts, even while using these concepts to characterize not being itself, but the activity of thinking.[26]

The form par excellence, which is no longer itself the matter for a form of higher level, is the *system*. Kant believed that this form surreptitiously governs all our judging activity. The requirement of systematicity is a properly logical requirement, since it concerns the mere form of thought, irrespective of its object. This requirement is stated in the second part of the *Logic*, the Universal Doctrine of Method: "As the doctrine of elements in logic has for its content the elements and conditions of the perfection of a cognition, so the universal doctrine of method, as the other part of logic, has to deal with *the form of a science in general*, or with the ways of acting so as to connect the manifold of cognition in a science."[27] Systematic perfection, the form of a science in general, depends above all on the "distinctness of concepts both in regard to what is contained *in* them

[25] Matter and form of *concepts*: *Logik*, §2; of *judgments*, §18; of *syllogisms*, §59; the universal doctrine of method deals with the form of a science in general: §96. When Kant states that the *Logic* deals with the form of thought alone, the matter for this form is the matter of concepts, mentioned in §2: the object. Concepts, judgments, inferences, and system are together the form of thought (all of which, as we saw in chapter 4, are as it were engrained in the form of judgment itself). Of course, saying that the object is the 'matter' for the 'form' provided by our discursive functions, escapes absurdity only if one remembers that the object here considered is either the "object in general," the mere form of an object; or the object "interiorized to representation," the *appearance* or "undetermined [and thus *determinable*] object of sensible intuition." Cf. chapter 5.

[26] This internalization within thought of the relation between *matter* and *form* is not, on the whole, a complete novelty. One precedent is to be found in Lambert, who wrote to Kant (February 3, 1766): "I wanted to make some more general remarks. The first concerns the question whether or to what extent cognition of the *form* leads to cognition of the *matter* of our knowledge. . . . Our cognition of the form, as it is in logic, is as incontestable and right as geometry itself" (Ak. X, 64; 51). In his *Architectonic*, Lambert deals with the "logical form," "derived from the *operations of the understanding* alone" (cf. *Neues Organon* II, *Architectonic*, introd. XXII). The idea of logical form appears in Kant from 1764 on: "the form is the manner in which I must compare the subject and the predicate" (*Met. Herder*, Ak. XXVIII-1, 8). In contrast, the use of the concepts of matter and form in the *Dissertation* remains ontological (cf. *Diss.* I, §2, I and II, Ak. II, 389; 380: matter, "that is the *parts*, which are here taken to be substances"; form, "which consists in the *co-ordination*, not in the subordination, of substances"). However, in the case of the sensible world, the notion of form was already internalized within representation, as the form *of our sensibility*, space and time.

[27] *Logik*, §96 (my emphasis).

and in respect of what is contained *under* them."[28] That is, it demands that concepts be as fully analyzed as possible with regard to their content, and as fully specified as possible with regard to their sphere or extension.

In the first *Critique*, we find this same requirement of systematicity expounded in the appendix to the Transcendental Dialectic. As an example of reason's striving to systematicity Kant then gives the search for a fundamental force in nature:

> Reason's logical principle [*das logische Vernunftprinzip*] calls upon us to bring about such unity as completely as possible; and the more the appearances of this and that force are found to be identical with one another, the more probable it becomes that they are simply different manifestations of one and the same force, which may be entitled, relatively to the more specific forces, the *fundamental force*. . . . The relatively fundamental forces must in turn be compared with one another, with a view to discovering their harmony, and so to bring them nearer to a single radical, that is, absolutely fundamental, force. (A649/B677)

Kant calls this fundamental force or highest genus "matter," thus reviving the Aristotelian sense of generic matter. But here again, "matter" first has a "logical" sense, referring to the matter *of thought*. The genus is the "logical matter," a generic concept determinable by a discursive process of specification. But, Kant adds, the *logical* meaning of "matter" becomes a *transcendental* meaning insofar as reason necessarily presupposes that generic unity exists in the things themselves, as appearances. Apart from this presupposition, the requirement of systematicity in knowledge would be empty. The logical form of a system thus becomes the regulative idea of a unified system of genera and species *in nature*, which makes possible the unity of nature under empirical laws. Thus "logical" matter reflects "real" matter, the matter of things, as phenomena.[29]

Kant develops a similar idea in the first introduction to the *Critique of Judgment* when he claims that reflective judgment, in ascending from the particular to the universal, proceeds according to the regulative idea of nature's conformity to the logical form of a system.

> The logical form of a system consists merely in the division of given universal concepts (here the concept of a nature as such); [we make this division] by thinking, in terms of a certain principle, the particular (here the empirical) in its manifold as contained under the universal. In order to do this we must, if we proceed empirically and ascend from the particular to the universal, *classify* the manifold, i.e., compare several classes, each falling under a definite concept; and, when these classes are completely enumerated in terms of their common characteristic, we must subsume them under higher classes (genera), until we reach the concept containing the principle of the entire classification (and constituting the highest genus). On the other hand, if we start from the universal concept, so as to descend to the particular by a complete division, we perform what is called the *specification* of the manifold under a given

---

[28] *Logik*, §98.

[29] I shall say more on matter and form of objects as appearances (*apparentiae*) and as phenomena later, in chapter 10.

concept. . . . It would be more correct to say, rather, that we *make the universal con-cept specific* by indicating the manifold that falls under it. For the genus is (logically considered) as it were the matter, or the crude [*roh*] substrate, that nature processes into particular species and subspecies by determining it multiply; and so we can say that *nature makes itself specific* in terms of a certain principle (or in terms of the idea of a system), by analogy with how teachers of law use this term when they talk about the specification of certain raw [*roh*] material. *

* The Aristotelian school too called the *genus* matter, and the *specific difference* the form.[30]

This shows again that the concepts of matter and form "underlie all other reflec-tion." Reflective judgment is a comparison of representations, whether to derive concepts from sensible representations or to form higher (more general) concepts from lower. According to Kant, all reflective judgment is guided by the logical representation of a system, that is, of a logical matter (highest concepts as logical genera) determined by logical form (complete specification).

In the Amphiboly chapter, Kant gives four examples of "matter" and "form," each an illustration of the general logical sense of these concepts: "determinable" and "determination" in respect of thought in general, whether it be logical reflec-tion in the narrow or in the broad sense. But if one supposes that all thought, in-cluding all knowledge of objects, can proceed by pure concepts in the intellect alone, then as with the other concepts of reflection, an amphibolous use of these concepts occurs. Unfortunately it is, in this case, often difficult to distinguish the legitimate, logical from the amphibolous, ontological use of the concepts men-tioned in Kant's examples. Yet, by dint of careful analysis, and some anticipation of Kant's refutation of the rationalist amphiboly (which we shall pursue in the next section), we can attempt to clarify this distinction.

Here are the four examples Kant gives for "matter" and "form" (the numbers in brackets are added):

[1] Logicians formerly gave the name 'matter' to the universal, and the name 'form' to the specific difference. [2] In any judgment we can call the given concepts logical matter (*i.e.* matter for the judgment), and their relation (by means of the copula) the form of the judgment. [3] In every being the constituent elements (*essentialia*) are the matter, the mode in which they are combined in one thing the essential form. [4] Also, as regards things in general, unlimited reality was viewed as the matter of all possibility, and its limitation (negation) as the form by which one thing is distin-guished from others according to transcendental concepts. (A266–67/B322–23)

The second and third of these examples might well have come straight out of the *Logic*. I mentioned earlier the second example ("matter" and "form" of judg-ment), and I cited its treatment in the *Logic*.[31] The third example, *being* or *essence* (*Wesen*) and *essentialia*, is also treated in the *Logic*. There Kant explains that *es-*

[30] *Erste Einl.*, V, Ak. XX, 214–15; 402–3.
[31] *Logik*, §18; cf. note 25.

sential marks, or *essentialia*, are "those that must always be there to be found in the thing represented," and moreover "belong to the thing *as grounds* of other marks of one and the same thing." Kant then specifies that the essence (*Wesen*) so defined is only logical, not real. It is an *esse conceptus*, containing the marks that together constitute a sufficiently distinct concept of the thing, not an *esse rei* or *real essence* of the thing, which is unknowable by us. Thus this logical definition of the essence and its *essentialia*, despite the terminological similarity to Wolff's definitions, avoids the lure of rational ontology and the illusion that things are cognizable by pure concepts. It is compatible with Kant's own view, that *essentialia* are not properties of things known by pure intellect, but marks reflecting the "rules of our apprehension" of objects as appearances. Given this view, one can still treat marks as the *matter* which, together with their *form* or combination, define the essence (*esse conceptus*) of the thing.[32]

The first and fourth examples belong to the representation of form as a *system*. Curiously, Kant formulates each of these examples in the past tense, as if he doubted whether the modes of thought they present can be legitimately sustained from the critical standpoint: "Logicians *formerly gave* the name 'matter' to the universal, and the name 'form' to the specific difference.... Unlimited reality *was viewed* as the matter of all possibility, and its limitation ... as being the form by which one thing is distinguished from others" (my emphasis). Yet, the first example is not entirely relegated to the past. For Kant himself, the division of universals into specific differences is the logical form of a system, guiding all comparison and reflection. Therefore, such a representation is not the exclusive property of a mode of thinking the *Critique* discredits. Nevertheless, it is apt to attribute illusory ontological import to the merely logical form of a system. That is, it tempts one to construe a relation of matter and form *that is itself a mere form of thought*, as a given whole of logical *matter* (a complete whole of completely determined concepts accessible to pure intellect) by means of which things as they are in themselves are cognized in their real essence. The form of a system is thus particularly liable to amphibolous misinterpretation. It is this amphibolous temptation Kant relegates to the past when he uses the past tense in the text quoted earlier. As always, the rationalist illusion has two related aspects. First, the rationalist thinks that the matter of thought is constituted by pure concepts given in the intellect alone, independently of any sensible condition, its form being the various possible logical combinations of these concepts. And, second, he thinks that the matter and form of thought are also matter and form of things themselves, as noumena.

Kant's first three examples thus culminate in the fourth: the *ens realissimum* as the *matter* of all possibility, its limitation the *form* by which each thing is distinguished from all others. What we have here is both a logical representation of the system (a complete logical *matter*, together with its *form* as the complete whole of its determinations, i.e., limitations) and the locus par excellence of the amphiboly one runs into if this representation, instead of being itself interpreted as a

---

[32] *Logik*, Introduction, VIII-5, Ak. IX, 60; 566. *Essence* and *essentialia* appear in other texts of Kant, for instance *Anfangsgründe*, Ak. IV, 467n3; *Entdeckung*, Ak. VIII, 229; 141–42.

merely logical (conceptual) *form* guiding all concept formation, is viewed as the ontological foundation providing the *matter* of every being. The latter idea is precisely what Kant himself espoused in his text of 1763, *The Only Possible Argument in Support of a Demonstration of the Existence of God*. Hence, in this case, the use of the past tense is above all autobiographical—a reference to Kant's own precritical philosophy. Yet, even here the past is not entirely rejected: in the *Critique*, the *ens realissimum* is granted a legitimate status as a mere ideal of pure reason.

This is where the link between "matter" and "form" and the notion of the *possible* finds its fullest clarification. However, in order to understand this link and to perceive how Kant, in the critical period, opposes his own definition of possible *experience* to the rationalist amphiboly on matter and form of possibility, it will be helpful to recall the 1763 text. There, Kant begins by defining the conditions under which something is possible in general, that is, is thinkable or conceivable. The first condition, he says, is *formal*, or *logical*: something is thinkable if it is in agreement with the principle of contradiction. The second condition is *material*: "something" must be thought. Whatever is thinkable thus involves a "formal element," which is "the agreement between the data according to the principle of contradiction," and a "material" or "real" element, the *data* of which the thinkable is composed. These data themselves can be analyzed according to their formal possibility as well as their material possibility, until one arrives at the simplest *data*, the basic elements of everything thinkable. On what condition are these data themselves thinkable? On the condition that *something* is thought in them; and this condition can be met, according to the precritical Kant, only if a being exists that contains all of reality and is the ground of all that can be thought. Thus does the analysis of possibility as thinkability yield the only possible argument for the existence of God.[33]

Gérard Lebrun has convincingly shown that, already in 1763, the originality of Kant's position lies in his interpreting the *possible* not as a *being* but as a "complex of meanings." This is why for Kant no existence can be deduced from the possible. The existence of the *ens realissimum* is not deduced from its concept (its possibility) as one of its characters (as it is in the Anselmian/Cartesian proof for which Kant coined the expression *ontological proof* in the first *Critique*), but is proved to be a condition for the thinkability of concepts in general, or, in Kant's terms, a condition for the *material* aspect of possibility. In this sense, the 1763 proof already heralds the end of Wolffian/Leibnizian ontology.[34] Nonetheless, by defining the *matter* of the possible as conceptual data and its *form* as logical noncontradiction, *The Only Possible Argument* is caught in the rationalist amphiboly.

[33] *Beweisgr.*, I, 1–4, Ak. II, 77–81; 122–26.

[34] Lebrun, *Kant*, 130–34. "'Reality' in Leibniz's sense refers to the perfection contained in the essence, the degree of which will be one of the criteria of God's choice (*Monadology*, §54). What does the word 'reality' stand for in Kant? It means that I know what I am talking about when I say the name. 'Reality', first of all, is the meaning as I represent it to myself. . . . Second, whereas for Leibniz, essence is 'possible' before it enters into existence, Kant no longer thinks of an essence which would only be lacking existence. The complex of meanings which fits *a given thing*: such is the 'possible'— it is what I have in mind when I say about *this* that it is a triangle" (ibid., 132).

By reducing the possible to what is thinkable through pure concepts, it hypostatizes the "matter of all possibility" into a being itself thinkable by pure concepts. By constrast, in the Ideal of Pure Reason of the first *Critique*, the critical analysis of the *ens realissimum* consists in recognizing that such a representation is the hypostatization of a mere *logical form*, namely, the major premise of a disjunctive syllogism in which all possible determinations of things are supposed to result from the limitation of a presupposed whole of reality, or complete set of positive determinations. Such a supposition, Kant argues, is inconsistent with the result proved in the Transcendental Analytic, that realities—that is, positive determinations of things as appearances—can be thought only insofar as they are reflected from what is given in experience.[35]

I gave this preview of Kant's argument in the Transcendental Dialectic because I think it helps us understand his denunciation of the rationalist amphiboly on matter and form in the Amphiboly chapter. The critical analysis of the *ens realissimum* achieved in the Transcendental Dialectic gives us some idea of what a legitimate, logical use of the concepts of matter and form amounts to in the case of Kant's fourth example. It involves acceptance of only the *logical form* of the "*matter* of all possibility," namely the *regulative* representation of a concept of the "whole of reality" from which every particular concept could be obtained by limitation. The Transcendental Ideal, in the Transcendental Dialectic, is concerned with criticizing the hypostatization of this mere form into the concept of an *ens realissimum* whose existence one then assumes as a necessary ground of all possibility. For its part, the Amphiboly is concerned simply with showing that the relation of the *matter* and the *form* of all possibility, if considered (as it should be) as itself a mere *logical form*, does not allow the presupposition of a given whole of "logical matter," a matter of thought given by pure concepts, independently of any sensible condition. Still less does it allow matter and form in appearances to be assimilated with matter and form in pure thought—which, as we shall now see, is the main target of Kant's criticism of the rationalist amphiboly on the concepts of matter and form.

So far we have seen in what sense, for Kant, "matter" and "form" are "concepts of reflection" by means of which we may characterize all activity of thinking. We

[35] In a *Reflexion* for which Adickes suggests the dates 1783–84, Kant writes: "The *ens realissimum* must be given prior to any possibility . . . not as object, but as the *mere form of reason* [my emphasis], to think the difference of any possible thing in its thoroughgoing determination [*in ihrer durchgängigen Bestimmung*], thus as an Idea which is (subjectively) actual [*wirklich*] before something is thought as possible" (*Refl.* 6289, Ak. XVIII, 559). From this it is clear that the representation of a "matter of all possibility," whose complete set of possible limitations would be the "form" of possibility, *is itself merely a form*, and as such a regulative idea guiding all use of reason. In the portion I omitted (marked by ellipsis), Kant compares the role of space as a *form* of sensibility with the role of the *ens realissimum* as the *form* for the complete determination of things in the understanding. On this comparison, and the interpretation of the passage in its entirety, see Lebrun's commentary, *Kant*, chap. 7, 183–86. In part III, I will again consider the idea of an *ens realissimum* in its relation to the logical forms of infinite and disjunctive judgments, on the one hand, and to the *quantum infinitum* of space as the form of all possible experience, on the other hand (see chapters 10 and 11). For a further analysis of this point, see Longuenesse, "Transcendental Ideal."

have seen how the form of all thinking culminates in the form of a system, and how this is apt to give rise to amphibolous use (including an amphibological notion of possibility). I now consider Kant's denunciation of the amphiboly. I will then show in the final two sections how the correct use Kant recommends for the concepts of reflection "matter" and "form" brings us close to the use of *reflective judgment* he describes a few years later, in the *Critique of Judgment*.

Criticism of the Amphiboly

If thought proceeded by means of purely intellectual concepts, its *matter* would be prior to its *form*. *Genera*, simple concepts into which analysis might resolve all cognition, would be prior to their *specific differences*. *Concepts* would be prior to their combinations in *judgments*; *essentialia* would be prior to the essence into which they would be combined; and the *ens realissimum*, the unlimited whole of possible essences, would be prior to all its *determinations and limitations*. Irrespective of the psychological chronology of our acquisition of cognitions, the logical order here described would be at once the ontological order of the constitution of essences and the order according to which an infinite understanding would cognize things as noumena. Further, it would be the norm of order to which our finite understanding should tend insofar as its own limitations would permit. As before, the rationalist illusion is here twofold. First, it consists in believing that a cognition through pure concepts, independently of any sensible condition, is in principle possible. Second, it consists in believing that logical reflection on the relations between concepts mirrors the real relations holding between objects, as noumena. Hence the primacy of matter over form in *concepts* is also a primacy of matter (noumenal substances, monads) over form (the order of coexistents, i.e., space; and the order of successives, i.e., time) in *things*. Kant's antidote is none other than the doctrine expounded in the Transcendental Analytic and Transcendental Aesthetic. To a purely intelligible *determinable* whose *determination* consists in (purely intellectual) combinations, he opposes a sensible *determinable*, sensations, and a sensible *determination*, the a priori forms of space and time, synthesized in accordance with the schemata of the categories.[36]

This definition of a phenomenal order characterized by the primacy of its form over its matter yields a new meaning for the concept of the possible. Whereas the exposition of matter and form in concepts culminated in a definition of unlimited reality as the *matter of all possibility*, the exposition of matter and form in appearances supposes the background of *possible experience* as the condition for the possibility of any object, as appearance:

[36] Note that the criticism of the rationalist amphiboly on the concepts of matter and form retrospectively clarifies Kant's use of these concepts throughout the *Critique*, starting with the Transcendental Aesthetic. Kant indicates, in effect, that their use in the Transcendental Aesthetic and Transcendental Analytic belongs to transcendental reflection, and thus clarifies the overturning of Leibnizian rationalism he started in the transcendental aesthetic.

If [space and time] are only sensible intuitions in which we determine all objects merely as appearances, then the form of intuition (as a subjective property of sensibility) is prior to all matter (sensations); space and time come before all appearances and before all data of experience, and are indeed what makes the latter at all possible. The intellectualist philosopher could not endure to think of the form as preceding the things themselves and determining their possibility. . . . But . . . the form is given by itself, and so far is the matter (or the things themselves which appear) from serving as the foundation (as we should have to judge if we followed mere concepts) that on the contrary its own possibility presupposes a formal intuition (time and space) as antecedently given. (A267–68/B323–24)[37]

What is possible is so not because its matter results from a specific limitation of the matter of all possibility (as in *The Only Possible Argument in Support of a Demonstration of the Existence of God*). Nor is it because it is contained, together with infinitely many other possible essences, in God's infinite intellect (as in the Leibnizian version of the primacy of intelligible "matter"). Rather, the possible is so only because it *is representable*, that is, because its concept is in agreement with the universal form of experience (forms of intuition and categories, with their schemata). This does not mean, however, that all reference to a *matter* of possibility is eliminated from Kant's definition of the possible. On the contrary, the *form of experience*, that is, *possible experience*, determines the realm of the possible in general only because it is the form for a *matter*, first sensation, then appearances.

As I did with the previous concepts of comparison, I shall now try to extend Kant's argument beyond its explicit development in the Amphiboly of Concepts of Reflection. Kant's primary purpose is to show that the relation between matter and form is reversed when one moves from objects of pure intellect (noumena) to objects of sensibility (phaenomena). I will show that this reversal in the relation of matter and form holds also for understanding itself *when it is conditioned by a sensible given*. In other words, it is not only in sensibility, but also in the understanding that *the form precedes the matter*. Kant's redefinition of the modalities of judgment is a result of this reversal.

Matter and Form of Thought, and Modalities of Judgment: Kant's Argument, Continued

In Kant's terminology, the rationalist holds that the *form* of judgment (i.e., the manner in which concepts are combined) depends on its *matter* (the conceptual data). The *modality* of the combination thus also depends on the matter of judgment. The

---

[37] A267–68/B323–24. Note that Kant says, on the one hand, that form (space and time) precedes all matter, *that is, sensations*, and, on the other hand, that form precedes *things*, as appearances. Space and time "precede" sensations in that their representation does not find its origin in the combinations of our sensations, but in our a priori representational capacities (in this case our receptivity or sensibility). But sensation is needed for the a priori forms of sensibility to become forms *of appearances*, "indeterminate objects of empirical intuition." These are in turn the "matter," or determinable, for the

combination is "possible" or "impossible," "necessary" or "contingent" depending on the marks contained in the concepts combined.[38] Kant, on the contrary, holds that the *form* of judgment has primacy over its *matter*. This means, where modality is concerned, that the modality of judgment is not dependent on its matter (the concepts combined), but on its form (the manner in which the particular combination of concepts in a given judgment is related to "the unity of thought in general"). This first aspect of Kant's opposition to Leibniz and Wolff is inseparable from a second. For the rationalist, modal determinations are primarily ontological. The modalities of combinations of concepts in judgments express the modalities of the relations between individual things and their essential and accidental properties. For Kant, on the contrary, there is a specifically logical characterization of modality, distinct from the modal determinations of empirical objects. Indeed, he uses a different vocabulary for the modalities of judgments "considered in their mere form" (problematic, assertoric, and apodeictic) and for the modal determinations of empirical objects (possible or impossible, actual, necessary, or contingent).

Let us now consider Kant's "formal" modalities, specifically.

When Kant explains his table of logical forms of judgment, he defines the three modalities of judgment (problematic, assertoric, apodeictic) not by the contradiction or noncontradiction of the concepts combined, but by the place the relevant judgment holds in the activity of thought in general:

> The *modality* of judgments . . . concerns only the value of the copula in relation to thought in general. . . .
>
> Thus the two judgments, the relation of which constitutes the hypothetical judgment (*antecedens et consequens*), and likewise the judgments, the reciprocal relation of which forms the disjunctive judgment (members of the division), are one and all

---

"form," or determination through spatiotemporal syntheses in accordance with the categories (schematism). Kant's conception of space, time, and schematism will be discussed in part III of this work. See also Waxman, *Model*, 196–98.

[38] 'A is B' is *possible* if B does not contradict A (no mark belonging to B is the negation of a mark belonging to A). It is *impossible* if B does contradict A. 'A is B' is *necessary* if its negation is contradictory (if B is contained in A as part of its marks), *contingent* if its negation is not contradictory. There are major differences between Leibniz's and Wolff's conceptions of modalities when one moves from the modalities of *relations of essences and modes* and their expression in judgments, to modalities of *existence*. I do not want to enter into these issues here, since my purpose is simply to explain how Kant, in his characterization of the modalities of judgment, replaces the rationalist primacy of matter over form with his own conception of the primacy of form over matter (for a more detailed exposition of Leibniz's and Wolff's views on modality, see Longuenesse, *Kant et le pouvoir de juger*, 201–2). Kant would have been familiar with Leibniz's conception of modalities at least through the *Theodicy* (cf. §413–14) and the *New Essays* (bk. IV, chap. II, §1, and bk. II, chap. 21, §13). And he certainly knew Wolff's treatment of modal concepts in his *Philosophia prima sive ontologia* (see in particular §§79–80, 85, 171–76, 279, 294). It is, however, worth remarking that Wolff expounds modal notions in his *Ontologia* but not in his *Philosophia rationalis sive logica*, even though the examples he gives in the *Ontologia* concern concepts and judgments. Not one line is devoted to the modalities of judgment in the *Philosophia rationalis sive Logica*. This confirms, I think, the primacy of ontology over logic in the rationalist conception of modality.

problematic only. . . . The assertoric proposition deals with logical actuality [*die lo-gische Wirklichkeit*] or truth. Thus, for instance, in a hypothetical syllogism the an-tecedent is in the major premise problematic, in the minor assertoric, and the syllogism shows that the consequence follows in accordance with the laws of the understanding. The apodeictic proposition thinks the assertoric as determined by these laws of the un-derstanding, and therefore as affirming *a priori*; and in this manner it expresses logi-cal necessity. Since everything is thus incorporated in the understanding step by step—inasmuch as we first judge something problematically, then maintain its truth assertorically, and finally affirm it as inseparably united with the understanding, that is, as necessary and apodeictic—we are justified in regarding these three functions of modality as so many moments of thought. (A74–76/B99–101)

One can see here that in each of the modalities considered, the "value of the cop-ula," and thus the modality of judgment, is determined by its "relation to thought in general." A proposition is *problematic* if it is merely a component in another (hypothetical or disjunctive) proposition. The assertion of its truth is thus "sus-pended": only the composite proposition to which it belongs is asserted. A propo-sition is *assertoric* if it holds the position of a minor premise in a hypothetical syl-logism, that is, if it is an instantiation of the condition of a rule (e.g., 'if the sun shines on the stone, the stone gets warm; *but the sun shines on the stone* [asser-toric]; therefore, the stone gets warm'). A proposition is *apodeictic* if it is asserted under a universal principle. In each of these cases, the modality of judgment is determined by its relation to the forms of thought involved in deductive reason-ing (judgments and syllogisms), not by its internal components (its "matter").

It may be objected that we have here only one part of Kant's definition of the "formal" modalities of judgment. Indeed, at the beginning of the text just quoted I omitted a passage where Kant specifies that

Problematic judgments are those in which affirmation and negation is taken as merely possible (optional [*beliebig*]). In assertoric judgments, affirmation or nega-tion is viewed as *actual* [*wirklich*] (true), and in *apodeictic* judgments as necessary.

Similarly, in the *Logic* Kant says:

As to modality, through which moment the relation of the whole judgment [*des ganzen Urteils*] to the faculty of cognition is determined, judgments are either *prob-lematic* or *assertoric* or *apodeictic*. The problematic ones are accompanied with the consciousness of the mere possibility of the judging, the assertoric ones with the con-sciousness of its actuality [*der Wirklichkeit*], the apodeictic ones, finally, with the consciousness of its necessity.[39]

One may therefore object that the explanation I just gave places too much stock on Kant's characterization of logical modalities as determined by the place the judgment holds in another judgment or in reasoning. After all, is it implausible to suppose that this place itself results from the judgment being either "reflected as

[39] *Logik*, §30.

possible," "reflected as actual," or "reflected as necessary"? If such is the case, it would be this "reflection" that stands in need of clarification.

Yet, Kant's explanations make clear that it is precisely *the place of a judgment in relation to the activity of thought in general* that determines whether a judgment is "reflected as possible" (*problematic*), "reflected as true (or actual)" (*assertoric*), or "reflected as necessary" (*apodeictic*). Indeed, defining the modality of judgment through its position in the unity of thought in general is what makes it possible to apply one and the same (formal) definition of modal determinations to all judgments, whether analytic or synthetic, empirical or a priori. This universal applicability of the definition is what makes it purely formal. Only after the *content* of the concepts combined is taken into account, does it become relevant to distinguish between analytic and synthetic judgments: between judgments where reflection is "merely logical in the narrow sense," and judgments where reflection is "logical in the broad sense" (i.e., conditioned by the sensible given represented by the term "x" in the logical form of judgment).

Consider Kant's example: "If there is a perfect justice, the obstinately wicked are punished" (A73/B98, A75/B100). Kant claims that the proposition "there is a perfect justice" is *problematic* because it functions as the antecedent in a hypothetical proposition. Now, one might expect him to have called it "problematic" because the concept of perfect justice, if analyzed by merely logical reflection in the narrow sense (the mere comparison of concepts in the understanding), turns out to be a noncontradictory concept. In logical reflection in the narrow sense, a judgment is termed 'problematic' if the concepts it combines do not contradict each other, and 'apodeictic' if negating the attribution of the predicate to the subject yields contradiction (a negative judgment is apodeictic if asserting the predicate of the subject yields a contradiction). In such logical reflection in the narrow sense, the logical matter does indeed determine the modality of the combination. But were we to suppose that all of our judgments are of this sort, we would fall into the rationalist amphiboly that presumes that every combination of concepts takes place in the understanding alone and opens the way to a complete knowledge of the combinations of marks in things. In my view, the reason Kant does not define the problematic character of judgment *in general* by its noncontradictory character is precisely to avoid this amphiboly. For him, a judgment is problematic, in the most general sense, only if *used* as a merely problematic judgment—that is, only insofar as it functions as the component of another judgment, which itself is used assertorically, or even apodeictically. That this definition of 'problematic' is applicable to all judgments, whether analytic or synthetic, is precisely what makes it a *formal* definition, properly consigned to general logic. *Once this formal definition is given*, one may go on to consider not just the *form*, but also the *content* of the judgment, and thus differentiate between logical reflection in the narrow sense (in the understanding alone) and logical reflection in the broad sense (in relation to the sensible represented by x in the logical form). In the former, the judgment will be problematic ("reflected as possible," *i.e., used as such*) if it is noncontradictory, and its negation (e.g., 'there is no perfect justice') is also noncontradictory. In the latter, the noncontradictory character of the concepts combined in a judgment is not a sufficient condition for the judgment to be admitted for use even as problematic. For the judgment must fulfill a further condition, namely, that of not contradicting the universal principles of the possibility of experience stated in the Transcendental Analytic. But in *both* species of logical reflection, that is, in *both* analytic and synthetic judgment, a problematic judgment is present as such in the form of our thought in general, either as one of the components of a disjunctive judgment, or as the antecedent or consequent of a hypothetical judgment.

Similarly, a proposition is apodeictic "merely as to its form" not if its negation is contradictory (this condition is too strong, and can hold only in the context of logical reflection in the narrow sense) but more generally if it is thought of as "determined by [the] laws of the understanding," that is, if it is deducible from universal laws. What these laws are remains undecided in the context of the formal definition. They may be purely logical laws (in which case the apodeictic proposition belongs to logical reflection in the narrow sense). But they may also be, and indeed in most cases are, universal principles of the possibility of experience, or even particular laws derived under empirical conditions. In the latter sort of case, the proposition is apodeictic in the context of logical reflection in the broad sense, under the condition of the sensible given represented by the term x in the logical form of judgment.

I would certainly not claim to have given an exhaustive account of Kant's conception of the modalities of judgment, or even to have begun to explain the relation between Kant's "formal" modalities of judgments and his modal categories. But I hope to have given force to the thesis advanced at the beginning of this exposition. Instead of modalities of judgment determined by their logical *matter* (the concepts combined, and their combinations' conformity to the principle of contradiction), Kant propounds modalities of judgment considered merely as to their form. The factor determining these modalities is the *form of thought*, that is, the relation of a particular judgment to the complete system of propositions that either reflects the whole of our experience (in the case of judgments belonging to logical reflection in the broad sense, i.e., under sensible conditions) or results from the combinations of our concepts in pure thought (in the case of judgments belonging to logical reflection in the narrow sense, i.e., in the understanding alone). Kant's novel definition of the "formal" modalities of judgment thus displays in striking fashion the precedence he grants the form of thought over its matter.

Matter and Form, and the Generation of Concepts through Comparison/Reflection/Abstraction

For all three pairs of concepts of comparison previously examined (identity/diversity, agreement/conflict, inner/outer) I showed that these concepts not only guide the comparison of concepts in judgments but also guide the initial generation of concepts from the sensible given. Now, the concepts "matter" and "form" serve to reflect the very activity of thought described in the three other pairs of concepts of comparison. The thesis that the concepts of comparison, "inner" and "outer," "agreement" and "conflict," "identity" and "difference," guide the formation of concepts from the sensible given is equivalent to saying that the *matter* of all thought (viz. concepts) is generated by the very activity that combines concepts in accordance with its proper *form* (the forms of judgment).

But we can go even further in our use of the concepts "matter" and "form" to reflect the generation of concepts through comparison/reflection/abstraction. (1) We can go further down, toward the determinable, and consider the *matter* for which the concepts themselves are the *form*, namely the object. (2) We can go further up, toward the determination, and consider the *form* for which judgments are the *matter*, namely forms of inference, and the form of a system in general.

1. Further down, form determines matter not only insofar as the forms of judgment determine the formation of concepts as the matter for judgment, but also insofar as they contribute to generating the representation of objects as the "matter" for concepts.[40] We saw that the object to which concepts are related in judgment is represented by "x" in Kant's analysis of the logical form of judgment. And we saw that according to Kant, this "x" actually designates an object only insofar as the act of judging determines the object as *phenomenon* (object of the appearance thought under concepts), under the supposition of a *transcendental object* $= X$.[41] Now, to say that phenomena are reflected under concepts in judgment only insofar as we suppose them to be related to a "transcendental object" is to say that we cannot consider the "matter" of concepts (the object) to be arbitrarily generated by our concepts. The object, even granted its status as object-of-representation, depends on more than just the activity of thought. Nevertheless, the *form* (the *determination, i.e., the activity of thinking*) is prior to and determinative of its own proper *matter*, the empirical object (phenomenon), insofar as the latter does not exist "as" object unless it is first synthesized in intuition, then reflected under concepts in judgment. This means that the very same activity of thinking that generates concepts as "that form required for the power of judgment" also generates the substitutional instances for the term "x" in Kant's logical form of judgment: singular objects, synthesized in such a way that they may be reflected under concepts in judgments, and thereby serve as the "matter" for concepts.[42]

2) Further up, the generation of judgments depends on the forms of thought for which they are themselves the matter. We saw that it is an intrinsic feature of judgment, by virtue of its very form, to be a potential element in the *ratiocinatio prosyllogistica*, the chain of syllogistic reasonings, by means of which its condition is subsumed under the condition of a more and more universal rule.[43] We also saw that the concepts combined in judgments are formed under the regulative rep-

[40] *Logik*, §2. Cf. note 25.

[41] See chapter 5.

[42] The object itself, as *sensible* object (appearance as the "undetermined object of an empirical intuition") is the outcome of the determination of a *matter* (sensation) by a *form* (the forms of sensibility). The variety of contexts for the pair of concepts "matter/form" results in a variety of specific meanings for the primacy of form over matter, which need to be specially analyzed in each case. On "matter" and "form" of appearances, see chapter 10, note 14.

[43] Cf. chapter 4, pp. 90–93.

resentation of a universal scale of genera and species, and thus subordinated to the regulative idea of a whole of reality, the "matter of all possibility," in relation to which each singular object might be completely determined by concepts. Consequently, if the logical forms of judgment guide reflection upon the sensible given and thus guide the generation of the matter of judgments (concepts and their proper matter, phenomena), the activity of judging is itself guided by the search for rules and for systematic unity, that is, by the forms of inference and the form of a system.

It thus becomes evident that the analysis of concepts of comparison in the first *Critique* brings us right to the threshhold of the conception of judgment Kant was later to expound in his *Critique of Judgment*.

THE UNITY OF THE *CRITIQUE OF PURE REASON* AND THE *CRITIQUE OF JUDGMENT*

Our analysis of the concepts of reflection, "matter" and "form," showed that the acts of comparison/reflection/abstraction whereby concepts are generated from the sensible given are guided, according to Kant, by the forms of judgment, and that the activity of forming judgments is intrinsically geared toward the form of a system. How could one fail to recognize, in this presentation of the activity of judgment, the features of reflective judgment later described by Kant in the first introduction to the *Critique of Judgment*? Indeed, I borrowed from this introduction one of the texts cited earlier, concerning the ordering of logical *matter*, the genera, in the *form* of the system.[44] This proximity confirms one of the theses I advanced at the beginning of this work: at the heart of the first *Critique* we find a conception of judgment in which *reflection* plays an essential role, contrary to the common view that *reflection* is a theme exclusive to the third *Critique*. Admittedly, in the first *Critique* the reflective aspect is somewhat obscured by the predominantly determinative focus of the Transcendental Deduction of the Categories, and one may easily be tempted to conclude that the *Critique of Pure Reason* is exclusively devoted to *determinative* judgment, while the *Critique of Judgment* alone is occupied with *reflective* judgment (a distinction Kant did not even see fit to announce until the third *Critique*). On such a reading, the first *Critique*'s concern with the legitimate use of the categories is presumed to relate only to the *application* of universal concepts, and so to determinative judgments, the function of which is to "find the particular for the universal." The third *Critique*, for its part, is supposed to deal with the hitherto neglected topic of reflective judgments, whose function is to "find the universal for the particular."[45] But opposing the two *Critiques* in this way seems to me both mistaken and seriously misleading, for two reasons.

In the first place, such an opposition ignores the fact that Kant was careful to characterize the judgments on which he focused in the third *Critique* (aesthetic

[44] Cf. note 30. *Erste Einl.*, V, Ak. XX, 211–17; 399–404. See also *KU*, introd., IV, Ak. V, 179–81; 18–20.

[45] *Erste Einl.* V, Ak. XX, 211; 399–400. *K.U.*, Einl. IV, Ak.V, 179; 18–19.

judgments and teleological judgments) as *merely* reflective judgments (*nur re-flektierende, bloß reflektierende*).[46] This restrictive modifier is meant to deny that these judgments are in any sense determinative; they are *purely* reflective. They differ in this regard from other judgments relating to the sensible given, which are not *merely* reflective, but determinative *as well*. What makes judgments *merely* reflective is that in them, the effort of the activity of judgment to form concepts *fails*. And it fails because it *cannot* succeed. This is the case in "merely reflective" *aesthetic* judgment, where the agreement of imagination and understanding is of such a nature that it cannot be reflected under any concept. And it is the case also in "merely reflective" *teleological* judgment, where no cognitive concept of a final cause can legitimately be employed to account for the objective purposiveness of organisms, or the systematic unity of nature as a whole (what Kant calls the "subjective purposiveness" of nature). Thus, the peculiar feature of aesthetic and teleological judgments is not that they are reflective judgments (*for every judgment on empirical objects as such is reflective*); it is rather that they are *merely* reflective judgments, judgments in which reflection can never arrive at conceptual *determination*.[47]

Second, to suppose that the first *Critique* is concerned only with *determinative* and not with *reflective* judgment is to miss the fact that even in the first *Critique*, the *application* of the categories is inseparable from a thought process that has a *reflective* aspect. For it presupposes a progress from sensible representations to discursive thought: the formation of concepts through comparison/reflection/

---

[46] Cf. esp. *Erste Einl.*, VII, Ak. XX, 220–21; 408–9: "Clearly, then, in a *merely reflective* judgment imagination and understanding are considered . . . Imagination and understanding are—in mere reflection—in mutual harmony, a harmony that furthers the task of these powers. . . . A judgment about the objective purposiveness of nature is called *teleological*. It is a *cognitive judgment*, yet it belongs *only to reflective and not to determinative judgment*" (my emphasis). Also, "Every *determinative* judgment is *logical*, because its predicate is a given objective concept. But a merely *reflective* judgment about a given individual object *can be aesthetic*, if . . . the power of judgment, having no concept ready for the given intuition, holds the imagination (as it merely apprehends the object) up to the understanding" (ibid., VIII, Ak. 223–24; 412; my emphasis). And cf. the entire third *Critique*.

[47] On reflection failing to reach determination under a concept in aesthetic judgments, cf. *Erste Einl.* VI, Ak. XX, 220–21; 408–409. On the impossibility of reaching the concept of an objective ground (a final cause) for objects represented as natural ends in teleological judgments, ibid. Ak. XX, 221; 409. The same impossibility holds for the "subjective purposiveness" of nature, namely the representation of nature as a system for the benefit of our faculty of judgment; cf. *Erste Einl.* V, Ak. XX, 213–14; 401. The supposition that nature constitutes a system of empirical concepts and empirical laws is itself only a necessary supposition for our faculty of judgment in its reflective use, not an objective concept (ibid.). The "merely reflective" use of the power of judgment thus concerns aesthetic judgments, teleological judgments, and the representation of nature as a system ("subjective purposiveness" of nature). "Merely reflective" means in all three cases reflective *and not* determinative, but this general description covers three specifically different "merely reflective judgments." The third kind is the condition for all *empirical* judgments, that is, a condition for all judgments where judgment is "*in its reflection, at the same time determinative*" (XX, 212). This last case, I think, can already be found in the first *Critique*. What is new in the third *Critique* is the systematic correlation it establishes between this case and the first two, and by this means, between the cognitive and the practical use of reason. I develop this argument in more detail in Longuenesse, "Transcendental Ideal."

abstraction, which is just what *reflective judgment* is: finding the universal for the particular. When Kant, in section 19 of the Transcendental Deduction, describes judgment as "the manner in which given cognitions are brought to the objective unity of apperception," this *reflective* procedure is what should first come to mind. The logical form of each empirical judgment results from an activity of *reflection* on the sensible, guided by *concepts of comparison* that "do not present the object according to what constitutes its concept . . . but only serve to describe in all its manifoldness the comparison of representations which is prior to the concept of things."⁴⁸ But this reflective procedure, unlike the third *Critique*'s "merely reflective" judgments, is *determinative* as well: first, because it consists not only in forming empirical concepts but also *applying* them (remember: "a concept becomes clear only when it is applied in a comparison"),⁴⁹ and second, and most important, because it is an essential link in the *application of the categories*. To apply the categories, as "universal representations of synthesis," to empirical objects, one must first have reflected these objects under concepts in empirical judgments.

Judgments in which categories are *not* applied are called by Kant "judgments of perception," those judgments in which they are applied, "judgments of experience." It is impossible to understand this distinction unless one remembers that empirical judgments are first formed *not* by *application* of the categories, as full-fledged *concepts*, but by *reflection* of the empirical given under empirical concepts, themselves combined in accordance with the logical forms of judgment. There is however another dimension to the "application" of categories, which has to be taken into account even in the judgments Kant calls "judgments of perception." For although judgments of perception do not *apply* categories in the sense that they do not subsume empirical objects under categories understood as "universal and reflected representations" (Kant's definition for *concepts* in general), they nevertheless do presuppose *synthesis according to the categories*, those "blind" syntheses of imagination that the categories, as full-fledged discursive *concepts*, "universally represent."⁵⁰

Analyzing the two kinds of empirical judgments will provide the transition to the third part of this work, where I will expound Kant's conception of the *forms of synthesis necessary for any analysis*, that is, the transcendental syntheses of imagination which must have occurred in order for any empirical judgment to be formed, be it judgment of perception or judgment of experience. In the present chapter I was concerned only with Kant's conception of the *analysis of the sensible given*. I argued that the logical forms of judgment listed in Kant's metaphysical deduction of the categories, being forms of combination of concepts that, in empirical cognition, are related to sensible objects, are also a priori forms proper to an activity of *reflection upon the sensible given* in order to form concepts. It is very significant indeed that Kant should have listed "concepts of comparison,"

⁴⁸ A269/B 325.

⁴⁹ Cf. chapter 5 (citation referenced in note 30).

⁵⁰ Cf. A78/B104: "Pure synthesis, universally represented [*allgemein vorgestellt*], gives us the pure concept of the understanding."

also called "concepts of reflection," corresponding to each of his logical forms of judgment. Let me once again cite the passage in which these concepts are contrasted with the categories:

> These concepts differ from the categories by the fact that they do not present the object according to what constitutes its concept (quantity, reality) but serve only to describe in all its manifoldness the comparison of representations *which is prior to the concept of things*. (A269/B325, my emphasis)

Here Kant states explicitly that concepts of comparison, and empirical judgments as *reflective* judgments, are "prior to concepts of things" and thus also prior to the *subsumption of empirical objects under categories*, as universal concepts of objects. In this chapter I have shown how he must have conceived this reflection in the case of the four "titles" of logical form. In so doing, I have laid particular stress on the final pair of concepts of comparison, "matter" and "form." Kant's argument culminates with these concepts because they reflect the structure of every act of thinking in general, and therefore the structure of the acts effected by means of the other concepts of comparison. With this, the hitherto unnoticed proximity and accord between the theories of judgment in the first and third *Critiques* became apparent. I shall argue in the next chapter that this proximity is confirmed when we examine Kant's notions of judgment of perception and judgment of experience.

Judgments of Perception and
Judgments of Experience

IN THE PREVIOUS chapter I have argued that empirical judgments are *not* formed, according to Kant, by application of the categories, if by this application one means, for instance, that we generate (empirical) hypothetical judgments by applying the concept of cause (in which case the antecedent of an empirical hypothetical judgment would always be thought as a cause, which is absurd). I have argued that according to Kant, empirical judgments are formed by comparison/reflection/abstraction on the sensible given, and these operations are oriented toward the discursive forms of combination of concepts in judgments. I have thus argued that the "concepts of comparison" or "concepts of reflection" corresponding to each logical form of judgment, expounded in the Amphiboly, should be understood not merely as concepts according to which, "before any objective judgment, we compare concepts" (cf. A262/B317), but also as concepts according to which "before any concept of things" (cf. A269/B325), we compare *our sensible representations in general, in order to form empirical concepts to be combined according to the logical forms of judgment.* But one may raise the obvious objection that my account ends up depriving the categories of any role whatsoever.

In examining the distinction Kant draws between judgments of perception and judgments of experience, my main purpose is to answer precisely this objection. In the *Prolegomena*, Kant explicitly distinguishes between judgments formed by mere "logical connection of perceptions" (which he calls "judgments of perception") and judgments formed by application of pure concepts of the understanding (which he calls "judgments of experience"):

> In the first place we must state that while all judgments of experience are empirical (i.e., have their ground in immediate sense-perception), yet conversely, all empirical judgments are not therefore judgments of experience; but, besides the empirical and besides what is given to sensible intuition in general, special concepts must yet be added—concepts which have their origin entirely *a priori* in the pure understanding, and under which every perception must first of all be subsumed and then by their means changed into experience.
>
> Empirical judgments, so far as they have objective validity, are *judgments of experience*; but those which are only subjectively valid I name mere *judgments of perception*. The latter require no pure concept of the understanding, *but only the logical*

connection of perceptions in a thinking subject [my emphasis]. But the former always require, besides the representation of the sensible intuition, special *concepts
originally generated in the understanding*, which make the judgment of experience
objectively valid.[1]

In the "logical connection of perceptions in a thinking subject," we can recognize the operations of comparison/reflection/abstraction that, according to Kant's
Logic, are the source of all concepts as "the form required by the power of judgment." Indeed, only a few pages after the passage just cited, Kant notes that in
judgments of perception "I may merely compare perceptions and combine them
in a consciousness of my state."[2] Only subsumption of perceptions under the categories insures the "universal validity and necessity" of the judgments first
formed by mere comparison, and thus elevates them to the dignity of judgments
of experience:

> Hence it is not, as is commonly imagined, enough to yield experience to compare
> perceptions and connect them in consciousness by judging; there arises no universal
> validity and necessity, by virtue of which alone consciousness can become objec-
> tively valid and be called experience.
>
> Quite another judgment therefore is required before perception can become expe-
> rience. The given intuition must be subsumed under a concept which determines the
> form of the act of judging in general with regard to the intuition, connects the em-
> pirical consciousness of the intuition in consciousness in general, and thereby grants
> universal validity to empirical judgments. A concept of this nature is a pure *a priori*
> concept of the understanding, which does nothing but determine for an intuition the
> general way in which it can be used for judging.[3]

Kant's distinction, however, seems only to raise new difficulties. It is hard to
see how a "logical connection of perceptions" with merely subjective validity can
miraculously be endowed with universal, and therefore objective, validity by subsuming an intuition analyzed and discursively synthesized under a category.[4]
Moreover, should this claim be conceded, one would then have to wonder why
Kant himself seems to have espoused it so fleetingly. For a mere four years after
the publication of the *Prolegomena*, the distinction between judgments of per-

---

[1] *Prol.*, §18, Ak. IV, 297–98; 41.
[2] *Prol.*, §20, Ak. IV, 300; 43.
[3] Ibid.
[4] 'Universal' means here: *subjectively* universal. When we take our judgment to be *objective* (= in
conformity with the empirical object) as opposed to *subjective* (= valid only from a particular point
of view at a particular time), we claim for it *subjective* universal validity, that is, as Kant says, we
claim that it should "hold good *for us at all times, and also for everyone*" (cf. Ak. IV, 298). Similarly,
we claim for it *subjective* necessity, in that "the judgments *of other men* [should] necessarily agree
with *mine*." Now, Kant's point about judgments of experience is that we can make such a claim to *subjective* universality and necessity only if we also claim *objective* universality and necessity for our
judgment, either because we think it as being itself (objectively) universal and necessary, or because
we think it as a particular instantiation of an (objectively) universal and necessary judgment. When
Kant characterizes judgments of experience as having "strict necessity and universality," we should

ception and judgments of experience seems to disappear in favor of that between merely empirical associations and judgments, advanced in section 19 of the B Transcendental Deduction. There, all judgments, judgments as such, seem to be equated with objective thinking, whereas "subjective" combinations are confined to associative imagination alone; no place seems to remain for judgments of perception. The distinction does remain present in Kant's later writings, however: we find it expounded in *Reflexionen* and Lectures on Logic well into the 1790s, as well as in the *Logic* collated by Jäsche. But this only provides us with a new source of puzzlement. For in the latter texts, the examples Kant provides to illustrate his distinction are quite different from the ones he provides in the *Prolegomena*. In the *Prolegomena*, judgments of perception are judgments *about spatiotemporal objects*, albeit valid "only for me." In the *Logic*, on the contrary, judgments of perception appear to be judgments *about my own subjective states*. Indeed, the examples suposed to illustrate judgments of perception in the *Logic* seem closer to the empirical association in section 19 of the *Critique* than to the judgments of perception in the *Prolegomena*.

Given this apparent confusion, it is no surprise to see many commentators treat Kant's distinction with great suspicion.[5] I shall argue that the analysis I proposed of the reflective function of judgment, specified according to its logical forms, is an indispensible tool for dealing with the difficulties commonly perceived in Kant's distinction. To support my contention I will first examine in some detail the examples Kant gives in the *Prolegomena* to illustrate the transition from *judgments of perception* to *judgments of experience*. This will be the first section of the chapter. In the second, I will explain why the distinction is not mentioned

then undertand these "necessity and universality" as *both* subjective and objective, in the sense just outlined. These various aspects of Kant's view on "judgments of experience" will unfold in what follows. Note finally that this explanation puts "judgments of experience" in an interesting relation to the aesthetic judgments of the third *Critique*: the paradox presented by the latter judgments, according to Kant, is that for them we claim *subjective*, although we make no claim to *objective* universality and necessity.

[5] For instance Paul Guyer thinks that the distinction, in the *Prolegomena*, between judgments of perception and judgments of experience, belongs to the context of one of Kant's many unsuccessful attempts at providing a transcendental deduction of the categories. In this particular case Kant assumes as a premise the universal validity of some empirical judgments (the judgments he calls 'judgments of experience') and then proves the objective validity of the categories as the necessary condition for the possibility of such judgments. But, says Guyer, by making the categories the conditions for judgments of experience Kant contradicts the view he defends in the *Critique*, according to which categories are the conditions for *all* judgments, and of unity of apperception in general (*Claims*, 91–120). Similarly, Allison thinks that the distinction between judgments of perception and judgments of experience is eliminated in the second edition of the *Critique* in favor of the distinction between subjective unity of consciousness (associations of imagination) and objective unity of consciousness in judgment in general (*Idealism*, 148–53). For earlier defenses of similar views, see Cassirer, *Substance*, 279–80; Lachièze-Rey, *Idéalisme*, 311–20, and n. 2, p. 318 for a bibliography of earlier references. On the contrary, Gerold Prauss (*Erscheinung*) and Hansgeorg Hoppe (*Synthesis*) have given prominent importance to Kant's distinction. But their interpretations differ significantly from one another, and both differ from mine. See notes 26, 32, 36. Prauss gives an interesting summary of previous German and Anglo-American literature on the topic (*Erscheinung*, 139–58). Among more recent interpretations, see also Jürg Freudiger, *Wahrnehmungsurteile*; Thöle, *Gesetzmäßigkeit*, 90–95, 305–7; Mohr, *Wahrnehmungsurteile*. See also Longuenesse, *Jugements empiriques*. No interpretation before mine considers reflection according to the logical forms of judgment as the key to Kant's notion of a judgment of perception.

in section 19 of the B edition of the *Critique*. In the third, I will compare Kant's distinction in the *Prolegomena* with the explanation and examples he gives for it in the lectures and *Reflexionen* on logic. I will show how each of these texts contributes to clarifying the nature of the categories and their relation to acts of judging in general. From these explanations it will again become apparent that Kant's conception of judgment in the first *Critique* is more closely related to that of the third *Critique* than is usually suspected: this will be the conclusion of the chapter.

With this, our examination of Kant's conception of judgment as *analysis* of the sensible given will be completed. We shall then, in part III, turn to the *synthesis* that, according to Kant, necessarily precedes all analysis, and provides the ultimate ground for the objectivity of the categories.

JUDGMENTS OF PERCEPTION AND JUDGMENTS OF EXPERIENCE IN THE
PROLEGOMENA: FROM THE MERE "LOGICAL CONNECTION OF
PERCEPTIONS" TO SUBSUMPTION UNDER THE CATEGORIES

The presence of a distinction in the *Prolegomena* that is almost completely absent from Kant's other published writings needs to be understood in light of the peculiar method of this work. Kant describes it as "analytic" and opposes it to the "synthetic" method of the *Critique*.[6] By this he means that in the *Prolegomena*, unlike the *Critique of Pure Reason*, he is not trying to explain how synthetic a priori cognitions are possible by gradually building them up from their elements (forms of sensibility, categories, schemata, application of the categories in synthetic a priori judgments). Instead, he starts with the assumption that some empirical propositions have strict universality and necessity,[7] and makes it his goal to show that they presuppose conditions of possibility which must therefore be granted along with them. Hence Kant contends, first, that mathematics presupposes a priori forms of sensible intuition and, second, that natural science presupposes a priori concepts without which its judgments, however objective in their form, would remain merely subjective connections of representations (= connections of perceptions holding only for me, in the present state of my perceptions). As we saw, Kant calls these subjective connections *judgments of perception*. He calls the logical connections of perceptions whose objectivity is guaranteed by the subsumption of intuition under the categories, *judgments of experience*. Unlike the *Critique*, the *Prolegomena* contains no attempt to prove the legitimacy of such subsumption. Kant is satisfied with noting that it would be impossible to grant our judgments of experience the objectivity and universality we actually claim for them if we did not presuppose "quite another judgment . . . before perception can become experience"—that is, if we did not presuppose a principle, or rather several principles, in relation to which particular and contingent combinations of perceptions can be converted into universal and necessary connections.

[6] Cf. Ak. IV, 279; 24.
[7] Cf. note 4.

We convert our judgments, which are at first merely judgments of perception, into judgments of experience, because we presuppose other judgments applying to appearances "concepts of intuitions in general so far as these are determined in themselves, i.e., necessarily and universally, with respect to [*in Ansehung*] one or the other of [the] moments of judging."[8] Thus a judgment valid "for myself" (a judgment of perception) becomes a judgment valid "for everybody," or "in itself" (judgment of experience).

It is beneficial for purposes of clarification to abandon any attempt at justification and focus instead on the de facto components of our cognitions. This approach allows Kant to explain in some detail the difference between what judgment might be if it was left to empirical comparison alone, and by what means it becomes the assertion of a universal and necessary connection. But there are also significant drawbacks to this carefully circumscribed ambition. We are not told what makes it legitimate to subsume connected perceptions under the categories and move from judgment of perception to judgment of experience. Thus the relation between the two kinds of judgments remains obscure. The transition from one to the other—or, better, their organic unity—remains unexplained. To get such an explanation we need to return to the *Critique* and its synthetic procedure. This is what we shall do when we consider again section 19 in the B Deduction (in the next section of this chapter). I shall then show why the distinction between the two types of judgment is absent in the *Critique*, and I shall argue that this does not entail Kant intended to disavow the distinction he made in the *Prolegomena*.

To understand Kant's distinction let us first consider his examples. Kant is clearly uneasy about these illustrations, and his uneasiness is indicative of the difficulties he faced. Twice he substitutes for an earlier example another one he hopes will prove more satisfactory. We shall thus have to analyze three examples (or series of examples). The first deals with judgments of perception which, according to Kant, cannot lead to judgments of experience: 'The room is warm, sugar sweet, and wormwood unpleasant'. They have limited worth because they serve only to illustrate the first component of the distinction, the judgment of perception. Kant therefore offers another example, 'Air is elastic', to show how the transition from the first to the second type of judgment can take place. But the drawback of this example is that the same formulation is used for both types of judgment. One judgment, 'Air is elastic', alternatively expresses a "merely logical connection of perceptions" (judgment of perception) or a judgment whose objectivity is guaranteed by subsumption of the perceptions under a category. Accordingly, Kant furnishes a third and final example which seems at last to satisfy him, and which, moreover, allows him to complete the explanation of the previous one. In this last example, judgment of perception and judgment of experience are clearly distinguished by their very formulation: 'If the sun shines on the stone, it grows warm' Kant describes as a judgment of perception, 'The sun warms the stone' he describes as a judgment of experience.[9]

---

[8] *Prol.*, §21, Ak. IV, 302; 45.
[9] *Prol.*, §19, 20, Ak. IV, 299–302; 42–44.

Let us now consider each example in greater detail.

The main function of the first series of examples is to illustrate what a "merely subjective" connection of representations in a judgment may be. To this end Kant chooses predicates that can only express, he says, "my present state of perception":

When we say 'The room is warm, sugar sweet, and wormwood unpleasant', we have only subjectively valid judgments. I do not at all expect that I or any other person shall always find it as I now do; each of these sentences expresses only a reference of two sensations to the same subject, i.e., myself, and that only in my present state of perception; consequently, they are not intended to be valid of the object. Such are judgments of perception.[10]

The statements considered have the logical form of judgments. As such, like all judgments they express the relation of the concepts combined in them to a term x representing the object thought under the subject-concept. 'To this x, to which the concept "room" belongs, the concept "warm" also belongs'; 'To this x, to which the concept "sugar" belongs, the concept "sweet" also belongs'; and so on.[11] But insofar as the predicate of these judgments reflects the sensation impressed in me by the object rather than a determination holding independently of my particular state, such judgments cannot hold of the object considered in itself: "I do not at all expect that I or any other person shall always find it as I now do." The logical form of judgment, whose function is to express the relation of representations to an object, is no sufficient ground for me to claim that my judgment is actually true of the empirical object, that is, valid at all times, for every empirical subject, in any circumstances.

Interestingly, the situation described here is the same as the one portrayed in *Reflexion* 3051 analyzed in chapter 4. In this *Reflexion*, Kant states that the form of judgment expresses a combination valid for "a consciousness (in general, not only my own)." But, he continues, if a judgment is generated according to the rules of imagination only, that is, according to the rules of empirical association of subjective states, the function manifested in its form is not fulfilled.[12]

One might object that in the passage from the *Prolegomena*, Kant denies that the judgment of perception makes any claim to universal validity, and thus objectivity; so that it is inappropriate to relate it to *Reflexion* 3051 where he says that the very form of judgment carries a claim to validity for "a consciousness in general (not merely my own)." I would respond that, on the contrary, this *Reflexion*

[10] *Prol.*, §19, Ak. IV, 299; 42–43.

[11] The present examples can involve only singular judgments, since Kant describes them as logical combinations of "my *present* [*diesmaligen*] state of perception." But the other examples seem to indicate that a judgment of perception might also be a universal judgment, where the universality is not "strict universality," but mere inductive generality.

[12] Cf. *Refl.* 3051, Ak. XVI, 633: "The representation of the manner in which various concepts (as such) belong to a consciousness (in general not only my own) is judgment. They [the concepts] belong to a consciousness in part according to the laws of the imagination, and hence subjectively, or according to the laws of the understanding, that is, in a manner which is universally valid for any being possessing an understanding." Cf. chapter 4, pp. 88–90.

is in accord with the very ambiguity of the examples mentioned. Insofar as they result from acts of judging, Kant's examples tend to fulfill the function of judgments, "bringing given cognitions to the objective unity of apperception." Yet these judgments make no claim to hold at all times, for every subject, in any circumstances. For their predicate is understood as expressing a subjective state of myself at the present time. This is why they are described as mere judgments of perception.[13]

However, Kant readily acknowledges that this first series of examples is insufficient to clarify the distinction he has in mind:

> I freely grant that these examples do not represent such judgments of perception as ever could become judgments of experience, even though a concept of the understanding were superadded, because they refer merely to feeling, which everybody knows to be merely subjective and which, of course, can never be attributed to the object and, consequently, never can become objective. I only wished to give here an example of a judgment that is merely subjectively valid, containing no ground for necessary universal validity and thereby for a relation to the object.[14]

The most that could be achieved by a reflection on the judgments in Kant's examples in relation to the whole of experience would be to recognize their inalterably subjective character.

Thus if Kant's first examples clarify the nature of some at least of the judgments we may call 'judgments of perception', they teach us nothing about the move from judgments of perception to judgments of experience. To explicate this, which is what really matters to his argument, Kant provides another example:

> What experience teaches me under certain circumstances, it must always teach me and everybody; and its validity is not limited to the subject nor to its state at a particular time. Hence I pronounce all such judgments as being objectively valid. For instance, when I say the air is elastic, this judgment is as yet a judgment of perception only—I do nothing but refer two sensations in my senses to one another. But if I would have it called a judgment of experience, I require this connection to stand under a condition which makes it universally valid. I desire therefore that I and everybody else should always necessarily connect the same perceptions under the same circumstances.[15]

---

[13] One way to express the merely subjective validity of these judgments of perception would be, as Prauss suggests, to reformulate them as "sugar tastes sweet, the room feels warm, wormwood tastes bitter" (cf. *Erscheinung*, 197). However, from this Prauss concludes that these judgments are really not about the objects themselves, but about our own "subjective-private" states. But I do not think it is Kant's intention to say this, at least in the *Prolegomena*. What he intends to say is that our judgments about empirical objects are at first deprived of any claim to subjective universality, that is, objective validity, *although* they do relate given cognitions to the objective unity of apperception The most obvious case in point is the one treated in this first series of examples, that of judgments attributing to the object a predicate that really expresses a feeling of pleasure and displeasure in us. For further treatment of these examples, see pp. 190–93.

[14] *Prol.*, §19n, Ak. IV, 299; 42–43, n. 11.

[15] Ak. IV, 299–300; 43.

In this second example, one and the same judgment, with the same logical form, combining the same concepts, is raised from judgment of perception to judgment of experience. When it is "merely" a judgment of perception, it is a logical combination (i.e., a combination of concepts) that reflects an association of impressions in me, in particular circumstances at a given time. When it becomes a judgment of experience, the combination "stands under a condition that makes it universally valid," so that I claim it should hold not only for myself, now, but also for "everybody, always." What allows me to make such a claim, however, and what guarantees the objective validity of the judgment of experience, remains as yet unclear. In fact, even what is meant by the judgment 'Air is elastic' is unexplained.

In the *Metaphysical Foundations of Natural Science*, Kant calls *elasticity* one of the two fundamental properties of matter, that is, of "the moveable insofar as it *fills a space*."[16] The property of filling space is grounded in a fundamental repulsive force by which matter resists the penetration of its space by other matter and tends to expand in space. This is why repulsive force is also called force of extension, or expansive force (*Ausdehnungskraft, expansive Kraft*), or finally *elasticity*: "The expansive force of matter is also called *elasticity*. Now, since this force is the basis upon which rests the filling of space as an essential property of all matter, this elasticity must be termed *original*, because it cannot be derived from any other property of matter. All matter is, accordingly, originally elastic."[17] A mechanical device can limit the expansion of matter, as is the case for instance when air is compressed in an air pump. Thus the property of elasticity, which manifests itself as resistance of all matter to penetration, also manifests itself as the property of returning to its initial volume once a force of compression has been removed.[18]

This may give us some indication of what Kant means when he gives 'Air is elastic' as an example of judgment of perception that can become a judgment of experience. The judgment of perception expresses the "logical connection of perceptions" obtained when one generalizes the common observation that air compressed in a pump resists this compression and tends to return to its initial volume as soon as the force compressing it diminishes. When I say 'air is elastic', I may thus mean 'air *feels* resistant to compression', just like when I say 'the room is warm' I may mean 'the room *feels* warm'. In other words, I may suspend at least provisionally any claim to objective validity of my judgment, and just state how things *seem* to me. Nevertheless, to obtain such a judgment I make use of the logical function of judgment, according to its logical form, to guide the combination and comparison of my representations, and thus obtain a "logical connec-

---

[16] This is the definition of matter in the *Dynamics*. Cf. *Anfangsgründe*, II, Explication 1, Ak. IV, 496; 40.

[17] *Anfangsgründe*, Proposition 2, Note 1, Ak. IV, 500; 44–45.

[18] Ibid., Observation on Explication 3, Ak. IV, 500; 45. And General Observation on Dynamics, §3, Ak. IV, 529–30; 86–87. Here Kant is probably making use of Euler's exposition of the elasticity of air in the *Lettres à une princesse d'Allemagne* (cf. letters 9 to 14; letter 9 explains the compression of air in a pump; letter 14 explains the expansion of air because of heat). I am considering here only the use Kant makes of these examples in the context of his distinction between judgments of perception and judgments of experience. An analysis of their place in Kant's philosophy of material nature would require a different study.

tion of perceptions," namely a connection of concepts related to an object thought under the subject-concept. The judgment becomes a judgment of experience, on the other hand, when the concept 'expansion of air', or 'resistance to compression', is subsumed under the more general concept 'elasticity' or 'fundamental repulsive force', which is itself, Kant argues in the *Metaphysical Foundations*, the result of subsuming the empirical (dynamical) concept of matter under the category of causality. In fact, only a metaphysics of nature can fully justify the move from a judgment of perception to a judgment of experience. And it can do this because its own universal principles rely on a prior demonstration of the objectivity of the categories (the demonstration provided in the *Critique*) and thus on the demonstration of our *right* to convert our judgments of perception into judgments of experience. But again, in the *Prolegomena* Kant only tells us that we convert judgments of perception into judgments of experience because we de facto give ourselves this right, we de facto presuppose the universal validity of the categories under which the intuitions analyzed and combined in our particular judgment (of perception) are subsumed. For further explanation of what justifies this presupposition, we are referred to the *Critique*.

What the contribution of the *Critique* is, we shall see in a moment. The present example, however, provides an additional reason for perplexity. The judgment 'Air is elastic' is categorical. It attributes the predicate 'elastic' to the subject 'air'. We therefore expect Kant to explain that it becomes a judgment of experience by subsumption of the analyzed intuition under the category of substance or what he also calls the relation of *inherence/subsistence*. 'Air' would then be subsumed under the category of *substance*, 'elasticity' under that of *property* or *accident*. But Kant says nothing of the sort. He explains the move from the judgment of perception 'Air is elastic' to the same judgment, considered this time as a judgment of experience, by the subsumption of 'air' under the category of *cause*:

> Before, therefore, a judgment of perception can become a judgment of experience, it is requisite that the perception should be subsumed under some such [pure] concept of the understanding; *for instance, air belongs under the concept of cause, which determines our judgment about it with regard to its expansion as hypothetical.* Thereby the expansion of the air is represented, not as merely belonging to the perception of the air in my present state or in several states of mine, or in the state of perception of others, but as belonging to it *necessarily*. The judgment that air is elastic becomes universally valid and a judgment of experience *only because certain judgments precede it which subsume the intuition of air under the concepts of cause and effect*; and they thereby determine the perceptions, not merely as regards one another in me, but as regards the form of judging in general (*which is here hypothetical*), and in this way they render the empirical judgment universally valid.[19]

The unexpected privilege granted to the category of causality and hypothetical judgment can perhaps be understood in the following way. If the elasticity of air is manifested at first by its resistance to compression in a pump, or again by its

---

[19] *Prol.*, §20, Ak. IV, 301; 44–45.

tendency to increase its volume when heated, one may make use of hypothetical judgments of perception such as 'If air is heated, then it expands', or 'If air is compressed, then it resists this compression', or again 'If air ceases to be compressed, then it expands'.[20] Such judgments are mere "connections of perceptions in relation to one another, only in myself as a subject," which can in turn be generalized into 'If the *x* of my intuition is air, it tends to expand in volume'. Now, informed by the multiplicity of concurrent observations, we may conclude that the perceptions under consideration are "determined in themselves with respect to the logical form of the (hypothetical) judgment." The perceptions thought under the concept of 'air' are consequently to be subsumed under the concept of *cause*, those thought under the concept of 'expansion' under that of *effect*, and we transform our judgments of perception into judgments of experience.[21]

Giving pride of place to the hypothetical form of judgment and the corresponding category of cause is in agreement with the experimental method described in the second preface to the *Critique of Pure Reason*. It a striking fact that in this text Kant should have referred to Francis Bacon. For what we owe to Bacon, which Kant does not mention but which is, I think, the most plausible reason for his enthusiastically invoking his name immediately before those of Galileo, Torricelli, and (less felicitously) Stahl, is the explicit formulation of rules of method for testing hypotheses *concerning causal determinations*.[22] According

[20] It may be objected that these judgments are in fact composed of judgments of experience, since "resisting compression" or even "compression" contains a representation of causality. In fact it is difficult to find a judgment of perception free from any causal representation. The same remark can be made about the judgment of perception 'If the sun shines on the stone, it grows warm'. Isn't the category of causality already present in the judgment 'The sun shines on the stone'? My view is that in order to understand Kant's analysis of the move from judgment of perception to judgment of experience, we must consider not the components, but the connective in the judgment ('If . . . then'). The question then becomes, How does the merely logical combination of perceptions expressed by this connective lead to the subsumption of intuition under the corresponding category? If the judgments making up the hypothetical judgment express a causal connection ('The sun shines on the stone', 'Air is compressed', etc.), they have been generated in the same way, and then become components in a more complex judgment.

[21] We saw earlier Kant insist that the so-called inner determinations of matter are inner only in a relative sense. "All that we know in matter are merely relations, . . . but among these relations some are self-subsistent and permanent, and through these we are given a determinate object" (A285/B341). When expounding Kant's view I quoted the property of *impenetrability* as a typical exemple of an "inner" determination (a property to be attributed to all matter *nulla adjecta conditione*) which is entirely relational (known merely through relations in space, and reflected by means of hypothetical judgments expressing the state of a given matter *sub adjecta conditione*): cf. chapter 6, note 17. The same can be said of 'Air is elastic': the property of elasticity universally asserted of 'air' in a categorical judgment is a relational property first known by means of hypothetical judgments expressing the state of the air *under added conditions*. This state is itself manifested as occupation of space, that is, relation to other objects in space. We shall see, when we consider the *categories* of substance and causality and the related *principles*, that Kant similarly insists that *substance is known through causality*. See for instance A204/B249–50: "I must not leave unconsidered the empirical criterion of a substance, insofar as substance appears to manifest itself not through permanence of appearance, but more adequately and easily through action. Wherever there is action—and therefore activity and force—there is also substance, and it is in substance alone that the seat of this fruitful source of appearance must be sought." I must postpone further analysis of this point until chapter 11.

[22] Cf. Francis Bacon, *Novum Organum*, II, particularly aph. 21, 36 (on the *instantiae crucis*).

to the B preface, such a method is characteristic of reason approaching nature "holding in one hand its principles, according to which alone concordant appearances can be equivalent to laws, and in the other hand the experiment which it has devised in conformity with these principles" (Bxiii). According to the *Prolegomena* and its distinction between two kinds of empirical judgments, only a method such as this can lead us beyond judgments of perception to judgments of experience, by confronting every judgment of perception with many others whose connections constitute the totality of experience. Categorical judgments such as 'Air is elastic' can thereby also acquire the status of judgments of experience. But they require the mediation of hypothetical judgments, the true guides of an experimental method whose main goal is the discovery of causal connections.[23]

This is why the third example is ultimately the most adequate, or, in Kant's terms, "easier to understand:"

> As an easier example, we may take the following: if the sun shines on the stone, it grows warm [*Wenn die Sonne den Stein bescheint, so wird er warm*]. This judgment, however often I and others may have perceived this sequence, is a mere judgment of perception and contains no necessity; perceptions are only usually combined in this manner. But if I say: the sun warms the stone [*die Sonne erwärmt den Stein*], I add to the perception a concept of the understanding, viz., that of cause, which necessarily connects with the concept of sunshine that of heat, and the synthetic judgment becomes of necessity universally valid, viz., objective, and is converted from a perception into experience.[24]

This example is "easier to understand" than the previous one because it clearly distinguishes the logical connection and the full-fledged application of the category. The hypothetical judgment 'If the sun shines on the stone, it grows warm' results from the operations of comparison/reflection/abstraction by means of which the light of the sun is reflected as the *external condition* of the warming of the stone. As in all previous cases, the logical form already expresses a relation of representations to objects. Under the condition expressed in judgment A ('The sun shines on the stone'), judgment B can be asserted ('the stone grows warm').

---

[23] Of course, this is only the beginning of an account of judgments of experience. Once again, to understand what makes the move from empirical generalizations to strictly universal judgments possible, we need to know what, according to Kant, makes it possible to suppose that intuitions are "in themselves determined with respect to logical functions of judgment." Only the *Critique* provides this explanation and also shows why, for such universalization to occur, empirical reflection must often collaborate with mathematical construction (as shown in the example of Galileo in the B preface). These points will be considered in chapters 9 and 11. See also my paper: "Kant on Causality: What was he trying to prove?" Finally, it should be noted that Kant's reference to Bacon at Bxii–xiii is something of a paradox. For Bacon's conception of the method of empirical science is strictly inductive. Kant, on the other hand, introduces Bacon as having "partly initiated [a] discovery, partly inspired fresh vigour in those who were already on the way to it." The "discovery" in question is that of the cooperation of a priori principles and experiment in empirical science, as indicated in the text quoted earlier: the contrary of a strictly inductive method. But again, I suggest that Kant's main point here might be the role of systematically tested hypothetical judgments in generating causal judgments, that is, empirical judgments having (according to Kant) a claim to strict universality and necessity.

[24] *Prol.*, §20n, Ak. IV, 301; 44.

Nonetheless, even if the relation of assertion B to condition A is intended as a relation between *objects* reflected under concepts in the antecedent and consequent of the hypothetical judgment, the mere form of judgment is not sufficient to insure that the relation does hold of the empirical objects "in themselves." But if, in conformity with the definition of the categories, I think the intuition as "determined in relation to the form of judgment" (here, *hypothetical* judgment), then the relation this judgment expresses is not only logical but real, and the judgment 'If the sun shines on the stone, it grows warm', reflected as universally and necessarily true, can be converted into this other judgment: 'The sun warms the stone'. The latter formulation expresses the subsumption of perceptions (reflected under concepts combined in the logical form of a hypothetical judgment) under the category of causality or "concept of an object, by means of which the intuition of this object is considered as determined with respect to the logical form of [hypothetical] judgment." [25]

If the explanation I just gave is correct, in this third example the hypothetical form of the judgment of perception is of primary importance. Yet all translators render the '*wenn*' of the copula as 'when' and not 'if', even though in section 29 of the *Prolegomena* Kant makes the hypothetical form quite explicit:

> But it is possible that in perception we may meet with a rule of relation which runs thus: that a certain appearance is constantly followed by another (though not conversely); and this is a case for me to use the hypothetical judgment and, for instance, to say that if the sun shines long enough upon a body it grows warm. Here there is indeed as yet no necessity of connection, or concept of cause. But I proceed and say that if this proposition, which is merely a subjective connection of perceptions, is to be a judgment of experience, it must be regarded as necessary and universally valid. Such a proposition would be that the sun is by its light the cause of heat. The empirical rule is now considered as a law, and as valid not merely of appearances but valid of them for the purposes of a possible experience which requires universal and therefore necessarily valid rules.[26]

[25] There remains an ambiguity, however. What exactly is the judgment of experience in this case? Should 'The sun warms the stone' be understood as a universal rule, which means it would be equivalent to the judgment 'If the sun shines on the stone, it grows warm' (or "all stones, if shone upon by the sun, get warm"), where the hypothetical connection is *thought as objectively valid* (holding "for everyone, always"), that is, as reflecting a connection in the things themselves (as appearances)? Or should we understand 'The sun warms the stone' as referring to a singular case (this stone, at the present moment, is warmed by the sun)? Then its meaning would be that of the entire syllogism 'If the sun shines on the stone, it grows warm; now, the sun, at the present moment, is shining on this stone, here; therefore, this stone grows warm', in which the major premise is considered once again as expressing a connection in the things themselves—and thus as being valid "for everybody, always." As we shall see in chapter 11, this second sense would agree with Kant's understanding of causal connection. Thinking a causal connection in any given case is thinking an event as *taking place in conformity with a universal rule*. On this point, see also Longuenesse, "Logique et Métaphysique"; and "Causality."

[26] *Prol.*, §29, Ak. IV, 312; 54–55. Here the translator renders "*wenn*" as "if," which is obviously correct since Kant describes the judgment as hypothetical. But why then should the same "*wenn*" be translated as "when" in the first occurrence of the example (§20n)? True, the German language maintains an ambiguity that cannot be preserved in English: *wenn* may mean "when" as well as "if." In-

The judgment of perception analyzes repeated temporal succession into a discursive connection between antecedent and consequent of a hypothetical judgment. But this connection is weak, because insufficiently determined. The most it expresses is that if the sun shining on the stone is among the objects I perceive at a given time, the stone getting warm is among the objects I perceive at a succeeding time. But the relation of ground to consequence is so far a mere "logical connection of perceptions" which remains to be further determined. This will be done by confronting the correlations already obtained with many more, while perhaps also using the resources of mathematical construction to anticipate and test further possible empirical correlations. Only after such a method has been systematically applied can a causal connection be asserted: 'the sun warms the stone'.[27]

If the analyses just proposed are correct, Kant's distinction between judgments of perception and judgments of experience in the *Prolegomena*, and his statement that judgments of perception are "the logical connection of perceptions," confirm the thesis that I have been advocating. Empirical judgments are formed by operations of comparison/reflection/abstraction by means of which empirical perceptions and their reproductive associations are reflected under concepts combined in judgment. Judgments of experience occur when the intuitions so analyzed are subsumed under the categories.

But as I said earlier, this distinction between a "merely subjective" and an "objective" connection in judgment may seem blatantly to contradict the B edition of

deed, Kant gives systematic significance to this linguistic ambiguity: in the Second Analogy of Experience, he argues that whenever we perceive a temporal succession as objective, we make implicit use of the hypothetical form of judgment, because we suppose a rule (unknown to us) for the temporal succession. The presence of this implicit, unreflected rule in the perception of a particular case of objective succession explains that a succession that has become *customary* should give rise to hypothetical judgment (transition from "when," which might refer to a mere association of imagination, to "if," a logical connection) and then eventually to a hypothetical judgment for which we claim universal validity: the representation of a causal connection. The argument of the Second Analogy will be analyzed in detail in chapter 11. In any case, hesitancy to translate *wenn* by "if," in Kant's example of judgment of perception, is significant of a widespread resistance to the very idea of a "judgment of perception." The same problem occurs with French translations, and most German commentators have the same misgivings with respect to the nature of logical connection in judgments of perception. Here are two examples. Cassirer wrote that in judgment of perception, "we establish only the coexistence of two contents, without setting them in any relation of mutual dependence" (*Substance*, 245). More recently, Prauss declared that "according to Kant's own doctrine, a hypothetical judgment such as 'If the sun shines on the stone, it grows warm', however it is understood, can be valid only as a judgment of experience, bearing on objects [*das über objektive Gegenstände urteilt*], not subjective appearances [*über subjektive Erscheinungen*]" (*Erscheinung*, 180). He concluded that Kant was unable to find a satisfactory formulation for judgments of perception (181). Both Prauss's and Cassirer's positions will be discussed later.

[27] Michael Friedman has pointed out to me that in this regard Kant's third example is far from trivial. According to Friedman, Kant has in mind Wilhelm Scheele's theory of radiant heat presented in his *Chemische Abhandlung von der Luft und dem Feuer* of 1777. I gratefully quote Friedman's written indication to me: "Scheele discovered that in addition to ordinary conduction and convection, heat is also communicated in *rays* obeying the laws of geometrical optics (reflection and refraction). At normal temperatures these rays are not visible—they fall in what we now call the infra-red part of the spectrum. At high temperatures such as those of the sun, however, rays of radiant heat fall in the visible part of the spectrum—light rays themselves become rays of radiant heat. Hence, that the sun is

the Transcendental Deduction, according to which the logical form of judgment expresses "the relation of given cognitions to the objective unity of apperception." Many commentators thus conclude that Kant had no choice but to renounce a distinction fundamentally incompatible with the transcendental deduction of the categories. According to them, section 19 of the *Critique* substitutes for the distinction between judgments of perception and judgments of experience that between empirical associations of imagination, on the one hand, and on the other hand judgment *in general*, which by virtue of its logical form alone expresses a claim to objective validity. I shall argue, on the contrary, that the distinction put forth in the *Prolegomena* is not contradicted by the argument of the B Deduction, but rather contributes to clarifying its actual import.

JUDGMENT IN SECTION 19 OF THE *CRITIQUE*

From Kant's distinction between judgments of perception and judgments of experience we can conclude that even though every judgment expresses the relation of representations to objects, this relation may remain "subjective" if it expresses connections holding only "for myself," "in the present state of my perception." This cautionary assessment of the function of judgment should be kept in mind when we read Kant's definition of judgment as "the form of the objective unity of apperception" in section 19 of the B Deduction. Indeed, immediately after propounding this definition, Kant emphasizes the empirical conditions under which objective unity of apperception is realized.

> A judgment is nothing but the manner in which given cognitions are brought to the objective unity of apperception. This is what is intended by the copula 'is'. It is employed to distinguish the objective unity of given representations from the subjective. It indicates their relation to original apperception and its *necessary unity*. It holds good *even if the judgment is itself empirical and therefore contingent, as for example in the judgment 'Bodies are heavy'*. (B141–42)

As I suggested in chapter 4, a judgment such as 'Bodies are heavy' may be at first only a judgment of perception (where it really means "bodies *feel* heavy").[28] But like the judgment 'Air is elastic' in the *Prolegomena*, it can become a judgment of experience if the intuition reflected under concepts in the empirical judgment

---

through its light the cause of heat is a highly non-trivial proposition. It is based on Scheele's experimental investigation and thereby brought into connection with the mathematics of geometrical optics." I should add that the example of sunshine, stone, and heat was previously used by Wolff as an example of hypothetical judgment, and by Aristotle as an example of causal relation. Kant's notion of a "judgment of experience" is broader, I think, than the contemporary scientific discovery cited by Friedman. The latter is simply the most sophisticated development he would have available. I shall argue later that the *Prolegomena*'s distinction is in many cases a relative one: most empirical judgments combine the contribution of mere empirical associations of imagination, of understanding or *Vermögen zu urteilen*, and of *Urteilskraft*, which subsumes logically connected perceptions under the categories.

[28] See chapter 4, p. 83.

is also subsumed under a category. In the case of 'Air is elastic', the judgment of perception becomes a judgment of experience when the logically connected perceptions are subsumed under the concept 'force of repulsion', which is itself thought under the concept of cause. In the case of 'All bodies are heavy', the logically connected perceptions can be subsumed under the concept 'force of attraction', which is itself thought under the concept of cause. All that matters in the context of section 19 is that, whatever the status of the empirical judgment, that is, even if it is a mere judgment of perception, *insofar as it is a judgment* it is to be related to the original unity of apperception.

The modal determinations in the passage cited are puzzling. What exactly does Kant mean when he says that the unity of apperception, to which the copula 'is' tends to bring given cognitions, is "necessary"? What does he mean by the "contingent" character that may nevertheless pertain to empirical judgment? I think that one important step toward clarifying Kant's intention here is to recognize that *necessity* and *contingency* characterize on the one hand the *act* of synthesis necessary for any judgment to occur, on the other hand the *propositions* that result from this act.

1. *Necessity of the act.* For all our representations to relate to objects, *one and the same act* of synthesis *must* combine them. As we saw, this has been stated in the initial paragraphs of the B Deduction, and in greater detail in the A Deduction.[29] In section 15 of the B Deduction, for instance, Kant wrote: "This act [of spontaneity] is original and *must be* the same for all combination [*und für alle Verbindung gleichgeltend sein müsse*], and . . . its dissolution, analysis, which seems to be its contrary, always presupposes it" (B131, emphasis mine). And again, in section 16: "This principle of the *necessary* unity of apperception . . . reveals *the necessity of a synthesis* of the manifold given in intuition" (B135, emphasis mine). When Kant says in section 19 that the copula 'is' is employed to express "the relation [of given representations] to original apperception and its *necessary unity*," what is described as *necessary* is first the very fact *that* there is unity of an act, as he argued in the previous sections. Note also that the necessity at stake here is neither logical necessity, nor the *category* of necessity (which applies only to empirical objects given in space and time). It is the necessity of a transcendental condition, here the necessity of the unified act that conditions any representation of object. Now, which *empirical* acts of judging result from this (necessary) transcendental condition being satisfied remains contingent with respect to it. Empirical acts of judging do not derive from the transcendental unity of apperception alone but depend on the individual or collective histories of empirical cognitive subjects in their relation to what is given to them in the forms of space and time.

2. Necessity of the *propositions* resulting from the act. The a priori principles that derive from the necessary unity of apperception are themselves *necessary* propositions, propositions expressing combinations of appearances that cannot fail to occur whenever an empirical object is represented. This, I think, is what Kant indicates when he writes:

[29] Cf. chapter 3, pp. 61–64.

Representations . . . belong to one another in virtue of the necessary unity of apperception in the synthesis of intuition, *that is, according to principles of the objective determination of all representations, insofar as knowledge can be acquired by means of these representations—principles which are all derived from the fundamental principle of the transcendental unity of apperception.* (B142, my emphasis)

For instance, by virtue of the relation of all objective representations to the necessary (necessity 1) unity of apperception, we can assert as necessary (necessity 2) the following propositions (which will be demonstrated in the Analytic of Principles, and analyzed in part III of this work): "all appearances are extensive magnitudes" (principle of the axioms of intuition); "all appearances are intensive magnitudes" (principle of the anticipations of perception); "all alterations in appearances occur according to the law of connection of cause and effect" (second analogy of experience); and so on. By contrast with these propositions, empirical judgments are *contingent* in that their truth depends on empirical data for which we can imagine any number of alternative possibilities. Even the Newtonian law of gravitation is *contingent* in this sense, in that a world of objects perceivable and knowable by us (by virtue of the unity of apperception and its discursive and intuitive forms) *could be* a world where attraction was not a fundamental property of matter, or where gravitation failed to obey the inverse square law. On the contrary, the causal law (enunciated by Kant as the principle of the Second Analogy of Experience) is *necessary* in that (assuming Kant's proofs are correct) a world of objects perceivable and knowable by us *could not be* a world where an event occurred without being causally determined.

In short, the *necessity* Kant mentions in section 19 is (1) the necessity, as a condition for cognition of objects, of the original unity of apperception and its forms of judgment and (2) the derived necessity of the propositions expressing the combinations of appearances resulting from the unity of apperception. The *contingency* is (1) the contingency (with respect to the original unity of apperception) of empirical acts of judging and (2) the contingency of the propositions expressing the empirical properties of matter. I think that keeping in mind these two meanings for necessity and contingency is by itself quite sufficient to understand Kant's argument in section 19 of the B deduction. However, the situation becomes more complex if we try to relate what Kant says in section 19 to his characterization of empirical judgments in the *Prolegomena*. In the latter text, Kant does not simply associate *necessity* with the original unity of apperception and *contingency* with empirical judgments. He makes quite clear that subsuming appearances under categories in judgments of experience results in empirical judgments which themselves "contain necessity." In a footnote to section 22 of the *Prolegomena*, Kant readily grants the difficulty of such a position: "But how does the proposition that judgments of experience contain necessity in the synthesis of perceptions agree with my statement so often before inculcated that experience, as cognition *a posteriori*, can afford contingent judgments only?" His response:

When I say that experience teaches me something, I mean only the perception that lies in experience—for example, that heat always follows the shining of the sun on a stone; consequently, the proposition of experience is always so far contingent. That

this heat necessarily follows the shining of the sun is contained indeed in the judgment of experience (by means of the concept of cause), yet is a fact not learned by
experience; for, conversely, experience is first of all generated by this addition of the
concept of the understanding (of cause) to perception. How perception attains this
addition may be seen by referring in the *Critique* itself to the section on the transcendental power of judgment [*Urteilskraft*], B176 *et seq.*[30]

The necessity Kant is talking about here is the necessity of the *connection* between the light of the sun and the heat of the stone. Hence, Kant does claim not
only that (1) unity of apperception is necessary, and that (2) the universal principles based upon it are necessary propositions, but also that (3) some empirical
propositions (judgments of experience), although contingent with respect to the
unity of apperception, express a necessary connection (between light of the sun
and heat of the stone; between impenetrability of the air and its expansion; between attraction of the earth and free fall of the body; and so on); and so are themselves, as propositions, necessary in a third sense. Kant claims, moreover, that
these empirical propositions express necessary connection when they apply categories to empirical objects. And we proceed to such an application because "experience is first of all generated by . . . addition of the concept of the understanding . . . to perception." However, if we ask how this is so, then Kant makes clear,
in the text just cited, that the answer to this question is given not in the *Prolegomena*, nor indeed in the Transcendental Deduction, but in the Schematism and
System of Principles of the *Critique of Pure Reason.*[31]

We shall therefore have to postpone consideration of the necessity proper to
empirical judgments until we examine the Principles of Pure Understanding, in
part III of this work. The present remarks at least suggest again that as far as section 19 of the Deduction is concerned, it is sufficient for Kant's purpose to state
that empirical judgments, *even if they are contingent* (i.e., without the question of
their specific brand of necessity even being raised at this point), are "related to
original apperception and its necessary unity."[32]

[30] *Prol.* §22n, Ak. IV, 305; 305, n. 15. Kant's reference to the *Critique* sends us to the chapter on
the Schematism of the Pure Concepts of the Understanding, which opens the Analytic of Principles.

[31] In "Causal Laws and Natural Science," Friedman shows how Kant's analysis of the passage from
Kepler's laws to Newton's universal law of gravitation, in the Phenomenology of the *Metaphysical
Foundations of Natural Science*, illustrates the passage from mere empirical regularities to necessary
causal laws (see "Causal Laws," 175–80). His analysis is illuminating in that it shows what Kant
means when he claims that only application of the categories makes possible the representation of
strictly universal *empirical* laws. But it does not answer the question, *what is it that legitimates the
application of the categories?* In other words, Friedman does not address the question '*quid juris ?*'
proper to the *Critique*. The answer to this question is given in the Transcendental Deduction of the
Categories, and the full development of this answer for each of the categories is provided in the
Schematism and Principles of Pure Understanding.

[32] The position I am advancing here bears some resemblance to that defended by Hansgeorg Hoppe
in his book, *Synthesis bei Kant.* I have distinguished the point of view of §19 of the *Critique*, in which
what is considered is the logical function of judgment in general as the function relating representations to objects, and the point of view of the *Prolegomena*, where Kant distinguishes among our empirical judgments those that are (empirically) subjective (i.e., valid only "for me, in the present state
of my perceptions") and those that are (empirically) objective (i.e., valid "for everybody, always").
Similarly, Hoppe argues that Kant makes use of two different notions of "objectivity" and "subjectiv-

Already in section 18, that is, before the logical form of judgment is even mentioned, Kant insists that the empirical unity of consciousness, however dependent it may be on particular empirical conditions, and therefore however subjective and contingent, nevertheless results from the objective unity of apperception:

> Whether I can become *empirically* conscious of the manifold as simultaneous or as successive depends on circumstances or empirical conditions. Therefore the empirical unity of consciousness, through association of representations, itself concerns an appearance and is wholly contingent. But the pure form of intuition in time, merely as intuition in general which contains a given manifold, is subject to the original unity of consciousness, simply through the necessary relation of the manifold of the intuition to the one '*I think*', and so through the pure synthesis of understanding *which is the a priori underlying ground of the empirical synthesis*. Only the original unity is objectively valid; the empirical unity of apperception, upon which we are not here dwelling, *and which besides is merely derived from the former under given conditions in concreto*, has only subjective validity (B139–40; my emphasis on the last two sentences).

Here are some examples to illustrate the relation between empirical unity of apperception and the original unity from which it is derived. I am "empirically conscious of the manifold as simultaneous" when the stars appear to be shining simultaneously in the sky. I am "empirically conscious of the manifold as successive" when the sun appears successively in different positions or when I hear thunder after seeing lightning. In each case, the temporal determinations I assign to objects "depend on circumstances or empirical conditions" in which I find myself as an empirical subject. These temporal determinations constitute the empirical unity of my consciousness. But they "concern only appearances" not in the transcendental sense in which every empirical object is an appearance, but in the empirical sense in which what I perceive is "only" an appearance, for which judg-

---

ity", one Hoppe calls "categorial" (*kategorial*), the other "factual" (*faktisch*). "Categorial" objectivity is the intentional relation of representations to objects in general. "Categorial" subjectivity is the lack of any such relation (characterizing mere perceptual "flux"). "Factual" (*faktische*) objectivity and subjectivity *both* characterize representations that are "categorially" objective, that is, that bear intentional relation to objects in general. But this relation may remain (factually) subjective, dependent on the particular situation of the empirical subject (this is the case in judgments of perception); or it may be (factually) objective, as in intersubjectively valid scientific knowledge (judgments of experience) (see *Synthesis*, 5). Hoppe claims, however, that Kant does not hold consistently to his distinction between the two standpoints, and that this failure results in confusions in his handling of modal categories (48). The distinction between categorial and empirical standpoints is clear in §19 of the *Critique*: according to Hoppe, the *necessity* of the objective unity of apperception is *categorial*, the *contingency* of empirical judgments is *factual*. But the distinction is blurred in the *Prolegomena*, where the confusion between the two standpoints results in the openly contradictory statement that judgments of experience are both *necessary* and *contingent* (50–51). I agree with Hoppe on the distinction of standpoints (but differ from him in the importance I give, in explicating this distinction, to the role played by the logical function of judgment). I disagree with his charge that Kant's characterization of judgments of experience as contingent but expressing a necessary connection rests on a confusion of the two standpoints (although there is certainly difficulty accounting for the nature of this "necessity." For a unified account of the necessity of empirical judgments, see my "Logique et métaphysique" and "Causality." See also chapter 11, pp. 374–75.

ments of experience will determine the (empirical) thing-in-itself.[33] But even if the empirical appearance is subjective and contingent, it nonetheless depends on the *objective* unity of consciousness by means of which I am conscious of all simultaneity or succession in objects. This is why "the pure form of intuition in time [alone . . .] is objectively valid." Temporal relations of simultaneity and succession in general are objective. They are the very (sensible) form of empirical objectivity, even if their empirical "filling" is subjective, that is, even if I attribute succession to the positions of the sun, permanence to my own position, and simultaneity to the stars by virtue of the "circumstances or empirical conditions" in which I happen to perceive these objects.

Similarly, the logical form of judgment expresses relation to an object even if this form is "filled" in an empirical, contingent, and (empirically) subjective manner. The similarity I am stressing here between section 18 and section 19 is not fortuitous. Kant's purpose in section 19 is to argue that the logical form of judgment is precisely the *discursive (analytic) form* of the objective unity of apperception whose *intuitive (synthetic) form* he described in section 18 as preceding and determining all empirical-subjective unity of consciousness. This is what allows him to conclude in section 20 that the unity of empirical intuition, insofar as it necessarily stands under the original unity of apperception (as stated in sections 17 and 18), also stands under the logical form of judgment (section 19), *and thereby under the categories*, since the latter are nothing other than "concepts of an object in general, insofar as the intuition of that object is considered as determined with respect to one of the logical functions of judgments" (section 14), or "pure synthesis, universally represented." (section 10).[34] Note that I am *not* arguing that the synthetic unity of apperception, from which in section 18 empirical unity of consciousness is said to be derived, *already has the form of a discursive judgment.* What I am arguing is that the empirical unity of consciousness, which "concerns merely an appearance, is contingent and merely subjective" (section 18), depends on the original synthetic (intuitive) unity *just as* the judgment of perception that will eventually reflect it under concepts depends on the original unity of apperception, whose (discursive) form is judgment. And this is so because the empirical unity of consciousness is that initial unity produced in our representations with a view to reflecting them under concepts in empirical judgments.

To be sure, Kant's demonstration is incomplete at this point. We have no idea how the discursive unity of judgment is supposed to guide the unification of a sensible given which is not discursive but intuitive. Section 19 needs to be complemented with what Kant himself describes as the final step of the transcendental deduction, the explanation of "the possibility of cognizing *a priori* by means of *categories* whatever objects may *present themselves to our senses*" (B159).

---

[33] Another example of appearances in the *empirical* sense is that given in the Transcendental Aesthetic: the rainbow, for which the (empirical) "in itself" is the diffraction of light in the drops of rain (cf. A45–46/B62–63). In other words, by appearances we must here understand objects that are empirically given outside us (in space) although we cognize only the manner in which they appear to us in particular empirical circumstances.

[34] See §14, B128; §10, A78/B104. Cf. also §20, B143.

The need for such an explanation can be fully grasped only if one remembers that the categories, insofar as they are mere logical functions of judgment, are *discursive* functions, forms of *combination of concepts*. How can a discursive function enable us to cognize "whatever may be present to our senses," that is, what is present in forms (space and time) whose synthesis, if Kant is right, is quite different from a discursive synthesis such as that described in Kant's logical forms of judgment? This is the question section 26 of the Transcendental Deduction will have to answer.

Whatever the outcome of this second part of Kant's argument, we should by now have a better view of the difference between Kant's argument in section 19 of the *Critique* and in the *Prolegomena*. The issue in section 19 is the form of judgment as the form of the objective unity of apperception in general. This form is present in all judgments, whether they are judgments of perception, however (empirically) subjective they may be, or judgments of experience, which alone are (empirically) objective. In fact, our capacity to judge carries within its very forms (the logical forms of judgment, specified according to quantity, quality, relation) the norms that drive us to progress from judgments of perception to judgments of experience. The search for rules, which generates the "merely logical combination" of our perceptions in judgments, also eventually generates discursive connections "valid for all, always"—that is, empirically objective connections, judgments of experience. This is why Kant concludes that were it not for the original objective function of judgment "I could say only : 'if I carry a body, I feel a pressure of weight' and not: 'it, the body, is heavy', which means the same as: these two representations are linked in the object, whatever the state of the subject, and are not merely together in perception (however often it is repeated)."

This is a clear rejection of Humean associationism. What is not so clear is how exactly this rejection should be understood. There are two possible readings, the second, I think, more plausible than the first.

Here is the first. If we did not have objective unity of consciousness as an original capacity manifested in the form of our judgments, Hume's account of the combinations of our perceptions would be the only possible one. We would have to admit that empirical imagination produces customary associations of perceptions, which can be expressed discursively in combinations of ideas having merely nominal universality. But such associations could never give rise to judgments such as "It, the body, is heavy." "However often they be repeated," conjunctions of perceptions would give rise only to the discursive expression of their combinations in my subjective state, not in the object. Thus we could say only (we would be *able to* say only): "If I carry a body, I feel a pressure of weight," where the "if . . . then" expresses nothing more than the repeated conjunction (and thus expected joint repetition) of states of myself. Such an account, then, could not explain the actual form of our judgments, which do not relate my states to myself, but marks to objects. This incapacity of the empiricist genesis of the combinations of representations to account for the actual form of our judgments would thus be an additional argument in favor of the Kantian account of judgment, which makes every empirical judgment derive from an original capacity and not merely from empirical associations.

I think such a reading is implausible because, of course, Hume does have a story to tell about how we come to believe that our impressions and ideas represent properties of objects "whatever the state of the subject." He also has a story to tell about why we accordingly express the combinations of our impressions and ideas in the form of judgments expressing the relation of general marks to objects ("it, the body, is heavy").[35]

But Kant's text can be read another way, that does not make it an attempt at refuting Hume (the actual refutation starts earlier and ends later in the *Critique*, and depends on more than a mere consideration of the grammatical form of our judgments). On this second reading, Kant's concern is rather *what would result* if an associationist account of empirical judgment were the right one. If the form of our empirical judgments were not the form of the original objective unity of apperception—if instead empirical judgments were merely the result of empirical associations of imagination—then we would have to surrender to Hume's skeptical views. We would have to acknowledge that our judgments are deceptive when they express as objective connections what are really mere subjective expectations arising from habitual conjunctions. Where these expectations find expression in a judgment such as 'it, the body, is heavy', we could say only 'if I carry a body, I feel a pressure of weight'. 'We *could* say' here means 'we would *legitimately* say', or 'we would *be warranted* in saying'. This phrase does not express an incapacity (the incapacity even to utter a judgment such as 'it, the body, is heavy') that would condemn the empiricist account of the genesis of judgment, but merely the recommendation, inspired by empiricist-skeptical wisdom, to withdraw the illusory objectifications conveyed by our judgments, and to adopt instead the only formulation expressing what a Humean empiricist thinks we truly perceive: 'if I carry a body, I feel a pressure of weight'.

It is of course tempting to see in this confrontation between the two formulations ('it, the body, is heavy', and 'if I carry a body, I feel a pressure of weight') an echo of the distinction made in the *Prolegomena* between judgments of perception and judgments of experience. All the more so since Kant specifies that the meaning of the objective form, 'it, the body, is heavy', is that "[the] two representations are linked in the object, whatever the state of the subject," whereas the formulation of empirical association, "if I carry a body, I feel a pressure of weight" is said to hold "only in my perception." Because of the striking resemblance between these formulations and the way judgments of perception and judgment of experience are characterized in the *Prolegomena*, it is tempting to think that Kant here renounces the opposition between two kinds of judgment in favor of the opposition between mere empirical association and judgment. But I think this interpretation is mistaken because again, the *Critique* and the *Prolegomena* obey a different purpose. In the *Prolegomena*, Kant distinguishes between two types of empirical judgments. In the *Critique*, he shows what the combinations of our perceptions would be in the absence of a function of judging that we could consider as *original*, what they would be if our judgments merely derived from empirical associations. Then our representations would have no other

---

[35] Cf. Hume: *Treatise*, bk. I, pt. III, sect. 9, 108; bk. I, pt. IV, sec. 2.

connection than those derived from subjective associations, and the only adequate formulation for these combinations would be such as 'if I carry a body, I feel . . .' No combination would be adequately expressed by 'it, the body, is heavy', since no combination would hold "whatever the state of the subject," that is, as a judgment of experience. The *Critique* does not make use of the distinction of the *Prolegomena* because it opposes not two types of empirical judgments, but two origins of judgment. One origin would result in the fact that judgment is the expression of mere association according to laws of imagination (= Humean reduction of judgment, which indeed would oblige us to consider all our judgments as mere judgments of perception; it may explain the proximity in formulations between the two texts). The other origin, the one Kant argues for, relates judgment back to the original function of judging. It alone can explain the possibility for us to obtain those empirically objective judgments Kant calls, in the *Prolegomena*, "judgments of experience."

However, for my argument to be complete I still need to confront the explanations given in the *Prolegomena* with another series of texts in which Kant develops in some detail the distinction between the two types of judgment: Kant's *Reflexionen* and lectures on logic, and the *Logic* collated by Jäsche. These texts seem to contradict the *Prolegomena*, because the examples of judgments of perception they provide no longer attribute marks to empirical objects, but our own subjective states to ourselves. Only judgments of experience are presented as applying concepts to independent empirical objects. Gerold Prauss relies mainly on these texts to support his own interpretation of Kant's distinction. For him, judgments of perception are those particular judgments whose objects are our own "subjective-private" states of consciousness, whereas only judgments of experience express the attribution of properties to objects. Prauss concludes that in the *Prolegomena*, Kant does not provide adequate examples for the distinction he is trying to draw. According to him, only the *Logic* (in agreement with section 19 of the *Critique*!) provides adequate formulations for judgments of perception.[36] I shall argue, on the contrary, that just as the *Prolegomena* and the *Critique* could be shown to be in agreement once the difference in their perspective and method is taken into account, so the *Logic* can be shown to be in agreement with both *Critique* and *Prolegomena* if one takes into account its particular perspective and method.

JUDGMENTS OF PERCEPTION AND JUDGMENTS OF EXPERIENCE IN
THE *LOGIC:* FROM UNCRITICIZED OBJECTIFICATIONS
TO THEIR CORRECTIONS

It should first be remembered that the *Prolegomena* and the *Logic* are texts of a very different nature. The former was written and published by Kant himself, and the distinction between the two kinds of judgment plays an important role in the

---

[36] Cf. Prauss, *Erscheinung*, 175–88.

development of its argument. The latter, in contrast, is only a textbook put together by a student, albeit with Kant's consent. Here the distinction between the two kinds of judgment is mentioned only in passing and has no demonstrative function. Indeed, strictly speaking this distinction is not relevant to logic, since its function is to sort out what is empirical and what is a priori in our empirical judgments. The problem at stake is thus one of *origin*, and Kant characterizes such problems as metaphysical, not logical. Why, then, does he nevertheless mention this distinction, not only in the *Jäsche Logic* but also in most versions of his logic lectures and in the *Reflexionen* on logic? One reason may be that it takes the place of Meier's distinction between *intuitive* and *discursive judgments*.[37] And it is not unusual to see Kant in his lectures go beyond the boundaries he has set for general or formal logic and provide broader epistemological or metaphysical views.[38]

Nevertheless, the *Logic* does provide an original standpoint on judgments of perception and judgments of experience, a standpoint distinct from that of the *Prolegomena*. This, in my view, explains the difference in formulation between the two texts. In the *Logic*, Kant first gives a characterization of the two kinds of judgments which simply restates what was said in the *Prolegomena* ("A *judgment of perception* is merely *subjective*, an objective judgment from perceptions is a *judgment of experience*").[39] Then he goes on to provide not only examples, but also an intimation of the proper formulation of each kind of judgment:

[37] Cf. Meier, *Auszug*, §§313–23, Ak. XVI, 667–78. *Intuitive* judgments are judgments of "immediate experience," expressing what is immediately given to our senses. *Discursive* judgments are deduced by reasoning, whether a priori (purely rational judgments) or from "mediated experience," that is, depending ultimately on intuitive judgments. Kant's *judgments of perception* take over from Meier's *intuitive judgments*. In *Reflexionen* from the 1750s, Kant adopts Meier's distinction, but rejects as illusory the *immediate experience* Meier associates with intuitive judgments. Only singular things, says Kant, are objects of immediate experience (i.e., sensation). As for intuitive judgments, they do not express immediate experiences since they contain abstract concepts (cf. esp. *Refl.* 3138, Ak. XVI, 674). Only in later *Reflexionen* does the term '*judgment of perception*' replace '*intuitive judgment*' (*Refl.* 3145, 3146 [1790s], Ak. XVI, 678–79). In *Logik Dohna-Wundlacken* (1790s) we still find the two terms used as equivalent: "A judgment of perception is intuitive (not discursive). An empirical judgment is intuitive, but experience is nonetheless discursive" (Ak. XXIV-2, 767; 499). However, in his critical period Kant mainly uses the expression 'intuitive judgment' for pure mathematical judgments. *Judgments of experience* replace Meier's *discursive judgments of mediate experience*. What is interesting here is that Kant no longer gives primary emphasis, in the notion of experience, to sensuous immediacy (like in Meier's judgments of immediate experience), but to *discursive* connection of perceptions. The *Inaugural Dissertation* may be the turning point in Kant's use of the term 'experience': "But in the case of sensible things and phenomena [*phaenomenis*], what precedes the logical use of the understanding is called *appearance* [*apparentia*], while the reflective cognition, which arises when several appearances are compared by the understanding, is called *experience*. Thus, there is no way from appearance to experience, except by reflection in accordance with the logical use of the understanding [*Ab apparentia itaque ad experientiam via non est, nisi per reflexionem secundum usum intellectum logicum*]" (§5, Ak. II, 394; 386).

[38] Cf. *Logik Blomberg*, §319 (Ak. XXIV-1, 280; 225): "Now it belongs to metaphysics to investigate whether a judgment is a judgment of experience or not." The same held for the distinction between synthetic and analytic judgments, for the determination of the origin of concepts, and so on. These topics all belong, according to Kant, to metaphysics. Yet all are at least mentioned in the logic.

[39] *Logik*, §40, Ak. IX, 113; 608.

A judgment from mere perceptions *is not really possible* [*ist nicht wohl möglich*], except through the fact that I declare my representation *as perception*. I, who perceive a tower, perceive in it the red color. But *I cannot say: It is red*. For this would not be merely an empirical judgment, but a *judgment of experience*, i.e. an empirical judgment through which I get a concept of the object.[40]

Such normative remarks fulfill the proper aim of a general or formal logic, which is not to expound the manner in which we think, but the manner in which we *should* think, and so too the manner in which we should *speak* in order to give our thought its proper grammatical expression. Whereas the way we speak tends to endorse and fix the uncriticized objectifications produced by an understanding influenced by "the laws of imagination," logical reflection on the contrary counters the influence of imagination, provides the judgment of perception with an adequate grammatical form, and reserves the grammatical form of objective judgment for a thought that proceeds "according to the rules of the understanding."[41]

This is what we saw in the text cited earlier. According to the *Prolegomena*, a judgment of perception is a judgment in which the logical connection of my perceptions holds only "for myself, in my present state of perception." According to the *Logic*, it is therefore optimally expressed only if it is given a grammatical form exhibiting the fact that the marks we "naturally" attribute to the object are actually relative to the empirical subject. A judgment of perception is not entitled to the logical form of a judgment relating concepts to an object. Until it has become a judgment of experience, it must be cut down to the more modest claims of a mere coordination of perceptions. Instead of the grammatical form '(every, some, this) A (are, is) B', developed by Kant as, 'To (every, some, this) x, to which concept A belongs, concept B also belongs', we must resort to the form proper to subjective association, 'I, who perceive x (s) as A, also perceive it (them) as B' ('I, who perceive a tower, also perceive it as red', 'When touching the stone, I feel warmth').

Interestingly, this suggestion agrees with what Kant says in *Reflexion* 3051 examined in chapter 4 and mentioned earlier in this chapter.[42] According to this *Reflexion*, the logical form of judgment, as concept subordination, expresses that these concepts belong to "a consciousness in general (not only my own)." However, insofar as they are related to *my* consciousness *alone*, concepts can be only *coordinated* (like sensations): they are merely associated in my subjective state. When examining *Reflexion* 3051, I compared Kant's distinction between concept

---

[40] Ibid., note; 608–9 (my emphasis on "is not really possible" and "I cannot say"). The same formulation can be found in *Reflexion* 3145 (1790s), which Jäsche probably used (Ak. XVI, 678).

[41] *Logik*, introd. I, Ak. IX, 16; 531. Logic is "a science of the correct use of the understanding and of reason in general, not subjectively, however, i.e., not according to empirical (psychological) principles for how the understanding does think, but objectively, i.e., according to principles *a priori* for how it ought to think." Kant says little about the relation between thought and language, between logic and grammar. The chapter on "Judgment" has only this remark: "Without words, one would not judge at all." But the text quoted earlier, like others I will mention later, clearly indicates that among the functions of logical reflection is setting rules for the proper use of language.

[42] See note 13. And Ak. XVI, 633.

subordination (judgment) and coordination of sensations, with the distinction he makes in section 19 of the *Critique* between judgment and empirical association. Similarly, the examples of empirical association on the one hand ('When I support a body, I feel a pressure of weight') and judgment on the other hand ('It, the body, is heavy'), given in the *Critique*, are identical to the examples of judgment of perception in "normalized" form ('I, who perceive a tower, perceive in it the red color'; 'In touching the stone I sense warmth') and judgment of experience ('The tower is red'; 'The stone is warm') given in the *Logic*. As I suggested earlier when analyzing section 19, if the combinations of our representations were reduced to Humean empirical associations, then no judgment, if it is possible at all, could be more than a judgment of perception. The form of judgment as objective combination (combination of concepts related to an object = x) would really mean a combination relative to the subject. Conversely, the reason why the formulation of judgments of experience according to the *Logic* is the same as that of judgment *tout court* in section 19 of the *Critique* is that the logical form of judgment, as combination of concepts related to empirical objects, satisfies its function in cognition only when the judgment has become a judgment of experience.

All this being said, there is still reason to be surprised at the examples of judgments of experience Kant gives in the *Logic*: 'It (the tower) is red' and 'The stone is warm'. Their predicates are concepts of secondary qualities. And to make things worse, the second example is almost identical to one Kant described in the *Prolegomena* not only as a judgment of perception, but even as one unfit ever to become a judgment of experience. The only possible explanation for this divergence, I think, is that in the *Logic* the judgments 'The stone is warm' and 'The tower is red' are not taken by Kant to be formed in the same way as 'The room is warm, sugar sweet, and wormwood unpleasant' in the *Prolegomena*. About the latter, Kant wrote: "I do not at all expect that I or any other person shall always find it as I now do; each of these sentences only expresses a reference of two sensations to the same subject, i.e., myself, and that only in my present state of perception." Thus these judgments do nothing more than express the combination of my subjective sensations in a particular circumstance. On the contrary, we may assume that the judgments quoted in the *Logic*—'The stone is warm' or 'The tower is red'—are taken to be formed after a comparison of whole series of perceptions (not only my own), which eventually result in subsuming the given intuition under the relevant categories. Saying 'The stone is warm' because I now feel it to be warm is quite different from saying it after the complex process that may consist of (1) relating our judgment to other judgments on temperatures of different objects in different circumstances, (2) comparing variations of temperatures constructed as intensive magnitudes, (3) forming the judgment of perception 'if the sun shines on the stone, the stone gets warm', and finally (4) forming the judgment of experience 'the sun warms the stone'. In this last context a judgment such as 'the stone is warm' does not hold "for myself, in the present state of my perception." Now, this case is no different from at least one of the examples quoted from the *Prolegomena*: 'the room is warm'. This judgment is a mere judgment of perception if upon entering a room I have a feeling of warmth and say 'the room is warm'. But it is a judgment of experience if I think it in the context of compared and connected combinations of concepts, which make it the conclusion, for instance, of an inference such as 'If the stove is lit, the room grows warm'.[43]

Of course, this means that in the *Prolegomena*, Kant should not have described 'The room is warm' as a judgment of perception *unfit to become a judgment of experience*. This inconsistency is perhaps to be related to similar discrepancies in Kant's treatment of *sensation*. In the general classification of representations that opens the Transcendental Dialectic, sensation is defined as "perception which relates solely to the subject as the modification of its state." It is opposed to cognition, an "objective perception" which is in turn divided into intuition and concept. Yet according to the Transcendental Analytic, sensation is certainly related to objects, since we know the *degree* (intensive magnitude) of qualities in objects by means of the *degree* of sensation. In the *Critique of Judgment*, Kant has an interesting formulation for the twofold aspect of sensation, subjective and yet related to the object. He explains that "what is merely subjective in the representation of an object is its aesthetic character [*ästhetische Beschaffenheit*]." This aesthetic (i.e., sensible) character has a form, space, and time, and a matter, sensation. Now, however subjective both matter and form may be, they are employed in the cognition of objects. The only sensations that can in no way contribute to the cognition of the object, Kant goes on, are those of pleasure and pain, which should be called *feelings* rather than sensations so as to distinguish them from *objective sensations*.[44] This distinction between *sensation*, which relates to the object, and *feeling* of pleasure or displeasure, which is only my subjective state, might be implicit in the three examples of the *Prolegomena*. This would then resolve the seeming discrepancy between the *Prolegomena* and the *Logic*. According to the *Prolegomena*, the first three examples *cannot become judgments of experience* because all three must be understood as obeying the same pattern as the third ('wormwood is unpleasant'), namely as expressing our own subjective state. In this context 'Sugar is sweet' should be read as 'Sugar tastes sweet, its taste is pleasant'; 'The room is warm' should be read as 'It feels warm (pleasant) in the

---

[43] The relation between stove and warmth of the room is an example used by Kant in the Second Analogy of Experience: see A202/B247–48. An even clearer example of the difference between the use of the predicate 'warm' in a judgment of experience and its use in a judgment of perception is, of course, the difference between its use in a scientific assessment of the relation between light and heat such as Scheele's (cf. note 27), and in a judgment such as 'the room is warm' or 'the stone is warm'. Judgments of natural science are thus the most sophisticated of our "judgments of experience." They make use of mathematical construction and experimental method to anticipate the totality of experience which alone can provide the adequate context for asserting that the judgment should hold "for everyone, always," that is, claiming for it strict universality and necessity (cf. also the cases discussed earlier: 'air is elastic', 'bodies are heavy').

[44] For the definition of sensation in the Transcendental Dialectic, see A320/B377. For the relation between the degree of sensation and the degree of reality in the appearance, see A166/B207–8, and chapter 10. For the "aesthetic character" of the appearance, see *KU*, introd. VII, Ak. V, 188–89; 28. On the difference between *sensations* and *feelings*, see *Erste Einl.*, Ak. XX, 224; 412–13, and *KU*, §3, Ak. V, 206; 47.

room'. Read in this way, they cannot become judgments of experience, and the coherence of Kant's view is salvaged. I admit, though, that here Kant depends heavily on the charity of his reader.

Whatever amount of charity we are ready to spare, I would suggest that Kant's explanations in the *Logic* do not contradict the distinction made in the *Prolegomena*, but instead complement it by viewing it from the standpoint of a reflection on "the correct use of the understanding, i.e., that in which it agrees with itself."[45] To say, as the *Logic* does, that judgment of experience alone can "truly" fulfill the promise carried by the logical form of judgment is not to invalidate the analyses of the *Prolegomena*. Rather, it is to bring them together with the argument of section 19 in the B edition and present the logical form of judgment as the form proper to an activity of thinking that carries its own norm. In the *Prolegomena*, judgments of perception are the first empirical "filling" of such a logical form. In the *Logic*, their claim to objectivity is exposed as baseless by bestowing on them a grammatical form appropriate to their merely subjective meaning. Only judgments of experience carry out the requirement contained in the logical form. And even they are liable to the ever renewed corrections induced by further progress of empirical knowledge.

I have suggested that according to Kant, the logical function of judgment is present in judgments of perception, but adequately fulfills its goal or immanent norm only in judgments of experience. Such a view might seem to blur the very distinction between the two kinds of judgments. After all, on this reading, what else is judgment of perception but a potential judgment of experience? As for judgment of experience, if it is provisional and rectifiable, is it not relative and subjective, even if it is less so than the judgment of perception, so that the difference between the two kinds of judgment would again be only one of degree? Cassirer, for one, reached just this conclusion. He argued that the very notion of a judgment of perception was a concession on Kant's part to empiricism, made mainly for didactic purposes:

> The further the Kantian distinction proceeds, however, the more it appears that the judgment of perception is only meant to be a methodologically constructed limiting-case, to throw light upon the newly gained concept of scientific objectivity by force of contrast; but that the distinction carries with it no real separation of judgments into two heterogeneous classes. Every judgment claims a certain measure of objectivity within its self-chosen narrower sphere, no matter how limited its subject-concept. It is never satisfied with establishing a mere coexistence of representations, but it erects a functional coordination between them, so that whenever the one content is given, the other is taken as required. The "is" of the copula is the expression of this connection, and thus enters as a necessary factor into every assertion regarding an individual, empirical object. The proposition, that body is heavy, does not mean that as often as I have hitherto lifted a body, certain touch and pressure sensations have been felt, but it is meant to establish a connection, based in the object and independent of the condition of this or that sensing individual. Even the individual *a posteriori* judg-

---

[45] *Logik*, introd. I, 3, Ak. IX, 13; 529.

ment always contains an *a priori* element in the necessity of the connection, which
it affirms (cf. *Critique of Pure Reason*, B edition, §19). In the final conception of the
system of experience, the instrumental concept of the mere judgment of perception
is transcended and excluded.[46]

I do not think that Cassirer is correct. First of all, one main reason he believes
Kant's judgment of perception to be ultimately "transcended and excluded" is that
he has himself reduced it to empirical association of representations, without taking heed of Kant's description of this judgment as a "logical connection of perceptions."[47] According to Cassirer, in a judgment of perception "we only establish the
coexistence of two contents, without setting them in any relation of mutual dependence."[48] But this assertion does not agree with Kant's own statements. As we
saw, one of Kant's characterizations of the logical form of judgment is precisely
that this form expresses the relation of an assertion to its condition.[49] Cassirer
concludes from section 19 of the *Critique* that Kant "transcends and excludes"
the notion of a judgment of perception, but in fact, if my analysis is correct, what
should be rejected is rather Cassirer's reduction of judgments of perception to a
strictly associationist model.

One might grant me the foregoing argument against Cassirer while still observing that this is not sufficient to salvage Kant's distinction. Saying that judgments of perception involve more than mere empirical associations merely confirms, the objector will say, that Kant's distinction is a loose one from the outset,
and that there are simply more or less adequate empirical judgments. But I would
not accept this version of the objection either, for two reasons.

First, the importance Kant grants to judgment of perception as the initial step
of all objective cognition, *and yet a merely subjective connection of our perceptions*, is a necessary condition for avoiding any overly simplified interpretation of
the "application" of the categories. Certainly, in every judgment representations
are related to objects. Nevertheless, the empirical use of logical functions of judgment does not by itself entitle us to consider the intuition analyzed and discursively synthesized as being "determined in itself with respect to logical forms,"
that is, subsumable under the corresponding categories. This is the principal lesson to be drawn from Kant's distinction between two types of judgment. This lesson makes the distinction a radical and indispensable one, even if the judgment
of experience is itself provisional and ever in need of further correction.

But there is more. To say that all judgments concerned with appearances are at
first mere judgments of perception or "mere logical connections" of perceptions,
prior to any subsumption of appearances under categories, is to recognize the full

[46] Cassirer, *Substance*, 245–46.

[47] Cf. *Prol.*, §18, Ak. IV, 298; 41: "[Judgments of perception] require no pure concept of the understanding, but only the logical connection of perceptions in a thinking subject"; and §21a, Ak. IV,
304; 47: "The judgment of experience must therefore add to the sensible intuition and its logical connection in a judgment (after it has been rendered universal by comparison) something that determines
the synthetic judgment as necessary and therefore as universally valid."

[48] Cf. note 24. This sentence immediately precedes the passage I have just cited.

[49] Cf. chapter 4, pp. 93–99.

role of *mere logical forms of judgment*, as *forms of reflection*, in guiding the generation of perceptual schemata. If judgments of perception result from reflection on a sensible manifold given in circumstances that are quite contingent (depending on the biography of particular empirical subjects), the activity that produces this kind of judgment is also the activity that first generates in the sensible given the forms of synthesis Kant calls "*schemata* of the pure concepts of understanding." This is why I earlier related what Kant says in section 18 of the Transcendental Deduction, according to which "the empirical unity of consciousness depends on the objective unity," to what he says in section 19: all judgment, however "empirical, and therefore contingent," depends on the objective unity of consciousness. The effort of the mind to reflect the sensible given under empirical concepts combined in judgments—which can at first be only judgments "of perception," "valid for me, in the present state of my perception"—is precisely what generates the syntheses of appearances to be reflected under concepts combined in judgments, the "manner in which given cognitions are brought to the objective unity of apperception." For these syntheses *then* to make possible the subsumption of appearances under categories, further steps have to be taken in order to overcome the merely relative, empirically subjective character of judgments of perception, and generate judgments of experience.

DISCURSIVE JUDGMENTS AND SENSIBLE SYNTHESES: AND THE THIRD *CRITIQUE*, AGAIN

The foregoing argument brings us once again very close to the conception of judgment developed in the third *Critique*. What better confirmation do we have of the dependence of empirical syntheses on objective unity of self-consciousness, considered as an original *capacity to judge*, than this striking passage from the first introduction to the *Critique of Judgment*:

> With respect to the universal concepts of nature, under which in general a concept of experience (without any particular empirical determination) is possible, reflection has in the concept of a nature in general, i.e. in understanding, already its direction [*ihre Anweisung*] and *the power of judgment does not need a particular principle for its reflection, but schematizes it a priori* [*die Urteilskraft bedarf keines besonderen Prinzips der Reflection, sondern schematisiert dieselbe a priori*] and applies these schemata to each empirical synthesis, without which no judgment of experience would be possible. The power of judgment is here *in its reflection at the same time determinative*, and the transcendental schematism of the latter is at the same time a rule under which empirical intuitions are subsumed.[50]

[50] *Erste Einl.* V, Ak. XX, 212 (emphasis mine); 401. Note the expression, "in its reflection, at the same time determinative," which confirms the point I was making at the end of chapter 6. Teleological and aesthetic judgments are distinguished from cognitive judgments not insofar as they are reflective, but insofar as they are *merely* reflective. In cognitive judgments, namely in the application of categories (and empirical concepts), the power of judgment is "in its reflection, at the same time determinative." Cf. chapter 6, pp. 163–66.

This text immediately precedes the long passage discussed in chapter 6 in connection with the concepts of comparison, "matter" and "form," and the form of a system. There we saw Kant argue that the power of judgment in its reflective use necessarily formulates for itself a special principle stating that nature presents a systematic unity of genera and species.[51] In the text I cite here, Kant prefaces this point by indicating that where the subsumption of appearances under categories, and thus where the a priori laws of nature are concerned, the power of judgment does *not* need a specific principle for its reflective use. This is because, in this case, the power of judgment "schematizes [its reflective use] *a priori*." I think this peculiar expression should be taken quite literally. Where the universal laws of nature are concerned, the power of judgment [*Urteilskraft*] with its logical functions, which (as we saw) are functions of reflection oriented toward combining concepts according to logical forms of judgment, *schematizes its reflection*, that is, generates the schemata outlining in the sensible given the universal forms of the objects represented by "*x, y, z*" in Kant's logical forms of judgment. Objects are thus synthezised in the spatiotemporal forms of unity required for them to be reflected under concepts combined in judgments, and in the end subsumed under the categories as "concepts of an object in general, by means of which the intuition of the object is regarded as determined in respect of one of the logical functions of judgment."[52] In other words, if it is true that empirical judgments are formed by comparison/reflection/abstraction on the sensible given, it must also be added that, *in order for such reflection to be possible*, the sensible given must be "run through and held together" (A99) according to forms of synthesis that make it suitable for reflection under concepts combined in judgments and, eventually for subsumption under categories, "universal representations of synthesis" (A78/B104). Before they are such "universal representations," or concepts under which appearances can be subsumed, categories are nothing but mere logical functions of judgments, or forms of the *Vermögen zu urteilen* whose effort, or *conatus*, pervades the totality of our sensible perceptions.[53]

This means, then, that the categories have a role to play as it were at each end of the activity of judging. They are reflected as *concepts*, "universal and reflected representations" subsuming the perceptions first reflected in accordance with the logical forms of judgment, only as a result of the procedure that leads from judgments of perception to judgments of experience. But such a subsumption is legitimate only if it can be shown that the sensible given has always been "in itself" in agreement with these logical forms, that is, if it is shown that "with respect to

---

[51] *Erste Einl.* V, Ak. XX, 216; 403–404. Cf. chapter 6, pp. 151–59. And notes 30, 44.

[52] Cf. §14, B128.

[53] In "The Ground of the Distinction of All Objects in General into Phenomena and Noumena," Kant states most clearly that categories, when deprived of their schemata, are nothing but logical functions of judgment. See A242, A245, and esp. B305: "[Categories] are nothing but *forms of thought*, which contain the merely logical capacity [*das logische Vermögen*] to unite *a priori* in one consciousness the manifold given in intuition." Cf. also Transcendental Dialectic, A310/B367: "[Concepts of understanding] . . . contain nothing more than the unity of reflection upon appearances, insofar as these appearances must necessarily belong to a possible empirical consciousness." In a *Reflection* that Adickes dates in 1771, Kant defined categories as *conceptus reflectentes* (*Refl.* 5051, Ak. XVIII).

the universal concepts of nature, . . . the power of judgment schematizes its reflection *a priori* ." The *Critique of Judgment* can take this "*a priori* schematization" for granted because it is supposed to have been proved in the Tanscendental Analytic of the first *Critique*, from the Transcendental Deduction of the Categories to the System of Principles.

I have so far analyzed the activity of judging in its discursive form. I have inquired into the nature of those logical forms which, according to Kant, are the forms of the "manner in which we bring given cognitions to the objective unity of apperception." I have shown that this act could be fully understood only if we took into account its *reflective* nature. I have thus pointed to the profound accord between the first and third *Critique* in respect of their conception of judgment. It is now time to consider what makes those intellectual syntheses, or discursive judgments, possible in the first place. And for this we must retreat from the *synthesis intellectualis* to the *synthesis speciosa*, or the transcendental synthesis of imagination.

PART THREE

Synthesis Intellectualis, Synthesis Speciosa:
Transcendental Imagination and the
Foundation of the System of Principles

IN PART II I showed why, in order to understand Kant's table of the categories, we need to understand his definition and differentiation of the logical forms of judgment. These are the forms of discursive thought in general. Therefore the operations of comparison/reflection/abstraction, by means of which empirical concepts are derived from the sensible given, are also operations that ultimately combine these (empirical) concepts according to the logical forms of judgment. But this presupposes that the sensible given has been synthesized according to schemata "represented universally" in the categories, that is, in the "concepts of an object in general, by means of which the intuition of this object is regarded as determined in respect of one of the logical functions of judgment."[1] If this is correct, we must conclude that the categories, as full-fledged *concepts* or "universal and reflected representations,"[2] are in no way prior to the activity of judging. On the contrary, they result from this activity of generating and combining concepts according to the logical forms of judgment. Of course, all activity oriented toward these forms is also a potential reflection of the sensible given under the categories corresponding to them. This is why it can be said that in a sense every empirical judgment—and, similarly every synthesis of the sensible given in order to form judgments—is an "application" of the categories.[3] But from this one should not be misled into supposing that the categories are concepts ready to be "applied" prior to the activity of judgment. Such an interpretation is incompatible with Kant's consistent opposition to innatism of representations. On the contrary, acknowledging the primacy of the act of judging over the categories not only does

---

[1] B128.

[2] See *Logik*, §1.

[3] This is why I said, at the end of the previous chapter, that the categories have a role to play "at each end" of the activity of judging: as "mere logical functions of judgment," they play a role in guid-

justice to Kant's antiinnatism, but also, as I shall show in the next chapters, allows us to make sense of Kant's much maligned, because generally misunderstood, doctrine of the schematism of pure concepts of the understanding.

Kant makes clear the primacy of the activity of judging over the categories in the two extremely compact sentences with which he introduces and justifies the parallel tables of categories and forms of judgment in section 10 of the Analytic of Concepts. We are now in a position to provide a full analysis of these two sentences.

> The same function which gives unity to the various representations *in a judgment* also gives unity to the mere synthesis of various representations *in an intuition*, and this unity, universally represented, we entitle the pure concept of the understanding. The same understanding, through the same acts by which in concepts, by means of analytical unity, it produced the logical form of a judgment, also introduces a transcendental content into its representations, by means of the synthetic unity of the manifold in intuition. On this account we are entitled to call these representations pure concepts of the understanding, and to regard them as applying *a priori* to objects. (A79/B105)

Note the difference in construction between the first and second sentences. The first exhibits an exact symmetry between the discursive unity of representations in judgment on the one hand ("the same function, which gives *unity* to the *various representations* in a the *judgment*"), and the synthetic unity of representations in intuition on the other ("also gives *unity* to the *mere synthesis of representations* in *an intuition*"). If the interpretation developed here is correct, this symmetry expresses the fact that the acts of thinking the discursive unity of concepts in judgment are *the same* as the acts of combining and ordering the sensible given in order to reflect universal representations combined in judgments. These acts thus also generate sensible schemata or forms of "unity of the mere synthesis of representations in intuition," which, "represented universally, we entitle the pure concepts of the understanding."[4] The second sentence, in contrast, exhibits a twofold asymmetry. First, there is a disconcerting asymmetry in the tense of the verbs, first imperfect, then present: the understanding "produced" (*zustande brachte*) the logical form of the judgment in concepts; it "introduces" (*bringt*) a transcendental content into its representations, and hence the latter "are called" pure concepts of the understanding. Second, there is an asymmetry in what is thus generated: on the one hand, the understanding produces a *form*, the "logical form of a judgment"; on the other hand, it introduces a *content*, "a transcendental content into its representations." These two asymmetries are related, and highly significant.

Of course the difference in tenses might reflect merely the order of exposition

---

ing reflection of the sensible given with a view to forming empirical concepts, and for this they must first also guide *synthesis in view of reflection*. But as *concepts*, they are applied only in judgments of experience.

[4] Cf. B104, immediately preceding the passage just quoted.

of the Analytic of Concepts. The acts of understanding leading to judgments were discussed in section 1 (A67/B92: The Logical Use of the Understanding in General), the unity of the synthesis of the sensible is first mentioned in section 2. This order of exposition is what the imperfect and the present tenses might refer to. But I submit that the order of exposition is also an order of reasons or grounds, *in der Sache selbst.* Only insofar as we strive to form judgments (combinations of concepts) do we generate in the sensible given of intuition the forms of unity providing their content to the categories. There is no *chronological* priority here (we do not form discursive judgments *before* we synthesize the sensible). But there is a priority of determination. Reflection according to logical forms, *as a goal to be reached*, guides the acts of unification of the sensible and thereby introduces a transcendental content into the categories.

We see, here, the relation between the two asymmetries mentioned above. The progression from mere logical *form* ("The same understanding, through the same acts by which in concepts . . . it produced the logical form of a judgment . . ."), to transcendental *content* ("introduces a transcendental content into its representations") focuses attention on the generation of the categories or, more precisely, the generation of their *content*, which is indispensable to their status as "concepts of an object in general, by means of which the intuition of this object is regarded as *determined* with respect to one of the logical functions of judgment." The reason the second sentence is asymmetrical, whereas the first is not, is that the first expresses the identity between two acts of combination—the discursive combination of concepts and the intuitive combination of the sensible given—whereas the second sentence expresses the generation of their common result, the *original acquisition* of the categories.

The reason I dwell so long on the structure of these two sentences is that many interpreters have pointed to the assymetries just analyzed as one more obscurity, or even an outright inconsistency in Kant's thinking. The puzzlement they express stems in part from a misunderstanding of the terms "analytic unity" and "synthetic unity."[5] If "analytic unity" is understood as the unity expressed in the logical form of judgment, then considerable interpretive sleight of hand is required to explain that "the same acts" that realize this logical form (= *analytic* unity) also realize the *synthetic* unity of the sensible. But in fact, as we saw, the analytic unity of consciousness is attached to *concepts*, and it is only the *means* by which *synthetic* unity is established among representations in a judgment. What Kant is saying, then, is that the "same operation" that produces this (discursive) synthetic unity of judgments[6] also produces the (intuitive) synthetic unity of the sensible manifold, in order to subsume this manifold under concepts in judgment. And the (intuitive) synthetic unity of the sensible thus produced is in turn the means by which a transcendental content is introduced into the pure concepts of the understanding. Far from lacking rigor, the progression of Kant's exposition is, on the contrary, extremely precise. Its abuse by even the most careful

[5] See reference to this misunderstanding and its criticism by Reich, chapter 4, note 10.
[6] See B131.

of readers is therefore difficult to fathom. De Vleeschauwer speaks of a "dispar-
ity in equating the common function of unity in a judgment and in a concept,"[7]
and Kemp Smith, after having quoted the sentence I discussed ("The same understanding, through the same acts . . ."), declares that "Kant's exposition is extremely misleading . . . his real argument is by no means that which is here given
. . . Kant is unable to prove, and does not ultimately profess to prove, that it is "the
same understanding," and still less that it is "the *same* operations," which are exercised in discursive and in creative thinking."[8] Hoppe makes a similar reproach:
"Despite all his references to the specificity of transcendental thought, Kant ultimately has it rely on analytic and explicative thought [*das analytische und ex-
plizierende Denken*], and thereby considers the fundamental functions of analytic
thought and transcendental-synthetic thought as identical."[9]

If my reading is accurate, these harsh verdicts rest on a misunderstanding of
Kant's argument. However, they also point to a genuine difficulty. How are we to
understand Kant's claim that a *discursive* activity accounts for the combination of
a sensible given that on its part—Kant is emphatic enough on this point—is heterogeneous to any discursive form?

The principle for a solution to this problem lies in Kant's explanation of the relation between *synthesis intellectualis* and *synthesis speciosa* in section 24 of the
Transcendental Deduction.[10] The *synthesis intellectualis* is a "mere form of
thought," a form of combination thought in the categories independently of any
sensible given.[11] Although Kant does not say it explicitly here, this purely intellectual synthesis—*Verstandesverbindung*—can be nothing other than the synthesis performed in accordance with the logical forms of judgments. It corresponds
to the discursive aspect of the function of unity mentioned in section 10. The *synthesis speciosa* or transcendental synthesis of imagination is the "effect of the understanding on sensibility" or the "determination of inner sense" by the understanding. It is clearly equivalent to the intuitive aspect of the function of unity
mentioned in section 10. But Kant doesn't here just repeat the metaphysical deduction. Rather, he provides the ground for the correspondence between discursive and sensible "unity of synthesis" by making this correspondence more than
a mere parallelism: an actual *effect* of understanding on sensibility, or an *affection*
of sensibility by understanding. The reason for the correspondence between logical forms of judgment (forms of "intellectual synthesis," mere forms of thought

---

[7] De Vleeschauwer, *Déduction*, II, 92, n. 4.

[8] Kemp Smith, *Commentary*, 177. Describing as "creative thinking" the sensible synthesis under
the categories is, in any case, completely inappropriate.

[9] Hoppe, *Synthesis*, 153.

[10] Notice once again how the B Deduction builds on the Metaphysical Deduction of the Categories
(§10) more closely than the A Deduction did: §19 clarifies the parallelism between the table of the
categories and the table of judgments by defining judgment as the "act of bringing given cognitions
to the objective unity of apperception"; §24, then §26, explain the relation between intellectual syntheses and sensible syntheses. Thus it is apparent that the rewriting of the transcendental deduction
both takes its guidance from the metaphysical deduction and provides the support it needed, by transforming what was at first only a "guiding thread" into an actual justification of the categories.

[11] B150.

reflected in the categories) and sensible syntheses (which alone give a content to the categories, i.e., make them concepts of possible objects) is that the latter are the effects of the acts that tend to produce the former. The act of thinking whose *result* is judgment, because its *goal* is judgment, affects receptivity and thereby combines the sensible given with a view to judgments. This is how the capacity to form judgments introduces ordering into sensible perception: not by making clear what was already perceived in a confused way (as Leibniz thought), but by *generating* the sensible orderings (figure, succession, simultaneity . . .) that make possible reflection according to the forms of discursive combination.

In other words, instead of a mere parallelism between the two syntheses, as expounded in the metaphysical deduction, we are now offered an account of their organic unity, in which the one, the discursive synthesis or *synthesis intellectualis*, is the goal to be reached by means of the other, the intuitive synthesis or *synthesis speciosa*. This is not to say that the logical forms *themselves* affect sensibility and produce forms of sensible combination. Rather, sensibility is affected, the sensible given is combined, by an act whose *goal*, and thus whose proper *effect*, is to reflect representations under concepts combined according to logical forms of judgment. *What* this act is, we don't know, says Kant.[12] All we can say is that the activity of combination is *oriented toward* the forms of discursive combination in judgment.[13] This provides at least a partial answer to the difficulty raised earlier: how can a discursive act produce a sensible, intuitive synthesis? The answer, I think, is that in fact it is *not* judgment, in its discursive forms, that affects sensibility. But the *act of spontaneity* which affects sensibility has judgment for its *goal*—that is, discursive combination of concepts according to logical forms. Only in this way are we capable of using our understanding. Recall once again Kant's striking formulation in section 16: "An understanding in which through self-consciousness all the manifold would *eo ipso* be given, would be *intuitive*; our understanding can only *think*, and for intuition must look to the senses" (B135).

Without entering into a general confrontation that would require a study of its own, it is interesting to compare the conclusions I propose here with Heidegger's analysis, in *Kant and the Problem of Metaphysics*, of the two sentences from section 10 of the Analytic of Concepts quoted earlier. On several points my analysis is closer to his than to any other I am acquainted with. Heidegger recognizes the synthetic function of every judgment, even analytic judgment (section 3). He calls the categories *reflective concepts*—concepts "employed with, in and for reflection" (section 11). He is thus able to point out Kant's reasons for identifying discursive unity and intuitive (sensible) unity (section 13). Where I disagree with Heidegger is in his explanation of the "same function" which establishes, on the

[12] This is why, after the first part of §24 has expounded figurative synthesis as the effect of understanding on sensibility, the second part asserts that *the 'I think' does not cognize itself as it is "in itself," but only in the manner in which it affects itself in sensibility.*

[13] What allows us to say this, is transcendental cognition: a cognition "occupied not so much with objects as with our mode of cognition of objects [*unser Erkenntnisart von Gegenständen*], insofar as it must be possible *a priori*" (B25).

one hand, the unity of concepts in judgment, and on the other hand, the unity of sensible synthesis. He explains this function as being that of imagination, the "common root" of sensibility and understanding. I explain it as a function of thought aiming at the production of discursive forms. It is no use appealing to the authority of Kant's text to decide the issue here, for Heidegger quite explicitly and deliberately displaced Kant's problematic by granting pride of place to imagination. What interests me is the meaning of such a displacement, and the light it throws *a contrario* on Kant's position. Heidegger's view leads him to presuppose a unity always already given or, rather, projected (by the "transcendence" of original imagination), from which the unity of sensible intuition and that of the discursive forms emanate. For Kant, on the contrary, unity is not taken for granted, but produced by imagination *only if* it is *under the unity of apperception*, whose form is the logical form of judgment, or form of the *Vermögen zu urteilen* whose specifications make up the table of the forms of judgment. In his *Phenomenology of Perception*, Merleau-Ponty denounces in Kant's transcendental philosophy a revival of classical rationalism, which always assumes that "a total explication has already been achieved somewhere."[14] By this he means that Kant's transcendental unity of apperception functions as an a priori guarantee, given once and for all, that the sensible given is accessible to a priori concepts. But actually, such a reproach applies better to Heidegger, who does presuppose an original unity from which categories emerge. For Kant, as I understand him, unity is never taken for granted, but produced, as it were bit by bit and effort after effort. We have only as much unitary world as we are able to *produce* by the painstaking use of our *Vermögen zu urteilen*.

The gist of my disagreement with Heidegger can be summarized as follows: Heidegger considers the identity of sensible and discursive unity as grounded in an obscure "common root" and makes it the task of transcendental philosophy, understood as an analytic of *Dasein*, to explore this "common root." I find Kant's original position more interesting than what Heidegger makes of it. If my interpretation is correct, Kant considers the identity of sensible and discursive unity as the result of an act oriented toward an end, that of discursive thought. He thus makes it the task of transcendental philosophy to answer the question: "What is it to be *capable of judgment*," that is, capable of the clarity of discursive thought? And what kind of relation to being (to our own being as well as to the being of entities external to ourselves) does this capacity entail? To be sure, Kant is led to show that the clarity of discursive thought is itself dependent on the "blind but indispensable function" of imagination. My aim in the present work is so little to diminish the latter that, on the contrary, all of part III will be devoted to it. But imagination itself, in its transcendental function, is for Kant to be understood in light of its relation to discursive thinking and its logical forms, not the reverse.

Synthesis speciosa or figurative synthesis, although the "effect of understanding on sensibility," is nonetheless performed by *imagination*. Many commentators of the first *Critique* have argued that in B, imagination loses the independence or

[14] Merleau-Ponty, *Phénoménologie*, 75; 62.

even the primacy over intellectual functions granted to it in the A Deduction.[15] My view is that on this topic, as on most others, Kant merely clarifies rather than modifies his position in the B Deduction. In this case, new light is cast on the way in which Kant's reflection on the role of logical functions of judgment leads him to develop an original conception of imagination as the faculty generating in sensibility the represented manifolds (the objects) to be reflected under concepts in judgments. In other words, what becomes clearer is the relation between logic and psychology in Kant's transcendental endeavor.

It is interesting, in this respect, to compare the *synthesis speciosa* of section 24 with Kant's conception of imagination as expounded in his *Anthropology from a Pragmatic Standpoint*, a late publication of anthropology lectures Kant gave throughout his career. There Kant defines imagination as the "faculty of representing an object in intuition even when it is not present." The same definition appears in section 24 of the Transcendental Deduction, when Kant attributes figurative synthesis to imagination and thus distinguishes it from intellectual synthesis: "But the figurative synthesis . . . must, in order to be distinguished from the merely intellectual combination, be called the *transcendental synthesis of imagination. Imagination* is the faculty of representing in intuition an object *even when it is not present* [*auch ohne dessen Gegenwart*]" (B151, translation modified). This definition of imagination is close to that of the textbooks in empirical psychology Kant may have used. Thus Wolff: "The faculty of producing perceptions of absent sensible things is called the *faculty of imagining* [*facultas imaginandi*] or *imagination*."[16] Similarly, Baumgarten: "I possess a faculty of imagining or *imagination* [*phantasian*]. Even though my imaginings are perceptions of things which were once present, they are, while I imagine them, perceptions of absent things [*sensorum absentium*]."[17] But for the *Schulphilosophie* psychologists, this faculty of representing "absent sensible things" (*sensa absentia*) is essentially *reproductive*. Wolff and Baumgarten spend some time setting forth its *associative* rules.[18] Wolff expounds, in addition to reproduction, a *productive* function of imagination, which he calls *facultas fingendi*. But this function remains dependent on the elements provided by the senses, which it separates in order to combine them in different ways, thus producing configurations not found in nature.[19] The distinction between *production* and *reproduction* is in any case not very sharp, and Wolff often uses the first term in place of the second.

[15] Cf. chapter 3. This view, defended most forcefully by Heidegger, is developed in detail in Mörchen, *Einbildungskraft* (see esp. 49, 75). But it has also been widely shared outside the Heideggerian school, at least by commentators taking seriously the psychological aspect of Kant's argument. See, e.g., De Vleeschauwer, *Déduction*, 182; Lachièze-Rey, *Idéalisme*, 304.

[16] Wolff, *Psychologia empirica*, §92. Cf. Aristotle, *De Anima* 428a6–7.

[17] Baumgarten, *Psychologia empirica*, §558.

[18] See Wolff, *Psychologia empirica*, §§104–17; Baumgarten, *Psychologia empirica*, §§557–71.

[19] Wolff, *Psychologia empirica*, §141. Baumgarten, on his part, insists on the fact that the imagination can only *reproduce*, that is, recall to clear consciousness what was once present to the senses (*Psychologia empirica*, §559), even if these reproductions are often partial and deceptive, "empty illusions or false imaginings" (*vana phantasmata seu imaginationes falsae*, 571). He takes up Wolff's definition and description of the *facultas fingendi*, but views it as distinct from imagination (§§589–90).

Kant, on the contrary, even while invoking the school definition of imagination in section 24 of the Deduction, makes a clear distinction between its *productive* and its *reproductive* function. The latter belongs solely to psychology, while transcendental philosophy is concerned only with the former:

> Insofar as imagination is spontaneity, I also sometimes entitle it *productive* imagination, to distinguish it from *reproductive* imagination, whose synthesis is entirely subject to empirical laws, the laws, namely, of association, and which therefore contributes nothing to the explanation of the possibility of *a priori* cognition. The reproductive synthesis falls within the domain, not of transcendental philosophy, but of psychology. (B152)

The sharpness of Kant's distinction, which goes so far as to make the two uses of imagination the objects of two different inquiries, is of course due to the a priori character he assigns to *productive* synthesis. I will consider this point shortly. But it should first be noted that the fact that transcendental philosophy is not concerned with *reproductive* imagination does not mean that empirical psychology should not be concerned with *productive* imagination. On the contrary, in the *Anthropology*, immediately after defining imagination, Kant divides it into *productive* and *reproductive*:

> Imagination (*facultas imaginandi*), as the faculty of intuitions, even of an object that is not itself present, is either productive, viz., a faculty of original presentation of the latter (*exhibitio originaria*), which consequently precedes experience; or reproductive, a faculty of derivative presentation (*exhibitio derivativa*), which brings back to the mind an empirical intuition one has already had.[20]

There can be no doubt that the expression "*productive* imagination" refers to the capacity that generates the figurative synthesis explained in the *Critique*. Indeed, Kant immediately describes productive imagination as the source of "the pure representations of space and time," while all other sensible representations, he says, depend on empirical intuition and thus on *reproductive* imagination.[21] However, the initial distinction between two functions of imagination is lost in the empirical descriptions that follow. Under the title, *Von dem sinnlichen Dichtungsvermögen nach seinen verschiedenen Arten (On the Power of Sensible Invention and Its Different Species)*, Kant sets forth different activities of empirical imagination, which obviously depend as much on what he calls *production* of the intuitions of space and time as on the *reproduction* of sense-data. Thus the *productive synthesis* defined at the beginning of the chapter on imagination is never expounded for itself, but instead is implicitly present throughout the exposition of the empirical activity of imagination.[22]

[20] Kant, *Anthr.*, §28, Ak. VII, 167.

[21] "The pure intuitions of space and time belong to the first form of presentation [= the original presentation of productive imagination]; all others presuppose an empirical intuition which, when it is combined with the *concept* of the object, thus becoming an empirical cognition, is called experience" (ibid.). Kant does not mention reproductive imagination here, but clearly no empirical concept could be formed without it.

[22] The *Dichtungsvermögen* mentioned in the title quoted is to be related to the adjective *dichtend* that Kant uses earlier as an equivalent of *produktiv* (while *reproduktiv* is equivalent to *zurückrufend*, *Anthr.*, §28, Ak. VII, 167). The reader can verify for himself that the three aspects of this *Dich-*

One can understand why it should be so. The *synthesis speciosa*, figurative synthesis, does not belong to an empirical psychology because it can be identified and defined only if one admits the two theses that we have a priori forms of sensibility and that logical forms of judgment are the forms of an original function relating representations to objects. Neither of these assertions belongs to an empirical psychology, that is, to the empirical description or genesis of the combinations of our representations. Only a transcendental inquiry as Kant defines it can establish their necessity. This does not mean that they are of no use to psychological description. On the contrary, close scrutiny of Kant's *Anthropology from a Pragmatic Standpoint* shows that while neither the forms of space and time nor the objective unity of apperception (with its logical forms) is discussed in this work, both are in fact implicitly present and contribute to the originality of Kant's anthropological descriptions and analyses concerning the senses, understanding, self-consciousness. The same holds for the imagination. Kant accepts the traditional view according to which imagination is a mediator between sensation and intellect, a function reproducing sensations in the absence of any external affection, a source of phantasms and illusions but also an indispensable tool for the activity of discursive thought. But his conception of this function is transformed by his discovery of the *synthesis speciosa*, which reverberates through all aspects of the activity of imagination—its rules of association as well as what the *Schulphilosophen* called the *facultas fingendi*, the faculty of inventing images not given in nature. However, only a transcendental inquiry can expound the *synthesis speciosa* in and for itself, because only such an inquiry can recognize in this synthesis the activity in which the (associative or fictional) "free play" of imagination is appropriated by the *effort toward judgment* conditioning all representation of objects.[23]

To speak of an "appropriation" of imagination by understanding means that there is also an activity of imagination that is *not* appropriated by understanding, or even that many different degrees of "appropriation" or interaction between the laws of imagination and the laws of understanding may occur. We have encountered a similar situation where judgment is concerned: we have seen how the laws of imagination interfere with those of understanding and constantly threaten to

tungsvermögen Kant considers (*Bildung, Beigesellung*, and *Verwandtschaft*, Ak.VII, 174–77) have *both* a *productive* aspect, in which imagination must agree with the understanding, and a *reproductive* aspect, in which imagination is dependent on sensation. This may explain why even in the *Critique* one comes across the ambiguous expression '*empirical* power of *productive* imagination' (A141/B181). Production in the strict sense, that is, *pure* production, is the production of the pure intuitions of space and time. I will have more to say about this in chapter 8.

[23] It would be a worthwhile undertaking to examine in detail the ways in which, in Kant's *Anthropology*, empirical inquiry is informed by transcendental philosophy. Mörchen has some interesting suggestions on this point, but they concern only imagination, and even on this topic they are neither complete nor entirely accurate. See also Satura's *Kants Erkenntnispsychologie*. I explained earlier the collaboration of general logic and transcendental philosophy in Kant's elucidation of the logical functions of judgment (see the introduction to part II). Similarly, Kant's empirical psychology, or more precisely, his anthropology, is informed both by his logic and by his transcendental philosophy. These inquiries (together with the analysis of our moral imperatives and our aesthetic judgments) are part of one and the same endeavor to answer the question to which, according to Kant, all philosophical questions boil down: "What is man?" (see *Logic*, Ak. IX, 25; 538).

make a formally objective judgment the expression of a mere subjective association. The same holds at the other end for imagination. It belongs to *sensibility* or
receptivity, and as such obeys rules of passive association. These rules govern a
great deal of our representational combinations and hence a great deal of our be-
havior as living beings. But Kant is only marginally interested in this merely sen-
sible/associative/fictional activity of imagination. More important to him is the
manner in which it is appropriated by the requirements of understanding (*Vermögen zu urteilen*). This appropriation is the source of all objective representation,
including, as we shall see in detail, the mere *intuition* of objects.[24]

This is precisely where the *synthesis speciosa* of the B Deduction represents a
significant advance over the painstaking analyses of the A Deduction. It is no
longer necessary to list for each of the three syntheses (apprehension, reproduction, recognition) a corresponding "transcendental" synthesis. The one and only
condition for relating representations to objects is the capacity to form judgments.
The intentional relation of any of the three syntheses considered in the A Deduction to an object depends on this capacity. To borrow a term from Spinoza and
Leibniz, one might speak of an actual *conatus*, a continual effort, to shape the representation of what affects us in order to exercise our judgment. This *conatus* is
what makes our *apprehension* an act of "running through and holding together,"[25]
what orients the *reproductions* of imagination toward judgment, and finally what
enables these reproductions to be *recognized* under concepts. This does not mean
that apprehension and reproduction always lead to recognition. On the contrary,
we may be affected by sensations that we apprehend without reproducing them,
just as we may reproduce without the resulting reproductions leading to recognition, that is, to discursive judgment. But sensation leads to intuition of an object *only if* it is apprehended *in such a way as to be* reproduced, and reproduced
in such a way as to be recognized, by virtue of one and the same intellectual
conatus. The actualization of this *conatus* is the "action of understanding on sensibility,"[26] namely the *synthesis speciosa*, the figurative synthesis carried out by
imagination.

This figurative synthesis will be our concern in the following chapters. In chapter
8, I shall argue that Kant's doctrine of figurative synthesis completes the Transcendental Deduction of the Categories in the B edition by providing a reinterpretation of the "manner in which things are given to us"—in effect, a rereading

---

[24] A strictly associative imagination can be only an animal imagination, such as that described by
Kant in the *Logic* under the term *Kennen* (*Logik*, introd. VIII). Kant would probably admit that animals also have a rudimentary form of *dichtende Kraft*, in Wolff's sense of the term: an imagination
productive of fantasies (for instance in dream). We make abundant use of imagination under these two
aspects, in themselves inadequate for "unity of apperception." But the descriptions of imagination in
the *Anthropology* go well beyond such a merely associative function. I think we may conclude from
them that, for Kant, a strictly associative imagination could not produce *images*, if by image we mean
image *of an object* (and not merely blind reproduction of sensations). This accords with the relation
established in the Schematism chapter of the first *Critique*, between *image* and *schema* (A142/B181).
[25] Cf. A99.
[26] B152.

of the theory of space and time expounded in the Transcendental Aesthetic. In chapter 9, I will analyze the relation Kant established between the *synthesis speciosa* oriented toward the logical form of quantity of judgments, and the generation of homogeneous manifolds in sensibility. This a priori constitution of the form of homogeneous manifolds sheds light on Kant's view of the relation between logicodiscursive thought and mathematical thought. It also explains the primordial role Kant assigned to the categories of quantity in the constitution of experience, because, as we shall see, imagination must synthesize the sensible given as a homogeneous multiplicity for the other forms of figurative syntheses, geared toward the logical forms of *quality* and *relation*, also to be achieved. These forms will be analyzed in chapters 10 and 11.

Synthesis Speciosa and
Forms of Sensibility

THE EXPRESSION "figurative synthesis," *synthesis speciosa*, appears only briefly in the Transcendental Deduction of the Categories. After section 24, Kant does not use it again. In section 26 he does consider the role of imagination (and its dependence on intellectual synthesis), but he does not make use of the expression "figurative synthesis."[1] Yet the absence of the expression should not obscure the essential role played by the notion in Kant's argument. With the explanation of *synthesis speciosa*, Kant completes the Transcendental Deduction of the Categories by returning to what it presupposed, the forms of sensibility expounded in the Transcendental Aesthetic. Thus the notion of *synthesis speciosa* not only is Kant's major tool for bringing the Transcendental Deduction to completion, but also completes the theory of space and time whose first lineaments were expounded in the 1770 *Inaugural Dissertation*. This striking continuity from the *Dissertation* to the *Critique* is one reason I prefer to use the beautiful Latin expression *synthesis speciosa* together with its English equivalent, "figurative synthesis" (in German, *figürliche Synthesis*). In the *Inaugural Dissertation*, Kant argued that space and time are not properties or relations of things considered in themselves, but "*formae seu species*," forms or configurations which have their source in the particular constitution of our minds.[2] The *synthesis speciosa* harks back to these *species*: in the *Dissertation*, Kant attributed them to sensibility; now he argues that they are products of a synthesis of imagination, thus *synthesis speciosa*.

In the first section of the present chapter, I shall defend the thesis just stated and analyze the relation between *synthesis speciosa* in the Transcendental Deduction and space and time in the Transcendental Aesthetic. In the second section of the chapter, I will show that the explanation of *synthesis speciosa* in the B Deduction goes together with a new development of Kant's theory of *inner sense*, a theory essentially absent from the *Dissertation* and only briefly sketched out in the first edition of the *Critique*. We saw that Kant's explicit and systematic appeal to the logical forms of judgment to elucidate the relation of categories to an object is the major advance of the B Deduction over the A. It should now be added that the doctrine of *synthesis speciosa*, and the doctrine of inner sense that is its correlate, are decisive contributions to this advance. Logical forms of judgment on the side of the understanding, *synthesis speciosa*, and doctrine of inner sense

---

[1] See B164: "Now it is imagination that connects the manifold of sensible intuition; and imagination is dependent for the unity of its intellectual synthesis upon the understanding, and for the manifoldness of its apprehension upon sensibility."

[2] Cf. *Diss.*, §4, Ak. II, 392–93; 384–85.

on the side of sensibility are thus the twin pillars of the B Deduction. Together they support the demonstration of the objectivity of the categories and the elucidation of the way in which the categories relate to a sensible given.

SYNTHESIS SPECIOSA AND KANT'S COMPLETION OF
THE TRANSCENDENTAL DEDUCTION OF
THE CATEGORIES

I have mentioned earlier the perplexities occasioned by the second part of the B Deduction. It seems redundant. What more is there to prove? If we accept Kant's argument in sections 15 to 18 (every intuition I call mine is related to the original synthetic unity of apperception) and in sections 19 to 21 (this unity, whose logical form is that of judgment, relates our intuitions to objects that thereby stand under the categories), it seems that the relation of categories to objects in general has been fully established. Yet Kant insists that we still need to inquire into the "manner in which the empirical intuition is given in sensibility"(B144), or into "the possibility of knowing *a priori*, by means of *categories*, whatever objects may *present themselves to our senses*" (B159). This second step is announced as early as section 21:

> Since the categories have their source in the understanding alone, *independently of sensibility*, I must [in this deduction] abstract from the mode in which the manifold for an empirical intuition is given, and must direct attention solely to the unity which, in terms of the category and by means of the understanding, enters into the intuition. In what follows (cf. §26) it will be shown, from the mode in which the empirical intuition is given in sensibility, that its unity is no other than that which the category (according to §20) prescribes to the manifold of a given intuition in general. Only thus, by demonstration of the *a priori* validity of the categories in respect of all objects of our senses, will the purpose of the deduction be fully attained. (B144–45)

And again, at the beginning of section 26:

> In the *metaphysical deduction* the *a priori* origin of the categories has been proved through their complete agreement with the general logical functions of thought; in the *transcendental deduction* we have shown their possibility as *a priori* cognitions of objects of an intuition in general (cf. sections 20, 21). We have now to explain the possibility of cognizing *a priori*, by means of *categories*, whatever objects may *present themselves to our senses*, not indeed in respect of the form of their intuition, but in respect of the laws of their combination, and so, as it were, of prescribing laws to nature, and even of making nature possible. For unless the categories discharged this function, there could be no explaining why everything that can be presented to our senses must be subject to laws which have their origin *a priori* in the understanding alone. (B159–60)

It would be a mistake to interpret Kant as saying that in the first part of the deduction he considered the categories independently of their relation to sensibility, and that the goal of the deduction is "fully attained" only when this relation is taken into consideration. On the contrary, we saw that relation to a *sensible* intuition was at the heart of Kant's explanation of the logical forms of judgment and the functions they exhibit, and thus also at the heart of the a priori genesis of the categories.[3] It might seem, then, that the new contribution of the second part of the Deduction is the consideration now given, not to a sensible intuition in general, but to *our* sensible intuition. But why should this be necessary? If our intuition provides merely a particular case for a rule that has been proved universally (*all* sensible intuition is subordinate to the categories), it would seem superfluous to provide a specific proof for this case, and so too a mistake to regard such a proof as that by which the purpose of the deduction should be "fully attained."[4]

On closer scrutiny, however, the argument of section 26 turns out to be far more radical than the mere application, to the particular case of *our* intuition, of a proof first produced for all cases of sensible intuition. Kant's aim is not simply to winnow down the scope of his demonstration. His aim is rather to radicalize his deductive procedure by reinterpreting, in light of the demonstration he has just provided, *the manner in which things are given to us*, that is, the forms of intuition expounded in the Transcendental Aesthetic. He wants to reveal in these forms the manifestation of an activity that only the Transcendental Deduction of the Categories can make explicit. This is why the object of section 26 is neither the relation of the categories to sensible intuition in general, nor even their relation to *our* (spatiotemporal) sensible intuition, but *space and time themselves*, the forms in which things are given to us. The goal of the Transcendental Deduction of the Categories is "fully attained" only when it leads to a rereading of the Transcendental Aesthetic.

This rereading of the Transcendental Aesthetic is in part obscured or blurred by the two examples that conclude Kant's demonstration in section 26: the perception of a house, the perception of the freezing of water.[5] For these examples divert our attention from the intuitions of space and time *as such*, as singular and unlimited representations which precede and condition every particular intuition. Instead, the examples direct our attention to the manner in which particular acts of apprehension are governed by particular categories—the category of quantity

---

[3] Were our intuition not sensible (limited to what we receive from the senses), our understanding would not be discursive (limited to "universal or reflected representations"). Then we would not need the logical forms of judgment, and would have no occasion for a priori generation of our categories. True, the passage I just quoted from §26 is ambiguous on this point, since it mentions only the relation of the categories to "objects of an intuition *in general*," while in order to be consistent with what precedes it should have said "objects of a *sensible* intuition in general." The emphasis on the relation of the categories to the *sensible* given is present in the very title of §20: "*All Sensible Intuitions Are Subject to the Categories, As Conditions under Which Alone Their Manifold Can Come Together in One Consciousness*." This relation is even more strongly emphasized in §23: the categories could be related to an intuition unlike ours "*if only it be sensible* and not intellectual" (B148). This restriction is often understood as merely reiterating the *caveat* that we cognize only what is *given* to us in the forms of our sensibility. But we also need to recognize the important thesis that the forms of our thought, as forms of *discursive* thinking, have engrained in them, as it were, their necessary relation to a *sensible* given. Without this relation there would be no raison d'être for such forms (forms of a *discursive* understanding, an understanding whose concepts are "general and reflected representations").

[4] For references to discussions of the structure of the B Deduction, see chapter 3, note 17.

[5] B162–63.

for the perception of the house, of causality for the perception of freezing. But notice that Kant gives these examples only after he has finished his main proof.[6] The examples thus have no particular role to play in the proof itself. They simply serve to illustrate the result of the main argument, which is the following: (1) Every synthesis of apprehension presupposes the forms of space and time; (2) now, *these forms, being themselves unified intuitions, are under the transcendental unity of apperception, which is the source of the categories*; (3) therefore, every synthesis of apprehension, by the mere fact that it presupposes the forms of space and time, is capable of being thought under the categories. The burden of the proof in this reasoning is borne above all by the minor premise (2), that is, by the affirmation that space and time are under the original unity of apperception. Thus it matters little that the two examples given at the end, by invoking the schemata of quantity and causality, should anticipate explanations given only later, in the Schematism of the Pure Concepts of Understanding and the Principles of Pure Understanding. It matters even less that these examples should consider only two categories among the twelve laid out in section 10. Again, the real weight of the argument in section 26 lies in the reexamination of the two questions: what is space, and what is time?

Rereading the Transcendental Aesthetic

In point 3 of the Metaphysical Exposition of the Concept of Space in the Transcendental Aesthetic, Kant maintains that space is not a discursive concept but an intuition, that is, a representation that is both *singular* and *immediate*. The relation of *spaces*—shapes, volumes, and their relations—to the *one, undivided space* is not that of particular representations to the universal concept for which they might be supposed to provide the extension. Spatial representations are not thought *under* space as, for instance, the concept of force is thought *under* the concept of cause, or the concept of red *under* the concept of color, or as a given red object is subsumed *under* the concept of red thing. Nor is the relation of *spaces* to *space* that of elements to the sum or aggregate of these elements. Space, being *one*, precedes the determination of its parts, which are only its limitations.[7] Points 4 and 5 of the Metaphysical Exposition of the concept of time make a sim-

[6] This is indicated by the division of the section, at B161.

[7] A25/B39. Points 1 and 2 in the Metaphysical Exposition argue that space is (1) not empirical but (2) a priori. Point 3 (= point 4 in A) argues that it is not a discursive representation, but an intuition. Point 4 (5 in A) argues that this pure intuition is represented as an "infinite given magnitude." Point 3 in A treats issues that in B are reserved for the Transcendental Exposition of space. The same general structure is applied in the case of time. My concern in the present chapter is not to give a full account, even less an evaluation, of Kant's exposition of space and time in the Aesthetic, but only to show how his explanation of both as a priori intuitions is to be reread in light of the *synthesis speciosa* ("effect of understanding on sensibility") in the B Deduction. According to the latter, space and time, as pure intuitions, provide the forms of homogeneous multiplicities to be reflected under concepts in judgments. What was initially presented as mere forms of receptivity thus turn out to be the result of the affection of receptivity by the very same effort of the capacity to judge (*Vermögen zu urteilen*), which ultimately results in actual *judgments*. A full evaluation of Kant's view cannot be attempted until we

ilar point. Time is an undivided intuition, its parts are only limitations of it. Time is not a concept abstracted from temporal relations, but, on the contrary, the various temporal relations can be thought only as different ways in which the intuition of time (itself one and unlimited) is limited.[8]

Now, these same properties that, in the Transcendental Aesthetic, are arguments in favor of the *intuitive* rather than *discursive* nature of our representations of space and time, become, in section 26, reasons to assert that these intuitions are made possible by acts of a priori synthesis. And the a priori synthesis that generates space and time as a priori intuitions, also generates the conformity of the manifold of empirical intuitions to the *categories*. Kant explicitly invites his readers to return to the Transcendental Aesthetic and confirm for themselves that space and time, as presented there, indeed require such a synthesis:

> But space and time are represented *a priori* not merely as *forms* of sensible intuition, but as themselves *intuitions* which contain a manifold [of their own], and therefore are represented with the determination of the *unity* of this manifold (*vide* the Transcendental Aesthetic). Thus *unity of the synthesis* of the manifold, without or within us, and consequently also a *combination* to which everything that is to be represented as determined in space or time must conform, is given *a priori* as the condition of the synthesis of all *apprehension*—not indeed in, but with these intuitions. This synthetic unity can be no other than the unity of the combination of the manifold of a given *intuition in general* in an original consciousness, in accordance with the categories, insofar as the combination is applied to our *sensible intuition*. (B160–61)

Finally, in case the reader cannot or will not see that the space described here is the same as that discussed in the Transcendental Aesthetic, Kant adds a footnote:

> Space, represented as *object* (as we are required to do in geometry), contains more than mere form of intuition; it also contains the *gathering-together* [*Zusammenfassung*] of the manifold, given according to the form of sensibility, in an *intuitive* representation, so that the *form of intuition* gives only a manifold, the *formal intuition* gives unity of representation. In the Aesthetic I have treated this unity as belonging merely to sensibility, simply in order to emphasize that it precedes any concept, although as a matter of fact it presupposes a synthesis which does not belong to the senses but through which all concepts of space and time first become possible. For since by its means (in that the understanding determines the sensibility) space and time are first *given* as intuitions, the unity of this *a priori* intuition belongs to space and time, and not to the concept of the understanding (cf. §24). (B160–61n)

---

examine the use he makes of his theory of *synthesis speciosa* in the Principles of Pure Understanding. For this, see chapter 9, "The Primacy of Quantitative Syntheses," where I analyze Kant's conception of space and time in the context of his philosophy of mathematics; and chapter 11, "The Constitution of Experience." For a careful and illuminating evaluation of Kant's theory of intuition, space, and time in the Transcendental Aesthetic, and for references to major recent literature on the topic, see Parsons, "Transcendental Aesthetic."

[8] A31–32/B47–48.

The space "represented as object, as required in geometry" mentioned at the beginning of this note was also explicitly mentioned in the text of the Transcendental Aesthetic I referred to earlier. Only if space is a pure intuition, said Kant, can we account for the possibility of deducing a priori the properties of the triangle.[9] Now he declares that such an intuition is the effect of a synthesis by which "the understanding determines sensibility." This is clearly the *synthesis speciosa* expounded in section 24. Indeed, Kant refers to this section at the end of the text just quoted.

However discrete, this reference is the key to the rereading we are asked to perform. For the explanations given in section 24 help us understand the paradoxical or apparently contradictory aspects of the unity of sensible intuition in the text cited earlier. Kant reminds us that in the Transcendental Aesthetic this unity was described as "belonging merely to sensibility." This is because, he says, it "precedes any concept" and "belongs *a priori* to space and time." Yet it presupposes "a synthesis which does not belong to the senses," in which "the understanding determines sensibility." These features correspond to the description of the *synthesis speciosa* expounded in section 24: the latter is an "action of understanding on sensibility,"[10] that is, an action of the *Vermögen zu urteilen*, the capacity to form judgments. Nonetheless, it is prior to the actual production of any discursive judgment, hence prior to the reflection of any concept and a fortiori to the subsumption of intuitions under the categories. Kant can thus say that space and time are given only if understanding determines sensibility, and yet also that space and time are *intuitive* (immediate and singular representations) and *not discursive* (universal or reflected representations). They are *sensible*, the "manner in which things are *given* to us," and *not intellectual*, the manner in which we *think* things. Of course, they are *also* intellectual representations, but only mediately through the pure intuition of space and the pure intuition of time, "all concepts of space and time become possible."

If this analysis is correct, we should conclude that the space and time described in the Transcendental Aesthetic are products of the figurative synthesis of imagination, and as such are what Kant calls, in section 26, *formal intuitions*. Yet it might be objected that in the texts quoted here, Kant insists on the distinction between *forms of intuition* and *formal intuitions*. Only the second are "represented with the determination of the *unity* of [the] manifold," only they are expressly related to figurative synthesis. Perhaps, then, we should rather conclude that the *forms of intuition*, which are the proper object of the Transcendental Aesthetic, are *not* related to *synthesis speciosa*. Only *formal intuitions* are, and this is precisely why they are introduced only at the end of the Transcendental Deduction, and not in the Transcendental Aesthetic. Unlike the *forms of intuition*, they do not depend on receptivity alone, but also on a transcendental synthesis of imagination in accordance with the categories. If this is so, the argument of section 26 is less radical than I initially claimed. It does not bring into new light the "manner in

[9] A25/B39 (This belongs to point 3 of the Metaphysical Exposition of the Concept of Space, mentioned earlier. See also note 7).

[10] B152: "*eine Wirkung des Verstandes auf die Sinnlichkeit.*"

which things are given to us," but merely introduces a distinction Kant could not introduce in the Aesthetic, the distinction between what depends on sensibility or receptivity alone (space and time as forms of sensible intuition) and what depends on the transcendental synthesis of imagination or figurative synthesis (space and time as formal intuitions).

But in fact, if we follow Kant's suggestion and return to the Transcendental Aesthetic, we see that the objection does not hold. True, in the Transcendental Aesthetic Kant does not use the expression "formal intuition." He talks only of *form of intuition*, and of *pure intuition*. However, *both* notions are retrospectively clarified by the figurative synthesis of sections 24 and 26. Indeed, we are even faced with a new paradox. Section 26 distinguishes between form of intuition, which "only" gives the manifold, and formal intuition, in which figurative synthesis contributes unity to the manifold. By contrast, in the Transcendental Aesthetic both *form of intuition* and *pure intuition* are clearly *unified*; thus both seem to depend on *synthesis speciosa* just as much as the formal intuition of section 26. But if this is so, what is the form of intuition which, according to section 26, merely "gives the manifold"? I shall first consider form of intuition and pure intuition in the Aesthetic, and then propose a solution to this new difficulty.

In the Transcendental Aesthetic, the expression "form of intuition" is first introduced in relation to the constitution of *appearances*. *Form* is then paired with *matter*. But when form is considered for itself, it is referred to as *intuition*, or *pure intuition*:

That in the appearance which corresponds to sensation I term its *matter*; but that which so determines the manifold of appearance that it allows of being ordered in certain relations, I term the *form* of appearance. That in which alone the sensations can be posited and ordered in a certain form cannot itself be sensation; and therefore, while the matter of all appearance is given to us *a posteriori* only, its form must lie ready for the sensations *a priori* in the mind [*zu ihnen insgesamt im Gemüte a priori bereitliegen*], and so must allow of being considered apart from all sensation.

I term all representations *pure* (in the transcendental sense) in which there is nothing that belongs to sensation. *The pure form of sensible intuitions in general, in which all the manifold of intuition is intuited in certain relations, must be found in the mind* a priori. *This pure form of sensibility may also itself be called pure intuition.* (A20/B34, my emphasis on the last two sentences)

The constant [*beständige*] form of receptivity which we call sensibility is a necessary condition of all the relations in which objects are intuited as outside us; and if we abstract from these objects, it is a pure intuition, which bears the name of space. (A27/B43)

Note, in the first of the texts just quoted, the shift from "form of appearance" to "form of sensible intuitions" and finally "form of sensibility." The notion of *form* is properly a metaphysical rather than a psychological notion, which takes its meaning from its relation to the *matter* it determines, whose ordering and combining it provides. This is how it appeared in the *Inaugural Dissertation*, where

Kant distinguished between the form of the sensible and the form of the intelligible world. Similarly, here form is first introduced as the form *of the appearance*, that is, of the sensible object. But Kant's "Copernican revolution" makes this notion of *form* a mere concept of reflection referring to the *determination by the cognitive power*.[11] This is why Kant regresses so easily from object to subject, from the form of *appearances* to the form of *sensible intuitions* (representations) and finally to the form of *sensibility*: the spatiotemporal ordering of qualities in the object (form of appearance) characterizes it insofar as it is a *represented* object (form of sensible intuition), and thus depends on our sensible capacity to order what we receive in space and time (form of sensibility).[12]

This form of appearances, or form of sensible intuition, or form of sensibility, is defined as "that which makes the manifold of appearance capable of being ordered," or again as "that in which . . . the sensations can be . . . ordered." But that in which the manifold of appearance can be ordered is the undivided and unlimited intuition of space and of time. This means, then, that although the *pure intuition* of space and time may be distinguished from the *form of intuition* or form of appearances insofar as it is considered independently of the phenomenal *matter* (see the second text quoted earlier), considered in relation to the matter of appearances pure intuition is *itself* the form of appearances. Indeed Kant, at the end of the first text quoted earlier, fully identifies 'pure intuition' and 'form of sensibility':

> The pure form of sensible intuitions in general, in which all the manifold of intuition is intuited in certain relations, must be found in the mind *a priori*. This pure form of sensibility may also itself be called pure intuition. Thus, if I take away from the representation of a body that which the understanding thinks in regard to it, substance, force, divisibility, etc., and likewise what belongs to sensation, impenetrability, hardness, color, etc., something still remains over from this empirical intuition, namely

---

[11] Cf. chapter 6, pp. 149–50. On form and matter in the *Dissertation*, see Ak. II, 389–92 (*Diss.* I, §2).

[12] Allison suggests that what Kant calls 'form of intuition' should be understood in two ways: on the one hand, as form of intuit*ing*, and on the other hand, as form of the intuit*ed*. The first is the form of sensibility as a "mere capacity to intuit," the other is the "given, infinite, all-inclusive space which contains within it the manifold of spaces" (*Idealism*, 97). Allison argues that "form of intuition" in the Aesthetic is used mainly in the second sense, whereas the "form of intuition" of the footnote to §26 I quoted earlier has the first sense: form of intuit*ing*, mere capacity to intuit (Ibid.). I think Allison is correct to say that the form of intuition in the footnote to §26 is a mere "form of intuiting." But the point I am making here, concerning the regression from object to subject in the three uses of "form" I quoted *from the Aesthetic* (form of appearance, form of sensible intuition, form of sensibility) is different from his. Here, one and the same form is form of the intuit*ed* and form of intuit*ing* (although not the same as the "form of intuiting" of the footnote to §26). This form is the form of the object as represented object (form of the appearance as "indeterminate object of empirical intuition") *and* the form of a sensibility affected "from outside," by the thing in itself, as well as "from within," by the "effect of understanding on sensibility." This is how *one and the same form is form of the intuited and form of intuiting*. A relevant analogy might be: when I follow with a stick the outline of a drawing on the ground, the figure I draw (the form of my *drawing*) and the figure out there (the form of the *drawn*) are one and the same. The line out there is literally the meeting point between my own action and the resistance of the ground. Similarly, forms of intuiting and forms of intuited are, in the Aesthetic, one and the same. This is because, as "forms of sensibility" (forms of intuit*ing*), they are more than the mere "capacity to intuit." They are the forms of a sensibility *affected both by the thing in itself and by spontaneity*. I say more on this point in the following pages.

extension and figure. These belong to *pure intuition*, which, even without any actual object of the senses or of sensation, exists in the mind *a priori* as a mere *form of sensibility*. (A21/B35)[13]

Extension and figure belong to the "pure intuition" of space, which is "that in which the manifold of appearances can be ordered," that is, that *by limitation of which* the extension and figure of a given object are delineated. Therefore, space and time provide the form of appearances only insofar as they are themselves an intuition: a *pure* intuition, that is, an intuition preceding and conditioning all empirical intuition; and an *undivided* intuition, that is, an intuition that is presupposed by particular intuitions rather than resulting from their combinations. But this can be no other than the intuition that, according to the footnote to section 26 quoted earlier, "precedes any concept" and has a unity that "belongs to space and time, and not to the concept of the understanding." We must then conclude, in light of sections 24 and 26 of the Transcendental Deduction, that the figurative synthesis or "effect of understanding on sensibility" generates the *pure intuition* of space and time and thereby the *form of appearances*, or form of intuition, or form of sensibility, all of which were expounded in the Transcendental Aesthetic.

From this we can draw some interesting conclusions regarding the terms "sensibility" and "form of sensibility" in the Transcendental Aesthetic. Kant defines sensibility as "the capacity (receptivity) for receiving [*bekommen*] representations through the manner in which we are affected by objects." He goes on: "Objects are *given* to us by means of sensibility, and it alone yields us *intuitions*"(A19/B33). Now, intuition is not just any representation "received through the manner in which we are affected by objects." According to the "stepladder" (*Stufenleiter*) of representations given at the beginning of the Transcendental Dialectic, intuition is a species of *cognition* (*Erkenntnis*), that is, a conscious representation *related to an object*. As such, it is distinguished from mere *sensation*, which is a mere state of the subject, by itself unrelated to any object. Let us quickly recall the first steps in Kant's ladder. The generic concept is *representation*. A representation, says Kant, is either *without* or *with* consciousness (he calls the latter *perceptio*). A *perceptio* is in turn divided into *sensation* (*Empfindung, sensatio*), which "relates only to the subject as the modification of his state," and *cognition* (a *perceptio* related to an object). Finally, cognition is divided into *intuition* and *concept*, which are distinguished from one another by the fact that "the former relates immediately to the object and is singular, the latter refers to it mediately by means of a mark which several things may have in common" (A320/B377).[14] In contrast with sensation, then, intuition is a conscious representation *related to an object*, even if this relation is "immediate" and if the

---

[13] My emphasis. Cf. also A22/B36: in the Transcendental Aesthetic, we will abstract from everything the understanding thinks through its concepts, and from all sensation, "so that nothing may remain save *pure intuition* and the *mere form* of appearances."

[14] Kant gives the Latin term *perceptio* in parentheses, as an equivalent for the German term *Perzeption*, which is rarely used elsewhere. This probably indicates he uses the term in the sense of "perception" accepted in seventeenth- and eighteenth-century theory of ideas, where "perception" is conscious representation in general, even if only obscurely (cf. Leibniz's "petites perceptions"), whether related to an object or a merely subjective state. Kant sometimes uses the German *Wahrnehmung* in

representation is "singular," thus prior to any concept.[15] One might say that, in intuition, the object is *represented* even if it is not *recognized* (under a concept). Now, in the Transcendental Aesthetic Kant characterizes sensibility as the capacity that "yields us intuitions." This means that sensibility is not merely a capacity to be consciously affected, but a capacity for conscious representations *related to an object*. But we now know, after sections 24 and 26 of the Deduction, that if sensibility is such a capacity, then it must be receptive not merely to affections received from *outside*, but also to affection from *inside*, from the *spontaneity* of the mind, or the act of *figurative synthesis*, which alone can transform the outer affection into an intuition of object. Space and time are the forms of a sensibility (receptivity) capable of being affected not merely from "outside" but from "within."[16]

Thus the *form of intuition* expounded in the Transcendental Aesthetic does indeed appear, just as much as the *pure intuition*, to be the product of the *synthesis speciosa* analyzed in section 24 of the Transcendental Deduction. And we can understand why Kant should say that, in the second part of the Deduction, he revisits "the manner in which things are given to us." But we are then faced with the paradox I mentioned earlier: the *form of intuition* presented in section 26 does not seem to have the unified synthetic character it has in the Transcendental Aesthetic. Only *formal intuition* seems to have this character. This opposition is clearest at the beginning of the footnote I cited earlier:

> Space, represented as *object* (as we are required to do in geometry), contains more than a mere form of intuition; it also contains the *gathering-together* of the manifold, given according to the form of sensibility, in an *intuitive* representation, so that the *form of intuition gives only a manifold, the formal intuition gives unity of representation*. (B160–61n, my emphasis on last sentence)

---

this broad sense, but most often he uses *Wahrnehmung* in the more specific sense of an empirical *intuition*, a sensation *related to an object*. One may be surprised to see Kant refer to intuition as *cognition* (*Erkenntnis*), given his insistence elsewhere that cognition is the *determination* of an intuition by a concept (cf. A50/B74). Kant is in fact using the term *cognition* loosely here. He calls cognition any representation *relating to an object*, and this characterizes intuition as opposed to "mere" sensation. I noted in chapter 7 that the status of *sensation* is ambiguous. By itself sensation is only a conscious state of the subject, but in most cases it also relates to the object insofar as it is the "matter" of an empirical intuition.

[15] Kant's characterization of intuition as "immediate" representation essentially means, I think, that intuition does not require the mediation of another representation to relate to an object. A concept, on the other hand, relates to an object, at least cognitively, only by the mediation of intuition. Hintikka has claimed that Kant's "immediacy criterion" for intuition was in fact redundant, and that intuition was sufficiently distinguished from concept by its being characterized as a singular representation, namely the referent of a singular term (see Hintikka, "Intuition"). But I think that for Kant the two defining characters of intuition are inseparable. This seems clear if we remember what was said in chapter 5: a concept is the representation of a "rule of our apprehension." This means that there has to be apprehension (in intuition, thus "immediate" representation as well as referent for singular terms) for there to be rules and thus "general and reflected (mediated)" representations: concepts. I agree with Parsons, that the phenomenological component of the notion of intuition, as involving some "direct presence to the mind," is important to Kant. See Parsons's postcript to "Philosophy of Arithmetic"; and "Transcendental Aesthetic."

[16] Where "outside" and "within" should be understood in the sense of the concepts of reflection "inner" and "outer" elucidated in chapter 6.

What Kant here calls *form of intuition* seems to be the form of a mere capacity to take in a manifold, devoid of any power to unify the manifold. This agrees with the definition of sensibility Kant gives at the beginning of the Transcendental Aesthetic, a "capacity . . . for receiving representations through the mode in which we are affected by objects." But not with its further characterization as that which "yields intuitions," representations *related to an object.* But how can the mere capacity to receive representations be described as having a *form*? In the Transcendental Aesthetic, the form of appearances or of empirical intuition is described as "that which so determines the manifold of appearance that it *allows of being ordered.*" On section 26, the form of intuition is only described as *giving* the manifold, whereas formal intuition provides the "combination" of this manifold. What is a form that "gives the manifold" without "so [determining the latter] that it allows of being ordered?" How can this description of the "form of sensibility" be reconciled with that given in the Transcendental Aesthetic?

The solution to this difficulty lies in Kant's evolutionary, "epigenetic" conception of the conditions of representation. Space and time as presented in the Transcendental Aesthetic are products of a figurative synthesis. But for such a production to be possible, its potentiality must be contained in receptivity itself. The latter, which "gives the manifold," must be constituted in such a way that this manifold (of sensations, *perceptiones* but not intuitions, according to the *Stufenleiter* mentioned earlier) *potentially* "allows of being ordered" in space and time. Representational receptivity, the capacity to process affections into sensations (conscious representations), must also be able to present these sensations in an intuition of space and an intuition of time. This occurs when the affection *from outside* is the occasion for the affection *from inside*—the *figurative synthesis.* The form of the receptive capacity is thus a *merely potential form*, a form that is actualized only by means of the figurative synthesis. When Kant speaks of the "form of intuition" in section 26, I think he has in mind this potential form. He rarely uses the term "form" in such an elementary sense. Generally, the context or even his explicit statement indicates, as is the case in the Transcendental Aesthetic, that the form of sensibility is not this merely potential form, but an actualized form, a form synthesized by the intervention of spontaneity: a *formal intuition.*[17]

[17] See for example Transcendental Dialectic, B457n: "Space is merely the form of outer intuition (formal intuition)." I have referred to the development of a mere "potentiality of form" into a formal intuition or form of intuition as "epigenetic." Kant uses the expression "epigenesis of pure reason" as a metaphor to describe the origin of the categories in §27 of the Transcendental Deduction (B167). The "epigenetic" explanation in biology is the theory according to which the characteristics and structure of the mature organism are predetermined but not "preimprinted" in the embryo. They are acquired through gradual development in the course of which the embryo is transformed under the influence of the environment. The theory of *epigenesis* is thus opposed to the theory of *preformation*, according to which all the characteristics of the developed organism are "imprinted" in the embryo. In the *Critique of Judgment*, Kant explicitly favors the epigenetic theory in biology (§81, Ak. V, 422–23; 308–9). He uses this model early on in his work, to describe his conception of the origin of cognitions, as opposed to both empiricist and innatist theories (see *Refl.* 4275, Ak. XVII, 492; *Refl.* 4851 and 4859, Ak. XVIII, 8 and 12. Adickes locates all of these *Reflexionen* in 1771). Where the categories are concerned, I understand this model in the following manner: the categories are the "germ" which is present from the outset in experience, but which only discursive reflection can transform into a "developed or-

This explanation is confirmed by a famous text from Kant's response to Eberhard, where he considers the question whether the forms of intuition are *innate*. His answer is close to the one he gave already in the *Inaugural Dissertation*. The representations of space and time, he says, are not innate, but acquired. Yet they are acquired not *empirically*, but *originally*.[18] However, this answer now receives a more precise treatment than in the *Dissertation*. Kant distinguishes between the *first formal ground of intuition* (the constitution of receptivity, which alone, he says, is "innate") and *formal intuition*, which he also terms *form of outer objects* (intuitions of space and time). We recognize here the *pure intuition* of the Transcendental Aesthetic (or *formal intuition* of section 26). In contrast, the "first formal ground of intuition" is closer to the *form of intuition* Kant described in section 26:

> The ground of the possibility of sensible intuition is . . . the merely particular *receptivity* of the mind, whereby it receives representations in accordance with its subjective constitution, when affected by something (in sensation). Only this first formal ground, e.g., the possibility of a representation of space, is *innate*, not the spatial representation itself. For impressions are always required in order first to enable the cognitive power to represent an object (which is always its own act). Thus, the formal *intuition* which is called space emerges as an originally acquired representation (the form of outer objects in general), the ground of which (as mere receptivity) is nevertheless innate and the acquisition of which long precedes determinate concepts of things that are in accordance with this form.[19]

Kant clearly distinguishes here between what I have called the mere potentiality of form and the formal intuitions of space and time as forms of outer objects. Equally noteworthy is the assertion which concludes the text: "The acquisition of [the formal intuition] long precedes determinate concepts of things that are in accordance with this form." This assertion agrees with the note to section 26 quoted earlier: the formal intuition "precedes any concept," its unity "belongs to space and time, and not to the concept of the understanding."[20] But if this is the case, the *synthesis speciosa* that produced this intuition is also prior to any concept, and *even to the categories*, even though it is a "determination of sensibility by the un-

---

ganism"—namely, universal concepts governing a system of cognitions according to principles. I have extended the model of epigenesis to the forms of intuition, although Kant does not explicitly use the term in this case. Here, the "germ" is what I have called the "potentiality of form" contained in receptivity and thus in the manifold that it "gives." The developed organism is the form of sensible intuition or of appearances, "developed" under the influence of both outer affection (impressions) and the affection of spontaneity (the figurative synthesis). For a detailed analysis of the theme of epigenesis in Kant, see Waxman, *Model*, 249–67.

[18] *Entdeckung*, Ak.VII, 223; 137. Cf. *Diss.*, §15, Ak. II, 406; 400. Kant develops a similar thesis concerning the categories. I should note that Allison (correctly, I think) identifies what he calls "form of intuit*ing*" and what Kant calls "first formal ground of intuition" in the Response to Eberhard. See *Idealism*, 345, n. 32. I disagree with Allison in his interpreting formal intuition as intuition *determined by concepts*. See pp. 223–25, and note 21.

[19] *Entdeckung*, Ak. VII, 222; 136.

[20] B161n.

derstanding." If my earlier analyses are correct, this should be understood as follows: space and time, as formal intuitions, are the first, most original "effect of
the understanding on sensibility." Within these formal intuitions are achieved the
figurative syntheses generating the given multiplicities that are to be reflected
under concepts according to the logical forms of our judgments. Not only do
these intuitions precede any *determinate* concept (whether empirical or mathematical), they also precede the universal concepts (the *categories*). For they are
prior to (and a necessary condition of) each specific synthesis making possible reflection under one or the other of the logical forms of our judgments and thus, a
fortiori, prior to the categories, "universal representations of synthesis."

Kant's distinction between *forms of intuition* and *formal intuitions* has under-
standably given rise to much commentary. Whatever their differences, most
commentators have this in common: they interpret section 26 as distinguishing
indeterminate representations of space and time (the "mere forms of intuition,"
supposed to be the object of the Transcendental Aesthetic) from representation of
space and time *determined* by concepts (formal intuitions).[21] My analysis is obviously at odds with such a reading: I have argued that both the "form of intuition" and the "pure intuition" of the Transcendental Aesthetic are revealed, in the
second step of the Transcendental Deduction, to be the product of a unifying *synthesis speciosa*; that the "formal intuition" of section 26 can thus be identified
with both "form of intuition" and "pure intuition" of the Transcendental Aesthetic; and that when "form of intuition" is distinguished from "pure intuition" in
the Aesthetic, the reason for such distinction is mostly that *form* is paired with
matter (sensations, appearances), whereas "pure intuition" can be considered in
abstraction from all matter. I shall not repeat the reasons I have already given, but
I would like to make two additional remarks on behalf of the view I am defend-
ing. The first concerns *form of intuition*. The second, *formal intuition* and the
meaning of *synthesis speciosa* as an "effect of understanding on sensibility."

1. As we saw, the term "form" has meaning only in relation to the term "matter." Matter is the determinable, form the determination. Attempting to explain the
difference between "form of intuition" and "formal intuition" as a difference intrinsic to the representations of space and time, instead of considering the forms
in relation to the matter they determine, is misunderstanding the very notion of
form (which is then characterized by the fact that it is . . . *indeterminate*, quite a
paradoxical reversal of Kantian terminology!). This is, if I may borrow Kant's
formulation against Eberhard, wandering through the *Critique* "with the help of
a dictionary,"[22] in search of a fixed equivalent for the expression "form of intu-

---

[21] Cf. particularly Buchdahl, *Metaphysics*, 573, n. 2; 579–94; Allison, *Idealism*, 94–98. Heidegger's interpretation deserves special mention; I discuss it later. Waxman defends a view that is close
to the one defended here, in that he identifies the formal intuition of §26 with the form of intuition
and pure intuition of the Transcendental Aesthetic. He also gives an interesting account of recent literature on the topic. See Waxman, *Model*, 79–117. He might disagree, however, with my characterization of formal intuition as resulting from the affection of sensibility by the *Vermögen zu urteilen* or
capacity to form judgments.

[22] Cf. *Entdeckung*, Ak. VIII, 223; 136.

ition," whereas one should interpret it only in relation to its correlative *matter*. The latter can be (i) sensation, or (ii) "that which corresponds to sensation," or (iii) appearance. The corresponding *form of intuition* is then (i) the "first formal ground of sensibility" mentioned in Kant's response to Eberhard, or (ii) the form that results from the "effect of understanding on sensibility" or *synthesis speciosa* (form of appearance, whose matter is "that which corresponds to sensation"), or finally (iii) the form of the sensible world, whose matter is the appearances thought under the categories. For its part, "pure" or "formal" intuition is sometimes to be identified with "form of appearances" or even "form of the sensible world," sometimes to be understood as space and time considered *independently of any (phenomenal) matter*. This is why it provides the space "required in geometry."[23]

2. If, as I have argued, it is a mistake to suppose that "form of intuition" is opposed to "formal intuition" as being less determinate, it is also a mistake to suppose that "formal intuition" is determined *by concepts*. That this view should be so often defended is surprising, since Kant explicitly says, in section 26, that formal intuition is *prior to any concept*. The common view is based, I suggest, on a misunderstanding of Kant's assertion that in formal intuition, "the understanding determines sensibility." If one reads "the understanding" as "the pure concepts of the understanding," that is, the categories as universal and reflected representations (of pure synthesis), then indeed we have to conclude that formal intuition is generated by the application of the categories, or even by construction according to pure mathematical concepts. But then Kant's assertion, in the footnote to section 26, that formal intuition "precedes any concept" remains very mysterious indeed. However, if one reads "the understanding" as *das Vermögen zu urteilen*, the capacity to judge, then one can understand, as I suggested earlier, that the capacity to form judgments, "affecting sensibility," generates the pure intuitions of space and time as the necessary *intuitive* counterpart to our discursive capacity to reflect *universal* concepts, concepts whose extension (the multiplicities of singular objects thought under them) is potentially unlimited. When this original intuition is produced, no concept is thereby *yet* generated. Everything, as it were, remains to be done. But part of the minimal equipment that a human being, capable of discursive thought, has at his disposal, is the capacity to generate the "pure" intuitions of space and time as that in which empirical objects are instances of *concepts* (i.e., universal representations, representations whose logical extension is unlimited). This is how the *synthesis speciosa* can be said to be an "effect of the understanding on sensibility," *prior to any concept*, although *by it* all conceptual representation of empirical objects is made possible.

Here again it is worthwhile to compare my interpretation with Heidegger's.[24] Heidegger fully recognizes the *unity* Kant confers to forms of intuition in the

[23] For further development of this point, see chapter 9.
[24] See in particular Heidegger, *Phän. Int.*, §9.

Transcendental Aesthetic. He also recognizes the identity between space and time as *pure intuitions* and space and time as *forms of intuition*, and that the form of intuition has its own brand of (preconceptual) unity. But for him, this purely intuitive unity is distinct from the unity of formal intuition, which is determined *by concepts*. In other words, Heidegger grants unity to the form of intuition (identified with pure intuition) only at the cost of distinguishing *pure* intuition and *formal* intuition. Consequently, he pries apart the space and time of the Transcendental Aesthetic and the formal intuition of section 26. He thinks that the latter concerns only *conceptualized* spatiotemporal representations, most notably mathematical constructions. But as I pointed out, in section 26 Kant explicitly indicates that formal intuition is *prior to any concept*. And if *pure intuition* and *formal intuition* were different, Kant would have no reason to refer to the Transcendental Aesthetic when mentioning the unity of the formal intuition. My disagreement with Heidegger's reading is the same, I think, as the one I expressed earlier concerning the identity of intuitive and discursive synthesis as the ground of the metaphysical deduction of the categories. According to Heidegger, the unity of intuition is the result of a transcendental synthesis of imagination that, far from being the "effect of the understanding on sensibility," is the "common root" of intuition and pure thought. It is thus no surprise that he should distinguish pure intuition (the intuitive unity resulting from transcendental imagination alone) from formal intuition (which he interprets as conceptual production, and thus the result of the collaboration of intuitive unity and intellectual unity). But if we do not share his opposition to the idea of an "effect of understanding on sensibility," nothing stops us from accepting that pure intuition and formal intuition are one and the same intuition, produced by the *synthesis speciosa* or the effect of the understanding on sensibility.

I have argued that the second step of the B Deduction is a reexamination of the *manner in which things are given to us*. Here again, the B edition gives clearer expression to the radicality of Kant's view than the A. In the A Deduction, with its two recapitulations "from below" and "from above," Kant showed that all synthesis is ultimately subject to the transcendental unity of apperception. Now he says that *space and time themselves*, which might have been assumed prior to any synthesis, are on the contrary the result of a transcendental synthesis of imagination that is an "effect of understanding on sensibility."[25] How important this argument is, we can see if we recall how at the beginning of the Transcen-

---

[25] Although this thesis is not made as clear in the A Deduction, it fully agrees with Kant's intentions already there. See for instance the Preliminary Explanation of the Possibility of the Categories, as a priori Cognition: "There is *one single* experience in which all perceptions are represented as in thoroughgoing and orderly connection, *just as there is only one space and one time* in which all forms of appearance and all relation of being or not-being occur" (my emphasis). This sentence and the following paragraph introduce the idea of a transcendental ground of the unity of the synthesis of appearances (A110–11). The unity of space and time, just like that of experience, stems from their relation to this originary ground. See also A99–100, A107.

dental Deduction Kant contrasted the relative ease of his argument concerning space and time and the much greater difficulty of the argument concerning the categories:

> That objects of sensible intuition must conform to the formal conditions of sensibility which lie *a priori* in the mind is evident, because otherwise they would not be objects for us. But that they must likewise conform to the conditions which the understanding requires for the synthetic unity of thought is a conclusion the grounds of which are by no means so obvious. Appearances might very well be so constituted that the understanding should not find them to be in accordance with the conditions of its unity. Everything might be in such confusion that, for instance, in the series of appearances nothing presented itself which might yield a rule of synthesis and so answer to the concept of cause and effect. This concept would then be altogether empty, null, and meaningless. (A90/B123)

Cause and effect are concepts by means of which appearances are *thought* (reflected discursively in judgments of experience). They are not, like space and time, intuitive representations in which appearances are *given*. Thus it is conceivable, said Kant at the beginning of the Deduction, that appearances be such that they cannot be reflected under any concept of causal relation, whereas it is impossible that an appearance be given that did not conform to the conditions of space and time. But now, if we accept the argument of section 26, the very fact that appearances are given in space and time is a sufficient ground for their being in conformity with the categories, even though it remains true that they are not given *in* a category (as "in" an intuition) or even cognized *under* a category until the relevant operations of comparison/reflection/abstraction, together with a priori construction, have generated such cognition. Nevertheless, since the space and time of the Transcendental Aesthetic are, as intuitions, products of *synthesis speciosa* or "effects of understanding on sensibility," the fact that appearances are given in them is a sufficient warrant that they *can* be cognized as "determined [in themselves] with respect to one or the other of our forms of judgment," and thus subsumed under the categories.[26]

Kant gives two examples to illustrate the conformity to the categories of appearances apprehended in space and time: the perception of a house, the perception of the freezing of water. The former illustrates perception *in space*, the latter perception *in time*:

> When, for instance, by apprehension of the manifold of a house I make the empirical intuition of it into a perception, the *necessary unity* of space and outer sensible intuition in general lies at the basis of my apprehension, and I draw as it were the outline of the house in conformity with this synthetic unity of the manifold in space.

> When, to take another example, I perceive the freezing of water, I apprehend two states, fluidity and solidity, and these as standing to one another in a relation of time.

[26] *Prol.* §21; cf. B128 in the *Critique*.

But in time, which I place at the basis of the appearance [insofar] as [it is] inner *intuition*, I necessarily represent to myself synthetic *unity* of the manifold, without which that relation of time could not be given in an intuition as being *determined* (in respect of time-sequence). (B162–63)

Kant goes on to show that the apprehension of the house in space and the apprehension of the freezing of water in time conform respectively to the categories of quantity and causality. The category of quantity is the universal representation of the synthetic unity *in space* in conformity with which I draw the outline of the house. The category of cause is the universal representation of the synthetic unity *in time* in conformity with which I perceive the succession of the states of water. It is highly significant that Kant should have chosen these two categories for his examples, one an instance of *mathematical* synthesis (in this case, quantity), the other an instance of *dynamical* synthesis (in this case, causal relation). Nevertheless, these two examples are not essential to the argument itself. Their full explanation can be given only later, when Kant expounds the Schematism of the Concepts of Pure Understanding and the System of Principles.[27] To say the truth, the examples are even partly misleading, because it may seem that Kant is describing two distinct intuitions: on the one hand the intuition of *space*, in which *figures* are apprehended (apprehension of the house); on the other hand the intuition of *time*, in which *successions* are apprehended (apprehension of the freezing of water). But this is not how Kant has explained the intuitions of space and time as products of *synthesis speciosa.* He has explained *synthesis speciosa* as production of the intuition of space *by means of* production of the intuition of time, and conversely production of the intuition of time *by means of* production of the intuition of space, *outer sense* and *inner sense* being linked together by their common relation to the objective unity of apperception.[28] In order to elucidate the relation of space and time in our two empirical examples, we thus need to give closer consideration to the relation of outer sense and inner sense in *synthesis speciosa.*

[27] On the distinction between "mathematical" and "dynamical" synthesis, see A160/B199, B201–2n. This difference will be elucidated in detail in chapters 9, 10, and 11, together with the Schematism and Principle of Pure Understanding corresponding to each category.

[28] This combined production of the representation of space and that of time is most striking when Kant describes *synthesis speciosa* in the second part of §24: "We cannot think a line without *drawing* it in thought, or a circle without *describing* it. We cannot represent the three dimensions of space save by *positing* [*setzen*] three lines at right angle to one another, and we cannot represent time itself save insofar as we attend, in the *drawing* of a straight line (which has to serve as the outer figurative representation of time) merely to the act of synthesis of the manifold by which we successively determine inner sense, and in so doing attend to the succession of this determination in inner sense. Motion, as an act of the subject (not as a determination of an object) and therefore the synthesis of the manifold in space, first produces the concept of succession—if we abstract from this manifold and attend solely to the act through which we determine the inner sense according to its form. The understanding does not, therefore, find in inner sense such a combination of the manifold, but *produces* it, by *affecting* the sense [bringt sie hervor, *indem er ihn* affiziert]" (B154, Kant's emphasis).

SYNTHESIS SPECIOSA, OUTER SENSE, INNER SENSE

Kant characterizes the figurative synthesis as an "effect of the understanding on sensibility"[29] or as "the affection of *inner sense* by understanding."[30] This "affection" has two aspects. First, it is an act by which the understanding affects inner sense *with a given manifold*:

> But since there lies in us a certain form of *a priori* sensible intuition which depends on the receptivity of the faculty of representation (sensibility), the understanding, as spontaneity, is able to determine inner sense through the manifold of given representations, in accordance with the synthetic unity of apperception. . . . This synthesis of the manifold of sensible intuition . . . may be entitled *figurative* synthesis (*synthesis speciosa*). (B150–51)

Second, to say that the determination of inner sense takes place "in conformity with the synthetic unity of apperception" is to say that the understanding affects inner sense *with its own acts of combination*. These two aspects are interdependent. As spontaneity (understanding), the mind combines what it receives in the form of outer intuition; and it affects itself, as inner sense, with this combination. The proper function of this act of combination and self-affection is to synthesize an *empirical* given. Nevertheless, this act has a "pure" aspect, manifested in the a priori construction of geometrical concepts. The inseparability of temporal and spatial intuition, the fact that they are jointly produced, is most apparent in this "pure" aspect of the *synthesis speciosa*. The understanding produces the intuition of space only insofar as it affects inner sense with this production. It thereby also produces the intuition of time as the form in which it intuits its own act (of producing the spatial intuition). There would be no intuition of time were it not for the act of producing a figure in space. Both intuitions are the result of one and the same act of self-affection:

> We cannot think a line without *drawing* it in thought, or a circle without *describing* it. We cannot represent the three dimensions of space save by *setting* three lines at right angles to one another from the same point. Even time itself we cannot represent, save insofar as we attend, in the drawing of a straight line (which has to serve as the outer figurative representation of time), merely to the act of synthesis of the manifold whereby we successively determine inner sense, and in so doing attend to the succession of this determination in inner sense. (B154)

[29] The transcendental synthesis of imagination is "an effect of the understanding on sensibility" (B152); by means of this synthesis, "the understanding determines sensibility" (B161n).

[30] "What determines inner sense is the understanding and its originary power of combining the manifold of intuition, that is, of bringing it under an apperception, upon which the possibility of understanding itself rests" (B153). "Thus the understanding, under the title of a *transcendental synthesis of imagination*, performs this act upon the *passive* subject, whose *faculty* it is, and we are therefore justified in saying that inner sense is affected thereby" (B153–54).

Kant insists particularly on this original generation of the intuition of time. It means, he says, that we do not obtain this intuition from perceiving the motion of things in space, but rather from our own action, that is, from the "synthesis of the manifold in space . . . *if we abstract from this manifold and attend solely to the act* through which we determine the inner sense according to its form" (B155, my emphasis). The reason time is called form of *inner sense* is precisely that it is the form in which we intuit *our own act* of representation. But to say that it is the form of intuition of our *acts* is to say that we no more *find* time in inner sense than we *find* space in outer sense. The intuition of time, in which we perceive the successive character of the production of a figure, is, just like the intuition of space, generated originally by the *synthesis speciosa*. "The understanding does not, therefore, find in inner sense such a combination of the manifold, but *produces* it, in *affecting* that sense" (B155).

The two examples given in section 26 (the apprehension of a house, the apprehension of the freezing of water) obscure the original interdependence of the intuitions of space and of time because they do not illustrate pure figurative synthesis, but *synthesis of apprehension*, by means of which an *empirical* given is taken up into figurative synthesis. The perception of the house is a synthesis of the spatial configuration of an empirical object. The perception of the freezing of water is a synthesis of the succession of states of an empirical object. The case of apprehending the house by "drawing the outline" may perhaps illustrate the interdependence of space and time as it exists in the "pure" *synthesis speciosa* of section 24.[31] But the case of apprehending the freezing of water presents quite another problem with regard to time. In this example, time is not only the form of the apprehension of my act of representation, but also the form of *the object itself*. Paraphrasing Bergson, we might say that one must wait for water to solidify just as one must wait for sugar to melt.[32] Here the perception of succession is dependent on this expectation, not on an arbitrarily performed act of synthesis. In other words, with these two examples we are faced with two different temporalities. One is the temporal character of our act of representation, the other the temporal character of the empirical object. It is not at all clear how the *synthesis speciosa* of section 24 may account for this duality.

The Two Aspects of Time in the Inaugural Dissertation

This difficulty is not a new one. Already in the *Inaugural Dissertation*, Kant considered time under two aspects whose relation was not explicitly analyzed. In the first section of the *Dissertation*, time is presented as the form of our sensibility responsible for the fact that neither the idea of a totality of substantial compounds, nor that of their complete division, can be represented *in concreto*, that

---

[31] "I draw as it were the outline of the house" (B162), just as earlier, I drew the line, the circle, or the three dimensions of space.

[32] See Bergson, "Données immédiates," chap. 2.

is, generated in intuition, although both are necessary representations of the intellect. This impossibility of representing *in concreto* what is nonetheless thought *in abstracto* (in universal concepts) motivates Kant's distinction between sensible cognition and intellectual cognition, and thus between sensible and intelligible world. In this context, time appears as the sensible condition of all intuitively representable composition and division, which means also, of all mathematical operations.[33]

But on the other hand, time is, just as space is, a *forma seu sensibilium species*, form or configuration of sensible *things* (and not merely of our own operations of composition and decomposition, as in the previous case), imprinted on them by the particular nature of our minds.[34] From this point of view, time *and space* are to the same degree, and in the same way, *forms of the sensible world*. The third part of the *Dissertation* is devoted to these forms, which are expounded in exactly parallel ways. Both are prior to the relations whose representations they make possible, both are singular representations, both are intuitions, both are *quanta continua*, both are subjective, and if one attempts to posit either as a being or as the determination of a being *in itself*, for both the result is a purely imaginary being. The distinction between *outer* sense and *inner* sense plays no role in this exposition. Just as much as space, time is the form by means of which we coordinate *sensations*, that is, the effects of outer objects on our sensibility. This identity of function is most clear when Kant characterizes the domain of objects for which space and time provide the forms.

> Accordingly, whatever the principle of the form of the sensible world may, in the end, be, its embrace is limited to *actual things*, insofar as they are thought capable of *falling under the senses*. Accordingly, it embraces neither immaterial substances, which are already as such, by definition, excluded from the outer senses, nor the cause of the world. . . . These formal principles . . . are absolutely primary and universal; they are, so to speak, the schemata and conditions of everything sensitive in human cognition. I shall now show that there are two such principles, namely, space and time.[35]

In section 14, time is described as the "condition of the relations to be found in sensible things" and as the "principle of the laws of what is continuous in the changes of the universe."[36] Even when Kant says that the succession *of our representations* gives us the intuition of time, he mentions in the same breath *motion*, that is, the succession of positions of *things*: "we are able to calculate the *quantity* of time only in the concrete, namely either by *motion* or by *a series of thoughts*."[37]

[33] *Diss.*, §1, Ak. II, 387–89; 377–79.

[34] *Diss.*, §4, Ak. II, 392–93; 384–85.

[35] *Diss.*, §13, Ak. II, 398; 391.

[36] *Diss.*, §14, 3d and 4th points, Ak. II, 399; 392.

[37] *Diss.*, §14, 5th point, Ak. II, 401; 394. The only difference to be found between Kant's explanation of time and his explanation of space, is that in the latter case Kant speaks of *outer sensations*, whereas he speaks only of *sensations* in the case of time (§15, C and E). To be sure, he mentions "the doctrine of Leibniz and his followers," according to which time is "something real which has been ab-

In fact, both the exposition of space and the exposition of time have as their background the cosmological controversy stemming from the Leibniz-Clarke correspondence. There space and time were treated in parallel ways. For Leibniz, both space *and time* are only relations: "If space and time were anything absolute, that is, if they were anything else, besides certain orders of things; then indeed my assertion would be a contradiction."[38] For Clarke, the Newtonian, space and time are realities in themselves:

> Space and time are not the mere order of things, but real quantities (which order and succession are not).[39]

> If no creatures existed, yet the ubiquity of God, and the continuance of his existence, would make space and duration to be exactly the same as they are now.[40]

In this context, time is not fundamentally related to our inner states, or to the succession of ideas. In the *New Essays*, Philalethes asserts that we obtain the idea of duration from the succession of our ideas, and Theophilus answers that "a train of perceptions arouses the idea of duration, but it does not create it."[41] For Leibniz, what "creates" the idea of duration is the confused representation of an order of incompossibles; similarly, what "creates" the idea of space is the confused representation of an order of compossibles. In the *Dissertation*, Kant too treats space and time on the same footing. But his position is a compromise between the Leibnizian and Newtonian positions, which means it is also a rejection of both. Like Leibniz, Kant asserts that space and time *are only relations*, and that as such they are infinitely divisible and expandable. But like Newton, he asserts that the *one* space and the *one* time are ontologically prior to things, their states, and their relations. Against both Leibniz and Newton, he maintains that space and time are only forms of appearances, which tell us nothing about a world considered *in itself*.

Nonetheless, this strictly symmetrical treatment of space and of time is nuanced in the Corollary to the third part of the *Dissertation*. Kant considers again the representation of time and underlines its primacy over that of space. Time "embraces in its relations absolutely all things, namely, space itself and, in addition, the accidents which are not included in the relations of space, such as the thoughts of the mind." But here, unlike in the *Critique*, Kant does not relate this primacy of time over space to what I have called the "interiorization to represen-

---

stracted from the succession of internal states." But this is only to state his opposition to this view, which makes time an empirical and abstract, rather than a priori and intuitive representation. In fact, the doctrine he opposes here is surely not Leibniz's, but rather that of the *Schulphilosophen* who were under the influence of Locke as much as of Leibniz. Indeed the Lockian influence is manifest, I think, in Lambert's and Mendelssohn's argument when they deny Kant's assertion of the merely subjective and ideal character of time by invoking the undeniable reality of the succession of our representations. More on this later.

[38] Leibniz's fourth paper, §16, *Leibniz-Clarke Correspondence*, in *G* VII, 378; 39.

[39] Ibid., Clarke's fourth reply, §§16–17 (*G* VII, 385; 49).

[40] Ibid., §41 (*G* VII, 388; 52).

[41] Leibniz, *New Essays*, II, 14, §16.

tation of the object of representation." As is apparent in the passage I have just quoted, the "thoughts of the mind" are rather presented as a particular case of objects in time, another case being space and external objects. Time is the universal form in which *changes of state* are possible, whether the latter are representational or material:

> [Space and time] constitute *the underlying foundations upon which the understanding rests*, when, in accordance with the laws of logic and with the greatest possible certainty, it draws conclusions from the primary data of intuition. Indeed, of these concepts *the one* properly concerns the intuition of an *object*, while the other concerns its *state*, especially its *representational* state [. . . *alter proprie intuitum objecti, alter statum concernit, inprimis repraesentativum*].

Does this last assertion ("time . . . concerns its *state*, especially its *representational* state") finally point to an original relation between time and what Kant, in the *Critique*, calls *inner sense*? I do not think so. The most the preceding formulation might mean in this regard is that the intuition of time relates *primarily* to the succession of our representations, and only *secondarily* to the succession of states of things. In itself, this is not enough to make time a form of inner sense as Kant will understand it in the *Critique*. Again, time is the form of the sensible world in general, and within the sensible world it is the form of the succession of our representational states. This way of considering time is manifest also when Kant stresses the relation of time to causality: "the relation of cause and caused, at least in the case of external objects, requires relations of space. In the case of all objects, however, whether they be external or internal, it is only with the assistance of the relation of time that the mind can be instructed as to what is earlier and what is later, that is to say, as to what is cause and what is caused."

Only at the end of this recapitulation does Kant return to the relation between *time* and the intuition of *quantity*, which he discussed in the first section of the *Dissertation*: "And we can only render the *quantity* of space itself intelligible by expressing it numerically, having related it to a measure taken as a unity. This number itself is nothing but a multiplicity which is distinctly known by counting, that is to say, by successively adding one to one in a given time."[42] Here at last we are again presented with the aspect of time with which Kant began the *Dissertation*. But its relation to time as the form of the "coordination of our sensations" remains obscure. It would be comprehensible only if time, as the sensible condition of mathematical operations, were also understood as the form of a coordination of sensations. But what could these sensations be? They cannot be outer sensations, or mathematics would be empirical cognition. Hence they must be genuinely *inner* sensations, in which the mind affects *itself*. Without the notion of such an affection there is no possible unity between time considered as a necessary condition of mathematical thought and time as a condition of the coordination of outer sensations. But this solution is absent from the *Dissertation*. Kant

---

[42] All texts quoted are from the "Corollary" to section 3 of the *Dissertation*, Ak. II, 405–6; 399–400.

finds a distinct formulation for it only later. The association of time with *inner* sense is the first step in this direction. But only the doctrine of the *synthesis speciosa*, in the B edition of the *Critique*, provides an explicit and complete exposition of this solution.

Inner Sense: From the Dissertation to the Critique

Time is explicitly attributed to *inner* sense in the 1772 Letter to Herz, in which Kant replies to various criticisms of his *Dissertation*. I submit that even though Kant rejects these criticisms as misunderstandings, they nonetheless played an important role in the evolution that led him to specify that time is the form of *inner* sense and space the form of *outer* sense.

The reaction Kant's *Dissertation* received from Mendelssohn and Lambert is well known. Both found unacceptable the description of time as a *form of sensibility*, that is, as a determination of things *only insofar as they appear to us*. Granted, they said, one might doubt the reality of space. But the reality of time is as indubitable as the succession of our representations, which even the staunchest idealist would not think of denying.[43] Thus Kant's view, the import of which was primarily ontological—what is the being of space, what is the being of time?—and whose background was a discussion of rational cosmology, was criticized from a psychological standpoint, by an argument stressing the undeniable empirical reality of the succession of our representations. Kant was surprised by this objection: he took his own doctrine to be no other than the radicalization of the Leibnizian thesis that space and time are only *phenomena*. From this perspective, there is no reason to treat time any differently than space. However, Kant does take the objection seriously enough to answer it at length, not only in the Letter to Herz but again in the first edition of the *Critique*.[44] The reason he takes such pains is not only, as he says, that the objection will inevitably come to any reader's mind and thus requires a convincing refutation. It is also, I think, that the objection obliged him to pay closer attention to the relation between time and *inner* sense:

> An objection . . . has made me reflect considerably, because it seems to be the most serious objection that can be raised against the system, an objection that seems to occur naturally to everybody. . . . It runs like this: changes are something real (according to the testimony of inner sense). Now, they are possible only on the assumption of time; therefore time is something real that is involved in the determination of the things in themselves.

Kant's reply to this is well known: the objection is based on a misunderstanding: "I do not deny that changes are real, any more than I deny that bodies are real, even though by *real* I only mean that something real corresponds to the

---

[43] Letter from Lambert to Kant, October 13, 1770, Ak. X, 103–11 (esp. 107–9); 60–67. Letter from Mendelssohn to Kant, December 25, 1770, Ak. X, 113–17 (esp. 115); 67–70 (esp. 69).

[44] Letter to Herz of February 21, 1772, Ak. X, 129–35 (esp. 134); 70–76 (esp. 75); also *KrV*, A36–38/B53–54.

appearance."[45] Something real corresponds to the succession of our representations, just as something real corresponds to the spatial relations of objects. This answer is in tune with the proper standpoint of the *Dissertation*, in which what was discussed was not the psychological experience of time but its ontological status, which is the same as the ontological status of space: both are mere forms of appearances. However, accepting Lambert's assertion that thanks to the "testimony of inner sense" the reality of time is more immediately indubitable than the reality of space,[46] Kant was compelled to give further thought to the relation between space and time.

The outcome is to be found in the first edition of the *Critique*. In the Transcendental Aesthetic, space is presented as the form of *outer* sense, time as the form of *inner* sense:

> By means of outer sense, a property of our mind, we represent to ourselves objects as outside us, and all without exception in space. In space their shape, magnitude, and relation to one another are determined or determinable. Inner sense, by means of which the mind intuits itself or its inner state, yields indeed no intuition of the soul itself as an object; but there is nevertheless a determinate form [namely, time] in which alone the intuition of inner states is possible, and everything which belongs to inner determinations is therefore represented in relations of time. Time cannot be outwardly intuited, any more than space can be intuited as something in us. (A22–23/B37)

The notions of inner and outer sense are quite common in German *Schulphilosophie*.[47] But I suggest that, more than Baumgarten or Tetens, Kant's discussion here echoes Locke. For it is in Locke and not in the works of German philosophers that Kant could find outer sense (which Locke simply calls *sensation*) correlated with space, inner sense with time. Comparing Locke's analysis in the *Essay* and Kant's analysis in the Transcendental Aesthetic will thus be helpful to

---

[45] Ak. X, 134; 75.

[46] In fairness to Lambert, it should be added that, for him, asserting the indubitable reality of time in the name of the undeniable reality of the succession of our representations does not mean we should doubt the reality of space. The merely subjective character of the forms of sensibility seems equally unacceptable to him in both cases, but it seems particularly absurd in the case of time, for the reason mentioned (cf. Ak. X, 107; 63). On the whole, he prefers to abandon any ontological definition of space and time (107; 63), and refuses to bother with Leibniz and Clarke's "theological difficulties" (108; 64). This letter deserves to be read, for its wit and delightful exasperation with what Lambert holds to be the useless obscurities of metaphysics.

[47] It is to Locke, it seems, that we owe the notion of inner sense understood as the reflection of the mind on its own operations and representations. Inner sense and outer sense are not mentioned in Wolff's *Psychologia empirica*: the chapter on *sense* (sec. II, chap. 2: *De sensu*) deals only with *sensations*. However, in 535 of Baumgarten's *Psychologia empirica* (§§504–669 of his *Metaphysica*), which Kant used in his lectures, we find the following definitions: "I have a faculty of sensing, or *sense* [*sensum, der Sinn*]. *Sense* either represents the state of my soul, *inner* sense [*internus, der Innre*], or the state of my body, *outer* sense [*externus, die aüssre Sinnen*]. Consequently, *sensation* is either *inner*, through inner sense (consciousness in the strict sense), or *outer*, actualized through outer sense" (Ak. XV-1, 13; the italics correspond to capitals in the text Adickes transcribed; the German terms next to the Latin terms were Kant's addition in his copy of Baumgarten's textbook). Inner sense is analyzed in detail by Tetens, whose *Philosophische Versuche über die menschliche Natur und ihre Entwicklung* appeared in 1777. On the influence this work had on the development of Kant's thought,

clarify the two aspects of time (time as the form of our own acts of synthesis, time as a form of the object itself) in the *synthesis speciosa* expounded in the second edition of the *Critique*. This comparison will help us to evaluate the ways in which Kant combined his own metaphysical inspiration in the *Dissertation*, and the empiricopsychological inspiration of Lambert's and Mendelssohn's objection.

Time As the Form of Inner Sense: Kant and Locke

According to Locke, we acquire the idea of space through sight and touch—through what Kant later calls *outer* senses. But we acquire the idea of time through *inner* sense. More precisely, the idea of time is the idea of duration insofar as it can be measured; and the idea of duration, just like that of succession, is an idea of reflection, or inner sense:

> It is evident to anyone who will but observe what passes in his own mind, that there is a train of ideas which constantly succeed one another in his understanding, as long as he is awake. Reflection on these appearances of several ideas one after another in our minds, is that which furnishes us with the idea of *succession*: and the distance between any parts of that succession, or between the appearance of any two ideas in our minds, is that we call *duration*. For while we are thinking, or whilst we receive successively several ideas in our minds, we know that we do exist; and so we call the existence, or the continuation of the existence of ourselves, or anything else, commensurate to the succession of any ideas in our minds, the duration of ourselves, or any such other thing co-existent with our thinking.[48]

The original of which our ideas of succession and duration are derived is the "train of ideas" within us. When this train ceases—for example, when we are asleep—so does the perception of duration. Similarly, if someone fastens his attention on a single idea, duration will feel much shorter to him than it would to someone feeling a multiplicity of ideas passing through his mind. Only by the mediation of this inner awareness of the succession of our own ideas can the idea of duration also be applied to outer things:

> That we have our notion of succession and duration from this original, viz. from reflection on the train of ideas, which we find to appear one after another in our own minds, seems plain to me, in that we have no perception of duration but by considering the train of ideas that take their turns in our understandings.

> Indeed a man having, from reflecting on the succession and number of his own thoughts, got the notion or idea of duration, he can apply that notion to things which exist while he does not think; as he that has got the idea of extension from bodies by his sight or touch, can apply it to distances, where no body is seen or felt.[49]

---

see De Vleeschauwer, *Déduction*, I, 299–322. Note the shift from the singular (*sensus externus*) to the plural (*die aüssre Sinnen* [*sic*]). The same variation is present in the *Anthropology*, §15. For Kant, outer sense (in the *singular*), the form of which is space, combines the data of the five senses (outer senses, in the plural), which relate us to the objects external to our representations of them.

[48] Locke, *Essay*, bk. II, chap. xiv, §3.

[49] Ibid., bk. II, chap. xiv, §§4–5.

It might seem, Locke continues, that we acquire our idea of duration from the continuous change of things around us. But in fact this change itself is perceived only if it is commensurable with the perceptible succession and duration of our ideas. A change that is too slow, like the apparent movement of the sun in the sky or the turning of the hands of a watch, is not perceived as such. We perceive only its results, the different positions of the sun, or of the hand of the watch, at different moments. Similarly, a movement that is too fast, like that of a cannonball, is perceived as a continuous line. Only a change that occurs in things at a pace close enough to that of the succession of our ideas can be perceived. Thus the perceived succession *of ideas* is the means by which the succession of outer things and their states is perceived. Nevertheless, when it comes to *measuring* duration, the states of things external to ideas, and more particularly certain regular motions, are the means by which time can be measured. Because of the role played by motion in the *measurement* of time, motion has wrongly been considered as the *origin*, that is, the *original* of our idea of time.

Kant knew the *Essay Concerning Human Understanding*. He probably had Locke's explanations in mind when he wrote that "Time cannot be outwardly intuited, any more than space can be intuited as something in us" (A23/B37). This twofold restriction needs explanation, particularly its first clause: it is in no way self-evident that time cannot be "outwardly intuited," that is, intuited through the changes of state in outer objects. In the exposition of time, Kant makes clear what he means by saying that "[time] cannot be a determination of outer appearances; it has to do neither with shape nor position, but with the relation of representations in our inner state" (A33/B49–50). But this is not convincing. That time has to do neither with shape nor with position is not enough to prove that it is not a form of outer sense if one considers, as Kant did in the *Dissertation* (and as he never denied later), that shapes and positions themselves, along with the entirety of space, are *in time*. However, Kant's intention becomes clearer if we relate it to Locke's psychological analyses. Time is to be related to *inner sense*, not outer sense, if the only succession immediately present to us is the succession of our ideas. In order to be perceived, the succession of states of things must in some way or other be in tune with the succession of our ideas or, in Kantian terms, of our representations. So considered, the relation of time to inner sense is better expressed in the conclusion of the Aesthetic:

> Time is the formal *a priori* condition of all appearances whatsoever. . . . But since all representations, whether they have for their objects outer things or not, belong, in themselves, as determinations of the mind, to our inner state; and since this inner state stands under the formal condition of inner intuition, and so belongs to time, time is an *a priori* condition of all appearance whatsoever. It is the immediate condition of inner appearances (of our souls), and thereby the mediate condition of outer appearances. (A34/B50)

Here the shift from the *Dissertation* to the *Critique* is readily perceivable. Only by the mediation of its being *given in inner sense* does every appearance, whether "outer" or "inner," have temporal determination.

To be sure, the manner in which time is related to inner sense is quite different for Kant and for Locke. For the British empiricist, it means that the only succession we directly perceive is the succession of our ideas. The succession of states of things is perceptible only if it can be reflected in a perceptible succession of ideas. For Kant too, only the succession of our representations is immediately perceived.[50] But the relation between *inner* succession and *outer* succession is different in kind from Locke's image of two parallel chains of events proceeding at more or less comparable rates. For Kant, this relation belongs to the schematism of the categories, which I shall analyze in the following chapters. What matters here is that this difference in the way Kant and Locke understand the relation between *inner* and *outer* succession is related to a fundamental difference in their ontological characterizations of time. For Locke, succession, duration, and time may be perceived only by inner sense; they are nonetheless determinations "in themselves," both of representations and of the things they represent. For Kant, succession, duration, and time are no more determinations that exist "in themselves" in inner sense than they are in outward appearances. To say that time is the form of inner sense is not only to say that all perception of time is primarily perception of the succession of our representations in inner sense, but also to say that time is the form according to which inner sense apprehends what is represented in it. Thus the meaning of the relation between time and inner sense according to Kant is far more radical than it was in Locke's psychological analysis.

Nevertheless, Locke opened the way to this radicalization by treating inner sense as a *receptivity* to be understood on the model of outer receptivity. For

---

[50] This is stated most clearly in the Second Analogy of Experience: "The appearances, insofar as they are objects of consciousness simply in virtue of being representations, are not in any way distinct from their apprehension, that is, from their reception in the synthesis of imagination; and we must therefore agree that the manifold of appearances is always generated in the mind successively. Now if appearances were things in themselves, then since we have to deal solely with our representations, we could never determine from the succession of representations how their manifold may be connected in the object. . . . In spite of the fact that appearances are not things in themselves, and yet are what alone can be given to us to know, in spite also of the fact that their representation in apprehension is always successive, I have to show what sort of connection in time belongs to the manifold in the appearances themselves" (A190/B235). This text is not easy to interpret because of Kant's ambiguous use of the term *appearance*. In the first sentence, it means "representation," empirically given as object of inner sense; in the other three sentences, it means "object of representation," empirically distinct from the representation as object of inner sense. This text nevertheless makes quite clear that the succession in outer sense, in the *object of representation*, is accessible only through the succession of *representations* "generated in the mind." However, in the Refutation of Idealism, Kant will also argue that the succession of representations in the mind (*qua* phenomenal object of inner sense) is itself apprehended only under the supposition of a permanent that can be given only in outer sense. With this argument, he claims, "the game played by idealism has been turned against itself" (B276). In this respect also, even if Kant owes to Locke the relation of time to *inner sense*, he nevertheless profoundly transforms the relation of inner sense to *outer sense*: the objects of the second are not simply mirrored by the objects of the first, but both are *jointly* accessed, and when the whole story is told, *with equal immediacy*. This is because one and the same act of the mind (*synthesis speciosa*) generates awareness of self and awareness of outer objects. How much of a refutation of idealism this really is, however, remains dubious.

Locke, the mind is *inwardly* receptive, or receptive to itself, as much as it is *outwardly* receptive, or receptive to things external to it. Witness the terms in which he introduces inner sense as the "other fountain" of our ideas, the first being sensation, which relates us to outward things:

> Secondly, the other fountain from which experience furnisheth the understanding with ideas is, —the perception of the operations of our own mind within us, as it is employed about the ideas it has got; —which operations, when the soul comes to reflect on and consider, do furnish the understanding with another set of ideas, which could not be had from things without. And such are *perception, thinking, doubting, believing, reasoning, knowing, willing*, and all the different actings of our own minds; —which we being conscious of, and observing in ourselves, *do from these receive into our understandings as distinct ideas as we do from bodies affecting our senses* [my emphasis]. This source of ideas every man has wholly in himself; *and though it be not sense, as having nothing to do with external objects, yet it is very like it, and might properly enough be called internal sense* [my emphasis].[51]

This description of inner sense as an affection of the mind by its own acts, which alone allows it to "reflect" these acts, is confirmed in many other passages. For instance:

> Thus the first capacity of human intellect is, —that the mind is fitted to receive the impressions made on it; either through the senses by outward objects, or by its own operations when it reflects on them.

> In this part the understanding is merely passive; and whether or not it will have these beginnings, and as it were materials of knowledge, is not in its own power. For the objects of our senses do, many of them, obtrude their particular ideas upon our minds whether we will or not; and the operations of our minds will not let us be without, at least, some obscure notions of them.[52]

Note that in the earlier quote, the first idea received from internal affection is *perception*. Perception is the act by which the mind applies itself to the ideas it receives.[53] When the mind *perceives* the idea received from sensation, it adds to it an idea of reflection, or an idea stemming from inner sense—the idea of perception itself. This probably explains why, when Locke discusses the origin of our idea of time, he no longer views inner sense as a reflection on the *operations* of the mind, but as a reflection on the *ideas* contained in the mind. For him the idea of succession, and then the ideas of duration and time, are derived from the succession of *ideas*, not *operations*, in inner sense. This is surprising: the mind ap-

---

[51] Ibid., bk. II, chap. i, §4.

[52] Ibid., bk. II, chap. i, §§24–25.

[53] An "act" bordering on passivity. Cf. *Essay*, bk. II, chap. ix, §1: "*Perception*, as it is the first faculty of the mind exercised about our ideas; so it is the first and simplest idea we have from reflection, and is by some called thinking in general. Though thinking, in the propriety of the English tongue, signifies that sort of operation in the mind about its ideas, wherein the mind is active; where it, with some degree of voluntary attention, considers anything. For in bare naked perception, the mind is, for the most part, only passive; and what it perceives, it cannot avoid perceiving."

pears to be affected by ideas themselves, rather than by its own operations, which makes inner sense harder to distinguish from sensations, that is, from what Kant will later call outer sense. But the difficulty disappears if we recall that the idea itself is an object of *perception*, so that the representation of succession emerges from the succession of these *acts of perception*. Sensations alone—that is, ideas passively received from outside—would not suffice to generate the idea of succession, since, as Locke expressly indicates, the idea of succession could not be derived from ideas to which the act of perception did not apply.[54]

Last, it should be noted that, according to Locke, in this receptivity to its own acts the mind mirrors itself, just as in sensation it mirrors outer objects. This image of the mirror appears explicitly at the end of the passage I just quoted, when Locke stresses that the ideas we receive from the operations of our mind are just as involuntary as the ideas we receive from outward objects through sensation: "These simple ideas, when offered to the mind, the understanding can no more refuse to have, nor alter when they are imprinted, nor blot them out and make new ones itself, than a mirror can refuse, alter, or obliterate the images or ideas which the objects set before it do therein produce."[55]

Kant shares with Locke the conception of inner sense as receptivity, but he no longer considers the mind as a mirror, either in relation to itself or in relation to objects. The forms or configurations of sensible things, *formae, nempe sensibilium species*, described in the *Inaugural Dissertation* as "laws inherent in our minds" by means of which we coordinate our sense-data, must also be laws by means of which we coordinate the given of *inner* sense, understood as receptivity to oneself. More precisely, *time* holds for inner sense in the same way as *space* and *time* (*via* inner sense) hold for outer sense. Just as the thing in itself that affects me from outside is forever unknowable to me, I who affect myself from within by my own representative act am forever unknowable to me. Something corresponds outside me (i.e., distinct from myself and my representations) to what appears to me as a body in the form of space. Similarly something corresponds in me (as a subject of representations, the very being of these representations, or as Descartes would say, the source of their formal reality) to what appears to me as representations in the form of time. This "something" is known to me only through its phenomenal manifestation, the temporal continuity of my representational acts and their effects.[56]

[54] Ibid., bk. II, chap. xiv, §4.

[55] Ibid., bk. II, chap. i, §25.

[56] The originality of Kant's position is manifested in the terminological distinctions he devises. Against rationalist metaphysicians, he distinguishes *inner sense* from *apperception*. Inner sense is self-receptivity, "the manner in which the mind is affected through its own activity (namely, through this positing of its representation)" (B68), "the consciousness of what man *undergoes* when he is affected by the play of his own thoughts" (*Anthr.*, §24). Apperception is the consciousness of the act of thinking, the consciousness of the "spontaneity of my thought" (*KrV* B158n), the "consciousness of what man does, [which] belongs to the faculty of thought" (*Anthr.*, §24). But against Locke, Kant also distinguishes *inner sense* from *reflection*. In self-receptivity, the mind is not mirroring itself or its own actions; it perceives or intuits only the way in which it is affected by itself and its actions. For Kant, there is no *reflection* as Locke understood it—no psychological reflection. Kant's use of the term 're-

The complex relation thus established between *outer sense* and *inner sense* finally finds its full-fledged exposition with the *synthesis speciosa* of the B Deduction. Only then are we offered a full clarification of the role in the constitution of appearances played by by *external affection* on the one hand, by its *interiorization* in inner sense on the other hand. Kant's explanation is roughly this: our receptivity is constituted in such a way that objects are intuited as *outer* objects only in the form of space. But the form of space is itself intuited only insofar as an act, by which the "manifold of a given cognition is brought to the objective unity of apperception," affects *inner* sense. Thanks to this act the manifold becomes *consciously perceived*, and this occurs only in the form of time. Thus the B Transcendental Deduction leads not only to a rereading of the Transcendental Aesthetic, as I argued earlier, but even to a partial revision of it. In a passage added to section 7 of the Aesthetic in the B edition, Kant stresses the double character of the representations of inner sense. On the one hand, inner sense has no other material than what is given to outer senses; on the other hand, inner sense is nothing but "the manner in which the mind is affected through its own activity (namely, through [the] positing of its representation), and so is affected by itself" (B68). If the acts affecting inner sense by the given of outer sense have an empirical matter (*data* of perception), they are the synthesis of apprehension discussed in section 26 of the Transcendental Deduction. But if these acts are considered in themselves, independently of their empirical matter, they are none other than the *synthesis speciosa* described in section 24, which produces the forms of space and time in which the empirical given is combined.

The Two Aspects of Time in the Synthesis Speciosa

It can still be objected that no solution has been offered to the difficulty concerning the seeming discrepancy between, on the one hand, Kant's examples of *synthesis speciosa* or affection of inner sense by understanding in section 24 and, on the other hand, his two examples of synthesis of apprehension in section 26 of the Transcendental Deduction. In the latter, space and time are treated as two distinct intuitions, the perception of the house being an empirical intuition synthesized *in space*, the perception of freezing an empirical intuition synthesized *in time*. In the former, Kant describes the pure intuition of space and the pure intuition of time as jointly produced, for example, in the act of drawing a line. In following the development of Kant's conception of the forms of sensibility from the *Inaugural Dissertation* to the *Critique*, my main goal was to shed some light on this difficulty. We saw that, already in the *Dissertation*, time seemed to belong to two different contexts: the mathematical synthesis of magnitudes, the phenomenal world and its forms. It seemed that the two aspects of time were properly unified once

---

flection' alternates between the three following meanings: reflection is the act of relating representations to the unity of consciousness (= the act of forming universal concepts by way of the "merely reflective judgments" of the third *Critique*); it is the act of *comparing* these concepts (logical reflection, in the "Amphiboly" chapter); lastly, it is the act of relating every representation to its locus in the cognitive power (*transcendental* reflection). See chapter 5, note 22.

time was defined as the form of *inner* sense: for then, *both* the successive character of the intuition of (arithmetical or geometrical) magnitudes, and the temporal succession in which an empirical given (such as the freezing of water) is apprehended, have their source in the affection of the mind *by its own acts*. The difference between the pure and the empirical case, however, is that in the first, the affection is *purely* internal, as the mind intuits in the successive synthesis only *its own act of production*. In the second, on the contrary, the mind intuits, together with its own act, the *outer* empirical given with which this act affects inner sense. In both cases, the intuition of space and the intuition of time are completely dependent on each other. If in pure syntheses the generation of the line is successive and the enumeration quasi-spatial, similarly in empirical syntheses the spatial apprehension of the house is successive and the temporal apprehension of freezing presupposes a spatial configuration of water. Nonetheless, clearly the dependencies are not of the same kind in both cases, because the *temporalities* are not of the same kind. More precisely, the temporal character of the spatial apprehension of the house is of the same kind as the temporal character of the apprehension of a line in pure intuition—in both cases, time is a form of the affection of inner sense by the act of apprehension. But the temporal character of the freezing of water is of a different kind. It seems not to depend on our act of apprehension, but on the (empirical) object itself. Thus we are again faced with our initial problem: how do we account for the two aspects of time—the temporal character of the "pure" *synthesis speciosa*, and the temporal character of the empirical object with which the *synthesis speciosa* affects inner sense?

The answer to this question can be found only when we progress from the general definition of the *synthesis speciosa* to its specifications. Indeed, the difference just stressed between the two aspects of temporality will be at the heart of Kant's argument in the Second Analogy. More generally, we shall see that there are as many aspects of *synthesis speciosa*, the "effect of understanding on sensibility" or "determination of inner sense by understanding," as there are intellectual syntheses according to the logical forms of judgment. These different aspects are our next object of investigation.

In the present chapter, my main concern was to show how Kant's Transcendental Deduction of the Categories, in the B edition, is completed by his reexamination of "the manner in which things are given to us," that is, the forms of sensibility expounded in the Transcendental Aesthetic. Such a reexamination is the necessary counterpart to Kant's characterization of the logical form of judgments as "the objective unity of the apperception of the concepts which they contain" in section 19 of the Deduction. For by arguing that our spatiotemporal forms of sensibility are generated by the *synthesis speciosa* or "affection of inner sense by understanding," Kant provides the universal framework (space and time as qualitative unity, preceding and conditioning all unity according to the categories)[57]

[57] In §15, Kant stresses that one of the components of his notion of combination is the notion of *unity*. And he goes on: "The representation of this unity cannot *result* from the combination, but makes possible the concept of combination in that it is added to the manifold. This unity, which precedes

242   · CHAPTER 8 ·

within which empirical knowledge of objects may occur. How singular objects are apprehended in such a framework; how this apprehension occurs according to correlations generated so that objects can be recognized under concepts combined according to the logical forms of the *Vermögen zu urteilen*; how they are ultimately thought under the categories, "concepts of an object in general, insofar as the intuition of that object is considered as determined with respect to a logical function of judgment": the answer to these questions is not given in the Transcendental Deduction, but in the Schematism of pure Concepts of the Understanding and the System of Principles. There, the relation of *synthesis intellectualis* and *synthesis speciosa*, forms of reflection and forms of synthesis, *Vermögen zu urteilen* and *Urteilskraft*, finds its detailed elucidation.

---

a priori all concepts of the combination, is not the category of unity; for all categories are grounded on logical functions of judgment, but in these there is already combination, and thus unity of given concepts. Thus the category presupposes combination. We must seek this unity (as qualitative) even higher, i.e. in that which is itself the ground of the unity of various concepts in judgments, and thus of the possibility of understanding even in its logical use" (B131). This "qualitative unity" is no doubt the transcendental unity of apperception. But the transcendental unity of apperception generates the a priori representation of a complete unity of our representations, whose intuitive form is the unity of space and time.

The Primacy of Quantitative Syntheses

PRELIMINARY REMARKS: *SYNTHESIS SPECIOSA* AND SCHEMATISM OF THE PURE CONCEPTS OF UNDERSTANDING

The purpose of the Transcendental Deduction of the Categories is, in Kant's words, "fully attained" once he has shown, in section 26, that the manner in which things are given to us is a priori in accordance with the categories: space and time are given as pure intuitions and forms of appearances only by means of *synthesis speciosa*, the "effect of the understanding on sensibility."[1] The intuitive unity of space and time, in which appearances are given prior to any discursive judgment, is the effect of what I have called the *effort toward judgment* affecting inner sense.[2] Hence this intuitive unity is in a priori agreement with the categories, ready to be reflected under the categories or "pure concepts of the understanding." The respective function of the two main steps of the B Deduction is thus confirmed: in sections 19 and 20, Kant argues that because the logical forms of judgment are the forms of thought by means of which our representations are related to objects, empirical objects can be reflected under the categories. In section 26, he argues that even prior to such reflection, appearances are in themselves, as objects of empirical intuition, immediately in accordance with the categories, by virtue of the spatiotemporal forms in which they are given.[3] Thus proving not only the *discursive-intellectual* (sections 19–20) but also the *intuitive-sensible* (section 26) subordination of appearances under the categories is ensuring the objective validity of the latter, so that the purpose of the Transcendental Deduction is "fully attained" (B145): the categories are a priori applicable to the objects of empirical intuition because these objects, insofar as they are apprehended in space and time, are (intuitively) synthesized in such a way that they can be (discursively) reflected under empirical concepts according to the logical forms of judgment. They are therefore determinable in accordance with these forms and, ultimately, subsumable under the categories as "universal representations of synthesis" (A78/B104).

In this argument, the status of the categories is an evolving one. The very notion of an *epigenesis of reason* by which, in section 27, Kant sums up the meaning of the Transcendental Deduction,[4] indicates that the categories become full-

---

[1] B152. Cf. chapter 8.

[2] Cf. the introduction to part III.

[3] This means, of course, that the very notion of a "given" is relativized. What is "given" as object of empirical intuition is also generated by our own (passive and active) representational capacities. Cf. chapter 1, the "internalization of the object of representation to representation."

[4] B167. See the explanation of this notion in chapter 8, note 17.

fledged *concepts* (universal and reflected representations) only as the result of a process of "original acquisition." Kant's definition of the categories is given in section 14 of the B edition: categories are "concepts of an object in general, by means of which the intuition of the object is regarded as determined in respect of one of the logical functions of judgment" (B 128–29). With this definition, Kant is able to account for the various aspects of the categories as they appear in the argument of the Transcendental Deduction. The categories are, as it were, engrained in the mind as logical functions—that is, functions of discursive combination of concepts related to objects. The capacity for judgment guides sensible synthesis, and this *synthesis speciosa* is the initial "application" of the categories. However, in this appplication the categories are not reflected as concepts, so that the combinations guided by the *Vermögen zu urteilen* remain undetermined (undetermined by concepts, "blind" syntheses of imagination). Reflection under categories as *concepts* can occur only when empirical judgments, analyzing the figurative synthesis first presented in intuition, have been formed and systematically correlated. Categories are then "applied" in a second sense: "applying" a category then means claiming for a discursive combination objective validity, validity not only "for myself, in my present state of perception," but "for everybody, always."[5] Kant calls this second "application" of the categories, "subsumption of an object under a concept of pure understanding."

Kant discusses the relation between *synthesis* and *subsumption*, and the ways in which the former makes the latter possible, in the Schematism of the Pure Concepts of Understanding.[6] The judgments expressing the subsumption of objects, as appearances, under the categories, are expounded in the System of Principles of Pure Understanding.[7] These two chapters belong to the Analytic of Principles and are beyond the scope of the Transcendental Deduction proper. For if we accept Kant's argument concerning the role played by the logical functions of judgment and *synthesis speciosa*, the question of right (*quid juris*) has been resolved, and the meaning and scope of the categories are explained when the Analytic of Concepts has been completed. However, the Schematism and Principles do more than merely reap the benefits of Kant's proof in the Transcendental Deduction articulating its consequences in a doctrine of transcendental judgment as the "application" of the categories. They clarify, in turn, the meaning of the Transcendental Deduction itself: the *synthesis speciosa* is specified in the different schemata of the concepts of the pure understanding, and the a priori conformity of appearances to the categories is explained in the System of Principles. There is nothing surprising in the fact that the Analytic of Principles should thus retrospectively clarify the Transcendental Deduction: one of the reasons the Deduction was rewritten in the B edition may have been to make the transition to the Schematism and Principles more perspicuous than it was in the A Deduction. When this transition is achieved and the Principles are expounded, the import of the Deduction becomes fully explicit.

[5] Cf. chapter 7, the explanation of judgments of perception and judgments of experience.
[6] Chap. 1 of the Analytic of Principles: A137–47/B176–87.
[7] Chap. 2 of the Analytic of Principles: A148–235/B187–294.

Thus the Schematism and Principles give specific content to the relation between *synthesis intellectualis* (achieved by logical functions of judgment, according to its logical forms) and *synthesis speciosa* (productive syntheses of imagination), which has been stated in the most general manner in section 24 of the Transcendental Deduction. For the schemata enumerated in the Schematism of the Pure Concepts of the Understanding are nothing other than the specific results of the *synthesis speciosa*, that is, the results of the "determination of inner sense by the understanding" that aims at reflecting the sensible given under concepts combined according to the logical forms of judgment. In the Transcendental Deduction, Kant does not discuss the specific aspects of the *synthesis speciosa*, but merely gives a general description of it. The discussion does not occur in the Schematism chapter either, for here Kant has already moved beyond the description of *synthesis speciosa*. He lists the schemata of the pure concepts of the understanding only as an introduction to the Principles of the Pure Understanding, that is, to the transcendental judgments expressing the subsumption of objects (as appearances) under the categories. Yet, if the relation between *synthesis intellectualis* and *synthesis speciosa* stated in the Transcendental Deduction makes any sense at all, it must be possible to fill in the intermediate steps in Kant's argument, between the general explanation of *synthesis speciosa* (section 24) and the list of schemata (Schematism chapter) and provide a case-by-case explanation of the productive syntheses of imagination as they relate to the logicodiscursive forms for which they are produced, thus generating the schemata of pure concepts of the understanding.

Reading the Schematism chapter in this way not only allows a more complete elucidation of the Transcendental Deduction of the Categories, it also provides a solution to some of the difficulties and purported inconsistencies for which the Schematism chapter itself is often criticized. It helps clarify, in the first place, the relation between *subsumption* and *synthesis*. The schemata are first presented as the mediating elements by means of which the *subsumption* of sensible objects under the pure concept of the understanding is made possible. The Schematism chapter thus fulfills its principal function, which is to open the way to what *follows* it, the System of Principles of the Pure Understanding:

> Obviously there must be some third element [*ein Drittes*], which is homogeneous on the one hand with the category, and on the other hand with the appearance, and which thus makes the application of the former to the latter possible. This mediating representation must be pure, that is, void of all empirical content, and yet at the same time, while it must in one respect be *intellectual*, it must in another be *sensible*. Such a representation is the *transcendental schema*. (A138/B177)

Then Kant explains the nature of this "mediating representation": it is a transcendental determination of time, that is, a *pure synthesis* of time according to a rule of unity:

> [T]he schema of a *pure* concept of understanding . . . is simply the pure synthesis, in conformity with a rule of unity according to concepts in general, to which the category gives expression. It is a transcendental product of imagination, a product which

concerns the determination of inner sense in general according to conditions of its form (time), in respect of all representations, so far as these representations are to be connected *a priori* in one concept in conformity with the unity of apperception. (A142/B181)

This passage invites us, in effect, to look back to what *precedes* the Schematism chapter: to the Transcendental Deduction of the Categories and, more specifically, to the explanation of the *synthesis speciosa*—the determination of inner sense by the understanding. This return to the Deduction is important in that it alone can dispel the seemingly arbitrary character of the relation between the pure concepts and their respective schemata. For in order to understand why, for example, "succession of the manifold, insofar as it is subjected to a rule,"[8] allows appearances to be subsumed under the category of causality, one must understand how this succession according to a rule is *apprehended*: it is apprehended in an act of sensible synthesis (*synthesis speciosa*) performed with a view to subsuming appearances under concepts according to the discursive form of hypothetical judgment (*synthesis intellectualis*). A similar analysis can be provided for all the schemata. In each case, the rule of synthesis that will allow the subsumption of appearances under pure concepts of the understanding is first generated by the "blind" syntheses of imagination in view of reflecting appearances under (empirical) concepts according to the logical functions of judgment. If we content ourselves with Kant's enumeration of the schemata corresponding to each of the categories, we learn nothing about how these schemata are *produced*, nor do we obtain any justification of their mediating role in subsuming appearances under the categories. By contrast, if we bring together the teachings of the Deduction and the Schematism, and examine the schemata in light of the relation, elaborated in the Deduction, between *synthesis intellectualis* and *synthesis speciosa*, we can give life to Kant's conception of the activity of discursive thought and gain crucial insight into the role he assigns to transcendental imagination.

Kant opted not to provide this explanation himself, deeming it too "dry and tedious": "That we may not be further delayed by a dry and tedious analysis of the conditions demanded by transcendental schemata of the pure concepts of understanding in general, we shall now expound them according to the order of the categories and in connection with them" (A142/B181). But in fact, Kant's own introduction of *synthesis speciosa* in the B Deduction is testimony that we need to know more about "the conditions demanded by transcendental schemata of the pure concepts of understanding." For only *synthesis speciosa*, figurative synthesis, is able to account for the schematism as a production (the "determination of inner sense by the understanding"), not merely as a result (the correspondence between the schemata and the categories). In the remaining chapters of this book, I will examine precisely this production, beginning, in this chapter, with the case of quantity.

I will first analyze in the next section Kant's conception of the logical quantities of judgment, and then examine the schema of quantity in light of the relation

[8] The schema of causality: see A144/B183.

between *synthesis intellectualis* and *synthesis speciosa* expounded in the Transcendental Deduction. I argue that if we take this relation seriously, we should understand the schema of quantity as generated by the acts of synthesis (*synthesis speciosa*) generating the extensions of concepts, according to the logical forms of quantity in judgment (*synthesis intellectualis*). I will then show how this insight into the relation between *schema* of quantity and *logical* quantity throws new and interesting light on Kant's conception of number, on his characterization of space and time as *quanta infinita* and *quanta continua*, and finally on the role he assigns to quantitative synthesis in empirical intuition.

In the third section of the chapter, I will analyze Kant's conception of arithmetic and geometry in light of the relation between discursive thought (logical forms of judgment, *synthesis intellectualis*) and rules for a priori synthesis of homogeneous multiplicities (schemata, *synthesis speciosa*). I argue that read in this way, Kant's conception of mathematics is more powerful than is generally appreciated, and bears an interesting relation to conceptual revolutions yet to come.

QUANTITIES OF JUDGMENT, SCHEMATA, AND CATEGORIES OF QUANTITY

The Logical Forms of Quantity of Judgment

Kant defines the quantities of judgment by the relations of inclusion or exclusion between extensions or spheres of concepts: "In the *universal* judgment, the sphere of one concept is wholly enclosed within the sphere of another; in the *particular*, a part of the former is enclosed under the sphere of the other; and in the *singular* judgment, finally, a concept that has no sphere at all is enclosed, merely as part, under the sphere of another."[9] As we saw in chapters 5 and 6, the relations between extensions of concepts depend for Kant on acts of judging, which are acts of *comparing* concepts. I argued, moreover, that according to Kant, there are two kinds of logical comparison: "logical comparison in the narrow sense," where the relations between extensions of concepts depend on the mere explanation of these concepts (e.g., it follows from the explanation of the concept 'man' that its extension is wholly enclosed in the extension of the concept 'rational', while we may suppose that only part of the extension of the latter is included in the extension of the former); and "logical comparison in the broad sense," where concepts are compared in relation to the sensible "x, y, z's" thought under them (e.g., we need to compare the sensible "x, y, z's" thought under the concept 'body' in order

---

[9] *Logik*, §21; Ak. IX, 102; 598. These definitions are traditional, except for the description of the subject of singular judgment as a "concept without a sphere." Meier calls the subject of singular judgment, a singular concept (cf. *Auszug*, §301: "The subject of a judgment is either a singular concept, or an abstract concept. The former is a singular judgment (*judicium singulare*), and the latter is a common judgment (*judicium commune*)." But for Kant, at least in the critical period, there are no singular concepts (cf. *Logik*, §1). We may suppose, then, that the subject of a singular judgment is, as a representation, a concept referring to a singular intuition by means of its schema, and as a linguistic expression, either a proper name, or a description uniquely referring by means of a deictic or by means of spatiotemporal individuation.

first to assert, 'some bodies are heavy', then 'all bodies are heavy', a proposition for which we eventually claim strict universality by subsuming the categorical connection between the concept of body and the concept of weight under the categories of cause/effect and substance/accident.[10]

The distinction between these two ways of comparing concepts helps explain the two different orders in which Kant presents the logical quantities of judgment. In his Lectures on Logic, as well as in the table of logical functions of judgment in the *Critique* and in the *Prolegomena*, logical quantities are listed in the order: *universal, particular, singular*. But in the Lectures on Metaphysics, the logical quantities are often given in the reverse order: *singular, particular, universal*.[11] The former order agrees with the presentation traditional in logic textbooks, where particular judgment is listed after universal, and singular judgment may be listed either before or after the other two. This is because, in the Aristotelian tradition, one first distinguishes judgments in which the subject is a singular concept (singular judgments) from those in which the subject is a common concept (common judgments). Then common judgments are divided into universal, in which the extension of the subject is completely contained in the extension of the predicate, and particular, in which the extension of the subject is only partially contained in the sphere of the predicate. Thus universal judgment has priority over particular judgment, the latter being a limitation of the former, and therefore derivative with respect to it, just as negation is derivative with respect to affirmation.[12] The comparison I have called 'logical in a narrow sense' would privilege this order of priority: in this comparison, concepts are given in the understanding and compared in their whole extension; the extension of the one is "wholly" or "in part" contained in the extension of the other. In contrast, in a logical comparison in the broad sense, the x, y, z's represented under the concepts are the indispensable condition of the comparison. Hence singular judgment comes first, expressing the attribution of a concept to a singular object given in intuition ('This body is heavy'), then particular judgment, in which a concept is attributed to several objects ('Some bodies are heavy'), and lastly universal judgment, which may or may not deserve to be called a judgment of experience.

The *categories* of quantity are always presented in the order: *unity, plurality, totality*. Since Kant meanwhile preserves, at least in his published writings, the traditional order (*universal, particular, singular*) for the logical quantities of judgment, this raises a problem for the parallelism of the two tables of quantity, which has occasioned a great deal of discussion. Is Kant asserting a correspon-

---

[10] On the distinction between logical comparison in the narrow sense and logical comparison in the broad sense, see chapters 5, and 6. On claiming strict universality for the proposition 'all bodies are heavy' see chapter 7, the explanation of judgments of experience.

[11] For *universal, particular, singular*, cf. *Logik*, §21; *KrV* A70/B95; *Prol.*, §21; *Met. Pölitz*, Ak. XXVIII-2, 747. This order is also found in all of Kant's Lectures on Logic. For *singular, particular, universal*, cf. *Refl.* 4700 (1773–75), Ak. XVII, 679; *Met. Volckmann* (1784–85), Ak. XXVIII-1, 396; *Met. von Schön*, Ak. XXVIII-1, 480; *Met. Dohna* (1792–93), Ak. XXVIII-2, 626.

[12] For the origin of these distinctions, see Aristotle, *De Interpretatione*, 7. Regarding singular and common judgments, then universal and particular judgments, see Meier, *Auszug*, §301, Ak. XVI, 647. I am indebted for these analyses to Frede and Krüger, *Quantitäten*.

dence between, on the one hand, universal judgment and unity, and on the other, singular judgment and totality? Or should one of the tables be reversed (and then, which one?), the correspondence then being singular judgment/unity, universal judgment/totality? In my view, this question is answered conclusively in an important note of the *Prolegomena*, concerning the interpretation of *particular* judgment. This judgment, says Kant, should more appropriately be termed *judicium plurativum*, "plurative judgment":

> This name [*judica plurativa*] seems preferable to the term *particularia*, which is used for these judgments in logic. For the latter already contains the thought that they are not universal. But when I start from unity (in singular judgments) and proceed to totality, I must not [even indirectly and negatively] include any reference to totality. I think plurality merely without totality, and not the exclusion of totality. This is necessary, if the logical moments are to underlie the pure concepts of the understanding. In logical usage one may leave things as they were.[13]

From this note one must conclude that to understand the categories of quantity one must consider their genesis as parallel to the progression from singular to particular, then to universal judgment. Furthermore, the particular judgment should not be understood as a restriction of a possible universal judgment ("some, not all"), but rather as equivalent to a plurality of singular judgments ('This body is heavy', 'This body is heavy', etc., and thus 'Some bodies are heavy'). Thus the categories of quantity, in the order *unity, plurality, totality*, do not correspond respectively to *universal, particular, singular* judgments, as the parallelism of the two tables in both editions of the *Critique* and in the *Prolegomena* might lead us to believe, but rather to *singular, particular* and *universal* judgments.[14] This is the correspondence we must consider in order to understand the genesis and meaning of the schemata and categories of quantity.

The Schema of Quantity

The schema of quantity involves "the successive addition of (homogeneous) units."[15] Now, synthesizing homogeneous units is precisely what is required in order to generate the form of logical quantity in an empirical judgment. For instance, to be able to say 'Some bodies are heavy' or 'All trees in this garden bear fruits', I must run through the elements thought under the subject-concept

---

[13] *Prol.* §20n, Ak. IV, 302; 45, n. 13.

[14] For a helpful discussion of the problem posed by the presentation of the two tables of quantity (logical and categorial), see again Frede and Krüger, "Quantitäten."

[15] A142–143/B182. The complete formulation is: "The pure *schema* of magnitude (*quantitatis*), as a concept of the understanding, is *number*, a representation which gathers together [*zusammenfaßt*] the successive addition of homogeneous units." Here *Magnitude* [*Größe*] is equivalent to *Quantity* [*Quantität*], as confirmed by the Latin *Quantitas* given in parenthesis. *Größe* may have another meaning, that of the Latin *quantum*. (See the section on *quantity* and *quantum*.) I provisionally restrict my analysis of the schema of quantity to the phrase: "successive addition of homogeneous units" in order to clarify the relation of the schema to the logical forms of quantity in judgment. The full sentence shall be analyzed later.

('body', or 'tree in this garden'), and compare them with respect to the predicate-concept ('heavy', or 'bearing fruit'). Then I must successively 'affect inner sense' with their representations, considered as elements of a homogeneous manifold (a manifold thought under the same concept).[16] Thus we may understand the schema of quantity as resulting from the determination of inner sense by the understanding, aiming at the logical form of the quantity of a judgment. This synthesis of the homogeneous is not necessarily reflected as a category. If it is achieved only for the sake, so to speak, of the logical form of judgment, this synthesis is not reflected as such, in a concept. When generating the proposition, 'Some trees are in this garden', I perform the successive synthesis of the elements thought under the concept 'tree' (thus *homogeneous*), but I do not reflect this synthesis itself, as such. Its function is only to determine the logical quantity of the judgment in which I include (part of) the extension of the concept 'tree' in that of the concept 'located in this garden'. However, if the schema of quantity, that is, the synthesis that serves to generate a judgment according to its logical quantity, is reflected as the specific kind of synthesis it is, then the *category* of quantity is reflected.

This analysis is confirmed, I think, by a text from *Metaphysik von Schön*, echoing the definition of the categories in the *Critique* I have quoted several times, and will quote once again:

> [The categories] are concepts of an object in general, by means of which the intuition of an object is regarded as determined in respect of one of the logical functions of judgment. Thus the function of the categorical judgment is that of the relation of subject to predicate; for example, 'All bodies are divisible'. But as regards the merely logical use of the understanding, it remains undetermined to which of the two concepts the function of the subject, and to which the function of predicate, is to be assigned. For we can also say, 'Something divisible is a body'. But when the concept of body is brought under the category of substance, it is thereby determined that its empirical intuition in experience must always be considered as subject and never as mere predicate. Similarly with all the other categories. (B128–29)

[16] The classic mathematical definition of homogeneity was given by Archimedes: "Two magnitudes are homogeneous when the smaller magnitude multiplied a finite number of times can exceed the larger one" (cf. Couturat, *Logique de Leibniz*, 306). Leibniz analyzes this mathematical notion of homogeneity at length in relation to the problems of continuous magnitudes. He distinguishes *homogeneous* magnitudes, which can be made *similar* through a transformation, for instance from a line to a curve, from *homogonous* magnitudes, which can be made similar only by moving from one genus to another, for example, from point to plane, or from instant to time (cf. Belaval, *Leibniz*, 333–34). *Units* are homogeneous if they are generically identical. Arithmetical addition presupposes the homogeneity of the elements added, that is, it presupposes their generic identity, even if the genus they fall under is the broadest of all, for example, the idea of a "thing." Cf. Belaval, *Leibniz*, 247: "'Things' (God, angel, man, motion, body, mind . . .) can therefore be added together, i.e., are homogeneous in the mathematical sense, only if through abstraction they are brought from heterogeneity to homogeneity, by moving up to the highest genus." In my opinion, Kant means the same when he defines number as the "successive addition of homogeneous units." This allows him to relate number, as the schema of quantity, to the logical quantity of judgment, and this is why I take "homogeneous" to mean "thought under the same concept." I discuss the relation between discrete and continuous quantity according to Kant in the section on *quantitas* and *quantum*.

Kant's rather cavalier conclusion, "Similarly with all the other categories," is perplexing. One can perhaps understand what Kant means when he says that substance is what is thought under the subject rather than the predicate in a categorical judgment, or cause what is thought under the antecedent rather than the consequent in a hypothetical judgment. But no such choice is available in the case of the categories of quantity, since unlike the categories of relation, they have no correlate. One then wonders what "regarding the intuition as determined in respect of one of the logical functions of judgment" might mean in this case. Now in *Metaphysik von Schön*, Kant gives an explanation similar to that of the *Critique*, but this time he takes quantity as his example:

> When we survey the concepts of the understanding, at bottom they mean nothing else than the relation of the understanding to a representation insofar as the latter is determined in respect of one or the other of the logical functions. When I say 'Some men are sinners', this 'some' is a plurality, to be sure, but it is determined only logically in comparison with the representation, and I do not think a synthetic unity. But when I represent to myself a being, in such a way that a One [*ein Eines*] contains several, I have the concept of magnitude. For example, 'Some men are learned' and 'Some learned individuals are men', I can reverse the proposition. But if the proposition is determined in such a way that it cannot be reversed, then it is a magnitude.[17]

The last two sentences can be interpreted in the following manner. If I consider only the logical form of the proposition 'Some men are learned', this proposition can be converted into another, 'Some learned individuals are men'. In other words, it "can be reversed." But if I consider the act of thinking by which the proposition was formed, then I recognize that this act consists of the successive consideration of the x's reflected under the concept 'man', in order to compare them to the concept 'learned', not the reverse. From this viewpoint, just as (following Kant's explanation in section 14 of the *Critique*) the x reflected under the concept 'man' can be only subject, not predicate, similarly the successive synthesis of such x's is what generated the judgment considered in its logical quantity: 'Some men are learned'. I did not perform the successive synthesis of the units thought under the concept 'learned' in order to determine which of them are also subsumed under the concept 'man', but on the contrary, I successively considered the units thought under 'man' and compared them with respect to the concept 'learned'. Thus if I reflect the act through which the judgment, considered in its logical quantity, was generated, "the proposition cannot be reversed."

At the end of part II, I argued that according to Kant, in the production of schemata for the categories, the power of judgment (*Urteilskraft*) schematizes for its reflective use.[18] This claim holds for the schema of quantity just as much as for the other schemata—however strange this might seem, as we expect Kant to as-

[17] *Met. von Schön*, Ak. XXVIII-1, 472. Gerhard Lehmann, the editor of this volume, considers these notes to be later than those from *Metaphysik Volckmann*, which are from 1784–85. Of course, the magnitude is not the proposition, but what is thought under it. Remember that these are students' lecture notes!

[18] See the concluding section of chapter 7.

sociate quantity with *construction* rather than *reflection*.[19] Nevertheless, I maintain that according to Kant, even the category of quantity is originally acquired
insofar as the power of judgment, reflecting on the sensible given in order to subordinate representations to empirical concepts combined in judgments, generates
the *schema* of quantity—that is, a successive synthesis of homogeneous elements
(where 'homogeneous' means 'reflected under the same concept'). One may object that this genesis of the categories of quantity seems strangely empirical. But
recall what Kant says of *acquisitio originaria* in the Eberhard controversy: original acquisition presupposes an innate capacity of the mind, but the acquisition
actually occurs only under the effect of sensible impressions. Not only the a priori forms of space and time, but also the categories, are thus *originally acquired*:

> For impressions are always required in order first to enable the cognitive power to rep-
> resent an object (which is always its own act). Thus, the formal *intuition* which is
> called space emerges as an originally acquired representation (the form of outer objects
> in general) . . . the acquisition of which long precedes determinate *concepts* of things
> that are in accordance with this form. The acquisition of these concepts is an *acquisi-
> tio derivativa*, as it already presupposes universal transcendental concepts of the un-
> derstanding. *These likewise are acquired and not innate, but their acquisition, like that
> of space, is* originaria *and presupposes nothing innate except the subjective conditions
> of the spontaneity of thought (in accordance with the unity of apperception).*[20]

In the preceding chapter I proposed an explanation of what "original acquisition" means in the case of space and time: what is "original" in their case is the
"first formal ground" pertaining to the innate *receptive* capacity of the mind.
What is "acquired" is the form of intuition or formal intuition, as form of appearances which "precedes all concepts of things." The latter is *acquired* in that,
as Kant says in the text I quote again here, "impressions are always required in
order first to enable the cognitive power to represent an object" (see chapter 8).
But it is *originally acquired* in that) the form of intuition (formal intuition) has an
a priori ground in the capacity of the mind, and it precedes and conditions all empirical acquisition of (objective) representation.

Similarly, in the case of the categories what is "original" is the *discursive* (intellectual, spontaneous) capacity, with its logical forms as forms of the objective
unity of apperception. What is "acquired" are the categories as "concepts of an

---

[19] Cf. A717/B745: "Mathematical cognition is the cognition gained by reason from the *construction* of concepts. To *construct* a concept means to exhibit *a priori* the intuition which corresponds to
the concept." I say more on Kant's conception of construction of concepts in mathematics in the section on number. I am not arguing that according to Kant, mathematics proceeds by reflection rather
than construction. I am arguing, however, that according to him the *original acquisition* of the quantitative categories and their schemata is possible only when synthesis with a view to reflection is, as
it were, "triggered" by sensory stimulation. The ability to *construct* concepts (anticipate experience
by presentation of concepts in a priori intuition) is then also acquired, together with the representations of space and time "needed for geometry," that is, pure space and time as "infinite given magnitudes." I say more on this later in this chapter, in the section on geometry.

[20] *Entdeckung*, Ak. VIII, 222–23; 136 (my emphasis on last sentence). On the *acquisitio originaria*
of the forms of sensible intuition, cf. chapter 8, p. 221.

object, insofar as its intuition is considered as *determined* with respect to the logical functions of judgment." In other words, what is acquired are categories as concepts of the *unity of synthesis* achieved with a view to analysis according to the logical functions of judgment. I would claim that according to Kant, categories so considered are acquired in exactly the same sense as forms or intuition (= formal intuitions) are acquired: "Impressions are always required in order first to enable the cognitive power to represent an object." However, they are *originally* acquired, in that they have their ground in an a priori (intellectual, spontaneous) capacity of the mind; and their acquisition precedes and conditions all other acquisition of (objective) representation. Now, this acquisition results in two "applications" of the categories, corresponding to the two steps described at the beginning of this chapter: (1) They are applied as *schemata*, that is, as rules of sensible synthesis generated with a view to forming judgments. In this first application, they are, again, "originally acquired": they are *acquired* because they would not come forth as rules of synthesis unless synthesis according to these rules were occasioned by sensible impressions; but they are *originally* acquired because the capacity for judgment must be innate in order for syntheses according to these rules to be generated. (2) They are applied as "clear concepts," that is, as "universal representations" of pure synthesis according to rules (for instance, when we apply to empirical objects concepts of number, or of continuous magnitude, or of cause and effect, and so on). In this second application too they are "originally acquired": *acquired* not only because they would not be reflected as concepts unless impressions had struck our senses and given rise to acts of sensible synthesis, but also because they presuppose the empirical concepts under which appearances are thought, as well as the combination of these concepts in empirical judgments. But they are *originally* acquired, for the same reason as before: because they are grounded a priori in the forms of the objective unity of apperception, that is, in our capacity to form judgments.

If we apply the preceding remarks to the case of the categories of quantity, we can say the following: what is "original" about them are the logical functions of quantity in judgment. The *categories* of quantity are originally acquired as "concepts of an object, insofar as the intuition of this object is considered as determined with respect to the logical functions of quantity in judgment": pure concepts of unity, plurality, totality. They are *acquired* in that "impressions are required" for us to strive to recognize such concepts, and thus to implement the forms of syntheses that generate *schemata* for the categories of quantity. But they are *originally* acquired in that they have an a priori ground in the (discursive and intuitive) capacities of our minds; and in that their acquisition (together with the original acquisition of all other categories) precedes and conditions all objective representations.

Here, however, we run into a difficulty. Kant defines only one schema for three logical forms and three categories of quantity. Perhaps one solution to this difficulty is to say that in fact, all three logical forms of quantity, as well as all three categories of quantity, appear in this one schema. To see this, consider now the full definition of the schema, as Kant gives it in the Schematism chapter: "The pure *schema* of magnitude (*quantitatis*), as a concept of the understanding, is . . .

a representation that gathers together [*zusammenfaßt*] the successive addition of homogeneous units" (A142–43/B182). So far, I have discussed only the "successive addition of homogeneous units," because this part of the definition made clear the relation between the generation of a manifold of elements thought under the same concept (and thus of the logical form of quantity in judgment) and the schema of quantity. But the complete definition is important in that it exhibits all three moments of quantity: unity ("units"), plurality ("successive addition of homogeneous units"), and totality ("representation which gathers together the successive addition of homogeneous units").

Yet this observation does not completely remove the difficulty. True, the full definition of the schema presents us with the three aspects or moments of the category of quantity. But this seems to make the schema, properly speaking, that of *totality*. Unity and plurality would then be mere mediating elements in the generation of the schema of totality. I suggest, in fact, that this is indeed Kant's intention. To reflect in a concept the mere synthesis of a (homogeneous) manifold *is thereby to totalize this manifold*, that is, to think the unity of a plurality: totality.

Consider again the logical quantities of judgment, for example 'This stone is shiny', 'Some bodies are shiny', 'All bodies are heavy'. The category of plurality corresponds to particular judgment ('Some bodies are shiny'), the category of totality corresponds to universal judgment ('All bodies are heavy'). But reflecting the act of successive synthesis by which *some* of the elements thought under the concept 'body' are thought as identical with respect to the concept 'shiny' is precisely constituting them as a *totality*: the totality, which I can reflect in a number, of just those elements, thought under the concept of body, that also have the accidental property of being shiny. I thus obtain a totality in this case just as I obtain a totality when reflecting the manifold of elements contained under the concept of body taken in its whole extension, as the subject of a universal judgment. In both cases, the notion of totality is different from the merely discursive notion of universality (= a concept taken in its whole extension). It reflects a rule of sensible synthesis, the unity of successive synthesis of (homogeneous) elements. When we think such unity of synthesis, it matters little whether the (homogeneous) manifold was initially reflected in view of a particular judgment ('Some bodies are shiny') or a universal judgment ('All bodies are heavy'). In both cases, the "representation which gathers together the successive addition of homogeneous units" is generated when the synthesis of the manifold is achieved not for the sake of discursive judgment and its logical quantity any more, but so that it is *itself* reflected, so that it receives numerical determination. This also provides the key to the role of "unity" in the generation of the schema of quantity: "unity" is then properly the unit, the arbitrarily chosen element providing the successive synthesis with the x it iterates. Reflecting an object as a unit is reflecting it as a singular x posited in intuition and reflected under a concept, the iteration of which constitutes the successive synthesis of a (homogeneous) multiplicity.[21]

21 This role of the unit is explicit in Kant's presentation of the table of the categories in the *Prolegomena*: next to unity, he adds *Maß* in parentheses (i.e., *measure*, or rather *unit of measure*; cf. Ak. IV, 302; 46). Hence in this context, *quantity* is inseparable from the *quantum* it measures. I discuss this aspect of quantity in the section *quantitas* and *quantum*.

Thus the reason Kant presents only one schema for quantity is that regardless of the logical quantity considered, it presupposes that a multiplicity of (homogeneous) units has been posited in intuition through a successive synthesis. The *category* of quantity is the concept reflecting this successive synthesis of homogeneous units *as a whole*. It remains true, however, that we cannot be completely satisfied by this identification of plurality and totality in the schema of quantity. After all, Kant himself argues, in the solution to the Antinomies of Pure Reason, that some pluralities *cannot* be reflected as totalities: there is, according to him, no possible *complete* synthesis of appearances in space and time, although we can form the representation of this synthesis as indefinitely pursuable, and thus as a *quantity* (albeit indeterminate). His presentation of the schema of quantity would be less puzzling if it explicitly mentioned this possibility of a plurality *without* unity.[22]

Leaving this particular problem aside, we now see better, I hope, why Kant says that the schema of quantity is "a representation that gathers together the successive addition of homogeneous units." However, additional problems arise from the fact that he identifies this schema with *number*: "The pure *schema* of magnitude (*quantitatis*), as a concept of the understanding, is *number*, which is a representation that gathers together [*zusammenbefaßt*] the successive addition of homogeneous units. Number is thus nothing other than the unity of the synthesis of the manifold of homogeneous intuition in general." The first problem raised by this identification of the schema of quantity with number is that Kant also talks, in several places, of a *concept* of number.[23] But if number is the schema for the category of quantity, what is the schema for the *concept* of number? And what can we make, more generally, of the assertion that number itself is "nothing other" than a *schema*?

I think the solution is something like the following. When Kant says that number is the schema of the category of quantity, he is not thereby denying that there is also a *concept* of number (indeed, that there are concept*s* of particular numbers). Rather, he is insisting that the schema corresponding to the concept of number is not an empirical schema, but a result of *synthesis speciosa*, that is, of the "effect of the understanding [*Vermögen zu urteilen*] on sensibility." Number is the schema of quantity in that it is a rule of synthesis we are able to produce by virtue of our faculty of constituting the extensions of concepts when generating judgments determined with respect to the logical form of quantity. We saw Kant define the logical quantity of judgment by the inclusion of all or part of the sphere of a concept in the sphere of another concept. In empirical judgments, reflecting according to the logical quantity of judgment presupposes "going through and as-

[22] Cf. Critical Solution to the Cosmological Conflict of Reason with Itself, A498/B526–27. In the remarks to the table of categories, added in B, Kant did consider the difference between plurality and totality: "The concept of a *number* (which belongs to the category of totality) is not always possible simply upon the presence of concepts of plurality and unity (for instance in the representation of the infinite)" (B111). I will say more on Kant's conception of number immediately.

[23] See B111: "The concept of a number (which belongs to the category of totality) . . ." A103: "The generation of multiplicity by successive addition of unit to unit is number. For this concept consists exclusively in the consciousness of this unity of synthesis." See also the letters to Schultz and Rehberg referenced in notes 36 and 40.

sembling" a multiplicity of homogeneous elements. The representation of the unity of such an act of "going through and assembling" is number as a *schema*. Thinking a *concept* of number is reflecting the specific rule for generating a given homogeneous multiplicity. Then we have not only a schema (number as a "representation gathering together the successive addition of homogeneous units"), but also a concept reflecting the schema (a concept of number). How can number, as a schema, be the schema for both the category of quantity, and the concept of number? Perhaps Kant should have said that the concept of number is the concept of a *determinate* quantity, and that number as a schema is the schema of *determinate* quantity. But this added precision is hardly necessary, if it is true, as I suggested, that reflecting as it were "for its own sake" the act of synthesizing the homogeneous manifold just *is* generating the "representation which gathers together the successive addition of homogeneous units"—except, as we have seen, in the case where the manifold cannot be "gathered together" and where the quantity cannot be reflected as *determinate* quantity, namely as number.[24]

Because commentators tend not to pay sufficient attention to the relation between number and the category of quantity, as well as to the relation between the latter and the logical forms of quantity in judgment, they often end up simplifying or distorting Kant's conception of number and arithmetic. Admittedly, Kant is himself the main culprit, for his elliptical or ambiguous indications make it difficult to develop a coherent interpretation of his thought. But the difficulty does not stem only from imperfect exposition. Rather, it is inherent in Kant's notion of number, in which pure understanding and pure synthesis of imagination are more closely conjoined than in any other concept. This is because Kant is trying to define a concept quite different from the "universal or reflected representations" inherited from the School logic. To see this, we need to consider his conception of number more closely.

---

[24] In his thoughtful discussion of Kant's conception of number in relation to the categories of quantity, Charles Parsons suggests that Kant wavered between two conceptions of number, one according to which it is thought by purely intellectual concepts, the other according to which it is a sensible representation (a schema). According to Parsons, the first conception was present in the *Inaugural Dissertation* and appears again in the lectures on Metaphysics posterior to the first edition of the *Critique*; it appears also in the second edition of the *Critique* and in the Letters to Schultz and Rehberg on number and arithmetic (discussed later). On the contrary, according to Parsons, in the first edition of the *Critique* the relation of number to the pure categories is less prominent. In particular, "Kant appears in the Schematism to reject the idea expressed in the *Dissertation* and implicit, though not consistently held to, in the *Metaphysics Lectures*, of describing the concept of number in terms of the pure categories" (Parsons, "Categories," 146). This is a strange thing to say if we recall that in the Schematism chapter, Kant writes that number is the schema *of the category of quantity*. Thus he does not abandon the definition of number "in terms of the pure categories," unless "pure" is understood as meaning "having no relation to the sensible" (unschematized). But if one understands it in this way, then one has to say that Kant did not define number in terms of the "pure" categories at any point since 1770, or even in the *Dissertation* itself (see in particular *Diss.* §1n, Ak.II, 388n; 379). Nevertheless, I agree with Parsons that the relation between intellectual synthesis (*synthesis intellectualis*) and figurative synthesis (*synthesis speciosa*) elaborated in the B Transcendental Deduction helps clarify the relation between schema and category in the definition of number (see Parsons, "Categories," 149).

Number

Kant's generation of number from the logical function of quantity in judgment shows at least that his conception of number is less naive than is often believed. A superficial reading of the introduction to the first *Critique* or of the Axioms of Intuition may lead the reader to think that, for Kant, the concept of number is formed by such process as counting one's fingers or lining up points on paper.[25] In contrast, if we consider seriously the relation of number to the category of quantity, and the relation of the latter to the logical quantities of judgment, we should conclude that for Kant, forming the concept of number depends on constituting *sets of objects thought under the same concept.* Kant's concept of number then appears to belong to the path leading to Frege's definition of number as the property of a concept.[26] This proximity has been noted by Charles Parsons, who, in relation to this point, cites the following passage from the Schematism chapter:

> If five points be set alongside one another, thus, ... , I have an image of the number five. But if, on the other hand, I think only a number in general, whether it be five or a hundred, this thought is rather the representation of a method whereby a multiplicity [*eine Menge*], for instance a thousand, may be represented in an image in conformity with a certain concept, than the image itself. (A140/B179)

25 Cf. Couturat, "Mathématiques de Kant," 338, for the claim that Kant had a "crudely empiricist" notion of arithmetic. On this point, Couturat refers to Vaihinger's commentary, according to which Kant viewed the concept '5' as "a mere name, which only receives content when it is converted into an intuition" (Vaihinger, *Commentar*, I, 296, n. 1). Kemp Smith finds Kant's notion of arithmetic to be inconsistent (*Commentary*, 40: "An appeal to our fingers or to points is as little capable, in and by itself, of justifying any *a priori* judgment as are the sense-contents of grounding an empirical judgment"), and Bennett considers it to be "wrong in a thoroughly boring way" (*Kant's Analytic*, 52). R. and M. Kneale object to Kant that the truth of the equation '135664 + 37863 = 173527' cannot be proved by counting on one's fingers (see Kneale, *The Development of Logic*, 447). Many other examples could be given.

26 Cf. Frege, *Grundlagen*, 46: "It should throw some light on the matter [of the nature of number] to consider number in the context of a judgment which brings out its basic use [*ihre ursprüngliche Anwendungsweise*]. While looking at one and the same external phenomenon, I can say with equal truth both 'It is a copse' and 'It is five trees', or both 'Here are four companies' and 'Here are 500 men'. Now what changes here from one judgment to the other is neither any individual object [*das Einzelne*], nor the whole, the agglomeration of them, but rather my terminology [*meine Benennung*]. But that is itself only a sign that one concept has been substituted for another. This suggests as the answer to the first of the questions left open in our last paragraph, that the content of a statement of number is an assertion about a concept. This is perhaps clearest with the number 0. If I say 'Venus has 0 moons', there simply does not exist any moon or agglomeration of moons for anything to be asserted of; but what happens is that a property is assigned to the *concept* 'moon of Venus', namely that of including nothing under it [*nichts unter sich zu befassen*]. If I say 'the King's carriage is drawn by four horses', then I assign the number four to the concept 'horse that draws the King's carriage'." My attempt to bring together Kant and Frege may seem implausible, considering how strongly Frege criticizes Kant's conception of arithmetic. Frege reproaches Kant for appealing to intuition in order to ground arithmetical propositions (§5, certainly a direct inspiration for Kneale's objection mentioned in the previous note; also §12, §89). He draws attention to the weakness of Kant's definition of a con-

Parsons comments this passage as follows:

> However, even for a number like 5, for which there is no difficulty in obtaining the sort of thing Kant calls an image, we do *not* have a "method of representing a multiplicity in an image in conformity with a certain concept," unless the multiplicity itself is determined by a concept, in the example at hand something like *dot on the page*. This is just Frege's point that a number attaches to a concept.[27]

Even while remarking that some texts might confirm this interpretation, particularly in Kant's *Reflexionen* and Lectures on Metaphysics, however, Parsons doubts that Kant was clearly aware of any such relation between number and a concept under which a multiplicity is thought.[28] I think, on the contrary, that Kant's generation of number from logical quantity reveals that this relation is an essential aspect of Kant's notion of number: we would acquire no representation of number were it not for our capacity to generate and reflect the unity of a multiplicity under a concept.

To be sure, this parallel quickly finds its limit. Kant nowhere approaches the definition of number from the relation of equinumericity between concepts, or a purely logical definition of the series of numbers, two essential elements in Frege's analysis of number.[29] For Kant, numbers are generated a priori by the "successive addition of homogeneous units" in the form of inner sense, time. This recourse to temporal intuition in order to think both the series of numbers and any individual number leaves Kant's doctrine very far from modern set-theoretical definitions of number. Nevertheless, Kant's recourse to temporal intuition to ground number series does not mean that he gives secondary importance to the intellectual/conceptual aspect of number. On the contrary, the genesis of number through "successive addition of (homogeneous) units" finds its explanation in the metaphysical deduction of the category of quantity. The concept of number is the concept of a determinate quantity, namely the reflection of the specific unity of a (homogeneous) manifold. This relation to the pure concept of quantity

---

cept as a composite of marks (§88), and generally criticizes the weakness of Kant's logic, which made Kant's distinction between analytic and synthetic judgments ineffectual and prevented him from recognizing the analytic character of arithmetic (§87–88). But Frege's reading of Kant on arithmetic, for example, the explanation of addition he attributes to Kant in §5, is sometimes unfair, and certainly one-sided. Like most readers of the *Critique*, Frege pays attention only to Kant's appeal to intuition as the ground of arithmetic statements, and fails to consider the meaning given to number by the transcendental account of the category of quantity. Only such an account can give force to the parallel I am suggesting here. In my opinion, this parallel, however limited, is indispensable to evaluating Kant's notion of number and its function in transcendental philosophy, which on the contrary remains completely obscure if Kant's position is reduced to an unacknowledged empiricism.

[27] Parsons, "Categories," 115. The concept Kant is referring to in the text quoted ("a multiplicity ... may be represented ... *in conformity with a certain concept*") is not the concept of a "point on the page," but rather the concept of number itself. A multiplicity is presented in intuition *in conformity with the concept of number*. Parsons is merely asserting (in my view, rightly) that such a conformity presupposes the constitution of a multiplicity under a concept, here, the concept 'point on the page'.

[28] See ibid., 142–43. Parsons provides a very helpful discussion of the ways in which Kant approaches, without clearly articulating, the distinction between whole/part and set/element.

[29] Cf. Frege, *Grundlagen*, §§69, 79.

is Kant's *rationale* for the relation of number to time: the *synthesis speciosa* in which the understanding "affects inner sense" with a manifold to be reflected under concepts combined according to the logical form of quantity of judgment generates the successive synthesis of homogeneous units, whose determinate unity can be reflected as a concept of number. Temporal synthesis is necessary for the constitution of the extension of a concept by the "effect of the understanding on sensibility," and the concept of number reflects this act of constituting a sensible multiplicity reflected under the same concept.

Now, relating the concept of number (and number itself, as a schema) in this way to the generation, through *synthesis speciosa*, of the extension of concepts, has two important consequences. First, the function of number in the activity of the understanding is as universal and unavoidable as the form of discursive concepts itself, that is, discursive universality, since a number is "nothing other than the schema of quantity," that is, the specific rule of synthesis generating the *extension* of a (discursive) concept. But second, the *concept* of number, which reflects this rule of synthesis, is very different from the discursive concepts whose extension is generated according to this rule. The concept of number is not a synthesis or aggregate of marks, but the reflection of the rule generating the sphere, or extension, of concepts (themselves syntheses or aggregates of marks).[30] Admittedly, Kant never explicitly draws attention to this difference, which I can claim only to extract from his transcendental genesis of quantity and number. But I shall argue that this irreducibility of the concept of number to an aggregate of marks is essential for understanding Kant's analysis of the propositions of arithmetic.

Because Kant, in the *Critique*, puts primary emphasis on the intuitive/sensible aspect of number, his analysis acquires a peculiarly empiricist tone, for instance in the famous passage of the introduction where he explains that adding five to seven means adding one by one, to the number seven, the units given in the image of the number five provided by the fingers of one hand or five points on paper.[31] But in fact, in this explanation fingers or points serve only to present intuitively given units as the extension of an arbitrarily chosen concept. They are intended as an aid to exhibit the act of synthesis of discrete units, which is the meaning of the concept of number. Moreover, we should not conclude from these examples that a number can be formed only by the addition of empirical elements (fingers of the hand or points on a page): an immediate objection would, of course, be that large numbers cannot be generated in this way. But in counting, anything can serve as a unit, including a numbered multiplicity of elements (for instance, a ten). In large numbers, I no longer add up merely simple units, but tens, hundreds, thousands, which constitute new units added together according to the same rule used in adding primitive units. Surprisingly, Kant explicitly refers to this procedure not in his discussion of arithmetic, but in the metaphysical deduction of the categories: "Thus our counting, as is easily seen in the case of larger numbers, is

---

[30] On concepts as "syntheses" or "aggregates" of marks, or again as "combinations of coordinated marks" see *Logik*, introd. VIII, 58–59.

[31] B15; cf. also A140/B179.

a synthesis according to concepts, because it is executed according to a common ground of unity, as, for instance, the decade. In terms of this concept, the unity of the synthesis of the manifold is rendered necessary" (A78/B104). The concepts mentioned here are not ordinary common concepts, syntheses of marks, but number concepts, reflections of the rule of synthesis of a determinate multiplicity, in which a determinate multiplicity can itself serve as a unit. Just as I add a unit to a unit, I can add ten to ten, and a hundred to a hundred, and so forth, because thanks to the intuitive presentation of the addition of discrete units, which is the ground of the concept of number, any number (small or large) can become meaningful so long as a relation to the unit can be ascribed to it. Number does not acquire its meaning from an image, but from a schema, which is the rule for the formation of a multiplicity.

It is interesting to compare this explanation with Locke's in the *Essay Concerning Human Understanding*.[32] According to Locke, the idea of unity naturally accompanies every object of our senses, and the idea of number arises from repeating the idea of unity and associating a sign with each collection thus generated by addition of units. Any collection bearing a sign can then in turn serve as a unit, which allows us to form the larger numbers. Locke even suggests additional signs for the collections of millions (billions, trillions, quatrillions) in order, as he says, to make our calculations clearer.[33] When Vaihinger claims that, for Kant, numbers are mere signs whose referent is a collection of units in intuition,[34] he describes Kant's conception of number as if it were Locke's. But for Kant, the idea (the concept) of a unit is not given with each sensory object. It presupposes an act of constituting a homogeneous multiplicity, which requires an a priori form of our imagination (a rule of the *synthesis speciosa* producing "time itself" in the sensible presentation of a homogeneous multiplicity) and of our understanding (a rule of the *synthesis intellectualis*, namely the discursive act of thinking the logical quantity of judgment). Thus the idea of number is not the idea of a collection of given units to which we associate a sign, but the reflected representation of a rule for synthesis, that is, for the act of constituting a homogeneous multiplicity. When such an act is presented a priori in intuition, a concept of number is *constructed*. The sensible signs associated with numbers are tools to help this construction, in which each sign stands for the rule for generating a determinate collection of units. The choice of a numerical base (in current numerical systems, ten) allows for the representation of the rule for generating a determinate collection of units as a larger unit. Similarly, signs also serve to represent the relations between numbers and the operations performed on them. Because of this role played by signs, Kant describes the construction of concepts in arithmetic (and also in algebra) as *symbolic*, while the construction of concepts in geometry is described as *ostensive*. In geometry, the act of constituting a (spatial) multiplicity is given direct sensible presentation in the figure, while in arithmetic the act of constituting a multiplicity ("the successive addition of homogeneous

[32] Locke, *Essay* II, xvi, §§1–6.
[33] Ibid., §6.
[34] See note 25.

units") is symbolically represented by signs. The relations between these signs are those of the multiplicities they represent, or rather of their schemata (the rules for the constitution of a multiplicity). Each number is symbolically represented by a sensible sign, that is, a digit. The latter makes the schema of number directly visible (*augenscheinlich*, says Kant). This schema is the rule of the constitution of the multiplicity reflected under a concept of number.[35]

It would thus be a mistake to reduce Kant's notion of number to the image of points on a page or fingers on a hand. Even the temporal character of the genesis of the manifold reflected in a number should not let us forget the *purely intellectual* origin of the capacity of thinking and thus of constructing (presenting a priori in intuition) a homogeneous multiplicity. This is, I think, what Kant meant when he wrote, in a letter to Schultz, that "time has no influence on the properties of numbers":

> Time, as you correctly notice, has no influence on the properties of numbers (as pure determinations of magnitude), as it has, on the contrary, on the character of all alteration (as a *quantum*), which is itself possible only relative to a specific disposition of inner sense and its form (time). The science of numbers, notwithstanding the succession that every construction of magnitude requires, is a purely intellectual synthesis, which we represent to ourselves in thought. But insofar as specific magnitudes (*quanta*) are to be determined in accordance with this science, they must be given to us in such a way that we can grasp their intuition successively; and this grasping must be subjected to the condition of time. So that when all is said and done, we cannot subject any object other than an object of a possible *sensible* intuition to quantitative, numerical assessment, and it thus remains a principle without exception that mathematics can be applied only to *sensibilia*.[36]

The science of numbers is a "pure intellectual synthesis, which we represent to ourselves in thought." The notion of a (homogeneous) multiplicity, like that of the determinate unity of this multiplicity, is a pure concept of the understanding, dependent on one of its original logical functions. Time plays a role only insofar as the representation of this multiplicity as a *quantum*—that is, as an object—depends on the condition of inner sense. Even then, however, time itself is not an object of arithmetic. This is what Kant means when, at the beginning of the passage, he distinguishes between the science of numbers and the science of alter-

[35] Kant explains the distinction between symbolic construction and ostensive construction in the Transcendental Doctrine of Method (A717/B745). True, Kant then restricts the term 'symbolic construction' to algebra (*Buchstabenrechnung*). But I believe that the explanation he gives there applies just as well to arithmetic, in which magnitudes and their relations are represented by sensible signs. Algebra only introduces generality—the consideration of indeterminate magnitudes represented by letters, and the greater complexity of possible operations—into the science of magnitudes and their relations. Indeed, Kant often calls it "general arithmetic" (see *Deutlichkeit*, §2, Ak. II, 278; Letter to Schultz, November 25, 1788, Ak. XI, 555). For a helpful account of construction in arithmetic, see Young: "Arithmetical Concepts."

[36] Letter to Schultz, November 25, 1788, Ak. X, 556–57; 130–31. I translate as "alteration" the German *Veränderung*. This is the term Kant uses in the second Analogy to refer to any objective succession. See the second part of chapter 11.

ations. In the latter, time itself is a property of the object as *quantum*, that is, as an object to be determined quantitatively. In the science of numbers, time is only a subjective condition of the representation of number as a *quantum*, a multiplicity given as an object.

The correspondence between Kant and Rehberg makes this point even clearer. Rehberg, astonished that Kant, in the *Critique*, should maintain that mathematical propositions are grounded in intuition, asserts that this is correct in the case of geometry, where the proofs depend on the intuition of space. But the same does not hold for arithmetic:

> Even if it is undeniable that sensible appearances are subject to the application of arithmetic truths only to the extent that time, insofar as it is their universal form, is subjected to the application of the concepts of the understanding by the transcendental synthesis of imagination, it seems however that the truth of arithmetical propositions themselves does not arise from the intuition of the pure form of sensibility. [This is so] because no intuition of time is necessary to guide arithmetical and algebraic proofs. On the contrary, these proofs arise immediately from the concepts of numbers, and require only sensible signs by which they are recognized, during and after the operation of the understanding. Unlike geometry, they do not require pure images to guide the proofs at all.[37]

However, Rehberg allows, asserting that arithmetical concepts and demonstrations are purely intellectual raises a difficulty: how are we then to explain the fact that the understanding, which arbitrarily (*willkürlich*) creates for itself concepts of numbers, cannot determine by numbers a concept such as $\sqrt{2}$?[38] The ground of this impossibility probably lies, he writes, in "the nature of the *transcendental* faculty of *imagination* and *its connection to the understanding*, which are incomprehensible to any human capacity of understanding."[39]

Kant's answer is significant. On the one hand, he writes, it is true that I can consider any number as the product of two factors. I can also search for the second factor when the first is given to me. I can represent a number as the product of two *equal* factors, even if these factors are not, and cannot be, given as numbers. Thus, given a number algebraically represented by a, I can represent each of the equal factors as $\sqrt{a}$. But on the other hand, it is also true that even though I can always *think* $\sqrt{a}$ in this way, I cannot thereby produce it—that is, determine it completely as a multiplicity of units. Thus I can *think* $\sqrt{2}$, and I can even ascertain that this concept is not empty, since it can be represented geometrically by a *quantum*, the diagonal of a square. But from this concept alone, I cannot deter-

[37] Letter from Rehberg to Kant, September 1790, Ak. XI, 205; 164.

[38] Ibid., 206; 165. Rehberg specifically asks "Since the understanding has the power to create numbers arbitrarily [*willkürlich*], why is it incapable of thinking $\sqrt{2}$ in numbers?" By "thinking in numbers," he means thinking in multiples or fractions of the unit, that is, in rational numbers.

[39] Ibid. Rehberg's appeal to imagination may seem similar to Kant's, but it is not. His "transcendental imagination" has no spatial or temporal character. The rest of the letter shows that he views imagination merely as the capacity to make use of sensible signs to solve equations concerning relations of magnitude. Kant of course understood this. At the beginning of his reply, he describes Rehberg as appealing to imagination "independently even of space and time" (ibid., 207; 166).

mine a denumerable relation to the unit, a *quantitas*. This last impossibility manifests with particular clarity the relation of number to time:

> But the reason why the understanding, which arbitrarily [*willkürlich*] creates for it-
> self the concept of √2, must content itself, as if it were guided by another faculty
> [*gleichsam von einem andern Vermögen geleitet*] with an indefinite approximation of
> the number √2 and cannot also produce the complete numerical concept (the rational
> relation of √2 to unity)—the ground for this has to do with the successive progres-
> sion as the form of all counting and of all numerical magnitudes, namely time, for
> time is the basic condition of all this producing of magnitudes.[40]

Because time is the condition under which a multiplicity can be presented in intuition and reflected as determinate, *thinking* the concept of a number is not sufficient for this presentation and reflection. If I think √2 as the number that, multiplied by itself, is equal to 2, I have a clear concept of √2, but this is not enough
to determine the multiplicity reflected in √2. This multiplicity can be determined
only by successive approximations of the relation between √2 and the unit. The
reason the concept is not enough to guarantee the completion of these approximations is that representing the multiplicity does not depend on the concept
alone, but also on its presentation in intuition under the condition of time. There
is, however, a compensation for this limitation: even though the temporal condition signals the incapacity of the concept to determine the magnitude represented
symbolically as √2, nevertheless this incapacity is alleviated by the fact that the
formal intuition of time as an "infinite given magnitude" allows us to think the *indefinite approximation* of the numerical value of √2. This is why Kant makes the
striking remark that here the understanding is "guided by another faculty." This
other faculty is imagination, which presents a priori not only the schema for any
determinate multiplicity, but also the possibility of pursuing indefinitely, in the
formal intuition of time as an "infinite given magnitude," the approximation of √2
to a number—that is, to a magnitude having a determinate relation to the unit.[41]

Quantitas *and* Quantum

I have said nothing so far about the most important aspect of the category of quantity, namely the role it plays in the determination of a *quantum*. Kant's most explicit definition of the relation between a *quantum* and a *quantitas* is found in his
Lectures on Metaphysics:

[40] Letter to Rehberg, Ak. XI, 208; 167.
[41] Thus Kant has what Parsons ("Categories," 144) calls a "pre-Cantorian" view of numbers: only
rational numbers may properly be called numbers, an infinite number is an impossibility. The latter
point is asserted with greatest emphasis in the *Inaugural Dissertation* (§1n, Ak. II, 388n; 378n) and
repeated in the *Critique* (B111). As to the former point, note that in the letter to Rehberg Kant does
refer to the concept of √2 as the concept of a number. But this is a borderline case, a concept not representable as a determinate multiplicity of units but only as a figure in space (as the diagonal of a
square whose side is equal to one), that is, as a *quantum continuum*. I discuss the relation between
number and *quantum continuum*, and the role of the formal intuitions of space and time as "infinite
given magnitudes" in the next section.

Quantity: determination of a being, how many times it is posited [*Quantitas: deter-minatio entis, quoties sit positum*].

Quantum: it is one thing, in which there is quantity [*Quantum: est unum, in quo est quantitas*].[42]

Something identical posited several times is called a multiplicity [*etliche mahl einerlei gesetzt, heißt eine Menge, aliquoties facta positio ejusdem est multitudo*].

In every *quantum* there is a multiplicity [*eine Menge*], for that which is entirely simple cannot be called a *quantum*. Where there is no homogeneity there cannot be a *quantum* either, for if we wish to think a heterogeneous composite as a *quantum*, we must allow for a certain homogeneity.[43]

A *quantum* is a single entity (*unum*) that can be quantitatively determined (*in quo est quantitas*). For this to be possible, the entity must not be simple: it must contain a multiplicity, and this multiplicity must be made up of homogeneous parts. Otherwise, the entity would be a *compositum*, but not a *quantum*, because only insofar as the parts are homogeneous can their multiplicity be quantitatively determined.

Kant distinguishes *quantum continuum* and *quantum discretum*, and defines number as the representation of a *quantum discretum*:

Every *quantum* is either *continuum*, or *discretum*. A *quantum* whose magnitude leaves the multiplicity of parts indeterminate is called *continuum*. It has as many parts as I wish to give it. A *quantum discretum* is a *quantum* by the magnitude of which the multiplicity of parts is determined. . . . A *quantum discretum* must be distinguished from a *quantum* represented as *discretum*. Through a number, we represent every *quantum* as *discretum*. When I acquire a concept of the *quantum discretum*, I think a number.[44]

From this text one may conclude that Kant distinguishes three kinds of *quanta*: (1) *quantum continuum*, which I can divide into as many parts as I wish (*continuum* thus means infinitely divisible;[45] (2) *quantum* "in itself" *discretum*, a collection of discrete units built into a totality by the act of counting; (3) *quantum* "in itself"*continuum*, but which I can represent as *discretum* by choosing a unit of measurement to determine the *quantitas* of this *quantum*—that is, *quoties in eo unum sit positum*, how many times the unit is posited in it. Note, however, that in the *Critique*, Kant seems to exclude the second sense of *quantum* just listed. He denies that a mere collection of discrete elements can be called a *quantum*. He reserves this term for the *quantum continuum*, which only the arbitrary choice of a

[42] *Met. Herder* (1762–64), Ak. XXVIII-1, 21. The text of the *Lectures on Metaphysics* (of which we have only student notes) is partly in Latin, partly in German, sometimes both. The Latin is often directly borrowed from Baumgarten's *Metaphysica*, used by Kant in his lectures.

[43] *Met. Volckmann* (1784–85), Ak. XXVIII-1, 422–23. Note that Kant's *Menge* is *multitudo* in Latin.

[44] *Met. Pölitz* (1790), Ak. XXVIII-2, 560.

[45] On the difference between Kant's notion of a *quantum continuum* and the contemporary notion of continuity, see note 57.

unit of measurement can eventually represent as *quantum discretum* determinable by numbers.[46]

This issue—the measurement of *quanta continua*—is I think what matters most to Kant in his analysis of the category of quantity and its schema, number. It appears explicitly in the table of the categories of quantity, in the *Prolegomena*:

Unity (Measure) [*das Maß*]
Plurality (Quantity) [*die Größe*]
Totality (Whole) [*das Ganze*].[47]

In the same work, Kant uses the example of the measurement of a *quantum continuum* (a line) to illustrate the transition from the logical form of quantity of judgment to the category of quantity:

The principle that a straight line is the shortest distance between two points presupposes that the line is subsumed under the concept of quantity, which certainly is no mere intuition but has its seat in the understanding alone and serves to determine the intuition (of the line) with regard to the judgments which may be made about it in respect to the quantity, that is, to plurality [*der Vielheit*] (as *judicia plurativa*). For under them it is understood [*verstanden*] that in a given intuition there is contained a plurality of homogeneous parts.[48]

This text can be explained in light of the relation between the logical form of quantity in judgments and the category of quantity analyzed previously. Thanks to the logical form of "plurative" judgments, says Kant, "it is understood that in a given intuition there is contained a plurality of homogeneous parts." He means, I think, that the same capacity to judge that makes us capable of reflecting our intuitions according to the logical form of quantity also makes us capable of recognizing in the line a plurality of homogeneous segments, thought under the concept "equal to segment *s*, the unit of measurement." To "subsume under the concept of quantity" is to count these segments, that is, to reflect the unity of this plurality of homogeneous elements. What we have here is a typical case of determining the *quantitas* of a *quantum*. The line is not a *quantum* "in itself *discretum*," for the quantitative determination of which we would only need to enumerate its discrete units. It is a *quantum continuum*, which we need to represent as a *quantum discretum* for its *quantitas* to be determined (thought in a number). The *quantum* is immediately given as an intuition. But the determination of its *quantitas* requires the activity of the discursive function capable of generating the logical form of the quantity of judgment. However, in this particular use, the discursive function

[46] A170–71/B212. Kant does not hold with great constancy to the use of the term *quantum* (restricted to *quantum continuum*) he recommends in this text. *Metaphysik Pölitz*, quoted earlier, is posterior to the *Critique*. And in the letter to Schultz quoted earlier (see note 37) the term *quantum* could refer to either sense of the *quantum discretum*.

[47] *Prol.*, §21, Ak. IV, 303; 46.

[48] Ak. IV, 301–2; 45. See my comment on Kant's expression "*judicia plurativa*," earlier in this chapter, and note 13. For a discussion of the "principle" grounded, according to Kant, in the subsumption of the line under the concept of a magnitude, see the section on geometry.

generates not a discursive judgment, but instead the thought of the rule for generating a homogeneous plurality.

The immediacy of the *quantum*, as well as the mediate character of the determination of its *quantitas*, are asserted repeatedly in Kant's *Lectures on Metaphysics*. Here is an example from *Metaphysik Dohna*: "*Quantum*, in which there is quantity [*Quantum, in quo est quantitas*]. *Quantum*, I can cognize it immediately. But not quantity, how large it is."[49] Kant uses the German term *Größe* (magnitude) to translate the Latin *quantum* as well as the Latin *quantitas*. In the first case, "magnitude" (= *Größe* as *quantum*) refers to an object immediately given in intuition, which is called a *quantum* because we recognize the possibility of determining its *quantitas*. In the second case, "magnitude" (*Größe* as *quantitas*) is a predicate, referring to a quantitative determination of the *quantum*. Only the second case is strictly speaking an instance of the *category* of quantity. Now, it is quite significant that throughout the *Critique*, the term *Größe* should tend to replace the term *Quantität*, and that Kant should speak of the "category of magnitude" rather than the "category of quantity."[50] The reason, in my view, is that the category of quantity (*Quantität*) finds its most fruitful use when it serves to determine the *quantitas* of a *quantum*, that is, the *Größe*, the *magnitude* of an object itself given as a continous magnitude, a *quantum continuum* in space and time.

This relation between *quantum* and *quantitas* helps clarify Kant's terminology in the Schematism chapter, where he describes space and time as "pure images of all magnitudes" (where "magnitudes," *Größen*, should be understood as *quanta*), before explaining that number is the schema of magnitude (where *Größe* should be understood as *quantitas*):

> The pure image of all magnitudes (*quantorum*) for outer sense is space; that of all objects of the senses in general is time. But the pure *schema* of magnitude (*quantitatis*), as a concept of the understanding, is *number*, a representation which gathers together the successive addition of homogeneous units. Number is therefore simply the unity of the synthesis of the manifold of a homogeneous intuition, a unity due to my generating time itself in the apprehension of intuition. (A142–43/B182. The Latin terms in parenthesis are Kant's; 'magnitude' is always *Größe*)

It is important that even before defining the schema of magnitude (*quantitatis*), Kant should mention the "pure image of all magnitudes (*quantorum*)," namely space and time. The categories of quantity (unity, plurality, totality) are thus given a meaning they would not have by being merely related to the logical forms of quantity in judgment, and number is given a relation to continuity and infinity that

---

[49] *Met. Dohna* (1792–93), Ak. XXVIII-2, 630. The same idea appears in the *Critique of Judgment*, §25: "That something is a magnitude (*quantum*) can be cognized from the thing itself without any comparison of it with others, namely, if a multiplicity of the homogeneous together constitutes a unity. On the other hand, [to judge] *how large* something is we always need something else, which is also a magnitude, as its measure" (Ak. V, 248; 104).

[50] See B115, A245, B201, B293, etc. In these cases Kemp Smith translates *Größe* sometimes by 'magnitude', sometimes by 'quantity'. It is better, I think, to translate *Größe* always by 'magnitude', leaving it to the reader (as Kant does when he uses *Größe*) to discern from the context whether it is equivalent to *quantum* or to *quantitas*.

could not be obtained from its mere definition as "a representation which gathers together the successive addition of homogeneous units."

To see this, consider Kant's statement that space and time are the "pure images of all magnitudes." Already in the Transcendental Aesthetic, they are presented as *unum, in quo est quantitas*, one, in which there is quantity:[51] a single space "within which" (not "under which," as with a concept) there are spaces, or more precisely, spatial relations, capable of being measured,[52] and a single time "within" which there are temporal relations, capable of being measured. Indeed, Kant already uses the term *Größe* to characterize space and time: both are described as *infinite given magnitudes*, an expression we are now in a position to understand. Note, first, how this confirms the thesis I defended in the previous chapter: space and time as presented in the Transcendental Aesthetic are already *entia imaginaria*, products of the *synthesis speciosa* of transcendental imagination, the determination of inner sense by the understanding. There would be no space and no time as *quanta* if they were not an "effect of the understanding on sensibility," which presents them as an intuition in which the "successive addition of homogeneous units" (*quantitas*) can be reflected. But conversely, there would be no pure synthesis of *quantitas* if a pure intuition (which for us happens to be spatiotemporal) did not provide it with the material for a "successive synthesis of homogeneous units," a representation of the repetition of unit as many times as one wishes. Space and time are "pure images of all magnitudes (*quantorum*)" because every object (as appearance) is a magnitude (*quantum*) only insofar as it has a spatiotemporal form; and because an object has spatiotemporal form only insofar as it belongs, as a part, to the unified intuition of space and time, themselves magnitudes, *quanta*.

Now, this pure intuition of space and time as *quanta, in quibus est quantitas, quanta* in which there is quantity, presents us with a totality different from the category of *totalitas* we have elucidated earlier (the third category of quantity): a *totum* distinct from *totalitas* in the same way as *quantum* differs from *quantitas*, an intuitively given whole that conditions the determination of its own parts, and thus transcends any "representation which gathers together the successive addition of homogeneous units." This explains in what sense Kant calls space and time *quanta infinita*: any *quantitas* determined in them will be a part, not a whole, relative to the one space and time that precede and make possible their parts. In other words, according to the definitions of 'larger' and 'smaller' given in Kant's *Lectures on Metaphysics*, space and time are *larger* than any *quantitas*.[53] This is

[51] For this expression, see the text referenced in note 42.

[52] In this regard, Kant is certainly on the side of Leibniz arguing against Clarke that space as treated in geometry consists only of relations, to which quantity applies (cf. *Leibniz-Clarke Correspondence*, 4th reply of Clarke, and 5th paper of Leibniz, 47–54). Where Kant differs from Leibniz is in his conception of the space of the metaphysician, that is, his conception of the single space that grounds the spatial relations apprehended by imagination. For Leibniz, its ultimate nature is an order of compossibles accessible to an *intellectus archetypus*. For Kant it is the pure form of sensible intuition, or formal intuition. See chapter 6 and chapter 8.

[53] See *Met. Dohna* (1792–93): "A thing is larger than another thing when a part of this thing is equal to the other thing. A thing is smaller than another thing when it is equal to a part of this other thing" (Ak. XXVII-2, 626).

why, on the one hand, space and time must be termed *infinite given magnitudes* (*quanta infinita*), and on the other hand, any determination of a *quantitas* in space and time can be *indefinitely pursued*. These two points are most clearly stated in Kant's comments about Kästner, published in Eberhard's *Philosophisches Magasin*:

> Thus, the geometer, as well as the metaphysician, represents original space as infinite and more precisely, as an infinite *given*. For the representation of space (together with that of time) has a peculiarity found in no other concept, viz., that all spaces are possible and thinkable only as parts of one single space, so that the representation of parts already presupposes that of the whole. Now, if the geometer says that a straight line, no matter how far it has been extended, can still be extended further . . . this means that *the space in which I describe the line is greater than any line which I might describe in it.* Thus, the geometer expressly grounds the possibility of his problem [*seiner Aufgabe*] of infinitely increasing a space (of which there are many) on the original representation of a single infinite space, as a singular representation, in which alone the possibility of all spaces, proceeding to infinity, is given.[54]

We find similar statements in Kant's *Lectures on Metaphysics*:

> The mathematical infinite is infinite magnitude, given or giveable [*quantum infinitum datum s. dabile*]. If given, space. If giveable, number [*Datum: Raum. Dabile Zahl*].[55]

> We represent space to ourselves as a mathematical infinite; [this does not mean] that we can always draw a line further, which is the indefinite. Rather, the imaginary being [*ens imaginarium*] we call space is infinite.[56]

Just as space and time, as original magnitudes [*quanta*], are infinite [*infinita*]—that is, larger than any quantitative synthesis of a *quantum*—similarly their parts are not discrete elements preceding their collection as a whole. On the contrary, they are limitations of this whole, which can be arbitrarily (*willkürlich*) determined. In other words, space and time are not only *quanta infinita*, but also *quanta continua* (continuous magnitudes), where *continuous* has the definition quoted earlier, which Kant inherits from Baumgarten. We find similar versions of that definition in all the *Lectures on Metaphysics*, as well as in the *Critique*:

> Every *quantum* is either *continuum*, or *discretum*. . . . A *quantum continuum* is not made up of simple parts. . . . The multiplicity of parts of which it is made up is not determined by its magnitude, and I can allow the multiplicity I wish [*eine Menge, wie und soviel ich will*].[57]

[54] Ak. XX, 419–20; this text is reproduced in Allison's edition of *The Kant-Eberhard Controversy*, 176.
[55] *Met. Pölitz* (1790), Ak. XXVIII-2, 568.
[56] *Met. Dohna* (1792–93), Ak. XXVIII-2, 644.
[57] *Met. Volckmann* (1784–85), Ak. XXVIII-1, 423. Kant gives similar definitions in all the versions of these lectures available to us. This notion of a *quantum continuum* is different from the modern notion of a *continuum* for which a rigorous formulation was provided at the end of the nineteenth century by Dedekind. As Friedman explains, what Kant calls continuity in the text quoted here corresponds to what today would be called denseness. For a helpful clarification of this point, see

The property of magnitudes by virtue of which no part of them is the smallest possible, that is, by virtue of which no part is simple, is called their continuity. Space and time are *quanta continua*, because no part of them can be given save as enclosed between limits (points or instants), and therefore only in such fashion that this part is itself again a space or a time. (A169/B211)

But this also means that every *quantitas* generated in them by means of a successive synthesis can itself be generated in a continuous manner, that is, not as an aggregate of discrete elements but through the continuous increase of a magnitude of which no part is the smallest possible. Following Newton, Kant calls the magnitudes thus generated by continuous increase, *flowing magnitudes*:

> Space therefore consists solely of spaces, time solely of times. Points and instants are only limits, that is, mere positions which limit space and time. But positions always presuppose the intuitions which they limit or are intended to limit; and out of mere positions, viewed as components capable of being given prior to space or time, neither space nor time can be constructed. Such magnitudes may also be called *flowing*, since the synthesis of productive imagination involved in their production is a progression in time, and the continuity of time is ordinarily designated by the term flowing or flowing away. (A169–70/B211–12)

We started by considering quantitative synthesis as the synthesis of a discrete magnitude, that is, of a multiplicity whose determination can be thought in a rational number. From there we moved, through the application of *quantitas* to space and time as original *quanta*, to a quantitative synthesis that can be indefinitely iterated and whose parts are arbitrarily delimited; finally, we considered continuous magnitudes whose genesis can be thought as an integration of infinitesimal increases.[58]

Friedman, *Kant*, 60–62. Friedman shows, moreover, that when Kant goes on to relate *quantum continuum* and Newton's notion of fluent magnitude (see next quotation), he comes closer to the notion of continuity defined forty years later by Bolzano and Cauchy in terms of convergence and limit of an infinite series. But again he gives only an intuitive formulation of this notion by appealing, like Newton, to the variability of a magnitude through time. See Friedman, *Kant*, 71–75; also Coffa, *Semantic Tradition*, 28–29.

[58] Thus the *flowing magnitudes* refer to Newton's *calculus of fluxions*. Kant certainly knew it through Newton's *Principia mathematica Philosophiae naturalis*, which he studied while he was working on the *Critique*. Newton sums up his conception of fluxions ("speeds of augmentation or diminishment") of quantities in book II, lemma 2 of the *Principia*, where he speaks of the "motion" and "flux" of magnitudes, both terms that Kant takes up in the text just quoted. Kant may also have known the main treatises in analytic geometry in which Newton first expounded his method of fluxions, that is, his discovery of calculus: *De Analysi per aequationes numero terminorum infinitas* (written in 1669, and first published in 1711 by William Jones, then frequently reprinted); *Methodus fluxionum et serierum infinitarum* (written in 1671, published in 1676, frequently reprinted, then translated into French by Buffon in 1740); lastly, the *Tractatus de quadratura curvarum*, which was reprinted many times in Latin and in English from 1704 onward. For the history of these texts, see Derek Whiteside's introduction to his edition of Newton. Generally speaking, the importance of calculus in Kant's reflection on mathematics should not be underestimated. It is difficult to say exactly what Kant read of Leibniz, but Cassirer rightfully insists on the importance for Kant of Dutens's 1768 edition of Leibniz's philosophical and scientific works (see Cassirer, *Kant*, 98). Equally important was the 1765

Now, this synthesis corresponds word for word to the *synthesis speciosa* Kant describes in section 24 of the Transcendental Deduction. Recall Kant's examples:

> We cannot think a line without *drawing* it in thought, or a circle without *describing* it. We cannot represent the three dimensions of space save by *setting* three lines at right angles to one another from the same point. Even time itself we cannot represent, save insofar as we attend, in the *drawing* of a straight line (which has to serve as the outer figurative representation of time), merely to the act of the synthesis of the manifold whereby we successively determine inner sense, and in so doing attend to the succession of this determination in inner sense. (B154)

In the previous chapter, I expressed surprise at the fact that, although Kant presents the relation between *synthesis speciosa* and *synthesis intellectualis* as concerning all the categories, the examples in section 24 (a priori synthesis of figures in space, a priori generation of time) concern only mathematical synthesis of magnitudes.[59] But after elucidating the category of quantity, we have less reason for surprise. For as we saw, what is reflected in the category of quantity is the synthesis of homogeneous multiplicity in general, that is, the form of the *exhibition of the x* without which there would be no judgment on appearances (and hence no cognitive use of the categories). The syntheses according to all other categories are dependent on this original presentation: the synthesis of quality (reality) "fills" the form thus constituted, and the syntheses of relation delineate in it an order of reasons. None of this would be possible, were not the form of homogeneous multiplicity constituted by the schematism of quantity—that is, the "determination of inner sense by the understanding" that also constitutes space and time as infinite and continuous magnitudes, *quanta continua infinita*—meanwhile also generating number, the schema of *quantitas*.

The schema of quantity thus allows Kant to kill three birds with one stone. First, he can argue that all empirical apprehension, to the extent that it consists in the successive synthesis of a homogeneous multiplicity, is subject to *synthesis speciosa* in accordance with the category of quantity. Second, he can argue that this *synthesis speciosa* makes possible synthetic a priori judgments in pure mathematics. Third, he can argue that mathematics is applicable to appearances. The first was announced in section 26 of the Transcendental Deduction ("When I make the empirical intuition of a house into a perception . . .").[60] I analyzed it in

---

Raspe edition, through which Kant became acquainted with Leibniz's *New Essays on Human Understanding*. And finally, many of Leibniz's works on calculus were published in the Leipzig *Acta eruditorum*. Kant's admiration for Euler is also well known. What is less known is that Michelsen dedicated his German translation of the *Introductio in Analysin infinitorum* to Kant (the translation appeared in 1788, but Euler's *Introductio* is from 1748). It is therefore surprising to see Gottfried Martin assert that "Kant was not interested in calculus" (Martin, *Zahl*, 91), even if it is true that in the *Critique*, Kant's interest in the problem of "conditions of possibility" leads him to focus mainly on elementary operations (addition in arithmetic, drawing figures in geometry). For more careful assessments of Kant's relation to the mathematics of his time, see Büchel, *Geometrie*; Schulthess, *Relation*; and again Friedman, *Kant*.

[59] See chapter 8, pp. 227, 241.
[60] B162.

the previous chapter when explaining *synthesis speciosa*, and will now complete the analysis. The second shall be examined in the last section of this chapter. The third can be fully explained only when the other categories are examined. This will be done in the final two chapters of the book.

"When I make the empirical intuition of a house into a perception . . ."

When, for instance, by apprehension of the manifold of a house, I make the empirical intuition of it into a perception, the *necessary unity* of space and of outer sensible intuition in general lies at the basis of my apprehension, and I draw as it were the outline of the house in conformity with this synthetic unity of the manifold in space. But if I abstract from the form of space, this same synthetic unity has its seat in the understanding, and is the category of the synthesis of the homogeneous in an intuition in general, that is, the category of *quantity* [*Größe*]. To this category, therefore, the synthesis of apprehension, that is to say, the perception, must completely conform. (B162)

The relation Kant draws here between "empirical intuition" and "perception" parallels the relation between *quantum* and *quantitas* I just explained. We saw that the *quantum* is "immediately cognized," but also that it is *in quo est quantitas*, something "in which there is quantity," or that can be measured by a successive synthesis of homogeneous units. Similarly, "making the empirical intuition of [a house] into a perception" means subjecting the immediate sensible given (the intuition of the house as a *quantum*) to the act of attention by which it can also eventually be measured. With this act, "I draw as it were the outline of the house" just as in the earlier example I drew the line or the circle. Nonetheless, as an empirical intuition, the house is first given to me as an immediately present whole. Note in passing that some objections classically raised against Kant are dispelled here. If the analyses I have just expounded are correct, it is a mistake to attribute to Kant the idea that perception is a combination of simple sense-data.[61] For Kant, what is immediately "given" is the whole of intuition, which then is "run through and combined" by an act of synthesis. This act, "if I abstract from the form of space . . . , is the category of the synthesis of the homogeneous in an intuition in general, that is, the category of magnitude." Should one then criticize Kant for maintaining that the mere sensible perception of the house contains intellectual representations of quantity or magnitude? Should one complain, as Merleau-Ponty does, that when all is said and done, Kant endorses the principle that "everything is already there," which Merleau-Ponty views as the motto of what he calls "intellectualism"?[62] This too would be a mistake. Far from "everything already being there," according to Kant our own synthesizing acts introduce into

[61] See for instance Henrich, *Identität*, 17.

[62] See the introduction to part III and note 14. Saying that for Kant "everything is already there" is, in effect, accusing him of the same amphiboly he accuses Leibniz of commiting: intellectualizing the sensible (cf. A271/B327).

intuition the forms of combination we shall eventually reflect in quantitative concepts. The representational act through which we generate the perception of the house (no longer as an immediate intuition, but as a perception of which we are conscious) is governed by an *effort to form judgments*, whose logical function of quantity generates the *schema* of quantity, that is, the affection of inner sense by a combination of homogeneous elements, eventually reflected in a number. We shall then say, for instance, that the house is twenty feet high, that it has four front windows, and so on. I might add that the quantitative synthesis of an intuition given as a *quantum* can also have the form of a continuous generation (generation of a "flowing" magnitude), in which the choice of a unit is arbitrary. This again shows that Kant does not hold a sense-atomist conception of perception. The "manifold" (*das Mannigfaltige*) given in intuition is not a discrete multiplicity of sensory atoms, but a manifold first given as an intuitive whole and then synthesized in imagination as a continuous magnitude, which thus can eventually be cognized either as a sum of discrete units, or as a magnitude that has no assignable relation to a unit but can only be figured in space, or even as resulting from the continuous generation of a "flowing" magnitude.[63]

Kant's conception of the role played by quantitative synthesis in our acts of perception is confirmed in the third *Critique*, at the beginning of the Analytic of the Sublime. In analyzing the perception of a *quantum*, he distinguishes two acts of imagination, apprehension (*Auffassung, apprehensio*) and comprehension (*Zusammenfassung, comprehensio aesthetica*).[64] Apprehension, Kant writes, consists in successively surveying the partial representations whose totality constitutes the *quantum*. Comprehension consists in gathering these partial representations into the unity of the complete representation. This gathering up is not always possible: the imagination may run up against its own limitation. If the object to be represented is too large, the partial representations are erased from imagination before the complete representation can be taken in. When confronted with an object that pushes to the limit the capacity of our imagination to take in as a whole what we have first apprehended, we experience the kind of feeling that leads us to describe the object as "sublime." Kant cites as examples the experiences of watching Saint Peter's Basilica in Rome and the pyramids in Egypt, and he quotes a comment from the traveler Savary, according to whom one can experience the full emotional effect of the pyramids only if one stays "neither too close nor too far away":

> For if one stays too far away, then the apprehended parts (the stones on top of one another) are presented only obscurely, and hence their presentation has no effect on the subject's aesthetic judgment; and if one gets too close, then the eye needs some time to complete the apprehension from the base to the peak, but during that time some of the earlier parts are invariably extinguished in the imagination before it has apprehended the later ones, and hence the comprehension [*die Zusammenfassun*] is never complete.[65]

[63] This point will be further elaborated in the next chapter, when we examine Kant's account of appearances as both "extensive" and "intensive" magnitudes.

[64] *KU*, §26, Ak. V, 251; 107–8.

[65] Ibid., Ak. V, 252; 108.

According to this description, in perceiving an object as imposing in size as a pyramid, imagination gives itself an implicit unit that it can absorb "in one glance"[66] (here, the monumental slabs of stone of which the pyramid is made), and successively surveys the elements thus arbitrarily chosen before taking in the totality of the object. In perceiving the house mentioned in section 26 of the Transcendental Deduction, we proceed no differently. In both cases, imagination gives itself a unit, which serves as it were to underpin the act of *apprehensio*, and then the act of *comprehensio aesthetica*. This implicit, "blind" admission of a unit, by means of which an object is apprehended as a *quantum*, requires an act of attention governed by an *effort to form judgments*, whose logical form of *quantity* generates the representation of a plurality of homogeneous elements, that is, elements reflected under the same concept. The only difference between the case of the house and that of the pyramid is that, in the latter, the imagination is pushed to the limit of its ability to embrace (*zusammenfassen*) what it had initially apprehended (*aufgefaßt*), whereas in the former no such limit is reached.[67]

This explanation of the way in which imagination may be pushed to its limit agrees with Kant's analysis of the difference between *image* and *schema* of a magnitude. Imagination, he writes in the third *Critique*, may be limited in its capacity of *comprehensio aesthetica* (which is, in effect, an activity of producing an image). But this limitation in no way prevents it from providing the understanding, for the sake of *comprehensio logica* of an object as a *quantum*, that is, for the sake of measurement, with units that may be larger than anything imagination itself can encompass in an intuition. For example, imagination cannot encompass "in one glance" a German mile, much less the diameter of the earth, but it can nevertheless offer them as units of measurement, for it ensures the meaningfulness of the rule according to which a mile is obtained by a determinate synthesis of units, perhaps themselves thought as a synthesis of units, and so on until we arrive at a final unit, arbitrarily chosen, which can be grasped through *comprehensio aesthetica*.

> This mathematical estimation of magnitude serves and satisfies the understanding equally well, whether the imagination selects as the unit a magnitude that we can take in in one glance, such as a foot or a rod, or whether it selects a German mile, or even an earth diameter, which the imagination can apprehend but cannot comprehend in one intuition (by a *comprehensio aesthetica*, though it can comprehend it in a numerical concept by a *comprehensio logica*).[68]

The difference between a unit that the imagination can grasp "in one glance," and a unit for which it provides only the intuitive presentation of a rule for apprehension, is a familiar one. It is the difference between an image and a schema

[66] This is Kant's expression, Ak. V, 254; 110. See the text I quote later, cited in note 68.

[67] Thus the *apprehension* Kant describes in §26 of the Transcendental Deduction (in the first *Critique*) includes in itself the two operations he describes in §26 of the Analytic of the Sublime (in the third *Critique*) as *apprehensio* and *comprehensio aesthetica*, or *Auffassung* and *Zusammenfassung*. This agrees with the description of the *synthesis of apprehension in intuition* in the A Transcendental Deduction: it includes the two acts of *Durchlaufen* and *Zusammennehmung*, running through and holding together (A99).

[68] Ak. V, 254; 110–11.

described in the Schematism chapter. We have an image of a foot or a meter, but we have only a schema of a mile or of the diameter of the earth. However, both can serve as a unit in the *comprehensio logica* of magnitude, that is, in its determination by a concept of number. This numerical determination, on its part, can be pursued as far as one wishes. Whatever the initial unit, whether or not it allows of a *comprehensio aesthetica*, "In either case the logical estimation of magnitude progresses without hindrance to infinity."[69] By presenting the rule of a synthesis that can be iterated indefinitely, and which is applicable to its own result (in turn taken as unit), the imagination gives meaning to as large a number of these units as one wishes. Consequently, it allows us to determine by means of a number the magnitude of any empirical object, however large.

How Is Pure Mathematics Possible? Kant's Principle of the Axioms of Intuition

According to Kant, explaining the quantitative synthesis that presides over conscious perception is also explaining what makes mathematical thinking possible. This is not at all because mathematical thinking merely reflects and generalizes what we empirically perceive, but, on the contrary, because the mental acts by means of which we are capable of perceiving a homogeneous multiplicity— which is never merely given, but is the result of a successive synthesis of apprehension, governed by *synthesis speciosa* in accordance with the category of quantity—these mental acts are also what enables us to generate an a priori science of multiplicities and their relations. In other words, Kant considers that the same mental capacities that generate appearances as *quanta* (= *in quibus est quantitas*, things in which there is quantity) also generate the objects of the mathematical sciences. This is why, in the System of Principles, his exposition of the Principle of the Axioms of Intuition deals with the property of being an *extensive magnitude* that characterizes appearances as objects of sensible intuition; the nature of mathematical propositions in geometry and arithmetic; and, finally, the application of mathematics to appearances.[70] Owing to the close link Kant claims thus to establish between mathematical objects and objects of experience (appearances), a standard criticism addressed to his view is that he confused "pure" and "applied" mathematics (i.e., mathematics applied to science of nature).[71] But such

---

[69] Ak. V, 254; 111. "In either case" means, whether or not the unit chosen can be grasped through *comprehensio aesthetica*. This statement immediately follows the passage quoted earlier.

[70] These four points correspond to the four paragraphs of the Axioms of Intuition in the A edition, maintained without change in the B edition. In the B edition, Kant prefaces these four paragraphs with a "proof" (B202–3) which repeats the argument concerning the apprehension of a house in 26 of the Transcendental Deduction (B162). Or rather, §26 in B repeats the argument given only in the Analytic of Principles in the A edition. This confirms what I said earlier of the relation between the B Deduction and the Analytic of Principles: see the first section of this chapter.

[71] Cf. Vaihinger, *Commentar*, II, 88. According to Vaihinger, Kant's view amounts to a confusion between "pure" mathematics and its application in physics (= "applied" mathematics). The distinction between "pure" and "applied" mathematics has a second meaning, according to which one should dis-

criticism rests, I think, on a misunderstanding of Kant's position. For Kant, explaining the possibility of pure mathematics and deducing the possibility of its application to appearances in a pure (mathematical) natural science are one and the same procedure, not because pure mathematics (i.e., that which deals with "the mere form of an object") and mathematics applied to empirical objects are the same science, but because explaining the possibility of pure mathematics is also explaining the possibility of its use in empirical science—that is, the transcendental basis of its application to appearances.

As we saw, the possibility of mathematical thinking depends, according to Kant, on the a priori generation of the form of homogeneous multiplicity, or the form of the extension of any arbitrarily chosen concept. Mathematical concepts can be constructed—that is, presented a priori in pure intuition—because they are nothing other than concepts of (i.e., concepts reflecting the rules for generating) determinate homogeneous multiplicities and their relations. No one among Kant's commentators seems to have noticed that such a view amounts to turning inside out the very predicative logic on which Kant grounds his account of mathematical concepts. On his account, moving from logic to mathematics is moving from considering "universal or reflected representations" and their relations, to considering homogeneous multiplicities originally constituted as the extensions of universal or reflected representations (concepts), and the relations between these multiplicities. Because of this inversion of the form of thought, where one switches from the form of universal and reflected representations to the pure form of (homogeneous) multiplicity, Kant characterizes mathematical thinking as founded on, and inextricably bound up with, the transcendental synthesis of imagination, which alone can produce the representation of pure multiplicities. This is what makes mathematical thinking irreducible to the mere analysis of concepts considered as universal or reflected representations or combinations of marks.

I will now examine this reversal more closely: first, in the case of arithmetic, which deals with pure *quantitas*; and, second, in the case of geometry, which deals with a pure *quantum*, space.

Arithmetic

To clarify what Kant means when he asserts that propositions of arithmetic are synthetic, it is useful to recall the terms in which he defines analytic and synthetic propositions in the *Logic*:

> An example of an *analytic* proposition is, To everything *x*, to which the concept of body (*a + b*) belongs, belongs also *extension* (*b*).

---

tinguish between a formal axiomatized system ("pure" mathematics) and its possible models ("applied" mathematics). This second meaning too gives occasion for a criticism of Kant's position. The criticism is that Kant presented as "pure" geometry what is only one model among other possible models of a formal axiomatized system, which alone can be said "pure." I discuss this problem at the end of this chapter. The issue I am discussing here concerns only the problem raised by Vaihinger.

An example of a *synthetic* proposition is, To everything *x*, to which the concept of body (*a* + *b*) belongs, belongs also *attraction* (*c*).[72]

According to this explanation, an analytic proposition is a proposition in which attributing a predicate to an object *x* results from the *mere analysis of the marks* attributed to the object *x* by means of the subject-concept. A synthetic proposition, on the contrary, is a proposition in which the predicate-concept can be asserted of the object *x* not because it is "contained" in a concept already attributed to it (the subject-concept in the proposition), but only by consideration of the *x*'s given in intuition and thought under the subject-concept. Thus the predicate-concept is attributed to all the *x*'s ('All bodies are heavy') or to some of the *x*'s ('Some bodies are animate') to which the subject-concept is attributed. Now, with respect to this distinction, the status of the concept of number is quite unique. A concept of number, according to Kant, is nothing other than the representation of the rule for constituting the extension of any concept, that is, the rule for the act of successively taking up and bringing together the *x*'s of judgment. This act constitutes the *Menge*, the multiplicity of the *x*'s of judgment constituted as (what we call) a set by being subsumed under a concept (body, point, finger, etc.). Hence an arithmetical proposition is essentially, by its very nature, irreducible to an analysis of marks. For this to be fully clear, Kant should have said that the concept of number is not an ordinary concept, that is, not a "common concept" that can be predicated, as a mark or a combination of marks, of another concept. It is different from "common concepts," since it reflects as such (as multiplicities or, as Cantor will say, as sets having a determinate 'power') sets of objects defined by a concept.[73] Or rather, it reflects the "unity of the act" that generates such sets. Kant never explicitly distinguishes between different orders of concepts in this way, but I would suggest that such a distinction is implicitly at work in the famous

---

[72] Kant, *Logik*, §36, Ak. IX, 111; 607.

[73] Cf. Cantor, *Beiträge zur Begründung der transfiniten Mengenlehre*, §1: "I term the power or the cardinal number of a set the universal concept which, thanks to our active power of thought, emerges from the multiplicity [*Menge*] when one abstracts from the constitution of its various elements and from the order in which they are given." However, Kant would reject the view that the act of thinking resulting in a number is an act of abstraction. For him, the multiplicity is not given, but constituted, and a number concept reflects just this act of constitution. In the article cited earlier, Parsons relates some of Kant's formulations to Cantor's. He stresses the importance of the notion of *Menge*—multiplicity—and the similarity between Kant's definition of totality, "plurality considered as unity [*die Vielheit als Einheit betrachtet*]" (B111), and Cantor's explanation of the notion of a set: "every plurality which lets itself be thought as unity [*jedes Vieles, welches sich als Eines denken läßt*]" (cf. Cantor, *Grundlagen einer allgemeinen Mannigfaltigkeitslehre*, 204). However, Parsons rightfully warns that this similarity should not be taken to mean that Kant anticipated Cantor, but rather that "Cantor's explanations are based on older ways of thought" ("Categories," 155, n. 22). In any case, the restrictions I formulated earlier when comparing Kant with Frege also hold, *mutatis mutandis*, for the comparison with Cantor. Obviously Kant does not have a notion of sets and their relations of equivalence, as Cantor does. It is nevertheless remarkable, I think, that he should consider number as the *rule for generating a multiplicity*, a rule common to multiplicities defined under arbitrarily chosen concepts. But as Parsons remarks, Kant does not always clearly distinguish between a multiplicity with cardinal number n, and the number n itself (see Parsons, "Categories," 139, 146)—in Kantian terms, between the "image" of a number and number itself as a schema (a rule for generating multiplicity, common to multiplicities defined under different concepts).

passage from the introduction to the first *Critique* where he explains the synthetic
a priori nature of the proposition: $7 + 5 = 12$. In his explanation, reference to the
use of five fingers or five points in elementary operations of addition—that is, reference to the *intuition of a (homogeneous) multiplicity*—is meant to demonstrate
the impossibility of reducing an arithmetical concept to an aggregate of marks,
and thus the impossibility of considering a proposition of arithmetic as an analysis of concepts understood as aggregates of marks.

> We might, indeed, at first suppose that the proposition $7 + 5 = 12$ is a merely analytic
> proposition, and follows by the principle of contradiction from the concept of a sum
> of 7 and 5. But if we look more closely we find that the concept of the sum of 7 and
> 5 contains nothing save the union of the two numbers into one, and in this no thought
> is being taken as to what that single number may be which combines both. The con-
> cept of 12 is by no means already thought in merely thinking this union of 7 and 5;
> and I may analyze my concept of such a possible sum as long as I please, still I shall
> never find the 12 in it. We have to go outside these concepts, and call in the aid of the
> intuition which corresponds to one of them, our five fingers, for instance, or, as Seg-
> ner does in his *Arithmetic*, five points, adding to the concept of 7, unit by unit, the
> five given in intuition. For starting with the number 7, and for the concept of 5 call-
> ing in the aid of the fingers of my hand as intuition, I now add one by one to the num-
> ber 7 the units which I previously took together to form the number 5, and with the
> aid of that figure [the hand] see the number 12 come into being. That 5 *should* be
> added to 7, I have indeed already thought in the concept of a sum $= 7 + 5$, but not
> that this sum is equivalent to the number 12. Arithmetical propositions are therefore
> always synthetic. This is still more evident if we take larger numbers. For it is then
> obvious that, however we might turn and twist our concepts, we could never, by the
> mere analysis of them, and without the aid of intuition, discover what [the number is
> that] is the sum. (B15–16)

One might think, says Kant at the beginning of the text, that "the proposition $7 +$
$5 = 12 \ldots$ follows by the principle of contradiction from the concept of a sum of
7 and 5." This would make it similar to the proposition 'man is a rational animal',
which follows analytically from the concept of a man. But 7, 5, and 12 are not
marks (*notae*) and arithmetical addition is not a combination of marks, but the
generation of a multiplicity from two given multiplicities, by means of an operation which has nothing in common with the combination of marks making up the
content of a concept.

One may object that I am giving Kant too much credit. If he had actually recognized that concepts of number are not aggregates of marks, he would not have
argued as he does in the text just quoted, where he relies explicitly on the traditional conception of concepts as aggregates of marks, and of propositions as
combinations of just such concepts, to assert that propositions of arithmetic are
synthetic. Indeed, this objection is one Couturat directed long ago at Kant's explanation of arithmetic propositions. According to Couturat, Kant's explanation
depends entirely on the "narrow and simplistic" conception of logic according to
which every concept is "composed" of partial concepts that can be discovered

through analysis or decomposition. Because the concepts of arithmetic do not allow such analysis, Kant concludes that the propositions of arithmetic are synthetic. But actually, says Couturat, all this proves is the inadequacy of classical logic. When Kant claims that we have to "go outside" the combination of the concepts '7' and '5' to find '12', he simply means that 12 is not obtained by combining the two numbers like marks, but by disjoint union of the classes that correspond to '7' and '5': in modern terms, by logical addition, not by logical product.[74] This is correct, says Couturat. Nevertheless, one does not have to "go outside" the concept of '7 + 5' to obtain '12'. On the contrary, the identity of these concepts ('7 + 5' and '12') follows from their definition in set-theoretical terms. It would be incorrect, he continues, to retort that when we replace concepts as marks by concepts defining classes, judgment is made dependent on intuition. For the psychological origin of the concept is of no interest. Whatever its psychological origin, what results from the definition of the concept in accordance with the laws of logic must, in Kant's own terms, be considered as analytically contained in the concept. Kant himself asserts that even though the origin of the concept of gold is empirical (and thus relies on empirical *intuition*), once the concept is formed the proposition 'Gold is yellow' is an analytic proposition; similarly, he asserts that even though the concept of body is empirical and the concept of extension depends on pure intuition, the proposition 'All bodies are extended' is analytic. In the same way, the concept '7 + 5', regardless of its psychological origin, is identical to the concept '12' by virtue of its definition. Couturat proceeds to show this by expounding a proof of the proposition '7 + 5 = 12' inspired by Leibniz's proof of '2 + 2 = 4' in the *New Essays*.[75]

But to throw back at Kant his own treatment of 'Gold is yellow' or 'Bodies are extended' misses the point since in these judgments, concepts are combined as aggregates of marks, whereas if I am correct, Kant's entire account of arithmetic rests on his awareness (however imperfectly expressed) that numbers are *not* such concepts and are *not* so combined. One might, of course, still retort that whatever the nature of number concepts, a logical proof of addition was possible, as shown by Leibniz's example in the *New Essays*. But this too would be a dubious argument to raise against Kant. For not only did he know the *New Essays*, but moreover, in his early Lectures on Mathematics, he gave a demonstration of '8 + 4 = 12' analogous to Leibniz's proof of '2 + 2 = 4'. Thus when he maintains, in the critical period, that arithmetical propositions are synthetic, he clearly knows what the objection of a Leibnizian logician would be. To understand how he came to hold the critical view, it is interesting to compare the passage from the introduction to the *Critique*, cited earlier, with the proof in Leibnizian style of his 1760s' lectures, as we have it from Herder's notes.

[74] Kant's "aggregate of marks," in terms of set-theoretical logic, is a logical product, that is, on the example given earlier, the intersection of the sets defined by the marks 'animal' and 'reasonable'. Conversely, what corresponds to arithmetical addition is logical sum, that is, the disjoint union of sets.

[75] Couturat, "Mathématiques de Kant," 338–47; he summarizes the proof of 7 + 5 = 12 on p. 338. See note 76. Cf. Leibniz, *New Essays*, IV, chap. 7, §6.

Kant's proof ran as follows:

Theorem: $8 + 4 = 12$

Proof:

$8 = 8$ §20 [every magnitude is equal to itself]

$\underline{4 = 3 + 1}$ definition

$8 + 4 = 8 + 3 + 1$ §24 [equal added to equal makes equal sum]

$\underline{8 + 1 = 9}$

$8 + 4 = 9 + 3$

$\underline{3 = 2 + 1}$

$8 + 4 = 9 + 2 + 1$

$\underline{9 + 1 = 10}$

$8 + 4 = 10 + 2$

$\underline{10 + 2 = 12}$

$8 + 4 = 12.$[76]

Just like Leibniz's proof, this proof proceeds by successive substitutions of terms equivalent by definition ($3 + 1$ replaces 4, then 9 replaces $8 + 1$; $2 + 1$ replaces 3, then 10 replaces $9 + 1$; lastly, 12 replaces $10 + 2$). This series of substitutions corresponds to what Kant describes in the *Critique* as one synthetic operation ($7 + 5 = 12$). In both cases, the first term remains unchanged: "$8 = 8$" (*Mathematik Herder*); "starting with the number 7" (*Critique*). The second term is added to the first, unit by unit. In *Mathematik Herder*, this occurs through substitutions based on definitions: 4 is replaced by the addition equivalent to it by definition ($3 + 1$), which allows replacing $8 + 4$ by $8 + 3 + 1$, and then replacing $8 + 1$ by its equivalent, 9.

[76] Cf. Ak. XXIX, 1–1, 57. The equations underlined are definitions, as Kant indicates for the first instance. §§20 and 24, mentioned in the proof, are earlier sections in the lecture notes (the proof itself is §36). I have cited in brackets the principles referred to in the relevant sections. Kant's proof is shorter than Couturat's because besides the law of associativity, it also implicitly uses the law of commutativity of addition. Thus Kant can move directly from $8 + 3 + 1$ to $8 + 1 + 3 = 9 + 3$. Similarly, he moves directly from $9 + 2 + 1$ to $9 + 1 + 2 = 10 + 2 = 12$. On the contrary, Couturat's demonstration of $7 + 5 = 12$ uses only associativity, and therefore he must successively replace (by virtue of the definitions of 5, 4, 3, and 2) $7 + 5$ with $7 + (4 + 1)$, that is, $(7 + 4) + 1$, then replace $7 + 4$ with $7 + (3 + 1)$, that is, $(7 + 3) + 1$, then replace $7 + 3$ with $7 + (2 + 1)$, that is, $(7 + 2) + 1$, and lastly replace $7 + 2$ with $7 + (1 + 1)$, that is, $(7 + 1) + 1$, before he can run the series again and (by virtue of the definitions of 8, 9, 10, 11, and 12) write: $7 + 1 = 8$, $7 + 2 = 8 + 1$, $7 + 3 = (7 + 2) + 1 = (8 + 1) + 1 = 9 + 1 = 10$; $7 + 4 = (7 + 3) + 1 = 10 + 1 = 11$; $7 + 5 = (7 + 4) + 1 = 11 + 1 = 12$. In Leibniz's proof, the problem of whether to use the property of commutativity did not arise because $2 + 2 = 4$ is a simpler operation. Couturat, inspired by Frege (cf. *Grundlagen*, §6), makes explicit his use of associativity by putting in the necessary brackets, which both Leibniz and Kant neglected to do. Since Herder attended Kant's lectures from 1762 to 1764, Kant's proof predates the publication of the *New Essays*, in 1765. This does not mean that Kant's proof is an independent discovery. The proof was probably well known before Leibniz's *New Essays* was finally published.

Then the operation is repeated: $3 = 2 + 1$, $9 + 3 = 9 + 2 + 1$, $9 + 1 = 10$, and finally $10 + 2 = 12$.[77] This series of substitutions corresponds to what Kant describes in the *Critique* as the act of adding the units of the second term to the first term of the addition: "for the concept of 5 calling in the aid of the fingers of my hand as intuition, I now add one by one to the number 7 the units which I previously took together to form the number 5, and with the aid of that figure [the hand] see the number 12 come into being." Thus it is not through logical substitution of equivalent terms, but by means of intuition, that the number 5 is decomposed in order to add its units one by one to the number 7 and "see the number 12 come into being." This "coming into being" of the number 12 was also apparent in *Mathematik Herder*, in which the gradual decomposition of 4 ($4 = 3 + 1$, $3 = 2 + 1$) made possible the composition of 12 ($8 + 1 = 9$, $9 + 1 = 10$, $10 + 2 = 12$). We must then ask why this series of purely logical substitutions was replaced, in the *Critique*, by the genesis of the sum through the successive addition of units in intuition.

Leibniz's proof in the *New Essays* is defective, as was noticed long before Frege drew attention to its shortcoming. Leibniz does not insert the brackets that would be necessary to make clear his use of the law of associativity of addition; nor does he explicitly state this law as an axiom at the head of his proof. Kant's proof in *Mathematik Herder* compounds this flaw. Not only does Kant, like Leibniz, fail to make explicit his use of associativity; he fails moreover to mention commutativity, also used in his proof. Should we then conclude that the reason Kant, in the critical period, asserted that arithmetic is synthetic was that he discovered for the first time the axiomatic character of his proof? This thesis was defended by Gottfried Martin. According to Martin, Kant's defense of the synthetic character of arithmetic was a defense of its axiomatic (instead of purely logical) character. Martin does not rest his case on Kant's own statements, but rather on the works of Kant's disciples, primarily the mathematician Johann Schultz, who wrote a *Prüfung der Kantischen Kritik der reinen Vernunft* (*Examination of Kant's Critique of Pure Reason*) under Kant's close supervision. Commutativity and associativity of addition are mentioned for the first time in this work, and Schultz begins his later *Anfangsgründe der reinen Mathesis* with the statement of these properties as axioms. Martin, who has studied the manuscript, tells us that the draft of the *Prüfung* that Schultz presented to Kant defined arithmetic as analytic. Only after Kant criticized the manuscript on this point did Schultz, in his final draft, define arithmetic as synthetic and state its two axioms. After quoting the letter in which Kant argues in favor of the synthetic character of arithmetic and asks Schultz to reconsider the relevant part of his book, Martin concludes: "Schultz allowed himself to be convinced by Kant. The *Prüfung* takes the point that arithmetic judgments are synthetic, and that this synthetic character of arithmetic judgments is grounded in the axiomatic character of arithmetic, newly discovered and expounded."[78]

---

[77] Notice that this time Kant does not mention '$10 + 1 = 11$' or '$11 + 1 = 12$'. The rule for constituting a ten and for adding units to tens is sufficient here, and the substitutions already established are not repeated.

[78] G. Martin, *Arithmetik*, 64. And see Parsons's criticism of Martin's view in *Arithmetic*, III. Also Friedman, *Kant* 83–84.

In fact, however, a close look at Kant's published texts does not warrant so straightforward a conclusion. Neither in the *Prolegomena* nor in the *Critique* does Kant make any allusion to an axiomatic grounding of the propositions of arithmetic. In the Axioms of Intuition, he even explicitly denies that arithmetic has axioms.[79] Moreover, if the synthetic character of addition had meant for him that commutativity and associativity of addition are stated as synthetic a priori principles, Kant could have maintained the proof of *Mathematik Herder*, simply adding explicit reference to these axioms. But Kant does not analyze the proposition 7 + 5 = 12 in these terms, either in the *Prolegomena* or in the *Critique*. Rather, he presents the truth of the proposition as immediately grounded in the operation of addition itself. Thus even if Kant, as seems undeniable, convinced Schultz of the synthetic character of arithmetic, Schultz drew his own conclusion, not Kant's, when he translated this synthetic character into an axiomatic presentation. The difference between Kant and Schultz in this regard is obvious if we look at the letter in which Kant tries to convince Schultz that arithmetic is synthetic *even though, he admits, it has no axioms*:

> Certainly arithmetic has no axioms, since its object is actually not any *quantum*, that is, any quantitative object of intuition, but rather *quantity as such*, that is, it considers the concept of a thing in general by means of quantitative determination. On the other hand, arithmetic has *postulates*, that is, immediately certain practical judgments. For if I regard 3 + 4 as the setting of a problem, namely, to find a third number (7) such that the one number will be seen as the *complementum ad totum* of the other, the solution is found by means of the simplest operation, requiring no special prescription, namely by the successive addition that the number 4 proposes simply as a continuation of the counting up to 3. The judgment '3 + 4 = 7' does seem to be a purely theoretical judgment, and objectively regarded, that is what it is; but subjectively, the sign '+' signifies the synthesis involved in getting a third number out of two other numbers, and it signifies a task to be done, requiring no instruction or proof. Consequently the judgment is a postulate.[80]

The beginning of this text implicitly refers to the difference between arithmetic and geometry. To be sure, Kant says, arithmetic has no axioms, because its object is not a *quantum*. The principles of the science of numbers, unlike the principles of geometry, are not dictated by the formal intuition that is its object, but are contained in the very act of constituting quantity or magnitude. Because of this difference between arithmetic and geometry, on the one hand Kant calls the principles of arithmetic postulates ("immediately certain practical judgments") rather

[79] A164/B204–5.

[80] Letter to Schultz, November 25, 1788, Ak. X, 555–56; 129–30. The debate between Schultz and Kant can thus be reconstructed as follows. For Schultz, 'synthetic' is synonymous with 'axiomatic'. Since arithmetic, unlike geometry, is not axiomatic, it is thus not synthetic either. Kant grants Schultz that arithmetic has no axioms, but tries to show him that it nonetheless is synthetic. He succeeds so well that Schultz immediately sets out to develop an axiomatic presentation of arithmetic. But for Kant, 'synthetic' and 'axiomatic' were always two distinct notions, and if arithmetic is synthetic, it is so in a different way than geometry. The text where Kant grants Schultz that "Time . . . has no influence on the properties of numbers" is in the same letter, immediately after the passage cited here (cf. note 36).

than axioms, and on the other hand he does not formulate them as universal principles, but rather considers each singular operation as a "special prescription,"
and the equation resulting from it as a postulate. In arithmetic, the act dictates its
own rule, and the concept of a *quantitas* is constituted and presented in intuition
by virtue of this rule.

Thus Gottfried Martin is correct in claiming that Kant's dissatisfaction with the
Leibnizian proof is due to his new awareness of operational rules irreducible to
the logical principle of contradiction. But he is mistaken in thinking that for Kant,
these operational rules are to be stated as axioms. Why Kant would refuse this
may become clearer if we compare the associativity and commutativity of addition (which Schultz states as axioms of arithmetic) with some of the axioms of
geometry mentioned in the *Critique* : "there is only one straight line between two
points," "three points always lie in a plane," "space has three dimensions."[81]
These axioms state the properties of space "represented as an object," which is
the condition for any demonstration in geometry. However, associativity and
commutativity are not properties of an object, and certainly not properties of time
"represented as an object," but properties pertaining to the very act of generating
quantity. In fact, this illustrates Kant's assertion in a passage of his Letter to
Schultz quoted earlier, that "time has no influence on the properties of numbers."
Addition does not owe its laws of associativity and commutativity to its temporal
condition, but to the rules proper to the act generating a homogeneous multiplicity. Thus, according to the critical Kant, the proof of *Mathematik Herder* was both
useless and deceptive, for its validity was derived from the very operation whose
validity it was supposed to ground. This is what Kant's presentation of addition
in the introduction to the *Critique* makes apparent. He follows the same progression as in the logical proof of *Metaphysik Herder*, but he describes number concepts as concepts reflecting rules for generating multiplicities, and arithmetic
propositions as stating the identity between multiplicities generated by acts of
construction that carry within themselves, together with their own rules, the
ground of the validity of arithmetical propositions.

This conception of arithmetic and the dissimilarity between arithmetic and
geometry implicit in Kant's discussion with Schultz are in agreement with a point
Kant always insisted upon: arithmetic is the most universal of all mathematical
sciences because it is the most closely related to the laws of pure thought.[82] I have
proposed an explanation of what this universality means for Kant in his critical
period: the rules of arithmetical thought are the flip side of the rules of general
logic (as Kant delimits it). The rules of addition are rules of acts of constructing
(homogeneous) multiplicities, and these multiplicities are the flip side of universal or reflected representations, namely the concepts that are the "matter" of general or formal logic. Seen in this light, Kant's position bears a striking structural
resemblance to that of Frege, who grants the synthetic character of geometry but
maintains, by appealing to a logic more powerful than Kant's, the analytic char-

---

[81] For references, see note 85.
[82] Cf. *Deutlichkeit*, I, §4, Ak. II, 282; 255. *Diss.*, II, §12, Ak. II, 397; 390.

acter of arithmetic.[83] Hence one may suppose that if a set-theoretical definition of number and a Fregean-Russellian extensional logic had been available to Kant, he would not have described arithmetical judgments as "immediately certain practical judgments," but as judgments resulting from the definition of number by deductive proof in accordance with the laws of logic. In other words, Kant might then have described the propositions of arithmetic as analytic. This is certainly what Frege himself thought, at least in the *Grundlagen*. But we should not be too quick in satisfying ourselves with such a conclusion. For another point needs to be considered. The synthetic character of arithmetic, for Kant, consists in the fact that arithmetical operations rely on the *construction* of the concept of number—that is, on its *presentation in pure intuition*, as a rule for generating (homogeneous) multiplicities. Now, in Kant's view, this dependence cannot be ignored, for without pure intuition there would be no relation between the category of quantity (and thereby mathematical thought) and *experience*. For him, the multiplicities posited in pure intuition are "merely possible" multiplicities lending their form to every object of experience (every actual multiplicity). Discarding the relation of arithmetic to pure intuition and its temporal form would mean discarding the whole project of a transcendental deduction of the categories, and thus the whole critical project.

Of course, one might retort that this is precisely what later developments in logic, in philosophy of mathematics, and in natural science have given us ample reason to do. Even more than Kant's view of the role of temporal intuition in arithmetic, his view of the role of spatial intuition and the apodeictic truth it is supposed to lend Euclidean geometry would seem amply to justify such a reply.[84] But I would suggest that later developments in mathematics have not so much provided sufficient reason to dismiss Kant's views as they have contributed to the emergence of philosophical projects quite distinct from his. Before pursuing this point, however, we need first to consider the case of geometry.

Geometry

According to Kant, the reason geometry has axioms is that, unlike arithmetic, it is not a science of mere quantity but a science of *quantum*, applying quantitative syntheses to the formal intuition of space. The axioms of geometry state the marks of this formal intuition, and as such they provide the principles of an a priori science of figures and their positions in space. However, Kant nowhere provides an exhaustive or systematic list of these axioms; here again his approach differs from that of a mathematician like Schultz. Kant's aim is not to give an axiomatic presentation of geometry, but rather to elucidate the nature of axioms and what makes them possible.[85] The importance of this question for him is made ob-

---

[83] Cf. Frege, *Grundlagen*, §§14, 17, 88.

[84] Cf., for instance, Coffa's scathing criticism of neo-Kantian attempts to salvage Kant's views in the face of new developments in geometry: *Semantic Tradition*, 57–61.

[85] The examples of "fundamental propositions" (*Grundsätze*) supporting Kant's claim that geometry is synthetic a priori are scattered throughout the *Critique*. Not all of them are axioms in the sense given to this term in standard presentations of Euclidean geometry already in Kant's time: in these

vious by the fact that it appears in a new form with each major division of the *Critique*. Considering each of these appearances helps us understand what Kant means by 'axiom' and the significance of the synthetic character of geometry for transcendental philosophy. I shall thus consider (1) the grounding of the axioms in pure intuition according to the Transcendental Aesthetic, which becomes (2) their grounding in *synthesis speciosa* according to the Transcendental Analytic; and finally I shall consider (3) the difference between the "intuitive" principles of geometry and the purely rational principles, according to the Transcendental Dialectic.

1. According to the Transcendental Aesthetic, the principles of geometry are grounded in the pure intuition of space. Kant insists on the fact that this intuition must be distinguished from perception, which is empirical and thus cannot ground a universal science of spatial relations:

---

presentations, axioms are indemonstrable propositions providing, together with the definitions, the premises from which theorems are deduced. Euclid himself does not call the indemonstrable propositions *axioms*, but some of them *postulates*, others *common notions*. Kant considered Euclid's common notions to be analytic propositions (A164/B204–5), which belong to mathematics only insofar as they can be presented in intuition (B16–17). These shall not be discussed here. Kant's *axioms* are closer to Euclid's *postulates*, in keeping with the usage of his time as well as of ours. Yet it must be emphasized that for Euclid, only two of Kant's examples might count as axioms (or rather as Euclid's postulates): "between two points there is only one straight line" (cf. A24, A163/B204, A300/B356); and "two straight lines do not enclose a space" (cf. A163/B204). Both these examples are variations on Euclid's first postulate (see Heath's remarks in his edition of Euclid's *Elements*, I, 232). Another of Kant's examples merely results from the definition of a plane: "three points always lie in a plane" (B760). A third expresses an intuitive presupposition which Euclid never made explicit: "Space has three dimensions" (A24). This proposition was central to Kant's reflection on the nature of space already in his early essay on "living forces" (for a helpful account of the evolution of Kant's thinking on this question, see Büchel, *Geometrie*, 159–85; also Friedman, *Kant*, 5–14). Another example is: "In a triangle two sides together are greater than the third" (A25/B39, A164/B205). It is in fact not an axiom but a theorem (Euclid, I, 20), as Kant certainly knew. Lastly, in the introduction to the first *Critique* and in the *Prolegomena*, Kant gives the example: "the straight line between two points is the shortest" (B16). This example does not appear in Euclid, either as an axiom or as a theorem. Archimedes admits it as an *assumption* (cf. Heath's comment in Euclid, *Elements*, I, 166). Friedman comments that Kant might have chosen this example with Euler's method of variations in mind, through which Euler attempted to prove this Archimedian "assumption" (Friedman, *Kant*, 87, n. 54). Indeed, it is quite plausible to suppose that for Kant there was a *proof* of this proposition. The way he presents it in the *Prolegomena* (see Ak. IV, 301–2; 45) would confirm such a suggestion: he presents the proposition as universally valid by virtue of the subsumption of the line under the category of quantity. This "subsumption" might mean the application of *quantitas* to *quantum* in a method of infinitesimal variations or "flowing magnitudes" (see the earlier section on quantum). In drawing attention to the variety of Kant's examples, I do not mean to argue that Kant's analysis of the foundations of geometry cancels out any distinction between axioms and theorems. Kant does believe that geometry contains "immediately certain" apodeictic propositions, which are *principles* from which all other propositions are deduced. Those principles alone are axioms for Kant, and they certainly correspond to what a mathematician like Schultz calls axioms. But it is also true, as I shall show, that from Kant's *transcendental* standpoint, the distinction between axioms and theorems is relativized, because all geometrical propositions share some fundamental characters with the ones that alone are strictly speaking axioms: all are grounded in intuition, yet are universally valid and thus can serve as principles; and all can serve as principles for a science of natural phenomena.

The apodeictic certainty of all geometrical principles [*Grundsätze*], and the possibility of their *a priori* construction, is grounded in this *a priori* necessity of space. Were this representation of space a concept acquired *a posteriori* and derived from outer experience in general, the first principles [*Grundsätze*] of mathematical determination would be nothing but perceptions. They would therefore all share in the contingent character of perception; that there should be only one straight line between two points would not be necessary, but only what experience always teaches (A24).[86]

2. In the Transcendental Analytic (Principle of the Axioms of Intuition), the principles of geometry are called *axioms*, and their grounding in the pure intuition of space becomes (i.e., is further explained as being) their grounding in the productive synthesis of imagination.

The mathematics of extension (geometry) is based upon this successive synthesis of the productive imagination in the generation of figures. This is the basis of the axioms which formulate the conditions of sensible *a priori* intuition under which alone the schema of a pure concept of outer appearance can arise—for instance, that between two points only one straight line is possible, or that two straight lines cannot enclose a space, etc. These are the axioms which, strictly, relate only to magnitudes (*quanta*) as such. (A163/B204)

Axioms reflect the properties of space resulting from productive syntheses of imagination, governed by the categories of quantity (unity, plurality, totality). Pure intuition, which in the Transcendental Aesthetic grounds the axioms of geometry, becomes pure intuition *resulting from the productive syntheses of imagination, in accordance with the categories of quantity*. Axioms are the result of discursive reflection on the figurative synthesis that is the source of the form of multiplicity (*Menge*) in general, and thus the source of the possibility of reflecting space, whose intuition we have produced, as determinate multiplicity. In this figurative synthesis, the forms of understanding (the logical forms of quantity of judgment) are the source of the form of multiplicity, but the form of outer sensibility is the source of the spatial character of the multiplicity thus produced, and thus the source of the properties of *spatial* quantum, reflected by the axioms.

This is where the difference between arithmetic and geometry acquires its full meaning. While in arithmetic—that is, the science of *quantitas*—the object (number) is completely defined by the act that generates it (the successive synthesis of homogeneous units), in geometry, *quantitas* is applied to an object as *quantum*, *unit* becomes *(unit of) measure*, and the rules of the act of quantitative synthesis do not suffice to define the object, since units of many different kinds (differing in quantity as well as quality) can be used as (units of) measure. This is why the properties of space are expressed by axioms, that is, universal propositions under

[86] Here, the term *Grundsatz* can be translated as 'principle' (although Kemp Smith gives "proposition" for the first occurrence), because in its second occurrence it is qualified by the adjective "first," and because the example makes clear that Kant has in mind what in geometry would be called an axiom. It is true, however, that *Grundsatz* can also be applied to mere theorems (see previous note), in which case the best translation would probably be 'fundamental proposition'.

which an infinite variety of particular cases can be subsumed. Kant points to this peculiarity of geometry when, in the Axioms of Intuition, he opposes the "numerical formulas" of arithmetic, which, he says, are singular, to the axioms of geometry, which are universal:

> On the other hand, the evident propositions of numerical relation are indeed synthetic, but are not universal like those of geometry, and cannot, therefore, be called axioms but only numerical formulas [*Zahlformeln*]. . . . But although the proposition [7 + 5 equals 12] is synthetic, it is also only singular. So far as we are here attending merely to the synthesis of the homogeneous (of units), that synthesis can take place only in one way, although the *employment* of these numbers is universal. If I assert that through three lines, two of which taken together are greater than the third, a triangle can be described, I have expressed merely the function of productive imagination whereby the lines can be drawn greater or smaller, and so can be made to meet at any and every possible angle. (A164–65/B205)[87]

If we compare the Transcendental Analytic and the Letter to Schultz analyzed earlier,[88] we may conclude that, according to Kant, principles of geometry differ from propositions of arithmetic in two ways. First, they are immediately certain *theoretical* propositions, based on pure intuition, whereas the propositions of arithmetic are immediately certain *practical* propositions, based on acts of generation of quantity. Second, principles of geometry are *universal*, while the propositions of arithmetic are *singular*. These two features make geometrical propositions *axioms*, whereas the fundamental propositions of arithmetic are said to be *postulates* insofar as they are *practical*, and *numerical formulas* insofar as they are *singular*.

3. In the introduction to the Transcendental Dialectic, Kant draws on this twofold character of axioms (universal, based on pure intuition) to specify the sense in which they can be termed *principles*:

> The term 'principle' [*eines Prinzips*] is ambiguous, and commonly signifies any cognition which can be used as a principle, although in itself, and as regards its proper origin, it is no principle. Every universal proposition, even one derived from experience through induction, can serve as major premiss in a syllogism; but it is not therefore itself a principle. The mathematical axioms (*e.g.* that there can be only one straight line between two points) are instances of universal *a priori* cognitions, and are therefore rightly called principles relatively to the cases which can be subsumed under them. But I cannot therefore say that I apprehend this property of straight lines in general and in itself, from principles; I apprehend it only in pure intuition. (A300/B356–57)

---

[87] Here Kant's example of a geometrical proposition is not an axiom, but a theorem. Yet he uses it to illustrate the difference between an axiom (in geometry) and a "numerical formula" (in arithmetic; on this point, see also note 92). Notice also the difference between the proposition as formulated here, where Kant stresses the grounding of the proposition in the figurative synthesis *producing* the formal intuition of space, and the proposition given in the Transcendental Aesthetic, where space is treated as *given*: "In a triangle two sides together are greater than the third" (A25/B39). The "given" space of the Aesthetic is revealed, in the Analytic, as really produced by transcendental imagination. On this point, see chapter 8.

[88] See p. 281.

Mathematics has no principles in the absolute sense required by reason. Axioms are not universal propositions cognized by means of pure concepts. They may be universally and apodeictically true, but their truth is based on the pure intuition of space, not derived from pure concepts according to the principle of contradiction. For instance (to take up Kant's example in the text quoted here), it is logically possible that several straight lines should pass between two points; but this is incompatible with our pure intuition of space. This aspect of Kant's view has given rise to opposed commentaries: some take argument from Kant's assertion of the nonanalytic character of the properties of Euclidean space to credit him with an opening toward non-Euclidean geometries. Others, on the contrary, denounce Kant's assertion of the apodeicticity of the properties of Euclidean space as closing off the possibility of non-Euclidean geometries. My own view is that Kant's transcendental account of the pure intuition of space provides no reason to assert that space is necessarily Euclidean, so that Kant needlessly limits the scope of his transcendental Aesthetic and Analytic when he claims that the representation of space they ground is that of Euclidean geometry. I will return to this problem in the conclusion of this chapter.

First I should add that not only the axioms but also the *proofs* of geometry rely, according to Kant, on pure intuition. In the Transcendental Doctrine of Method, Kant shows this by using as an example the proof of the equality of the three angles of a triangle to two right angles. A philosophical method, he says, proceeding by mere analysis of the concept of a triangle, would be unable to produce such a proof. It can be produced only by a mathematical method, proceeding by construction of concepts (their presentation *in concreto*, in singular representations, i.e., intuitions). Kant gives a brief summary of the proof, which we can better understand by comparing it with the Euclidean proof itself:

> Now let the geometrician take up these questions. He at once begins by constructing a triangle. Since he knows that the sum of two right angles is exactly equal to the sum of all the adjacent angles which can be constructed from a single point on a straight line, he prolongs one side of his triangle and obtains two adjacent angles, which together are equal to two right angles. (A716/B744)

The proof stated in Euclid's *Elements* begins with constructing the triangle and then prolonging the side BC: "Let ABC be a triangle, and let one side of it BC be prolonged to D."[89] Even though the proof itself does not state it, we know that the triangle is constructed in conformity with definitions 19 and 20, and prolonging BC is justified by postulate 2. The construction is therefore the presentation *in concreto* of a universal concept and the instantiation of an axiom. In Kant's words, the universal is cognized in the singular, while a philosophical proof would attempt to cognize the singular (any "case" of a triangle) under the universal (the concept of a triangle).[90] Furthermore, Kant specifies that prolonging BC is carried out because the geometrician knows that "the sum of two right

[89] Euclid, *Elements*, I, prop. 32.
[90] Cf. A714/B742.

angles is exactly equal to the sum of all the adjacent angles which can be constructed from a single point on a straight line." This is indeed established in proposition 13 of the *Elements*, to which Kant appeals at the end of his proof. That Kant should mention it from the beginning is characteristic of his conception of method. The geometrician knows what he wants to prove, and his constructions are justified by the end they serve in the proof and the principles he will have to use. The choice of these principles, and hence the choice of the constructions that present them *in concreto*, depends on that particular aspect of the power of judgment (*Urteilskraft*) which, as Kant says at the beginning of the Analytic of Principles, cannot be taught, because it depends on a mother wit (*Mutterwitz*), a talent that no learning of scholarly rule can replace.[91]

Kant continues: "[The geometrician] then divides the external angle by drawing a line parallel to the opposite side of the triangle, and observes that he has thus obtained an external adjacent angle which is equal to an internal angle—and so on."

Euclid's proof is stated as follows:

For let CE be drawn through the point C, parallel to the straight line AB [I, 31]. Then, since AB is parallel to CE, and AC has fallen upon them, the alternate angles BAC, ACE are equal to one another [I, 29]. Again, since AB is parallel to CE and the straight line BD has fallen upon them, the exterior angle ECD is equal to the interior and opposite angle ABC [I, 29].

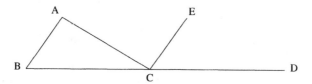

Once again, we see that the construction performed (segment CE) is presented as conforming to (subsumed under) a universal proposition (proposition 31 stated that through a point one can draw a line parallel to a given straight line). But, most importantly, this text helps us understand what Kant means by "observe" in his explanation of the proof. When the geometrician "*observes* that he has thus obtained an external adjacent angle [here, ACE] which is equal to an internal angle [here, BAC]," what he "observes" is the possibility of subsuming the singular intuitions he produced under the principle stating the properties of equality of the angles determined by a secant to two parallel lines. This "observing" is again a judging, in which the productive synthesis of imagination is reflected with a view to subsuming its result under a universal principle.

Finally, Euclid's proof concludes in the following manner:

Therefore [i.e., by virtue of the equality that has just been established between the two angles] the whole angle ACD is equal to the two interior and opposite angles BAC, ABC.

[91] Cf. A133/B172.

Let the angle ACB be added to each; therefore the angles ACD, ACB are equal to the three angles ABC, BCA, CAB.

But the angles ACD, ACB are equal to two right angles [I, 13]; therefore angles ABC, BCA, CAB are also equal to two right angles, etc.

The final stage of the proof thus consists in applying simple operations of addition to the figures, and then subsuming the result thus obtained under a universal principle (proposition 13, mentioned by Kant at the outset). Kant describes this completion of the proof as follows: "Through a chain of inferences guided throughout by intuition [*durch eine Kette von Schlüssen, immer von der Anschauung geleitet*], [the geometrician] arrives at a fully evident and universally valid solution of the problem" (A717/B745). The demonstration is a "chain of inferences" because all the intermediate propositions were obtained by the subsumption of the constructed figures under axioms or universal propositions previously proved. Yet these inferences are "guided by intuition" (sensible intuition) because the application of the principles is made possible by subsidiary constructions and additive operations.[92]

Michael Friedman provides a penetrating analysis of the role Kant assigns to construction of concepts in geometry. He explains, first of all, why Kant had to emphasize the indispensability of constructions of figures in geometrical proofs. Euclid's *Elements*, the model for all axiomatic presentations of geometry until the end of the nineteenth century, is not an axiomatic system as we understand it after Hilbert. In particular, the relations stated by Hilbert in the axioms of order and continuity have no axiomatic expression in Euclidean geometry. Instead they have an intuitive counterpart in the construction of figures.[93] Thus it is correct to say, as Kant does, that in a geometry such as Euclid's, axioms alone, without intermediate constructions, are not sufficient to prove the theorems. In saying this, Friedman in a way does nothing more than reiterate Russell's thesis: Russell held that an axiomatic like Hilbert's, together with a quantificational logic of relations, render irrelevant the role Kant granted to pure intuition in geometry. Geometry

---

[92] This analysis sheds light on the passage from the introduction to the *Critique of Pure Reason* in which Kant criticizes the mistaken view that, because "all mathematical inferences proceed in accordance with the principle of contradiction" (*die Schlüsse der Mathematiker alle nach dem Satze des Widerspruchs fortgehen*, B14), the "fundamental propositions" (*Grundsätze*) are cognized by means of the principle of contradiction. Actually, he writes, "though a synthetic proposition can indeed be discerned in accordance with the principle of contradiction, this can be only if another synthetic proposition is presupposed, and if it can then be apprehended as following from this other proposition" (B14). For some interpreters (Martin, L. W. Beck), this passage expresses an axiomatic conception of geometry, according to which the synthetic character of geometry is the synthetic character of its *axioms*; its demonstrations, however, can proceed exclusively according to the laws of logic that is, "in accordance with the principle of contradiction." The analysis of the proof I have just mentioned shows that its proceeding "in accordance with the principle of contradiction" does not stop it from also appealing to constructions of concepts. In this sense, the proof itself has an intuitive character, where the universal must be presented *in concreto*. Geometry and arithmetic may differ in that the former, but not the latter, has axioms. But they are similar in that both proceed by construction of concepts: symbolic for arithmetic, ostensive for geometry. I agree here with Friedman (*Kant*) and Parsons ("Philosophy of Arithmetic").

[93] Friedman, *Kant*, 56–61.

now proceeds by strictly deductive inference from definitions and axioms according to the laws of logic. But Friedman's version of this thesis is more positive than Russell's. The lesson he draws from the history of geometry and logic after Kant is not so much that Kant's views are outdated, as that Kant perceived with exceptional acuity the nature of the mathematical procedures he had at his disposal, and the ways in which they transcend the limits of his general or formal logic.[94] I agree with this diagnosis. I would even suggest that although Kant, unlike Leibniz or Lambert, for instance, certainly underestimated the potential fecundity of formal languages and logical procedures, he was more sensitive than they were to the irreducibility of mathematical concepts and methods to the concepts and methods employed in classical predicative logic.

But this is not all. What I said earlier about arithmetic, I would say also about geometry. Kant's conception of geometry, and the role he assigns in it to pure intuition, can be fully appreciated only in the context provided by the transcendental deduction of the categories. From this standpoint, the following, I think, can be said. If a formal expression of mathematical thought-procedures had been available to Kant (axiomatic presentation, logic of relations, quantification, and especially, as Friedman insists, multiple quantification), he would probably not have granted the importance he did to intuitive construction of concepts in the method of geometry. However, this would in no way have solved the transcendental question, which concerns the relation of propositions of geometry (axioms and theorems) to objects: not only mathematical objects (constructions in pure intuition), but above all objects of experience. The problem of the nature of mathematical thinking interests Kant only insofar as solving it might help clarify the conditions of possibility of experience and thus, more generally, the relation between cognitive subjects and objects of cognition and of thought. The role Kant grants to the pure intuition of space in positing the objects of geometry (the "mere form" of objects) is, in his mind, an essential element in such clarification, and this is a role for which no progress in conceptualization or formalization provides sufficient ground to make Kant's appeal to intuition redundant. Nor do I believe his appeal to pure intuition in solving transcendental problems to be incompatible with modern formalizations of geometry. This can be said, however, only with a huge reservation: it is true only if Kant's a priori spatial intuition is stripped of the Euclidean features Kant considered as necessarily belonging to it. But, in fact, these features do not result from the transcendental genesis of space achieved in the Transcendental Aesthetic and Analytic of the *Critique of Pure Reason*. If we take into account only the qualification of the form of outer receptivity as *spatial*, plus the qualification of the *synthesis speciosa* generating the formal intuition of space as a synthesis *according to the category of quantity*, the characters that result for pure intuition are (1) the quality of spatiality as a primitive, undefinable quality (the form of *Auseinandersein* or, as Leibniz would have said, of *situs*), (2) the fact that it is a *quantum* (*unum, in quo est quantitas*: one, in which there is quantity), and (3) continuity and infinity (insofar as it is an intuition, space is a

---

[94] Ibid., 55–56, 63–66, 95. Cf. Russell, *Principles of Mathematics*, §434.

quantum continuum infinitum, a continuous and infinite magnitude, namely a magnitude in which divisions can be iterated indefinitely, and which is larger than any determinate spatial magnitude). Kant overstepped what he had actually deduced (but not the method of the geometry he knew) when he thought he could assert that the form of pure intuition, of which he had provided a transcendental genesis, necessarily possessed the features associated with the space of Euclidean geometry: three-dimensionality, postulate of parallels, and all the properties of figures depending on these features.

If this is correct, it proves the importance of a detailed elucidation of the relation between *synthesis speciosa* and *synthesis intellectualis* as defined in the Transcendental Deduction of the Categories. Following Kant's systematic argument, one discovers that he provides an analysis of the relation between discursive thinking and sensible intuition more powerful and of broader scope than would appear from the ways in which he links its fate to a particular moment in the history of human knowledge.

The Real as Appearance:
Imagination and Sensation

IN THIS CHAPTER, I shall first analyze the relation between the logical forms of quality in judgment and the corresponding categories. I shall then examine the nature of the *synthesis speciosa* or "affection of inner sense by the understanding," which makes possible the reflection of an empirical manifold according to the logical form of quality in judgment—that is, generates the *schema* for quality. Finally, I shall consider Kant's principle of the Anticipations of Perception, also known as the "principle of intensive magnitudes." I shall show how Kant's argument for this principle depends on the previous account of the categories of quality and the *synthesis speciosa*, or figurative synthesis oriented toward the forms of quality in judgment.

My account of Kant's categories of quality thus differs from other accounts once again in the importance I accord to the systematic unity of logical functions, figurative synthesis (in the schematism of the categories of quality), and the principle of the pure understanding (principle of the Anticipations of Perception, grounded in the schematized categories of quality). This approach to Kant's argument is original, moreover, not only in its method, but also in its outcome: one of its major results is the importance granted to the third moment of quality—the logical function of "infinite" judgment and the corresponding category of limitation—a moment generally neglected by commentators, or even rejected as "spurious."[1] I shall argue that, on the contrary, elucidation of this third moment is essential to understanding Kant's "principle of intensive magnitudes" and its relation, on the one hand, to the principle of the Axioms of Intuition that precedes it and, on the other hand, to the Analogies of Experience that follow it.

LOGICAL FORMS AND CATEGORIES OF QUALITY

Logical Forms of Affirmative and Negative Judgment, and Categories of Reality and Negation

In relating the categories of quality to the logical forms of affirmative and negative judgment, Kant was clearly influenced by his rationalist predecessors. Baumgarten, for instance, defined reality and negation in the following way:

What is posited in something to determine it (marks and predicates) [*quae determinando ponuntur in aliquo (notae et praedicata)*] are its *determinations*; these are either

[1] See Bennett, *Analytic*, 165.

positive and affirmative—and if they are truly so, they are *realities*—or negative—and if they are truly so, are *negations*. A merely apparent negation is a *hidden reality* [*realitas cryptica*], a merely apparent reality is a vacuity [*vanitas*].[2]

Meier, whose metaphysics textbook was influenced by Baumgarten, is even more explicit:

> Through every determination, something is either asserted or denied of the thing thus determined [*Durch eine jedwede Bestimmung wird von der dadurch bestimmten Sache entweder etwas bejahet oder verneinet*]. An affirmative determination which does not merely appear to be affirmative, but is truly so, is called a reality or a real determination. . . . If one justifiably asserts something about a thing [*wenn man etwas von einer Sache mit Recht bejahet*], this something belongs to and is contained in the thing. A reality is therefore a genuine addition [*ein wahrer Zusatz*] to a thing, through which it in fact receives something and is broadened or enlarged.

> If one denies something about a thing, one thinks that this something is lacking. Consequently, a negation is in fact a diminishment, and something is diminished when it is subjected to a negation.[3]

Two aspects of these definitions are worth noticing: first, the correspondence between *reality* and *negation*, as determinations of things, and logical forms of affirmative and negative judgments; and, second, the distinction between "merely apparent" and "true" affirmation and negation. According to the latter distinction, a logically negative judgment may ontologically mean the attribution of a reality (a "truly affirmative" determination) to a thing, in case the negated determination is itself a negative determination (a privation or imperfection). Conversely, a logically affirmative judgment may ontologically mean the negation of a reality, in case what is asserted is a negative determination, that is, a privation or imperfection. Hence, in elaborating his view on the categories of quality, Kant relies on a generally accepted correspondence between ontological determinations (reality and negation) and forms of predication (affirmation and negation in judgment). But he transforms the meaning of this correspondence by making the latter the origin of the former, and by claiming further that logical forms give rise to ontological determinations only if they are related to a sensible given. If we recall again Kant's definition of the categories in section 14 of the Deduction and apply it to the category of reality, we thus should say that "reality" is the "concept of an

[2] Baumgarten, *Metaphysica*, Ak. XVII, 34. Particularly important in this passage are the terms "determine" and "determination." To "determine" a subject with respect to a predicate is to assert *or* negate the predicate of the given subject. On the other hand, a subject is *indeterminate* with respect to a predicate when the predicate could either be asserted or negated of it (for instance, a general concept is *indeterminate*, although *determinable*, with respect to any of its possible specifications: the concept 'man' is indeterminate with respect to 'Athenian' or 'non-Athenian'. But any individual man is *determined* with respect to these predicates: an individual man either *is*, or *is not* Athenian). Kant makes use of this notion of determination in the "principle of complete determination" he enunciates in the opening section of the Transcendental Ideal. I consider this point on pp. 295–98; and pp. 306–8. On Kant's use of the terms "determine" and "determination," see also note 26.

[3] G.W.F. Meier, *Metaphysik*, §46, 48, quoted by Anneliese Maier, *Qualitätskategorien*, 15.

object in general, by means of which the intuition of this object is regarded as determined *in respect of the logical function of affirmation in a judgment,*" and that "negation" is the "concept of an object in general, by means of which the intuition of this object is regarded as determined *in respect of the logical function of negation in a judgment.*" It is thus the "concept of the absence of an object," or of a "privation" (A291/B347). So construed, these categories take the place of Baumgarten's and Meier's conception of reality and negation as "truly affirmative" and "truly negative" determinations. However, since, for Kant, objects are given to us only through the senses, a determination can be considered as "truly affirmative" only if its concept results from reflection upon some sensory given. Conversely, a determination is "truly negative" only if its concept reflects the *absence* of a sensory given.[4] In other words, if regarded a priori, the category of reality is reduced to the mere logical form of affirmative judgment unless it is related to the schema generated by the *synthesis speciosa,* or "affection of inner sense by the understanding," aiming at the logical form of affirmative judgment. Similarly, the category of negation is a merely logical negation unless the affection of inner sense by understanding, aiming at the logical form of negation in judgment, gives it a transcendental meaning. What exactly these figurative syntheses might be, and how the representation of "truly" (transcendentally) affirmative and "truly" (transcendentally) negative determinations of things might be generated, we shall see in greater detail.

Infinite Judgment and Category of Limitation

Besides the logical forms of affimative and negative judgment, Kant considers a third form, which he calls (after Wolff and Meier) *infinite* judgment. Its copula is affirmative, but its predicate is a determination which is itself *negated.* Kant's example is taken from Meier's *Auszug:* "the soul is non-mortal." Kant also follows Meier in acknowledging that, from the point of view of general logic, infinite and affirmative judgments are indistinguishable.[5] But the remainder of Kant's explanation is original, and clearly related to his goals in the *Critique*:

> Now by the proposition, 'The soul is non-mortal', I have, so far as the logical form is concerned, really made an affirmation, by positing the soul in the unlimited sphere [*in den unbeschränkten Umfang*] of non-mortal beings. Since the mortal constitutes

[4] Kant's most frequent examples of "reality" and "negation" are light and darkness, heat and cold. Cf., for instance: "Reality is *something*; negation is *nothing*, namely, a concept of the absence of an object, such as shadow, cold" (A291/B347). These examples will be analyzed later, particularly the case of negation.

[5] Cf. Meier, *Auszug*, §294 (Ak. XVI, 635): "If, in a judgment, there is a negation, either in the subject or in the predicate, or in both at once, but the copula is not negated, the judgment is affirmative; it is called an *infinite judgment* [*judicium infinitum*]. All negative judgments can therefore be transformed into affirmative judgments if the negation is moved from the copula to the predicate. For example, 'the soul is not mortal, the soul is non-mortal'." Thus, not only does Meier equate the infinite with the affirmative judgment, but moreover his purpose in mentioning it is precisely to point out the possibility of transforming a negative judgment ('the soul is not mortal') into an affirmative one ('the soul is non-mortal') by moving the negation from the copula to the predicate. Kant denies the logical

one part of the whole extension of possible beings, and the non-mortal the other, nothing more is said by my proposition than that the soul is one of the infinite multiplicity [*von der unendlichen Menge*] of things which remain over when I take away all that is mortal. The infinite sphere of all that is possible is thereby only so far limited [*beschränkt*] that what is mortal is separated from it, and the soul is posited in the remaining sphere of its space. (A72/B97–98)

The infinite judgment 'S is non-A', asserts that the sphere of the subject-concept 'S' is included in the infinite sphere external to that of the concept 'A', whose negation, 'non-A', is the predicate of the judgment.

In view of this explanation, the infinite judgment would appear to obey what Kant elsewhere calls the "principle of complete determination." According to this principle, given the totality of possible predicates, any individual thing either falls under a predicate A or under its negation non-A: in other words, each thing, as the substitutional instance of the term "*x*" in judgment, is *either* within the sphere of any given concept *or* within the infinite sphere *outside* the sphere of this concept.[6] If one could have cognition of the exhaustive division of the "infinite sphere of all possible determinations," and could exhaustively specify all the subspheres to which the thing belongs *and* to which it does *not* belong, then one would know the thing in its complete determination and, thus, as the *individual* thing it is. In several *Reflexionen*, Kant does indeed explain infinite judgment in relation to the principle of complete determination:

[The infinite judgment] is performed according to the principle of complete determination, which is required with regard to a thing in general. It determines with respect to thinghood [*Sachheit*] in general, i.e., reality [*Realität*], and introduces, outside of the sphere of a concept, an infinite sphere of the determination of all things, namely, of thinghood, i.e., reality. Outside the sphere of a concept, there is room for an infinity of spheres [*außer der Sphaera eines Begriffes ist Raum zu einer Unendlichkeit von Sphäris*].

The proposition '*anima est non-mortalis*' is a judgment of determination, which

---

validity of this operation, which bears not only on the form of the judgment (the copula) but also on its content (the predicate). Kant holds that from the point of view of general logic, an infinite judgment must simply be considered as affirmative, and no consideration must be taken of its negative predicate (cf. *Logik*, §22, notes 2 and 3, Ak. IX, 104; 600; also *Refl*. 3070, Ak. XVI, 641). Only from the point of view of transcendental logic does the "act of the understanding" in the infinite judgment deserve particular attention; in fact, as we shall see, Kant's entire analysis of the categories of quality hinges on this. Finally, it should be noted that the "infinite" judgment discussed here is different from Aristotle's indefinite judgment, which is a judgment whose *quantity* is undetermined (cf. *De Interpretatione* 7, 17b30; *Prior Analytics* 7, 29a27). Kant's infinite judgment is the attribution to a subject of what Aristotle calls an *indefinite term* (cf. *De Interpretatione* 2, 16a30).

6 Cf. Kant's formulation of the principle of complete determination at the beginning of the Transcendental Ideal: "[E]very *thing*, as regards its possibility, is . . . subject to the principle of *complete* determination, according to which if *all the possible* predicates of *things* be taken together with their contrary opposites, then one of each pair of contradictory opposites must belong to it" (A571–72/B599–600). For a more complete analysis of Kant's "principle of complete determination" and its relation to infinite judgment, see Longuenesse, *Transcendental Ideal*.

states that of two opposed predicates, *a* and not-*a*, the second belongs to the soul. All judgments of determination are infinite, in order to determine a thing completely, and not merely the relation of combination or opposition.[7]

So considered, Kant's analysis of the act of the understanding in infinite judgment is the first step toward the critical reduction of the notions of a "whole of reality" (*totum realitatis*) and "maximally real being" (*ens realissimum*), which were the primary focus of his analysis of the concepts of *reality* and *negation* in the precritical writings. There, Kant maintained that all positive determinations of things (i.e., all "realities") are possible (thinkable) only as limitations of one whole of reality (*totum realitatis*), whose ground is one being possessing *all* reality, the "maximally real being" (*ens realissimum*): God.[8] But in the *Critique*, just as Kant argues that the logical functions of understanding in affirmative and negative judgment are the origin of the metaphysical notions of *reality* and *negation*, so he argues that the act of the understanding in infinite judgment is the origin of the representation of every determination of a thing (reality) as a *limitation*. Thus to think every determination as a limitation is not to presuppose a whole of reality (a whole of positive determinations of things), or even less its hypostatization in a maximally real being (*ens realissimum*). It is merely to say that the sphere of every particular concept should be thought of as a limitation of the sphere of the concept of "possible determination"; and to think the sphere of any concept in this way (as a subsphere of the one sphere, the exhaustive division of which should yield all possible conceptual spheres) is merely to set oneself the task of generating, through one's discursive activity, the complete logical space in which to think everything that is or may be. The "infinite sphere of all possible determination" is therefore a "merely logical" representation, and the concept of an *ens realissimum* is the illusory hypostatization of the totality of discursive determinations, specifying the concept of 'possible determination of thing' in relation to which every singular thing is determined (either positively or negatively).

So, whereas rationalist metaphysicians of the Wolffian school, and the precritical Kant himself, believed that with the idea of the *ens realissimum* they had a "concept of what possesses all reality" (A576/B604) as the purely intelligible ground of all possible realities in things, the later Kant analyzes the act of understanding in infinite judgment as merely positing the thing, reflected under the subject-concept, in the "infinite sphere of all possible determinations" outside the sphere of the concept whose negation is the predicate. An infinite judgment is thus essentially *indeterminate*:

> The infinite sphere of the possible is only so far limited [by the proposition 'the soul is non-mortal'] that the mortal is excluded from it, and that the soul is located in the remaining part of its extension. But, even allowing for such exclusion, this extension

[7] *Refl.* 3063 (1776–8?), Ak. XVI, 638.

[8] On the "whole of reality" (*totum realitatis*) and "most real being" (*ens realissimum*) in the precritical writings and in the critical period, cf. chapter 6, p. 154.

still remains infinite, and several more parts of it may be taken away without the concept of the soul being thereby in the least increased, or determined in an affirmative manner. (A72–73/B97–98)

For the "infinite sphere" to provide for the complete determination of the thing belonging to it, one would have to have actually achieved the exhaustive division by means of which each thing would be thought as completely determined. But this, as Kant argues in the Transcendental Ideal, is impossible: we do not have at our disposal the complete totality of discursive concepts (concepts of "realities") from which to pick out the combination of realities and negations belonging to a given thing. We generate our concepts of empirical things by means of a never-ending process of empirical cognition, which supplies the ground for specifying (determining) our universal concepts. Only if our concepts are ever further specified (and thus the "infinite sphere of possible determinations" ever more exhaustively divided into its subspheres) can we attain a more determinate cognition of objects. This is certainly why, in the *Critique*, Kant ascribes to *disjunctive syllogism*, not infinite judgment, the function of thinking individual things according to the principle of complete determination.[9] Nevertheless, infinite judgment remains the act of understanding that posits the infinite sphere within which one must think (for the complete determination of any given thing) the complete division of the spheres of discursive concepts under which all things have to be thought.

The relation between infinite judgment and category of limitation should now begin to be clear. Returning once again to the general definition of the categories in section 14 of the Transcendental Deduction, we may say that limitation is the "concept of an object in general insofar as the intuition of this object is considered as determined with respect to the logical function of *infinite* judgment": an object is thought under the category of *limitation* if its intuition is reflected in such a way that it is determined as belonging to the infinite sphere outside the sphere of a given concept. Now, in respect of the conditions of our cognition, such a sphere is none other than the sphere that contains *everything given in the forms of intuition, space and time*. If so, then the "determination of inner sense by the understanding" or *synthesis speciosa*, aiming at infinite judgment, would be the act by means of which any empirical given is posited in the infinite sphere of every possible (empirical) determination—that is, *reflected as an object given in the forms of intuition, space, and time* and, within this sphere, compared with all the *realities* ("truly affirmative determinations") either already cognized, or to be cognized. The category of limitation thus becomes pivotal for the other two categories of quality. Indeed, it is *the* category of quality. For, by its means, all positive determinations (realities) of any object as appearance are thought as delimited against the background of all the determinations that do *not* belong to it (negations), all of which, however, belong to the common infinite sphere of the concept "given in the forms of space and time."

[9] Cf. the role Kant assigns the form of disjunctive syllogism in the generation of the Transcendental Ideal: cf. for instance A323/B379; A576–77/B604–5.

For further clarification, we now need to turn to the *synthesis speciosa*, or "affection of inner sense by the understanding," aiming at the logical forms of quality in judgment and thereby producing the schemata for the categories of quality.

REALITY, NEGATION, AND LIMITATION IN APPEARANCE: SENSATION AND IMAGINATION

Reality

As a pure category, *reality* is the mere form of (affirmative) predicate. Or, as Kant puts it in the chapter on Phenomena and Noumena, "Reality is [the determination] that can be thought only by an affirmative judgment" (A246). But this "affirmation" remains empty unless a content is given to it, and this can be done only by sensation. Thus the schematism of the categories of quality: "sensation is reality as appearance" (*sensatio realitas phaenomenon*, A146/B186).

This view is in fact not entirely new. Already in a *Reflexion* from the 1770s, Kant writes: "*Realitas phaenomenon* or *noumenon*. The former is, in the appearance, what corresponds to perception (sensation). . . . Reality as *noumenon* is positedness in the object in itself."[10] But in the *Critique*, Kant denies any possibility of cognizing *realitas noumenon*, and asserts that what makes us capable of cognizing something as *realitas phaenomenon* is the logical function of affirmative judgment. This also means, then, that the sensible given is determined as *realitas* (truly affirmative determination of a thing, *determinatio rei vere affirmativa*) only insofar as a *synthesis speciosa* "affects inner sense through the manifold of given representations,"[11] for this alone permits it to be reflected according to the logical form of affirmative judgment. Thus, for the category of reality to be applicable, three conditions must be satisfied: that something affect the senses in sensation, that this sensation/affection be "taken up" (apprehended) in figurative synthesis, *synthesis speciosa*, and that it be reflected under concepts according to the logical form of quality in judgment.

One might wonder what exactly the specific contribution of imagination is supposed to be here: what, in the present case, is the nature of the *synthesis speciosa*? From what Kant says of the schema of reality in the Schematism of the Concepts of Pure Understanding, I think we may conclude that the figurative synthesis corresponding to the category of reality is the act of *representing in time* "that which corresponds to sensation." Or it is synthesizing sensation *with* time, as "the form of inner sense." For Kant defines reality, in the Schematism, as "being (in time)":

> Reality, in the pure concept of the understanding, is that which corresponds to a sensation in general; it is that, therefore, the concept of which in itself points to a being (in time) [*dasjenige, dessen Begriff an sich selbst ein Sein (in der Zeit) anzeigt*].

[10] *Refl.* 4817 (1775–76), Ak. XVII, 737.
[11] Cf. §24, B150, and my analysis of *synthesis speciosa* in chapter 8.

Negation is that, the concept of which represents a non-being (in time) [*dessen Be-griff ein Nichtsein (in der Zeit) vorstellt*]. The opposition of these two thus rests upon the distinction of one and the same time as filled and as empty. (A143/B182)

This coheres with Kant's general presentation of *synthesis speciosa* in section 24 of the Transcendental Deduction. For "affecting inner sense" through the manifold of given representations means positing the latter *in time* (the form of inner sense) and thus achieving, as it were, the *configuration* of the sensation—making it the content of an inner intuition. This "positing in time" is a necessary condition for relating sensations to "what corresponds to them" in objects (another condition is the application of the categories of relation to generate the representation of the objective order of time—see chapter 11). This is how "what corresponds" to sensation can be reflected under concepts in judgments, as properties of things subsumable under the category of reality (*Sacheit, Realität*). We should beware, then, of a possible misunderstanding of Kant's formulation: *sensatio, realitas phaenomenon*. Sensation *itself* is not what is reflected as *reality*. What is reflected as reality is that in the appearance which "corresponds" to sensation, and the representation of this "correspondence" results from (is made possible by) the synthesis of imagination that first bestows on our awareness of sensation a temporal determination.

Here again, the Transcendental Analytic induces a rereading of Kant's formulations in the Transcendental Aesthetic, concerning the *matter* of appearances—a rereading analogous to the one I suggested earlier (in chapter 8) with respect to their *form*. In the Aesthetic, Kant writes: "That in the appearance which corresponds to sensation I term its *matter*; but that which so makes the manifold of appearance that it allows of being ordered in certain relations, I term the *form* of appearance" (A20/B34). We saw in chapter 8 that in light of Kant's explanation of *synthesis speciosa*, the form of appearance should be considered as itself the product of transcendental synthesis of imagination. The Transcendental Deduction thus required a rereading of the Transcendental Aesthetic, in which the "form of intuition" and "pure intuition" expounded in the latter were shown to be generated by the *synthesis speciosa* expounded in section 26 of the B Deduction.[12] Similarly, we should now conclude that the "matter of appearances" can be represented as "what corresponds to sensation" only insofar as it is represented as such by means of the "determination of inner sense by the understanding," the *synthesis speciosa* of imagination performed with a view to forming judgments. This claim may cause some eyebrows to raise: does it not amount to erasing the very distinction between *matter* and *form* of appearances Kant is so adamant to draw in the transcendental Aesthetic? It already took some effort to grant that the form of appearances, as presented in the Transcendental Aesthetic, was a product of *synthesis speciosa*, the reader might impatiently remark. If we now have to admit that even the *matter* of appearances, that which "corresponds to sensation," depends on a synthesis of imagination, then not only does the distinction between

12 Cf. chapter 8, p. 215; *KrV*, B160–61n.

receptivity and spontaneity seem altogether to disappear, but so too that between what is *empirically given* (the *matter* of appearances) and what is *generated a priori* by the constitution of the subject (the *form* of appearances). This is drawing Kant too close toward Fichtean and Hegelian idealism, which no one will grant in good faith to be true to Kant's intention.

But this impression is mistaken. It is not my intention to deny that, for Kant, the matter of appearances has to be *received*, or that receptivity remains radically distinct from spontaneity. Let me be more specific: in the Transcendental Aesthetic, Kant calls "matter" of appearances (i.e., matter of the "undetermined objects of empirical intuition") "that which corresponds to sensation." And "sensation" is defined as "the effect of an object on the capacity of representation, insofar as we are affected by it." The most plausible way of interpreting the notion of "affection," in these initial paragraphs of the *Critique*, is to understand it as the affection of the representational capacities *by a thing in itself*, that is, by something external to our representational capacities (something that functions as an "added condition" to our representational capacities in the grounding of representations).[13] *Sensation* so considered is strictly *given*, in no way a product of synthesis. But "what corresponds to sensation" becomes *matter* of the appearance only insofar as sensation itself is "apprehended," and insofar as figurative synthesis "affects inner sense" with the given *and apprehended* manifold of sensation. Finally, *reality*, defined in the passage cited earlier as "that which corresponds to sensation," is what is thus "posited in time" in such a way that the logical form of affirmative judgment allows us to reflect it as the *property of a thing* [*Sachheit, Realität*]. Rereading Kant's description of the "matter of appearances," in the Aesthetic, in light of the schematism of reality expounded in the Analytic, is therefore *not* minimizing the importance of what is simply *given*. Rather, it is saying that in the context of our empirical cognition, the "given" appears *as* given only insofar as it is *also synthesized* by imagination under the unity of apperception (*synthesis speciosa*); and *synthesis speciosa* itself has for its raison d'être the function it fulfills in "affecting inner sense" with a "given" manifold (which is represented "as" given only insofar as it is synthesized by imagination), to be reflected under concepts. Thus, if the Transcendental Analytic involves a rereading of the Transcendental Aesthetic, conversely the latter is the necessary presupposition of the former.[14]

Bringing together the lessons of the Transcendental Analytic and Aesthetic may help us understand a particularly puzzling passage of the Schematism chap-

---

[13] On this point I agree with Allison: cf. *Idealism*, 249. However, the notion of an "added condition" is original to my explanation of this point. On this notion and its relation to the logical form of hypothetical judgment, cf. chapter 6. pp. 141–42. If I am correct in my analysis of this relation, the mere form of hypothetical judgment allows us to think the thing in itself as an "added condition" to our own representational capacities, although we do not know this "added condition" as a (schematized) *cause* of representations.

[14] Just as I suggested, in chapter 8, that we should distinguish between space and time as the "original formal ground" of sensibility as receptivity, and space and time as form of intuition/formal intuition (generated by *synthesis speciosa*), I would here suggest that we should distinguish sensation as the original *affection* of sensibility by a thing in itself and as *apprehended* sensation. The matter of appearance (i.e., the matter of the "indeterminate object of empirical intuition") "corresponds" to the *apprehended* sensation, that is, to the sensation with which *synthesis speciosa* "affects inner sense,"

ter, which immediately follows the one cited earlier in this section.[15] After characterizing the opposition between reality and negation as "the distinction of one and the same time as filled and as empty," Kant continues: "While time is merely the form of intuition, and so of objects as appearances, that in the objects which corresponds to sensation is the transcendental matter of all objects as things in themselves (thinghood, reality [*Sachheit, Realität*])" (A143/B182). What is puzzling about this passage is the description of "what corresponds to sensation" as "the transcendental matter of all objects *as things in themselves*" (my emphasis). According to the Aesthetic, previously cited, "what corresponds to sensation" is the matter "*of appearances* [my emphasis]." It is thus natural to suppose that "things in themselves," in the passage from the Schematism, should be understood as *empirical* things in themselves, objects we represent to ourselves as distinct from our representations, but which nonetheless are given only as appearances (phenomena) "corresponding to" our representations.[16] What is reflected as *reality* would thus be the transcendental matter of *empirical* things in themselves, namely, that which "corresponds" to sensation in empirical objects recognized under concepts and represented as distinct from our representations of them. Comparing the Schematism with the Aesthetic thus encourages a weak interpretation of the expression "things in themselves" in A143/B182. But on the other hand, reference to the Transcendental Aesthetic also allows us to relate the *empirical* to the *transcendental* thing in itself. For according to the Aesthetic, the *matter* of appearances depends on *affection*, and, as already remarked, the most plausible way to interpret "affection" in the context of the Aesthetic is to interpret

---

thus positing it in time. "Correspondence" here should not be understood in the context of any kind of mind/body, or representation/object of representation dualism, where something in the object "corresponds to" something in the mind. In fact, as I insisted in chapters 1 and 2 of this book, at this point object and intuition-of-the-object, and similarly "matter" of the appearance and (apprehended) sensation, are identical. Saying that the matter of appearance "corresponds to" sensation simply means, I think, that *whenever there is* (apprehended) sensation there is a "matter" (i.e., a "determinable"; cf. chapter 6) of appearance. On the other hand, application of the category of reality takes us one step further toward a distinction between (empirical) object and (empirical) representation: reality is that *in the object* (of outer sense) which "corresponds" to sensation, which on its part is an object of inner sense: with the categories of quality we have reached the level of the *determination* of an object, and thus of the distinction between inner sense and outer sense, sensation and the reality (property of the empirical object) that "corresponds" to it. The categories of quality (reality, negation, limitation) are not sufficient, however, to account for this distinction: insofar as they reflect properties of *objects* they do not function independently of the categories of relation, as I shall argue in what follows.

[15] See p. 298.

[16] Compare a strikingly similar characterization of "reality" in the Transcendental Ideal: "That which constitutes the thing itself, namely, the real in the [field of] appearance, must be given—otherwise the thing could not be conceived at all—and since that wherein the real of all appearances is given is experience, considered as single and all-embracing, the material for the possibility of all objects of the senses must be presupposed as given in one whole" (A581–582/B609–10). Here Kant describes reality as "that which constitutes the thing itself." But it is quite clear that he means "the thing itself *as appearance*." I would suggest that the "thing in itself" in the text from the Schematism, should *first* be understood in a similar way, as the *empirical* thing in itself. But as I shall add shortly, it *also* points toward the thing in itself in the *transcendental* sense: the *external* condition, or ground, for our representations. The text from the Transcendental Ideal will be analyzed later in this chapter.

it as the relation of our receptivity to a thing in itself in the strong sense, a thing we suppose to exist "outside" our representational faculties. Thus the *synthesis speciosa* reflected in the category of reality should be understood as an act of "filling" our temporal intuition with a "matter" whose ground is ultimately the thing in itself.[17]

Finally, if the category of reality reflects, not sensation *simpliciter*, but sensation *related to an object*, or the matter of appearance as "that which corresponds to sensation," the category of reality (*Realität*) cannot be considered apart from the categories of relation. For relating subjective representations to what "corresponds" to them in empirical objects (considered as (empirical) things in themselves, distinct from empirical representations) is the function of the logical forms, categories, and schemata *of relation*.[18] Any attempt to characterize the category of reality, either in its schema, or as a concept, thus seems to point in the direction of the categories of relation. This is clearly apparent in the 1787 "proof" of the Anticipations of Perception. In the opening section of the System of Principles, Kant has insisted on the distinction between "mathematical" categories (quantity and quality) and "dynamical" categories (relation and modality). He has stressed that the former have to do with the constitution of our (pure or empirical) intuitions, while the latter alone have to do with the *existence* of the objects represented in our intuitions. But in the proof of the Anticipations of Perception he relates "the real of sensation" to "something *existing* in space or time" (my emphasis): "Appearances, as objects of perception . . . contain in addition to intuition the matter for some object in general (whereby something existing in space or time is represented); they contain, that is to say, the real of sensation as merely subjective representation, which gives only the consciousness that the subject is affected, and which we relate to an object in general" (B207–8). The correlation between the two sets of categories, *quality* (reality, negation, and limitation) and *relation* (substance/accident, cause/effect, and community) will be confirmed and further explained when we consider the categories of relation themselves. At this point, however, we need to grasp what is *proper* to the synthesis according to the category of reality. What is proper to it, I think, is the mere act of *positing* what is apprehended *in time*. This "positing in time" conditions the further synthesis according to the categories of relation, which *determines* the temporal form—that is, generates the principles of ordering without which the "positing in time" would remain a mere successive apprehension of sensory contents, a mere aware-

[17] The interpretive difficulties associated with A143/B182 have prompted some commentators to suggest the sentence be changed to its exact contrary: "that in the object which corresponds to sensation is *not* the transcendental matter of all objects, as things in themselves" (see Kemp Smith's translation, p.184; the modification is originally suggested by Wille: see Immanuel Kant, *Kritik der reinen Vernunft* [Hamburg: Felix Meiner, 1956], 201). If I am correct in the interpretation I have suggested, there is no need for such a reversal. Interestingly, in his *Commentary* (prior to his translation), Kemp Smith commented on Kant's original text, unchanged. He thought, however, that it was yet another example of Kant's hesitation between phenomenalism and subjectivism (351).

[18] I shall discuss this point in detail in the following chapter.

ness of the temporal "flux" of perceptions, from which no objective order of appearances would ever emerge.

We shall see that this "positing in time" is also what allows reality to be thought as intensive magnitude. But before considering this, we need to examine the *synthesis speciosa* generating the schema for the second category of quality, *negation*.

Negation

As a pure concept of the understanding, negation is the concept of a "privation" or "lack" of a real determination. "Reality is *something*, negation is *nothing*, a concept of the lack of an object, as shadow, cold (*nihil privativum*)" (A291/B347). Even in his precritical writings—most notably in the 1763 *Attempt to Introduce the Concept of Negative Magnitudes into Philosophy*—Kant argued that negation, as a predicate, means the *absence* of a positive or "real" determination.[19] In the *Critique*, Kant also maintains this view, while at the same time limiting the objective meaning of the concept of *negation* just as he did the objective meaning of *reality*. For just as reality is reduced to the mere logical form of affirmative judgment unless it receives a content from the sensations with which *synthesis speciosa* affects inner sense, so too the category of *negation* is reduced to the merely logical form of negative judgment unless it represents the lack of a real determination, that is, the lack of some determination "corresponding to sensation." Hence, cognizing a *negation* depends on cognizing the corresponding *reality*. That is, we would form no concept of darkness unless we had a concept of light, and in general form no concept of the *absence* of what "corresponds to sensation" without some concept of the opposed *presence*.

Anything sensibly giveable that is *not*, as a matter of fact, given, is *negation*, or *nothing*. Kant's table of the divisions of the concept "nothing," at the end of the Transcendental Analytic, offers an interesting development of this point.[20] Kant defines "nothing" according to the four headings of his table of categories. According to quantity, he says, "nothing" is "the object of a concept to which no assignable intuition whatsoever corresponds": the empty extension of a concept. According to quality, it is the "absence of an object, such as shadow, cold": this is the category of negation we are presently concerned with. According to relation, *nothing* is "the mere form of intuition, without substance," namely pure space and time. According to modality, *nothing* is "the object of a concept which contradicts itself." I shall consider the first and fourth descriptions of 'nothing' only briefly, as they do not primarily concern us here: in them, 'nothing' is defined independently of any relation to sensation, even before the question whether anything is *given* can be raised. In the first case ('nothing' according to quantity), a concept for which no intuition can be given has a fortiori no relation to sensation: what corresponds to it is the absence of any intuition at all, whether pure or

---

[19] See note 22.
[20] See A290–91/B347–48.

empirical. Interestingly, Kant's first example of a concept thus "without an object" is the concept of noumena. Kant thereby settles the case of all *entia* of rational metaphysics: they are mere *entia rationis*, which from a cognitive standpoint are *nothing*, empty extension for concepts.[21]

Like the first concept of 'nothing', the fourth ("nothing" according to modality) is also defined independently of any relation to sensation: the object of a contradictory concept is *nothing* even for reason. It is a nonconcept, *nihil negativum*; a fortiori no sensation can give it a content. In short, nothing as *ens rationis* (first case of nothing, empty extension of a concept) is what is thinkable, but not representable in sensibility. Nothing as *nihil negativum* (fourth case of nothing, object of a contradictory concept) is what is radically unthinkable. Therefore, neither of these concepts relates to *synthesis speciosa* according to the categories of quality, neither is to be taken into account in the schematism of *reality* and *negation*.

On the contrary, the second and third cases do relate to schematism of *reality* and *negation*, since both are concepts of the *absence* of determinations *which might be given in sensibility*. They are therefore relevant to our elucidation of Kant's concept of negation as an objective predicate.

Under the heading of quality, we find the category of *negation*, which is our main concern here. Negation is *nothing* as the mere lack of a determination we know to be giveable in sensation. Kant's expression for it, *nihil privativum*, should remind us of his analysis of negation in the pre-Critical *Attempt to Introduce the Concept of Negative Magnitude into Philosophy*. There he distinguished two kinds of negation (understood as the absence of a determination): the one he called simply "lack" (*defectus*), the other, "privation" (*privatio*). The first is the mere absence of a determination; the second is the absence of a determination resulting from the conflict of *opposed* determinations. For instance, rest (absence of movement) may be the effect of two moving forces of opposed directions.[22] The *nihil privativum* considered in the *Critique* might be either of the two cases considered in the precritical text: *defectus* or *privatio*. The second case (*privatio*) is the more interesting, however, for it relates both *reality* and *negation* to the third category of quality: *limitation*. Indeed, as we shall see, *all* reality and negation, determination of a thing (*Sachheit, Realität*) and absence of such a determination, *is nothing but limitation*: the determinations of each thing given in space and time are nothing but reciprocal *limitations* of determinations universally opposing each other (*limiting* each other) in space and time.

Under the heading of relation, "nothing" is *ens imaginarium*, which Kant identifies with the forms of intuition when they are deprived of any empirical content: "The mere form of intuition, without substance, is in itself no object, but the

---

[21] A292/B348. Kant gives as a second example "certain new fundamental forces, which though entertained in thought without self-contradiction are yet also in our thinking unsupported by any example from experience, and are therefore not to be counted as possible." Compare what he says on the same topic in the Postulates of Empirical Thought: A222/B269–70.

[22] A related point is that so-called negative magnitudes by which we express, for instance, forces of opposed directions are, metaphysically speaking, always *positive*, that is, *real*. Metaphysically speaking, we may call negation only the *absence* = 0 of a determination. See *Neg. Gr.*, Ak. II, 175–76; 214–15. On *defectus* and *privatio*, see *Neg. Gr.*, Ak. II, 178; 217.

merely formal condition of an object (as appearance), as pure space and pure time (*ens imaginarium*). These are indeed something, as forms of intuition, but are not themselves objects which are intuited" (A291/B347). Thus *nihil privativum* (under quality) and *ens imaginarium* (under relation) have this in common, that both of them are *nothing* by virtue of the mere *absence of a sensory given*. Kant emphasizes this proximity a few lines further: "the *nihil privativum* and the *ens imaginarium* are empty *data* for concepts. If light were not given to the senses we could not represent darkness, and if extended beings were not perceived we could not represent space. Negation and the mere form of intuition, in the absence of something real, are not objects" (A292/B349). That Kant should define space and time, considered as "the mere form of intuition, without substance," as being, metaphysically speaking, nothing, is striking. This characterization of space and time is related to Kant's assertion, in the Transcendental Aesthetic and the *Prolegomena*, of their transcendental ideality *and* empirical reality.[23] Space and time are "real" only insofar as they are cognized as relations of things, whose *reality* is "what corresponds to sensation." Outside this function of ordering sensations, space and time are nothing: they are purely ideal. Yet they are not a mere *nihil privativum*, because they are still beings *for imagination*, products of *synthesis speciosa* and as such, *entia imaginaria*, just as under the first title of "nothing," noumena were beings *for reason* (*entia rationis*), although they were not realities, "truly affirmative beings or determinations, *entia sive determinationes vere affirmativae*."

It is interesting that Kant should list *ens imaginarium* as falling under the category of relation. The explanation for this might be as follows: as we saw, it is difficult to separate the categories of quality from those of relation, since reality is defined as "that which corresponds to sensation," or as that through which our sensations are related to "something existing in space and time": but "something" is determined as "existing in space and time" by means of the categories of *relation*. Indeed, as we shall see in chapter 11, realities, negations, and limitations can be reflected only as properties of substances interacting in space and time. Now, we may radicalize in thought our concept of negation or *nihil privativum* to the point of supposing, not the absence of *some* particular determination (say, darkness as the absence of light; silence as the absence of sound, etc.) but the absence of *every* real determination. Then substance itself disappears. So do space and time as empirically real. What remains are space and time as *entia imaginaria*, *beings of imagination*, or metaphysically speaking: *nothing*.

Limitation

Surprisingly, the category of "limitation" seems at first to be missing in the Schematism chapter as well as in the Anticipations of Perception. Even the word "limitation" is absent from the Schematism: after Kant has expounded the schemata of reality and negation, he goes on to consider, not "limitation," but "re-

[23] Cf. A28/B44, A36/B52–53; *Prol.*, §13-III, Ak. 293; 36–37.

ality, as the quantity of something insofar as it fills time."[24] In the Anticipations, the word "limitation" occurs only once, almost as an afterthought, in a passage where Kant describes space and time as *quanta continua*:

> The property of magnitudes by which no part of them is the smallest possible, that is, by which no part is simple, is called their continuity. Space and time are *quanta continua*, because no part of them can be given save as enclosed between limits [*Grenzen*] (points or instants), and therefore only in such fashion that this part is itself again a space or a time. Space therefore consists solely of spaces, time solely of times. *Points and instants are only limits, that is, mere places for the limitation of space and time* [*Stellen ihrer Einschränkung*]. (A169/B211)

In fact, this text does give us an important indication concerning the category of limitation. For I want to argue that limitation (*Einschränkung*) in space and time—that is, enclosing of a reality within limits (*Grenzen*)—is the sensible manifestation of the *category* of limitation (called *Limitation* in the *Critique*, and *Einschränkung* in the *Prolegomena*).[25] It is also, as we shall see in the third section of this chapter, what makes possible the quantitative determination of the *degree of reality* of appearances (their intensive magnitude).

Let me start with limitation in space and time. Recall first the analysis I gave earlier of the relation between the "act of the understanding in infinite judgment" and the category of limitation. I argued that the "infinite sphere of every possible determination," posited by the predicate of infinite judgment, is indeterminate, save for one determination: in the conditions proper to our (sensible) cognition, it is determined as the sphere of the concept 'given in space and time'. Now, in an infinite judgment, the subject-concept is determined (a predicate is asserted of it)[26] only insofar as it is posited somewhere in the infinite sphere external to the sphere of the concept whose negation is the predicate. In other words, it is determined insofar as the part of the infinite sphere it belongs to is gradually *limited* by exclusion of the subspheres to which it does *not* belong. But for this *discursive* limitation to be possible, transcendental imagination must present an *intuitive* limitation, where objects as appearances reciprocally determine each other's situation in space and time and qualitative properties.

We can confirm and specify this relation between *discursive* and *intuitive* limitation by considering the only text where the concept of *limitation* is given extensive consideration: the Ideal of Pure Reason in the Transcendental Dialectic. In this text, Kant opposes to the hypostasis, by rationalist metaphysicians, of the purely rational concept of *totum realitatis*, supposed to be the ground of the complete determination of every individual thing, a *critical* concept of the *totum re-*

---

[24] A143/B183.

[25] A80/B206, *Prol.*, §21, Ak. IV, 303.

[26] In the 1755 *Nova dilucidatio*, Kant says that "to determine is to posit a predicate while excluding its opposite." This notion of determination remains unchanged in the critical period, although Kant's account of what makes it possible to "assert a predicate while excluding its opposite" of course changes drastically. This will be particularly important in the discussion of his treatment of the "principle of reason": see chapter 11.

alitatis which he takes to have been established by the Transcendental Analytic. This gives him occasion to oppose, to the dogmatic-rationalist concept of *limitation*, his own critical concept, in fact the only minimally developed account of this concept we find in the *Critique*. Let us briefly consider this account, which provides a useful complement to the frustratingly scarce explanations Kant provides in the Schematism and in the Anticipations of Perception.

I commented earlier on the relation between the logical form of infinite judgment and the precritical notion of a whole of reality, *totum realitatis*. We saw that instead of presupposing a whole of realities, or positive determinations, of which each singular thing might be thought as a specific limitation, Kant, in the critical period, merely asserts that every singular thing is thought as belonging somewhere in the infinite sphere of the concept 'object given in space and time'.[27] Nevertheless, the idea of a *totum realitatis*, a "concept of all reality" (*Inbegriff aller Realität*)—a concept of all possible positive determinations thought by concepts, of which every singular thing is a completely specified (completely determined) limitation—is, Kant maintains, perfectly legitimate as long as it is acknowledged for what it is: a mere *ens rationis*, an idea of reason with no more than a regulative use. Its sole legitimate use is to guide the cognizing understanding in the direction of ever increasing specificity of determination, on the one hand, and ever greater universality, on the other. Its use becomes illegitimate only when we suppose a *totum realitatis*, a whole of positive determinations to be *actually given*, or, even worse, when we hypostatize this whole by supposing an *ens realissimum* as the ground of all positive determination in finite things (i.e., the God of rational theology). But then, why is reason forever drawn toward this illusory hypostasis? Kant's answer is that the presupposition of a whole of reality, not only as an idea (which, as *ens rationis*, is "nothing"),[28] but also as something "which corresponds to sensation," namely as something *existent*—this presupposition *too* is legitimate, and even indispensable. But as an *existent* being, it is not a discursively, conceptually definable individual any more. It is merely the whole of reality one has to presuppose as "filling" space and time, and in relation to which every finite intuitively given thing is also given. We can find these two aspects of the "whole of reality"—the *merely regulative* idea of a discursive whole of positive determinations, and the *conceptually indeterminable* whole of reality, presupposed as given in space and time—in this text from the Transcendental Ideal:

> The possibility of the objects of the senses is a relation of these objects to our thought, in which something (namely, the empirical form) can be thought *a priori*, while that which constitutes the matter, reality in appearance (that which corresponds to sensation), must be given, since otherwise it could not even be thought, nor its possibility represented. *Now an object of the senses can be completely determined only when it is compared with all the predicates that are possible in the appearance, and by means of them is represented either affirmatively or negatively.* (my emphasis)

[27] Cf. pp. 294–98.
[28] Cf. p. 305.

This last sentence refers us to the *totum realitatis* described under the first aspect: the merely regulative idea of a totality of positive determinations of things. Such a whole can never be actually given, since our cognition of objects is sensibly conditioned and empirical, and concepts of "realities"—that is, concepts of positive determinations of things, can be generated only in our never-ending progress of empirical cognition. Kant, however, continues:

> But since that which constitutes the thing itself, namely, the real in appearance, must be given—otherwise the thing could not be conceived at all—and since that wherein the real of all appearances is given is experience, considered as single and all-embracing, *the material for the possibility of all objects of the senses must be presupposed as given in one whole; and it is upon the limitation of this whole that all possibility of empirical objects, their distinction from each other and their complete determination, can alone be based* [my emphasis]. No other objects, besides those of the senses, can, as a matter of fact, be given to us, and nowhere save in the context of a possible experience; and consequently nothing is an object *for us, unless it presupposes the sum of all empirical reality as the condition of its possibility* [my emphasis on clause following the comma]. (A582/B609–10)[29]

This time, Kant states that every empirical thing, given in intuition, is related to a presupposed whole of reality in experience. Hence, it is true that the complete determination of the objects of the senses presupposes a *totum realitatis* not only as an idea, but as something really existing. But this is quite different from the illusory concept of the *ens realissimum*. It is a sensible, conceptually indeterminate whole necessarily presupposed as the background of any empirically given. The concepts under which this whole of reality may be cognized are not themselves given as a whole, but are formed by empirical cognition. Or, as Kant says, the *totum* of positive determinations of things, or realities, *discursively thought by concepts*, does not have the collective unity of a thing, but rather the distributive unity of the "empirical use of the understanding" (A582/B610).

Thus the concept of an individual thing should not be thought as the limitation of a *totum realitatis* given to a pure intellect, but as the reflection of a sensory given, delimited in space and time, before being discursively determined by concepts. Kant expresses this view in a very striking *Reflexion* where he opposes the point of view of rational metaphysics, according to which reality is determined as a shadow on the background of universal light, to his own critical point of view, according to which reality is rather like light emerging from darkness. To be sure, Kant adds, as a *concept* reality always precedes negation, as light darkness. One can have a concept of negation or privation only if one already has formed a concept of reality, to which this privation is opposed. But it is illusory to conclude from this *logical* (conceptual) primacy of reality to its *ontological* primacy, and so believe that the whole of reality is given prior to its limitations, namely prior to particular realities. Reality is not given to pure intellect, as noumenon, but to

---

[29] In the second line of the quoted text, "empirical form" obviously means "form of the empirical object."

sensibility, as phenomenon. Hence even though concepts of reality necessarily precede concepts of negation, nevertheless *nothing* (the mere forms of space and time in which sensations are ordered) is ontologically, in the sense established in the Transcendental Analytic, prior to *reality* (what corresponds to the sensory given, reflected under concepts):

> If I represent the intellect that thinks reality, as light, and when it negates reality, as darkness, then complete determination can be represented either as the introduction of light into darkness, or as darkness which is a mere limitation [*Einschränkung*] of universal light, so that things are distinguished only by shadows, and reality is the ground, a single universal reality. In the opposite case, things are distinguished only by their light, as if they had originally sprung from darkness. Now I can indeed represent a negation when I have a reality, but not when no reality is given. Reality is therefore logically first, and from this, I conclude that it is also metaphysically and objectively first. But because the objects of the senses are not given by the understanding (and are not given *a priori* at all), negation, and the darkness from which the light of experience develops its figures, are what is first.[30]

The "negation" that for a merely sensible knowledge is "first" is of course what the appendix to the Transcendental Analytic describes as *nothing* under the category of relation: space and time as *entia imaginaria*. For our sensible cognition, *nothing* is prior to *something*: space and time, which in themselves are mere *entia imaginaria*, are the condition for representing any reality at all. This is why Kant says that for us, determination is not darkness delineated against universal light (finite determination of things as limitation of a *totum realitatis* thought by pure intellect), but on the contrary light emerging from darkness: sensible reality appearing in space and time.

There is something quite disconcerting in this assertion of the priority of *nothing* (space and time as *entia imaginaria*) over any reality, if one remembers that after all, in the text from the Analytic just quoted, Kant insists that negation cannot be represented prior to the reality it is the negation of, and similarly space and time, as *entia imaginaria* or *nothing*, cannot be represented unless substance has been represented. I think this apparent contradiction can be resolved in the following way: we would form no representation of "pure" space and "pure" time unless sensations were to be ordered "in" space and time, thus generating the "matter" of appearances, as "that which corresponds to sensation." In this sense, there definitely would be no representation of space and time without a sensory given. But on the other hand, reality would not appear as such (as "that which corresponds to sensation") unless it were ordered in space and time, and even in space and time as "infinite given magnitudes," as described in the Transcendental Aesthetic. The primacy of negation (space and time) over affirmation (reality) affirmed in the *Reflexion* just quoted is thus no other than the primacy of sensible form over sensible matter, which I analyzed in chapter 6. This priority is a transcendental priority, characteristic of the very standpoint of transcendental ideal-

---

[30] *Refl.* 5270, Ak. XVIII, 138.

ism: an intuition of space and time as "infinite given magnitudes" is the a priori condition for the representation of any empirical object, although space and time would not emerge, as intuitive representations, unless empirical realities were to be ordered in them, and representation of "pure" space and "pure" time are possible only as *entia imaginaria*, that is, in the *absence* of any apprehended and ordered empirical realities.

We now perhaps have all we need to understand Kant's category of *limitation*. It involves two correlated aspects: *discursive* limitation and limitation *in intuition*. Discursively, or by concepts, every particular empirical thing is determined (reflected under concepts) by *limitation* of the infinite sphere of the concept of 'object given in space and time'. And *prior to* this discursive limitation, *in order for* such discursive limitation to be *thinkable*, every particular thing is (intuitively) represented as *limited in space and time*: in the "infinite given magnitudes" of space and time, each thing occupies a delimited (*einbeschränkt*) space and time, enclosed within limits (*Grenzen*). The role of the *synthesis speciosa* that the category of limitation reflects is to present this limitation in intuition. The *category of limitation*, according to which sensible objects are considered as "determined in themselves with regard to the logical function of the infinite judgment," thus reflects their *intuitive/sensible* limitation—the fact that they are given within spatial and temporal limits—as well as their *discursive* limitation, the fact that the sphere of the concepts under which they are thought are limited subspheres of the infinite sphere of the concept, 'object given in space and time', or, again, what they *are* is thought only against the background of what they are *not*.

If this elucidation of the category of limitation is correct, it should help us to understand the principle of the Anticipations of Perception, or "principle of intensive magnitudes," in which Kant attempts to explain what makes possible the quantitative determination of quality, that is, the quantitative determination of "the real of appearances."

"THE SCHEMA OF REALITY, AS THE QUANTITY OF SOMETHING
INSOFAR AS IT FILLS TIME" AND THE PRINCIPLE
OF INTENSIVE MAGNITUDES

Reality as Intensive Magnitude

In the Schematism of the Pure Concepts of Understanding, Kant defines the schema of reality as "being (in time)," that of negation as "not-being (in time)" and the opposition between reality and negation as a "distinction of one and the same time as filled and as empty" (A143/B182). We then expect him to define the schema of *limitation*. Yet as noted earlier, Kant makes no mention of this category, but instead proceeds to consider the possibility of thinking the *quantitative determination* of reality:

> Now every sensation has a degree or magnitude whereby, in respect of its representation of an object otherwise remaining the same, it can fill out one and the same time, that is, occupy inner sense more or less completely, down to its cessation in

nothingness (= 0 = *negatio*). There therefore exists a relation and connection between reality and negation, or rather a transition from the one to the other, *which makes every reality representable as a quantum*. The schema of a reality, as the quantity of something insofar as it fills time, is just this continuous and uniform production of that reality in time as we successively descend from a sensation which has a certain degree to its vanishing point, or progressively ascend from its negation to some magnitude of it. (A143/B182–83, my emphasis)

Thus we have moved from the schema of *reality* to the schema of reality *as a quantum* (which, as we saw in chapter 9, means "a unity, in which there is quantity [*unum, in quo est quantitas*].") The latter schema is the "continuous and uniform production" of reality in time. This schema, and the resulting capacity to determine quantitatively not only the *form* of appearances, but also their *matter*, grounds "the second application of mathematics (*mathesis intensorum*) to natural science."[31] For insofar as they are synthesized in conformity with this schema, all appearances have an intensive magnitude, as Kant states in the principle of the Anticipations of Perception: "In all appearances, the real that is an object of sensation has intensive magnitude, that is, a degree" (B207).[32]

Kant's "proof" for this principle consists in stating that all appearances can be represented as synthesized in accordance with the schema of "reality, as the quantity of something," stated in the text from the Schematism cited earlier. That is to say, the real in all appearances can be represented as "continuously produced in time":

From empirical consciousness to pure consciousness a gradual alteration is possible, the real in the former completely vanishing and a merely formal *a priori* consciousness of the manifold in space and time remaining. Consequently a synthesis in the process of generating the magnitude of a sensation is also possible, from its beginning in pure intuition = 0, up to any magnitude. Since, however, sensation is not in itself an objective representation, and since neither the intuition of space nor that of time is to be met within it, no extensive magnitude belongs to it, but nevertheless it does have a magnitude (namely, through the apprehension of it, whereby the empirical consciousness of the sensation can increase in a certain time from nothing = 0 to its given measure), but an *intensive* one. Corresponding to this intensity of sensation, an *intensive magnitude*, that is, a degree of influence on the sense, must be ascribed to all objects of perception, insofar as the latter contains sensation. (B208)[33]

[31] *Prol.*, §24, Ak. IV, 307; 50.
[32] In the A edition, the principle is formulated as follows: "In all appearances sensation, and the *real* which corresponds to it in the object (*realitas phaenomenon*), has an *intensive magnitude*, that is, a degree." I comment on this small difference in formulation later.
[33] This citation belongs to the "proof" added in B. But the proof is similar in A: from the possibility of representing "the uniform and continuous production" of sensation, Kant concludes that sensation has intensive magnitude, and from this he in turn concludes that intensive magnitude also pertains to the "real which corresponds to sensation." In A, this proof is given twice: in A167–68/B209–10, and again in A176/B217–18. Contrary to Kemp Smith (*Commentary*, 349), I do not think there is a significant difference between the first proof of A on the one hand, and the second proof of A and proof of B on the other hand.

Kant is by no means the first to state that qualities, *qua* qualities, have their own kind of magnitude, defined as *degree* or *intensive magnitude*. This notion is a familiar one in German *Schulphilosophie*. Wolff, for instance, defines *degree* as

> that by which the same qualities may differ, while keeping their identity [*quo qualitates eaedem salva identitate differre possunt*], either at the same time in different subjects, or at different times in the same subject.

> *Degrees are the quantities of qualities.*[34]

Like every quantitative proportion, says Wolff, the proportion between the degrees of a quality can be represented by the proportion between two segments of a line:

> For example, just as a line is double, triple, quadruple, etc. with regard to another, so the degree of heat in a subject is double, triple, quadruple, etc., with regard to the degree of heat in another subject, and similarly the speed [*celeritas*] of a moving force in a movable is double, quadruple, etc., with regard to the moving force of another movable.[35]

A given degree may be considered as made up of other smaller degrees (its parts) just as a line is made up of smaller segments of lines taken as units. However, the "parts" of a quality are not external to one another, and cannot be juxtaposed in space like the segments of a line; qualities are not extensive magnitudes, but intensive magnitudes. Wolff describes their parts as "imaginary," and calls intensive magnitude or degree *magnitudo imaginaria*.[36] Nonetheless, degrees can be represented by extensive magnitudes (straight lines), and the correlated variations of two degrees can be represented by a the curve of a function. Wolff's description of the "mathematical cognition of qualities" thus clearly refers to the methods of algebra and analytic geometry: "Degrees may be represented by lines, and their mutual relations can be drawn and are distinctly conceived as the relations of lines, determining curved lines; the relation of the one to the other is given by rational or irrational numbers. It is therefore obvious that mathematical cognition of qualities is possible."[37] Wolff then gives examples: the intensity of light (for which he refers the reader to his *Optics*), the "density and rarity of bodies," the weight of solids in fluids (for which he refers to his *Elements of Hydrostatics*), the "condensation and rarefaction of air" (discussed in his *Elementa aerometriae*). Finally, he indicates that intensive and extensive magnitude are related not only because the former is geometrically represented by means of the latter; but also, and even more importantly, because we can have determinate cognition of the degree or intensive magnitude of a reality only through its relation to an extensive magnitude of which it is the ground: for instance, heat is measured by the height of the mercury in a thermometer, a moving force is measured by the acceleration of a moving body, thus by the space traveled in a given time, and so on.

[34] Wolff, *Philosophia prima*, §§746–47.
[35] Ibid., §749.
[36] Ibid., §§753–54.
[37] Ibid., §755.

Kant thus takes his inspiration from the Wolffian school when, in his early Lectures on Metaphysics, he characterizes extensive magnitude as one *in which* there is a manifold, intensive magnitude as one that *grounds* a manifold:

> A *quantum* is considered either intensively—that which has a quantity insofar as it is a ground—or extensively—that which has a quantity, but not insofar as it is a ground, for example space, the size of the army. Quantity is considered either intensively, insofar as something posits something else a given number of times; or extensively, insofar as in something, something else is posited a given number of times.[38]

Although the notion of intensive magnitude is no innovation of the *Critique*, what *is* new is Kant's attempt to answer the question, What allows us to consider as a magnitude, not only the *form* of appearances (their shapes and positions in space and time, as explained in the Axioms of Intuition) but *the real itself* ("that which corresponds to sensation")? How is this application of mathematics, not only to the form but also to the matter of appearances, anything other than a convenient fiction of imagination? The schema of quantity was explained in the Schematism and in the principle of the Axioms of Intuition. It requires a successive synthesis, whether applied to discrete units or to a *continuum* such as space and time. But the real is given to us only through sensation. And even though sensation "fills" time, it is not itself, as a sensation, spread out in space or time, it is not apprehended by successive synthesis. How could it have a magnitude?

According to the Schematism and Anticipations, cited earlier, the reason is this: although no sensation is successively synthesized, every sensation can at least be reflected, as the *quale* it is, under the concept of a *unit*, by comparison with which its absence is *nothing*: zero. Both this reality = one, and this negation = zero, are posited in time. But between zero and one, and between one and zero, an infinite number of intermediate quantitative determinations can be posited. For since time is a *quantum continuum*, any magnitude altering from 0 to 1 can be conceived as generated, from one instant to the next, by an indefinite series of intermediate instants (and thus intermediate states between 0 and 1). But this means representing sensation (and with it, the real that "corresponds to it") *as quantitatively synthesized*. Kant's highly compressed elucidations in the Anticipations may be usefully complemented here by two *Reflexionen*, both contemporary with the *Critique*:

> The magnitude of a thing insofar as it is not intuited as composite, *whose emergence and disappearance may be considered as composite (in time)*, is a degree.

---

[38] *Met. Herder* (1762–64), Ak. XXVIII-1, 22. In *Met. Volckmann*, we also find: "Every magnitude (quantity) can be considered either extensively, or intensively. The quantity which, as manifold, is contained in the thing, is *extensive*. And the quantity which is represented by the manifold which is posited by the thing is *intensive*. Some things are *quanta* because they contain a manifold of parts, and some things are *quanta* by which, as grounds, a multiplicity is posited. For example, the luminous capacity [*die leuchtende Kraft*] of the candle is intensively greater than that of the oil lamp, for with the former we can read from a distance of two feet, and with the latter, from a distance of one foot. The former is the ground of a greater consequence, and the latter the ground of a smaller consequence" (Ak. XXVIII-1, 425).

Possibility of applied mathematics. For all things (as appearances) have a magnitude, extensive or intensive. Thereby, mathematics acquires objective reality. It does not apply to *entia rationis*.[39]

The principle of intensive magnitudes, by relating the "real of appearances" to sensation and grounding our ability to represent any sensation as continuously generated from 0 to any given intensity, thus explains what makes the "real of appearance" a magnitude, not only mediately (i.e., by virtue of its association with the extensive magnitudes it grounds), but even *in itself*, as appearance (i.e., by virtue of the character imparted to it by our representational capacities—receptivity to affection, and *synthesis speciosa* generating the representation of a *quantum*). Sensation, like the space and time in which it is posited by the *synthesis speciosa* relating it to an object, is a *quantum continuum*. Space and time are *continua* as *extensive* magnitudes, in which the whole is made up of parts external to one another—this is why the *continuum* may be represented as *discretum*. Sensation, on the other hand, is a *quantum continuum* as an *intensive* magnitude, one that cannot be presented by a successive synthesis of parts, whether discrete or continuous; but one whose successive degrees can be represented as continuously generated through time.

Yet, even if one accepts Kant's argument for the *possibility* of representing sensation as a *quantum* (= as continuously generated from 0 to 1 between two instants in time), why should this be supposed to justify the assertion that sensation (and thus the real that "corresponds to it") *is* a *quantum continuum*? Admitting that we can treat sensation (and the real) as an *intensive magnitude* makes it possible to anticipate experience by determining, at least in some cases, mathematical functions representing the continuous variation of the intensity of a given reality through time. But whether reality is *actually* a continuous magnitude should be confirmed or falsified only empirically. Indeed, Kant says just this in the case of the continuity of *change*. Whether change is continuous, he says, can be established only empirically:

> Since all appearances, alike in their extensive and in their intensive aspect, are thus continuous magnitudes, it might seem to be an easy matter to prove with mathematical conclusiveness the proposition that all alteration (transition of a thing from one state to another) is continuous. But the causality of an alteration in general, presupposing, as it does, empirical principles, lies altogether outside the limits of a transcendental philosophy. For upon the question as to whether a cause capable of altering the state of a thing, that is, of determining it to the oposite of a certain given state, may be possible, the *a priori* understanding casts no light. . . . Since in our present inquiry we have no *data* of which we can make use save only the pure fundamental concepts of all possible experience, in which there must be absolutely nothing that is empirical, we cannot, without destroying the unity of our system, anticipate general natural science, which is based on certain fundamental experiences [*welche auf gewisse Grunderfahrungen gebaut ist*]. (A171–72/B212–13)

[39] *Refl.* 5588 and 5589, Ak. XVIII, 241 (my emphasis).

Now, one might expect this caution to extend to the continuity of reality itself. For it is quite different to say that we can *represent* reality *as* a continuous magnitude (namely, *imagine* or *construct* a priori its continuous variation through time), and to say that it *is*, *as* reality, namely as an *empirical given*, a continuous magnitude. When Kant asserts this, he seems to extend to the *matter* of appearance the continuity of its *form*: his whole argument for *asserting* the continuity of reality as an intensive magnitude rests on the continuity of the *time* (as formal intuition) through which reality can be constructed a priori as varying.

Of course, in the principle of the Anticipations of Perception itself Kant does *not* assert that the real that "corresponds to sensation" is a continuous magnitude. He only asserts that it is an *intensive* magnitude. And it seems sufficient, for something to be an intensive magnitude, that it be represented as what *can* vary continuously through time. But why then does Kant, in the course of his exposition of the Anticipations, actually extend to sensation and the real that "corresponds" to it the property of continuity that pertains to pure space and pure time? This seems to mean that he does after all deny the irreducible duality of *matter* and *form* of appearances, thereby contradicting a cardinal tenet of critical philosophy.

Kant might perhaps respond that there would be no unity of time (whether "pure" time or time as the form of appearances) unless time were continuous (between two instants of time, whether pure or empirically determined, there is a time-magnitude, no time "void," as it were); and there is no unity of experience unless there were unity of time as the form of appearances; hence, the continuity of time should be understood, not merely as the continuity of pure, "transcendentally ideal" time, but as the continuity of "empirically real" time, time as the form of appearances. And this means the continuity of the real in appearances themselves: the real should actually *be* such that it is a priori representable as susceptible of continuous variation through time. But whether the real *does* so vary, the response would go on, depends not only on the nature of reality (as intensive/continuous magnitude), but on the causes of alteration, which are empirically given.

Perhaps this is a possible defense for Kant's view that the continuity of the real as intensive magnitude (although not the continuity of change) can be asserted a priori, as a universal principle. I can do no better at this point than leave this question open. But only after two additional remarks. The first is that such a defense would mean assigning a very strong sense indeed to the priority of *form* over *matter* in appearances: the *matter* of appearances thus owes to its being taken up, by means of *synthesis speciosa*, into the *form* of intuition not merely its property of being a magnitude (albeit intensive, not extensive), but even that of being a *continuous* magnitude. In fact, Kant indicates just this when he writes, at the end of his exposition of the Anticipations of Perception: "It is remarkable that of magnitudes in general we can know *a priori* only a single quality, namely, that of continuity, and that in all quality (the real in appearances) we can know *a priori* nothing save their intensive *quantity*, namely that they have a degree. Everything else has to be left to experience" (A176/B218). According to this text, because reality is intuited in time, it can be represented as a quantity (or rather, a quantum); and because it can be represented as a quantum it can also be represented as a continuous magnitude: thus reality itself ("what corresponds to sensation," the matter of appearances synthesized in order to be reflected in judgment) has properties imparted to it by the form of intuition.

My second remark is that not only the continuity of the real as intensive magnitude, but the continuity of *change* itself will in the end be asserted as an a priori principle, in the Second Analogy of Experience. This certainly adds to our difficulties: the assertion seems impossible to reconcile with Kant's *denial*, in the Anticipations, that we can state the continuity of change as an a priori principle. I shall argue in chapter 11 that this discrepancy might at least confirm what I suggested to be the true ground for Kant's assertion of the continuity of *reality*, as intensive magnitude. This ground may be understood through the following reasoning: (1) there is unity of experience only if there is unity of empirically real time ; (2) there is unity of time only if there is *continuity* of (empirically real) time; (3) there is continuity of (empirically real) time only if there is continuity of change; (4) there is continuity of change only if reality itself is a *continuous* intensive magnitude. If it is correct to attribute this reasoning to Kant, then this confirms once more the very close link between Anticipations of Perception and Analogies of Experience—indeed, between all three sets of "objective" categories and principles: quantity, quality, and relation.[40]

What we should think of this a priori assertion of the principle of continuity of change, however, is a question I again have to leave open at this point. I shall take up the matter once more when analyzing Kant's argument for the necessity of causal connections in the Second Analogy of Experience.[41]

Reality as Intensive Magnitude, and Newton's Calculus of Fluxions

The continuous generation of degrees, or intensive magnitudes, finds its mathematical formulation in Newton's calculus of fluxions. Kant alludes to this calculus when he uses the expression "*flowing* magnitudes" to describe extensive as well as intensive magnitudes:

> The property of magnitudes by which no part of them is the smallest possible, that is, by which no part is simple, is called their continuity. . . . Such magnitudes may also be called *flowing*, since the synthesis of productive imagination involved in their production is a progression in time, and the continuity of time is ordinarily designated by the term flowing or flowing away.

---

[40] Quantity, quality, and relation are "objective" as distinguished from modality, which is "subjective"' in that through modal categories "no additional determinations are thought in the object itself; the question is only how the object, together with all its determinations, is related to the understanding and its empirical employment, to empirical judgment, and to reason in its application to experience" (A219/B266).

[41] See chapter 11, pp. 374–75, and note 85.

All appearances, then, are continuous magnitudes, alike in their intuition, as extensive, and in their mere perception (sensation, and with it reality) as intensive (A169–70/B211–12).[42]

The influence of the Newtonian model is also noticeable in Kant's assertion that we can represent sensation as "vanishing towards 0" and "increasing from 0." As we saw, such representation is what, according to Kant, allows us to attribute intensive magnitude to sensation, and thus to the real which "corresponds to it." In this "vanishing" and "increase" we find an echo of the *ratio ultima* or "evanescent augment," and *ratio prima* or "nascent augment," which, according to Newton, are the limits of the fluxions of two continuously varying magnitudes.

These concepts are expounded in Newton's *Treatise on the Quadrature of Curves* (*Tractatus de Quadratura Curvarum*). The context is the following: Newton sets himself the task of determining the relation of the "fluxions," that is, rates of variation ("augments of the fluents, generated in equal, but infinitely small parts of time") of two magnitudes x and y, where y is a function of x. This relation would today be called the *derivative* of the function $y = f(x)$. In order to obtain this relation, Newton assumes an augment or "increment" of x, which he calls o. When x becomes $x + o$, y becomes $f(x + o)$. Newton sets down the ratio of the two increments, and determines its value when o tends toward 0, that is, when the *time* during which the magnitudes vary tends toward 0. He calls the ratio of *instantaneous* variations *ratio prima* or *ratio ultima*: it is the ratio of fluxions at any moment in time—at any moment of the increase of the two magnitudes, or at any point of the curve representing the function $y = f(x)$. This ratio is thus also the ratio of the fluxions *at the initial beginning of their growth*, as well as *at the moment of their vanishing*.[43]

Newton's "method of fluxions" is quite clearly what Kant had in mind when he described sensation as something that can increase continuously from zero as well as decrease continuously to zero. If one can represent the continuous variation of any sensation to its disappearance = 0, and from its absence = 0 to a given degree, then sensation can be represented as a *flowing* magnitude in Newton's sense, as generated through continuous variation (or fluxion). Sensation thus has the character of the magnitudes to which Newton applies his calculus of fluxions,

[42] Compare this text with Newtons's *Tractatus de quadratura curvarum*: "I don't here consider Mathematical Quantities as composed of parts *extremely small*, but as *generated by a continual motion*. Lines are described, and by describing are generated, not by any apposition of parts, but by a continual motion of points. Surfaces are generated by the motion of Lines, Solids by the motion of Surfaces, Angles by the Rotation of their Legs, Time by a continual flux, and so on in the rest" (ed. Whiteside, 141). On Kant's relation to Newton, see chapter 9, notes 57, 58.

[43] *Tractatus de quadratura curvarum*, 142. Newton discusses the example of the fluxion of x^n. Having dealt with the first question (given the flowing magnitudes, find the fluxions), Newton then discusses the reverse problem (given the fluxions, find the flowing magnitudes). Thus he grounds the relation of what today we call the *derivative* and the *integral*, which is the fundamental theorem of infinitesimal calculus. On the difficulties surrounding the notion of "fluxion," and the roles of time and continuous generation in Newton's presentation of calculus, cf. Friedman, *Kant*, 75–76; Boyer, *Calculus*, 189–202.

and it then becomes legitimate to suppose that this calculus is a priori (i.e., universally) applicable to the real of appearances. The "application of mathematics" to natural science thus concerns not only the form, but also the matter of appearances (although the latter in its specific, concrete character is strictly empirical).

There is something very strange indeed in Kant's attempt to prove that reality is a *quantum* (= "a unity, in which there is quantity [*unum, in quo est quantitas*]") by arguing that our *sensations* are *quanta*. Hermann Cohen seems only too justified when he charges Kant with psychologistic confusion for attributing to *sensation* an intensive magnitude that can belong only to the *object of* sensation, *reality*, for it alone is a priori constructible in pure intuition of space and time. Indeed, Cohen insists, attributing quantity to sensation is so blatantly misguided that Kant himself acknowledged his mistake, and modified his formulation of the principle of the Anticipations of Perception in the second edition of the *Critique* accordingly: whereas in A, intensive magnitude is attributed to "sensation, and the real corresponding to it," in the B edition it is attributed only to "the real that is an object of sensation."[44] Unfortunately, Cohen adds, Kant never completely renounced his psychologistic mistake, since even in the proof added in B, he makes the intensive magnitude of *sensation* the ground for universally asserting the intensive magnitude of *the real of appearance*. This is confusing transcendental and psychological "proof." In Cohen's eyes, such confusion contradicts the fundamentally antiempiricist and antipsychologistic inspiration of the *Critique*. A particularly damning example of this regression from transcendental to psychological method is, according to Cohen, Kant's treatment of the forms of intuition: when Kant discusses the "gradual alteration" from "empirical consciousness to pure consciousness . . . a merely formal consciousness of the manifold in space and time," and conversely from "pure intuition = 0 to any magnitude of sensation," he treats the transcendental forms of space and time as mere psychological *data* (or absence thereof).[45]

But Cohen's criticism disregards what *precedes* the principle of the Anticipations of Perception and its proof: Kant's metaphysical and transcendental deduction of the categories of quality, his explanation of *synthesis speciosa*, and his doctrine of the schematism of pure concepts of the understanding. Only if we take into account these earlier developments can we make sense of Kant's description of the forms of intuition as "zero" or "nothing," as well as of his description of "the real in appearance" as "what corresponds to sensation." In this context, "zero" is (if one will forgive the strangeness of the expression) a *metaphysical* zero: the absence of reality. It is so far from being an empiricopsychological *datum* that, on the contrary, when expounding the principle of the Anticipations of Perception, Kant insists that *no empirical/psychological state—no absence of perception or conscious sensation—*provides any sufficient ground to assert that

---

[44] A166: "In all appearances sensation, and the *real* which corresponds to it in the object (*realitas phaenomenon*), has an *intensive magnitude*, that is, a degree." B207: "In all appearances, the real that is an object of sensation has intensive magnitude, that is, a degree."

[45] Cohen, *Erfahrung*, 553–54. The formulations he quotes are from B208, that is, from the proof Kant added in B.

this zero, the complete absence of any reality, has been reached. Empty space and empty time may indeed exist, but they cannot be proved from a mere rarefaction of sensation.[46] Similarly, sensation "filling out time," and thereby providing the schema for the *real of appearance*, is not *only* an empirically given psychological state. It is a psychological state whose transcendental aspect has been explicated by the metaphysical deduction of the categories of quality, by the transcendental deduction of the categories and its explanation of *synthesis speciosa*, and finally by the doctrine of schematism. As for the representation of sensation as capable of passing through an infinite number of intermediate degrees before disappearing into *nothing* = 0, and similarly capable of continuously increasing from 0 to its present state, it is certainly not a psychological *datum*, but a mere possibility, whose representation is generated a priori by the application of mathematical synthesis to the *continuum* of the temporal form in which sensation is posited.[47]

Cohen is certainly right in linking intensive magnitude and determination *of an object* (the "real in appearance"). But he is doubly mistaken, I think, when (1) he interprets *sensation*, in the Anticipations of Perception, as a mere empirical and psychological given, without taking into account its function in the analysis of the a priori conditions of our representations of objects; and (2) he restricts the scope of intensive magnitude to the object of mathematical physics, ignoring the fact that the very possibility of applying mathematics to empirical objects is the problem Kant is trying to solve.[48] In the principle of the Anticipations of Perception, Kant attempts to solve this problem by attributing intensive magnitude to sensation as related to an object, and *consequently* to the "real that corresponds to it." Thus there is no reason to oppose, like Cohen does, the A and B presentations of the principle of the Anticipations of Perception. What is true, however, is that in B, Kant places greater emphasis on the ultimate goal of his demonstration: grounding the possibility of applying the mathematics of continuity to the "real of appearances." This is the reason, I think, for the change in formulation of the principle itself from A to B. The first formulation was: "In all appearances sensa-

[46] See A172/B214.

[47] Notice that Kant speaks only of the *possibility* of representing sensation as having been generated in a "continuous and uniform" manner. "From empirical consciousness to pure consciousness a gradual transition is *possible* . . . the empirical consciousness of it *can* in a certain time increase from nothing = 0 to its given measure" (B208); "Between reality and negation there is a continuity of *possible* realities and of *possible* smaller perceptions" (A169/B211) (my emphasis). This explains Kant's caution when he states the principle of continuity of alteration in the "real of appearance." That the generation of reality *can be represented* (*and mathematically constructed*) as *continuous* is not an adequate basis on which to assert that this generation is *empirically* continuous: this requires empirical cognition (A171/B213–14). However, Kant is not so cautious in the Second Analogy: there he affirms a universal principle of the continuity of alterations in appearances (A209/B254). Cf. my comment on this point earlier, p. 316, and in chapter 11, note 85.

[48] Robert Paul Wolff makes a similar mistake, it seems to me, when he explains the Anticipations of Perception as Kant's "dynamic theory of matter" (cf. *Mental Activity*, 232–33). Kant's reference to physics is indeed crucial, for it shows us *where Kant wanted to end up*: his demonstration was geared toward explaining the possibility of a mathematical physics of forces. But precisely for this reason, this physics cannot serve as a *proof* or a *ground* for the principle, even if keeping it in mind is crucial for grasping Kant's meaning.

tion, and the *real* which corresponds to it in the object (*realitas phaenomenon*), has an *intensive magnitude*, that is, a degree" (A166). The second formulation attributes intensive magnitude directly to the real in appearances: "In all appearances, the real that is an object of sensation has intensive magnitude, that is, a degree" (B207).

Indeed, *only* the "real of appearances," *not* sensation, is accessible to mathematical cognition. In other words, saying that sensation is ultimately our only source of cognition of the intensive magnitude of the real of appearances is certainly *not* saying that we can apply quantitative *determination* (i.e., *measure*) to sensation itself. The latter, according to Kant, is impossible, for quantitative determination relies on "successive synthesis of the homogeneous manifold," that is, on the determination of *extensive* magnitude. Intensive magnitude itself can be measured only by means of its relation to an extensive magnitude, and such a relation can be established in the case of the "real of appearances" that "corresponds" to sensation (gravity, heat, light, etc.) because this real is given in *space*. But no such relation can be established in the case of sensation itself, to which the real "corresponds." Therefore, the real of appearance alone, not sensation as such, is an object of mathematical cognition, and it is so only insofar as we can relate it to the variation of a *spatial* magnitude.[49]

But then, does this not take us back to Cohen's objection? Does it make any sense at all to speak of the magnitude of *sensation*? We find the elements of a reply in Kant's *Lectures on Metaphysics*. After stating that intensive magnitude is the "ground of a multiplicity," Kant continues: "For example, when a representation has inhibited many others, we say that this has made a great impression [*z.E wenn eine Vorstellung viele andere verdrängt, so sagt man, das hat eine große Sensation verursacht*]."[50] Even states of consciousness can thus be considered as "grounds of multiplicities," and therefore in some sense *compared* as to their magnitude. A representation is "more or less intense" according to the multiplicity of representations it inhibits; a very great pain makes one deaf and blind toward any other representation. But unlike spatial multiplicities, such multiplicities cannot receive quantitative determination.

It is interesting to compare Kant's position to Bergson's. Bergson denies any possibility of attributing an intensity to states of consciousness, and asserts that such attribution takes place only because one associates these states with *physical* causes and effects, to which alone quantitative determinations properly belong. Bergson would doubtless have been discomfitted to know that, on this point at least, his position was close to that of a neo-Kantian such as Cohen.[51] But Cohen's position is not Kant's. For Kant, it is true that sensations cannot by themselves be *determined* quantitatively.[52] Yet it is perfectly possible to attribute a

---

[49] Kant takes up this point again in the *Metaphysical Foundations of Natural Science*: cf. his discussion of the "empirical theory of the soul" in the preface (Ak. IV, 471; 8).

[50] *Met. von Schön*, Ak. XXVIII-1, 495.

[51] Cf. Bergson, *Essai sur les données immédiates de la conscience*, chap. 1.

[52] The method of "threshholds", as first experimented by Fechner, in determining the variation of intensity of sensations in relation to the continuous varation of stimuli, does not, I think contradict Kant's point as it stands: what is actually *measured* by this method (and thus has *determinate* magni-

magnitude to them, for two reasons: we can think of them as continuously generated from 0 to whichever magnitude they have at any instant; and, if sensations are associated with their mental effects (where, again, the concept of intensive magnitude is inseparable from the categories of relation), they can be compared with one another and termed *greater* or *lesser*. Therefore it makes sense to assert that our immediate access to the "real of appearances" *and its intensive magnitude* is our perception of the (indeterminate) intensive magnitude of our sensations. Naturally, this does not mean that our immediate representation of the magnitude of a reality, grounded in the intensity of our sensation, is adequate. Here as elsewhere, true cognition is possible only when we progress from *perception* to *judgments* of perception, and from these to *judgments of experience*.

Intensive Magnitude, Limitation, and the Transition from Quality to Relation

We should now have a better grasp of the way in which the "principle of intensive magnitudes" relates to the category of *limitation*. We saw earlier that for a thing to be thought under concepts that are a (discursive) limitation of the "infinite sphere of any possible determination," it must first be posited (in respect of its reality) as an (intuitive) limitation of the "infinite given magnitudes," the formal intuitions of space and time. This intuitive limitation is what Kant refers to in the only passage from the Anticipations of Perception where the term "limitation" occurs: the passage where Kant explains that space and time are *quanta continua* in which each part is only a *limitation* (*Einschränkung*) contained within limits (*Grenzen*) (A169/B211). Now, if the analysis I have just completed is correct, it is precisely the *positing of the real between limits* (*Grenzen*), both temporal and spatial, and the possibility of thinking a continuous variation of these limits, that allows us to cognize the quantitative determination of the real as intensive magnitude. *Discursive* limitation thus presupposes a limitation *in intuition*, exhibited by *synthesis speciosa*. This limitation in intuition is what allows the "*a priori* science of multiplicities," pure mathematics (in its most fruitful development, infinitesimal calculus), to be applied to the "real of appearances."

This application of pure mathematics to intensive magnitude is possible insofar as the latter is considered as the "ground" of an extensive magnitude. Gravity is the ground of the acceleration of motion in free fall, and thereby the ground of the space covered by the body in free fall; heat is the ground of the expansion of the volume of a liquid or a gas; elasticity is the ground of the transmission of

tude) is the stimulus, not the sensation; nevertheless, it makes sense, as Kant maintains (contrary to Cohen and Bergson) to attribute a greater or lesser "intensity" to the sensation. Moreover, the de facto *discontinuity* of our capacity to discern *continuous* variations of intensities of the stimuli, seems to me not to contradict Kant's transcendental point (related to the a priori intuition of time as *quantum continuum*) that sensation, and "the real that corresponds to it," *can* be represented as continuous magnitudes. Where there is a problem, it seems to me, is in his further a priori claim that sensation and "the real that corresponds to it" just *are* such continuous magnitudes. And this last point boils down to a blurring of the distinction between form (which relates to imagination) and matter (which relates to sensation) of appearances.

322 • CHAPTER 10 •

motion when a body hits another body. With this quantitative determination of the "real of appearance as *quantum*," we see once again the correlation between the categories of *quality* and those of *relation*—here, cause and effect. This correlation is stated explicitly in the following passage from the Anticipations of Perception:

> Every reality in appearance has therefore intensive magnitude, i.e. a degree. If this reality is viewed as cause, either of sensation or of some other reality in appearance, such as alteration, the degree of the reality as cause is then entitled a moment, for instance the moment of gravity. It is so named because degree signifies only that magnitude the apprehension of which is not successive, but instantaneous. This, however, I touch on only in passing; for with causality I am not at present dealing. (A168–69/B210)

Notice that the causal relation Kant mentions here involves not only the relation of the "reality in appearance" to an "alteration in appearance," but also the relation of this reality to *sensation* itself. This is a striking shift in point of view: whereas *sensation* was the transcendental ground for attributing intensive magnitude to the "real" in appearance, now the real is described as the *cause* of sensation. We started with the consideration of sensation and its intentional relation (insofar as it is the "matter" of an empirical intuition) to an object, and from there we have moved to considering the causal relation of "reality," as "that which corresponds to sensation," to sensation itself. Such a shift in point of view can be seen also in the sentence concluding the "proof" of the Anticipations, added in B: "Corresponding to this intensity of sensation, an *intensive magnitude*, that is, a degree of influence on the sense, must be ascribed to all objects of perception, insofar as the perception contains sensation" (B208). In one and the same sentence, an "intensive magnitude" is attributed to the "object of perception," *first* insofar as it "corresponds to" sensation, *second* insofar as it "influences the sense": thus as *object* of perception and as *cause* of sensation (the "matter" of perception, "corresponding to which" we represent the "matter" of appearance). Kant's account of this latter point, however—his account of how, when we relate our sensory perceptions to objects, we are aware of the causal determination of the former by the latter—is not given before the Third Analogy of Experience. There Kant will explain how our awareness of a universal order of time is conditioned by our awareness of the universal "community" or interaction of the objects we perceive in space. This includes an awareness of their interaction with *our own body*, and thus of their *causal* determination of the "matter" of our perceptions: sensations.[53]

As stated at the outset of this chapter, a systematic elucidation of the categories of quality makes clear their inseparability, not only from the first set of categories (quantity) but also from the next (relation). Equally inseparable, we now see, are

[53] See below, chapter 11, pp. 391–93.

Kant's account of the intentional relation of sensation to its empirical object (the reality that "corresponds to it") and his account of our representation of the (empirical) causal relation of the (empirical) object to sensation. For further examination of this point, we now need to consider Kant's argument in the Analogies of Experience.

The Constitution of Experience

JUST AS THE FORMS of relation in judgment are the discursive forms by means of which concepts are related to objects, so the figurative syntheses that generate combinations of appearances with a view to these forms are just those sensible syntheses by means of which perceptions are related to objects. Kant calls the perceptions so combined *experience*, and says that the principles by which relational categories are universally predicated of appearances are *regulative of intuition*, but *constitutive of experience*.[1]

In the introduction to the *Critique of Pure Reason*, Kant explains what he means by "experience": knowledge of objects by means of discursive combination of concepts. Kant's goal in the Analogies is to establish that experience thus characterized *presupposes* experience in a further sense: experience as *synthesis of perceptions in accordance with a priori (relational) categories*. He thus argues that a synthesis of perceptions (*synthesis speciosa*) according to a priori forms, which are forms of the objective unity of apperception, is the necessary precondition for all experience understood as empirical (discursive) knowledge of objects. His main line of argument for this point consists in showing that without such an a priori synthesis, no distinction between the subjective succession of perceptions and the temporal order of empirical objects would ever occur. Thus what he means, when he says that the Analogies of Experience are "constitutive of experience," is that they are universal propositions expressing the way experience—synthesis of perceptions, relating perceptions to objects so that we can reflect these objects under concepts—is constituted. For the Analogies are principles that predicate of appearances just those concepts that reflect the universal forms of synthesis by means of which perceptions are related to objects (or, appearances are related to phenomena) and thus by means of which experience as discursive knowledge of objects is made possible.

In the present chapter I shall attempt to elucidate Kant's argument in all three Analogies of Experience. A distinct part of the chapter will be devoted to each of the relational categories, and thus to each Analogy. In each case, I will first analyze the relation of the category to the corresponding logical form; I will then analyze Kant's explanation of the synthesis of imagination with a view to the relevant logical form, and thus his argument for each Analogy of Experience. This mode of presentation has a significant drawback: it forces us to divide the analysis of the Analogies, and thus to break the unity of Kant's account of the *order of time*, which is constituted, according to him, by the schemata of all three categories of relation *together*. But it seemed to me that taking seriously the relation

[1] Cf. A179–80/B221–23, A236/B296, A664/B692.

between metaphysics (doctrine of the categories as universal predicates of objects as appearances), logic (logical forms of judgment, *synthesis intellectualis*), and transcendental psychology (sensible/perceptual synthesis, *synthesis speciosa*) not only yields greater clarity for each Analogy individually, but also makes their unity perspicuous to a degree not otherwise achievable. Moreover, I think this method sheds unprecedented light on Kant's settling of accounts with rational metaphysics. It shows once again how, by means of his doctrine of imagination and *synthesis speciosa*, he moves from traditional predicative logic to a consideration of *extensions*, or the *objects* thought under concepts. This calls for interesting comparisons between Kant's conception of logic (and its relation to metaphysics) and modern, extensional logic.

SUBJECT AND PREDICATE, SUBSTANCE AND ACCIDENT, PERMANENT AND TRANSITORY

Subject and Predicate, Substance and Accident

When Kant explains the relation of the categories to the logical forms of judgment in general, he typically uses as his example the correspondence between the logical relation of subject and predicate, and the transcendental relation of substance and accident. Thus in section 14 of the Transcendental Deduction, Kant explains the nature of the categories as follows:

> [The categories] are concepts of an object in general, by means of which the intuition of an object is regarded as *determined* in respect of one of the *logical functions* of judgment. Thus the function of the *categorical* judgment is that of the relation of subject to predicate; for example, 'All bodies are divisible'. But as regards the merely logical use of the understanding, it remains undetermined to which of the two concepts the function of the subject, and to which the function of predicate, is to be assigned. For we can also say, 'Something divisible is a body'. But when the concept of body is brought under the category of substance, it is thereby determined that its empirical intuition in experience must always be considered as subject and never as mere predicate. Similarly with all the other categories. (B128–29)[2]

That Kant chose the category of substance to illustrate his point should come as no surprise, since the correspondence between *substance* and *subject* of predication was stated as early as Aristotle's exposition of the categories. Although Kant takes pride in having, contrary to Aristotle's random list, given systematic unity to the categories by relating them to logical functions of judgment, his explanation of the category of substance is nevertheless inspired by Aristotle, via Wolff and German *Schulphilosophie*.[3] Still, the primacy he gives to logical function

---

[2] See also B149 and A147/B186.

[3] A81/B106–7. For Aristotle's definitions of the category of substance or essence (*ousia*), see *Categories* 5, 2a11–20; *Metaphysics* IV, 1017b13 on accidental predication, *Posterior Analytics* I, 22, 83a4–17; on accident, *Metaphysics* IV, 1025a13–14. For Wolff's notion of substance, see *Philosophia prima*, §768f–69. For Baumgarten, see *Metaphysica*, §191f–92 (Ak. XVII, 66–67).

over ontological predicate allows him to assign an entirely new meaning to the category of substance.

We saw earlier how Kant distanced himself from Wolff's conception of the categorical proposition as expressing the ontological relation between a thing and its essential determinations (*essentialia*) and attributes (*attributa*), and considered instead the "mere form" of the categorical proposition, manifesting the discursive act that relates a predicate to a subject under a condition "internal" to the subject of predication, regardless of the ontological significance of the terms combined.[4] Indeed, from the logical point of view any concept may be used either as subject or as predicate in a judgment. We may write 'All bodies are divisible' but also 'Some divisibles are bodies', 'All Athenians are human' but also 'Some humans are Athenians'. From the transcendental standpoint, by contrast, we call *substance* or *accident* that whose intuition is "determined in respect of the logical form of the relation of subject and predicate in judgment."[5] We call substance that which (as a phenomenal determination) is to be reflected as the condition of predication, and whose concept thus rightfully occupies the position of subject in a categorical judgment. We call accident that which is to be reflected as predicate only under the condition of what is thought in the subject, and thus rightfully occupies the position of predicate in a categorical judgment. But what do these characterizations mean? How do we determine what should be reflected as subject, and not predicate, and what as predicate, and not subject?

A first answer might be provided by the expanded formulation of the categorical judgment analyzed in chapter 4: 'To everything x, to which the concept A belongs, there also belongs the concept B'. From this formulation we might conclude that only the object corresponding to the term x in Kant's logical form of judgment, can be called 'substance'. The concepts combined in judgment, for their part, regardless of their grammatical position, are always predicates, and thus refer to accidents. Only the term x is always subject, never predicate of something else. More precisely, following the analysis of reality and negation in the preceding chapter, we can say that since the only real predicates (*determinationes vere affirmativae*, truly positive determinations) are those reflecting what corresponds to our sensations when we relate the latter to an object, substance, for its part, is the object to which we relate our sensations so that the determinations corresponding to them are reflected as *realities* (*realitates phaenomena*, positive determinations as appearances). So understood, the concept of substance is indeed the "concept of an object in general, insofar as its intuition is regarded as determined in respect of the logical function of [categorical] judgment." It is the concept of the object represented by the term x, which we cognize through the predicates combined in our judgment. By contrast, since the concepts related to the term x are always predicates and never subjects properly so called, the realities they designate are never anything else than *accidents*. We thus cognize substance only through its accidents, as Kant maintains in his Lectures as well as several *Reflexionen* on Metaphysics: "A thing can be cognized only by means of judgments, i.e. by predicates. Substances can be cognized only

4 See chapter 4.
5 This is a variation on the definition of the categories at B128–29. See also *Prol.*, §28, Ak.311; 54.

by means of accidents. We cognize only by concepts, and therefore by predicates, and thus accidents."[6]

However, we cannot be satisfied with the conclusion that for Kant, substance is no other than what corresponds to the term x in judgment. For then there would be no reason at all for us to consider one concept rather than another as the subject and not the predicate in a given judgment (or on the contrary, as the predicate and not the subject). The example given in section 14 of the Transcendental Deduction would lose all significance, for it would not then matter, from a transcendental standpoint no less than from a logical standpoint, whether one said 'All bodies are divisible' or 'Some divisibles are bodies'. The only "true" subject would be the x to which both concepts are related as a predicates, thus representing accidents. But this is obviously not what Kant means to say. Hence, we must expect Kant to make a move analogous to Aristotle's distinction between primary and secondary substance, or to Wolff's between the individual substance and its essence, between the *substantiale* and its *essentialia*. In Kant's case, it takes the form of the determination of one concept as subject in relation to all others as predicate: "That which absolutely (from every point of view) (in itself, not logically) is a subject, the final subject, which no longer presupposes another subject as a predicate, is substance. The predicate for which no other universal concept can be given as a subject is that by which substance is immediately represented as something to which the predicate belongs."[7]

The "final subject, which no longer presupposes another subject as a predicate" is the x of judgment. But we are told here that this "final subject" is "immediately represented" by a predicate "for which another universal concept can no longer be given as a subject." What could this predicate be, "by means of which substance is immediately represented," or how do we recognize it? A text from the *Duisburgscher Nachlaß* provides a clue. Kant is clearly groping in it, but nevertheless this text helps us understand the nature of the problem he is posing to himself and the manner in which he is trying to solve it. He distinguishes three ways in which we may compare concepts in judgments. (i) We may compare only concepts, without any consideration of objects. We then compare "according to the principles of identity or contradiction," the comparison is "merely logical." Or (ii) we may compare concepts in relation to empirical objects where none of the concepts we compare refers to a substance. Or, finally, (iii) we may compare concepts in relation to empirical objects where one concept clearly refers to a substance. What makes this text interesting is the way Kant distinguishes between the three cases:

i) The principle of identity and contradiction contains the comparison of two predicates a and b with x, but only in such a way that concept a of x is compared with b and thus x is useless. It is a principle of form, not of content, and thus merely logical. A principle of analysis, from which nothing may be cognized *of an object*. . . .[8]

---

[6] *Metaphysik L,*[2] Ak. XXVIII-2 (1), 562.

[7] *Refl.* 5297 (1776–78), Ak. XVII, 146.

[8] The expression in italic is my translation for Kant's Latin adverbial form: *objective*. Kant gives no German equivalent. The rest of the text is in German.

ii) If I relate the two predicates to the x, and thereby to each other, this is synthetic, no x who is learned is ignorant, for here the limitation of time is required, viz. at the same time. To be sure, ignorance contradicts learning, but not the man x who is learned, except insofar as he is learned. Consequently, the contradiction is either with respect to the concept a that I have of x, or with respect to x, to which this concept does not of necessity belong. The synthetic validity of b and non-b with respect to the x that can be thought by concept a or not-a is called change [*Wechsel*].

iii) But if a cannot be separated from b in x, i.e. no x which is a body is indivisible, then one must see that the x which is thought through a can never be thought through non-a, that no being which has the nature of a body can become incorporeal, and that the a in itself is not a predicate in respect of x, but a reciprocal concept [*sondern mit ihm ein Wechselbegriff sei*] and thus holds *of a substance*.[9]

Let us look at the three different cases of predication discussed in this text:

1. Kant first discusses a comparison of concepts where the object represented by x is not taken into consideration: this comparison is what I called earlier a logical comparison in the narrow sense,[10] where concepts are known to be identical or opposed by virtue of the principles of identity and contradiction alone. If we take up in this context the example given by Kant in (ii), we might say that in 'Noone learned is ignorant', concepts may be compared in this way. It is contradictory to predicate of the concept 'learned' the concept 'ignorant'. The judgment is here an analytic truth, where the analysis of the subject-concept is sufficient to exclude the predicate-concept. However, any such analytic truth says nothing "of an object": the principles of identity and contradiction are "principles of analysis, from which nothing may be cognized *of an object*."

2. What Kant means by this becomes apparent in his second point, where he distinguishes between this "merely logical comparison" of concepts and their comparison *under the condition of the x of judgment*. If the predicates 'learned' and 'ignorant' are compared to one another *in relation to the object = x*, the temporal condition of the opposition must now be specified. One must say 'No x who is learned is *at the same time* ignorant'. This is because "ignorance contradicts learning, but not the man x who is learned, except insofar as he is learned." Mentioning the temporal condition brings to light the fact that neither of the two contradictory predicates is necessarily connected to the term x in the judgment. Kant expresses this by saying that they are *both* "synthetically valid" with respect to x. This is a rather surprising expression. What is the "synthetic validity" of a concept with respect to an x, if we suppose x refers to an intuition? The answer lies in the specification 'the man x'. The intuition (the x) to which the opposed predicates 'learned' and 'ignorant' are related, is itself thought under the concept of man. The "synthetic validity" of the concepts 'learned' and 'ignorant' with re-

---

[9] *Refl.* 4676 (1773–75: *Duisburgscher Nachlaß*), Ak. XVII, 653–54. In Kant's notes, the text is unbroken. I have divided it into numbered paragraphs that correspond to the divisions of my analysis. "*of a substance*" at the end of the text is my translation for Kant's Latin adverbial form: *substantive*.

[10] See chapter 5, and note 58. And chapter 6.

spect to the x is their synthetic validity with respect to the concept 'man' under which the object = x is thought. Neither of the two concepts is an analytic predicate of the concept 'man', but both can be attributed *successively* to the object thought under this concept, just as both their *negations* can be attributed to this object successively. For instance: a man can be learned *and then* forget his learning. This makes him knowledgeable *and then* ignorant. The predicate 'ignorant' contradicts the subject 'learned' (the "concept that I have of x"), but not the object x ("the x, to which the concept a does not necessarily belong" [and which I think under the concept 'man']). "The synthetic validity of b and non-b [ignorant and not-ignorant] with respect to the x that can be thought under a and not-a [learned and not-learned], is called *change*." This too is a surprising formulation. It can, I think, be explained as follows. The reason both a and non-a, and both b and not-b, may be true of x, is that both can be attributed synthetically (but not at the same time) to the concept (here: man) under which x is thought. This successive validity of two synthetic predicates is called *change*. Thus the way is prepared for Kant's analysis, in the First Analogy, of all change (*Wechsel*, disappearance of a sensible determination and appearance of its opposite) as the *alteration* (*Veränderung*) of a substance.[11]

3. But consider now the other example, 'No x which is a body is indivisible'. There is no need here to specify any temporal condition when the opposition of the two predicates is stated under the condition of their relation to x. x which is thought under the concept of body cannot cease at any time to be opposed to the concept 'indivisible', *because it cannot cease to be thought under the concept of body, which has 'divisible' as one of its analytic marks.*[12] Or, as Kant writes, the concept of body is a *concept reciprocal with the x* itself, and thus must be considered *as a concept of substance*: "No being which has the nature of a body can become incorporeal, and . . . the a itself [here, the concept of body] is not a predicate with respect to x, but a concept which is reciprocal with this x and thus holds *of a substance* [Kant's Latin adverb: *substantive*]." Thus Kant preserves the classic Aristotelian distinctions, while at the same time reviving in his own terms and for his own purposes Aristotle's inquiry concerning the ontological import of predication: the Copernican revolution achieved in the *Critique* means that the categories of substance and accident arise from our acts of discursive reflection, our acts of judging applied to the sensible given. As a result of these acts, on the one hand, only the object represented by x in the form of judgment should be called substance "most strictly, primarily and most of all," as Aristotle said of pri-

---

[11] Note that the same example is used in the *Critique* to caution against the common mistake of introducing a temporal condition in the expression of the principle of contradiction itself (see A152–53/B191–92). As is often the case, the "mistake" was in fact the precritical Kant's own: see *Inaugural Dissertation*, Ak. II, 401; 394.

[12] See letter to Reinhold, May 12, 1789, where Kant describes 'divisibility' as an *analytic* mark of 'body', derived from that of 'extension' (Ak. XI, 34–35). On the other hand, he says in the *Anfangsgründe* that divisibility is a necessary, although *synthetic* mark of the concept 'matter': cf. *Anfangsgründe*, II, Lehrsatz 4, Ak. IV, 503. The difficulties this might raise shall not be considered here. What matters is that divisibility should be a *necessary* mark of the concept of body, which is "reciprocal with x."

mary substance.[13] But on the other hand, every concept "reciprocal with the x," in the sense we saw above, is a concept of substance. In a judgment such as 'No body is indivisible', the concept of body is, from a transcendental standpoint, subject rather than predicate because it is "reciprocal with the x" and, as such, the sufficient ground for negating of x the predicate 'indivisible' (without any temporal condition). In a judgment such as 'No learned man is at the same time devoid of learning', both concepts are predicated of x by accident, and x is implicitly thought under the predicate 'man', "reciprocal with x." Successively attributing to x thought under the concept 'man' the predicates 'ignorant' and 'learned', and thus 'deprived of learning' and 'nonignorant' is a *change* (*Wechsel*) of these predicates, that is, an alteration (*Veränderung*) of the singular substance thought under the concept 'man' (Aristotle's 'secondary substance').

Just as we must distinguish two senses of 'substance', then, we must distinguish two senses of 'accident'. According to the first, all concepts are concepts of accidents, since all are, in judgments, predicates of the term x. Nevertheless, in a second and narrower sense, as we just saw, some concepts, but not all, are concepts of accidents. They are the concepts attributed to x only as synthetic (and changeable, hence contingent) predicates of the concepts "reciprocal with x," which are, for their part, concepts *of substance*. But what, in this view, is the status of predicates that are synthetic but *not* changeable, such as the predicate 'heavy' in the judgment: 'all bodies are heavy'? Such a predicate is neither an accident in the narrow sense just outlined (a synthetic *and changeable* predicate), nor a predicate belonging to the essence of the object thought under the concept 'body'. In fact, it seems to have the status of what Wolff and his followers called an attribute: a predicate that does not belong to the essence of the object (an *essentiale*) but nevertheless can be derived from this essence as a necessary predicate (an *attributum*).[14] The difference between Kant's view and the Wolffian view is of course that for Kant the predicate 'heavy' is not derivable from the mere *concept* of 'body', but is predicated of it only *under the condition of empirical intuition*.[15]

Compare Kant's view with Locke's. For Locke, the idea of substance arises from the constant conjunction of simple ideas, which we presume to hold to-

[13] See Aristotle, *Categories* 5, 2a12–13.

[14] Indeed, in the letter to Reinhold quoted earlier (note 12) Kant describes all predicates a priori derived from essential predicates, whether analytically or synthetically, as 'attributes'. 'Divisible' would thus be an analytic attribute (derived from 'extension') of 'body'. 'Heaviness' would be a synthetic attribute (derived in accordance with a synthetic principle from the essential marks 'impenetrable' and 'limited in space': see *Anfangsgründe*, II, Lehrsatz 5, Anm., Ak. IV, 509.

[15] Something along this line seems to be expressed in this *Reflexion* from the 1770s: "The difference between a logical subject and a real subject is the following. The former contains the logical ground for positing the predicate, but the latter contains the real ground (something else which is positive). . . . Ultimately we find that everything in the object is *accidentia*. The first subject is thus something by means of which are the accidents. Thus arise synthetic judgments, for example, something that I cognize through the persistent accidents of impenetrability also contains the [persistent accidents] of attraction" (*Refl.* 4412 (1771–78), Ak. XVII, 536–37). On Kant's conception of the relation between impenetrability and attractive force in the critical period, see *Anfangsgründe*, II, Lehrsatz 5, Anm., Ak. IV, 509; 57.

gether because they represent (i.e., are jointly caused by) qualities of one persisting thing. But actually we have no idea of what this "something," the subject of inherence, might be:

> So that if anyone will examine himself concerning his notion of pure substance in general, he will find he has no other idea of it at all, but only a supposition of he knows not what *support* of such qualities which are capable of producing simple ideas in us; which qualities are commonly called accidents. If anyone should be asked, what is the subject wherein colour or weight inheres, he would have nothing to say, but the solid extended parts; and if he were demanded, what is it that solidity and extension adhere in, he would not be in a much better case than the Indian before mentioned who, saying that the world was supported by a great elephant, was asked what the elephant rested on; to which his answer was—a great tortoise: but being again pressed to know what gave support to the broad-backed tortoise, replied—*something, he knew not what.* And thus here, as in all other cases where we use words without having clear and distinct ideas, we talk like children: who, being questioned what such a thing is, which they know not, readily give this satisfactory answer, that it is *something*: which in truth signifies no more, when so used, either by children or men, but that they know not what; and that the thing they pretend to know, and talk of, is what they have no distinct idea of at all, and so are perfectly ignorant of it, and in the dark.[16]

But like Theophilus in Leibniz's *New Essays*, Kant would grow impatient with Philalethes' (Locke's) irony. It is pointless to say that all we know are accidents, and that substance remains unknown to us. For the concept of substance has no other meaning than that of being the referent of the term *x* to which all concepts of real determinations are attributed in judgment. Outside this relation to accidents, there is no substance, just as outside their relation to a substance there are no accidents. Accidents just are the manner in which substance exists, and substance just is what the accidents reveal it to be. Locke supposes a regression toward an unknown substratum because he replaces the logical-transcendental notion of substance (an object whose intuition is determined in such a way that it is reflected under a subject-concept in a categorical judgment) with the imaginary notion of a support of accidents. "The sensory concept of support [*Sustentation*] is a misunderstanding. Accidents are only the substance's manner of existing according to what is positive."[17] Similarly, in the First Analogy Kant writes that

> The determinations of a substance, which are nothing but special ways in which it exists, are called *accidents*. They are always real, because they concern the existence of substance. (Negations are only determinations which assert the non-existence of something in substance). If we ascribe a special [kind of] existence to this real in substance . . . this existence is entitled inherence, in distinction from the existence of

[16] Locke, *Essay*, bk. II, chap. xxiii, 2. See also Leibniz, *New Essays*, II, xxiii, 2.

[17] *Refl.* 5861 (1783–84), Ak. XVIII, 371. Kant's opposition to Locke regarding his conception of substance is to be related to what I have called Kant's "Copernican realism" and his assertion that we know 'logical' rather merely nominal essence. See chapter 5, note 42.

substance which is entitled subsistence. But this occasions many misunderstandings; it is more exact and more correct to describe an accident as being simply the way in which the existence of a substance is positively determined. (A186–87/B229–30)

No less hopeless than Locke's position is that of rational metaphysics, according to which an absolute *substantiale* (the monad) can be asserted beyond its sensible accidents, *realitates phaenomena*. For us, there are no other real determinations than sensible ones, and consequently no other real subject than the subject of these sensible determinations: "An absolute subject which would remain once we had abandoned all predicates cannot be thought and is thus impossible, because it is contrary to human nature, for we cognize everything discursively."[18] Nevertheless, by relating the *logical* relation between subject and predicate to the *ontological* relation between substance and accident, Kant takes the side of rational metaphysics and Wolff's heritage against Locke's "imaginary" conception of substance.[19] But he has to reinvent the ground of this correspondence between logic and ontology. How is it possible for "realities" which are given to us only through the arbitrary and contingent interplay of our sensations, to be "determined" in respect of the relation between subject and predicate in judgment?

Once again, the answer to this question lies in *synthesis speciosa*, the affection of inner sense by the understanding, aiming at the discursive forms of judgment. The result of the *synthesis speciosa* is given in the Schematism of the Pure Concepts of Understanding: "The schema of substance is permanence of the real in time." (A144/B183). More precisely, one should say that the schema of the relation between substance and accidents is the temporal relation between a real that is permanent and a real that changes. The correspondence between this schema and the discursive relation of subject and predicate, and thus the complete chain: subject predicate, permanent changing, substance accident, appears quite clearly in a *Reflexion* from the late 1760s, in which Kant first articulates the various aspects of the substance-accident relation as I have analyzed them, then the sensible character by which this relation may be "recognized" (which in the *Critique* he calls its schema):

> The logical relation between substance and accident is synthetic. The subject itself is a predicate (for everything is thought through predicates, except the I), but it is termed 'subject', i.e. something which is no longer a predicate, because 1) no subject is thought for it, 2) it is the presupposition and the substratum of the others. The latter mark can be deduced only from duration, while the rest changes. Durability thus belongs to the essence of a substance. If we allow that substance ceases, then

[18] *Met. Volckmann*, Ak. XXVIII-1, 429–30. In my view, this can be read as an opposition to the rationalists' conception of a *substantiale* beyond the *phaenomena substantiata*, a purely intelligible substance beyond the sensible accidents that appear as self-subsistent, *phaenomena substantiata*. See Baumgarten, *Metaphysica*, chap. 7 (*Substantia et accidens*), §§193, 196, Ak. XVII, 67, and chap. X (*Monas*), §§230–45, Ak. XVII, 78–80; Wolff, *Philosophia prima*, §§789–95.

[19] Wolff's characterization of Locke's conception of substance: see *Philosophia prima*, §157.

this interruption would prove that it is not a substance, and since no substratum of this appearance is thought, the predicates are without a subject; there are neither judgments nor thoughts.[20]

We must now turn to the *synthesis speciosa*, the transcendental synthesis of imagination which exhibits this schema in sensible intuition.

Synthesis Speciosa *and Relation between*
Permanent and Transitory

Attributing permanence to substance is not particularly original: defining substance as the subject or substratum of determinations has always meant characterizing it as what persists through the change of its predicates or accidents. Kant's claim to originality lies rather in the status he gives to permanence. Permanence is a necessary mark of the concept of substance (and thus a mark by which we recognize what should be subsumed under this concept) only because it reflects the *schema* of substance. And what holds of the other transcendental schemata holds also of permanence: permanence is a schema for substance only because this schema was first produced by the *synthesis speciosa* of transcendental imagination, in order to reflect the sensible given under concepts combined according to the logical form of categorical judgment. Consequently, just as Kant inverted the classical relation between substance and logical subject by making the logical form the origin of the ontological determination, similarly he considers the "permanence of the real in time" not as the determination of a thing in itself, but as the determination of things as appearances, resulting from a transcendental synthesis of imagination that generates the ways in which objects of intuition are "determined in respect of the relation between subject and predicate in judgments."

Now according to Kant, only such a shift of perspective makes it possible to give a positive answer to the question metaphysicians took to be resolved before they even asked it: *is there* a permanent "substratum" of transitory determinations?

> I find that in all ages, not only philosophers, but even the common understanding, have recognized this permanence as a *substratum* of all change of appearances, and always assume it to be indubitable. . . . the philosopher expresses himself somewhat more definitely, asserting that throughout all alterations in the world *substance* remains, and that only the *accidents* change. But I nowhere find even the attempt at a proof of this obviously synthetic proposition. . . . Certainly the proposition, that substance is permanent, is tautological. For this permanence is our sole ground for applying the category of substance to appearance; and *we ought first to have proved that in all appearances there is something permanent on which* [an welchem] *the transitory is nothing but determination of its existence.* (A184/B227, my emphasis)

[20] *Refl.* 5297 (1776–78), Ak. XVIII, 146.

Actually, Kant was far from the first to question this last proposition. Already Locke's analysis, mentioned earlier, tended toward a moderate skepticism regarding the meaning of our notion of substance, and the existence of substance as the substratum of accidents. Hume radicalized the skeptical trend in Locke's analysis and considered the idea of substance as a fiction of the imagination supposed to reconcile the plurality of constantly conjoined qualities and their unity (for which a common substratum is presupposed), their variability and the continuity of their changes (which leads to the presupposition of something that remains "the same under all these variations").[21] Although we have no reason to suppose that Kant was familiar with Hume's discussion of substance in the *Treatise Concerning Human Nature*, he might have learned of it indirectly, and he was certainly acquainted with the skeptical conclusions of the *Enquiry Concerning Human Understanding*. In any case, Kant's description of the "permanence of the real in time" as the result of a synthesis of imagination is certainly reminiscent of Hume's argument to the effect that the idea of substance, like that of cause, is a concoction of imagination. Yet Kant reverses Hume's skeptical view in two respects. First, he defines the transcendental synthesis of imagination as an "effect of the understanding on sensibility," and thus defines the relation between substance and accident in appearances not merely as the result of the empirical associations of imagination, but also as the result, first and foremost, of an a priori rule of synthesis guiding these associations in order to reflect them under concepts according to the logical form of categorical judgment. Second, Kant argues that the presupposition of a permanent substratum of transitory determinations is itself not a result (whether fictitious or not), but a *condition* for perceiving the objective change as well as the objective simultaneity of sensible qualities—that is, a condition for precisely those temporal relations whose reality no skeptic has put into doubt.

Kant's reasoning concerning the role of the category of substance in our perception of objective temporal relations is most explicit in the second paragraph of the First Analogy in A.[22] The paragraph opens with a reminder of the ever suc-

---

[21] Cf. Hume, *Treatise*, bk. I, pt. IV, sec. 3, 220.

[22] The general structure of Kant's argument in the First Analogy is, I think, the following: (1) All appearances are in time, as the unified intuition in which their temporal relations (simultaneity and succession) are perceived. (2) Time itself is not perceived. All we perceive is the subjective succession of our perceptions in apprehension. (3) Objective temporal relations are perceivable only if changing appearances are related to a permanent substrate, which is the substrate of appearances themselves. (4) Therefore, all changing appearances are related, as accidents, to permanent substances. Premise (1) is stated in the first paragraph in A (A182, given in footnote in Kemp Smith's translation as well as in the Meiner edition) and in the first two sentences (the first three in Kemp Smith's translation) in the proof added in B. Premise (2) is the third (in Kemp Smith, fourth) sentence of the proof added in B, and was oddly placed in A (A183, toward the end of the second paragraph), although we can find an explanation of the point already in the first and second sentences of this same paragraph. Premise (3) is developed in the bulk of the second paragraph in A (from the second half of the second sentence—*"wo an ihr nicht etwas zum Grunde liegt . . . ,"* which becomes the third sentence in Kemp Smith: "For such determination we require an underlying ground"—to its second to last sentence). It is stated in the fourth and fifth (fifth and sixth for Kemp Smith) sentences in the B proof. Premise (4) is the last sentence of the second paragraph in A, and the last two sentences of the

cessive character of our apprehension, which makes impossible any direct perception of objective simultaneity or succession. By thus breaking the deceptive familiarity of temporal relations, Kant delineates the place of the *synthesis speciosa* according to the category of substance. Only in relation to an object supposed to be permanent can the subjective succession of our perceptions be interpreted in such a way as to distinguish between simultaneous and successive determinations in things:

> Our *apprehension* of the manifold of appearance is always successive, and is therefore always changing. Through it alone we can never determine whether this manifold, as object of experience, is simultaneous or successive. For such determination we require an underlying ground which exists *at all times* [*jederzeit*], that is, something *abiding* and *permanent*, of which all change and simultaneity are only so many ways (modes of time) in which the permanent exists. (A182/B225–26)

We believe that we perceive the succession or simultaneity of the states of things. Actually, all we perceive (apprehend) is the succession of our representations, whereas the simultaneity and succession in states of things are not directly perceived. Rather, the representation we have of objective simultaneity and succession is the result of the way we interpret the succession of perceptions in our apprehension. Now this interpretation, together with the resulting distinction between simultaneous and successive, is possible only if we relate the representations we apprehend successively to a permanent substratum. In this regard, the First Analogy is only the first step of a continuous argument that Kant pursues in the Second and Third Analogies, where he respectively accounts for the representations of objective succession and simultaneity. Thus the First Analogy remains extremely obscure if considered in isolation from the Second and Third. We shall be able to grasp how, according to Kant, the relation to a permanent substratum conditions any distinction between successive and simultaneous phenomenal determinations

---

proof added in B. There is no question that the proof is more clearly structured in B than in A, but I do not think there is any significant discrepancy between the two editions. The complete proof is given in the first two paragraphs in A, and repeated in the initial proof added in B. The rest of the text of the First Analogy develops particular aspects or consequences of the proof, but does not offer new proofs or new arguments for the initial proof. On this I differ from Guyer, who thinks that Kant gives three different proofs for the First Analogy (cf. notes 24, 27). I agree with Allison and Guyer that Kant's argument is not an argument on the conditions of time *measurement*, but on the conditions of time *determination* (see Allison, *Idealism*, 199–200; Guyer, *Claims*, 218). The opposite view was defended by Melnick, *Analogies*, 58–71. I discuss it in the section "Confrontation". I also agree with Allison and Guyer in thinking that it is unfair to accuse Kant, as Bennett does (*Analytic*, 200) of switching subreptitiously and uncritically from the notion of substance as bearer of properties to the notion of substance as sempiternal (see Allison, 212–15; Guyer, 220). Kant moves from unity of time, to permanent substrate for this unity, to substance as substrate of appearances by an explicit argument. Finally, my approach differs from all others in the importance I grant to the metaphysical deduction of the categories (i.e., categories as originally forms of *synthesis intellectualis*), and to schematism considered as the result of *synthesis speciosa*, "affection of inner sense by understanding." In other words, I give unprecedented importance, in Kant's argument, to the idea that we generate our own representations of objective temporal determinations by discursive + imaginative acts of the mind, relating all representations to the objective unity of apperception.

only when he also explains how these temporal relations are themselves products of figurative syntheses according to the relations of causality and community. Yet we have no choice but to consider the *synthesis speciosa* according to the relation between substance and accident before explaining the other two forms of figurative synthesis.

A comparison of Kant's reasoning with Descartes's analysis of our perception of a piece of wax in the Second Meditation might prove helpful here. Descartes argues that the piece of wax, which we think we cognize through our sensations of it, is actually distinctly cognized only if it is "perceived by the mind alone," through which we perceive "the wax itself" (*ceram ipsammet*) beyond the variability of its sensory qualities and in the infinite variety of its possible configurations. The idea of substance, which allows us to judge that "the same wax" (*eadem cera*) remains throughout all the alterations it undergoes when heated, is itself a purely intellectual idea, thus accessible to the mind alone. Now, the example of the piece of wax could also be used to illustrate Kant's argument, but it would be analyzed differently. Kant would first observe that in the synthesis of our apprehension, the perceptions are always successive. From this point of view, there is no difference between the apprehension of an object that remains unaltered but whose parts we successively run through, like the apprehension of a house in the Second Analogy,[23] and the apprehension of an altering object like the wax exposed to the heat of the fire. In *both* cases we have a *succession* of qualitatively different *perceptions*.

Only by relating these successive perceptions to a supposedly permanent object do we distinguish the case in which the succession is merely subjective (as in the case of the house, in which the determinations successively apprehended are objectively simultaneous, and the succession is only that of the subjective act of quantitative synthesis of a figure in space) from the case in which the succession is objective (the alteration of the piece of wax). In the latter case, we perceive that a state (*a*), which was not, came about, and that a state (*b*), which was, is no longer. But no negation is directly perceived, only the sequence of real determinations. This sequence is represented as change, as a determination *which was not* replacing a determination which preceded it and *is no longer*, only because we relate these determinations to the same thing, about which we assert or deny a real determination, and thereby acknowledge that a real determination which *is* now *was not* a moment before. Consequently, just as the imagination reproduces and preserves the apprehended determinations and represents them as simultaneous only if it relates them to the same supposedly permanent object, similarly, it presents a multiplicity of *real determinations* ("that which corresponds to sensation") as an alteration in the object only if it relates them to one and the same permanent. The representation of this relation to a permanent is generated by the search for an order in the succession of sensible perceptions, a search tending toward discursive judgment relating representations to objects. Without such combination of our representations oriented toward judgment, and hence without the

---

[23] Cf. A190–91/B235–36.

presupposition of their relation to a permanent, there would be neither perception of change, nor perception of the simultaneity of determinations in the object. Instead, our mind would be occupied with a multiplicity of perceptions, on which it might perform a great variety of associative combinations; but no objective temporal order would ever appear to us.

We presuppose a permanent (empirical) object even when the real determinations under the concept of which we cognize it disappear completely. Suppose we throw the wax into the fire, or suppose a candle is completely consumed, we will not assume that the wax has simply disappeared, but that it was transformed, regardless of how rudimentary or mistaken our understanding of this transformation might be (evaporation, transformation into hot air or smoke, emanation of phlogiston, etc.). This is the true source, according to Kant, of the general belief that the outright annihilation of matter (or, similarly, its creation out of nothing) could be achieved only by a miracle: such creation out of nothing or return to nothing is taken to be incompatible with any "natural" process only because it would contradict the conditions of the constitution of our experience, that is, the conditions for unified and determinate temporal relations between appearances (simultaneity or succession: existence at the same time, or existence at different times). If we did not suppose that the identical thing that is in a given place, in a given shape, at time t_1, is necessarily in some place (whether the same or another) in some shape (whether the same or another), at time t_2, we would be unable to grant any temporal unity to our experience, because we would be unable to represent the subjective succession of our perceptions in such a way as to distinguish what is "really" simultaneous (although we perceive it only successively, because our sole access to the real in space is through an act of successive synthesis), from what is "really" successive (i.e., what is a change in states of what is permanent). Thus Kant does not simply argue for the necessity of supposing the relative permanence of some persisting objects that serve as substrate for change, but for the necessity of supposing the absolute permanence of some ultimate substrate for all change. Only under the presupposition of such an absolute permanent can we generate for ourselves a unified representation of time—that is, suppose the unity of the complete web of temporal relations (succession and simultaneity) between appearances.[24] The presupposition of something permanent as the condition of

[24] Guyer offers an interesting analysis of Kant's argument for this point: *Claims*, 230. However, he interprets Kant's argument as an epistemic argument concerning the verifiability of empirical statements of objective time-determinations: "[Kant's] argument . . . implies that there is nothing which can count as empirical evidence for the cessation of the existence of *any* substance" (*Claims*, 231). I think there is a more fundamental level to Kant's claim: we would not even *perceive* a change *as* an objective change unless we were able to judge it to be the change of states of a substance. That we can also *empirically verify* a change (namely, test and confirm or disconfirm our judgments about objective change) only in relation to permanent substance, is a further claim that depends on the first (like the conditions for forming judgments of experience depend on the conditions for forming experience in the more elementary sense of the term: "synthesis of perceptions, related to objects"). In other words, Kant's argument for the conditions of our representing objective change is prior, in my view, to any *epistemic* argument for the empirical verifiability of our belief that this or that objective change has occurred. Guyer recognizes the former dimension in Kant's argument, but takes it to be an independent argument, which is invalid because it rests, according to him, on a conception of the "rep-

every experience of objective simultaneity and succession finds expression in the "two propositions of the ancients," namely "*Gigni de nihilo nihil, in nihilum nil posse reverti*" (Nothing is generated from nothing, nothing returns to nothing). These propositions can have only a transcendental proof, for they do not express the nature of the things considered in themselves, but the a priori conditions of our experience of temporal relations between appearances:

> *Gigni de nihilo nihil, in nihilum nil posse reverti*, were two propositions which the ancients always connected together, but which are now sometimes mistakenly separated owing to the belief that they apply to things in themselves, and that the first would run counter to the dependence of the world—even in respect of its substance—upon a supreme cause. But such apprehension is unnecessary. For we have here to deal only with appearances in the field of experience; and the unity of experience would never be possible if we were willing to allow that new things, that is, new *substances*, could come into existence. For we should then lose that which alone can represent the unity of time, namely, the identity of the substratum, wherein alone all change has thoroughgoing unity. This permanence is, however, simply the mode in which we represent to ourselves the existence of things in the appearance. (A186/B229)

If the permanent is nothing other than the condition of the representation of relations of simultaneity and succession between appearances, we cognize the permanent only through these relations between transitory determinations. Conversely, we cognize the transitory (with its relations of simultaneity and succession) only as a determination of the permanent. Kant's conclusion, which he will fully explain in the Second Analogy, is that every *change* (*Wechsel*) of phenomenal determinations, regardless of what it is (alteration of wax, "disappearance" of wax, freezing of water, evaporation of water, movement of a body, rotation of the earth, trajectory of planets, etc.) is nothing other than the *alteration* (*Veränderung*) of the substance(s), which on their part are absolutely permanent:

> On this permanence rests also the correct understanding [*Berichtigung*] of the concept of *alteration* [*Veränderung*]. Coming to be and ceasing to be [*Entstehen und Vergehen*] are not alterations of that which comes to be or ceases to be. Alteration is a way of existing which follows upon another way of existing of the same object. All that alters *persists*, and only its *state changes*. Since this change thus concerns only the determinations, which can cease to be or begin to be, we can say, using what may seem a somewhat paradoxical expression, that only the permanent (substance) is altered, and that the transitory [*das Wandelbare*] suffers no alteration but only a *change* [*Wechsel*], inasmuch as certain determinations cease to be and others begin to be. (A187/B230–31, translation modified)

---

resentation" of permanence both unsustainable and in fact elsewhere rejected by Kant himself (according to this conception, the permanence of time, which is unperceivable, is supposed to be "represented" by the permanence of substance) (*Claims*, 216–21). But I think Guyer's reading rests on a misunderstanding. Substance does not "represent" the permanence of time as a kind of substitute for it. What Kant argues is that our discursive acts of recognition, or better, our efforts toward recognition (*conatus* of the *Vermögen zu urteilen*) lead us to generate for ourselves the distinction between permanent and changing that we ultimately reflect under the categories of substance and accident.

The assertion that (permanent) substance alone alters, while what is transitory only appears and disappears, is not original with Kant. It may be read as a direct reference to Wolff, who stated in his *Philosophia prima sive Ontologia* that substance alone is *modifiable* (*modificabilis*), while accidents are *mutable* (*mutabilia*).[25] Kant's attempt at a "correct understanding" of the concept of alteration is thus the continuation of his effort to provide a rigorous elucidation of what rational metaphysics affirmed without adequate proof, that is, without an accurate elucidation of the status of its ontological statements.

Kant's elucidation of the concept of alteration is significant in two ways. First, it points back toward the logical elucidation of the relation between substance and accident discussed in the previous section: we saw that Kant called *Wechsel*, change, the synthetic attribution of opposite marks to the same subject. From the logical relation we have now moved to the sensible exhibition of this relation. When we perceive a change in phenomenal determinations, we presuppose a permanent object of which we successively state the affirmation and then the negation, or the negation and then the affirmation, of determinate properties.[26]

Second, the idea that every change (*Wechsel*) is perceived only as an alteration (*Veränderung*) of a permanent substance opens the way to the Second Analogy, in which Kant argues that this presupposition is inseparable from the recognition of the *regularities* in the successions of determinations in appearances, because it is inseparable from the presupposition of, and hence the search for, these regularities.[27] To assert successively opposite predicates of the same object presupposes that experience has given us occasion to generate and reflect sufficiently regular occurrences of such successions for them to be compatible with the concept we formed of the object. By virtue of such regularities, we can recognize the same object (e.g., "the wax itself") under the many different aspects it may have. For example, if we look away from the wax for a moment, then turn back toward it, we are able to recognize that the object 'wax' has not been replaced by another object, but instead has remained *the same*, while only its determinations have changed. On the contrary, if we find a rabbit where the moment before we had left a hat, we do not assume that there was a gradual transformation of the hat into a rabbit, but only that both changed places so that the rabbit came to the place occupied by the hat a moment before, without either of them being otherwise qualitatively altered. This capacity to represent the succession of our perceptions in

---

[25] Wolff, *Philosophia prima*, §§768, 779.

[26] See above, pp. 328–29, and note 9.

[27] In B, Kant makes this connection between the First Analogy and Second Analogy explicit by beginning the proof of the latter with a reminder that every change has been shown in the former to be the alteration of a substance (B232–33). I shall argue later that, already in A, this equation of 'change' and 'alteration of a substance' is an essential element in Kant's proof for the Second Analogy. I disagree with Guyer when he sees Kant's explanation of the concept of alteration as an independent (and invalid) argument for the First Analogy (see *Claims*, 221). Kant makes quite clear that his explanation on this point *results* from the previously developed argument for the permanence of substance: "(On this permanence [i.e. the permanence of substance. for which Kant has just provided an argument] rests also the correct understanding of the concept of *alteration* [*Auf dieser Beharrlichkeit gründet sich nun auch die Berichtigung des Begriffs von Veränderung*]" (A187/B230).

one way or the other presupposes the recognition of—that is, first of all, the *presupposition and the search for*—regularities in the possible changes of sensible determinations. These regularities are based on the anticipation of two possible kinds of marks to be attributed to supposedly permanent objects: on the one hand, marks proper to these objects, the "permanent accidents" discussed in the previous section, which constitute the "reciprocal concept" of the x of judgment; and on the other hand, "synthetic changing marks," which on their part are dependent on determinate conditions *external to* the subject of the determinations. This is where the Second Analogy connects up with the First, as the presupposition of *conditions external to* the subject of the alteration (Second Analogy) hooks up to the definition of every change as the alteration of a substance (First Analogy). All determinations of objective temporal relations rest on this fundamental distinction between permanent marks and marks subject to change under determinate conditions that are external to the altering subject, or substance.

Further examination of temporal relations must be postponed until we turn to the Second and Third Analogies. At this point we have at least some idea of the relation Kant seeks to establish between the permanence of substance and the unity of time. Like space, time is nothing but relations, and the unity of time is the unity of the relations of succession and simultaneity between appearances. But every perception of objective succession, just like every perception of objective simultaneity, depends on the presupposition of the relation of phenomenal determinations to a permanent substratum, which is "altered" only in determinate conditions, according to rules. Thus the unity of time (unified temporal relations between all appearances) presupposes the permanence of substance. This does not mean that time itself is substance or the representation of substance, but rather that the unified fabric of temporal relations between appearances rests on the presupposition of a permanent substratum of transitory determinations. This explains Kant's *prima facie* surprising assertion, in the Schematism chapter, that time "does not pass away," but rather "the existence of [appearances] passes away in time"; or again his description, in the proof of the First Analogy, of time as a "substratum (as permanent form of inner intuition)." Time is permanent insofar as it is the sensible form *of the permanent substance*, or *substances* (in the plural, as will be shown in the Third Analogy) presupposed for any temporal relation between appearances.

> The schema of substance is permanence of the real in time, that is, the representation of the real as a substrate of empirical determination of time in general, and so as abiding while all else changes. (The existence of what is transitory passes away in time but not time itself. To time, itself non-transitory and abiding, there corresponds in the appearance what is non-transitory in its existence, that is, substance. Only in substance can the succession and simultaneity of appearances be determined in time.) (A144/B183)

> All appearances are in time; and in it alone, as substratum (as permanent form of inner intuition), can either *simultaneity* or *succession* be represented. (B224–25)

From Time in the Transcendental Aesthetic to Time in the
Analogies of Experience

By asserting that the unity of time depends on the schematism of substance, Kant sends us back once again, in effect, to his discussion of the a priori intuition of time in the Transcendental Aesthetic. And the conclusion we reached in chapter 8 ("*Synthesis Speciosa* and Forms of Sensibility") is thus once more confirmed: the form of temporal intuition expounded in the Transcendental Aesthetic results from the *synthesis speciosa* of transcendental imagination, and is thus a priori in accordance not only with the forms of mathematical synthesis, but also with the forms of dynamical synthesis, leading to the logicotranscendental forms of relation in judgment. Indeed, there is a striking similarity between the text quoted earlier from the B Proof of the First Analogy—"All appearances are in time; and in it alone, as substratum (as permanent form of inner intuition), can either *simultaneity* or *succession* be represented"—and the Metaphysical Exposition of the Concept of Time in the Transcendental Aesthetic: "For neither simultaneity nor succession would ever come within our perception if the representation of time were not presupposed as underlying them *a priori*. Only on the presupposition of time can we represent to ourselves a number of things as existing at one and the same time (simultaneously) or at different times (successively)" (A30/B46).

Let me recapitulate the various aspects of time we have encountered, from the Transcendental Aesthetic to the First Analogy of Experience. According to the Transcendental Aesthetic, the form of intuition, or pure intuition of time, is the condition of the representations of simultaneity and succession in appearances. In the B Deduction, Kant argues that this pure intuition is itself the result of a figurative synthesis or "affection of inner sense by the understanding," which results in a "formal intuition" prior to any concept. According to the Axioms of Intuition and Anticipations of Perception, space and time as "infinite given magnitudes" are the original unity "by limitation of which" all schematism of quantity (extensive magnitude and intensive magnitude) is generated. We may now add that this formal intuition of time as "infinite given magnitude" is also the precondition for the representation of objective simultaneity and succession among appearances, both of which presuppose that the realities apprehended are related to a permanent, or, better, are "nothing but special ways in which the permanent exists," or "ways in which its existence is positively determined."[28]

The continuity in Kant's exposition of time, from the Transcendental Aesthetic, to the Axioms and Anticipations, to the First Analogy, is confirmed by the fact that in all cases time is defined as a *magnitude*. According to the Transcendental Aesthetic, time is (like space) an *infinite given magnitude* of which any determinate magnitude of time (any duration) is a limitation: "The infinitude of time sig-

[28] Cf. A186–87/B229–30.

342 • *C H A P T E R 1 1* •

nifies nothing more than that every determinate magnitude of time is possible
only through limitations [*Einschränkungen*] of one single time that underlies it"
(A32/B47–48). Now, according to Kant's recapitulation of the three Analogies of
Experience, the First Analogy deals specifically with *the relation of appearances
to time as magnitude*: the three analogies of experience "are simply principles of
the determination of the existence of appearances in time, according to all its
three modes, *viz. the relation to time itself as a magnitude* [my emphasis] (the
magnitude of existence, that is, *duration*), the relation to time as a *successive* series, and finally the relation in time as a sum of all *simultaneous* existence"
(A215/B262).

Of course, one must be careful to heed the necessary distinctions here. The
Analogies of Experience are concerned with the *existence* of appearances, the
Transcendental Aesthetic with the *mere form* of their sensible intuition. Only the
latter is an "infinite given magnitude." Like space, time is an infinite magnitude,
a *quantum infinitum*, only insofar as it is a *pure* intuition—as such, a "pure
image" of every temporal *quantum*, and the condition of any quantitative synthesis of time (any quantitative determination of a duration).[29] But time in the Analogies of Experience is a form inseparable from a *matter*. In *empirical* objects there
is no more "infinite given time" than there is "infinite given space." Instead, experience allows only for an indefinite approximation, through successive empirical syntheses, of a whole of physically determined space and time which in relation to empirically given space and time are only regulative ideas.[30] Nevertheless,
following the explanation of the schema of substance and the proof of the First
Analogy, if the representations of simultaneity and succession presuppose the
representation of a permanent real as the substratum of time, then the *form of intuition* expounded in the Transcendental Aesthetic is the (sensible) *determination*
for a *determinable*, or *matter*, which is the real thus represented as permanent.
When this form (whether time or space) is represented in and for itself, it is an
"infinite given magnitude"—a magnitude such that in relation to it any successively synthesized temporal (or spatial) magnitude is *smaller* than it, and any successive synthesis can be pursued *indefinitely*.

Confrontation

Some interpreters of the First Analogy have supposed that Kant's argument concerns the constitution of a frame of reference for situating appearances in time
and measuring their duration. Such intepretations neglect the opening premise of

[29] On space and time as *quanta infinita* and as "pure images of all magnitude," see chapter 9. On
form of intuition, pure intuition, formal intuition, see chapter 8, "Rereading the Transcendental Aesthetic."

[30] This will of course be the core of Kant's solution to the Antinomy of Pure Reason, in the Transcendental Dialectic: see A497/B525, "Critical Solution of the Cosmological Conflict of Reason With
Itself": the synthesis of the manifold "in" space and "in" time can be indefinitely pursued, and thus
the idea of a world-whole is a merely regulative idea of reason. On the representation of absolute
space as *itself* an idea of reason, which relative (empirical) spatial frames of reference indefinitely ap-
proximate, see also *Anfangsgründe*, chap I, Ak. IV, 482; 20.

Kant's argument at A182 ("Our apprehension . . . is always successive") and take for granted precisely what, according to Kant, is in need of explanation: the very possibility that appearances should present themselves to us in relations of simultaneity and succession. Their concern then is not how we generate for ourselves the representation of these relations, but how we are able to assign a place to appearances in a temporal frame of reference. Such interpretations may rely above all on the proof Kant added at the beginning of the First Analogy in the B edition. In this short proof, the premise stated in A ("Our apprehension is always successive . . .") is not explicitly repeated (although it does remain at the head of the second paragraph, unchanged from A to B), and the argument appears more directly concerned with *objective* time relations.[31] There seems to be no sign of the reasoning I analyzed, which progresses from the successive character of representations in apprehension to the distinction between succession and simultaneity in things.

In *Kant's Analogies of Experience*, Arthur Melnick presents a careful analysis of Kant's argument construed along these lines. Its progression is presented as the following. Simultaneity and succession are in time; but time itself is not perceived; call "*substratum*" of the representation of time some feature of appearances that allows us to determine temporal relations: for instance, the relative motion of the sun and the earth, or—to take a contemporary example—the degradation of a radioactive element. These features of appearances can be described as substrata of the representation of time because we can situate any event in time by its relation of simultaneity to a particular position of the sun or to a state of radioactive degradation. According to Melnick, Kant's goal is to show that only *substances* can provide such *substrata of time determination*.[32] They can do so because they are both *permanent* and *centers of action*. Here Kant's argument in the First Analogy anticipates, says Melnick, the Second Analogy and its claim that "the empirical criterion of substance is action."[33] We determine the magnitude of time intervals in terms of certain *actions* of a substance or substances—the most common example being the mechanism of a clock. It is precisely because action is the action of *something that persists through time* that it

---

[31] On the steps of the proof in B, see note 22. As I indicated there, I see no essential difference between the structure of the argument in A and in B.

[32] Melnick, *Analogies*, 61–62, esp. 62: "A substance is not defined as that which can serve as a substratum for the determination of time magnitude. Rather, it is defined in terms of permanence. . . . That substances are what can serve as substrata of time-determination is a synthetic claim. If we can show that only substances (the permanent in appearance) can serve as substrata, we will have shown that substances are required for the determination of the time magnitude (and thus that the application of the category of substance is required for any time determination)." Cf. *KrV*, A183/B226: "The permanent is the *substratum* of the empirical representation of time itself."

[33] Ibid., 63: "Kant says, in an important passage at the end of the First Analogy, 'We shall have occasion in what follows to make such observations as may seem necessary in regard to the empirical criterion of this necessary permanence—the criterion, consequently, of the substantiality of appearances' (A189/B232). This criterion of substantiality or permanence turns out to be action. 'But I must not leave unconsidered the empirical criterion of a substance insofar as substance appears to manifest itself not through permanence of appearance, but more adequately and easily through action' (A204/B249)."

can be used to determine the magnitude of a time interval. If the existence of the clock were interrupted, it could not be used as a measure for time determination. However, Melnick concludes, this analysis shows that the permanence of substance is necessary only for as long as it provides the substratum for time determination. But different substances can, as it were, take over from one another in fulfilling this role. Hence determining temporal relations depends on the presupposition of *relatively*, not *absolutely*, permanent substances. Nor can one conclude from this argument, as Kant does, that all *change* (*Wechsel*) is the *alteration* (*Veränderung*) of permanent substance(s):

> If I determine the magnitude of the time interval between *a* and *b* in terms, say, of the motion of the earth in its orbit about the sun, it does not follow that *a* and *b* are determinations (accidents) of the earth or the sun or, for that matter, of any substance at all that persists through the time interval of succession. From the fact that "the permanent in appearances is therefore the substratum of all determination of time" (A188/B231), it does not follow that "All existence and all change have thus to be viewed simply as a mode of the existence of that which remains." (A184/B227)[34]

Melnick's objections would be correct if Kant's argument were the one he attributes to him. But I do not think it is. Kant's problem is not how we situate appearances in time, but how we generate our representation of a unified time in the first place. In order for the sun in the sky, or the hands on the face of the clock, to provide a frame of reference for situating events in time or measuring duration, they must first themselves be represented as *successive*, and the event whose temporal position is thus determined must be represented as *simultaneous* with them. To explain the temporal determination of events by their relation to the successive states of a permanent object is to presuppose what is to be explained: how do we first perceive *this succession itself*, and how do we perceive anything as *simultaneous* with one of these successive states? Kant's thesis in the First Analogy is that these perceptions are possible only if we presuppose a permanent object (or more precisely, permanent objects, in the plural, as will become apparent in the Third Analogy), and this is what allows us to assert as a universal principle of experience that "in all appearances the substance persists" or that "All appearances contain the permanent (substance) as the object itself, and the transitory as its mere determination, that is, as a way in which the object exists." This, of course, does not allow us to assert of any particular empirical object (sun, wax, etc.) that it is absolutely permanent, even though some are "more permanent" than others and may thus be reflected under concepts thought to be "reciprocal with" permanent substances. Kant's point is simply that we discern objective relations of simultaneity and succession only if we relate the subjective succession of our perceptions to objective changes occurring according to rules, and thus cognizable as alterations of absolutely permanent substances, occurring according to rules (whereby the First Analogy opens the way to the Second and Third). This pre-

[34] Ibid., 70. This criticism is shared by many interpreters of the First Analogy, whatever their differences may be on other accounts. See for instance Kemp Smith, *Commentary*, 360; Strawson, *Bounds of Sense*, 130; Hoppe, *Synthesis*, 233–34.

supposition is at work, according to Kant, at the most elementary, original level of our temporal experience, and on this original experience depend the more sophisticated aspects of our ability to determine the temporal relations of appearances (constituting temporal frames of reference, calculating duration, elaborating a mathematical science of motion . . .).

Of course, by insisting as I have on the importance, in Kant's argument, of the acts by means of which we constitute our representation of time, I did not account for all the aspects of the First Analogy. It could be objected, in particular, that not only in the B edition, but also already in A, the tone is more "objectivist" than my interpretation would lead one to believe. It is *in things themselves* (albeit as appearances) that Kant affirms the presence of a permanent as "substrate" of the representation of time. However, my point is that we can understand the meaning and coherence of the principles, as well as the proof Kant attempts to give for them, only if we read them against the background of the metaphysical and transcendental deduction of the categories and if we acknowledge in the objects themselves the results of the acts of synthesis that make them, according to the *Critique*, objects *for us*.[35]

GROUND AND CONSEQUENCE, CAUSE AND EFFECT, ANTERIOR AND POSTERIOR

Our analysis of the First Analogy already pointed us in the direction of the Second. The unity of the two might be outlined as follows: in the First Analogy, Kant argues that we perceive objective change in appearances only as alterations of a

---

[35] I should add that in my view, the "objective" tone of the First Analogy rests sometimes on a confusion between the task of the Critique and that of the metaphysics of nature (as understood by Kant). This is the case, it seems to me, when Kant refers to the *quantitative* conservation of substance in the formulation and proof of the first Analogy in B (B224). This reference is absent from the principle and its proof in A, although we may find an allusion to it in the question, "how much does smoke weigh?" (cf. A185/B228). Actually, the question only expresses a common assumption, which a critical examination might reveal to be essentially illusory (in case it should be shown that conservation *cannot* and *need not* be quantitative, as Kant claims in the case of the soul). In spite of Allison's defense of the contrary thesis (*Idealism*, 210–12), my view is that the statement of a *quantitative* conservation principle cannot be made in the Analytic of Principles, because it presupposes an explanation of the quantity of material substance that Kant does not give in the *Critique* but in the *Metaphysical Foundations*, and to which he then applies the principle of permanence established in the *Critique* (Ak. IV, 537–41; 96–101). In the same place he goes on to argue that quantitative conservation holds for *corporeal* substance, defined as *Menge des Beweglichen* (literally, the multiplicity of what is movable), but could not be proved in the case of spiritual substance. To be sure, the Analogies themselves concern only corporeal substance, since experience of the permanent (as will appear clearly from the overall argument of all three Analogies and is confirmed in the Refutation of Idealism) is proved only with respect to temporal relations of objects in space. Nevertheless, defining corporeal substance as *Menge des Beweglichen* and showing that, as such, it is quantitatively determinable by the "degree of its force" depend on the *empirical* concept of body expounded in the Mechanics (part III of the *Metaphysical Foundations*). So, although Kant would have a right to claim that his proof of the quantitative conservation of material substance in the *Metaphysical Foundations* is an application of the first Analogy, it is nevertheless a *metaphysical* application, which presupposes

permanent substance. In the Second Analogy, he argues that this principle is inseparable from another: every change (as the alteration of a permanent substance) occurs in conformity with a rule. Thus Kant argues that the principle of causality—"Everything that happens, that is, begins to be, presupposes something upon which it follows according to a rule" (A189)—governs our very perception of objective change.

I will once again start my analysis of Kant's argument by examining the relation between logical form of judgment and category—in the present case, the logical form of hypothetical judgment and the causal relation. Then I shall analyze Kant's argument in the Second Analogy, and the role he assigns to synthesis of imagination in our representation of temporal succession. This new detour through Kant's analysis of judgment has a drawback: it breaks the continuity of Kant's account of temporal relations in the Analogies of Experience. But this drawback will be compensated, I hope, by the insight we thereby gain into the convoluted argument structure of Kant's Second Analogy.

Logical Form of Hypothetical Judgment and Relation of Cause to Effect

In *Metaphysik Volckmann* (Kant's Lectures on Metaphysics of 1784), hypothetical judgment and cause/effect are related in the following terms:

> According to relation, [judgments] are:
>
>   1) categorical: all humans are mortal. In which one asserts a predicate of a subject. Substance, accident;
>
>   2) hypothetical: if a being is an animal, it is mortal. Which indicates [*anzeigt*] the relation of ground [*Grund*] to consequence [*Folge*]. Antecedens, consequens, causa or causatum.
>
>   3) disjunctive: a triangle is either right-angled or not right-angled [. . .].[36]

Kant mentions the relation of ground and consequence before that of cause and effect, and relates both to the logical form of hypothetical judgment. This form, he says, "indicates the relation of ground to consequence" (*das Verhältnis des Grundes zur Folge anzeigt*). A ground is what we reflect under concepts in the antecedent, a consequence what we reflect under concepts in the consequent of a hypothetical proposition. Or more precisely, the *relation* of ground to consequence (*ratio/rationatum, Grund/Folge*) has no other meaning than that generated by the act of the understanding in a hypothetical judgment.

With this explanation, Kant's opposition to Wolff and Baumgarten on the notion of ground or reason, and on the so-called principle of sufficient reason (*Satz*

---

an *empirical* concept of matter, to which the *Critique* has shown we may legitimately apply a strong principle of conservation: *if* it is possible to reduce *all* material substances to one concept which makes it homogeneous and thus quantifiable, then the principle of conservation enunciated in the First Analogy becomes a principle of conservation of a (homogeneous) quantity.

[36] *Met. Volckmann* (1783–84), Ak. XXVIII-1, 397. I shall translate the German *Grund*, which corresponds to the Latin *ratio*, sometimes by 'ground', sometimes by 'reason'. In the latter case, I shall sometimes add 'ground' in parenthesis, to avoid confusion with the *faculty* of reason, *Vernunft*.

des zureichenden Grundes, principium rationis sufficientis), attains its final form. But it is noteworthy that, through its successive variations and corrections, Kant's view is always expounded in the context of an analysis of judgment (proposition). Thus at the time of its greatest proximity with rationalist metaphysics (in the 1755 *New Elucidation*), his position is nevertheless distinctive because of the privilege he grants to the analysis of *proposition* over that of *ens, being*. Similarly, at the time of his greater proximity to the anti-Wolffian inspiration of Crusius (early 1760s), Kant confines his questioning of what he then calls "real ground" within the context of an analysis of judgment. Because of this continuity of analytical framework, even writings that are remote from Kant's mature position are helpful in understanding how he ultimately arrived at his critical definitions of reason (ground) and cause, and why he structured the argument of the Second Analogy as he did.

In what follows, I first analyze Kant's discussion of "reason" and the "principle of reason" in the precritical writings. I show how his analysis of reason (ground) as reason of the truth of propositions influenced his formulation of the problem of "real ground" and thus his confrontation with "Hume's problem." I then use the results thus obtained, together with Kant's explanation of *synthesis speciosa* as "affection of inner sense by understanding" (B Transcendental Deduction, section 24), to embark on the analysis of Kant's argument in the Second Analogy.

THE NOTION OF REASON (GROUND) IN THE PRECRITICAL WRITINGS, AND KANT'S DEBATE WITH RATIONAL METAPHYSICS

In his *Metaphysica*, Baumgarten gives the following definition of reason or ground (*ratio*): "A reason is that from which it is possible to know *why* something is."[37] Baumgarten then proceeds to demonstrate the principle of reason (*principium rationis*), which he formulates thus: "Nothing is without a reason, or if something is posited, something is posited as its reason."[38] His "proof" is as follows: if an *ens*, or a *possibile*, was without a reason, then its reason would be *nothing*, that is, (following the definition of 'reason'), one could know, from *nothing*, why something is. *Nothing* would then itself be representable, i.e. it would be *some thing*, which is contradictory.[39]

---

[37] Baumgarten, *Metaphysica*, §14, Ak. XVII, 27: "*Ratio est id, ex quo cognoscibile est, cur aliquid sit.*" This definition is inspired by §56 of Wolff's *Philosophia prima*: "By sufficient reason, I mean that from which one understands why something is (*Per rationem sufficientem intelligimus id, unde intelligitur, cur aliquid sit*)."

[38] *Metaphysics*, §20, Ak. XVII, 31: "*nihil est sine ratione, seu, posito aliquo, ponitur aliquid ejus ratio.*" Compare with Leibniz: "nothing happens without a reason why it should be so, rather than otherwise" (*G* VII, 356; *Leibniz-Clarke Correspondence*, second paper, 16).

[39] This "proof" is circular: Baumgarten shows that the hypothesis (denying that everything has a reason) leads to an absurd conclusion ('nothing' is 'something'), only because (i) contrary to the hypothesis, he assumes that there has to be a reason, so that saying that some X has no reason is saying that *nothing is, positively, its reason*, and (ii) instead of interpreting the hypothesis (that X has no reason) as meaning that the extension of the concept 'reason for X' is empty, he concludes that if 'nothing' is a reason, it has to be an entity. It is strange that both Wolff and Baumgarten should have defended such a "proof." Leibniz, on his part, abstained from any attempt at "proving" the principle of reason.

Baumgarten then distinguishes the "*sufficient (complete, total)*" reason from the "*insufficient (incomplete, partial)*" reason. The former grounds the totality of marks by which a thing is individuated, whereas the latter grounds only some marks of a thing. From the statement of the principle of reason, he derives the statement of the principle of *sufficient* reason, or principle of "harmony" (*convenientiae*):[40] nothing is without a sufficient reason, or, if something is posited, something is posited as its sufficient reason. Both the sufficient and the insufficient reason are also described as *determining* ("sufficiently determining," or "insufficiently determining"), for to *determine* is to posit a predicate, and the reason (ground) makes knowable why a predicate is posited rather than its opposite.[41]

In the 1755 *New Elucidation*, Kant denounces the circularity of Baumgarten's (and Wolff's) definition of the reason (ground) ("A reason is that from which it is possible to cognize *why* something is"). In the word 'why', he says, we already have the notion of a reason. One might as well say that the *ratio* is that from which one knows the *ratio* of something.[42] Kant substitutes for this definition the following: a reason is "that which determines a subject in respect of any predicate," where "to determine" means "to posit a predicate while excluding its opposite": "To determine is to posit a predicate while excluding its opposite. That which determines a subject in respect of any of its predicates is called the *reason*."[43]

This terminology is inherited from Baumgarten, who called all reason a *determining* reason, and specified that *to determine* means "to posit that something is A, or not-A."[44] But Kant brings the logical aspect of determination into the foreground—even though at this period it is still the case for him, just as for the rational metaphysician, that *ratio* is indissolubly logical *and ontological*. Properly speaking, there is no other reason than the reason *for attributing a predicate to a subject*.

> The reason [*ratio*] . . . establishes a connection and a conjunction between the subject and some predicate or other. A reason thus always requires a subject; and it also requires a predicate, which it can unite with the subject. If you ask for the reason of a circle I shall not at all understand what you are asking for, unless you add a predicate, for example that it is, of all the figures which have a perimeter of the same length, the one which embraces the greatest area.[45]

For a proposition to be true, there must be a reason that determines the subject with respect to the predicate—that is, a reason that not only makes the predicate

---

[40] *Metaphysica*, §22.

[41] Ibid., §§34–35, Ak. XVII, 33.

[42] *Dilucidatio*, Ak. I, 393; 13. Kant also criticizes severely Wolff's and Baumgarten's "proof" of the principle of reason. There is no absurdity, he claims, in saying that the reason of something is nothing: it just means that "the only reason which can be attributed to the thing is one to which no concept corresponds at all" (Ak. I, 397–98; 19); by this Kant means, I think, no concept of anything at all is thought under the concept 'reason of X'.

[43] *Dilucidatio*, Proposition 4, Ak. I, 391–92; 11.

[44] See note 41.

[45] *Dilucidatio*, Ak. I, 392; 11–12.

noncontradictory with the subject (then, the proposition would be merely possible), but also excludes its opposite. Thus without a reason for *excluding the opposite* of a given predicate, the proposition would lack truth:

> Since all truth results from the determination of the predicate in a subject, the determining reason is not only the criterion of truth, but also its source. If one abandoned it, one would indeed discover a great deal which was possible, but nothing at all which was true. Thus it is indeterminate for us whether the planet Mercury revolves on its axis or not, for we lack a reason which would posit one of the two predicates to the exclusion of its opposite. Each of the two predicates remains possible, neither being established as true in respect of our knowledge.[46]

From this necessity of a reason for excluding the opposite of the predicate asserted of the subject in a true proposition, Kant concludes to the universal validity of the principle of reason: "Nothing is true without a determining reason."[47] But here, "nothing" means *no proposition*. The principle of reason is a principle of reason for the *truth of propositions*. The attribution of a predicate to a subject is true only if the predicate is *determined* (posited to the exclusion of its opposite), or if the subject is *determined with respect to the predicate*.[48]

Now, when introducing his definition of "reason" Kant distinguished two kinds of determining reasons: the "*antecedently* determining" reason (*ratio antecedenter determinans*) and the "*consequently* determining" reason (*ratio consequenter determinans*). The first kind may be either reason of essence (*ratio essendi*) or reason of existence (*ratio fiendi*). The second kind is reason of cognition (*ratio cognoscendi*):

> An *antecedently* determining reason is one, the notion of which precedes that which is determined. That is to say, an antecedently determining reason is one, in the absence of which what is determined would be unintelligible.* A consequently determining reason is that which would not be posited unless the notion determined by it was already posited. One might also call the first . . . reason of essence or of existence [*rationem essendi vel fiendi*], and the second . . . reason of cognition [*rationem cognoscendi*].

> * In addition to this one may mention the *identical* reason, where the concept of the subject determines the predicate by means of its own complete identity with the predicate.

---

[46] Ibid., Ak. I, 392; 12. One may remark that here Kant seems to make no distinction between the reason for the truth of the proposition and the reason for *our* knowing it as true. This is because a proposition is true just in case the full notion of its subject "determines" its predicate, and we *know* it as true just in case we recognize this determination of the subject with respect to the predicate. Cf. Wolff, in chapter 4, p. 95. Nevertheless, we shall see shortly that already in the *New Elucidation*, Kant introduces a *ratio cognoscendi*, or reason for our knowing the truth of a proposition, which threatens to undermine the rationalist confidence in the perfect isomorphism between reason for cognition (*ratio cognoscendi*) and reason for being (reason of the essence or reason of the coming into existence, *ratio essendi*, or *fiendi*).

[47] *Dilucidatio*, Proposition V, Ak. I, 393; 13.

[48] As we can see from the texts quoted, Kant uses both expressions: to "determine the predicate," that is, to assert it of the subject while excluding its opposite; and to "determine the subject with respect to the predicate," that is, to assert of it the predicate while excluding its opposite.

Take for example: a triangle has three sides. Here, the concept of what is determined neither follows nor precedes the determining concept.[49]

For example, the eclipses of the satellites of Jupiter are a *ratio cognoscendi* of the noninstantaneous propagation of light, but they do not give the reason of its existence, its efficient cause [*ratio fiendi*], which is the elasticity of the globules of air in which light is propagated.[50]

Defining the notion of reason in relation to propositions, plus distinguishing between the *reason of cognition* (*ratio consequenter determinans*) and the *reason of essence* or of *existence* (*ratio antecedenter determinans*) is potentially a powerful tool against rational metaphysics. For if we often have mere reasons for cognition, understood as "consequently determining reasons" (= experience), it is hard to see why we should assert that there is in all cases a *ratio antecedenter determinans*, a reason for asserting a predicate of a subject either from the essence of the subject, or from an antecedent cause. In other words, it would seem that nothing obliges one to admit the universal validity of a principle of reason in the rationalist sense. Yet, far from drawing this prudent conclusion, Kant asserts that even if we are often obliged to make do with consequently determining reasons (*rationes cognoscendi*, reasons of cognition), there is always a reason *antecedenter determinans*.

It has been established by the common opinion of all mortals that knowledge of the truth is always based upon a representation of the reason. However, when we are only concerned with certainty, we very frequently rest satisfied with a consequentially determining reason. But if one takes the theorem adduced above along with the definition and considers them together, it can easily be seen that there is always an antecedently determining reason, or if you prefer, a genetic or at least an identical reason; for, of course, a consequently determining reason does not bring the truth into being; it only displays it.[51]

Only a short while after the New Elucidation, however, Kant came to have doubts about the assumption that there is an antecedently determining reason for every true proposition, that is, for asserting a predicate of a subject to the exclusion of its opposite. For if the reason of a predication is (relatively) easy to grasp when the subject itself contains it (when subject and predicate are connected by identity), much more difficult to understand is the connection between, say, the elasticity of the globules of air and the noninstantaneous propagation of light. At the time of the *New Elucidation*, Kant did not wonder about this case and had no difficulty presenting his principle of reason as universally asserting an *antecedently determining* reason for the truth of all propositions. He remained essentially in agreement with rational metaphysics, and indeed went as far as to argue against Crusius in support of a "proof" of the principle of reason understood not only as a principle of (antecedently determining) reason for the truth of propositions, but also as a principle of reason for *the existence of contingent*

[49] *Dilucidatio*, Proposition IV, Ak. I, 392; 11.
[50] Ibid., Ak. I, 392–93; 12–13.
[51] Ibid., Proposition 5, Scholium, Ak. I, 394; 14.

things.[52] Nevertheless, by giving pride of place to the analysis of the reason *for asserting a predicate of a subject*, he has already opened the door to difficulties as well as developed some of the tools he will need for overcoming them.

In *Metaphysik Herder*, from the early 1760s, Kant introduces a new distinction, that between logical reason (*ratio logica*) and real reason (real ground) (*ratio realis*). The example he gives is 'the reason of evil in the world':

> Every reason is either logical—and thereby the consequence is posited *per regulam identitatis*, a consequence which is identical to it, like a predicate. Or it is real—and thereby the consequence is not posited *per regulam identitatis*, a consequence which is not identical to it.
>
> For example, from whence the evil in the world? *Responsio* as to the logical ground: because in the world there is a series of finite things [*auf einer Welt ist eine series endlicher Dinge*] which bear imperfections. If we search for the real ground, we search for the being that produces evil in the world.[53]

Both logical and real ground are distinct from the mere ground of cognition (our experience of evil, in the *New Elucidation*). Both, then, are what the *New Elucidation* called antecedently determining reason, *ratio antecedenter determinans*. In fact, Kant's example of *ratio logica* is what he called, in the *New Elucidation*, reason of the essence, *ratio essendi*—the world's containing a series of finite things is a *ratio essendi*, a reason of for all features belonging to its essence, among which, imperfection. His example of *ratio realis* is what he called *ratio fiendi or existendi*—the being that produces evil in the world is *ratio existendi*, or cause, of the existence of evil. Kant now calls this reason 'real reason' (or real ground: *ratio realis*), and remarks that the connection between ground and grounded is easily understood in the case of the logical ground, but not in that of the real ground:

> The connection between the logical ground and the logical consequence goes without saying [*ist wohl*], but not the connection between the real ground—that if something is posited, something else is posited at the same time [*wenn etwas gesetzt werde, zugleich was andres gesetzt werde*]. For example, 'God wills!'—'And there was the world!', 'Julius Caesar!'. The name brings to mind the thought of the master of Rome—what connection?[54]

The connection between hearing the name 'Julius Caesar' and forming the idea of Julius Caesar, and the connection between God's will and the existence of the world, present the same difficulty: in neither case are ground and grounded connected by identity.

---

[52] Ibid., Proposition 8, Ak. I, 396; 17 (Kant's proof is a proof *ad absurdum* from the concept of a contingent thing).

[53] Ak. XXVIII-1, 12. In the *Dilucidatio*, Kant did mention *ratio realis*, but only when describing Crusius's opposition to the principle of reason (see Ak. I, 398; 20). He did not formulate the distinction between *ratio logica* and *ratio realis*, or the difficulty proper to real ground or reason, *ratio realis*.

[54] Ibid. (question mark at the end added by me). Kant gives similar examples of 'real ground' in the Final Remark of the *Attempt to Introduce the Concept of Negative Magnitudes into Philosophy*, contemporary with *Metaphysik Herder* (cf. *Neg. Gr.*, Ak. II, 202–3; 239–40).

Now, the terms in which Kant states the difficulty are worth noticing. What is difficult to understand, he says, is how "if something is posited, something else is posited at the same time." What does this mean? Two things require explanation here: the term "posited," and the nature of the connection between the two "posited."

In texts from the same period, Kant distinguishes *existence* from *predication* and characterizes the former as "absolute positedness."[55] One might then suppose that in formulating his question about real ground, Kant is spotlighting the difficulty of thinking a relation of ground and grounded *between existents*: since existence is not a predicate, but an "absolute positedness," a connection between existents cannot be thought as a connection between concepts, in which one concept might be contained in the other. Kant's formulation would thus mean that one should beware of rationalist confusions between the connection of concepts and the connection of existents.

However, such a reading would only partly explain what Kant means by "posited." For the verb "to posit" may have a broader sense than the one it has in the expression "absolute positedness." At the beginning of the passage from *Metaphysik Herder* cited earlier, Kant describes the relation of *logical* ground as the relation of a subject to a predicate, in which "the predicate is posited by the rule of identity." In the *New Elucidation*, we saw that he defined "ground" as "that which determines a subject in respect of its predicate," that is, that which "posits a predicate while excluding its opposite." Hence the verb "to posit" may be understood not only as referring to "absolute positedness" (i.e., existence), but also to what Kant calls "relative positedness" (i.e., predication): a predicate A is "posited" relative to a subject insofar as the subject is determined with respect to A—that is, A is actually asserted of it (as opposed to being a merely possible predicate, whose negation, non-A, is also a possible predicate of the subject-concept, thereby leaving the latter "undetermined" with respect to A and non-A). "Posited," in the broader sense, thus simply means "asserted." And what may be asserted is either existence (= "absolute positedness") or the relation of a predicate to a subject (= "relative positedness").[56]

Now this helps to clarify Kant's main question, concerning the *connection* between the two "posited." Interestingly, the terms in which Kant considers this connection are the same as those in which the logic textbooks of the period characterize *modus ponens*, the first rule of inference from a hypothetical premise. In such an inference, *positing* the antecedent (whether this "positing" is "absolute," in an existential judgment, or "relative," in the "determination" of a subject with respect to a predicate) provides the reason for *positing* the consequent. Every hypothetical judgment is thus a possible major premise for a hypothetical syllogism in which, *if* the antecedent is posited (asserted as a minor premise), *then* the consequent should be posited (asserted as a conclusion).[57]

---

[55] *Beweisgr.*, Ak. II, 73; 118.

[56] On the distinction between the two kinds of "positedness," absolute (existence) and relative (predication), cf. *Beweisgr.* cited in note 55.

[57] Kant's formulation, "if something is posited, something else must be posited at the same time," is virtually a *verbatim* repetition of Wolff's definition of the rule of *modus ponens* : "If in a hypothet-

In the *Reflexionen* from the 1760s, one finds several occurrences of the problem of the real ground formulated in terms of *modus ponens*. These texts are also among the first known instances of Kant's distinction between *analytic* and *synthetic* connection:

> The relation of reason *ponens* is connection, *tollens* is opposition [*Respectus rationis ponentis est nexus, tollentis est oppositio*].

> The relation of logical reason *ponens or tollens* is analytic—rational. [*Respectus rationis logicae vel ponendi vel tollendi est analyticus—rationalis*].

> The relation of real reason *ponens or tollens* is synthetic—empirical [*Respectus rationis realis vel ponendi vel tollendi est syntheticus—empiricus*].[58]

If we apply this distinction to Kant's examples given earlier, we get, for the analytic relation of *ratio ponens*: "If the world is a series of finite things, then it is imperfect (contains evil). But the world is a series of finite things. Therefore, the world is imperfect (contains evil)." And for the synthetic relation: "If air is elastic, then light does not travel instantaneously. But air is elastic. Therefore, light does not travel instantaneously." Kant's question is, How do we have a necessary connection, and thus a premise for modus ponens, a *respectus rationis ponentis*, in the second case?

However, in the 1760s Kant derived no great result from this peculiar formulation of the problem of "real ground." No answer is offered to the question cited earlier ("How is it possible that, something being posited, something else should be posited?"), and the synthetic *modus ponens* remains incomprehensible. It will become comprehensible *only when it is no longer thought as depending on the connection of the concepts combined*—as is the case when the major premise of the *modus ponens* expresses an analytic connection between antecedent and consequent—but instead, *the concepts combined are themselves dependent on the act of generating a ratio ponens*, that is, when the act of the understanding in the hypothetical judgment is understood as *governing the formation of* (empirical) *concepts* and, even prior to this, as generating *the order of the sensible representations it is called upon to connect*. Not only the concept of a real ground, but the concept of a ground in general, whether "logical" (*nexus analyticus*) or "real" (*nexus syntheticus*), will then be assigned its origin in the act of the understanding in a hypothetical judgment (which may become the major premise of a syllo-

---

ical syllogism the antecedent is posited, the consequent must also be posited [*Si in syllogismo hypothetico antecedens ponitur, ponendum quoque est consequens*]" (Wolff, *Philosophia rationalis*, §407). "The antecedent being posited in the minor, the consequent must also be posited in the conclusion [*posito antecedente in minore, ponendum quoque consequens in conclusione*]" (§408). Note that Wolff and Baumgarten used this same formulation in their statement of the principle of reason: "Something being posited, soemthing else is posited as its reason [*Posito aliquo, ponitur aliud ejus ratio*]." But of course they reversed the relation of antecedent and consequent, since the principle of reason, formulated in this way, asserts that something being posited, something thought as its *antecedent* is posited. Kant uses the formula of *modus ponens* not to assert anything at all (let alone a necessary regression from consequent to antecedent) but only to elucidate the *relation* between ground and grounded (*ratio* and *rationatum*), cause and effect.

[58] *Refl.* 3753 (1764–66), Ak. XVII, 283. Cf. also *Refl.* 3738, 3744, 3756.

gism in *modus ponens*). Nevertheless, Kant's discovery of the difficulty concerning the real ground, and his formulation of this problem in terms of a synthetic
modus ponens, were in my view an essential step toward asserting that the concept of reason (ground) *in general* has its source in the logical form of hypothetical judgment.[59]

GROUND AND LOGICAL FORM OF HYPOTHETICAL
JUDGMENT IN THE CRITICAL PERIOD

We can now return to the critical period, and the text from *Metaphysik Volckmann*
cited earlier. We saw Kant explain that all relations of ground and grounded are
expressed in the logical form of hypothetical judgment:

> According to relation, [judgments] are:
>
> . . . .
>
> 2 / hypothetical: if a being is an animal, it is mortal. Which shows the relation of ground
> [*Grund*] to consequence [*Folge*]. *Antecedens, consequens, causa* or *causatum*.[60]

Further on, Kant repeats his critique of the Wolff-Baumgarten definition of
'ground'—"a ground is that [which explains] why something is [*ratio est id, cur
aliquid sit*]"—and offers his own definition: a ground is "what [is such that], if it
is posited, something else is posited [*id, quo posito, ponitur aliud*]." Because this
definition is now explicitly related to the logical form of hypothetical judgment,
its meaning comes into full view: positing the ground (. . . *id, quo posito* . . .)
leads to positing the grounded (. . . *ponitur aliud*), just as in a *modus ponens* syllogism, asserting in the minor premise the antecedent of the major hypothetical
premise implies the assertion of its consequent in the conclusion.[61]

The relation of ground to grounded may be either that of logical ground to logical consequence, where "the connection is established by means of identity," and
so is analytic, or that of real ground to real consequence, where the connection is
synthetic. The text cited provides an example of the first case: 'If a being is an animal [*ein Tier*], it is mortal.' In a letter to Reinhold from the late 1780s, Kant gives
another example: 'If bodies are extended, then they are divisible'. After having
stated his definition of the ground, "that which is such that, if it is posited, something else is posited" (*id, quo posito, ponitur aliud*), Kant explains in this letter
that the merely logical distinction between ground and consequence, provided by
the form of hypothetical judgment ('If bodies are extended, then they are divisible') is sufficient to distinguish ground from grounded and thus to justify the word
'else' (*aliud*)—something *else* is posited (*ponitur aliud*)—even though in content

---

[59] In the 1760s, Kant is still far from such a solution, since his conclusion at this point is that the
relation of real ground cannot be thought in a judgment. The logical ground is thought in a judgment
(attribution of a predicate to a subject in which it is analytically contained—for instance, 'a world
composed of finite beings is imperfect'), but the real ground is an unanalyzable concept. Cf. *Neg. Gr.*,
Ak. II, 204; 241, and *Refl.* 3755, Ak. XVII, 283. In *Reflexionen* from the late 1760s, we also find Kant
saying that cognition of the real ground is merely empirical, from habit (cf. *Refl.* 3756, Ak. XVII,
284).

[60] *Met. Volckmann* (1783–84), Ak. XXVIII-1, 397. I quoted the full text earlier, p. 346.

[61] Cf. Ak. XXVIII-1, 401.

the two "posited" are not distinct, since the predicate belongs to the subject as one of its marks.[62] Indeed, both the propositions cited as examples of logical ground/consequence could be replaced by a categorical proposition: 'All animals are mortal', 'All bodies are divisible'. This takes us back to Kant's statement in *Metaphysik Herder*, according to which a relation of logical ground is that of a predicate to a subject, where the former is connected to the latter "by the rule of identity."[63] Does that mean the form of hypothetical judgment is here superfluous? No; for in this form the ground of predication is as it were picked out from the other marks thought in the subject-concept and thus made explicit. More importantly, by tracing back the relation of ground to grounded to the logical form of hypothetical judgment, Kant is thus able to avoid the circularity in the rationalist definition of 'ground': a ground is not that which allows us to understand *why* something is—as Kant said as early as 1755, this would be tantamount to saying that a ground is that which allows us to understand the ground, a circular statement. Rather, a ground (reason) is defined as what can be reflected under the antecedent of a hypothetical judgment. In other words, something is a ground only by virtue of its being synthesized and reflected according to an original form of discursive connection between representations, proper to our understanding. Whatever the particular nature of Wolff's and Baumgarten's *why*, that is, whether it expresses a "logical" or a "real" ground, it derives its meaning from the logical form of our thought, namely from the act of understanding in a hypothetical judgment, the potential major premise of a hypothetical syllogism.

The relation of ground to grounded is that of "real" ground when the components of the hypothetical judgment (under which ground and grounded are reflected) are *not* analytically connected. This is the case in empirical judgments:

> A real ground is: *that which, if it is posited, something else is posited, but not according to the principle of identity*; this relation of ground to consequence is then *if something really different is posited*, whereas in the logical ground, it is *that by which something logically, but not really different is posited*. For example, if I say that butter melts in the sun, I first posit the ray of sunlight, and thereby at the same time posit that butter melts. I cannot see this by means of any analysis. Logically, two concepts are only partially, not totally different. One cannot say what the real ground properly rests on. Something A being posited, something really different B is posited. Yet there are many real grounds in physics, for instance when I have been exposed to cold, I posit that I am coming down with the flu, yet this concept is completely different from being exposed to cold. Despite this it seems impossible to think that because something is, something else which is not at all in the concept of this thing is posited.

> In the concept of a real ground there is a synthetic connection; in the concept of a logical ground there is only an analytic connection. The possibility of the latter requires no explanation, because it is possible according to the principle of contradiction. But the possibility of the connection between a real ground and its consequence poses a great problem.

[62] Letter to Reinhold, May 12 1789, Ak. XI-2, 35–36; 138.
[63] See earlier discussion, with citation referenced in note 53.

Now, this "problem" is the familiar one that, as we saw, Kant was unable to re-solve in his 1760s' *Reflexionen*. In the present text from *Metaphysik Volckmann*, Kant goes on to relate this difficulty to Humean skepticism:

> What contains the real ground of a consequence is called the cause. Hume con-structed a skeptical philosophy on the question of how I arrive at the concept of cause. The cause is what contains the real ground by virtue of which something is. It is completely identical with the real ground, for example, the wind is the cause of the motion of the ship, but how is it that if you posit the wind, something quite different, i.e., motion, follows? What is the connection between the wind and motion? Hume argues that all concepts of cause and consequence come from experience. Necessity, he says, would be something imaginary, and a long habit, but he saw no other way out, because he could not derive the relation from reason, and he viewed the concept of real ground as an empirical concept.[64]

We see here how Kant's long-standing confrontation with rational metaphysics on the problem of real ground and the principle of sufficient reason merges into his confrontation with Hume on the origin of our concept of cause. I shall argue that keeping in mind this twofold ancestry is essential to our understanding of Kant's reasoning in the Second Analogy of Experience.

THE CONCEPT OF A REAL GROUND AND "HUME'S PROBLEM"

In the preface to the *Prolegomena to Any Future Metaphysics* (contemporaneous with *Metaphysik Volckmann*), Kant calls the problem of causality "Hume's prob-lem," and states that Hume "awoke him from his dogmatic slumber." What does this mean? Probably not that he owes to Hume his discovery of the *problem* of the causal relation (even if Hume greatly contributed to this discovery: the *Re-flexionen* from the 1760s, in which Kant attributes our cognition of real ground to "habit," might indicate that Kant had read Hume or was at least familiar with Hume's theses in the *Enquiry Concerning Human Understanding*). But if we con-sider the particular sense Kant gives the term 'dogmatism', the conclusion to be drawn is rather that Hume had a key role, not so much in Kant's discovery of the *problem* of causality, as in the discovery of the *only possible locus of its solution*, namely the elucidation of the activity of imagination. Indeed, Hume's stating that *imagination*, not *reason*, is the source of our representation of the causal connec-tion is what Kant, in the preface to the *Prolegomena*, describes as the welcome shock that jolted him out of his slumber:

> [Hume] challenged reason, which pretends to have given birth to this concept of her-self, to answer him by what right she thinks anything could be so constituted that if that thing be posited, something else must also necessarily be posited; for this is the meaning of the concept of cause. . . .
>
> Hence he inferred that reason was altogether deluded with reference to this con-cept, which she erroneously considered as one of her children, whereas in reality it

---

[64] Ak. XXVIII-1, 404.

was nothing but a bastard of imagination, impregnated by experience, which subsumed certain representations under the law of association, and mistook a subjective
necessity (custom) for an objective necessity arising from insight.[65]

The power of Hume's explanation of the idea of cause in terms of a subjective
tendency of imagination generated by habit consists in its ability to account for
the universal validity and necessity implicit in the concept of cause even while depriving it of any objective validity. Hence if one is to take up Hume's challenge,
one must reckon with his thesis that imagination is the source of our idea of
causal connection: this, I believe, is the alarm that awakened Kant from his "dogmatic slumber."[66]

But Kant embarks on this confrontation fully equipped from his twenty-year-
long debate with rational metaphysics. This explains the bizarre, un-Humean terminology he uses when presenting "Hume's problem" in the passage from the
Prolegomena cited earlier: how can one think "that anything could be so constituted that if that thing be posited, something else must also necessarily be
posited"? This is the vocabulary Kant used in formulating the problem of the real
ground as early as the 1760s. By presenting "Hume's problem" in these terms, he
indicates that according to him, Hume's account of causal representations
amounts to making empirical associations of imagination the source of the synthetic *modus ponens* in which we think a real ground, and thus the source of the
idea of necessity tied to this *modus ponens*. Kant's response in the Second Analogy, prepared by the metaphysical and transcendental deductions of the categories, is to say that the associations of imagination which lead to the formulation of a hypothetical relation and thus to the *modus ponens* derived from it, are
possible only because empirical imagination is itself guided a priori by the effort
of our *Vermögen zu urteilen*, our capacity to form judgments. Thus the very representation of an objective succession, and a fortiori the representation of a *constant* succession, presuppose a *synthesis speciosa* of imagination or an affection
of inner sense by understanding, aiming at combining representations so that they
may be reflected under concepts combined according to the logical form of hypothetical judgment.

Such at least is the argument Kant advances in the Second Analogy. It is no surprise, then, that in each exposition of this argument we should find juxtaposed the

[65] *Prol.*, preface, Ak. IV, 257; 3.

[66] There is general agreement among Kant scholars on the fact that Kant's interest in Hume, present
throughout his philosophical career, peaked on two occasions: in the early 1760s, with Kant's recognition of the problem of "real ground" (Sulzer's translation of Hume's *Enquiry* appeared in 1755); and the
early 1770s, immediately after Kant wrote the *Dissertation*. Kant's statement in the preface to the *Prolegomena* would then refer to this second period. The occasion of Kant's "awakening from a dogmatic
slumber" may have been, as Erdmann, Vaihinger, and Beck have contended, the translation in 1772 of
Beattie's *Essay on the Nature and Immutability of Truth*, which introduced some of Hume's arguments
in the *Treatise* to German audience (see Vaihinger, *Commentar*, 427–28; Beck, *Kant and Hume*, 117).
Manfred Kühn has drawn attention to another possible source for Kant's knowledge of Hume: a translation of the final section of book I of Hume's *Treatise* (cf. bk. I, 4th part, sec. 7: "Conclusion of This
Book"), which appeared in the *Königsberger Zeitung*, July 1771. Cf. Kühn, "Kant's Hume," 185.

vocabulary gathered in the course of its twofold genealogy: on the one hand, "real ground" and *modus ponens* from a synthetic premise; on the other hand, combinations of imagination. Kant draws on both inspirations to argue that even prior to Hume's empiricoassociative combinations, imagination achieves a *synthesis speciosa* oriented toward judgment, which generates the representations of temporal order from which we derive associative combinations, and finally our empirical cognition of causal connections. This is how what corresponds to the empirical manifold of our sensations can be thought as "in itself determined" in accordance with the hypothetical form of judgment, and thus can eventually be reflected under the category of causal connection.

Keeping this background in mind, I shall now analyze Kant's argument in the Second Analogy.

Synthesis Speciosa *and Temporal Succession: Kant's Argument in the Second Analogy of Experience*

PERCEPTION OF OBJECTIVE SUCCESSION

Let us start with Kant's well-known example, in which he analyzes the difference between perceiving a house by successively apprehending its parts, and perceiving the movement of a ship by successively apprehending its positions as it sails down a river. In both cases, says Kant, our apprehension is *successive*. We perceive the base of the house before its top, the right side before the left, and so on. Similarly, we perceive the ship upstream before we perceive it downstream, then again further downstream, and so on. Yet no one would suppose for a minute that "the manifold of the house is also in itself successive,"[67] and conversely, no one would doubt that not only the apprehension of the positions of the ship, but these positions themselves, are successive. Why? Because, says Kant, in the case of the house we are aware that we can invert the succession of our perceptions and, for example, perceive the base *after* we perceive the top, while we had first perceived the latter *before* the former. In the case of the ship, on the contrary, we are aware that the perceptions could not be repeated in the reverse order. If our gaze goes back from the point at which we now see the ship, to the point at which we saw it a moment before, we shall find the latter point occupied by something other than the ship. We cannot repeat the apprehended perceptions at will, reversing their initial temporal succession. Of course, things would be different if the ship suddenly changed directions and started to sail upstream. But in this case too we would be aware that the order of our apprehension is irreversible, we would know that a perception B (perception of the position of the boat upstream) following a perception A (of its position downstream) could not be followed again by a perception qualitatively identical to A, unless the ship changed directions again. On the contrary, if there is no succession in the object itself, we can return at will to a perception qualitatively identical to a perception A after a perception B which followed A.

[67] A190/B235.

The general premise for Kant's analysis of these examples is the premise he stated at the outset of the A Deduction and repeats in the proof of each Analogy: all perception (synthesis of apprehension) *is*, as such, *successive*, regardless of the objective temporal relations we can experience by means of this apprehension. Here Kant is in effect asking us to suspend for a moment our belief in the familiar temporal relations of the world we inhabit, and inquire into the way in which these relations appear to us. We will then become aware, he argues, that *both* the perception of an unchanging object, one in which no objective succession of determinations is perceived (e.g., the house), and the perception of an object that is altered, one in which an objective succession of determinations is perceived (e.g., the ship), *are successive*. Thus our perceiving an objective succession is a more complex operation than we are naturally aware of, and we must ask *what* in our representation makes a *successive perception* the *perception of a succession*.[68] This is the question Kant sets about answering when contrasting the reversible character of our apprehension of a house and the irreversible character of our apprehension of a ship going downstream.

One may retort that this distinction between reversibility and irreversibility of a sequence of perceptions is both inadequate and unnecessary: if we perceive the house at one glance, *uno (sensibili) intuitu*, the perception of its parts is not successive. It becomes successive only when we detail these parts one by one. And even then, to know that they are unchanging parts rather than changing states of an object, all we need is an awareness of the whole in relation to which the position of each part is determined. This provides sufficient assurance that the parts are not in themselves successive, even while their apprehension, when they are considered one by one, is successive. Similarly, in the case of the ship, if we perceive at one glance the course of the river, and apprehend the positions of the ship on the river one by one, we just *see* that these positions have changed in relation

[68] For the answer to be complete, one must also ask about the reverse case: what makes a *successive perception* the *perception of a simultaneity* (e.g., the perception of the simultaneous parts of the house). Kant will answer this question in the Third Analogy. As far as the Second Analogy is concerned, the example of the house has only a negative function. It illustrates a "merely subjective" succession, in contrast with a succession which is also objective. But Kant does not at this point ask what *objective* temporality corresponds in this case to the subjective succession of perceptions. It should also be recalled that *subjective* succession, on its part, is governed by synthesis according to the category of quantity (cf. Transcendental Deduction, §26, B162). We must conclude that the problem of the relation between subjective succession and objective succession arises *because* we are capable of quantitative syntheses, that is, synthesis by means of which we "run through and gather up" (A99) a homogeneous (spatiotemporal) given. Finally, it should be noted that 'perception' (*Wahrnehmung*) has several meanings in the Second Analogy. Perception is (1) what we are conscious of at each moment (perception as "sensation accompanied by consciousness," discussed in the Anticipations of Perception: call this p1); (2) the *subjective synthesis* of a manifold of p1: call this p2; (3) perception *of an object*, which is the result of the subjective synthesis (p2) of p1, *subjected to a rule*. In this third sense (p3), perception is synonymous with experience. When Kant writes, in the first sentence of the B edition proof, "I perceive [*ich nehme wahr*] that appearances follow one another, that is, that there is a state *of things* [my emphasis] at one time the opposite of which was in the preceding time," this *perceiving* is an *experience* (= p3) which presupposes synthesis according to the schema of causality. Kant mostly leaves it to the reader to discern which of the three meanings of 'perception' is being referred to from one sentence to the next, sometimes even within the same sentence.

to the whole. Thus what makes us aware of the difference between a succession of perceptions and the perception of a succession is the relation, in each case, of what we perceive successively to a permanent frame of reference provided by the intuition of a spatial whole.

But actually, none of this, it seems to me, constitutes an objection to Kant's analysis. As we saw when examining the category of quantity, Kant explicitly grants that the perception of a sensible multiplicity is possible at one glance before it is laid out in a successive synthesis of apprehension.[69] He would grant just as easily that one perceives the movement of the boat as the alteration of a permanent object (the boat) in a material frame of reference that is itself permanent (the river, the surrounding landscape) and can be taken in at one glance. Note, however, that this is not always possible: the house may be too large, the river too long, for all parts to be taken in at one glance. I would think Kant had this sort of situation primarily in mind. In any case, even if one presupposes an intuition of the whole, it remains true that *when one successively lays out the parts of this single intuition*, the difference between the merely subjective succession in apprehension (the case of the house) and the apprehension of an objective succession (the case of the boat) is exhibited *in the subjective apprehension itself* in the following way. In the case of the house, the apprehension is thought to be reversible: we are aware that we could, if we would, return to a perception qualitatively identical to the first, one that may differ from it only by its temporal position in the succession of our apprehension. In the case of the ship, our apprehension is *not* reversible: if our glance returned to the position at which it was fixed a moment before, it would not find it "filled" by a qualitatively identical object.

What is specific to the apprehension of an objective succession, then, is that the synthesis of imagination conforms to a rule that "requires a certain mode of combination of the manifold." Kant states this rule as follows: "In an appearance which contains a happening (the preceding state of the perception we may entitle A, and the succeeding B), B can only follow A in the apprehension; but the perception A cannot follow upon B, but only precede it" (A192/B237). One should

---

[69] See above, chapter 9, pp. 271–72. The intuition of a house and that of a pyramid can be immediately given as *quanta* before they are the object of a successive synthesis of apprehension, which is necessary for the apprehension of their *quantitas*. Thus I do not agree with Vuillemin (*Physique*, 279, n.1) when he presents as an objection to Kant the fact, established by psychophysiological studies of instantaneous perception, that one may perceive a complex object such as a house at one glance. Kant explicitly admits this possibility, albeit not on the basis of psychophysiological explanation, but on the basis of his transcendental analysis of perceptual experience. One must therefore understand why this possibility is, according to him, not sufficient to account for, or solve the problem posed by, the difference between consciousness of the temporal determination of the house, and that of the moving ship. Again contrary to Vuillemin (ibid.), I do not think that Kant ignored the dependence of perceptual successions or simultaneities on "material speed of signals": as we shall see, he says in the Third Analogy that our perception of simultaneity depends on material transmission of light rays. But the problem posed in the *Analogies* is different from that of the empirical (material) conditions of perception. The problem is to know what constitutes our *consciousness of* objective temporal relations, prior to any empirical theorization of perception and its physical determinants. Kant's thesis is that such consciousness is not merely receptive but depends on imaginative and discursive syntheses, which it is the task of the Analogies to lay out.

pay due attention to the modality of necessity in these statements (B *"can* be apprehended *only* as following upon A," and A *"cannot* follow upon B *but only* precede it"). Such modal characterization exceeds the mere description of a de facto succession of our perceptions. The mere fact that in perceiving the movement of the ship we do not return to a perception qualitatively identical to the one previously apprehended is not by itself sufficient ground to assert the *impossibility* of such a return, or the *necessity* of the succession that in fact obtains. If the perception of the movement, as well as that of any objective succession, is accompanied by the consciousness of an *impossibility*, or of a *necessity*, this modal aspect requires explanation, which mere receptivity to what is present in apprehension cannot provide. What needs explanation is that I do not merely register, at time t_2 or t_3 following t_1, that I no longer have perception A (the ship I perceived at point x_1 at t_1), but I am also aware that *I cannot* have it, or that at t_2 *I can only have* perception B (the ship at point x_2), which is the kind of awareness I have when I take the succession to pertain not only to my apprehension, but also to the object itself.

IRREVERSIBILITY OF SUBJECTIVE SUCCESSION
AND RELATION TO AN OBJECT

Kant's next step is to explain what makes possible the awareness of the necessity of subjective succession (characteristic of the apprehension of an objective succession, as in the case of the moving ship). Now, the explanation he provides seems suspiciously circular: what leads us to reflect the succession of perceptions in empirical consciousness as *irreversible*, that is, as a *necessary succession* of our perceptions, he says, is that we relate it to an object. Thus to the previous question—how do we make the difference between merely subjective succession in apprehension, and apprehension of objective succession, that is, succession *in the object* (for instance, positions of the boat)?—Kant's answer was that in one case we are aware of the succession of perceptions in apprehension as reversible (order-indifferent), while in the other we are aware of it as irreversible. And now to the question, how is awareness of a succession of perceptions in apprehension awareness of an irreversible succession, his answer is that this is made possible by the relation we establish between the succession of our perceptions and an object. Perception of objective succession (succession in an object) is awareness of irreversibility, awareness of irreversibility is made possible by our relating our representations to objects: is this not circular?

It is not. We have to distinguish between representing an objective succession and relating subjective succession to an object, in general. Representing an objective succession just *is* being aware of subjective succession as irreversible, and being aware of subjective succession as irreversible *results* from the cognitive act of relating subjective succession to an object. Kant's point, more precisely, is that relating representations to objects may result in *either* recognizing coexisting (although successively apprehended) determinations of objects, *or* recognizing changing determinations of objects, and thus objective succession. The cognitive act is thus what generates awareness of reversibility (order-indifference) or irreversibility (order-determinateness) of subjective apprehension, which are phenomenological features of our awareness of objective temporal determinations (which on their part may be *either* objective simultaneity *or* objective succession). The seeming circularity, but also its resolution, are visible in the following passage:

> If we enquire what new character [*Beschaffenheit*] *relation to an object* [this is the second case mentioned earlier: relating subjective succession to an object, in general] confers upon our representations, what dignity they thereby acquire, we find that it results only in subjecting the representations to a rule, and so in necessitating us to connect them in some one specific manner; and conversely, that only insofar as our representations are necessitated in a certain order as regards their time-relations do they acquire objective meaning [this is the first case mentioned earlier: objective succession—or, as the case may be, objective simultaneity]. (A197/B242–43)

The act of thinking that relates the succession of apprehended perceptions to an object *is* the act that leads us to reflect this succession as (eventually) necessary (order-determinate), or as (eventually) arbitrary (order-indifferent), *which is the way in which* we perceive (cognize) objective temporal relations. If our act of apprehension did not aim at establishing a relation between the sequence of our perceptions and an object that we represent by means of these perceptions and recognize under a concept, the succession would remain a mere de facto succession, and it would be recognized neither as order-indifferent nor as order-determinate. Note that Kant is not claiming that we are aware of an irreversible succession of perceptions *prior* to recognizing an objective succession, or that we *conclude* from the irreversibility of the subjective succession that it is a succession not only in our apprehension, but also in things. According to Kant, we have a natural and immediate certainty of temporal succession in things, without having ever asked ourselves what relation this succession has to the succession of our representations. Only the critical procedure, presupposing the suspension of belief Kant demands of his reader (prepared by the Transcendental Aesthetic and Analytic), analyzes this immediate certainty of objective succession into an awareness of the irreversible character of the succession of our perceptions in apprehension. Irreversibility is the manner in which we recognize that the succession of our representations is a succession in the object, but the act of relating our representations to an object is what allows us (eventually) to reflect the succession of our representations as irreversible. What we need to understand, then, is how the act of relating our representations to an object can generate at one stroke the representation of an objective succession and a rule of succession (irreversibility) in our subjective representations—or, as the case may be, the representation of objective simultaneity and a rule of reversibility or order-indifference: the focus of the Third Analogy.

From the First Analogy, we have learned a few things regarding the relation of our representations to an object in general, and even regarding our representation of objective succession. Every objective succession of determinations, Kant argued, is the alteration of a substance that remains permanent. We have a representation of objective succession only if we represent a numerically *identical* thing that becomes *different*. Without the relation to a permanent *of which it is the alteration*, nothing would be an objective change. We also know that relating the transitory to a permanent of which it is the alteration means recognizing an object intuited under a concept "reciprocal with it," to which the marks it successively acquires in the course of its alteration are attributed. In the Second Analogy, Kant wants to argue that the *regularity of change itself* is what allows us to recognize such a relation between (relatively) permanent determinations and changing determinations, in the indefinite multiplicity of our sensations and intuitions. We can attribute permanent marks to an object only if we presuppose that every alteration of this object itself takes place under external conditions which can be recognized according to a rule. In other words, to say that we experience an objective change only as the alteration of a substance *is* to say that we always presuppose that such a change, when it takes place, does so *according to a rule*.

OBJECTIVE SUCCESSION AND "CONFORMITY WITH A RULE"

The presupposition of a rule according to which change occurs is indeed the main feature Kant assigns to our perception of "what changes," in each of the four expositions of his argument in the Second Analogy (he adds a fifth exposition under the title "proof" in the B edition). We perceive that "something happens" only if we presuppose that *it follows from the previous state in accordance with a rule*.

> When, therefore, I perceive that something happens, this representation first of all contains: that something precedes because only with respect to this does the appearance acquire its time-relation, namely, that of existing after a preceding time in which it itself was not. But it can acquire this determinate temporal position only insofar as something is presupposed in the preceding state upon which it follows invariably [*jederzeit*], that is, in accordance with a rule. From this there results [*woraus sich denn ergibt*] a twofold consequence. In the first place, I cannot reverse the series, placing that which happens prior to that upon which it follows. And secondly, if the state which precedes is posited, this determinate event follows inevitably and necessarily. (A198/B243–44)

This is the core of Kant's argument. We need to analyze it in some detail.

Let me first recapitulate the initial steps of the argument as I have analyzed them so far:

1. Our apprehension is always successive; this by itself does not tell us whether the succession of perceptions in our apprehension is perception of an objective succession (a change of objective states).

2. We become aware of the succession in our apprehension as perception of a change of states in an object when we take this subjective succession to be irreversible.

3. We take the subjective succession to be irreversible when, relating it to an object, we presuppose a rule according to which a change of states occurs in the object.

4. Therefore, perceiving (experiencing)[70] an objective succession (a change of states in an object) is presupposing a preceding state upon which the change of states follows according to a rule.

[70] See note 68.

I discussed (1) and (2) in the preceding sections. I discuss (3) in the present section. It is expounded in the text just cited, which I now proceed to analyze.[71]

The perception of what happens "contains: that something precedes, because only with respect to this does the appearance acquire its time-relation, namely, that of existing after a preceding time in which it itself was not." This brings us back to a situation already examined in the First Analogy. Perceiving that something changes (and 'something happens' means nothing else than 'some state of affairs changes at time t') is perceiving that something is at time t_2 that was not at time t_1 preceding t_2. The ship is at time t_2 in position b, in which it was not at time t_1, when it was in position a. The wax is at time t_2 in a liquid state, whereas at time t_1 it was hard. Water is at time t_2 in a solid state, whereas at time t_1 it was liquid. And so on. The thesis of the First Analogy is thus to be kept in mind as the background of the present argument: the perception of "something that happens" rests on the presupposition of a permanent object, whose state alone changes.

Any awareness of the alteration of a permanent—that is, every shift from one

---

[71] See A197/B242–43, cited earlier. Similar statements can be found at A194/B239, A195/B240, A200/B245, A201/B247. One of the problems posed by the Second Analogy is the repetitiveness of Kant's exposition. In the A edition, the argument is stated four times. It is stated a fifth time in the B edition. As I understand it, however, the general progression remains essentially the same in all expositions. If we number the paragraphs of the Second Analogy from 1 to 28 (paragraph 1 being the first paragraph under the title "proof" added in B), Kant's five expositions of the argument occupy the first 16 paragraphs. They are: (i) paragraphs 1 and 2 (added in B); (ii) 3 to 6 (= the first four paragraphs in A); (iii) 7–8 (5–6 in A): negative proof, taking as a premise the negation of the thesis to be proved (A194/B239: "Let us suppose that there is nothing antecedent to an event, upon which it must follow according to rule . . ."); 9 and 10 are transition paragraphs, restating the problem and leading to (iv) 11 to 15 (9 to 13 in A), in which the "principle of sufficient reason" is stated explicitly (A 200–201/B 245–46); (v) 16 (14 in A). The remainder of Kant's text addresses related issues (problem of the simultaneity of cause and effect, the concept of action, the principle of continuity). As we shall see, they are not part of the proof, but nevertheless they are important for clarifying its meaning. The proof added in B simply repeats the A proof in a more condensed form. The division of the text I am suggesting here agrees in its main lines with those of Adickes (*Kritik*, 211–12) and Kemp Smith (*Commentary*, 376–77), with one important difference: these authors both think that paragraphs 11 to 13 of the A edition (13 to 15 in B) give a different proof than the main one (of which all other expositions give some version), relating the concept of cause to the *order of time*. I hold, on the contrary, that these two paragraphs simply conclude the fourth exposition of the proof, just outlined. On this point I agree with Guyer (see *Claims*, 241). See also Allison, *Idealism*, 227. An interesting analysis of the different expositions of the argument and their correlation is provided by Thöle (*Gesetzmäßigkeit*, 189–90). Thöle shows convincingly that there is a specific rationale for each exposition, and thus succeeds in giving unprecedented clarity to the overall exposition of the Second Analogy. Like Kemp Smith and Adickes, however, he defends the view that there are two different proofs. One, he says, is an "analytic argument," an epistemological argument on the conditions of justification of our empirical judgments of objective succession (128–205, with an analysis of possible alternative readings of this argument, and discussion of relevant literature); Kant, according to Thöle, realized the shortcomings of the "analytic argument" and complemented it with a "synthetic argument" (developed, according to him, in exposition (iv) listed earlier) on the conditions for representing objects in conformity with the formal properties of time (205–11). But I think that Kant's argument is never merely an epistemological argument on the conditions of *confirmation, justification,* or *verification* of our judgments. It is a metaphysical argument of a new kind: an argument on the nature of objects as appearances, developed as an argument on the conditions of generation of *"judgeable"* perception (*synthesis speciosa*). Thus, the whole point of the argument is that (i) con-

"synthetic predication" to another "synthetic predication"[72]—presupposes a reason for asserting a predicate of a subject, a reason that cannot be contained in the subject-concept of predication. For otherwise moving from a predicate to its opposite would be impossible: if a subject A contains in itself the sufficient reason of the attribution of a predicate B, the opposite of B cannot be asserted of A. Thus if, as was stated in the First Analogy, we generate our representation of the relation between permanent and changing when we strive to reflect objects under concepts according to the form of categorical judgment, we must now add that we can attribute changing marks to *the same supposedly permanent object* only if we presuppose that there is a reason for asserting a predicate and then its opposite, a ground of change that can be stated according to the form of a hypothetical judgment. For example, the wax, if held close to a source of heat, from hard at time t_1 becomes soft at time t_2. The ship, if carried by the flow of the river, from point p_1 at time t_1 has moved to point p_2 at time t_2. If the logical forms of our judgments govern the formation of the schema of substance (the permanence of the real in time), then they must also govern the formation of a schema that makes the *alteration* of substance thinkable—that is, the attribution of a predicate contrary to a given predicate, which, according to the logical forms of our discursive thinking, can take place only *under an added condition*. This is precisely what the second sentence of the passage cited asserts: "But [something that happens] can acquire this determinate temporal position *only insofar as something is presupposed in the preceding state upon which it follows invariably, that is, in accordance with a rule*" (my emphasis). The "determinate position in this relation of time" is the fact that predicate B is attributed to the object at time t_2 following t_1 at which predicate A was attributed to it. This temporal position is given in my apprehension: I perceive predicate B after predicate A, not before. But as we saw, the mere succession in apprehension is not sufficient to determine awareness of a temporal succession in the object. The latter is determined only "insofar as something is presupposed in the preceding state upon which it follows invariably, that is, in accordance with a rule." Earlier in the same paragraph, Kant is still more explicit:

In the synthesis of appearances the manifold of representations is always successive. Now no object is hereby represented, since through this succession, which is common to all apprehensions, nothing is distinguished from anything else. But immediately I perceive or presuppose [*vorausannehme*] that in this succession there is a relation to the preceding state, from which the representation follows in conformity with a rule, something presents itself as an event, as something that happens; that is to say, I apprehend an object to which I must ascribe a certain determinate position in time—a position which, in view of the preceding state, cannot be otherwise assigned. (A198/B243–44)[73]

---

ditions for forming (empirical) judgments (*and*, yes, ultimately *also* identifying conditions for justification thereof) and (ii) conditions for objective time determination of appearances are *inseparable*.

[72] Cf. p. 329.

[73] Notice the expression "immediately I perceive *or presuppose*." The rule is not necessarily cognized. It is enough that it be presupposed (while it has yet to be determinately known) for an objective succession to be determined.

This explanation is disconcerting in that it tells us, in effect, that an event, which is *singular*, is perceived as such—as something, which was not, coming into being at a determinate point in time—only if we presuppose its relation to a rule, which is *universal*. Or, to stress even more the paradox contained in Kant's thesis: we perceive that something happens *in the present case* only if we presuppose something by virtue of which it would occur *in all cases*. Perceiving a singular event is mediated by the presupposition of the *universality* of a rule. However, we must be careful in our evaluation of this assertion. It does not mean that we actually cognize the event under a general rule, or that we know under which general rule it should be subsumed. Rather, it means that *the manner in which we perceive it* (as an attribution to a singular substance, e.g., the ship or the piece of wax, of a predicate which it did not have one moment before) presupposes the activity of a *synthesis speciosa* by virtue of which the appearance is "determined in itself," not only with respect to the relation between subject and predicate in a judgment, but also, inseparably—for the one would not be possible without the other—with respect to the relation between antecedent and consequent in a hypothetical judgment. In the synthesis of the manifold of our sensible intuitions, it would not be possible to reflect according to the form of categorical judgment (an object with relatively permanent predicates "reciprocal with it") if the form of hypothetical judgment were not also being used (thus allowing recognition of the alteration of the permanent object under "added" conditions, reflected in the antecedents of hypothetical judgments serving as rules). The statement that "everything that happens presupposes something else upon which it follows according to a rule" does not mean that we *cognize* this rule, but that we are so constituted as to search for it, for its presupposition alone allows us to recognize a permanent to which we attribute changing properties.[74] This presupposition of a universal, namely of *conformity with a rule*, in perception of the singular *as such*—that is, of an event as *this* objective succession I now perceive—is,

---

[74] Commentators often disregard the fact that the rule presupposed in the representation of an objective succession remains *indeterminate*. Thus according to Paul Guyer, Kant's argument is that we "have sufficient evidence to interpret our representation of the boat to mean that it *is* sailing downstream" only if we are in possession of causal laws that dictate this interpretation of our perceptions as the only possible one in the given circumstances—the position of the sails, the wind, the current, and the like (see Guyer, *Claims*, 252). But this would mean that we not only have to have already perceived this movement, but also have to have acquired a knowledge of its laws—before we "have sufficient evidence" that this movement occurs! To extricate himself from this difficulty, Guyer declares that the argument of the Second Analogy should be understood "not as a psychological model of the generation of beliefs but as an epistemological model of the confirmation of beliefs" (258). What Kant wants to show, according to Guyer, is not how we perceive an objective succession (or rather, how we believe that what we perceive is an objective succession), but how we *confirm* that a succession we perceive as objective *is* actually objective. Now, I think he is led to this watered down version of Kant's argument in part because he has initially overdetermined what Kant means by the "conformity to a rule" we have to presuppose to interpret subjective succession as perception of objective succession. I agree with him, though, in thinking that *presupposing* a rule also means that we will *confirm* the objectivity of our perception only if we *find* the rule. But I think Kant's argument is that our *perception itself* (in the third sense explained in note 68) is, in a sense, *already a striving to find the rule*, and that this striving is also what generates our awareness of the unity of objective time determinations.

of course, at the heart of Kant's solution to "Hume's problem" (I shall return to this point shortly).

The order-determinateness of *subjective* succession is thus inseparable from the order-determinateness of *objective* succession. *The (empirical) object* is where we identify the condition of a rule by virtue of which what follows can only follow, not precede, and what precedes can only precede, not follow. The sequence of states *in the object* is that for which the presupposition of a rule allows us to conclude that "in the first place, I cannot reverse the series, placing that which happens prior to that upon which it follows. And secondly, if the state which precedes is posited, this determinate event follows inevitably and necessarily." But, because we reflect such an order in the succession of determinations *in the object*, we attribute the same irreversibility to the subjective succession *of our perceptions*. Now this means that not only do we not *deduce* the objective character of the succession from the irreversibility of the succession of our perceptions, but, on the contrary, we derive our certainty of the irreversibility of the order of our perceptions from the recognition of an order of the succession of determinations *in the object*, that is, from the presupposition that *in the object*, state B follows state A, in conformity with a rule: "In this case, therefore, I shall have to derive the *subjective succession* of apprehension from the *objective succession* of appearances. Otherwise the succession of apprehension is entirely undetermined, and does not distinguish one appearance from another" (A193/B238). That the synthesis of apprehension is rule-bound (by virtue of which rule the subjective succession is recognized as order-determinate) depends on the presupposition that, in the object, state B follows state A "in conformity with a rule." But notice that here we are presented with two different senses of the term 'rule'. In the first sense, the rule is a *rule of sensible synthesis* (here, the irreversibility of subjective succession). In the second sense, it is a *discursive rule* (a hypothetical judgment as the major of a syllogism which remains to be determined, and whose conclusion would reflect the "following state," or rather the event: the transition from one state, which was and is no more, to the next, which was not and comes into being). The first rule—the rule of sensible synthesis—is dependent on the presupposition of the second rule, the discursive rule presupposed in the perception of an event. Because we presuppose that the object conforms to a discursive rule (although we do not necessarily cognize this rule), we recognize a sensible rule-governedness in the synthesis of our apprehension—the irreversibility of succession.[75]

---

[75] So interpreted, the relation Kant establishes between the *irreversibility* of subjective succession and the representation of an objective succession as *conforming to a rule*, and thus as *necessary*, is not the "*non sequitur* of numbing grossness" that Strawson (following Lovejoy) attributed to Kant. Strawson thinks that Kant concludes from the irreversibility of the succession of perceptions to the causal necessity of the objective succession. His reconstruction of Kant's argument is, I think, mistaken, both in what he approves (representing a subjective succession [*a*, then *b*] as order-determinate is thinking it as being *caused by* an objective succession [*A*, then *B*]) and in what he disapproves (Kant then fallaciously concludes from the order-determinateness of subjective succession, to the purported necessity of the objective succession it represents); see Strawson, *Bounds of Sense*, 28, 136–38. Kant's argument is in fact not grounded on a causal theory of perception (this would be circular from the out-

To these two senses of the term 'rule', we must add a third, in which the rule becomes a *principle*: the Second Analogy of Experience. From the analysis I have just elaborated, one must conclude that, in the realm of appearances, it is an absolutely universal rule (hence a principle) that "everything that happens presupposes something upon which it follows in according to a rule."

Let us now consider the three senses of "rule" in more detail.

THREE SENSES OF "RULE"

I shall call R the universal rule or principle stating that "everything that happens presupposes something else upon which it follows according to a rule," r the particular (empirical) objective rule, and r* the rule of sensible synthesis (awareness of irreversibility of subjective succession).

The correlation between the universal principle R and particular rules r is apparent for instance in this passage: "In conformity with such a rule there must lie in what precedes an event the condition of a rule according to which this event invariably and necessarily follows" (A193/B238–39). In conformity with R, there must lie in what precedes the condition of a rule r, that is, some event to be reflected under concepts in the antecedent of a hypothetical judgment such as 'if p, then A is altered from state S_1 to state S_2. Or more precisely: 'All As, if they are B, are altered from state S_1 to state S_2.[76] The universal rule (principle) R thus states that for any event one can find a rule r. For example, for the event: the stone grows warm, there is a rule r to be found by comparison/reflection/abstraction. This rule may be 'all stones, if lit by the sun, get warm', or 'all stones, if a fire burns under them, get warm', or 'all stones, if a hot source runs under them, get warm', and so on. If such a judgment is taken to be valid "for everybody, always," then it expresses a causal connection. In any case, the very fact that I perceive, in any singular case, *that the stone grows warm* (which is a different attitude from that of simply reacting to a sensation and then another, one of cold and then one of heat, so that for instance I avoid or on the contrary seek out the source of this

---

set, since it would presuppose the very concept whose objective validity is to be proved), but on an analysis of the conditions of the relation of our representations to an object (= the logical forms of judgment and the syntheses of imagination guided by the unity of apperception with a view to reflecting appearances according to these forms). By virtue of these conditions, representing an objective succession is *synonymous* with implicitly, confusedly (i.e., preconceptually) representing this succession as necessary, that is, as conforming to a rule. This awareness of necessity is what immediately (i.e., prior to any causal theory of perception) translates into awareness of the irreversibility (p3) of the subjective succession (p2) of our perceptions (p1) (on p1, p2, and p3, see note 68).

[76] As I showed in chapter 4, Kant's hypothetical judgment should be understood as a predication "under an added condition." This explains why he can describe a hypothetical, just as much as a categorical judgment, as a "universal rule." The hypothetical judgment "If a stone is lit by the sun, it gets warm," might be expressed more adequately as: "All stones, if lit by the sun, get warm." Subsuming a particular case under the rule would then be subsuming a particular object (this stone) *and* the particular "added condition" it is now subjected to (the sun shining now) under the subject *and* the added condition of the universal rule. Thinking a causal connection in a particular case is thus thinking the conjunction of two particular states of affairs as subsumed under a universal rule: "All stones, if lit by the sun, get warm. This stone is now lit by the sun. Therefore, this stone gets warm." On this point, see also Longuenesse, "Kant on Causality."

sensation)—this very fact means that *I presuppose a rule* in conformity with which one and the same object, the stone, was such that it could acquire opposed predicates: cold, then warm.

The correlation between r (the particular discursive rule for a given event) and R (the universal principle of causality stating that each event presupposes a rule r) can help us understand the difference in Kant's formulation of the Second Analogy from the A to the B edition. In A, the principle is: "Everything that happens, that is, begins to be, presupposes something upon which it follows according to a rule" (A189). The "rule" mentioned here is r, and the principle itself is R: the universal principle that states of "everything that happens" that it obeys a rule r.

In B, the principle is: "All alterations take place in conformity with the law of the connection [*Verknüpfung*] of cause and effect" (B232). The term 'alteration' reminds us that every event is a change in the state of a permanent substance. Thus the continuity between the First and Second Analogies is made explicit. The "law of the connection of cause and effect" is R. Every event, that is, every alteration of a substance, is subordinated to R, the universal principle that states of every singular event that it has a cause, that is, presupposes something to be reflected under the antecedent of a discursive rule r.[77]

The proof of R, in the Second Analogy, consists in showing that presupposing a rule r is a condition for any experience of objective succession. This means that the presupposition of some rule r is the condition for a rule r* in the field of appearance: a rule that is not discursive, but intuitive, a rule for the sensible synthesis of our perceptions. This rule r* is the awareness of the irreversibility of the succession in apprehension.

This helps to clarify the meaning of the *schema* of causality, in the Schematism of the Pure Concepts of Understanding: "The schema of cause, and of the causality of a thing in general, is the real upon which, whenever posited, something else always follows. It consists, therefore, in the succession of the manifold, insofar as that succession is subject to a rule" (A144/B183). To say that "the real upon which, whenever posited, something else always follows" is the schema of causality is to say that the presupposition of chronological anteriority in a regularly repeated succession is what allows us to *recognize* a cause. Or, as Kant would have us think of it, this situation tells us that a series of appearances is "determined in itself in respect of the logical function of hypothetical judgment." But the reason we are thus entitled to translate a regular succession into a causal connection is that the experience (the perception, p₃) of what happens, prior to any *repeated* experience of its temporal succession with respect to another appearance, is possible only if we presuppose something else "upon which it follows *according to a rule*." For example, when I perceive that the ship, which was at po-

---

[77] Thus contrary to Beck ("A Prussian Hume and a Scottish Kant," in *Kant and Hume*, 111–29) and Allison (*Idealism*, 216), I do not think one can dissociate, in Kant's Second Analogy, the universal causal principle ("For every event, there is a cause") from the assertion that there are regularities in nature ("same cause, same effect") . As I understand it, Kant's argument for the universal causal principle is an argument for *both* aspects of the causal principle. For he proves the universal principle ("for every event, some cause") precisely by proving that we would not perceive a particular event without presupposing that it obeys a rule ("same cause, same effect").

sition p₁, is now at another position p₂, the perception of this change is in itself the presupposition of a rule for the alteration (here, the change in position) of one and the same ship. When I perceive that the wax, which was cold, odorless, and hard is now warm, scented, and soft, the perception of this change is in itself (i.e., prereflectively) the presupposition of a rule for the alteration of one and the same wax. Because I have always already *presupposed a rule* for "what happens," I am thus entitled to translate the repeated succession of "something preceding" and "what happens" into an *empirical determination of this rule*, and thus an empirical causal connection.

This, then, is Kant's solution to "Hume's problem." And here it is important to note how close it remains, in many respects, to Hume's own solution, even while Kant reverses Hume's answer to the main question, that of the origin of the concept of cause. Like Hume, Kant considers that we cognize particular causal connections only empirically.[78] Like Hume, he considers that causal connections give us no access to "hidden powers" of substances: they are nothing but relations. Like Hume, he takes these relations to reflect a "natural tendency" of our mind. But *unlike* Hume, Kant considers that this tendency is not that of associative imagination, generating (as Hume supposes) our reasonings on matters of fact, but rather that of the understanding (the capacity for discursivity, the capacity to judge or *Vermögen zu urteilen*) guiding the syntheses of imagination a priori. And this is why, to the question posed in *Metaphysik Volckmann* ("What is the connection between the wind and the movement of the ship?"), one must respond, on the one hand, as Hume does: between the one and the other, *what is given to our senses and imagination is nothing more than a regularly repeated succession*. But on the other hand, *contrary to Hume*, we must say that our concluding from a constant succession to a causal relation does not *add* to the succession we perceive a merely subjective element (a universalization stemming from a subjective tendency of the imagination, mistaken for an objective connection). Rather, asserting a causal relation is merely supplying what we knew to be missing in our perception of objective succession (e.g., the successive positions of the ship): the antecedent of the rule that the succession obeys insofar as it is perceived as an objective succession. In other words, perceiving an event (the alteration of a substance) is, in a way, always a conclusion without a premise, the conclusion of a hypothetical syllogism whose major premise we do not know. The *constant* succession between this event and another event preceding it allows us to determine the premise (or premises) of which it is the conclusion, and thus to establish a causal relation, in which appearances are taken to be "determined in themselves in respect of the form of hypothetical judgment."

[78] On this point the Second Analogy is quite explicit: "Only through the perception and comparison of events repeatedly following in a uniform manner upon preceding appearances are we enabled to discover a rule according to which certain events always follow upon certain appearances, and . . . this is the way in which we are first led to construct for ourselves the concept of cause" (A195–96/B240–41). However, Kant insists that this should not lead us to believe that the concept of cause itself has an empirical origin. In the "Transcendental Doctrine of Method," Kant reproaches Hume for having confused the undeniable contingency of all particular causal laws with the contingency of the *principle of causality* itself (A766/B794).

THE PROBLEM OF THE TEMPORAL RELATION OF CAUSE TO EFFECT:
ORDER OF TIME AND COURSE OF TIME

Here, however, we run up against a difficulty: if the explanations I have given are correct, Kant argues in the Second Analogy that every perception of an objective change—the alteration of a substance—presupposes that this change occurs according to a rule. When the rule is specified and shown to be valid "for everybody, always," a causal relation is determined. This is why the schema of causality is "the real upon which, whenever posited, something else always follows, . . . [i.e.,] the succession of the manifold, insofar as that succession is subject to a rule." However, this schema actually introduces another succession than that of the states of a substance (alteration): what the description of the schema refers to is the regularly repeated succession between the alteration of a substance (an event) and *something else which precedes it*, and which ultimately will be reflected as the *cause* of the alteration. But then we are back where we started: how do we perceive *this* succession? Presumably not as the alteration of a substance.

Only after completing the five expositions of his argument does Kant provide an answer to this question. And this answer, when it finally comes, is quite surprising: actually, cause and effect are in the general case *not* successive, but *simultaneous*. Although regularly repeated succession is the sensible sign—the schema—through which we recognize a causal connection, this does not mean that the *cause* precedes the *effect*. On the contrary, at least in the first moment of its actualization, the cause is always *simultaneous* with the effect. The reason there is nevertheless a relation of temporal succession is that the *effect*—the alteration—*is not produced in one moment*. Like all realities, it is generated continuously through time:

> The great majority of efficient natural causes are simultaneous with their effects, and the sequence in time of the latter is due only to the fact that the cause cannot achieve its complete effect in one moment. But in the moment in which the effect first comes to be, it is invariably simultaneous with the causality of its cause. If this cause should have ceased to exist a moment before, the effect would never have come to be. (A203/B248)

Kant's examples of the simultaneity of cause and effect are well known: the leaden ball and the hollow in a cushion, a heated stove and the heat in a room, the sides of a container and the curved surface of a liquid.[79] Notice that only with these examples, mentioned *after* the completion of the proof, are we given actual instances of causal connections. The example of the moving ship with which the argument began was an *effect* for which we did not have a determinate *cause* It was an alteration whose very perception, Kant argued, implicitly presupposes something reflected under the condition of a rule—for example, the wind mentioned in *Metaphysik Volckmann*. Yet, neither wind nor any concrete cause is mentioned in the argument of the Second Analogy. Only at the very end of his expo-

---

[79] A202–4/B248–49.

sition does Kant provide examples of *complete* causal connections, conclusions *with their premises*. We then see clearly that succession (and *regular* succession, "the schema of causality") is not so much the succession of cause and effect as the succession between the state of the substance *before* the activity of the cause which alters it, and its state *after* this activity. The cushion is smooth and flat, then tumbled and hollowed. We presuppose a cause for this alteration—something to be reflected under the condition of a rule—and indeed find it in the presence of the ball. Kant specifies that the time between the cause (laying down the ball) and its effect (the hollow in the cushion) is "*vanishing*." If an order of temporal succession between cause and effect is nevertheless thought, this is because a relation exists between them, such that if the one (the cause, the ball on the cushion) is posited, the other (the effect, the hollow in the cushion) is posited, but not the reverse: if the hollow is posited, the ball is not necessarily posited:

> If I view as a cause a ball which impresses a hollow as it lies on a stuffed cushion, the cause is simultaneous with the effect. But I still distinguish the two through the time-relation of their dynamical connection. For if I lay the ball on the cushion, a hollow follows upon the previous flat smooth shape; but if (for any reason) there previously exists a hollow in the cushion, a leaden ball does not follow upon it. (A203/B248–49)

Here it is clear that the succession is above all the succession *of the states of the cushion*: "a hollow follows upon the *previous flat* smooth shape." But this succession (alteration) is linked to the difference between the presence and the absence of the ball. Hence the temporal location of the ball as a cause is determined in relation to the alteration to which it is linked. Significantly, Kant uses the terms of the *modus ponens* to describe this connection and its asymmetry. If the antecedent ("a ball lies on the cushion") is posited, the consequence ("the cushion is hollowed") is posited. But the reverse is not true: the consequent being posited, the antecedent is not posited at all. Thus the same *synthesis speciosa* aiming at the categorical and hypothetical forms of judgment, which guides the empirical reproductions required for the perception of a succession of states, also guides the empirical reproductions required for the determination of the rule of this succession, that is, for the determination of its cause.

The "succession of the manifold insofar as it obeys a rule" is the schema of causality because a real ground (or cause) can be *recognized* only in relation to the alteration of a substance, and thus in relation to an objective succession. But this in no way contradicts the fact that the cause is simultaneous with its effect, or that the time interval between the one and the other is "vanishing." The ship begins to move the moment the wind begins to blow, the cushion is hollowed the moment the ball enters into contact with it, the surface of the water curves the moment it is contained within the glass. And if the cause is continued during a time interval, the effect is continued at least through that same time interval. Thus Kant distinguishes between the *order of time* (*Zeitordnung*) and the *course of time* (*Zeitablauf*). The former is determined by the dynamical standpoint of relation (antecedent/consequent, cause/effect), according to which appearances mutually assign each other their place in time, however brief the interval between what is determined as "before" and what is determined as "after" may be. The latter, on the other hand, must be understood from the mathematical standpoint of *reality*, which, in the Schematism chapter and in the Anticipations of Perception, was described as a "continuous and uniform production in time."[80]

With the specification of these two aspects of time, Kant gives us a first glimpse into the overall unity of his system of principles: in the schematism of relation, appearances mutually assign each other their place in time (simultaneity and succession). This presupposes the formal intuition of time as a *quantum continuum*, in which the genesis of all reality as an intensive magnitude can be represented. This unified consideration (relations of appearances in time, formal intuition of time as a whole) opens the way to the Third Analogy, in which Kant's analysis of the relation of simultaneity brings back into the foreground the discussion of the *totum realitatis* we already encountered in the Anticipations of Perception: the whole of reality under the presupposition of which all determinations of appearances are synthesized, and recognized.

Kant and the Principle of Reason

Before taking leave of the Second Analogy, we may want to ask what remains of the "principle of reason" which, thirty years prior to the *Critique*, was the starting point for Kant's inquiry into the concept of cause. Kant claims that in the Second Analogy he provided the only possible proof for the principle of reason.[81] But what principle is he talking about here? Only a principle of reason for the *alteration of substances*. For the alteration of any (relatively permanent) object given in space and time, there has to be a reason, or cause. Otherwise the object would be neither recognizable nor locatable in relation to other objects in space and time. This is a very modest claim indeed, and one which addresses only one aspect of the 1755 principle of reason (the *principium rationis fiendi*, principle of reason of existence). Neither for the essence, nor for the existence of substances, does Kant now state, or prove, a principle of reason. All we have is a principle of reason of the alteration of substances whose own existence we must presuppose, and cannot explain by any reason.

Nevertheless, Kant does in a sense salvage all three aspects of the principle of reason stated in his 1755 *New Elucidation*. He maintains that, for all true (empirical) propositions, there is a reason for their truth. We may know only a *consequently determining reason* (when all we have is empirical knowledge that the proposition is de facto true). But the Second Analogy also entitles us always to posit an *antecedently determining reason*, because for any object, the properties attributed to it either belong to its essence (analytically or by synthetic a priori judgments such as those of Kant's metaphysics of nature), or, if changeable properties, satisfy the principle of causality stated and proved in the Second Analogy:

---

[80] Guyer misses this point when he takes the simultaneity of cause and effect to be an exception that Kant needs to explain away rather than the usual case. See *Claims*, 259–62.

[81] A200–201/B246–47; also A217/B265.

"Everything that happens presupposes something else upon which it follows according to a rule," or "All alteration occurs in accordance with the principle of connection of causes and effects." Thus even though the Second Analogy specifically proves only *one* aspect of *one* of the three "principles of reason" of 1755—the principle of coming into existence (*principium fiendi*) and only as a principle of the existence of *alterations of* (*relatively permanent*) *substances*—its proof is inseparable from a reinterpretation and, modulo this (deflationary) reinterpretation, a preservation of *all three* aspects of the 1755 principle of reason. The reinterpretation consists in saying that we do not know real essences, the essences of things as they are in themselves, but only "logical essences," concepts under which alone we are able to generate our representation of reidentifiable, and thus cognizable, empirical objects.[82] The (deflationary) preservation consists in saying that, given these essences, any mark we attribute to an object (a mark we may at first know only empirically, by a *ratio consequenter determinans* or *ratio cognoscendi*) has to be either derivable (analytically or synthetically) from its (logical) essence, or relatable to "something else, upon which it follows, according to a rule."[83]

How does this furnish the answer to Kant's worry in the 1760s, that we understand the necessity of the connection in an analytic *ratio ponens*, but not in a synthetic one? Is it not still the case that we see how we have a universal rule on which to build a *modus ponens* in 'God, if perfectly just, punishes the wicked' but not in 'all stones, if lit by the sun, get warm' or 'all ships, if the wind blows, are set into motion'?[84] For it is an analytic character of the concept of perfect justice that it involves punishment of the wicked; but it is not an analytic character of 'being lit by the sun', or of the combination of 'being a stone' and 'being lit by the sun' that it involves the warming of the stone. Kant's solution is, I think, this: in the synthetic (empirical) rule, what takes the place of the analytic connection of concepts is (1) the necessary supposition *that there is* an antecedently determining reason (*ratio fiendi*) for all alteration, and (2) the supposition of the *continuous preservation through time* of the synthetic connection (regularly repeated conjunction) to which only experience gives us access. This supposition itself de-

---

[82] Cf. Letter to Reinhold, May 12, 1789: "For I can easily find the logical essence, by the analysis of my concepts into all that I think under them, that is, I can find the primary *constitutiva* of a given concept, as well as the attributes, as *rationata logica* of this essence. But the *real* essence (the nature) of any object, that is, the primary *inner* ground of all that necessarily belongs to a given thing, this is impossible for man to discover" (Ak. XI-2, 36–37; 139–40. Cf. also chapter 5, note 42, and chapter 11, note 17).

[83] I should specify that Kant distinguishes between this principle of reason, which in a limited sense is a principle of the reason of existences (for every event—that is, for the coming into existence of any real determination—there is a real ground or cause), and the "logical" principle of reason, a principle of reason for assertoric propositions, which he states as follows: "all (assertoric) judgments must have a reason" (see Letter to Reinhold of May 12, 1789, Ak. XI-2, 36; 139). This principle is reminiscent of the broadest statement of the principle of reason of propositions in the *New Elucidation*. For any proposition to be true, there must be a reason that makes the predicate, not merely noncontradictory with the subject—then the proposition would be only problematic—but also asserted of the subject while excluding its opposite.

[84] On this formulation of the hypothetical rule, see note 76.

pends on our a priori intuition of time as a *quantum continuum infinitum*, as well as on the principle, demonstrated in the Anticipations of Perception, that reality is represented as *continuously generated through time.*[85] So, *synthesis speciosa* with a view to hypothetical judgment (which generates recognition of regularly repeated succession), together with formal intuition of time and Anticipations of Perception, compensates for the analytic connection of concepts that fails to obtain in the synthetic *modus ponens.* Thus, as I announced earlier, Kant solves the problem he posed himself in the 1760s by arguing that the necessity of the synthetic hypothetical rule does not depend on the concepts combined, but on the contrary the concepts combined are themselves dependent on the act of generating the representation of a *ratio ponens*, a necessary rule for a modus ponens. This act first generates a representation of the order of sensible representations (*synthesis speciosa*), then discursive rules (*synthesis intellectualis*), that is, possible major premises for *modus ponens* reflecting the sensible order of time.

As we saw, in this representation of the order of time, objective *succession* is represented in contradistinction to objective *simultaneity* (as shown in the opposition between perceiving the successive positions of the ship sailing down the river, and perceiving the simultaneously existing parts of the house). If the former depends on the category of causal relation (i.e., the relation of objects "in themselves determined" with respect to the form of hypothetical judgment), the latter depends, Kant will argue in the Third Analogy, on the category of *community*, or reciprocal interaction. Thus we now need to consider this third category in order to have a full view of Kant's argument in the Analogies of Experience.

LOGICAL DISJUNCTION, SIMULTANEITY, COMMUNITY

According to Kant's explanations in the Second Analogy, a causal action is always simultaneous with the initial emergence of its effect. In the Third Analogy, Kant takes one more step and states that the temporal relation of simultaneity presupposes a relation of *reciprocal* action between substances, so that all substances

[85] However, there remains a difficulty here. As I noted in chapter 10, in the Anticipations of Perception Kant warns us that the representation of reality as *continously generated through time* is the representation of a mere *possibility*, which in turn makes possible the "anticipation" of experience by mathematical construction. But whether changes are *actually* continuous can be known only empirically (A171–72/B212–13; cf. chapter 10, note 47). However, in the Second Analogy, Kant *asserts* the principle of the continuity of change (A208–9/B254). And indeed, he needs to assert it if I am correct in my suggestion that it serves, in the synthetic *ratio ponens*, as a substitute for the necessity of the connection of concepts in the analytic *ratio ponens*. I think that Kant's realization of this difficulty is one reason for his remarks concerning the necessity of empirical laws in the introduction to the third *Critique*: only an additional principle of reflective judgment, which allows us to think the continuity of forms in nature, also allows us to think that empirical laws, which are contingent with respect to pure understanding, are nevertheless *necessary* laws—that is, express necessary connections (strictly universal rules). See *KU*, Ak. V, 185; 24. I suggest there is an important relation between the (discursive) continuity of forms asserted as a principle of reflective judgment, in the third *Critique*, and the (intuitive) continuity of alteration, and thus of empirical time, in the first *Critique*. On this point, see also Longuenesse, "Logique et Métaphysique," and "Kant on Causality."

we perceive as simultaneous are in a relation of universal community (*Gemein-schaft*) or interaction (*Wechselwirkung*). Thus Kant completes his system of the Analogies of Experience, as an explanation of the transcendental conditions of objective temporal determinations.

In the Metaphysical Deduction of the Categories, Kant traces back the category of community to the logical form of disjunctive judgment. This parallelism is generally taken to be the most artificial of all.[86] Kant justifies it by claiming that in a logical disjunction, concepts are *coordinated* to each other, while at the same time *excluding* each other, just as in the relation of community, objects are coordinated in space according to universal attractive and repulsive forces.[87] Now, prima facie such a parallelism seems at best to have merely metaphorical value, at worst to be guilty of precisely the kind of amphiboly Kant denounces in the appendix to the Transcendental Analytic, between *logical* relations of concepts and *real* relations of objects given in space and time.[88] Yet I shall argue that despite this unpromising aspect, the relation Kant tries to establish between logical disjunction and category of community is an important and significant one. It provides an indispensable key to understanding Kant's handling of general logic, his conception of the relation between general and transcendental logic, and finally the role he assigns to transcendental imagination.

As I understand it, Kant's argument concerning the category of community, if we follow it from the Metaphysical Deduction of the Categories, to the Schematism, to the Third Analogy, has the following overall structure: (1) the logical form of disjunctive judgment is the form proper to the act of understanding that generates the representation of the universal subordination of *genera* and *species* in nature; but (2) this presupposes the representation of material substances as in relation of reciprocal action, or community; and (3) this, in turn, depends on a *synthesis speciosa* by means of which things are represented as simultaneously existing in space. Now, all of this means that conversely, representing things as simultaneously existing in space is from the outset guided by the capacity to represent their reciprocal interaction *and* by the capacity to represent nature under a universal scale of genera and species.

There are two main reasons, I think, for the particular difficulty we face in trying to grasp the correspondence Kant establishes between logical form (in this case, the logical form of disjunctive judgment) and category (in this case, community or reciprocal action of substances). The first reason is that, in fact, the transcendental role of the form of disjunctive judgment (its role in guiding the *synthesis speciosa* that generates the representation of multiplicities to be reflected under concepts in judgments) cannot be considered apart from that of the

---

[86] Cf. Adickes: "The explanation of the relation between disjunctive judgment and reciprocal action (§11 d) is extraordinarily contrived" (*Kritik*, 125). Guyer, *Claims*, 452 (n.14 to chap. 11): "As is often pointed out, Kant's connection of the real relation of reciprocal influence with the logical notion of an exclusive disjunction is the most tenuous of all."

[87] Cf. B112, which I analyze in detail in the next section.

[88] Cf. A274–75/B330–31, the amphiboly on the third pair of concepts of reflection, inner and outer. See my analysis in chapter 6.

other two forms of relation in judgment: categorical and hypothetical. We saw this earlier when, in chapter 4, we considered the logical forms of relation in judgment: already then it was emphasized that forming a disjunctive judgment supposes that concepts have previously been obtained (since disjunctive judgment expresses the division of a concept into its species). But the formation of empirical concepts depends itself on reflection according to the forms of categorical and hypothetical judgment. This means, if my general explanation of *synthesis speciosa* is correct, that *synthesis speciosa* with a view to the logical form of disjunctive judgment, and thus Kant's explanation of *simultaneity* as the schema of community, can be understood only if we clarify the collaboration of all three forms of relation in generating this schema. This is apparent in the brief sketch of Kant's argument in the previous paragraph: I stated that the *logical disjunction* of concepts applied to empirical objects presupposes the representation of these objects as in relations of reciprocal *interaction*, which in turn supposes their representation as *existing simultaneously* in space. I shall attempt, in what follows, to develop and clarify the general structure of Kant's argument so understood.

The second reason for the difficulty we face in trying to understand the relation Kant wants to establish between the logical form of disjunctive judgment and the category of community (with its schema, simultaneity) is that we are here at the heart of Kant's coming to terms with his rationalist predecessors as well as with his own rationalist background. Kant needs to show that *although* empirical objects, being given in intuition, are not knowable as *infimae species*, as the ultimate specification of universal concepts known by pure intellect, nevertheless the form of disjunctive judgment, and thus the representation of the complete division of concepts, plays an essential role in generating what we might call the 'logical space' with respect to which empirical objects are recognized and individualized. But again, the other two forms of relation in judgment, and the schemata they contribute to generate, play a mediating role in ensuring that the singularity of intuition and the universality of concepts are related to one another, so that individual objects (given in space and time) can be thought as susceptible to being reflected according to the systematic division of genera and species, i.e., according to the logical form of disjunctive judgment.

In the first part of this section, I shall consider the relation Kant claims to establish between the logical form of disjunctive judgment and the category of community. I shall argue that this relation rests on a change of perspective analogous to the one in the case of the categories of quantity: Kant progresses from the context of the *logical form* to the context of the *category* when he progresses from characterizing a *discursive relation of concepts* (here, the form of disjunctive judgment) to characterizing the *sensible manifolds* reflected under concepts combined according to this discursive form (here, multiplicities of objects as coexisting in space and time). The *category* of community is the universal concept reflecting the *synthesis speciosa* by means of which we generate the representation of these sensible manifolds.

In the second part of this section, I shall consider this *synthesis speciosa* itself: the transcendental synthesis of imagination generating the representation of things coexisting in space and time and susceptible to being reflected under common concepts. This *synthesis speciosa* is at the heart of Kant's argument for the Third Analogy of Experience. I shall show that, in his argument, Kant calls upon all three forms of relation in judgment, and thus all three categories of relation together with their schemata, to account for our generating our own representation of a unified space and time in which empirical objects may be cognized through their relations of universal interaction. One particularly striking aspect of this argument is Kant's claim that we thus also situate *ourselves*, as empirical unities of consciousness associated to a body we represent as our own, in the unified empirical space and time whose representation we thereby generate.

Logical Disjunction and the Category of Community

We saw in the preceding chapter that when he comments on the logical forms of quality in judgment, *infinite* judgment is the only title Kant considers in some detail. Similarly, when he comments on the forms of relation, he gives detailed explanations only concerning *disjunctive* judgment:

> Disjunctive judgment contains a relation of two or more propositions to each other, a relation not, however, of logical sequence, but of logical opposition, insofar as the sphere of the one excludes the sphere of the other, and yet at the same time of community [*Gemeinschaft*], insofar as the propositions taken together occupy the whole sphere of the cognition in question. Disjunctive judgment expresses, therefore, a relation of the parts of the sphere of such cognition, since the sphere of each part is a complement of the sphere of the others, yielding together the sum-total of the divided cognition. . . . There is, therefore, in a disjunctive judgment a certain community of the cognized constituents, such that they mutually exclude each other, and yet thereby determine *in their totality* the true cognition. For, when taken together, they constitute the whole content of one given cognition. This is all that need here be considered for our purpose in what follows. (A74/B99)

We can see here that, in defining disjunctive judgment, Kant privileges the point of view of *extension*. In a disjunctive judgment, "the sphere of a cognition," that is, the extension of a concept, is divided into the mutually exclusive spheres of its various subspecies, which together constitute the whole sphere of the divided cognition.[89]

This privileging of extension is even more explicit in the *Jäsche Logic*: the disjunctive judgment '*a* is either *b*, *c*, *d*, or *e*' is pictured by the division of a rectangular surface *a* (representing the extension of the divided concept) into four surfaces *b*, *c*, *d*, and *e* (which respectively represent the extensions of the subspecies of *a*). Disjunctive judgment, says Kant, asserts that the "*x* thought under the concept *a*" belongs to one or the other of the divisions *b*, *c*, *d*, or *e*. He prefaces this explanation by a comparison between categorical judgment and disjunctive judgment:

[89] I take it here that when Kant says that "the sphere of the one excludes the sphere of the other," he means the sphere of the *concepts* defined by the specification of the divided concept in the disjunctive proposition: for instance, in '*a* is either *b* or *c*' the reciprocally excluding spheres are the respective spheres of the concepts '*ab*' (*a* specified as being *b*) and '*ac*' (*a* specified as being *c*).

In categorical judgments, *x*, which is contained under *b*, is also contained under *a*:

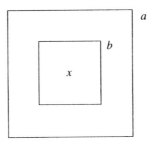

In disjunctive ones *x*, which is contained under *a*, is contained either under *b* or *c*, etc.:

Thus the division in disjunctive judgments indicates . . . all the parts of [the whole concept's] sphere.[90]

Kant then gives as an example: "A scholar is either a chronicler or a reasoner [*ein Gelehrter ist entweder ein historischer, oder ein Vernunftgelehrter*]." If we grant that 'chronicler' and 'reasoner' are mutually exclusive concepts, whose extensions taken together encompass the whole sphere of the concept 'scholar',[91] then, following what Kant says in the passage from the *Critique* cited earlier, these two concepts are at once in a relation of opposition (one and the same *x* cannot be included under these two concepts) and of community (their extensions together constitute two complementary parts of the whole extension of the concept 'scholar').

In the metaphysical deduction, Kant's example is more complex:

'The world exists either through blind chance, or through inner necessity, or through an external cause'. Each of these propositions occupies a part of the sphere of the possible cognition concerning the existence of a world in general; all of them together occupy the whole sphere. To take the cognition out of one of these spheres means placing it in one of the other spheres, and to place it in one sphere means taking it out of the others. (A74/B99)

[90] *Logik*, §29, Ak. IX, 108; 604.
[91] Cf. Kant's treatment of this disjunction in the preface to the *Anfangsgründe*, Ak. IV, 467–68; 3–4.

Here, the divided concept is the concept of 'existence of a world in general', or more specifically the concept 'modality of the existence of a world in general'.[92] This concept may be divided in two steps. First, 'existence of a world in general' is divided into 'contingent existence' ("through blind chance") or 'necessary existence'. Then, 'necessary existence' is further divided into 'internally necessary existence' and 'externally necessary existence' (= necessary "through an external cause"). Now, if the expression of the disjunctive judgment were formed on the same model as in the *Logic*, it should be "the existence of a world in general is either from blind chance, or from inner necessity, or from an external cause." But the judgment cited in the *Critique* is not this, since its subject is not the general concept of the existence of a world, but a singular term, *the* world (presumably, the phenomenal world as we know it).[93] The judgment 'The world exists either through blind chance, or through inner necessity, or through an external cause' thus states that the singular object thought under the concept 'world' (or, rather, the 'existence of the world') falls under one or the other of the divisions of the concept of the 'existence of a world in general.' If we return to Kant's example in the *Logic*, an equivalent case of disjunctive judgment would be, instead of 'A scholar is either a historical scholar or a rational scholar', 'Philalethes is either a historical scholar, or a rational scholar'. Instead of merely dividing the sphere of a concept into the spheres of two or more subconcepts with mutually exclusive extensions, we here describe a singular term as falling under one, and one only, of the subspecies of the divided concept. In other words, in the example from the *Critique* the judgment specifies a particular instantiation for the x mentioned in the analysis of disjunctive judgment given in the *Logic*. But in both cases (the simpler example of the *Logic* as well as the more complex one of the *Critique*), what is most significant is that Kant explains the logical form of disjunctive judgment in terms of the relation between the *extensions* or *spheres* of concepts—that is, as the division of the sphere of a concept into mutually exclusive spheres, which together constitute the whole sphere of the divided concept.

This is confirmed by the further comments Kant adds in the B edition of the *Critique*. There he insists that in order to make clearer the identity of the procedure of understanding at work in the logical form of disjunctive judgment and in the category of community, it is important to see disjunctive judgments as ex-

[92] It may seem strange to describe existence as a predicate, knowing Kant's warning against treating existence as a predicate in his refutation of the ontological proof (cf. A598–99/B626–27). But remember that in the same context, Kant also asserts that from a logical standpoint *anything* may be treated as a predicate. Existence is simply not a *real* predicate, that is, it adds no positive determination (*determinatio vere affirmativa*) to the concept of the thing. The same holds for the *modality* of existence. It adds no real determination to the concept of anything, but instead "expresses its relation to our cognitive capacity" (A219/B266). Nevertheless, it can be given expression as a predicate—a category—attributed to an object. The exposition of the logical form of disjunctive judgment is, in any case, not concerned with the content of the concepts combined.

[93] See A218/B265n. Of course, the conclusion of the fourth Antinomy in the Transcendental Dialectic will be that Kant's example of disjunctive judgment in the Transcendental Analytic is an illusory one: the world-whole is *not* the kind of object that can be thought as belonging to any of the subspheres of the concept 'modality of existence'. But this difficulty does not concern the logical from of the judgment, which is our sole consideration here.

pressing the coordinations of conceptual *spheres*, all of which, taken together, constitute the whole sphere of the divided concept. The sphere of the divided concept is thus a *whole* divided into *parts*. This relation is precisely the same, says Kant, as that between a "whole made up of things" and these things, or between a thing (e.g., a body) and its parts:

> To gain assurance that [the category of community and the form of a disjunctive judgment] do actually accord, we must observe that in all disjunctive judgments the sphere (that is, the multiplicity [*Menge*] which is contained in any one judgment) is represented as a whole divided into parts (the subordinate concepts), and that since no one of them can be contained under any other, they are thought as co-ordinated with, not subordinated to, each other, and so as determining each other, not in one direction only, as in a series, but reciprocally, as in an aggregate—if one member of the division is posited, all the rest are excluded, and conversely.
>
> Now in a *whole* which is made up of *things*, a similar connection [*Verknüpfung*] is being thought; for one thing is not subordinated, as effect, to another, as cause of its existence, but, simultaneously and reciprocally, is co-ordinated with it, as cause of the determination of the other (as, for instance, in a body the parts of which reciprocally attract and repel each other). (B112)[94]

Now, as I commented earlier, equating in this way the relation between extensions or spheres of concepts, on the one hand, and the relation of whole to parts in things, on the other hand, is a surprising move, suspiciously reminiscent of the Leibnizian amphiboly Kant himself vehemently rejects in the appendix to the Transcendental Analytic (On the Amphiboly of Concepts of Reflection). For regardless of how one interprets logical disjunction (from an extensional or from an intensional standpoint), identifying it with the "division of a thing into its parts" or with the "division of a whole made up of things" seems tantamount to identifying the relation of *things* with a relation of *concepts*. And in allowing himself such an amphiboly, Kant seems to violate a distinction he had carefully drawn in the Transcendental Aesthetic: that between the relation of a concept to a manifold of representations contained *under* it, and the relation of an intuition to a manifold of representations contained *in* it. Logical disjunction exemplifies the first type of relation, whereas the division of a thing into parts, or that of a "whole made up of things" into the multiplicity of things constituting its ultimate parts, exemplifies the second type of relation, since a thing or a "whole made up of things" is represented *in intuition*. The relation of a thing to its parts, just like the relation of a "whole made up of things" to these things as its parts, is homologous to the relation of an (empirical) intuition to the representations contained *in* it, whereas the logical division of a concept is the relation of a concept to the representations thought *under* it.

But actually, Kant's shift, in the description of disjunctive judgment, from consideration of *concepts* to consideration of their *extension*, does provide a defense

---

[94] Here again, when Kant talks about "the multiplicity contained in any one judgment" he means: the multiplicity *thought under each subspecies of the divided concept* (for instance, the multiplicity thought under *ab*, and the multiplicity thought under *ac*: cf. note 89).

against the charge of amphiboly. To see this, recall the terms in which, in the Aesthetic, Kant formulated the distinction between *concept* (containing representations *under* it) and *intuition* (containing representations *in* it):

> Now every concept must be thought as a representation which is contained in an infinite multiplicity [*in einer unendlichen Menge*] of different possible representations (as their common mark), and which therefore contains these *under* itself; but no concept, as such, can be thought as containing an infinite number of representations *within* itself. It is in this latter way, however, that space is thought. . . . Consequently, the original representation of space is an *a priori* intuition, not a concept. (B40)

This description of the concept (as a representation contained in things, and as thus containing the latter 'under' it) accords with Kant's definition of the *content* (*Inhalt*) and *extension* (*Umfang*) of a concept in the *Logic*: "Every concept, *as partial concept*, is contained in the representation of things; as *ground of cognition, i.e., as a mark* [*Merkmal*], these things are contained *under* it. In the former respect every concept has a *content*, in the other an *extension* [*einen Umfang*]."[95] When a concept is considered with respect to its *extension*, it is itself, as a *concept*, defined as a *mark*. This mark serves to identify a multiplicity (*Menge*) of things, which have this mark in common and thus are thought *under* it. But in the metaphysical deduction of the category of community, what is under consideration in the characterization of logical disjunction is not the concept as a mark. Rather, the discussion is directly concerned with the *extension* or *sphere* of the concept, as the multiplicity [*Menge*] of singular things thought under it. Now, following Kant's terminology, to say that the concept as mark does not contain the multiplicity of things *in* it, but *under* it, in no way prevents us from saying that its *extension* or *sphere* contains *within* it, as *parts* of which it is the *whole*, the respective extensions of the concepts that divide its sphere. Thus Kant does not assimilate the relation between the parts of a material whole to the relation of concepts defined as combinations of marks, but to the relation of the spheres of these concepts understood as the multiplicities [*Mengen*] of things thought under these concepts.

If this is correct, then the shift of perspective we have here is analogous to that already encountered in the case of the categories of quantity. I argued in chapter 9 that these categories reflect the intuitive exhibition of the "pure form" of the *extension* of concepts, that is, the "successive synthesis of homogeneous units" necessary for generating the logical form of quantity in judgment.[96] Similarly, the category of community reflects the intuitive exhibition of multiplicities to be reflected discursively under concepts combined in a disjunctive judgment. But here,

---

[95] *Logik*, §7 (Ak. IX, 95; 592). This text appears in Kant's notes as early as the 1760s, according to Adickes's dating: see *Refl.* 3096, Ak. XVI, 657–58. One might be confused by the fact that there is an 'in' relation in the case of concepts too: a concept is contained 'in' an infinity of representations, which are thus contained 'under' it. This 'in', however, should not be confused with the one that holds in the case of intuitions: "an infinite number of representations are contained 'in' an intuition." In the case of concepts, one concept is 'in' many representations (concepts or intuitions), as their common mark. In the second, many intuitions are 'in' one space, as its parts or occupants.

[96] Cf. chapter 9, pp. 249–55.

what we have is not the "pure form" of extension (homogeneous multiplicities, multiplicities thought under one and the same concept), but an extension consti- tuted by qualitatively determined individual things; not a *quantum*, but a *com- positum*.[97] This is what makes it possible for Kant to relate the logical form of dis- junctive judgment to the sensible intuition of "the whole made up of things" or "the whole and its parts," or again "the body and its parts," reflected under the cat- egory of community. The same procedure of understanding, Kant insists, is at work in both kinds of representations:

> The procedure which the understanding follows in representing to itself the sphere of
> a divided concept, it likewise follows when it thinks a thing as divisible; and just as,
> in the former case, the members of a division exclude each other, and yet are com-
> bined in one sphere, so the understanding represents to itself the parts of the latter as
> existing (as substances) in such a way that, while each exists independently of the
> others, they are yet combined together in one whole. (B112–13)

When considering quantity, I suggested that Kant's point was the following: the sensible exhibition of a homogeneous multiplicity depends on a *synthesis spe- ciosa* of imagination (determination of inner sense by the understanding) that pre- sents a sensible multiplicity to be reflected in accordance with the logical forms of quantity in judgment. Similarly with community, I think his point is that the sensible presentation of a *totum realitatis*, a whole of reality made up of hetero- geneous elements multiply and reciprocally correlated to each other, depends on a *synthesis speciosa*, a "determination of inner sense by the understanding," by means of which a sensible multiplicity is exhibited in such a way that it can be reflected in accordance with the logical form of disjunctive judgment. This dis- junctive judgment might be something like: 'The elements of the *totum realitatis* T are either A, or B, or C . . .' and so on. In other words, through such a synthe- sis, a *multiplicity of heterogeneous elements, correlated into a whole*, is presented

---

[97] This confirms once again how cautious one needs to be in interpreting Kant's notion of *exten- sion*. I indicated earlier that, from a strictly logical standpoint, Kant's notion of extension is essentially inherited from Port-Royal: the extension of a concept consists of the representations thought under it, whether these representations are universal or singular (in Kant's terms, whether they are concepts or intuitions). This is not the modern (Russellian) notion of extension as the class of individuals thought under a concept (on the "extension of an idea" in the Port-Royal Logic, and the ways in which it dif- fers from the modern notion of extension, see Pariente, *Port-Royal*, 230–32; also "Propositions," 248–49). But when general logic is considered in relation to transcendental logic, that is, in relation to the a priori conditions of representation of objects, then 'extension' tends to be identified with 'manifold of *individual things*', as is clearly the case in the texts we are considering now: here the spheres of the lower concepts are parts of the sphere of the higher concept, insofar as the multiplicity (*Menge*) of singular objects thought under them is part of the *Menge* of singular objects thought under the higher concept. Yet even in this case, one cannot straightforwardly identify Kant's notion of ex- tension with the modern notion. For the individuals which make up the extension of a concept in the Kantian sense play no role in the forms of logical inferences (they have no strictly logical status). Defining extensions in terms of manifolds of individuals when general logic is related to transcen- dental logic mainly serves to bring out the correlation between logical forms (forms of the combina- tions of concepts) and sensible syntheses (by which the representation of the individuals thought under the concepts is generated). Hence I cannot follow Schulthess (*Relation*, 11–13) when he sug- gests that Kant's conception of logic is a step toward an extensional logic in the modern sense.

in experience. This whole is none other than the *complete extension* of the concept, 'element of the *totum realitatis* T'.

But what does it mean for such a multiplicity to be exhibited in experience? We have already seen that things are recognized in two ways: by means of the concepts 'reciprocal with them', or concepts of essential characters, on the one hand; and by means of the concepts attributed to them only 'under an added condition', on the other hand.[98] This means that things can be fully identified only within the context of their universal interaction. Now, Kant's argument in the Third Analogy will be that the activity of thinking, by means of which we generate such recognition of individual things, is in turn the condition for our representation of their *simultaneous existence* in one (sensible) space. But if this is so, the *synthesis speciosa* corresponding to the category of community is more complex than any other. For on the one hand, we must say that *simultaneous existence in one spatial whole* is the sensible exhibition of things as "determined in themselves in respect of the logical form of disjunctive judgment." That is to say, it is the sensible exhibition of things in such a way that they may be reflected under concepts according to the form of the division of a generic concept. But on the other hand, what conditions this representation of things as so reflectable is a system of hypothetical judgments expressing the reciprocal determination of things in space and time. Indeed, Kant's argument in the Third Analogy will be that a *qualitatively determinate thing A*, and a *qualitatively determinate thing B* are represented as *simultaneous* just in case we can suppose a rule according to which if A (recognized under qualitative and quantitative determinations) is positcd, thcn B (similarly recognized) is posited, and reciprocally, if B is posited, then A is posited. According to Kant, only our capacity to think such a rule allows us to generate for ourselves both the representation of temporal relations of objective simultaneity, and a universal scale of genera and species (natural kinds) in nature.

We now perhaps have a better insight into the complex nature of the correspondence Kant wants to establish between the logical form of disjunctive judgment and the category of community. After having explained the logical form of disjunctive judgment, Kant turns to the corresponding category. But what he then describes is a relation of *interaction* or *reciprocal causality* between substances, namely a relation that seems more naturally in tune with *hypothetical* judgment (and the category of causality, which has now become *reciprocal* causality) than with disjunctive judgment. This is readily apparent in the passage from the Metaphysical Deduction cited earlier:

> In all disjunctive judgments, the sphere (that is, the multiplicity [*Menge*] which is contained in any one judgment) is represented as a whole divided into parts (the subordinate concepts), and . . . since no one of them can be contained under any other, they are thought as co-ordinated with, not subordinated to, each other, and so as determining each other, not in one direction only, as in a series, but reciprocally, as in an aggregate—*if one member of the division is posited, all the rest are excluded, and*

[98] See pp. 373–74.

conversely [my emphasis]. Now, in a *whole* which is made up of *things*, a similar connection [*Verknüpfung*] is being thought; for one thing is not subordinated, as effect, to another, as cause of its existence, but, simultaneously and reciprocally, is coordinated with it, as cause of the determination of the other (as, for instance, in a body the parts of which reciprocally attract and repel each other). (B112)

To be sure, immediately after this passage Kant insists that the relation of *reciprocal* causality, characterizing an *aggregate*, is of a "quite different nature" than the mere relation of cause to effect, in which "the consequence does not in its turn reciprocally determine the ground." But it is worth noticing that the example he gives of a relation of (*non*reciprocal) causality is the relation of the creator to the created world: "This [the relation of *reciprocal* causality] is a quite different kind of connection from that which is found in the mere relation of cause to effect (of ground to consequence), for in the latter relation the consequence does not in turn reciprocally determine the ground, and therefore does not constitute with it a whole—thus the world, for instance, does not with its creator constitute a whole" (B112). I suggest that in the sensible or phenomenal world, *all* causality is, by contrast, reciprocal causality—that is, the *succession* of effects (succession of objective *states* of substances) is causally determined only in the context provided by the *simultaneous existence* of substances themselves, as well as the *simultaneity* of cause and the initial production of its effect. But this, again, puts the category of *community* in more direct relation to (reciprocal) *hypothetical* than to *disjunctive* judgment.

One might object that it is wrong to *oppose* the two correspondences, or consider them as exclusive of each other, since after all Kant explains (quite classically) disjunctive judgment itself in terms of hypotheticals: "If one member of the division is posited, then all the rest is excluded, and conversely." However, these hypotheticals are quite different from the ones that would reflect the causal interaction Kant describes as the content of the category of community. For the hypotheticals he gives as equivalent to a disjunctive judgment (a is either b, or c) have the form: if a is b, then it is not c, and if a is not b, then it is c. Spheres of subspecies of the divided concept are in a relation of *exclusion* with respect to each other (the corresponding syllogism would be a syllogism in *modus ponendo tollens*, or *tollendo ponens*). On the contrary, the reciprocal causal relations between things are relations in which if a particular qualitative state of the one is *posited*, a particular qualitative state of the other *must be posited* (the corresponding syllogism would be in *modus ponendo ponens*). To take up the example that Kant uses in the third Analogy, a logical *disjunction* involving moon and earth might be: a celestial body in the earth's field of attraction is either the earth itself or the moon. The hypotheticals equivalent to this disjunction would be: if a celestial body in the earth's field of attraction is the earth, then it is not the moon; if it is not the earth, then it is the moon; and conversely, if it is the moon, then it is not the earth; if it is not the moon, then it is the earth. But the relation of community, or reciprocal interaction, between substances, is one where each *determines* the state of the other: the attractive force of the earth determines the rotation of the moon, the attractive force of the moon determines the tides of the sea on earth. We might express this by: "If earth with tides of such amplitude, then celestial body with such cyclic movement around the earth; if celestial body with such cyclic movement, then tides with such amplitude."

I suggest that what Kant is telling us, when he claims to establish a fundamental relation between logical disjunction and the category of community, is that the one (community) conditions the other (logical disjunction), which means that community reflects the *synthesis speciosa* performed by imagination with a view to reflecting material substances under concepts combined according to the logical form of disjunctive judgment. For reflecting material objects according to the form of disjunctive judgment is possible only if they are first reflected according to the form of hypothetical judgments so as to yield concepts forming a system of external relations by means of which we recognize their essential and inessential properties, and thus are able to constitute a system of concepts apt for reflecting natural kinds in nature.

The same pattern can be seen in the Schematism chapter, when Kant expounds the *schema* of community. For the latter is defined as a schema for *reciprocal causality*: "The schema of community or reciprocity [*Gemeinschaft (Wechselwirkung)*], the reciprocal causality [*wechselseitigen Kausalität*] of substances in respect of their accidents, is the simultaneity, according to a universal rule, of the determinations of the one substance with those of the other" (A144/B183–84). Here it is quite clear that, in community, determinations do not *exclude* each other (as do the spheres of concepts in logical disjunction), but on the contrary *posit* each other (as antecedent and consequent in hypothetical judgments). Nevertheless, this reciprocal causality does not make the relation between the category of community and the logical form of *disjunctive* judgment irrelevant. On the contrary, in thinking the category of community, logical disjunction and hypothetical judgments (and thus reciprocal causality) arc *equally* indispensable. Reciprocal causality is the relation by means of which substances are recognizable by their essential and accidental marks, and thus eventually reflectable in accordance with the form of *logical disjunction*. Conversely, only the logical form of disjunctive judgment can bestow on the category of community, as reciprocal interaction, its totalizing character. *The form of a complete logical disjunction of concepts is the discursive form of unity reflecting the unity of synthesis of appearances in space and time.* There would thus be no category of community in the full sense, as described in the Third Analogy—a system of the *universal* [*durchgehende*] reciprocal action of substances, generating the representation of a *world-whole*—unless the schema of simultaneity were guided a priori toward the logical form of disjunctive judgment, via hypothetical rules that Kant explicates in the Third Analogy.

Finally, one should note the intimate relation between the logical form of disjunctive judgment/category of *community*, on the one hand, and the logical form of infinite judgment/category of *limitation*, on the other. In chapter 10, I argued that in the sensible conditions proper to our cognition, the "infinite sphere of all possible determination" in which the subject of an infinite judgment is posited, is the infinite sphere of 'what is given in space and time'. The *intuitive* exhibition of this sphere is the whole of reality, the *totum realitatis* given in the forms of space and time as *quanta continua infinita*. As we saw in chapter 10, if an infinite judgment is to reflect an object as appearance, the *discursive* limitation thought in this judgment presupposes the reciprocal *intuitive* limitation of realities *represented in (spatiotemporal) sensible intuition*. Now, the logical form of disjunctive judgment and the universal community of substances are nothing other than the *determination* of what remained indeterminate in the infinite judgment and the spatiotemporal *totum realitatis* providing it with its sensible matter. Indeed, the logical form of disjunctive judgment is the form according to which the infinite sphere of all possible reality can be fully determined. Similarly, the reflection of a dynamical relation of reciprocal causality is the relation by means of which the intuitively given reciprocal limitation of realities in space and time can be determined, quantitatively and qualitatively.[99] Thus is Kant's attack on Leibniz's monadology in the Amphiboly of Concepts of Reflection fully confirmed and explained.[100] For a community of substances cannot be thought as a community of internal determinations of (fully determined) concepts, but only as a community of *external relations* (of reciprocal causality) between things, given in space and time. The logical form of universal subordination of genera and species can be obtained only by a never-ending reflection on the *totum realitatis* determined as a system of interaction of substances coexisting in space and time.

Kant's argument in the Third Analogy of Experience is an argument for the assertion that there *is*, indeed, such a system of universal interaction of substances in space and time. Just as in the Second Analogy he argued from our experience of objective succession to the assertion of the universal causal principle as the necessary condition for such an experience, similarly here his argument progresses from our experience of simultaneity to the supposition of universal causal interaction as the necessary condition for such an experience. I shall now consider this argument.

Synthesis Speciosa *and Simultaneity*

The pattern Kant follows in his proof for the Third Analogy is very similar to that of the Second Analogy. It rests on the same general premise: our apprehension of the manifold given in sensible intuition is always successive. In the Second Analogy, Kant asked, How do we tell what is successive in the object from what is not, since in either case our apprehension is successive? In the Third Analogy, the question becomes, How do we determine that things we apprehend only successively are objectively *simultaneous*? Kant's answer follows the same general line as before. (1) We perceive things as *simultaneous* when the order of succession in

---

[99] Cf. chapter 10, pp. 295–97. Note that in the *Metaphysical Foundations of Natural Science*, what corresponds to the category of *limitation* is the *reciprocal limitation of attractive and repulsive forces*. Thus the categories of quality are inseparable, in their application, from the categories of relation (cf. *Anfangsgründe*, General Note to Dynamics, Ak. IV, 523; 76).

[100] Cf. chapter 6, pp. 142–45.

the synthesis of our apprehension is indifferent, that is, when our apprehension can go from A to B to C, as well as from C to B to A, or A to C to B (in the Second Analogy, Kant stated that we perceive states of things as *successive* when the order of our apprehension *cannot* be reversed). (2) This reversibility (order-indifference) of our apprehension, however, is not sufficient by itself to generate the representation of simultaneity in things: "The synthesis of imagination in apprehension would only reveal that the one perception is in the subject when the other is not there, and reciprocally, but not that the objects are simultaneous, that is, that if the one is the other is at the same time, and that this is necessary for the perceptions to be able to follow one another reciprocally" (B257). The representation of the succession of perceptions in apprehension as a temporal re!ation of simultaneity in objects requires something more than the mere observation that, in our apprehension, the succession of perceptions of type A to type B is followed by a sequence from B to A (in the Second Analogy, Kant remarked that the de facto succession of our apprehension is not sufficient to generate the representation of an objective succession). (3) This "something more" is the pure concept of the reciprocal influence of substances, or the relation of community (in the Second Analogy, the "something more" was the concept of causal connection or, more precisely, the presupposition that the state of affairs we perceive follows "from the preceding state, according to a rule"). (4) We must therefore conclude that all appearances, insofar as we perceive them as simultaneous existents (substances) in space, are in a relation of universal reciprocal influence, or community (*Gemeinschaft*). This provides the proof of the principle stated as the Third Analogy of Experience: "All substances, insofar as they can be perceived in space as simultaneous, are in complete reciprocity [*in durchgängiger Wechselwirkung*]" (B256).[101]

Kant thus claims that perceiving things as simultaneously existing in space depends upon conceiving them as substances in relations of reciprocal interaction. Now, such a requirement seems prima facie implausibly strong. So, to understand better what Kant means, let us look at the example he gives in the "Proof" added in B:

> I can direct my perception first to the moon and then to the earth, or, conversely, first to the earth and then to the moon; and because the perceptions of these objects can follow each other reciprocally, I say that they are simultaneous. Now simultaneity is the existence of the manifold in one and the same time. But time itself cannot be perceived, and we are not, therefore, in a position to gather, simply from things being set in the same time, that their perceptions can follow each other reciprocally. . . . Consequently, in the case of things which are simultaneous externally to one another, an intellectual concept of the reciprocal sequence of their determinations is required,

[101] In the A edition, the principle is stated slightly differently: "All substances, so far as they are simultaneous, stand in thoroughgoing community, that is, in mutual interaction" (A 211). In the B edition, Kant emphasizes the *perception* (= p3, experience; cf. note 68) of simultaneity, thus already announcing what will be the core of his proof: this perception requires a rule of *synthesis speciosa* in imagination. Although he no longer mentions "community" in the statement of the principle, the term remains in the title of the Analogy: "Principle of Simultaneity, in accordance with the Law of Reciprocity or Community."

if we are to be able to say that the reciprocal sequence of the perceptions is grounded in the object, and so to represent the simultaneity as objective. But the relation of substances in which the one contains determinations the ground of which is contained in the other is the relation of influence; and when each substance reciprocally contains the ground of the determinations in the other, the relation is that of community or reciprocity. (B257–58)

To comprehend Kant's reasoning, we need to keep in mind the more detailed analysis he provided in the several expositions of his proof for the Second Analogy. There he argued that the de facto succession of perceptions in apprehension is reflected as irreversible (*necessary* succession) just in case, when it is intentionally related to an object, it is thought as exhibiting the alteration of a substance, which can occur only if it "follows upon something else according to a rule," that is, has a real ground, or cause. Thus to establish the relation between the perception of objective succession and the category of causality, one had to consider the act of the understanding guiding the *synthesis speciosa* of imagination, aiming at the discursive form of judgment and providing the origin and meaning of the category. The same applies here. Kant's argument is that the order-indifference of the succession of (generically identical) perceptions is reflected as objective simultaneity only if our *effort (conatus) toward judgment* leads us to think the reversible sequences of perceptions in *subjective* apprehension as a reciprocal conditioning of *objective* determinations. The subjective sequence of perceptions in my apprehension would by itself give me only a perception of the moon, then a perception of the earth, and then again a perception of the moon, then again a perception of the earth, and so on. But if these reversible and repeatable sequences of perceptions are reflected with a view to relating them to an object, that is, reflected under concepts combined in judgment, I form something like the judgment: 'If x (which I reflect under the determinations making up the concept "moon") is an element in the present whole of my perception/experience, then y (which I reflect under the determinations making up the concept "earth") is present in the same whole. And if y (which I reflect under the determinations making up the concept "earth") is present in the whole of my perception/experience, then x (which I reflect under the determinations making up the concept "moon") is present in the same whole'.[102] Simultaneity is not directly perceived: I do not perceive the moon at its zenith at the time I perceive the earth, nor do I perceive the earth at the time I perceive the moon; this temporal relation is only reflected when I relate the reversible succession of my perceptions to an object. What we represent as the *simultaneity* of things in space is then nothing other than the sensible form resulting from *synthesis speciosa* in accordance with the discursive form of a hypothetical judgment whose converse is also thought as true. In accordance with this discursive form, asserting the presence (existence, *Dasein*) of one of the objects perceived is represented as the condition for asserting the presence of the other, and conversely the presence of the latter is reflected as the condition for asserting the presence of the former. If A (with all the determinations I attribute to it—location in space, magnitude, qual-

---

[102] Here again "perception" should be understood as p3, "experience": see note 68.

ities) is present at time t_1, then B, with all the determinations I attribute to it, is also present at the same time t_1, but in another spatial location. Reciprocally, if B is present at time t_2, then A is also present at time t_2, but in another spatial location. What specific determination pertains to this reciprocal conditioning (i.e., specifically *what* conditions *what*), we do not know. We shall acquire a determinate cognition of it only by means of the indefinite, never-completed process of corrections and specifications of our discursive judgments in actual experience. Nonetheless, this process finds its initial impulse and its first step in the mere consciousness of the *simultaneous existence of things in space.*

That the category of community should thus reflect a *synthesis speciosa* geared toward the form of hypothetical judgment does not mean that there is no distinction any more between the respective arguments of the Second and Third Analogies. For hypothetical judgment is not assigned the same role in them. In the Second Analogy, Kant showed that the presupposition of a cause (of a real ground, "external" to the subject of changing determinations) is a necessary component in the representation of an objective succession of determinations, since this objective succession is perceived only insofar as it is reflected as the alteration of a substance. *What* actual existent the cause is, is not thereby determined. Perceiving the positions of the boat as successive means presupposing *a* cause of this succession, but not cognizing the *actual* cause. In the Third Analogy, Kant's argument is that each thing, with its specific determinations, is supposed to be the cause (as well as the effect) of the specific determinations of all the things perceived as simultaneous with it, while being itself (as far as its determinations are concerned) the effect all things simultaneous with it. Hence contrary to what was the case in the Second Analogy, *both* cause and effect are present in the very perception of simultaneity; but again, they are not *determined*, nor is the nature of their reciprocal conditioning (which actual existent causes which specific determinations in which other existents remains indeterminate in the mere perception—experience—of coexistence). There is thus no confusion, but rather a complementarity between the Second and Third Analogies: between Kant's explanation of our perception of objective succession, the succession of states in a substance, which we perceive only under the supposition that this succession "presupposes something else, upon which it follows according to a rule," and his explanation of our perception of objective simultaneity, the coexistence of substances, which we perceive only under the supposition that if the one is present, then so is the other, and if the other is present, then so is the first.[103]

---

[103] Guyer misses this point when he suggests that all Kant really established in the Third Analogy was causal relation, *not* interaction between substances (see *Claims*, 272). He is led to this mistake by his general insistence, in the case of the Third Analogy as previously in those of the first and second, that Kant's argument is an epistemological argument on how we *confirm* our beliefs about objective temporal relations, instead of—as it is really meant to be—a transcendental argument on the conditions *of our experience* of objective temporal determinations and thus *of the constitution of the phenomena themselves*, as temporally determinate existents. Thus Guyer claims that all Kant's argument in the Third Analogy entitles him to is the claim that in order to *confirm* that two substances are simultaneous, we need to know a law according to which if one is in a given state, then the other is coexisting with it, either as the cause or as the effect of the first in its present state. Now, if Kant's ar-

These complementary aspects of the causal connection (cause/effect on the one hand, community or *reciprocal* causality on the other hand) are thus together at work in our representation of the *order of time*. In the Second Analogy, Kant indicated that appearances mutually assign each other their place in time through their causal relations. This thesis is further developed and specified in the Third Analogy. As all causal relations belong to the context of the universal community of substances, the latter is the universal context in which appearances mutually determine for each other their relative positions in time and thereby also in space.

Strikingly, when explaining the relation between dynamical community (the interaction of substances), simultaneity, and spatial community, Kant stresses the role played by *our own body* as a necessary mediator in our apprehension of the universal community of substances:

> The word community is in the German language ambiguous. It may mean either *communio* or *commercium*. We here employ it in the latter sense, as signifying a dynamical community, without which even local community (*communio spatii*) could never be empirically known. We may easily recognize from our experiences that only the continuous influences in all parts of space can lead our senses from one object to another. The light, which plays between our eye and the celestial bodies, produces a mediate community between us and them, and thereby shows us that they coexist. We cannot empirically change our position, and perceive the change, unless matter in all parts of space makes perception of our position possible to us. For only thus by means of their reciprocal influence can the parts of matter establish their simultaneous existence, and thereby, though only mediately, their coexistence, even to the most remote objects. (A213/B260)

Our body appears to us as one substance among other substances, with which it is in a relation of dynamical community (*commercium*), simultaneity, and thereby spatial community (*communio*). Our experiencing the coexistence of other substances with our own body is the condition for our experiencing their respective relations of community. Through the light that strikes our eyes and "plays between the bodies," we perceive their respective positions. Each objective change of spatial position of our body is made evident to us by the alteration of its relation to other bodies. Their relative positions are associated with various sensory qualities affecting us. But who is this "we," or if you prefer, this "I" in the plural?

---

gument were of such a kind, then it would not, of course, furnish any ground to assert a *reciprocal* interaction between substances. But it would also leave unexplained how we *perceive* objective simultaneity in the first place—which is precisely the explanation the argument of the Third Analogy was designed to supply. It consists in showing that perception of objective simultaneity is made possible by a *synthesis speciosa* in accordance with reciprocal hypothetical judgments of the type: 'if A then B, and if B then A'. *Determinate* cognition of causal interaction will eventually emerge from the *determination* of these hypotheticals in empirical knowledge of objects thus represented as simultaneously existing in space and time. Just as I insisted, in the case of the Second Analogy, that according to Kant our very perception of objective succession is already a search for the rule governing this succession, similarly here I insist that, according to Kant, our very perception (experience) of objective simultaneity is a search for the rules of universal interaction that make things what they are, in any state of the world-whole.

I suggest it is the empirical unity of a consciousness whose states are associated with the states of a body it recognizes as its own, in a relation of spatial and dynamical community with other bodies in space. In section 18 of the Transcendental Deduction, Kant asserted that empirical unity of consciousness is "merely derived from the objective unity of self-consciousness under conditions given *in concreto.*" In section 19, he added that by means of the logical function of judgment, specified according to its logical forms, this empirical unity of consciousness can progress from the empirical consciousness that "If I support a body, I feel an impression of weight" to the objective judgment "Bodies are heavy."[104]

Now, this takes us back to the concluding sentence of the B "proof" of the Anticipations of Perception, whose analysis I left incomplete at the end of the preceding chapter: "Corresponding to this intensity of sensation, an *intensive magnitude,* that is, a degree of influence on the senses must be ascribed to all objects of perception, insofar as the perception contains sensation" (B208).[105] When discussing this text at the end of chapter 10, I remarked that Kant defines the relation of sensation to its object *first* as an intentional relation (where sensation is intentionally related to "objects of perception, insofar as the perception contains sensation"), *then* as a causal relation (in which sensation is thought to be the effect of the "influence on the sense" of the objects of perception). I suggested that the correlation between these two quite different types of relation could be fully explained only after the Analogies of Experience had been expounded. Now we are indeed in a better position to understand this correlation. The "objects of perception," that is, the objects to which sensations are intentionally related, are the substrates of changing determinations (relatively permanent objects, substances) in relations of community with all other substances in space. We cognize these objects only through their rule-governed relations, among which are their relations to our own body (itself cognized only through its relation to other bodies). The objects are the "causes" of the sensations we cognitively relate to them in experience, insofar as between the objects and the sensations we empirically cognize the temporal relation that is the schema of causality: for instance, the regularly repeated succession between my body's carrying another body and my feeling of weight; or the regularly repeated succession of rays of light shining on raindrops and sensations of rainbows of color. Thus the subjective manifold of our empirical representations is itself temporally determined in causal relation to the universal temporal order of the objects of experience, although we do not need to suppose any other community of reciprocal interaction than that of *corporeal* substances. For since only corporeal substances are given *in space,* only they can be cognized as simultaneous and thus in relations of universal *reciprocal* determination.

And this is how the astonishing edifice of Kant's Analogies of Experience comes to completion: by the location of "us" in the empirically given world. An

---

[104] Cf. Transcendental Deduction §18 (B 140) and §19 (B142).
[105] Cf. chapter 10, p. 322.

"us," that is, consisting of unities of empirical consciousness associated with a phenomenal body of our own, unities of consciousness both passive (receptive, capable of conscious sensation and associative imagination) and active (spontaneous, intellectual, capable of judgment and *synthesis speciosa*). And as such, the authors of the representation of the very world in which "we" locate "ourselves": transcendental subjects.

The Capacity to Judge and "Ontology
as Immanent Thinking"

UPON CONCLUDING his exposition of the three Analogies of Experience, Kant states that they "express nothing other than the relation of time to the unity of apperception":

> Our analogies therefore really portray the unity of nature in the combination of all appearances under certain exponents, which express nothing other than the relation of time (insofar as time comprehends in itself all existence) to the unity of apperception—such unity being possible only in synthesis according to rules. (A216/B263)

With this, the continuity of Kant's argument comes into full view, from the Transcendental Deduction of the Categories to the System of Principles. The transcendental unity of apperception was first introduced in the A Deduction, in the exposition of the "synthesis of recognition in the concept." There Kant argued that we could not recognize singular representations under common concepts unless they were taken up in one and the same act of combination and comparison, and unless we were (however dimly) conscious of the *numerical identity* of this act of combining our representations. This consciousness is what confers "logical form" upon our representations. And it "presupposes" or "includes" a synthesis of imagination.[1] In the B Deduction, Kant specified that the "logical form" thus given to our representations is that of *judgment*. The synthesis of imagination it presupposes is figurative synthesis (*synthesis speciosa*) or "affection of inner sense" by the understanding. I argued that this meant affection of inner sense not by categorial understanding (i.e., understanding already equipped with categories as full-fledged *concepts*), but by understanding as the mere *capacity to form judgments, Vermögen zu urteilen*. Thus, the "I think," or "transcendental unity of self-consciousness," has no other meaning or status than that of being the unified activity of combination and reflection on the sensible given. *There is no* unity of self-consciousness or "transcendental unity of apperception" apart from this effort, or *conatus* toward judgment, ceaselessly affirmed and ceaselessly threatened with dissolution in the "welter of appearances [*Gewühle der Erscheinungen*]."[2]

Now, this *effort toward judgment*, applied to the "welter of appearances," is precisely what Kant lays out in detail in the Analogies of Experience, which

---

[1] Cf. A117n. and A118.
[2] Cf. A111.

themselves presuppose the successive syntheses of intuition (reflected in the Axioms of intuition) and the "filling out of time" by the intensity of sensations (reflected in the Anticipations of Perception). Kant's argument in the System of Principles, as I understand it, is thus a continuous one, where no principle can be fully understood in isolation from the others. Kant argues that the successive apprehension (synthesis of multiplicities of homogeneous units, *quantitative* synthesis) of what first appears to us as a continuous and infinite whole of sensations of varying intensity (*totum realitatis*, intensive magnitude of the sensory given) is so rule-governed (by virtue of *relational* syntheses) that it results in our distinguishing singular objects under concepts. Among these singular objects is one we regard as our own body, associated to each and every state of the whole of reality present to our perception. These singular objects assign each other and assign our own body, delimit for each other and delimit for our own body, their location in space and time.[3] Thus not only is there no "transcendental unity of apperception" except through this unceasing effort toward judgment in the syntheses of our sensible representations. But also, this *transcendental* unity is itself inseparable from the *empirical* unity of consciousness associated with one's own body. For it is inseparable from the perpetual modification of consciousness by the "welter of appearances," under contingent circumstances peculiar to each empirical subject. Kant insists, in section 18 of the B Deduction, that what he is concerned with in the *Critique of Pure Reason* is *not* the *empirical*, but the *transcendental* unity of self-consciousness, namely just those universal forms of synthesis and analysis that make possible every one of our empirical judgments, and every one of our acts of perceptual synthesis oriented toward judgment. Nevertheless, his argument in the Analogies shows that any *empirical* unity of consciousness is grounded, irrespective of given empirical conditions and circumstances, in the *transcendental* unity of consciousness. Hence, Kant's transcendental unity of consciousness is not simply the "transcendental I that could be that of anybody else as well as my own" that Merleau-Ponty impatiently denounced in the "Critique of Pure Reason".[4] Kant's view is rather that unity of consciousness is always both "my own" *and*, insofar as it is "transcendental unity of self-consciousness" whose form is that of judgment, so constituted that it is capable of transcending the point of view of "myself, in the present state of my perception" to the point of view of "everybody, always."

Kant further maintains that the conscious *effort toward judgment*, that is, the transcendental unity of self-consciousness, is what makes possible consciousness of an objective temporal order. We have such consciousness only insofar as our perceptions are related to *realities*, to permanent or changing properties of singular things reciprocally determining each other's location in space and time. This is how the Analogies of Experience "portray the unity of nature in the combination of all appearances under certain exponents." When analyzing Kant's logical forms of judgment, we saw that the term "exponent" appears in Kant's notion of

[3] Cf. chapter 11, pp. 391–93.
[4] Cf. Merleau-Ponty, *Phénoménologie*, 75.

a *rule*. He calls the relation of the assertion to its condition the "*exponent*" of a rule, and the three possible "exponents" for rules are the three types of relation in judgment. Now, according to the Analogies of Experience, the capacity to attribute conceptual marks to a singular object (a boat, a piece of wax, a cushion, the surface of the water in a glass, the moon, the earth) that are either "reciprocal with the object" or belonging to it only *under an added condition*—this capacity is indeed what allows us to relate our successively apprehended perceptions to a system of objects correlated in time. It is in this way that the "combination of all appearances according to certain exponents" enables us to relate our subjective apprehension (the flux, the *Gewühle*) to an objective order of time. The capacity to represent discursively (thought) and the capacity to locate things, ourselves included, in time are thus one and the same. The "unity of self-consciousness" as the unity of the discursive *conatus*, and the unity of self-consciousness as the consciousness of an individuality located in time, are one and the same. Not because the discursive capacity *suffices* to generate a representation of objective time, since time is the form of *sensibility*. But sensibility, left to itself, is inadequate to exhibit things as located in relation to each other according to an independent order of time, any more than it would suffice to present things according to an order of space. This is possible only if the discursive effort exerted on the welter of appearances allows us to recognize things under concepts "reciprocal with them" (concepts of substances), as well as under concepts predicable of them only "under added condition" (concepts of changing properties or accidents, reflecting the *alterations* of substances).

The "guiding thread" that was the starting point of our inquiry thus finds its true meaning. For behind the deceptively rigid parallelism between logical forms of judgment and categories, what emerges is the cognitive effort of discursive beings confronting what is given to them in sensibility. This effort, *conatus* of the *Vermögen zu urteilen*, is according to Kant what essentially defines the kind of beings we are. It is also what generates the universal forms in which we think our world. My claim is that only if we accept to read the Transcendental Analytic under the "guiding thread" so understood will it cease to appear a cobbling together of an opaque argument (the Transcendental Deduction of the Categories) with diverse epistemological arguments (the Principles of Pure Understanding). Instead it will become what Kant intended it to be: a unified transcendental endeavor in which Kant displays under our eyes the genesis of the concepts of what once bore "the proud name of ontology," (B303) under the guidance of a question we might summarize as follows: how are there in general, for us, empirical objects representable as substitutional instances for the term "x" in the logical forms of our judgments?

The table of logical functions of judgments is retrospectively illuminated by the answer this question receives from the Transcendental Analytic as a whole. For what we learn from the System of Principles, especially the three Analogies of Experience, is that there would be for us no singular things recognizable under concepts reflecting their essence (concepts "reciprocal with x") unless we made systematic use of *all three* logical forms of relation in judgment (in combination with the forms of quantity and quality). In the First and Second Analogies of Experience, Kant argues that *things* (singular objects thought under concepts) are substitutional instances for "x" in the logical form of categorical judgments *only if they are also substitutional instances for "x" in hypothetical judgments* (whereby we are able to recognize their *alterations*). And in the Third Analogy, he completes his argument by showing that categorical and hypothetical judgment are formed under the supposition of the "infinite sphere" of the concept of 'object of experience', or 'object given in space and time' (which, in conjunction with the previous two forms, guides our recognition of things as universally interacting in space and time). The "simple" judgments (categorical judgments) by means of which we cognize things under concepts reflecting their essence, are thus possible only under the condition that we also generate "composite" or "complex" judgments (hypothetical and disjunctive judgments), by means of which we cognize a thing under its accidental marks, in universal correlation with all other things cognized in space and time. And finally, as we saw in chapters 9 and 10, the ability to reflect the sensible under concepts according to quantity and quality of judgment is also an ability to generate not only the representation of homogeneous *discrete* multiplicities, but also our representation of a spatiotemporal *continuum* within which all realities may be thought as possessing intensive magnitude.

The systematic combination of discursive forms presupposed in even the simplest categorical judgment about the things that constitute our world ('This body is heavy', 'Gold is a yellow metal', 'The river is frozen', etc.) is what Kant presents in the table of the logical forms of judgment providing its "leading thread" to the Metaphysical Deduction of the Categories. Hence, there is good reason to suppose that Kant's discovery of the table itself—that is, his selection and presentation of some, not all, of the logical forms he found in logic textbooks—was itself guided by a question that complements the one I formulated earlier: which logicodiscursive forms must we presuppose to be at work for the infinite manifold of our sensible impressions to result in representations of *things* capable of providing substitutional instances for the term "x" in the logical forms of our judgments? That is to say (taking up a term Kant will use in the third Critique), by means of which logical functions do we generate a "terrain" for our concepts? Only insofar as they were thus selected and organized under the guidance of the transcendental question (what are the a priori conditions for the representation of objects in general?) could logical functions of judgment serve as a guiding thread for the table of categories.

If we now take one last look at the passage from the *Prolegomena* I cited in beginning this book,[5] we may perhaps say the following: Kant found in logic textbooks a rhapsodic profusion of forms of judgment. Considering logicodiscursive forms in relation to the transcendental question, What are the a priori conditions for relating representations to objects given to the senses? led him to

---

[5] *Prol.*, §39, Ak. IV, 323–24; 65–66.

examine 1) judgment as concept-subordination and thus subsumption of objects under concepts (the various forms of which determine quantity and quality of judgment), 2) relation of an assertion to its "internal" or "external" condition (by means of which a judgment makes a claim to truth, and also by means of which judgments are related to one another in syllogistic inference, which includes *disjunctive* syllogism).[6] Having thus identified discursive forms by their role in relating representations to objects, Kant "referred these functions of judgment to objects in general, or rather to the condition of determining judgments as objectively valid," namely pure intuition, whose forms are for us space and time. This is how the table of logical functions became the principle for the table of categories, meanwhile also, I suggest, acquiring its definitive formulation. Those logical functions, characterized, on the one hand, as functions of a *pure understanding* and, on the other hand, as functions of an *understanding necessarily paired with a receptive capacity*, thus became not merely the guiding thread for the elucidation of the categories of an "ontology as immanent thinking,"[7] but also the architectonic principle for the entire critical system.

I certainly do not think that mounting a stronger defense of the systematic unity and coherence of Kant's project than has been done so far constitutes in itself a sufficient argument in favor of that project and its results. But I do think that unraveling the logical impetus of Kant's argument makes it a significantly more interesting one than has been often admitted. For Kant's table of logical functions of judgment turns out to be, according to its author, an exposition of the minimal norms of discursive thinking necessary for us to be able to recognize and reidentify objects under concepts. And the infamous "transcendental synthesis of imagination" turns out to be the complex web of perceptual combinations by means of which we take up sensible data into what we, in present times, have come to term "the space of reasons." One should thus not dismiss too readily the so-called psychological aspect of Kant's argument in the Transcendental Analytic. For as I have stressed many times, psychological hypotheses (hypotheses about the kinds of mental activities that are at work in our cognitive achievements) are always guided, in Kant's argument, by logical/transcendental hypotheses about what it means to give oneself norms for evaluating the truth and falsity of our judgments. Whatever the fate of the particular brand of descriptive psychology in which Kant dresses his views, the latter aspect of the argument should remain the main object of investigation.

I have indicated, while progressing through my analysis of Kant's argument in the Transcendental Analytic, what I took to be some of its unresolved difficulties.

---

[6] See chapter 4. The fourth title of the table, modality, concerns "the relation of our judgments to the unity of thought in general," which results in a specific "value of the copula." It makes no specific contribution to the activity of concept-combination (cf. B100).

[7] Cf. Letter to Beck, January 20, 1792, Ak. XI, 314; 182. In this letter Kant explains to Beck that he intends to write a "System of Metaphysics," which he will start with an exposition of his categories. He will then show that no experience of objects of sense is possible except insofar as these objects are thought under the categories (*and* given in space and time). From this he continues, "there emerges a whole science of ontology as *immanent* thinking, that is, a science of that thinking in which the objective reality of the concepts employed can be established with certainty."

Let me just recall a few: the ambiguity of Kant's notion of "appearance" and of what I called the "internalization within representation of the object of representation"; Kant's supposition that the "formal intuition" of space necessarily has the features of Euclidean space; his apparent inference from the continuity of the forms of intuition, space and time, to the continuity of change in nature; the use he seems to be making of this continuity in his defense of the necessity of empirical causal connections. One could show, case by case, that each one of these difficulties became a motivating factor in subsequent challenges to Kant's critical system, as were of course Kant's imprudent remarks on the definitive and perfected nature of Aristotelian logic. But again, even these difficulties or obscurities can best be addressed, I would like to claim, only if considered against the background of Kant's incredible systematic achievement, his overturning of rational metaphysics in favor of a completely new definition of what it means to think or know anything at all.

Adickes, Erich. *Immanuel Kants Kritik der reinen vernunft. Mit einer Einleitung und Anmerkungen* (Berlin: Mayer & Müller, 1889).

Allison, Henry. *Kant's Transcendental Idealism* (New Haven: Yale University Press, 1983).

Apel, Karl-Otto. "From Kant to Peirce: The Semiotical Transformations of Transcendental Logic," in *Proceedings of the Third International Kant Congress*, ed. L. W. Beck (Dordrecht: Reidel, 1972).

Aquila, Richard. *Matter in Mind, a Study of Kant's Transcendental Deduction* (Bloomington: Indiana University Press, 1989).

———. *Representational Mind, a Study of Kant's Theory of Knowledge* (Bloomington: Indiana University Press, 1983).

Arnauld, Antoine, and Nicole, Pierre. *La Logique ou l'art de penser*, ed. P. Clair and F. Girbal, 2d ed. (Paris: J. Vrin, 1981); *Logic or the Art of Thinking*, ed. Jill Vance Buroker (Cambridge: Cambridge University Press, 1996).

Bacon, Francis. *Norvum Organum*, trans. and ed. Peter Urbach and John Gibson (Chicago: Open Court, 1994).

Baumgarten, Alexander Gottlieb. *Metaphysica* (Halle, 1739), repr. in Kant, Ak. XVII; §§504–669 (*Psychologia empirica*), repr. in Kant, Ak. XV.

Beattie, James. *An Essay on the Nature and Immutability of Truth, in Opposition to Sophistry and Scepticism* (Edinburgh: A. Kincaid & J. Bell, 1770; repr., New York: Garland, 1983).

Beck, Lewis White, ed. *Essays on Kant and Hume* (New Haven: Yale University Press, 1978).

———. *Kant Studies Today* (LaSalle, Ill.: Open Court, 1969).

Belaval, Yvon. *Leibniz critique de Descartes* (Paris: Gallimard, 1960).

Bennett, Jonathan. *Kant's Analytic* (London: Cambridge University Press, 1966).

Bergson, Henri. *Essai sur les données immédiats de la conscience* (Paris: Presses Universitaires de France, 1985 (1st ed. 1927).

Berkeley, George. *Philosophical Writings*, ed. and introd. David M. Armstrong (London: Macmillan, 1974.

Beyssade, Jean-Marie. "L'Analyse cartésienne du morceau de cire," in Wagner, *Sinnlichkeit*, 3–25.

Blanché, Robert. *La Logique et son histoire* (Paris: Armand Colin, 1970).

Boyer, Carl. *The History of the Calculus and Its Conceptual Development* (New York: Dover, 1959).

Brandt, Reinhard. *Die Urteilstafel, Kritik der reinen Vernunft A67–76;B92–201* (Hamburg: Felix Meiner, 1991). *The Table of Judgments: Critique of Pure Reason A67–76; B92–101*, trans. Eric Watkins, North American Kant Society Studies in Philosophy, vol. 4 (1995).

Buchdahl, Gerd. *Metaphysics and the Philosophy of Science* (Oxford: Blackwell, 1969).

Büchel, Gregor. *Geometrie und Philosophie* (Berlin: De Gruyter, 1987).

Cantor, Georg. *Beiträge zur Begründung der transfiniten Mengenlehre* (1897). In Cantor, *Gesammelte Abhandlungen*, 283–356. *Contributions to the Founding of the Theory of Transfinite Numbers*, Trans. Philip E. B. Jourdain (Chicago: Open Court, 1915).

Cantor, Georg. *Gesammelte Abhandlungen mathematischen und philosophischen Inhalts*, ed. Ernst Zermelo, Nachdr. der Ausgabe Berlin 1932 (Hildesheim: G. Olms, 1962).

———. *Grundlagen einer allgemeinen Mannigfaltigkeitslehre* (1883), In Cantor, *Gesammelte Abhandlungen*, 165–209.

Carl, Wolfgang. *Der schweigende Kant. Die Entwürfe zu einer Deduktion der Kategorien vor 1781* (Göttingen: Vandenhoeck & Ruprecht, 1989).

———. *Die Transzendentale Deduktion der Kategorien in der ersten Auflage der Kritik der reinen Vernunft. Ein Kommentar* (Frankfurt am Main: Vittorio Klostermann, 1992).

Cassirer, Ernst. *Kants Leben und Lehre* (Berlin: B. Cassirer, 1911). *Kant's Life and Thought*, trans. J. Haden (New Haven: Yale University Press, 1981).

———. *Substanz und Begriff, Substance and Function*, trans. W. C. Swabey and M. C. Swabey (New York: Dover, 1953 [1923]).

Cavaillès, Jean. *Sur la logique et la théorie de la science*, 2d ed. (Paris: PUF, 1960).

Coffa, J. Alberto. *The Semantic Tradition from Kant to Carnap* (Cambridge: Cambridge University Press, 1991).

Cohen, Hermann. *Kants Theorie der Erfahrung*, 3d ed. (Berlin: B. Cassirer, 1918).

Couturat, Louis. *La Logique de Leibniz d'après des documents inédits* (Paris: Alcan, 1901).

———. "La Philosophie des mathématiques de Kant," *Revue de métaphysique et de morale* 12 (Paris, 1904), 321–383.

Crusius, Christian. *Dissertatio de usu et limitibus principii rationis determinantis vulgo sufficientis* (Leipzig, 1743), in Crusius, *Die philosophischen Hauptwerke*, IV-1, 182–324.

———. *Entwurf der notwendigen Vernunft-Wahrheiten wie sie den zufälligen entgegengesetzt werden* (Leipzig, 1745), in Crusius *Die philosophischen Hauptwerke*, II.

———. *Die philosophischen Hauptwerke*, ed. G. Tonelli, 4 vols. (Hildesheim: G. Olms, 1964–87).

Debru, Claude. *Analyse et représentation. De la méthodologie à la théorie de l'espace: Kant et Lambert* (Paris: Vrin, 1977).

Descartes, René. *Oeuvres*, ed. Charles Adam and Paul Tannery, new ed. with C.N.R.S., 11 vols. (Paris: Vrin, 1964–69).

———. *Philosophical Writings of Descartes*, trans. J. Cottingham, R. Stoothoff, and D. Murdoch, 2 vols. (Cambridge: Cambridge University Press, 1984).

De Vleeschauwer, H. J. *La Déduction transcendentale dans l'oeuvre de Kant*, 3 vols. (Anvers: De Sikkel, 1934–37; repr., New York: Garland, 1976).

Erdmann, Benno. *Kants Kritizismus in der ersten und in der zweiten Auflage der Kritik der reinen Vernunft; eine historische Untersuchung* (Leipzig: Voss, 1878; repr. Geisterberg, 1973).

Euclid. *The Thirteen Books of Euclid's Elements*, translated from Heiberg's text, with introd. and commentary by Sir Thomas Heath, 3 vols., 2d ed. (Cambridge: Cambridge University Press, 1926; repr., New York: Dover, 1956).

Euler, Leonhard. *Introduction in Analysin Infinitorum* (1748), in Euler, *Opera omnia*, I, 8–9. *Leonhard Eulers Einleitung in die Analysis des Unendlichen*, trans. Michelsen, 3 vols. (Berlin, 1788–91). *Introduction to the Analysis of the Infinite*, trans. J. D. Blanton, 2 vols. (New York: Springer Verlag, 1988–90).

———. *Lettres à une princesse d'Allemagne* (1768–72), in Euler, *Opera Omnia*, III, 11–12. *Letters of Euler on Different Subjects in Natural Philosophy, Addressed to a German Princess*, ed. and trans. D. Brewster (New York, 1833).

————. *Opera omnia* (Leipzig: Birkhauser, 1911–).

Förster, Eckart. "How Are Transcendental Arguments Possible?," in Schaper and Vossenkuhl, *Reading Kant*, 3–20.

Frede, Michael, and Krüger, Lorenz. "Über die Zuordnung der Quantitäten des Urteils und der Kategorien der Größe bei Kant," *Kant-Studien* 61 (1970), 28–49, repr. in Prauss, *Kant*, 130–50.

Frege, Gottlob. *Grundlagen der Arithmetik* (Hamburg: Felix Meiner, 1986). *The Foundations of Arithmetic*, trans. J. Austin (Oxford: Oxford University Press, 1950).

Freudiger, Jürg. "Zum Problem der Wahrnehmungsurteile in Kants theoretischer Philosophie," *Kant-Studien* 82 (1991), 414–35.

Friedman, Michael. "Causal Laws and Natural Science," in Guyer, *Companion*], 161–99.

————. *Kant and the Exact Sciences* (Cambridge, Mass.: Harvard University Press, 1992).

————. "Kant and the Twentieth Century," in Parrini, *Kant*, 27–46.

Gram, Moltke. "The Crisis of Syntheticity. The Kant-Eberhard Controversy," *Kant-Studien* 71 (1980), 155–80.

————. *Kant, Ontology, and the a priori* (Evanston, Ill.: Northwestern University Press, 1968).

Graubner, H. "Form und Wesen. Ein Beitrag zur Deutung der Formbegriffe in Kants Kritik der reinen Vernunft," *Kant-Studien*, Suppl. vol. 104 (Bonn: Bouvier Verlag, 1972).

Grondin, Jean. *Kant et le problème de la philosophie: l'a priori* (Paris: Vrin, 1989).

Gueroult, Martial. *Leibniz, dynamique et métaphysique*, 2d ed. (Paris: Aubier-Montaigne, 1967).

Guyer, Paul. *The Cambridge Companion to Kant* (Cambridge: Cambridge University Press, 1992).

————., ed. *Kant and the Claims of Knowledge* (Cambridge: Cambridge University Press, 1987).

Hegel, Georg Wilhelm Friedrich. *Gesammelte Werke*, with Deutsche Forschungsgemeinschaft, ed. Rhein-Westfäl. Akad. d. Wiss. (Hamburg: F. Meiner, 1968–).

————. *Glauben und Wissen*, in Hegel, *GW*, IV. *Faith and Knowledge*, trans. and ed. W. Cerf and H. S. Harris (Albany: SUNY Press, 1977).

————. *Science of Logic*, trans. A. V. Miller (Atlantic Highlands, N.J.: Humanities Press International, 1989).

————. *Wissenschaft der Logik*, I: *Die objektive Logik*, in Hegel, *GW*, XI.

————. *Wissenschaft der Logik*, II: *Die subjektive Logik*, in Hegel, *GW*, XII.

Heidegger, Martin. *Kant und das Problem der Metaphysik*, 4th ed. (Frankfurt am Main: Klostermann, 1973). *Kant and the Problem of Metaphysics*, trans. R. Taft (Bloomington: Indiana University Press, 1990).

————. *Phänomenologische Interpretation von Kants Kritik der reinen Vernunft* (Frankfurt am Main: Klostermann, 1977).

Heinrichs, Johannes. *Die Logik der Vernunftkritik: Kants Kategorientafel* (Tübingen: Francke Verlag, 1986).

Henrich, Dieter. "Die Beweisstruktur von Kants transzendentaler Deduktion," in Prauss, *Kant*, 90–105.

————. *Identität und Objektivität, Untersuchung über Kants transzendentale Deduktion* (Heidelberg: C. Winter, 1976).

Hintikka, Jaakko. "On Kant's Notion of Intuition (Anschauung)," in Penelhum and MacIntosh, *The First Critique*, 38–53.

Hoppe, Hansgeorg. *Synthesis bei Kant* (Berlin: De Gruyter, 1983).

Horstmann, Rolf-Peter. *Die metaphysische Deduktion in Kants* Kritik der reinen Vernunft, in Tuschling, *Probleme*, 15–34.

Hume, David. *An Enquiry Concerning Human Understanding*, ed. L. A. Selby-Bigge (New York: Oxford University Press, 1975).

———. *A Treatise Concerning Human Nature*, 6th ed. (Oxford: Clarendon Press, 1985).

Kaulbach, Friedrich, and Ritter, Joachim. *Kritik und Metaphysik. Heinz Heimsoeth zum achtzigsten Geburtstag* (Berlin: De Gruyter, 1966).

Kemp Smith, Norman. *A Commentary to Kant's Critique of Pure Reason* (London: Macmillan, 1918; repr. Atlantic Highlands, N.J.: Humanities Press, 1984).

Kitcher, Patricia. *Kant's Transcendental Psychology* (New York: Oxford University Press, 1990).

Kneale, William, and Kneale, Martha. *The Development of Logic* (Oxford: Clarendon Press, 1988 [1962]).

Krüger, Lorenz. "Wollte Kant die Vollständigkeit seiner Urteilstafel beweisen?," *Kant-Studien* 59 (1968), 333–56.

Kühn, Manfred. "Kant's Conception of 'Hume's Problem,'" *Journal of the History of Philosophy* 21 (1983), 175–93.

Lachièze-Rey, Pierre. *L'Idéalisme kantien*, 3d ed. (Paris: Vrin, 1972).

Lambert, J. H. *Anlage zur Architectonic, oder Theorie des Einfachen und des Ersten in der philosophischen und mathematischen Erkenntnis* (Riga, 1771).

———. *Neues Organon, oder Gedanken über die Erforschung und Bezeichnung des Wahren und dessen Unterscheidung vom Irrtum und Schein*, 2 vols. (Leipzig, 1764).

———. *Philosophische Schriften*, ed. H. W. Arndt (Hildesheim: G. Olms, 1965–).

Lebrun, Gérard. *Kant et la fin de la métaphysique* (Paris: Armand Colin, 1970).

Leibniz, G. W. *The Leibniz-Clarke Correspondence*, ed. H. G. Alexander (Manchester: Manchester University Press, 1956).

———. *New Essays on Human Understanding*, ed. and trans. P. Remnant and J. Bennett (Cambridge: Cambridge University Press, 1981).

———. *Opera omnia*, ed. Louis Dutens, 6 vols. (Geneva, 1768).

———. *Die philosophischen Schriften*, ed. G. J. Gerhardt, 7 vols. (Berlin, 1882; repr. Hildesheim: Georg Olms, 1978).

———. *Theodicy*, trans. E. M. Huggard (LaSalle, Ill.: Open Court, 1985).

Locke, John. *An Essay Concerning Human Understanding*, ed. A. C. Fraser, 2 vols. (New York: Dover, 1959).

Longuenesse, Béatrice. "Kant et les jugements empiriques," *Kant-Studien* 86 (1995), 278–307.

———. *Kant et le Pouvoir de Juger. Sensibilité et discursivité dans la Critique de la Raison Pure.* (Paris: Presses Universitaires de France, 1993).

———. "Kant on Causality: What Was He Trying to Prove?" Typescript.

———. "Logique et métaphysique dans le système critique. L'exemple de la causalité," *Bulletin de la Société Française de Philosophie* 3 (1994).

———. "The Transcendental Ideal, and the Unity of the Critical System," *Proceedings of the Eighth International Kant-Congress* (Milwaukee: Marquette University Press, 1995), I = 2, 521–38.

Maier, Anneliese. *Kants Qualitätskategorien, Kant-Studien*, Suppl. vol. 65 (Berlin, 1930).

Martin, Gottfried. *Arithmetik und Kombinatorik bei Kant* (Berlin: De Gruyter, 1972 [1938]). *Arithmetic and Combinatorics: Kant and His Contemporaries*, trans. J. Wubnig (Carbondale: Southern Illinois University Press, 1985).

———. *Immanuel Kant. Ontologie und Wissenschaftstheorie*, 4th ed. (Berlin: De Gruyter, 1969.) *Kant's Metaphysics and Theory of Science*, trans. P. Lucas (Manchester: Manchester University Press, 1955).

Meier, G.W.F. *Auszug aus der Vernunftlehre* (Halle, 1752), in Kant, Ak. XVI.

Melnick, Arthur. *Kant's Analogies of Experience* (Chicago: University of Chicago Press, 1973).

Merleau-Ponty, Maurice. *Phénoménologie de la perception* (repr., Paris: Gallimard-Tel, 1976). *Phenomenology of Perception*, trans. C. Smith (New York: Humanities Press, 1962).

Miles, Murray Lewis. *Logik und Metaphysik bei Kant. Zu Kants Lehre vom zweifachen Gebrauch des Verstandes und der Vernunft* (Frankfurt am Main: Klostermann, 1978).

Mohr, Georg. "Wahrnehmungsurteile und Schematismus," in Robinson, *Proceedings*, I-1, 331–41.

Mörchen, Hermann. *Die Einbildungskraft bei Kant* (Tübingen: Max Niemeyer Verlag, 1970).

Newton, Isaac. *The Mathematical Works of Isaac Newton*, ed. Derek Whiteside (New York: Johnson Repr. Corp., 2 vol., 1964–67).

———. *Philosophiae Naturalis Principia Mathematica*, 3d ed. with variant readings, assembled and ed. A. Koyré and B. Cohen, 2 vols. (Cambridge, Mass.: Harvard University Press, 1972).

Pariente, Jean-Claude. *L'Analyse du langage à Port-Royal. Six études logico-grammaticales* (Paris: Editions de Minuit, 1985).

———. "Le Système des propositions catégoriques à Port-Royal," in *Mérites et limites des méthodes logiques en philosophie,* ed. Fondation Singer Polinac (Paris: J. Vrin, 1986).

Parkinson, G.H.R. "Kant As a Critic of Leibniz: The Amphiboly of Concepts of Reflection," *Revue internationale de philosophie*, nos. 136–137 (1981), 302–14.

Parrini, Paolo, ed. *Kant and Contemporary Epistemology* (Dortrecht: Kluwer, 1994).

Parsons, Charles. "Arithmetic and the Categories," in Posy, *Mathematics*, 135–58.

———. "Kant's Philosophy of Arithmetic," in *Mathematics in Philosophy* (Ithaca: Cornell University Press, 1983), 110–49.

———. "The Transcendental Aesthetic," in Guyer, *Companion*, 62–100.

Paton, Herbert James. *Kant's Metaphysic of Experience: A Commentary on the First Half of the Kritik der reinen Vernunft*, 2 vols., 2d ed. (London: Macmillan, 1951 [1936]).

Patt, Walter. *Transzendentaler Idealismus. Kants Lehre von der Subjektivität der Anschauung in der Dissertation von 1770 und in der Kritik der reinen Vernunft* (Berlin: De Gruyter, 1987).

Penelhum, T., and J. J. MacIntosh, eds, *The First Critique: Reflections on Kant's Critique of Pure Reason*, (Belmont: Wadsworth, 1969).

Philonenko, Alexis. "Introduction à la *Lettre à Marcus Herz*," in Kant, *La Dissertation de 1770*, trans. P. Mouy, suivie de *Lettre à Marcus Herz*, trans. A. Philonenko (Paris: J. Vrin, 1976).

———. *L'Oeuvre de Kant. La philosophie critique*, 2 vols. (Paris: J. Vrin, 1969).

Pippin, Robert. *Kant's Theory of Form* (New Haven, Conn.: Yale University Press, 1982).

Posy, Carl J., ed. *Kant's Philosophy of Mathematics* (Dortrecht: Kluwer, 1992).

Prauss, Gerold. *Erscheinung bei Kant: Ein Problem der Kritik der reinen Vernunft* (Berlin: De Gruyter, 1971).

———. *Kant und das Problem der Dinge an sich* (Bonn: Bouvier Verlag, 1974).

———., ed. *Kant. Zur Deutung seiner Theorie von Erkennen und Handeln* (Cologne: Kiepenheuer & Witsch, 1973).

Raggio, Andres. "La concepcion kantiana de las modalidades," *Analisis filosofico* 4, no. 2 (1984), 27–30.

Reich, Klaus. *Die Vollständigkeit der kantischen Urteilstafel* (Berlin: Richard Schoetz, 1932). *The Completeness of Kant's Table of Judgments*, trans. J. Kneller and M. Losonsky (Stanford: Stanford University Press, 1992).

Reimarus, Hermann Samuel. *Vernunftlehre* (1756), repr., ed. F. Lötzsch (Munich: Hanser, 1979).

Robinson, Hoke, ed. *Proceedings of the Eighth International Kant Congress* (Milwaukee: Marquette University Press, 1995).

Rusnock, Paul, and George, Rolf. "A Last Shot at Incongruent Counterparts," *Kant-Studien* 3 (1995), 257–76.

Russell, Bertrand. *Principles of Mathematics* (New York: Norton, [1903]).

Satura, Vladimir. *Kants Erkenntnispsychologie in den Nachschriften seiner Vorlesungen über empirische Psychologie* (Bonn: Bouvier Verlag, 1971).

Schaper, Eva, and Vossenkuhl, Wilhelm, eds. *Reading Kant: New Perspective on Transcendental Arguments and Critical Philosophy* (New York: Basil Blackwell, 1989).

Scholz, H. *A Concise History of Logic*, trans. K. F. Leidecker (New York: Philosophical Library, 1961).

Schulthess, Peter. *Relation und Funktion. Eine systematische und entwicklungsgeschichtliche Untersuchung zur theoretischen Philosophie Kants* (Berlin: De Gruyter, 1981).

Steckelmacher, Moritz. *Die formale Logik Kants in ihren Beziehungen zur Transzendentalen* (Breslau: Köbner, 1879).

Strawson, Peter F. *The Bounds of Sense: An Essay on Kant's Critique of Pure Reason* (London: Methuen, 1966).

Stuhlmann-Laeisz, Rainer. *Kants Logik* (Berlin: De Gruyter, 1976).

Tetens, Johann Nikolaus. *Philosophische Versuche über die menschliche Natur und ihre Entwicklung* (Leipzig, 1777; repr. Hildesheim: G. Olms, 1979).

Thöle, Bernhard. *Kant und das Problem der Gesetzmäßigkeit der Natur* (Berlin: De Gruyter, 1991).

Thomson, Manley. "Singular Terms and Intuitions in Kant's Epistemology," *Review of Metaphysics* 26 (1980).

Tonelli, Giorgio. "Die Voraussetzungen zur Kantischen Urteilstafel in der Logik des 18. Jahrhunderts," in Kaulbach and Ritter, *Kritik*, 134–58.

Tuschling, Burkhard, ed. *Probleme der "Kritik der reinen Vernunft"* (Berlin: De Gruyter, 1984).

Vaihinger, Hans. *Commentar zur Kritik der reinen Vernunft*, 2 vols. (Stuttgart: Spemann, 1881; repr., New York: Garland, 1976).

Vuillemin, Jules. *Physique et métaphysique kantiennes* (Paris: PUF, 1955).

———. "Reflexionen über Kants Logik," *Kant-Studien* 52 (1960–61), 310–35.

Wagner, Hans. "Der Argumentationsgang in Kants Deduktion der Kategorien," *Kant-Studien* 71 (1980), 351–66.

———., ed. *Sinnlichkeit und Verstand in der deutschen und französischen Philosophie von Descartes bis Hegel* (Bonn: Bouvier Verlag, 1976).

Waxman, Wayne. *Kant's Model of the Mind* (New York: Oxford University Press, 1991).

Wolff, Christian, *Gesammelte Werke* (Hildesheim and New York: Georg Olms, 1962–).

———. *Philosophia prima sive Ontologia* (Frankfurt and Leipzig, 1736), in Wolff, *Gesammelte Werke*, II-3.

————. *Philosophia rationalis sive Logica* (Frankfurt and Leipzig, 1740), in Wolff, *Gesammelte Werke*, II-1, 3 vols.

————. *Psychologia empirica* (Frankfurt and Leipzig, 1736), in Wolff, *Gesammelte Werke*, II-5.

Wolff, Michael. *Die Vollständigkeit der kantischen Urteilstafel. Mit einem Essay über Freges Begriffschrift* (Frankfurt am Main: Vittorio Klostermann, 1995).

Wolff, Robert P. *Kant's Theory of Mental Activity: A Commentary on the Transcendental Analytic of the Critique of Pure Reason* (Cambridge, Mass.: Harvard University Press, 1963).

Young, J. Michael. "Kant on the Construction of Arithmetical Concepts," *Kant-Studien* 73 (1982), 17–46.

————. Preface to *Lectures on Logic*, in the *Cambridge Edition of the Works of Immanuel Kant* (Cambridge: Cambridge University Press, 1992), XV–XXXII.

Letters, Ak. X

LETTER TO HERTZ, FEBRUARY 21, 1772

Letters, Ak. XI

LETTER TO BECK, JANUARY 20, 1792

LETTER TO REINHOLD, MAY 12, 1789

About the Author

BÉATRICE LONGUENESSE is Professor of Philosophy at Princeton University, and has taught at various academic institutions in France. Her other books include *Hegel et la critique de la métaphysique*.